Of No Earthly Use

The 2nd Line Territorial Force Divisions and the Western Front 1914–18

K.W. Mitchinson

Helion & Company

To JB

For all those Welsh Ridge days

Helion & Company Limited
Unit 8 Amherst Business Centre
Budbrooke Road
Warwick
CV34 5WE
England
Tel. 01926 499 619
Email: info@helion.co.uk
Website: www.helion.co.uk
Twitter: @helionbooks
Visit our blog at blog.helion.co.uk

Published by Helion & Company 2021
Designed and typeset by Mach 3 Solutions (www.mach3solutions.co.uk)
Cover designed by Paul Hewitt, Battlefield Design (www.battlefield-design.co.uk)

Text and images © K.W. Mitchinson 2021
Maps drawn by George Anderson © Helion & Company Limited
Front cover: Second Line TF divisional insignia: Top (left to right) 62nd (West Riding) Division, 60th (London) Division, 58th (London) Division. Bottom (left to right) 57th (West Lancashire) Division, 61st (2nd South Midland) Division, 66th (2nd East Lancashire) Division, 59th (2nd North Midland) Division.

Every reasonable effort has been made to trace copyright holders and to obtain their permission for the use of copyright material. The author and publisher apologize for any errors or omissions in this work and would be grateful if notified of any corrections that should be incorporated in future reprints or editions of this book.

ISBN 978-1-914059-95-7

British Library Cataloguing-in-Publication Data.
A catalogue record for this book is available from the British Library.

All rights reserved. No part of this publication may be reproduced, stored in a retrieval system, or transmitted, in any form, or by any means, electronic, mechanical, photocopying, recording or otherwise, without the express written consent of Helion & Company Limited.

For details of other military history titles published by Helion & Company Limited contact the above address or visit our website: http://www.helion.co.uk.

We always welcome receipt of book proposals from prospective authors.

Contents

List of Maps		iv
List of Abbreviations		v
Introduction		vii
1	Formation	15
2	The Hiatus	29
3	Trench Acclimatization	64
4	Semi-open Warfare	95
5	Offensive Operations I: Third Ypres – The Middle Weeks	122
6	Offensive Operations II: Third Ypres – The Latter Weeks	164
7	Defensive Operations I: Rearguards	185
8	Defensive Operations II: Preparations for Battle	206
9	Defensive Operations III: Battle, 21-22 March 1918	232
Conclusion		269

Appendices

I	2nd Line Division Casualties, March 1918	280
II	Origins of Other Rank Fatalities, November-December 1917	285

Bibliography	289
Index	293

List of Maps

Note. Place name spellings on contemporary trench maps can vary considerably. For example, today's Poelkapelle can appear as Poelcapelle, Poelcappelle, or Poelcappele. Similarly, the stream called the Hanebeek can appear with that spelling and also as Hanebeke on the same map. Spellings used on maps in this volume are intended to be consistent.

1	184 Brigade attacks, March-April 1917.	109
2	Third Battle of Ypres, August 1917.	137
3	Aviatik Ridge, September 1917.	157
4	Poelcapelle sector, October 1917.	175
5	Welsh Ridge, December 1917.	197
6	Ecoust-St-Mein, March 1918.	210
7	Holnon sector, March 1918.	216
8	Hargicourt sector, March 1918.	235

List of Abbreviations

Several of the regiments mentioned in the volume have the prefix 'Royal'. These include the Warwickshire, Berkshire, and Sussex. In the text the prefix is omitted but no slight is, of course, intended.

A&Q	Adjutant and Quartermaster
AA&QMG	Assistant-Adjutant and Quartermaster-General
AAG	Assistant Adjutant-General
ACI	Army Council Instruction
ADMS	Assistant-Director Medical Services
ADS	Advanced Dressing Station
ADVS	Assistant-Director Veterinary Services
AG	Adjutant-General
AOD	Army Ordnance Department
ASC	Army Supply Corps
BEF	British Expeditionary Force
Bde	Brigade
Bde Maj.	Brigade Major
Brig Gen.	Brigadier General
BGGS	Brigadier General General Staff
BGRA	Brigadier-General Royal Artillery
CCS	Casualty Clearing Station
CIGS	Chief of the Imperial General Staff
C-in-C	Commander-in-Chief
CoS	Chief of Staff
CRA	Commanding Royal Artillery
CRE	Commanding Royal Engineers
CO	Commanding Officer
DAAG	Deputy Assistant Adjutant-General
DAC	Divisional Ammunition Column
DCLI	Duke of Cornwall's Light Infantry
DMS	Director of Medical Services
DDMS	Deputy Director Medical Services
DMO	Director of Military Operations
DRS	Divisional Rest Station
F Amb	Field Ambulance

F Coy	Field Company
FOO	Forward Observation Officer
GHQ	General Headquarters
GSO(s)	General Staff Officer(s)
GO(s)C	General Officer(s) Commanding
HAG	Heavy Artillery Group
LO(s)	Liaison Officer(s)
Lt Col	Lieutenant Colonel
Lt Gen	Lieutenant General
MBS	Man Battle Stations
Maj Gen	Major General
MDS	Main Dressing Station
MG Bn	Machine Gun Battalion
MG Coy	Machine-Gun Company
MO	Medical Officer
MVS	Mobile Veterinary Section
NCO	Non-Commissioned Officer
OP	Observation Post
ORs	Other Ranks
Pdr	Pounder
PUO	Pyrexia of Unknown Origin
PoW	Prisoner(s) of War
QMG	Quartermaster-General
RAMC	Royal Army Medical Corps
RASC	Royal Army Supply Corps
RAVC	Royal Army Veterinary Corps
RE	Royal Engineers
RFA	Royal Field Artillery
RHA	Royal Horse Artillery
RO	Record Office
RSF	Royal Scots Fusiliers
SAA	Small Arms Ammunition
SB(s)	Stretcher Bearer(s)
SMLE	Short Magazine Lee Enfield
TEWT	Tactical Exercise Without Troops
TF	Territorial Force
TM	Trench Mortar
TMB	Trench Mortar Battery
WO	War Office

Introduction

In May 1916, a frustrated and aggrieved Member of Parliament, Major Claud Hamilton, decried the existence of "thousands of men" who were "perfectly unfit and of no earthly use for military service."[1] The men to whom Hamilton referred were soldiers in 2nd Line units of the Territorial Force (TF). In voicing his discontent over the poor physical state and preparedness of the 2nd Line territorials, Hamilton, a former officer in the Grenadier Guards and Royal Irish Fusiliers, was merely echoing the thoughts of many within parliament and the military. There was perhaps a degree of exaggeration in Hamilton's comments but there was also an underlying and all too disquieting truth. Criticism and anxiety of the supposed inadequate state of the 2nd Line divisions had been aired frequently in parliament and the press. Furthermore, there was also significant discontent within the ranks of the battalions and other units of the 2nd Line divisions themselves.

The 2nd Line units had begun to form in early September 1914. Many of the infantry battalions filled up swiftly with men who had not been quick enough to enlist in the 1st Line units and with others who preferred for any number of reasons to join a unit which appeared to be intended for home defence. Some 2nd Line battalions did not reach establishment until later in the year, by which time the future equipping, purpose and deployment of their divisions had become a matter of debate and even conjecture. Demonstrating ambivalence towards the divisions, the War Office preferred instead to concentrate on training and equipping the swelling New Armies. This came as no surprise to many members of the pre-war TF who had, in their opinion and experience, suffered at the hands of a War Office which had long resented the money spent on the auxiliary. A few individual units did get up to and remain at full strength but the pre-war TF as a whole never reached establishment. Furthermore, annual reports by Regular Army inspectors frequently complained of the TF's "inexperience and youth", its failure to recruit and retain suitable men, its inadequate equipment, erratic training, and its indifferent leadership. The force was frequently ridiculed in the press and condemned both by its supporters and detractors in Parliament. Because it rapidly became apparent that the War Office was deliberately restricting enlistments in the reserve TF units and was clearly favouring the New Armies, many of the men who chose to enlist in the 2nd Line probably did so in the knowledge they were joining an organization that was likely to develop into even more of a Cinderella force than its parent units.

The unsurprising result was that by the spring of 1915 a collection of units grouped loosely into divisions struggled to find instructors, accommodation for their troops, uniforms to clothe

---

1 *Hansard* Vol. 82.129, 4 May 1916.

them, and weapons with which to train. Claud Hamilton's criticism could have been taken as a cry to the War Office to take the 2nd Line TF more seriously and to grant it equality with the New Armies in the supply of equipment. Alternatively, it could have been interpreted as an appeal to put the divisions out of their misery and to absorb them into the Regular Army. This is probably the route the War Office would have preferred, but until the introduction of conscription in 1916 the TF enjoyed a privileged status. Existing regulations stipulated that TF personnel could not be transferred to other corps without their consent. In addition, it was not until the spring of 1915 that enlistment purely for home service was prohibited. When their 1st Line units deployed overseas the 2nd Line usually replaced them at their war stations but, once the parent units began to sustain casualties many 2nd Line battalions were virtually drained of their trained men. What usually remained was a small core of fewer than 100 original recruits. These men might see their battalion several times made up almost to establishment before then again being stripped by the posting of men to France or Belgium. Morale and unit cohesion suffered from this regular haemorrhage of trained men. Many of those who remained in the UK were frustrated at the manner in which they were treated by the authorities and sought postings or commissions elsewhere. Others were happy enough to spend their time on coastal defence duties away from the dangers of shot and shell.

In 1916, however, the War Office made decisions about which of the remaining thirteen 2nd Line divisions should be deployed overseas and which should be retained in the United Kingdom for home defence and as training establishments. The first of the original 14 to deploy had been 2nd Wessex, a formation so embryonic when it sailed in December 1914 to be, to paraphrase Claud Hamilton's words, of little earthly use other than to begin its training and contribute to the imperial presence in India. One division and several independent units were sent to Ireland during the Easter Rebellion; the first two 2nd Line divisions to be sent to the Western Front embarked in June. They were to be followed between six and eight months later by a further five divisions. Because they were unsustainable, one division in the UK was broken up in 1916 and another a year later. For similar reasons five others never left the British Isles. Two of these five were even allocated for a time to Eighth New Army but by the end of 1917 those still in existence in the UK underwent major reorganizations. Such was the scale of these schemes that, in the dispassionate words of the official records, "in this way [they] lost [their] territorial association."[2] This was the final dashing of hopes of those who had long dreamt of a TF Army in France composed entirely of TF divisions.[3]

Generally, little was expected of those 2nd Line divisions deployed to the Western Front. This assumption was apparently quickly confirmed by the failure of 61st (2nd South Midland) Division to capture any ground during the Fromelles debacle. In the eyes of many long term detractors of the TF, the South Midlanders' failure merely confirmed the inadequate fighting power and resolution of the auxiliary as a whole. It came as something of a surprise, therefore,

---

2   A F Becke, *Order of Battle of Divisions*, (*ORBAT*) Part 2B, (London: HMSO, 1936) p37. The territorial element was also removed from the divisions' official titles. For example, 69th (2nd East Anglian) Division became simply, 69th Division.
3   Whilst serving as C-in-C Home Forces in 1914-15, General Sir Ian Hamilton had been an early advocate of such an army. Ignoring battles fought by corps that at the time contained only one division, and including 74th (Yeomanry) Division as a TF formation, on only six occasions were battles listed in *ORBAT* Part 4 fought by a corps consisting exclusively of TF divisions.

to those who had doubted the worth of the force when a 2nd Line division captured Bullecourt. Its tumbled ruins had previously frustrated the best efforts of a nominally regular division. A further surprise came when another 2nd Line formation burst into and through the formidable defences of the Hindenburg Line in November 1917.

When in early 1918 the War Office decided to reduce the number of battalions in the divisions of the British Expeditionary Force (BEF), the 2nd Line battalions were among the obvious choices for disbandment. Later that year, two 2nd Line divisions were reduced to training cadres and then reconstituted with several imported battalions which made them mere shadows of their former selves. When the armistice came and demobilization began, the 2nd Line units were disbanded and passed into history, albeit, temporary. They had served their purpose but now, as a period of disarmament and retrenchment dawned, they disappeared as surplus to requirements.

In 1918, a former instructor at the Royal Military College who had served as the General Staff Officer Grade 1 (GSO1) of 63rd (2nd Northumbrian) Division wrote an article[4] suggesting ways by which would-be authors of possible regimental histories might prepare themselves for the task. Lieutenant Colonel Augustus Ferryman Mockler-Ferryman became something of a prolific author himself but even he, with his entirely apposite background, failed to produce a volume on a 2nd Line battalion or division. Several battalions did publish accounts of their war experience, usually written either by one of its former officers or by an established author of military affairs. These range from the volume covering 2/1st Buckingham Battalion, which is little more than a roll of honour and lists of awards, to the very detailed account of 2/6th King's Liverpool. In addition to pages of rambling purple prose and bucolic description, the volume offers full coverage of the battalion's activities as well as a list and the fate of thousands of men who served with the unit.[5] Most TF regiments, however, opted to include their 2nd Line units within the volumes primarily dedicated to their 1st Line. Naturally enough because the 1st Line usually spent far more time overseas than the 2nd Line, their accounts take up many more pages. Nevertheless, the experiences of the 2nd Line are generally covered in detail and with empathy.

It is unclear precisely when Mockler-Ferryman wrote his article but it may have preceded or have been prompted by a letter to the TF county associations from Lord Dartmouth, President of the Staffordshire County Association. Dartmouth circulated all associations suggesting they should begin gathering material in preparation for producing post-war divisional or unit histories. The results were disappointing. By April 1919, fewer than 12 associations had submitted a positive response.[6] For the time being the idea was abandoned but associations were informed that publishers Kegan Paul retained an interest in the project. Interest revived shortly afterwards and eventually nine of the fourteen 1st Line divisions had a divisional history published after the

---

4 Lt. Col. A.F. Mockler-Ferryman, 'The Collection of Material for a Regimental Record of the War', *RUSI Journal* 63.449, pp. 113-119.
5 I. Liberty, *A Record of the 2nd Bucks Battalion TF 1914-1918*, (Chesham, n.d.); C. Wurtzburg, *The History of the 2/6th Battalion 'The Kings' (Liverpool Regiment) 1914-1919*, (London: Gale & Polden, 1920)
6 Correspondence from the Council of County Associations, April 1919, Lincolnshire Co. Record Office. TA5/1.

war. Another division produced a volume which covered the greater part of its overseas service.[7] Of the seven 2nd Line divisions that deployed abroad, three produced a history.[8] That of 59th (2nd North Midland) Division is a poorly edited affair, with chapters written by several former officers who seem not to have consulted each other in what they would submit.[9] The published history of 60th (2/2nd London) adopted a conventional approach covering most of the division's experiences in three theatres, while that of 62nd (2nd West Riding) is a two volume account offering a comprehensive history of the division's existence.[10] The motivation behind the changed attitude of the county associations towards producing volumes for what amounted to a substantial proportion of 1st and 2nd Line divisional histories, lay in their fears for the perceived future of the TF. At the end of the war and pending a decision about what role, if any, it might fulfil in the post-war world, the TF was put into suspended animation. The county associations were anxious to demonstrate how essential the work of their units had been in securing victory and viewed the publication of battalion and divisional histories as the means by which their units' achievements, valour and sacrifice could be disseminated. Knowledge of what the TF had done was seen as the key to securing a relevant and practicable future for the force.

The appearance of the histories was also a contribution to the long-running debate about the use of citizen auxiliaries in the modern world. Before the outbreak of war in 1914, military journals and the national press had devoted endless columns to how an army for home defence should be recruited and trained. Supporters of selective conscription argued that only a properly trained and resourced home army would be capable of repelling an invasion or substantial raid on vulnerable coastal points. Others, including the Liberal Government which came to power in 1906, believed a volunteer army supported and supplemented by elements of the Regular Army and the Royal Navy, would be adequate for what they considered to be a remote threat. The willingness of the bulk of the TF in August 1914 to agree to overseas' service and the speed with which the county associations raised their 2nd and 3rd Lines, despite the obstacles put in their way, were cited as evidence that a TF which agreed to wider terms and conditions of service than had existed before 1916 remained essential for home security. What persisted, however, was a belief in many quarters that although the TF as a whole had done vital work and performed beyond expectations during the war, raising the 2nd Line had been an error of judgement and policy. The fact that the divisions had not gone overseas until 1916-17, and the perception that they were little better than labour or line-holding formations, fuelled the continued assumption that their men and resources would have been better applied to divisions of the

---

7 Two of the formations deployed to India in 1914. Once there they essentially ceased to have any coherent divisional existence. Interestingly, the only 1st Line division that fought in France not to produce a history was 48th (South Midland). Furthermore, despite its being the first 2nd Line division to cross to France, and one which subsequently fought in several major battles, neither did 61st (2nd South Midland) Division publish a post-war account.
8 Two of the three 2nd Line histories were published at least half a decade later than those of the 1st Line.
9 Compiled, *59th Division 1915-1918*, (Chesterfield: Wilfred Evans, 1928). A former divisional commander made the point in his Foreword that the volume was "not intended to be a history of the 59th Division." Officers from five county associations were invited to offer contributions. This presumably accounts for its rather haphazard and repetitive composition.
10 P.H .Dalbiac, *History of the 60th Division (2/2nd London)* (London: Allen & Unwin, 1927); E. Wyrall, *The Story of the 62nd (West Riding) Division 1914-1919* (London: Bodley Head, 1924).

Regular Army. This contemporary view that the 2nd Line formations were, in reality, 'second division' formations endured long after the war. The legacy was to reassert itself within the BEF of a later generation. What was different about the circumstances of 1940 rather than those of 1917, was that the re-born 2nd Line divisions had been thrown into theatre inadequately trained and ill-prepared. In 1917, the 2nd Line divisions had been in existence for over two years and although few of their men had been in training for that length of time, the formations were equipped with modern weapons and functioned under a formal divisional structure.

The object of this volume is to assess whether the 2nd Line's reputation as 'second division' formations was deserved. Since it would be impracticable to examine all of the deployed divisions' actions throughout the two years or more they fought on the Western Front, selected engagements and battles, both offensive and defensive, will be analysed through the prisms of both contemporary and modern military doctrine. This is something of an artificial means because doctrine as we understand it today was, of course, unrecognized and unknown to the soldiers of 1917-1918. It was not, in fact, until 1989 that the British Army published what could be called its first pamphlet on modern doctrine. Furthermore, as a concept, 'doctrine' can be interpreted in different ways. The generally accepted modern views are that it provides the "central ideas of an army",[11] offers a framework or set of principles upon which an army could conduct operations, and affords options and guidance rather than a set of hard and fast prescriptive rules. Current NATO definition describes it as a collection of "Fundamental principles by which the military forces guide their actions in support of their objectives. It is authoritative but requires judgement in application."[12] Although definitions vary, there is a fairly universally accepted mantra of what it is *not*: doctrine is not, and should not become, dogma.

In 1914, many British officers of the BEF travelled to France with a handbook entitled *Field Service Regulations 1909 Part I (Operations) (FSR I)* tucked into their tunic pocket.[13] Despite its title, the book was not a bible on how officers should conduct themselves or command their units. It was instead guidance gathered from past experience and earlier lessons on how they might act and react in varied circumstances. Because it was not intended to be a document that officers should follow slavishly, it was in places a somewhat vague collection of thoughts, recommendations, advice, and suggestions. Like any such volume of guidance it relied very much on expecting readers to assert their inherent common sense and instinct. There was little advice covering how joint action between cavalry, infantry and artillery might be conducted, or even how command should be exercised at different levels. Given its manner and content it could be argued that *FSR I* should not be perceived or classified as doctrine. The book was written for a tiny army of professional volunteers whose officers, as 'gentlemen', appreciated that their primary concerns were the welfare, and thus the morale of their soldiers, and the maintenance of the Empire. The army's historic small size meant that in 1914 there were few serving officers

---

11 J.F.C. Fuller's definition of 1923 in Army Doctrine Publications *Operations* (*ADP*) E-2 (Shrivenham: DCDC, 2010). Von Clausewitz, *On War*, notes: "Doctrine is a guide for anyone who wants to learn about war from books: it will light their way, ease their progress, train their judgements and help them to avoid pitfalls. Doctrine is meant to educate the minds of future commanders ... not to accompany them to the battlefields."
12 AAP-6(V) NATO Glossary of Terms and Definitions.
13 *Field Service Regulations (1909) Part II (Organization and Administration)* dealt with issues for higher commands.

who had commanded anything as large as a division let alone anything bigger. In the far-flung reaches of the Empire, unit and sub-unit commanders had been accustomed to employing their initiative and making cooperative and effective use of any resources they might have to hand. When, as in 1914, they were confronted with situations that involved the deployment of large formations which had not before worked together, coupled with problems of alliance cohesion and differences in operational cultures, *FSR I* might have been considered by some to be essential reading. The reader would not, however, have found much enlightenment on many of the problems he was now about to face.

FSR I was very much the work of the later 1914 commander of I Corps, Lieutenant General Sir Douglas Haig. As Director of Staff Duties at the War Office, Haig had based the volume on his experience, knowledge, and belief that battles fell into four stages: the advance to contact; the establishment of a firing line, in which the British would achieve fire supremacy; the assault; and the pursuit. British practice in its colonial wars had generally adhered to these elements and, while the scope and scales of the armies and battles which were later to be fought in France and Belgium were unprecedented, the principles remained essentially unchanged. Because commanders were trained to consider and be guided by these principles, rather than to adhere to them whatever the situation, they were expected to demonstrate flexibility and pragmatism. They were also expected to know their senior commander's intent but, the means of achieving that intent or those objectives were open to a generous degree of what is now understood as 'mission command'.[14]

What became recognized in the 1990s as the BEF's 'learning curve' had become evident by mid-1916. By the time of the armistice the professionals, war time volunteers and conscripts had morphed into a skilled and capable organization which had learnt from its earlier mistakes. Doctrine had evolved substantially from *FSR I* and the other publications that had existed in 1914. The lessons hard learned on the Somme had been analyzed and incorporated within a series of instructional pamphlets published from the end of 1916. Two of these, SS135: *Instructions for the Training of Divisions for Offensive Action* (December 1916) and SS143: *Instructions for the Training of Platoons for Offensive Action* (February 1917), and their several updates, will be referred to throughout the volume. They, and the other similar publications, were crucial to the improvement of the BEF's combat effectiveness particularly from the early months of 1917, the date by which the bulk of the 2nd Line divisions were deploying to France. Although the vocabulary and the concepts enshrined in the manuals are different from those in use today, they do include several significant similarities to current British and NATO doctrine.

One of Europe's most revered nineteenth century strategists, Henri Jomini, noted: "There exists a small number of fundamental principles of war, which may not be deviated from without danger, and the application of which…has been in all times crowned with glory."[15] Modern doctrine has absorbed those fundamentals into ten contemporary Principles of War. Closely associated with this understanding of the need to consider these fundamentals is what is known as Fighting Power. This concept comprises three components: the conceptual, the physical, and the moral. Respectively, these cover the ideas of how to operate and fight; the means to operate and fight; and the ability to get people to operate and fight. Overall, therefore, they detail

---

14   The German word *auftragstaktik* is also widely employed.
15   H. Jomini, *The Art of War* (London: Greenhill Books, 1992)

current doctrine, emphasize the need to understand the type and character of any given conflict, stress how lessons should and could be learned, outline the requirement for sufficient manpower, equipment, and training, the need for adequate means to sustain the personnel, and also the development and understanding of moral cohesion and the ethical foundations on which the armed forces operate. These components all contribute to the British Army's capstone doctrine known as the Manoeuvrist Approach. This is a concept aimed first at understanding, and then targeting and ultimately destroying the three components of an enemy's fighting power. The ways and means of achieving this desired end are a combination of the Principles of War and the fundamental characteristics of the Manoeuvrist Approach. Thus, any operation will involve such essential elements as: concentration of force, understanding the situation, selection and maintenance of the aim, seizing and holding the initiative, breaking the enemy's cohesion and will (while at the same time protecting those of your own forces), offensive action, surprise, flexibility, and sustainability.

Corps and divisional commanders of the BEF might not have recognized all of the current terms but would certainly have appreciated what they represent. Deception, surprise, maintaining morale, applying strength against weakness, and ensuring adequate sustainment of your force have been apparent since earliest times. The advent of industrialized war, however, created additional problems of logistics and supply. All but one of the 2nd Line TF divisions deployed to the Western Front missed the worst of the Somme fighting but all were part of the gradual improvement in the BEF's fighting power and operational capability. By examining some of the actions in which they were engaged, certain conclusions can be drawn about the quality of the divisions' performances.

By the time the 2nd Line divisions were fully operational on the Western Front, the BEF's formations were organized into armies and corps. This study will largely ignore the influence of the army commanders on the divisions' activities but will of necessity often consider the role and influence of the corps level. Today, there is much debate about where the division between the operational and tactical levels of warfare lies, and even if the operational level does still exist. Although the idea was unknown at the time, most modern analysts would agree that during the Great War the operational level generally functioned at army and corps rather than at divisional levels. Important as corps commanders and staffs were, their influence on how the corps' component divisions performed varied both between the many corps, and over the course of the war. The discussion here will, therefore, concentrate primarily on how the individual divisions and their component infantry brigades and supporting arms performed. Where appropriate the analysis will sometimes be pitched at the operational level – how the forces were *directed* in an engagement, as well as at the tactical level – how the forces were *employed* in the action. There will also be some brief discussion of the effect those outcomes had on the military-strategic level of warfare.[16]

Although the divisional commander worked within the restrictions of the corps structure, he retained a reasonable degree of freedom to decide how and which units he would use to complete an operation ordered from higher authority. These were usually integrated or possibly joint operations in that they involved artillery, infantry and engineers, and frequently required

---

16 The doctrine of some European countries does not recognize the military-strategic level of warfare. Those states acknowledge only the strategic, operational, and tactical levels.

cooperation with neighbouring divisions. There was also increasingly regular involvement of the air component. The commander, therefore, had not only to identify what he intended his forces to achieve but also to recognize the boundaries or the restrictions imposed upon him by the needs of the particular action and his available capability. He had to manage a substantial number of men and their supporting equipment in such a way as to bring them to bear on an enemy who may well have been expecting them, who often enjoyed the protection of extensive defensive works and associated fire power, and who usually had the terrain in his favour. By forceful and possibly inspirational leadership, the commander had to impress on his subordinates at all levels the point of the mission and what he expected of them. Combat effectiveness, which is usually understood to mean the ability to achieve a mission with fewer casualties than has been inflicted on the enemy, can be defined and explained in several ways. Ultimately, however, success depends on a calculated assessment of the mission's inherent risks and the rational application and employment of units and sub-units in such a way as to maximize your own fighting power at the expense of your opponent's.

On deployment, all divisional commanders faced the same challenges but if there was a perception that the fighting power of 2nd Line formations was not the equal of other divisions, the commanders, their subordinates, and their men perhaps felt they had a point to prove. Their colleagues in the 1st Line had been in a similar position during the first years of the war and had largely proved their critics wrong. The strategy and tactics employed by the British and Dominion forces during the attritional battles of 1915-16 had offered few opportunities for any of the regular, Kitchener, or TF divisions really to make a name for themselves. Nonetheless, those 1st Line TF units which had sailed independently of their divisions and subsequently attached to Regular Army divisions were generally thought to have performed well in support of their regular hosts. When the deploying 2nd Line TF divisions took to the field in early 1917 there certainly were doubts, however, as to whether their fighting power and combat effectiveness would ever prove to be the equal of the more experienced divisions.

1

Formation

The 2nd Line TF was conceived as a war time necessity. Immediately it was born, however, several significant handicaps quickly became apparent. On 7 August 1914, Kitchener called for 100,000 men to enlist in the New Army; this was followed two weeks later by the call for a second 100,000. The Secretary of State predicted that the war would last considerably longer than a few months and decided to raise a completely new army untainted by the poor reputation and limiting terms of service of the TF. Having spent most of his service life overseas Kitchener had little understanding of, and empathy with, the TF. He believed it to be inherently inefficient and incapable of providing the foundations upon which a full continental army could be built and maintained. Naturally enough many in the TF disagreed profoundly with Kitchener's attitude. Nonetheless, in a spirit of patriotism they agreed to assist the War Office in raising the New Armies.[1] Kitchener's first call for volunteers was to have little effect on the 1st Line units currently in the process of reaching establishment but his second and subsequent calls for men to enlist, followed quickly by the creation of the locally-based Pals battalions, had a direct impact on recruiting for the TF's Reserve Battalions.

In addition to its anti-invasion role and as a force to defend against raids on vulnerable points and ports, Kitchener initially intended to use the TF to replace Regular Army garrisons in the Empire brought home for service in France. In mid-August he asked members of the TF to declare whether they were prepared to accept Imperial Service (IS) and serve abroad. Results varied between units but once the majority of soldiers had agreed to the extension of their terms of service, Kitchener began deploying several of the existing units and formations from their war stations. In September, 1 London Brigade was despatched to Malta and the East Lancashire Division left for Egypt. In October, the Wessex and Home Counties Divisions sailed for India.

On the same day as Kitchener appealed for the first 100,000 men he despatched a letter to the lords lieutenant who, in addition to their other duties, acted as presidents of the TF county associations. The Secretary of State's letter decreed that those TF units that had made themselves available for foreign service could recruit over establishment but in those where insufficient numbers had agreed to IS, excess men could not be recruited until the 100,000 regulars

---

1 After the war, criticism of Kitchener's failure to utilize the existing system was offered more openly. See, for example, C.H. Dudley Ward, *Regimental Records of The Royal Welch Fusiliers 1914-1918* (London: Forster Groom, 1928),Vol. III, p.25.

called for had been signed up. This was followed a week later by a further letter that instructed associations to divide their units into home and foreign service sections. The next day another letter arrived asking those associations whose original units had as a whole volunteered for foreign service to raise new units for home service (HS). This was not quite the start of the 2nd Line but a few days later another circular brought its formation a step closer. Units in which 80 percent had volunteered for IS were allowed to recruit up to overseas establishment and any surplus men would then form the nucleus of a new unit that would be completed with HS men. The final move came on 31 August when authorization was granted to units where 60 percent of the original men had agreed to IS to form a reserve unit. This reserve unit was to be raised and trained at the drill hall of the original unit under the supervision of a TF officer and a member of the permanent staff withdrawn from the parent. The unit was supposedly to be composed of both IS and HS men and was to replace the original – or what was to became known as the 1st Line – at its war station when the parent unit left for overseas. The dual function of the reserve unit was thus to provide a force for home defence and also to supply drafts to its IS unit. The new units were initially to be known as 'Reserve' but after several months and several alterations, they became officially the '2nd Line'.[2]

Not all county associations were immediately enthused with the idea of forming a 2nd Line. In September, the East Lancashire Association pointed out the grave difficulties to be overcome in creating and clothing new units. Owing to the shortages its home service men were already surrendering their kit in favour of those who had agreed to go overseas. Furthermore, the association claimed there was little point in recruiting a 2nd Line because not only would its units have no kit but there were also no officers and instructors available to command and train them.[3] In some respects it could be argued that the recruiting restrictions worked to the advantage of those associations which foresaw the immense difficulties they would encounter: Cambridgeshire, for example, initially refused to accept 17 year olds even for HS, a decision that may have been based on a realization that it would be unable to cope with the expected influx of recruits.[4] Other units that usually comprised divisional rather than brigaded troops were also restricted. They could recruit only to 60 percent of establishment, while the artillery brigades were restricted to a mere 25 percent. East Lancashire recorded that its 2nd Line artillery quota was easily filled immediately by gunners of its 1st Line brigades who had not sailed with the division to Egypt.[5]

Because the War Office had not yet specified that reserve units should only accept men who had agreed to IS, the future and eventual function of the 2nd Line remained muddied. In Kitchener's view the TF was an existing, albeit ill-equipped and indifferently trained force that could be utilized until his New Armies were ready for the field. It is likely that he foresaw their eventual use in France but it was not until the first engagements had taken place around Mons, followed swiftly by the retreat towards the Marne, that he began to consider their possible rapid deployment to the Continent. Despite an assurance that 1st Line units would not be deployed

---

2   The adoption of the title of '1st Line', '2nd Line' and '3rd Line' was not officially enacted until February 1915.
3   Manchester RO, M73/3/6, 11 Sep.1914.
4   Cambridgeshire RO, R.68/11, 7 Oct.1914. Existing TF regulations allowed for the enlistment of 17 year olds.
5   Manchester RO, M73/2/2, 6 Nov.1914.

abroad until their 2nd Line were up to establishment and fully trained, in September individual units began to cross the Channel independently of their division. As they departed, their under strength, very largely untrained and sparingly equipped 2nd Line unit usually replaced them at their war station.

There had long been an expectation that the TF would be allowed a six-month post-mobilization period during which it would reach establishment and complete its training. The TF's 14 divisions had been designated either as Local Force or Central Force formations. At their war stations, Local Force units were to confront the invader on or close to the beaches: the Central Force divisions would, meanwhile, march or be transported to support the Local Forces. If their 1st Line divisions deployed overseas, the 2nd Line units were to adopt the home defence role previously undertaken by their parent formation. When, however, events in France and Belgium had reduced the BEF and the number of reservists able to reinforce it to alarmingly low levels, the TF's battalions, batteries, field companies, field ambulances and yeomanry regiments were increasingly deployed to the Western Front. They were sent to plug the gaps and hold the line until the New Armies were trained and equipped. In other words, to Kitchener the TF was useful but, essentially, expendable.

It was quickly apparent that Kitchener did not want the TF to compete seriously with the New Armies for personnel, training grounds, equipment and kit. The TF could fulfil a vital, albeit temporary, role but once it had been deployed its battalions were to be kept deliberately under strength and recruitment to its feeder units restricted. When it had served its purpose of keeping a British presence on the Continent and contributing what military strength it could in support of the French, the TF would be superseded by the New Army divisions. When that point was reached, the TF would cease to be important or even worth retaining in its existing form. The opportunity would thus be created to absorb the TF, with its limiting terms of service, within a greater Regular Army. To emphasize his lack of faith in the TF's capability of attaining any real efficiency or viability as a permanent fighting force, Kitchener decreed that 2nd Line battalions could only recruit to 50 percent of establishment. The figure was not to be raised to 100 percent until early 1915.[6]

The limitations placed on recruiting meant that many men who wanted to join the territorials were compelled to enlist elsewhere. If they had queued at their local drill hall only to be told the battalion or unit was full, many had simply, but with regret, walked down the road to enlist at the town hall or other building currently occupied by recruiting teams of the Regular Army. Others became bored with waiting in queues at one battalion's HQ and joined the unit whose drill hall queues were shorter.[7] Many who wished but failed to join the London Scots' Reserve Battalion travelled to Bedford where the newly-arrived Highland Division was openly recruiting.[8] A significant number of men who had been frustrated in their wish to join their local territorial unit wrote to COs asking whether their names might stay on a reserve list. Although many of these had since enlisted in the New Army, the men requested that when gaps appeared in the TF unit they would be permitted to transfer across.[9] The War Office was aware of this trend and issued several circulars asking county associations not to form waiting lists

6   Becke, *ORBAT*, p.6.
7   O .Bailey & H. Hollier, '*The Kensingtons*', *13th London Regiment* (London: OCA, 1936), pp.210-11.
8   J.H. Lindsay, *The London Scottish in the Great War* (London: HQ, 1925) p.225.
9   See, for example, *Hansard*, Vol. 68.667, 20 Nov.1914

but to urge would-be recruits to join any unit that needed filling, irrespective of whether it was Regular Army or TF. There are a few reports of men who insisted that if they could not join a TF unit they would not enlist at all, but undoubtedly a number of men did do as the War Office wished.[10] The result was that an unknown number of recruits who might have formed an early and larger nucleus of what would have become a 2nd Line were lost to the TF. Yet, the number who did actually relinquish their ambition of joining a TF battalion or who agreed to transfer from the TF to a regular unit was probably quite small. In March 1915, the War Office decided to abandon the attempt at persuasion and decreed "no further action" was to be taken.[11]

The motivations driving men to enlist in the army in those first weeks of war are well known. Those who chose to join the TF, however, faced several disadvantages in addition to those concerning kit and equipment. Wages paid to TF specialists were lower than those awarded to recruits in the New Army. For example, farriers, wheelwrights, telegraphists and drivers in the New Army were all paid above the rate given to TF personnel with the same skill. This discrimination also applied to those doctors and veterinaries that elected to join the TF rather than the Regular Army. In view of these disadvantages, especially when the state's publicity was encouraging them to choose the Regular Army, it is perhaps surprising that many men still preferred to join the TF. There were several attempts to draw attention to the inequalities but they were generally explained away as being necessary for recruitment purposes or as unintentional anomalies that would be rectified in time. For obvious reasons government spokesmen in parliament, especially Harold Tennant, the Under-Secretary of State, could not publically deride the TF and its terms of service, but did little to remove the existing anomalies. While fully aware and apparently supportive of the War Office's decision to promote the New Armies over the TF, Tennant could not publically afford to alienate the county associations. He regularly thanked the associations for the work they were doing in helping to raise the Kitchener Armies and frequently rebutted accusations that the government was decrying the TF. He praised the men and the associations and tried to reassure the doubters that the TF was appreciated and was being treated no differently from the New Armies.[12]

The New Armies did possess a lure and attraction for many thousands of men. By the time their recruitment campaign swung into high gear, and also as a result of the restrictions imposed on TF recruitment, something like three men joined the New Armies for every one recruit who opted for the TF. The principal reasons behind the individual's decision to join a TF rather than a Kitchener unit probably had more to do with local and provincial loyalty and sentiment than with serving king and county. Although in pre-war years the TF as a whole had frequently been derided by officialdom, local populaces were usually proud of their battalion. It paraded on civic occasions, its drill halls were part of the local landscape, its band often played in the local park and was even available for private hire. Membership of the TF and the commitment it entailed might not have been attractive to young married men with growing families but the battalion or battery had become part of local society and culture. Units were also, of course, 'Pals' units in

10 *Hansard*, Vol. 68.665, 20 Nov 1915.
11 TNA WO 70/49721: 26 Mar.1915. Several battalions are known to have opened a waiting list for their 2nd Line. For example, when 2/5th Notts & Derby was full, despite having just despatched 124 men to its 1st Line, it announced names would be kept in reserve. Derbyshire RO, D530/1/2, 9 Nov.1914.
12 For example, *Hansard*, Vol.68.302, 16 Nov.1914; Vol. 69.289-90, 8 Feb.1915.

all but name. In the same way as the Rifle Volunteer units before them, TF units had long been filled by men from the same factory, mill, office, railway company, landed estate, and borough work force who wanted to serve together. The eight companies within a battalion had often been divided by social class, with student teachers in one, office clerks in another, and manual workers in a third. In other battalions, such as several units of the London Regiment, all members were drawn from the same social class or occupation. These traditions continued into the war time period and are apparent in the formation of 2nd Line units. For its Reserve Battalion the London Rifle Brigade, for example, continued to accept only men who were prepared to pay a subscription and who were of the clerical class. The CO of 2/7th Middlesex recalled that the essential and "first thing was to get a good 'tone'" and promptly accepted 115 elementary school masters who wanted to enlist *en masse*.[13] Several other battalions, too, continued their tradition of dividing their men into companies of manual and non-manual workers.

Despite the restrictions and disadvantages many 2nd Line battalions filled quickly: 2/12th London recorded it had reached establishment in a "remarkably short time"; 2/6th London claimed to have been "immediately overwhelmed" by recruits; 2/4th London enlisted 500 in 10 days; 2/10th Manchester reported 800 recruits in three days; 2/5th Loyal North Lancashire was up to strength in a week.[14] Many of the young men hastening to their local drill halls would have been inspired to join by the mass recruiting rallies taking place across the country. That addressed by Lloyd George in the Queen's Hall was typical of many. The Chancellor of the Exchequer urged young men to seize the "glow and thrill" of sacrifice and predicted a future society where the class divide would all but disappear and where the "great flood of luxury and sloth which had submerged the land" would be swept away.[15] To cope with the influx of new recruits the War Office instructed TF units at their war stations to send back up to four officers from the 1st Line to their HQ. The more fortunate battalions also managed to detach some of their permanent staff to assist in the process but not all battalions initially attracted huge numbers of new members. The four battalions of the Manchester Brigade reported uptake as "slow" with a total of only 700 men enlisting in the first two weeks. The two Worcestershire battalions needed three weeks to reach establishment, and 2/5th Sherwood Foresters had barely reached 50 percent strength after a month. In contrast, 2/6th West Yorkshire was reported to have signed up 1,500 men by the end of November. If this figure was accurate, the battalion had clearly broken the regulations.[16]

The type of man enlisting in their local 2nd Line battalion thus generally mirrored those who had traditionally joined the pre-war unit: 2/23rd London reported that "virtually all" of its recruits came from Clapham or Battersea; 2/7th and 2/8th Lancashire Fusiliers were largely filled, as were their parent battalions, by employees of Salford Corporation and with dockers from Trafford Park. Occasionally units' September recruits came from a social background which differed from the traditional member. The Civil Service Rifles' 2nd Line battalion noted

---

13 E. Wyrall, *The Die-Hards in the Great War* (London: Harrison, 1926), p.70.
14 Becke, *ORBAT*, p.81. On 22 October, 2/1st Middlesex Brigade paraded with 114 officers and 4,038 other ranks (ORs)
15 Lloyd George's published *Appeal to the Nation*, 19 Sept.1914
16 Becke, *ORBAT*, p.46. Although the battalion's 3rd Line was not officially created until 1915, it is possible 2/6th West Yorks was anticipating an earlier formation and recruited in excess in order to establish a nucleus.

a number of recruits reportedly wearing cloth caps, an adornment that was "not expected in the 1st Battalion" while, in a spirit of equalitarianism, 2/6th King's felt compelled to "discourage" a portion of its men from wearing bowler hats on parade.

Most of the recruits do seem to have come from their immediate locality although there is some evidence to suggest that groups of men who were working away from home enlisted together in their workplace's battalion. As in pre-war days there were occasional disputes between battalions within the same association and also between county associations about the right to recruit outside their usual catchment areas. North Yorkshire Association ordered 2/5th Green Howards to cease recruiting within 2/4th Battalion's area, and the Derbyshire Association wrote to the West Riding Association telling it to stop recruiting inside Derbyshire.[17] The East Lancashire Association went so far as to complain to the War Office when the Gordon Highlanders and Royal Scots sent recruiting teams to Manchester. The Scots refused to desist, insisting they did not need the permission of the local association to operate within the Manchester area. About 350 Mancunians were reported to have signed up for the Seaforth Highlanders in one day alone. The East Lancashire Association responded by noting that it did not object to the Scots recruiting in the city if the recruits were signing up for Scottish battalions of the Regular Army but its Chairman did, however, believe that, "If our force is to be a proper Territorial force, it should be drawn from local areas."[18] It was not until early 1915 that associations were instructed not to recruit in another's area without permission.[19]

Whichever style of hat the recruits to the two Leicestershire 2nd Line battalions were wearing was not noted, but the association was almost euphoric in praise of the type of man enlisting. The class of recruit was described as "wonderful", the numbers were "more than adequate", and there was an "unfailing supply" of men seeking commissions.[20] This obvious satisfaction with the way the battalions were filling was in contrast to that expressed by the Lincolnshire Association. Its committee felt criticism of the lower numbers in its two 2nd Line battalions (which served in the same brigade as the two Leicestershire battalions) was unwarranted. The committee pointed out that a large proportion of Lincolnshire men had already joined the navy and Royal Marines. Furthermore, Kitchener, it was claimed, had said that men working with horses, and fishermen, should not enlist. Another reason offered in explanation was that because Lincoln had not had a regiment based in the city for 50 years, "many people had never seen one" and consequently knew little of the army.[21] The report went on to emphasize the inequality built into the system, sentiments that would have been echoed by many other associations. It criticized the monetary rewards given to Regular Army recruiting teams for every man they signed up, it condemned the inequality in the height qualification that effectively prohibited TF bantam battalions, and opposed as unfair the practice which, under the terms of the existing Parliamentary Recruiting

---

17   North Yorkshire RO, NG/TA Mic.2196, 30 Dec.1914; Derbyshire RO, D530/1/2, 29 Mar.1915
18   Manchester RO, M73/3/6, 22 Jan.1915. In a reversal of roles, Captain Fairrie of the Liverpool Scots was sent to Edinburgh to sign up recruits for the 2nd Line. He apparently had "no difficulty in finding men." A.M. McGilchrist, *The Liverpool Scottish 1900-1919* (Liverpool: Henry Young & Sons, 1930) pp.190-91
19   TNA. WO70/48.640, 25 Feb.1915.
20   Leicestershire RO, DE819/1, 21 Sep.1914.
21   The two regular battalions of the Lincolnshire Regiment may have been elsewhere in the UK and overseas, but Lincoln housed the HQ of both the Lincolnshire Yeomanry and 4/Lincolnshire TF.

Scheme, sent eligible recruits directly to the Regular Army Recruiting Office.[22] Given the restrictions and the national propaganda campaign endorsed by the government for the New Armies, it is hardly surprising that some battalions did not fill as quickly as others. There is also evidence to suggest that some battalions were seen as outright competitors by their own 1st Line. Allegations were made that when 1st Line units were filled, their COs were making no attempt to instruct or persuade the disappointed men to enlist in the 2nd Line units.[23]

The 2nd Line TF attracted those men who, for whatever reasons, decided they wanted to demonstrate their patriotism and serve, but not necessarily overseas. In the febrile atmosphere of the war's early months there was much confusion over how many recruits had signed purely for home service. In September, official figures recorded that, for example, one 2nd Line London battalion had 695 recruits, all of whom had signed for IS; one battalion of the Manchester Regiment had 212 in its 2nd Line, all of whom had signed for HS. Of the total strength given for TF infantry battalions, 28 percent had signed for HS and 72 percent had opted for IS. Although official policy publically opposed the practice, it is evident some battalions stipulated that they would only enlist men who opted for IS. How widespread this practice was is unclear but in the infantry the proportion of HS and IS men had changed little by December.[24] Of the TF's infantry strength of almost 340,000, 70 percent had signed for IS and 30 percent for HS. The percentages for the Royal Field Artillery (RFA) and yeomanry regiments were a little more weighted towards IS.[25] Because the role of the 2nd Line was to defend the homeland as well as to provide drafts, the War Office did not seem unduly perturbed at this stage about the numbers signing for HS. But, if the proposed role were to change, and the 2nd Line units themselves were to be posted overseas, there would clearly have to be a rebalancing.

By early October, instructions had been issued about the grouping of 2nd Line units into brigades and divisions. Some tentative decisions had also been made about where those formations would train. Arrangements for the provision of staffs for the divisions and brigades were made in late November but it was left to the discretion of the GOsC as to where within a specified district the battalions and the supporting arms should be billeted and assembled. The already acute shortage of camp accommodation resulted in the War Office specifying that troops should be housed in billets. Essentially this meant that the War Office, overwhelmed by the response to the call for the New Armies, abdicated responsibility for providing any accommodation for the 2nd Line TF. The speed by which the various units would be able to concentrate within a larger formation thus depended on the availability of billets that the county associations or the formations' staffs could provide. The 2nd Line was to enjoy no privileges and unless a unit could move to its 1st Line's vacated war station the men lived at home, in the drill hall, or in any nearby rented building. The outbuildings of its CO's farm were occupied by 2/4th Berkshire and 2/4th London was given the run of two large mansions and their extensive

---

22 Lincolnshire RO, TA1/1, 18 Dec.1914.
23 TNA WO 955462, 2/7th Durham Light Infantry (DLI) Sep.1914.
24 Becke, *ORBAT*, Part 2, p.46 states the West Riding Division only accepted recruits who were prepared to sign for IS.
25 In December, the figures were 88 percent for IS in the yeomanry and 82 percent in the RFA for IS. TNA WO 114/43.

grounds to the north of the capital.[26] At first, those units which had to disperse their men in private houses were generally greeted by the householders with open arms and warm hospitality but, after a succession of battalions had passed through and the initial novelty had worn thin, the welcome could become somewhat cooler. By the time 2/4th Cameron Highlanders reached Norwich the local citizenry had had enough of billeted troops. The police were called to several streets where householders refused to accept a further compulsory allocation of soldiers.[27] The scattering of personnel did little to enhance unit *esprit a*nd cohesion and made the task of the newly appointed GOsC and their staff considerably more difficult. Yet, communal messing was not always an effective panacea. The historian of one battalion considered that even having secured an "early hold on the men, discipline did not come easily." This particular battalion's men were from "a good class… intelligent and quick to learn" which, in itself, created challenges for the officers. The writer ruefully recalled "one can remember the difficulty of obtaining silence when the orderly officer came round at meals asking, 'any complaints?'"[28] Whatever the state of discipline in a unit, one thing that all battalions did have in common was the almost complete lack of men with military experience. As one CO later remarked: "They were novices who were as keen as they were innocent of the military art.'[29]

The actual formation of the fourteen 2nd Line divisions was staggered over a period of seven months. In comparison, the 18 divisions of the first three Kitchener Armies were formed within two months of the declaration of war. Owing to the substantial strengths of several of its battalions, when it formed in early October some of the infantry of 2/2nd London Division was compelled to concentrate at the White City. The only other division to become officially formed in October was 2nd Wessex. Its units were largely raised after their parent battalions had left for India on 9 October; the 2nd Line division was created almost immediately afterwards. In December, and much reduced in establishment, the 2nd Line division also left for India. The 2nd Line division of the other 1st Line formation that had gone to India in October, the Home Counties Division, was not officially created until November 1914. Some of its units had begun recruiting in September while others did not begin to do so until the 1st Line division had sailed. In the same way as those infantry and gunners of 1st Wessex Division who had been left behind, a significant number of officers and men of 1st Home Counties Division were transferred to their 2nd Line. The 2nd Line Home Counties Division was destined never to cross to France, a fate that also befell another November- raised division, 2nd East Anglian.[30] The remaining three divisions which formed during November 1914 were all later to fight on the Western Front. As the 1st Line divisions of 2nd West Lancashire and 2/1st London had both been severely plundered to provide battalions and supporting units for other divisions it is unsurprising that these two 2nd Line formations received an early endorsement. Similarly, 2nd East Lancashire's 1st Line had sailed for Egypt in September and had already called for signifi-

---

26 F. Petrie, *The Royal Berkshire Regiment 1914-1918*, Vol. II (Reading: The Barracks, 1925), p.178; Compiled, *The History of the Old 2/4th (City of London) Battalion the London Regiment* (London: Westminster Press, 1919), p.7.
27 Compiled, *Historical Records of the Queen's Own Cameron Highlanders*, Vol.III (London: Blackwood & Sons, 1931), p.457.
28 Compiled, *21st London*, p.133.
29 Wyrall, *The Die-Hards*, p.71.
30 Together with 53rd (Welsh), 54th (East Anglian) Division was the last of the 1st Line TF divisions to go abroad. They both sailed for Gallipoli in July 1915.

cant numbers of drafts by the time the 2nd Line division was officially formed. Much of 2/1st London Division was able to occupy the war stations of its 1st Line units vacated when they left for France but the intended war stations for the 1st Line East and West Lancashire Divisions had been Ireland. Kitchener had decided in August not to send TF units to Ireland so their 2nd Line units could not now go to their 1st Lines' war stations. With so much of the available land in England having already been occupied by the New Armies, the East and West Lancashire 2nd Line units were initially scattered over a considerable area.

The first 2nd Line division to reach France, 2nd South Midland, was formed in January 1915, at the same time as 2nd North Midland. Two divisions that were eventually to lose their territorial affiliations, 2nd Highland and 2nd Welsh, were also created in that month, but 2nd West Riding, the one remaining of the seven divisions that were to fight on the Western Front, was not formed until February. During the period of their formation, the 14 divisions faced intense competition not only for kit but also for senior officers to command them. Taking only infantry divisions into consideration, by February 1915, 11 Regular Army, fourteen 1st Line TF, and 18 New Army divisions had been formed or assembled. Ignoring the substantial turnover of senior officers, many of whom stayed in command for very short periods, this meant that a minimum of 43 GOsC divisions, GSO1s, AA&QMGs, CRAs and CREs, and 172 GOsC infantry brigades had to be found and appointed. It is hardly surprising, therefore, to discover that the 2nd Line division were to be staffed and commanded by some quite elderly gentlemen.

Until permanent commanders arrived, four brigadier generals were appointed temporary acting GOsC divisions of the 2nd Line formations. Three of these had been GOsC brigades of 1st Line units. The temporary tenure of one of them, Adam of 2nd West Lancashire Division was eventually to last for five months.[31] These four brigadier generals were in their late forties or early fifties whereas seven of the permanent appointees had been brought out of retirement. Three of these officers had opted for retirement at least a decade before war was declared. At 52, the youngest permanent appointee was Stockwell. He was promoted from GOC Gordon Brigade in the Highland Division to become GOC 2nd Highland. Four of the GOsC were in their sixties, with two being in their seventies. MacCall of 2nd North Midland was 72 and Cavaye of 2nd East Anglian was two years younger. Given the rarity of such officers, and the consequent value placed upon them, it is a perhaps surprising that four of the 14 were Staff College graduates. Five of the total, and not all of the four Staff College graduates, had spent much their army careers in staff jobs in South Africa and India. Only three of the 14 are definitely known to have had non-infantry backgrounds, two having been GOsC of a TF infantry brigade before the war and one having held the same position in a brigade of militia. The two most experienced at senior command, and both in their mid-fifties, were Fry of 2/1st London, and Young of 2nd Home Counties Divisions. Fry, of the West Yorkshire Regiment, had served as adjutant to a Volunteer regiment in Burma and in 1908 was appointed as the first GOC of the TF East Lancashire Division. He then spent two years as Deputy Director General of the TF before being appointed GOC 1st London Division in 1912. He became GOC 2/1st London Division in 1915 when the 1st Line formation was broken up. Young had been a brigade

---

31   Frederick Adam had been a brigade commander in Malta before the war. He had apparently been earmarked for command of a division about to leave for France when he was involved in a riding accident. It seems he was unable to go overseas and retired in October 1915. He was awarded the honorary rank of major general in 1917. Wurtzburg, *2/6th King's*, p.6.

commander in India as well as Assistant Adjutant General before being appointed to command of the Home Counties Division. He took the division to India in 1914 but returned immediately to take command of its 2nd Line.

There was considerable experience amongst these largely 'dug out' GOsC, but much of it was gained during a previous era of warfare. Only one of the 14 was to go on to another senior position after his spell as GOC. These elderly men were not appointed, however, to take their divisions overseas but because several of them had some knowledge of working with volunteer auxiliaries and because there were few other available men of suitable rank. Those who might have been better suited had been appointed elsewhere. These first GOsC were there to develop the new divisions as efficiently as circumstances would allow and to get them into some sort of shape as personnel, kit, and training facilities became available. The average length of time they were retained in command was 13 months. This suggested that the authorities were not expecting to deploy the 2nd Line overseas for some considerable time, and also confirmed the divisions would remain at the bottom of the priority list for equipment. If their period in command is compared to those of the first GOsC divisions of the Second and Third New Armies which formed in September 1914, a significant difference becomes apparent. These GOsCs were also dug outs but their tenure was never intended to be lengthy. With the exception of two of the 12 GOsC, their average time in command was only six months.[32] They were clearly appointed to get the divisions started and then to make way when more suitable long term candidates became available. The second GOsC of those 10 divisions were to remain in command on average for almost 17 months. By the time the divisions of Fourth and Fifth New Armies were created between May and September 1915, war-experienced Regular Army battalion and brigade commanders of 1914 were available for promotion. Theirs were more considered appointments and even though two of the 12 had to relinquish command after only two months, the average period of 13 of those first GOC was almost 13 months.[33]

The newly appointed GOsC divisions of the 2nd Line, especially those who had been brought from retirement, would have relied heavily on their General Staff Officers for guidance and assistance. It is unknown how quickly the GSO2s and GSO3s were appointed or, indeed, how quickly the artillery and infantry brigades received their brigade majors and staff captains. The latter position could often be filled by a member of the TF but the more senior staff positions were the preserve of regular officers. Seven of the 13 divisions had a number of 'acting' GSO1s, usually captains who were appointed until a permanent officer could be a found. Fifteen individuals spent time in the acting capacity, five of whom had attended Staff College and eight brought from retirement. Several of these temporary appointees had previously worked with the auxiliaries and about 50 percent of them had had war time experience in South Africa and elsewhere. They usually served for a matter of weeks before moving to another post. The total period for which a division could thus have no permanent appointee could be substantial: 2nd West Lancashire, for example, was without for nine months, 2nd Welsh eight, and 2nd East Anglian seven months.

32 For statistical reasons Maj. Gen. Babington (23rd Division) and Maj. Gen. MacKenzie-Kennedy (26th Division) have been excluded. These two men remained in command for an unusually long and untypical period of 49 and 27 months respectively.
33 Maj. Gen. Lawford (41st Division) has been excluded from these calculations because he remained in command for the exceptionally long period of 42 months.

There is no pattern discernible in the length of tenure of the first permanent GSO1s. Only one was to hold office for over 12 months and just four in total reached double figures in terms of months. Of the 12 officers positively identified, none was older than 55 and eight had attended Staff College. That more than 50 percent of these youngish men had passed Staff College and were appointed to the TF 2nd Line rather than to one of the burgeoning number of Regular Army divisions is remarkable. Only two are known to have been brought from retirement, and two were probably Indian Army officers on home leave in the summer of 1914 and retained by the War Office for service in the UK. Unusually, one of the 12 was the holder of the Territorial Decoration, and another the Victoria Cross.[34] One was the former GSO1 of 1st London Division who, like Major General Fry and several of that formation's senior officers were posted to 2/1st London when their division was broken up. Within the ranks as a whole there was a significance degree of administrative, overseas, and war experience. This knowledge would certainly have aided the GOC division in raising and shaping the embryonic divisions. Their qualifications and experience suggest they were not appointed because they were unfit or unsuitable for posts with Regular Army divisions. They were possibly placed with the 2nd Line for a relatively short period in order to get the formation and the paperwork underway before, as four of them certainly were, being posted to a more prestigious appointment.

Most divisions were similarly slow in being able to appoint permanent AA&QMGs. Nine of the 13 divisions waited from between two weeks and eight months before a candidate was found. Of the 12 individuals who served in an acting capacity, seven had been brought from retirement. One, Monteith of 2nd Highland Division, served simultaneously as both GSO1 and AA&QMG for two weeks; another three initially appointed in an acting capacity were later promoted and made permanent. Of the 12 identified first permanent appointments, nine had been retired and two had passed Staff College. The oldest was 61, with most of the remainder being in their later fifties. Information about their experience is sketchy but two at least are known to have spent much of their army career in administrative posts. It is likely, however, that all of the permanent appointees had followed a similar career route. To them fell the thankless and almost impossible tasks of providing the troops with accommodation, rations, and clothing. Despite the complexity and difficulty of their responsibilities, the tenure of these first appointments was usually substantial. Three remained for under five months[35] but the others served an average period of 16 months. The longest service was that of Mathewes, one of the two Indian Army officers in the first group of appointees. He remained as AA&QMG of 2nd Lowland Division for 32 months.

While the AA&QMGs were liaising with county associations, manufacturers and the Army Clothing Department in the attempt to obtain whatever equipment might be available, the infantry brigadiers were trying to turn their disparate collection of recruits into something resembling an army. Sixteen of the first 21 colonels appointed to brigade GOC are identifiable with certainty. All of these officers had retired between 1901 and February 1914, one had passed Staff College and the great majority had served with the infantry. Two had commanded

---

34 Blair was a retired colonel of the Leicestershire Yeomanry. Sir Percival Marling had won his VC in the Sudan in 1884.
35 One of these three, Warner of 2nd Home Counties Division, remained in post for only two months. He was a lieutenant colonel in the Army Supply Corps and one of the Staff College graduates. Being only 50 years of age, it seems possible he was quickly transferred to a more pressing position.

Volunteer battalions and the three GOsC brigades of 2nd North Midland Division had all been commissioned into the Volunteers before transferring to the TF. It was unusual even during these early months of the war to appoint TF officers as GOC brigades, and unprecedented to have had three in one division. The fact that the War Office was prepared to sanction such appointments, albeit temporarily, and that it was placing so many officers who had been out of the army for over a decade as brigade commanders, is evidence of how stretched the supply of senior officers had become. While divisions of the New Army and of the 1st Line were also receiving brigade commanders who were no doubt enthusiastic and committed but somewhat long in the tooth, those appointed to the thirteen 2nd Line formations must have been a considerable way down the list of retired candidates suitable for further employment. At the time of the divisions' creation, however, few if any of the authorities had begun to consider the possibility of sending the 2nd Line overseas. Divisional staffs were incomplete, their units were generally far below establishment and scattered to the winds, and almost entirely without training equipment or facilities. If the authorities needed any further convincing that the units would be incapable of taking the field in the foreseeable future, they had only to consider the perceived abilities of the TF officers commanding the divisions' units.

One of the principal War Office motivations for disbanding the Volunteers was the alleged poor quality of unit COs. Many of them had attained command because it was 'their turn' or because they held a position of importance in local society. Inspectors' reports had regularly complained of Volunteer officers' lack of military knowledge, poor execution of command, inability to display initiative, an abhorrence of innovation and change, and reluctance to attend courses to improve leadership skills. As far as the military authorities were concerned, little had changed since the creation of the TF. Annual reports reiterated the same or similar faults. This was hardly surprising as the COs of TF units in 1914 had been very largely majors and second-in-commands at the end of the Volunteer era. In September 1914, many of the Volunteer COs who had resigned when or soon after the TF came into existence re-donned their uniforms and were appointed by their county associations as CO of the 2nd Line. An enormous number of these ageing individuals, many of them holders of the Volunteer Decoration (VD), who were eager to demonstrate their patriotism and loyalty to their former unit, and once more to feel valued, reported for duty in September 1914. Colonels Greig of the London Scottish, Hall of 5/Lancashire Fusiliers, Hanbury of 4/Berkshire, and Wheeler of 7/Worcestershire were among the dozens of former Volunteer COs who returned to service as COs of the 2nd Line. The first commanders of five of the six 2nd Line battalions of the Royal Scots were retired honorary colonels and holders of the VD.[36] Dunfee of 2/4th London had begun his career in the Royal London Militia before accepting a commission in the Tower Hamlets Rifle Volunteer Brigade in the early 1880s. Maclean, "That choleric but dearly-loved man" returned to become CO of 2/13th London, and Prince, former CO of a Manchester Volunteer battalion and currently the CO of the Manchester Brigade of the National Reserve, took command of 2/6th Lancashire Fusiliers. Like many other elderly COs Dunfee was assisted in his duties by a retired Volunteer and TF major appointed as his second-in-command.

---

36   The sixth had a Territorial Decoration (TD) which at that stage of the war meant that he, too, had served in the Volunteers.

At least two former pre-war COs of TF battalions and holders of the VD rejoined their regiment and served as CO of the 2nd Line before quickly being appointed to command overseas. Hanbury, formerly of 1/4th Royal Berkshire was posted from 2/4th Berkshire to command 1/7th Royal Warwickshire, and Fraser of 2/4th Cameron Highlanders was swiftly reappointed to command his old battalion, 1/4th Cameron Highlanders.[37] More common, however, was the acceptance by many COs of 1st Line battalions that they were personally too old or unfit to take their battalion abroad. Several, such as Wilton of 1/12th London and Watts of 1/9th King's, resigned and took command instead of the 2nd Line. Sometimes they took their second-in-command with them as well as more junior officers who had for the time being at least decided they could not accept foreign service. Three captains and nine sergeants of 1/6th King's Liverpool were sent back to the 2/6th, while two captains of 1/12th London returned from the 1st Battalion and were joined shortly by three of the battalion's former pre-war captains who rejoined in September. Those NCOs who returned from the 1st Line could assist the officers in raising and establishing an early discipline and ethos within the 2nd Line, but the most valued individuals who took command were generally those of the Regular Army who had previously served as adjutants to 1st Line TF units. When war was declared, the majority of serving adjutants quickly returned to their own regiments but several of those who remained were promoted to command. In pre-war days, Major Gordon-Clark of the King's Royal Rifle Corps had served first as adjutant and then CO of the Queen's Westminsters. In September 1914 he returned to Buckingham Gate and raised the 2nd Line. He was to remain in command of the battalion until February 1918.

The War Office wanted to see regulars such as Gordon-Clark in command of TF units. During the autumn of 1914 and the following winter significant numbers of COs in the 1st Line were in the process of being replaced by regulars in preparation for their unit or division to depart for overseas. In the eyes of the War Office the now deposed TF unit commanders could serve a purpose in raising the 2nd Line. They may not have possessed some of the military skills and knowledge preferred by the authorities, and their age may have been against them, but they did possess certain attributes which could be of use to the army. The annual reports on TF efficiency had never criticized the commitment and enthusiasm of most TF commanders, and the loyalty to their particular locality and to the unit were rarely questioned. They were invariably important people in the provincial and civic communities, be they solicitors, accountants, factory, mine or mill owners, bankers, or entrepreneurs. Their status and prestige could be used to attract men to their unit. Furthermore, unlike many regular officers they were used to dealing with volunteer auxiliaries. Many might be "choleric", pompous and distant from their men, as befitted employers and business men of their stature and social position, but often they had been fulfilling that familiar role for several decades. They understood the importance of building unit *esprit*, ethos and cohesion, whether it was constructed through a genuine concern for their men's welfare or whether through means of a paternalistic or employer-employee patrician model. Although the central emphasis remained on raising the New Armies, a numerically reasonably strong 2nd Line, whatever and wherever its future may eventually be or lie, had the advantage of providing reassurance that home defence was secure. Until the War Office made final decisions about what would be expected of the 2nd Line, having men undergo training and

---

37 Lt. Col. A. Fraser was killed whilst in command of 1/4th Cameron Highlanders in May 1915.

familiarization would in the meantime ultimately work to the benefit of the authorities. Because the War Office and TF county associations had historically not always enjoyed the most cordial of relations, difficulties were to be expected. These were further exacerbated when the depleted 1st Line battalions overseas began clamouring for drafts to replace their losses. The partially trained 2nd Line recruits about to be posted to their 1st Line in France were fully aware that the fundamental reason behind their ill-prepared state was the result of the War Office's apparent indifference, or at least indecision, about their future role. To those who had been in the TF for some years, such a realization was neither unsurprising nor unexpected.

2

The Hiatus

In the pre-war period clothing and equipping a territorial with his personal kit had been the responsibility of his county association. Arguments about funding, spending and who should provide what, were some of the several causes that had helped to create the difficult relationship between the associations and the authorities. Nonetheless, the associations had assumed that if mobilization was called, the War Office would quickly accept responsibility for equipping new recruits and providing *all* necessities. The threat of war would surely cause all parties to work in harmony towards a common purpose; previous antagonisms would be forgotten. When war came, however, and Kitchener decided to create a new army, it quickly became obvious that the War Office was favouring the New Armies at the expense of the TF. This favouritism became even more evident as the 2nd Line units formed.

Some of the envy felt by the 2nd Line towards the New Armies and the sense of disappointment over the way it had been treated was carried through into post-war histories. Wyrall wrote of how having "found favour with those in high places [Kitchener divisions] swept into their own ranks all the training ability of this country."[1] Similarly, Wurtzburg described the New Armies as "blue-eyed boys" of the War Office, "on whom everything seemed to be lavished."[2] In the Commons, Joynson-Hicks, who often spoke on TF issues, asked whether Harold Tennant, the Under-Secretary of State,[3] was aware of the dissatisfaction within the TF at the favouritism accorded to the New Armies. He demanded Tennant make an announcement to "relieve the minds of those men...in the TF who would feel deeply any aspersion on their military fitness and patriotic devotion."[4] Concern continued into the new year, with the Under-Secretary having frequently to field critical questions ranging from the lack of TF sports facilities and pay inequalities between the TF and regulars, to why commissioned TF sergeant majors were

---

1 E. Wyrall, *History of the 62nd Division (West Riding) Division 1914-1919*, Vol. I (London: Bodley Head, 1926),p.5.
2 Wurtzburg, *2/6th King's*, p.4.
3 Harold (Jack) Tennant had served as Financial Secretary to the War Office 1911-12. He was appointed Under-Secretary of State for War in 1912. He remained in that post until July 1916.
4 *Hansard*, Vol. 66.974-5, 17 Sep.1914.

punished financially and why the New Armies appeared to have preference even when it came to the distribution of stationary.[5]

The most obvious difficulty facing the associations in their quest to equip their 2nd Line was sourcing suits and boots. They were not only in competition with the War Office but also with other associations. Some associations had used the same suppliers for years but now found that the manufacturers complained of inadequate supplies of cloth and of a shortage of workers. Textile industries had traditionally employed women but they also relied on substantial numbers of men to work in the mills. With so many minders, piecers, and spinners having enlisted, production was severely hampered. Nonetheless, within the first nine months of the war, the supply of boots had increased from the pre-war annual production of 0.25m to 7.9m pairs, of jackets from 0.250m to 8.8m, and of greatcoats from a mere 0.06m to 3.6m.[6] The problem facing the associations and their 2nd Lines was how to get their hands on a share of this increased production.

Where possible, the associations had long relied on local textile producers and tailors; orders had been placed regularly and the goods paid for promptly. When permission had been granted to raise the 2nd Line the existing shortage of cloth caused one association member gloomily to predict that such was the demand, a day's delay in ordering would lead to a three week delay in delivery.[7] Matters were further complicated by contradictory instructions from the War Office about what, and what not, the associations should be supplying. For example, when the original order stipulating that the Army Ordnance Department (AOD) would provide replacement clothing and equipment was superseded by another that laid the responsibility on the associations, another scramble to order ensued. Producers capitalized on the difficulties by raising prices, refusing to entertain the idea of penal clauses for delayed deliveries and, in many cases, reducing the quality of the finished products. By October, with some 2nd Line battalions nearing establishment, the War Office exacerbated the associations' already severe difficulties by abdicating its own earlier responsibilities. Among other things it now instructed the associations to clothe and provide blankets for all men, even if the units moved to the 1st Line's vacated war station. This meant that to equip those troops who had agreed to foreign service, many existing members who had decided against leaving the UK, as well as the post-declaration home service recruits, were deprived of whatever kit they might so far have retained or received. For those long established territorial soldiers this was degrading and caused considerable resentment. After its members had suffered this humiliation, one 2nd Line battalion had subsequently managed to acquire a few pieces of replacement kit. The joy was short-lived as it was almost immediately instructed to hand over what little the men had received to another 1st Line battalion of the same regiment.[8] Such were the shortages that if a 3rd Line were to

---

5   *Hansard*, Vol. 71.496, 22 Apr.1915; 70.1858, 15 Mar.1915; 71.491, 22 Apr.1915; 76.2371. For further evidence of the feelings of inequality see, F. Bewsher, *The History of the 51st (Highland) Division 1914-1918* (Edinburgh & London: William Blackwood & Sons, 1921), p.30; P. Bales, *The History of the 1/4th Battalion, Duke of Wellington's Regiment* (Halifax: Mortimer, 1920), p.7; Compiled, *The War History of the 1/4th Battalion, The Loyal North Lancashire Regiment* (Preston: Toulmin & Sons, 1924), pp. 3-7.
6   TNA WO 107/19: 31 May 1915.
7   N. Riding RO. NG/TA Misc 2196. Precis of the Steps Taken by the Association, 14 Oct.1914
8   TNA WO 955462: 2/7th DLI, Sep. and Oct.1914

be raised, one association estimated its recruits would be without clothing until at least March 1915.⁹

Some of the associations' local suppliers did demonstrate loyalty and continued to meet the counties' demands. Unsurprisingly, those fortunate associations tended to advocate the retention of the existing system. Although their real fear was that a centralized system would erode their independence, they argued that their local contractors and tailors aided efficiency and kept costs down. Nottingham Association, which happily recorded that its orders for boots and clothing had been met "without delay," was one of those that supported the *status quo*. So successful had the association's ordering policy been that despite operating a system in which all clothing for its units deploying overseas was returned to the depot for cleaning and reissue, all new recruits were able to receive a completely new suit.¹⁰ Other associations, albeit reluctantly, believed a central system of supply would bring order to the chaos. They concluded a local system would involve higher costs because buildings needed to be rented as stores and, because 94 organizations were trying to buy the same articles and cloth, prices would inevitably continue to rise. To those associations the advantages of establishing universal standards of quality and establishing a degree of equitability of supply outweighed the threat to their independence. A series of consultations and conferences finally arrived at a compromise whereby associations would use up whatever stocks they possessed and then, with a few minor exceptions, ordering and supply would be conducted by the AOD.¹¹

These reforms, of course, took time to take effect. In January 1915, the continuing shortage of boots compelled the War Office to purchase a large number of inferior quality "trade" rather than the regulation pattern boots. These, the War Office insisted, would be suitable for the Reserve and Home Service units. ¹² Frequent disputes over rationing, accommodation, separation allowances, and implied accusations of nefarious practices at the White City punctuated the hectic winter months.¹³ When eventually billeted at their war stations, and like their 1st Line units they had replaced, 2nd Line battalions were frequently dispersed over considerable areas and engaged in a range of tasks. This made purposeful training difficult and also made it harder for battalions to develop unit *esprit*. Even if they possessed at least one suit, the supply of rifles, artillery pieces and just about every type of vehicle, horse and harness remained limited. Two of the few things that seemed to be in abundance were picks and spades. The majority of battalions based in and around London spent a great deal of their time digging the London Defences. Troops from the White City and elsewhere daily marched across London to board a train for Essex. There, hands were blistered and suits and boots worn out. In view of what was later to come in France some battalion officers tried to emphasize the positive and, wondering at the "remarkable" effect the digging had on the men's physiques, believed the experience "should

---

9   Manchester RO. M73/2/2, 4 Dec.,1914.
10 Nottinghamshire RO. DDTA/1/1, 27 Apr.1915
11 TNA WO32 11238, 20 May 1915
12 TNA WO 70/48 512: 8 Jan.1915. Permission was sought by 68th Division to obtain equipment and train men in the repair of boots. It explained that it had been informed by medical officers (MOs) that to avoid wet feet and consequent difficulties, the tongues of the men's boots needed to be stitched to their uppers.
13 *Hansard*,Vols.68.1306; 70.385; 69.142. A brigade of 2/2nd London Division was billeted in the White City. There were subsequent accusations of favouritism and corruption about the way the brigade was supplied.

prove of great use,"[14] Many of the troops remained less than convinced, expressing frustration at the lack of what they considered to be real military training.

The pre-war annual inspectors' reports had long criticised the standard of TF shooting. This was the result of a combination of obsolete weapons, a lack of available ranges, the prohibitive cost of obtaining more than the prescribed annual number of practice rounds, and qualification tests that were less demanding than those taken by the regulars. As the 1st Line battalions and divisions went to France still equipped with the Long Lee Enfield rather than the Short Magazine Lee Enfield (SMLE) it meant the 2nd Line at home suffered even more severely from inadequate weaponry.[15] Knowing that current British monthly output of SMLEs was approximately only about 8,000, the War Office placed an immediate order on the outbreak for almost four million rifles. Until industry could be geared up to produce the numbers required, and because no neutral country would sell arms to the belligerents, the government acquired 150,000 rifles from its ally Japan. Some of these were issued to 1st Line units until they were rearmed with improved marks of the Long Lee Enfield in early 1915. This, in turn, released a number of the Japanese weapons for the 2nd Line.[16] At first, the numbers were almost insignificant but they replaced an even smaller number of previously issued old Lee Enfields or Lee Metfords. Some of the 2nd Line battalions did manage to fire a few practice rounds, often at ranges constructed by their 1st Lines during their deployment at the war stations, before handing the weapons on to another unit. Inspections by visiting generals often necessitated having those troops actually in possession of a rifle standing within the general's eye sight or line of approach. Weaponless, the bulk of the brigade was drawn up behind.

When the first batches of Japanese weapons were issued to the three 2nd Line divisions and two additional battalions tasked to guard the East Coast, they turned out to be something of a mixed blessing.[17] Although useful for troops to become accustomed to drills and handling, the firing mechanism was so complicated that should one part be moved out of turn the whole thing was likely to fly to pieces. Too many of its parts were considered to be unduly delicate and easily lost when the weapon was stripped. There was no clear indication as to whether the weapon was loaded or not and .256 inch ammunition was not only thought to be too thin to cause significant damage to its intended victim but was also ill-suited to the 1908 and 1914 ammunition pouches. Because they were prone to fall out of pouches, cartridges were more usually kept in jacket or coat pockets.[18] One report condemned the Mark VI ammunition issued for the weapons because it was not what the troops would be using on active service and because the rifles were not sighted for it. Ruefully, it went on to explain, "Good scores can only be obtained by disregarding the fundamental principle of Aiming."[19] Because the Japanese rifle was no substitute

---

14 TNA WO 955464: 2/5th Suffolk, Sep.1915; TNA WO 953134, 197 Bde, 4 Sep.1915
15 Most of the 1st Line formations were not re-equipped with the SMLE until 1916.
16 The only 1st Line division still to be armed with the Japanese rifles in April 1915 was what was left of West Lancashire Division. TNAWO70/49.769, 17 Apr.1915
17 TNA WO 955453: Central Force, Assistant Director of Supply (ADOS) Dec. 1914.
18 TNA WO 953031 180 Bde, 2/17th London, Mar.1915; Becke, *ORBAT,* p.46; Compiled, *A War Record of the 21st London (First Surrey Rifles),* (London: Skinner, 1927), p.136. One chronicler pondered, "For what blasphemies and worry [the rifles] were responsible." W. Hall, *The Green Triangle. Being the History of the 2/5th Battalion Sherwood Foresters (Notts and Derby) in the Great European War 1914-1918,* (Letchworth: Garden City Press, 1920), p.11.
19 TNA WO 953031: 180 Bde, 2/17th London, Apr.1915

for the British field weapon one officer of 2/5th Loyal North Lancashire (LNL) noted his men were becoming "rusty" in the use of .303 weapons.[20] The need to possess the modern weapon was obvious to all and training was suffering as the consequence. There were even reports that National Reservists guarding vulnerable points were better armed than the anti-invasion forces. As precedence in distribution was given to infantry battalions, 2/2nd Home Counties Field Company described itself as still "entirely unarmed" but some field companies in other divisions were able to borrow from the infantry a small number for a few days at a time.[21] Useful as this might have been, when rifles were shared they tended to deteriorate even further because none of the sharers accepted responsibility for cleaning the borrowed weapon.[22]

In September, even allowing for the bias towards the infantry for any equipment that did become available, 202 Brigade reported it could do no firing because it had no ammunition. On a more positive note 2/4th Essex thought it was making progress in its training and provision of equipment when, in November 1915, all of its Japanese rifles were replaced. To the battalion's disappointment this proved, however, only to presage the demise of the battalion the following month.[23] In January 1916 battalions of 2nd West Lancashire and 2nd North Midland Divisions seem to have been particularly fortunate in receiving 100 SMLEs and, gradually, by the spring of 1916 the Japanese rifles were replaced by charger loading Long Lee Enfields or Lee Metfords.[24] A large proportion of the 'new' Long rifles, however, possessed no bayonets and slings and arrived in such poor condition that of the 440 Lee Metfords issued to 2/1st Sussex Yeomanry only 20 were reported capable of any degree of accuracy.[25] By March 1916, all battalions in 2/2nd London Division were training with a combination of about 600 Japanese and 100 Long Lee Enfields. Furthermore, and although there remained limitations on the number of available practice rounds, troops about to be drafted from 2/4th Yorkshire were granted an additional 10 rounds for their final target practice.[26] Even when battalions of 178 Brigade all received 800 SMLEs, the available Mark VI ammunition proved unsuitable because it caused the Short weapons to jam.[27] Troops of 2/5th Lancashire Fusiliers were annoyed because they had fired their course with the Japanese weapons and were then given no opportunity to practise before they deployed abroad with their newly-issued SMLEs.[28] They would no doubt have been envious of battalions in 2/2nd London Division who received their SMLEs in good time to become accustomed to them before sailing.[29]

Except for a small number borrowed from the local Church Lads' Brigade, field batteries in 2nd West Lancashire Division were reported in August 1915 to be "practically devoid" of carbines.[30] Of even greater importance, and in even shorter supply than serviceable rifles, was

---

20 TNA WO 952979: 2/5th LNL, Oct.1915
21 TNA WO 955463: Sep.1915; TNA WO 953015, Feb.1916
22 TNA WO 953005: 2/7th London, Aug.1815
23 TNA WO 955463: HQ 202 Bde, Sep.1915; WO 955464: 2/4th Essex, 11 Nov. 1915.
24 TNA WO 953012: A & G, 19 Jan. 1916.
25 TNA WO 953012: A & G, 19 Jan. 1916.
26 TNA WO 955462: 2/4th Yorkshire, 15 Nov. 1915.
27 TNA WO 953024: HQ 178 Bde, Mar. 1916
28 J.Latter, *The History of the Lancashire Fusiliers 1914-1919*, (London: Gale & Polden, 1949), p.87.
29 E.May, *Signal Corporal: The Story of the 2nd London Irish Rifles (2/18th London Regiment) 1914-1918*, (London: Johnson, n.d.).
30 TNA WO 952969: CRE, Aug. 1915

the provision of field pieces for the 2nd Line artillery. The 1st Line usually had to wait for up to a year for new 18 pdrs and 4.5 inch howitzers to replace their aged and obsolete 15 pdrs and 5 inch guns. Unsurprisingly, and ignoring for the time being the heavy artillery batteries which had a different existence from the field brigades, nearly all the 2nd Line Royal Field Artillery (RFA) brigades suffered equally badly. When the 1st Line received its new weapons the obsolete guns were sometimes handed on to the 2nd Line but the four 2nd Line divisions that were quickly allocated to the Central Force were fortunate enough to receive a very few old pieces as early as February 1915. The majority of divisions appear not to have been in possession of modern weapons until very late 1915 or early 1916. They could practise drills with any old ones they did manage to acquire but many were of necessity performed on so-called Quaker guns. These were generally wooden poles on wheels, pushed and pulled by the few men available in each battery. Rather more realistic training, albeit still with obsolete guns, was possible with the handful of 90mm French pieces loaned to the British. These weapons had been the standard French field gun until replaced by the 75mm from about 1897. The 90mm guns had lain in store since, as had a very limited amount of compatible ammunition. Although only 20 rounds per gun could be issued to the few brigades which received the weapons, and despite the absence of hand books and a complete lack of knowledge about how the guns should be sighted and the fuses set, these weapons did provide the opportunity for some 2nd Line units to practise with what was something bearing a vague resemblance to a modern gun.[31]

Becke's *ORBAT*[32] later chronicled the interrupted progress of 2nd Welsh Division's artillery brigades during this initial period of training. It was not until June 1915 that equipment began to arrive. The brigades were still without any guns but each brigade received 19 pieces of saddlery and during the following month one brigade received 278 horses of its intended establishment of a little over 300. In August, a number of harness were received and all brigades took possession of four 90mm guns. The brigades were all still approximately 200 men below establishment but in October eight more guns and wagons arrived for every brigade. Their arrival meant 2/4 Welsh Brigade RFA could return the wagons it had been hiring from Redhill's local traders. It also allowed the possibility of purposeful drills and the occasional opportunity to fire. In November, further progress was recorded when the 90mm guns were withdrawn and replaced by 15 pdrs and 5 inch howitzers. These pieces had been handed over by the 1st Line division when it left for Gallipoli in July. In December, with all units reporting they were about up to establishment in men and equipment, the 1st Line's old 15 pdrs were replaced by modern 18 pdrs.

The RFA brigades of 2/2nd London Division experienced a similar development. They had one live firing practice at Larkhill, and between April 1915 and May 1916, their strength grew from just over 1,000 to nearly 1,700, and from nine old 15 pdr to twenty-one 18 pdr guns.[33] Although the experience of 2nd Welsh and 2/2nd London Divisions were reasonably typical, as two of the formations allotted to the Central Force's First Army they did enjoy a degree of preferential treatment. Nevertheless, in September 1915, OC 2/5 London Brigade RFA reported he had no ammunition wagons, his limbers were obsolete, the ammunition column had only two general service (GS) wagons, and he possessed no fuse indicators, directors, or angle of sight

---

31 Becke, *ORBAT*, Part 2b, p.136.
32 Ibid., pp. 89-90.
33 TNA WO 953026: CRA May-Jun. 1915

instruments.[34] Central Force HQ responded by announcing that 800 GS wagons and 90 ambulance wagons were on order and as soon as they arrived (the first batch appeared in October) the impressed wagons could be replaced.[35] Other divisions had to wait considerably longer for guns, horses, and equipment. The artillery commander of 2nd Home Counties Division reported in September 1915 that should an emergency arise he would be able to turn out only four 90mm field guns. His howitzer brigade and heavy battery had neither guns nor ammunition.[36] When they had been fortunate enough to acquire guns of one description of another, brigades might spend three days firing at Larkhill, Orford, Southminster or Lydd, albeit very probably without sights and with faulty fuses.

In addition to the problems associated with the various types of guns and lack of equipment, several divisions had their artillery brigades scattered over a considerable geographical area. This dispersal effectively prohibited any possibility of joint training between infantry and artillery units. The artillery brigades of 2nd East Lancashire Division only managed finally to concentrate at their war stations in August 1915 and, even then, they were largely out of contact with the infantry brigades. Furthermore, even if a division's formations were able to effect an occasional training exercise with whatever limited equipment might be available, several divisions lost their artillery brigades fairly soon after formation. The brigades of 2nd Northumbrian, for example, went to the Royal Naval Division and thence to France; 2nd West Lancashire's artillery only eventually joined the rest of the division in October 1915 after its 1st Line batteries were released from attachment to the 2nd Line formation to go overseas with 2nd Canadian Division. Similarly, 2/1st London Division was served by its 1st Line artillery brigades until they were attached to 36th (Ulster) Division in September 1915. It was only then that the 2nd Line brigades were able to concentrate in East Anglia with the division's infantry. The drivers and gunners of some of the division's brigades had had at least a short opportunity to work with horses as they were briefly employed in handling remounts before the animals were despatched to 47th (2nd London) Division in France.[37]

Until remounts began to arrive in substantial numbers from South America and Ireland the provision of horses remained a significant problem for the entire army. Predictably, the 2nd Line units were again a low priority. One RFA brigade condemned the quality and suitability of many animals it received, accusing the authorities of "only wasting public money" by keeping them on strength. Those horses arriving with skin diseases had to be separated for two weeks, mange contracted from infected rugs was commonplace, ringworm was almost endemic, deliveries of fodder and straw were often late, and the provision of oats was frequently inadequate.[38] Because army vets remained very hard to acquire, any available civilian practitioners were employed at a rate of a half penny per animal per day. They frequently did not have access, however, to the numbers and types of drugs needed for such large concentrations of horses. Given the state of the horses and shortages of equipment such as field forges and iron and nails for shoeing, it is

---

34 TNA WO 953027: 2 Sep. 1915.
35 TNA WO 955454: Central Force ADOS, May 1915.
36 In Feb. 1916, the division's brigades were still 817 men and 716 horses short of establishment. See Becke, *ORBAT*, Part 2b, pp.81-82.
37 TNA WO 952994: CRA; WO 952995 290 Bde RFA, Oct.1915.
38 TNA WO 953027: 300 Bde, Dec.1915; WO 955456: ADVS, 68th Division Sep. 1915; AQMG, 69th Division, Nov.1915; WO 955461: 2/1st London Mounted Bde ASC, Nov.1915.

hardly surprising that a report on 2nd East Lancashire Division's artillery in August 1915 noted that individual riding, gun drills and the quality of remounts "left much to be desired."[39]

There was also a regular demand for drafts to reinforce the 1st Line artillery brigades. With the restriction against recruiting towards establishment in force into 1915,[40] this call was a particularly hard blow to units' attempts to secure a degree of efficiency. Several war diaries note a succession of subalterns travelling to France for a week to acquire experience and on return lecturing to their fellow officers in the 2nd Line. In order to allow a degree of practical training for the other ranks, 25 percent of 2nd Line gunners were attached to their 1st Line for a few weeks at a time. The first group then swapped with another 25 percent and returned to the 2nd Line to pass on what knowledge they had acquired. Whenever a group of 2nd Line gunners appeared to be approaching a point of efficiency there came the inevitable call for a permanent draft to the 1st Line. It was later pointed out that "even one draft of 250 trained gunners [to its 1st Line] considerably delayed the preparation of the [2nd East Lancashire] division for war."[41] Even before 2nd Welsh Division had received any guns, horses or saddlery, it was ordered to send over 100 officers and men to join its 1st Line ammunition column.[42]

The entire issue of drafting to the 1st Line developed into an extremely contentious issue during 1915. The loss of trained gunners was a blow to battery morale and preparedness, and the despatch of so many drafts of infantry also severely affected how well brigades could train and develop battalion and brigade cohesion. In June 1915, a War Office memo estimated that of the thirteen 2nd Line divisions in the UK, six would be ready to go overseas by July 1916, although not at full strength, with the remaining seven able to deploy within a further two months.[43] Written at a time when two 1st Line divisions were yet to go overseas it is evident from this and other internal estimates that the authorities assumed that the 2nd Line divisions would be capable of deployment by at least the end of the 1916 campaigning season. In view of the preference given to training and equipping the New Army divisions, the last of which crossed to France in June 1916, this may have sounded a reasonable assumption. The deficits in equipment then currently being experienced by the 2nd Line formations could probably be rectified as industrial capacity increased but the difficulty of manning those divisions, especially when they had already lost a substantial percentage of their early recruits, would remain.

From the time the order went out to form what would become known as the 2nd Line, there was some confusion as to what should happen to those men in the 1st Line units who had not agreed to serve overseas. The mid-August instruction to separate the HS from the IS men in the 1st Line had usually meant the creation of separate companies of HS men.[44] With the formation

39 TNA WO 953123: CRA, Nov.1915
40 Permission to increase to 100 percent establishment was initially not universally applied. The War Office refused permission for the West Lancashire Association to do so until March 1915 but the association itself continued the ban until May 1915. It then organized a recruiting campaign under the aegis of Lord Derby and quickly brought its brigades to strength.
41 Becke, *ORBAT,* Part 2b, p.73.
42 Ibid., p.89.
43 TNA WO 70/49 906, Jun.1915.
44 One brigade commander seems to have been dubious about the sincerity of this order and wondered whether it would not, like several previous dispatches from Whitehall, be quickly rescinded. He recorded that such a separation would be "a great improvement if carried out." TNA WO 953138: 198 Bde, Aug.1915.

of the 2nd Line those men could now, in theory, be posted to the 2nd Line and recruits there who had opted to take the IS option could be transferred in exchange. In practice, however, it was not as simple as that. A memo by the Chief of the Imperial General Staff (CIGS) claimed that the TF had "lost sight of its prime function" of home defence and that the separation of home and imperial service men had thrown it into a state of disorganization. What was needed, he decided, was a redistribution of several TF units. He especially targeted those around the Straits of Dover and the Thames estuary but optimistically insisted that during the process units should be kept in a "state of constant readiness to fight." He formally regretted the fact that those men who had opted for HS had been "looked down on and neglected" with a result that they were lacking kit and that some battalions were virtually unarmed. He predicted inevitable and protracted uncertainty and, if they were forced to take the field in their present state, chaos. Consequently, the CIGS instructed 1st Line units to retain all of their trained men until such a time that trained recruits from the 2nd Line could be exchanged with trained HS men from the 1st Line.[45]

For those units that were quickly to be sent abroad independently of their division, this exchange happened earlier than anticipated. The consequence was that many men sent to the 1st Line for those early deployments were far from fully trained; for those formations that were not to go overseas until well into 1915, the pace of exchange was somewhat slower. There was the occasional complaint from some men who on enlistment in those units which had stipulated agreement to accept IS subsequently claimed they never had agreed to it, but a significant development towards preparing the 2nd Line for overseas came in the spring of 1915 when it was decided to create provisional battalions from HS men.[46] Because they were largely to be stationed near to the coast, and would thus be the first to engage an invading or raiding enemy, these grossly under-armed units were to be expendable. By the end of May, many but by no means all 2nd Line divisions had posted their HS men to a provisional unit.[47] All men within the 2nd Line units should then, of course, have been working towards the common goal of overseas service. Nevertheless, the loss of the HS personnel did pose additional problems for the establishment and efficiency of the 2nd Line.

There were clearly mixed feelings within battalions about the decision made by these men and their subsequent transfer to the provisional battalions. In August 1914, when the 1st Line men had been asked to make a decision, epithets such as "The Stay-at-Homes" and "The Never Dies" were accorded first to the HS companies within the 1st Line, and then to the 2nd Line as a whole. In one 2nd Line unit, 2/21st London, a battalion parade was held in which the men were divided between those who had accepted foreign service and those who had declined. The IS men were apparently allowed to call to the HS men to cajole or persuade them to cross the divide. A "considerable number remained obstinate" and although the loss of 400 men was considered a blow to the unit the attempt did "settle at last a vexing and troublesome question."[48]

---

45 TNA WO 325266: 23 Sep.1914; WO 32 5267: 4 Oct.1914.
46 North Riding RO, NG/TA Misc. 2196, Emergency Comm. Meeting, 13 Feb.1915
47 TNA WO 955464: AQMG, Nov.1915. Owing to what it called a "misunderstanding," 2nd East Anglian Division reported that the HS men were still with it in November 1915. It seems likely that the original instruction to have all HS men in provisional battalions by the end of the summer was extended.
48 Compiled, *A War Record of the 21st London Regiment*, p.141.

Yet, a degree of empathy and understanding became apparent in later histories and reminiscences. Ernest May of 2/18th London was perhaps fairly typical. He recalled that he and his comrades "took a poor view of these people at the time" but mellowed later because, he asked, "Who knows what is in another man's mind?"[49]

In April 1915, just as the 2nd Line was told to transfer its HS troops to the new provisional units, there were 290,000 IS Territorial Force men training in the UK; a further 117,000 territorials had signed for HS only.[50] On receipt of the instruction to form provisional battalions, the County of Durham Association estimated it would need to recruit a further 2,400 IS troops to replace its HS men transferred from its 2nd Line to the new units.[51] The initial restrictions on recruiting to 2nd Line battalions was lifted early in 1915 yet even before then, 2nd East Lancashire Division had managed to recruit 78 percent of its officers and 88 percent of ORs.[52] The War Office prohibition on TF recruiting awards remained in place but between July 1914 and the end of January 1915, 358,903 men had enlisted in the TF.[53] Competition from the New Armies had resulted in one association recording its dissatisfaction at its recruitment figures and recommended "more drastic action" be taken. Another association blamed the negative impact of recruitment on the removal to a distant part of the country of its 2nd Line units to its now vacated 1st Line's war station.[54] In an attempt to maintain establishments, some battalions were certainly still accepting men fit enough only for HS if it was thought they would eventually become sufficiently able for IS. By June 1915, however, the War Office believed virtually all enlistments in 2nd Line units were for IS.[55]

The 3rd Line, too, was clearly concentrating on enlisting IS men. As early as November 1914, officers raising the 2nd Reserve were instructed to ensure that "at least" 80 percent of their recruits should have accepted foreign service.[56] The initial reluctance of Major General Bethune, the Director General of the TF, to allow some associations to raise a 3rd Line on the grounds that as the army was short of recruits there was "no use piling up Territorials", had been abandoned. Somewhat ironically, by April 1915 associations were reminded of the "urgent necessity" of bringing the 3rd Line to establishment.[57] Northumberland Association had already complained that because so many local men had joined the New Army, or were employed on

---

49 E. May, *Signal Corporal*, p.18.
50 TNA WO 70/49808: Ar.1915.
51 Durham RO, D/TA-4. Emergency Meeting 27 Apr.1915.
52 Manchester RO, M73/2/2, 8 Jan.1915
53 TNA WO 70/48, Feb.1915. The pre-war establishment of the TF had been a little over 315,000 all ranks.
54 North Riding RO, NG/TA Misc. 2196, letter date 26 Mar.1915; Hampshire RO, 37/M69/3. Chairman's Report 18 Dec.1914
55 TNA WO 70/49 989: 15 Jul.1915 and WO 70/49 949: 26 Jun.1915
56 TNA WO 70/48 365: 24 Nov.1914. In what seems a difficult statement fully to accept, the war diary of 2/4th KOYLI implies that from the outbreak recruits in the West Riding were required to sign for IS. See Latter, *Lancashire Fusiliers*, p.87 which makes a similar assertion for its 2/5th Battalion.
57 Manchester RO, M73/2/2, 1 Jan.1915 quoting letter of 18 Dec.1914; TNA WO 70/49.759, 13 Apr.1915. Bethune had been on the staff of General Sir Ian Hamilton, GOC Home Forces, while the latter had been GOC Southern Command 1905-09. Hamilton, as C-in-C Central Force, criticized Bethune, who "should have been looking after [TF] interests" but who had "finally chucked them in favour of Kitchener's New Army". Liddell Hart Centre for Military Archives (LHCMA), King's College, London. Hamilton Papers, 6/17, letter to Hampden, 21 Jan.1915.

government work or in the coal industry, raising the 3rd Line was "extremely difficult." Its 2nd Line was not up to establishment and the area had effectively been drained of potential recruits.[58] In contrast, East Lancashire Association, which was happy with the state of its 2nd Line and of its 3rd Line's growing strength, feared the War Office might place restrictions on further recruitment. It warned against such a possibility, pointing out that it remained "almost impossible" to get those recruits thwarted in their desire to join the TF to enlist instead in the Regular or New Armies[59] The point was also made that if all recruits had to enlist in the 3rd Line, the friends of those already in the 2nd Line would not bother to enlist.[60] Although there remained immense problems for the 2nd Line with the supply of weapons and kit, with the 3rd Line now recruiting there was a hope apparent by May 1915 that the 2nd Line might be relieved of the responsibility of providing drafts to the 1st Line. If that did prove to be the case it would thus be able to concentrate on getting all units to sufficient efficiency and strength to be considered capable of deployment. If a period of concerted training and stability could be secured for the 2nd Line divisions, it would also mean that the sniping expressions of dissatisfaction from the 1st Line about the quality of drafts sent to it by the 2nd Line might end.

Some battalion and regimental histories are coy about admitting how many 1st Line men decided they were unable to deploy overseas. It seems likely that about 80 percent of pre-war and August and early September enlistments opted to sail. This meant that about 200 men were required from the 2nd Line to maintain establishment. This figure of 200 appears in several histories and although it may be a convenient and neatly rounded total, it is probably reasonably close to the actual number initially transferred from the 2nd Line. Before their 1st Line units sailed, three battalions in 2/1st Staffordshire Brigade despatched between 200 and 250 men to their parent battalions; 2/4th Berkshire posted 200 to its 1/4th; 2/6th King's sent 240, and 2/15th London transferred 250. In 2/1st London Division, 2/12th London sent a smaller number, about 150, to its 1st Battalion in September, and 2/5th Gloucestershire in 2nd South Midland despatched 120 in November. These early transfers replaced 1st Line men who for medical reasons, being under age, or had work commitments, could not sail. Because they were transferred only a few weeks after their 1st Line had begun mobilization their standard of training would not have been too dissimilar from the August recruits to the 1st Line. Rather more problematic was, for example, the extent of the skills among the 166 ORs sent by 2/6th Warwickshire to its 1st Line just before 1/6th sailed, and the 247 from 2nd Line units transferred to the 1st Line Highland Division within ten days of its departure overseas.

Evidence of the limited training of 2nd Line draftees really started to become apparent in the early months of 1915. Those 1st Line battalions that had left for France in November and December 1914 quickly suffered from the onset of winter and from the wastage of trench warfare. Around the end of the year drafts to replace those who had succumbed to the conditions began to arrive. Sometimes the numbers were considerable. For example, 2/6th Cheshire, which had despatched 100 just before its 1st Line left for France, sent a further 243 in January 1915; 2/16th London sent 244 in February; 2/10th King's claims to have transferred in total about 600 to its 1st Line in the early months. The 2nd Line 'Shiny Seventh' London, recorded over 800 men sent to its 1st Line in 13 months, and 2/9th London despatched over 400 in four

---

58 Northumbria RO, 408/47. Minutes of 22 Jan.1915.
59 Manchester RO, M73/2/2/. Minutes of 14 Jun.1915.
60 TNA WO 955463: 2/5th Buffs, Sep.1915.

months. When the London Scottish, however, requested 300 from its 2nd Line to replace casualties taken at Messines on Halloween 1914, only 188 men were considered to be sufficiently trained to go. When referring to these transfers, unit histories generally write of these first drafts being a "very fine body" or "splendid material,"[61] and of how personal interviews were held to discern suitability because the numbers required could have been met "ten times over."[62]

In December 1914, the Adjutant General issued a memo to all Home Commands drawing attention to the "adverse reports" from the BEF about the quality of drafts being sent to France.[63] A few days later the Director of Military Training circulated a criticism of the TF units then being sent across the Channel. Their apparent faults were legion, ranging from the usual regulars' complaints about lax discipline and poor musketry, to inadequate basic trench skills. There were also complaints about the "untrained and immature lads" in the battalions and the lack of military knowledge and leadership among the officers and NCOs.[64] The memo was sent to all Home Commands so that standards and efficiency might improve as drafts were despatched from the 2nd Line. In response to another memo which indicated that if 2nd Line battalions did not have at least 200 trained men ready to be sent as replacements their 1st Line unit might have to be withdrawn from the BEF, most 2nd Line battalions established a separate drafting company.[65] These troops were earmarked for the next draft and received all the available kit and rifles in order that they could more rapidly develop their skills. Yet, even with this preferential treatment, GOC divisions in France continued to complain about the quality of drafts their TF battalions received and of the attitude allegedly held by senior officers of the 2nd Line units.

Various papers were written and circulated in January and February 1915 outlining the problems faced by regular divisions with attached TF units and suggesting ways by which the efficiency of the territorials could be improved. Sir William Robertson, for example, instructed that deployed TF battalions should no longer first spend time digging at GHQ. Instead they were to proceed directly to their allotted host division and receive instruction from that division's units.[66] Nonetheless, concern remained about the quality of the drafts and of their availability. Brigadier General Calley, GOC 2/2nd London Division, wrote to Sir Ian Hamilton, C-in-C Home Forces, about the assumed paucity of 2nd Line men who had signed for IS. Calley reported that COs of 2nd Line units had HS men who said they would agree to go if assurances were given they would deploy overseas with their own 2nd Line unit. In three battalions of 180 Brigade, an average of only 27 percent of ORs had agreed to a posting to their 1st Line; a mere seven, three and 10 of their officers had also agreed to such a move. In comparison, 65 percent of ORs in the brigade said they would accept foreign service provided they were posted with their current unit; 19, 26 and 22 of their officers were also prepared to go under that proviso.[67] What was apparently preventing them from agreeing to be posted to their 1st Line battalions were the "stories of the treatment of the men and the conditions of service at St Albans." It

---

61 J.Q. Henriques, *The War History of 1st Battalion the Queen's Westminster Rifles 1914-1918* (London: Medici, 1923), p.61.
62 Wurtzburg, *2/6th King's*, p.3; Bailey & Hollier *The Kensingtons*, p.213.
63 TNA WO 70/49 817: 18 Dec.1914
64 TNA WO70/48 458: 21 Dec.1914 and 458, 23 Dec.1914
65 TNA WO70/48 489: 4 Jan.1915
66 TNA WO 95590: 4 Feb.1915
67 TNA WO 953031.

was these tales of alleged poor treatment, the thought of having to break the cohesion of their existing platoon or company, and the fact that 2nd Line NCOs would lose their stripes if posted to the 1st Line that were, according to Calley, preventing men from agreeing to go overseas.[68] Hamilton was in a difficult position. He commanded the anti-invasion Central Force but was also partly responsible for overseeing the training of troops stationed in the UK. He had great faith in the TF, and a personal ambition to command a TF Army on the Continent, but he also accepted the necessity of providing the BEF with reinforcements. He had on several occasions urged that 2nd Line units replacing their parent unit in the Central Force should not be used as a go anywhere drafting pool and felt he "had to make a stand."[69] Such was the demand from the BEF, however, that although he might have prevented complete 2nd Line units from being despatched to France, those units did continue to supply reinforcements.[70]

It was not until mid-1915 that the authorities gave some indication that the 2nd Line divisions might eventually go overseas. This was welcome confirmatory news to the many men who had always assumed they would train and then deploy as discrete divisions. Indeed, the creation of the 3rd Line seemed to confirm that 2nd Line units were no longer mere draft finders. At least one GOC in France, however, still believed the 2nd Line units existed to support their parent units and that their perceived independence was not serving the interests of their 1st Line. Major General Barter and his 47th (2nd London) Division had sailed for France in March 1915. The division received what seems to have been a significant draft of men from its 2nd Line almost as it left the UK.[71] Once in France, Barter despatched a memo to GOC I Corps on the issue of possible reinforcements. He informed Lieutenant General Monro that there was little prospect of his units receiving a satisfactory flow of drafts for some considerable time. He explained that the 3rd Line would be unable to send trained men for many months but that this would not matter if the 2nd Line was "clearly enjoined…to provide efficient sufficient drafts in the meantime." This, he believed, was not the case because instructions existed to ensure that drafts from the 2nd Line were "to be restricted to what may be absolutely necessary." The problem with this, according to Barter, was that it allowed the COs of the 2nd Line to be the judges and assessors of what was "necessary". He believed they would make arbitrary decisions based not on the needs of the 1st Line but on those which served the purposes of their own units. This was apparent, he claimed, because COs of the 2nd line were actively discouraging their men from taking the IS commitment in order that the unit would later be able to volunteer en bloc.[72]

Monro passed on Barter's memo to the Adjutant General, adding, "The 2nd Line does not appear to consider themselves feeders …and hence relegate what should be their primary and most important function to 3rd Line units." Monro went on to criticize the inadequate number of instructors, the inexperienced cadre of officers and the youthful ORs of the 3rd Line, and

---

68 LHCMA, Hamilton Papers, 6/17, 13 Feb.1915. The 1st Line 2nd London Division was currently billeted in and around St Albans.
69 Ibid., 6/2, 3 Dec.1914,
70 Very few 2nd Line units had, however, gone overseas in 1915. For example, 2/5th Lancashire Fusiliers was sent to 51st (Highland) Division together with a 2nd Line field company and a field ambulance.
71 Becke, *ORBAT,* Part 2b, p.31 mentions "heavy drafts" from 2/2nd London Division to 47th (2nd London) Division in March 1915.
72 TNA WO 95590: 20 Mar.1915.

blamed the lack of sufficient drafts on the continuing discriminatory system of recruitment awards that encouraged recruiters to enlist men for the New Armies rather than the TF.[73] Barter returned to his theme in April when he noted "the evils of the present system of drafting" were now being recognized. If they had not arrived only a "few hours before" departure, Barter claimed the drafts that had joined as the division left the UK "would otherwise have been rejected." In response to what may have been an enquiry from higher authority, he condemned the inferior physiques of fresh drafts for 5 London Brigade, insisting it was neither his nor the fault of his COs that these men, too, were of "inferior quality."[74]

As 1915 wore on issues concerning the quality and supply of drafts from the 2nd Line remained contentious. Two 1st Line divisions and many TF battalions and field companies attached to regular formations had been heavily involved in 2nd Ypres and the subsequent summer battles. Enormous numbers of drafts were required from the 2nd Line but the War Office now appeared reluctant to maintain the strengths of the 1st Line at the expense of the 2nd. So long as there remained the possibility of invasion or, more likely, raids on vulnerable points, the civilian population wanted to see physical evidence of substantial home defence forces. The presence of 2nd Line formations was needed to sustain home front confidence. Furthermore, the War Office's ideas about the future use, status and deployment of the entire TF were becoming clearer. Rather than a mixture of regular, Kitchener and TF formations, the authorities wanted to create one *national* army. The terms and conditions of the TF were an obstacle to this ambition and moves were being made to bring them into line with the regular forces. Reducing the numbers of men sent from the 2nd Line to reinforce the 1st Line had caused a series of 1st Line amalgamations, some of which had led to political disquiet. The War Office had warned GOsC First and Second Armies in late May that it was unlikely that their TF divisions and attached TF units would receive drafts. This knowledge, as well as the practice of amalgamation and the conversion of some TF units to pioneer battalions, had caused considerable resentment within the TF. Although, however, some amalgamations continued, following a note sent to the Prime Minister by GOC First Army which more or less demanded drafts for his TF units, the authorities compromised.[75] The Under-Secretary of State insisted amalgamations had always intended to be only temporary expedients until more trained drafts became available. Despite this apparent reassurance there were, nonetheless, many who doubted whether his statement was itself merely a temporary expedient.[76]

In mid-June, the training period for recruits was reduced to 10 weeks. It was also announced that owing to the "emergency…exceptional measures" would be introduced whereby all trained men over a figure of 700 in 2nd Line battalions could be drafted. Fifty percent of those sent were to be replaced by men from the 3rd Line but if the 3rd Line could not provide the number required, the 2nd Line battalion should not be reduced to fewer than 800 men.[77] Nevertheless, strengths of the majority of 1st Line units overseas continued to be extremely low during the

---

73 Ibid., 23 Mar.1915 and 2 Apr.1915.
74 Ibid., 28 Apr.1915.
75 TNA WO 95181, 1 Jun.1915.
76 For example, *Hansard*, Vol. 72.1788, 30 Jun.1915 and 73.994, 15 Jul.1915.
77 TNA WO 70/49.934 and 972: Both 16 Jun.1915.

autumn and winter and it would not be until the spring and the approach of the Somme that 3rd Lines were in a position to make up the deficits.[78]

Several battalion historians later recorded that 2nd Line units were informed in May or June 1915 that they would no longer be required to send drafts to the 1st Line.[79] The history of 2/5th Sherwood Foresters went further and claimed that it was told in June it was now "definitely a service unit."[80] The war diary of one brigade confirmed the assumption in August by recording that under existing regulations the brigade would no longer be "available for drafts."[81] The precise date of the official decision is unclear but it is evident that drafts continued to leave some 2nd Line formations well into June and often considerably beyond. The London Rifle Brigade, 2/5th London, for example, which had already lost about 56 percent of its original recruits, sent almost another 150 to its 1st Line between July and September;[82] 2nd Line battalions of 2nd East Lancashire Division sent substantial numbers to their 1st Lines on Gallipoli well into the summer. The average number posted per battalion was about 200 but, for example, 2/9th Manchester sent 353, 2/4th East Lancashire 281, and 2/10th Manchester, 300.[83] In contrast, 52nd (Lowland) Division, which had also suffered huge casualties on Gallipoli, received only an average of 100 per battalion from its 2nd Lines during the summer.[84] Many of these were described as of "poor physique" whereas those who arrived at the East Lancashire Division were thought to be "mainly excellent material." The problem, according to one officer, was, "They seem to have practically no knowledge of musketry ... some of them have never seen a service rifle and as a result it is highly dangerous to be in the vicinity when they get their hands on one."[85] This may have been the somewhat naturally prejudiced thoughts of an officer grieving over the destruction of his old battalion and who believed that anyone or anything that replaced it was inevitably inferior. Tainted it may have been, but there was certainly an element of truth in the claim. Although in theory trained men, the opportunities to fire their old rifles on ranges at home had remained severely limited and they had only been issued with their modified 'new' weapons as they left the UK.

The disruption caused by the departure of large numbers of trained men, by the trickle of new recruits sent from the depot, and by the continuing shortage of equipment, made constructive and progressive unit training difficult. In the early summer of 1915, some battalions were

---

78   The 51st (Highland) Division probably only received about 1,000 reinforcements in the last six months of 1915. 49th (West Riding) Division seems to have taken a similar number despite having had about 5,600 killed and wounded, and another 3,800 sick.
79   A. McGilchrist, *Liverpool Scottish*, p.191.
80   W. Hall, *The Green Triangle*, p.11. Godfrey, *The Cast Iron Sixth*, p.34, records the battalion sent a "large" draft in September 1915 and was told that it would be its last.
81   TNA WO 953054: 182 Bde, Aug.1915.
82   K.W. Mitchinson, *Gentlemen and Officers* (London: IWM, 1995), p.41. This may have been one of several special cases because the summer drafts of 1915, together with substantial ones from the 3/5th, allowed the 1st Line to resume its separate identity. It had formed a composite battalion with 1/12th and 1/13th London after 2nd Ypres.
83   K.W. Mitchinson, *The Territorial Force at War, 1914-16* (Basingstoke: Palgrave Macmillan, 2014), pp.183-84.
84   The exceptions to this average were 1/6th and 1/7th Highland Light Infantry and 1/7th Royal Scots. The latter battalion received a huge draft of 436 ORs from its 2nd Line to help replace its losses in the Gretna train crash.
85   K.W. Mitchinson, *Amateur Soldiers* (Oldham: Jade, 1999), p.67.

reported to be as low as 300 men. In 2nd East Lancashire Division, 198 Brigade reported it was "reduced to a lamentable weakness" and 2/5th East Lancashire noted that it was receiving only between three and five recruits per week. Because its 1st and 3rd Lines were considerably under strength, the battalion declared there was no prospect of ever completing to establishment.[86] Then, on top of the existing difficulties, the HS men had been separated from the 2nd Line and sent to the forming provisional battalions. While this had been an encouraging move for those who wanted the 2nd Line to be deployed abroad as service units, it again reduced strengths. Something like 300 HS men had gone from the Liverpool Scottish to 49th Provisional Battalion and a similar number posted from 2/1st Brecknockshire to 50th Provisional Battalion. This posting left the Brecknockshire so weak that it necessitated a supposed temporary attachment of the remaining men to 2/7th Royal Welsh Fusiliers.[87] Several other battalions in 2nd Welsh Division also stated they had dropped below the minimum number required before drafts could be sent and were temporarily amalgamated.[88] In 2nd Northumbrian Division, GOC 189 Brigade reported that all COs, majors, and adjutants of his four battalions, and "a very large number of NCOs" had been transferred to provisional battalions. Similarly, 2/5th East Kent reported that "the majority" of its trained NCOs and men were HS only.[89] In addition to this drain, unit cohesion could also be impacted by significant numbers of men being interviewed by the Skilled Investigator and subsequently returned to industry or munitions.[90] This involved, for example, 130 from 2/10th Manchester and 268 in a four month period from 2nd East Anglian Division.[91] Officers and NCOs of the units struggled with few if any regular permanent staff to create an atmosphere where men could feel they were working together in a common cause and for a common outcome. Morale, as a consequence was reported in some battalions to be low.

Being a commander of troops in a 2nd Line formation, from GOC division down to platoon commander, was thus a demoralizing business. Somewhat belatedly, in July, the final two 1st Line divisions had left the UK, and between May and December, 23 New Army divisions had deployed overseas. Still only one 2nd Line division had left the UK. In reality, the GOsC of the remaining 13 divisions commanded what were little more than skeleton formations. Yet, there were still occasional pointers which suggested they might, eventually, go overseas. During the second half of the year, for example, rather than remaining as itinerants some of the divisions concentrated and stayed in a particular area. This increased degree of geographic stability and a gradual increase in the amount of available equipment helped the training process and the creation of a formational *esprit*. Confidence grew and at this stage of its still limited development, 2nd Line divisions now assumed they were working towards the ultimate objective of foreign service.

---

86 TNA WO 953138: Aug.1915; WO 953141: 31 Aug.1915.
87 A. McGilchrist, *Liverpool Scottish*, p.191; C.T. Atkinson, *The History of the South Wales Borderers* (London: Medici, 1931), p.181. The attachment was intended to be for a limited period but 2/1st Brecknockshire was absorbed by 2/7th RWF in November 1916.
88 TNA WO 955464: 2/5th Cheshire, Aug.1915; ibid. 2/2nd Monmouth, Aug.1915.
89 TNA WO 955462: HQ 189 Bde, 25 May 1915; TNA WO 955463: 2/5th East Kent, Aug.1915; WO 952999: 173 Bde lost its brigade major to 2nd Provision Battalion.
90 Even the adjutant of 2/4th Yorks requested discharge and returned to civilian employment. TNA WO 955462, Jun.1916 .
91 TNA WO 955464: AQMG, Oct.1915

It was explained earlier that the first permanent, as opposed to acting, GOC divisions and their GSO1s remained in post for several months. Towards the close of 1915 and into the new year, however, some of the older commanders were removed and replaced by officers with more relevant and recent experience. Until he was invalided home sick, Bulfin of 2/2nd London had commanded the regular 28th Division at 2nd Ypres and Loos; Forestier-Walker of 2nd Northumbrian had been Chief of Staff to II Corps before assuming command of 21st Division; Stephenson of 2nd Lowland had commanded both 2nd and 6th Divisions; Braithwaite of 2nd West Riding had been Hamilton's Chief of Staff during the Gallipoli campaign, and Bannatine-Allason of 2nd South Midland and then 2nd Highland had, until his dismissal in September 1915, been GOC of 51st (Highland) Division. Reade, a former Commandant of the Royal Military College of Canada and GOC Troops in the Strait Settlements, was appointed to 2nd North Midland but, as poor health prevented him from going overseas, in February 1916 he swapped places with Sandbach, GOC 2nd Welsh Division. Sandbach was former Chief Engineer, Second Army, and had commanded the 2nd Line Welsh Division since November 1915. As with the case of Bannatine-Allason, however, experience does not necessarily equate to efficiency or ability and not all of these GOsC had been bathed in previous glory.[92] Nonetheless, they had all commanded men, many of whom had been territorials, and had first-hand experienced of the war's evolving character.

During this period of dismissals and appointments in divisional command there was also something of a shake up among the GSO1s and GOsC brigades. Four of the first permanent GSO1 appointees remained in post until their divisions were broken up or reconstituted during 1916. They all later took up posts elsewhere. The ages of the nine first replacements tended to be a little younger than that of their predecessors and they remained in post for a longer period: two of them served for over 20 months and five for at least 10. Given the amount of time they were out and about visiting their dispersed units, their slightly younger age was probably an advantage. Lieutenant Colonel Dunlop, GSO1 2/2nd London Division, lectured frequently to the scattered batteries, battalions and field ambulances as well as chairing conferences about cooperation between the different arms. In addition, he spent six days in December in France with other senior officers on a tour to gain first-hand knowledge of conditions. Significantly all of the first replacement GSO1s had passed Staff College, two had served previously as GSO1s, and another was appointed, in turn, to two divisions. It is possible that one was a TF officer. If that was the case, it was an exceptionally rare if not unique appointment. Two of the men had spent most of their careers in India but as all the appointees had had considerable experience in senior administrative posts they could offer their GOC division invaluable help in trying to establish the formation on a war footing.

---

92 Similarly with Forestier-Walker. Although evidently a brave man, he had been unceremoniously sacked from command of 21st Division after Loos. His corps commander described him as being "very unpopular" and "positively inhuman to his troops." Lt. Col. K. Henderson, *Memoirs*, pp.154, 178-9; Henderson Papers DS/MISC/2 IWM quoted in S. Robbins, *British Generalship on the Western Front* (London: Frank Cass, 2005), pp.15, 60. Forestier-Walker was later moved from command of 63rd (2nd Northumbrian) Division to replace Major General Stephenson, who had given up command of 6th Division and then 65th (2nd Lowland) Division owing to ill health. Forestier-Walker was eventually given command of 27th Division in Salonika in December 1916.

The first and second replacements as GOsC infantry brigades also demonstrated the continuing but still restricted attempt to get men with recent overseas experience into post. In the seven divisions that were eventually to deploy overseas there remained a significant number of officers who had retired in the early years of the century and who had spent considerable parts of their careers in India or Egypt. Several of these, as well as some who had spent most of their service in the UK, had been largely administrators rather than senior field commanders. Nevertheless, some of their previous posts had been prestigious positions and a number of these commanders had in their earlier years served as adjutants to Rifle Volunteer units or the Militia. Four had held previous commands of a TF brigade, but the three TF colonels in 2nd North Midland Division were replaced, leaving only one TF officer as a GOC infantry brigade in any of the 13 divisions. In the divisions that were destined to remain in the UK, the first replacements tended to stay in post for a longer period than those formations which went to France. For example, Turner was to remain as GOC 195 Brigade from late 1915 until March 1918. The three first replacements in 2nd Welsh and 2nd East Anglian Divisions also served for relatively lengthy periods and were promoted to brigadier general from lieutenant colonel or full colonel while in post. The assertion by a member of 2/18th London that late 1915 and early 1916 was the period when "the elderly brigadiers" were replaced was thus to a large degree accurate, as was that of the historian of 2/21st London who thought the arrival of Brigadier General Watts added a "new liveliness and certainly made the brigade move more quickly."[93] Sometimes, however, the replacement process removed an intimacy which had existed for some time between brigadier and brigade. In August 1916, Brigadier General Macfie, "an old friend" and former pre-war CO of the Liverpool Scottish, was replaced as GOC 2/1st South Lancashire Brigade by Paynter of the Scots Guards.[94]

These senior divisional commanders must have sometimes felt unappreciated and vented their annoyance at the authorities for the indifference they believed their divisions were treated. Although no doubt committed to fulfilling their duty as well as circumstances allowed, they were in something of a privileged position. If they were so inclined they could make their presence felt and demonstrate leadership and command at parades and exercises. Yet, once he was sure his subordinates knew his commander intent, he could return to his brigade or divisional quarters and became again a remote and largely administrative figure to the mass of his troops. These GOsC might rail against the supposed lack of sympathy from the War Office and of the eccentricities and inadequacies of the TF, but this would have been done within the quiet of their own domain and to their own staff. The real frustration at their situation must have been felt more by the battalion, battery, and company commanders who, during 1915 and the first half of 1916, worked against the odds to get men trained only to see them posted away to other units. Their men, too, were frustrated by the system which had encouraged them to enlist in a particular unit composed largely of men from the same communities only for them to be denied their desire to serve overseas as a collective unit.

Inevitably during the course of 1915 and the turn of the year, there were changes in unit command and staffs. The uncertain future role of the 2nd Line meant there was not a great sense of urgency to replace existing TF commanders with Regular Army officers. The War

---

93 E. May, *Sapper Corporal*, p.21; Compiled. *War Record of the 21st London Regiment*, p.141.
94 A. McGilchrist, *Liverpool Scottish*, p.192.

Office seems to have been content to allow the county associations to continue to recommend and appoint senior unit officers well into 1915. There were, however, the usual complaints on the part of the associations about the administrative delays in getting their recommendations gazetted.[95] There are, nonetheless, a few examples of regulars, probably those who had been wounded or who were considered unfit for overseas service, being appointed when the position of CO fell vacant. Within the seven divisions that would eventually go overseas at least two battalion COs died in post in 1915, two resigned for reasons of ill health, and another four for private or commercial reasons. A further four infantry COs opted for HS and were posted to provisional battalions or the TF Reserve. There are also three known examples of captains and adjutants being promoted to command when, for whatever reason, the existing CO departed. Battalions of 2nd West Riding Division underwent possibly the greatest number of changes in command during 1915 and 1916. In a rare instance of noted emotion but expressing a sentiment probably common to other subordinates in his position, the diarist of 2/4th York & Lancs recorded the unit's "great regret" when the existing CO was replaced because he was too old to go abroad. The South African war experience of the new appointee, a retired regular captain of the Rifle Brigade was thought, however, to be "invaluable" for the future development of the battalion.[96] Similarly, when the long-serving former CO of the earlier Rifle Volunteer battalion and CO of 2/5th York & Lancs since its formation went off to the TF Reserve, his replacement was a regular captain with war experience who had previously served as adjutant to a TF battalion. The appointment of a new CO to 2/5th Gloucester, described as a "hustler" and whose "strong points were interior and exterior economy" led to several of the battalion's officers being quickly removed.[97] The appointment of these and other regular soldiers, although perhaps regretted by some, was an encouragement to others that the 2nd Line was finally being prepared for deployment.[98]

Encouraging as these and other moves may have been, frustration about the lack of more concrete progress towards overseas service is apparent in some war diaries. One noted in October the feeling apparently "rife among officers, NCOs and men" that no more TF units were to be sent overseas.[99] More publicly, questions continued to be raised in parliament about the force's future. Although probably referring to those few 1st Line units that had not yet deployed, Joynson-Hicks complained that because the New Armies were being favoured TF units were being "detained [in the UK] indefinitely" against their will.[100] Rather impractically he wanted the men to be allowed to transfer en masse to those units already overseas. His colleague, Lieutenant Colonel Carr-Gomm, himself the CO of a 2nd Line battalion, suggested an alternative means. In September, he demanded the authorities should make a decision about the future function of the 2nd Line because it was "very largely at a standstill." He said the men resented the things people were saying about them and "the idea exists that they have been

---

95 TNA WO 952994: CRE, Aug.1915
96 TNA WO 953090: 2/4th York & Lancs, Jul.1916
97 A. Barnes, *The Story of the 2/5th Battalion Gloucestershire Regiment 1914-1918* (Gloucester: Crypt House Press, 1930), p.26.
98 Comments on the worth of departing COs are more usually found in later battalion histories rather than in the war diaries.
99 TNA WO 953029: 2/4th F. Amb, Oct.1915.
100 *Hansard*, Vol. 72, 1934, 1 Jul.1915

widely overlooked." He argued that if they existed merely to supply drafts it was an expensive way of training reserves because the staffs continued to draw "very large salaries." He finished his lengthy question to the Under-Secretary by condemning the process which "wet blanketed" COs who dared to ask for skilled training staff.[101] In response, Tennant, who rarely offered a direct answer to any question, insisted that Carr-Gomm's assertions were untrue and that although the original drafting function of the 2nd Line had changed, "we now consider [the 2nd Line] to be of great importance in the military machine." It had, he insisted, the War Office's "fullest consideration." Significantly, he went on to say, "[The 2nd Line] will be utilized in all probability as fighting formations to go abroad when the time comes."[102] This statement gave encouragement not only to those who wanted the 2nd Line to go overseas but also to those who feared that if they did go, they would become merely labour or lines of communications formations.

Referring to the low morale in his battalion, Carr-Gomm questioned why his men had in the previous spring been induced to sign for foreign service when, nine months later, they were still kicking their heels at home. Colonel Yate, another long term supporter of the TF, announced that he had heard a 2nd Line division was to be posted to France in March. He asked how it could possibly be ready to go when the average size of the battalions was 400 rifles. Tennant again avoided a direct answer, claiming that although the situation was unsatisfactory the men were "happy to go as drafts," and expressed the hope that the Derby Scheme would quickly get the battalions up to strength.[103] He also several times fielded questions about why the 2nd Line yeomanry brigades had not yet been sent to France. His critics complained that the regiments were "between the devil and the deep blue sea" and that the 2nd Line as a whole was living "an absolutely stagnant life."[104] His usual response to questions about deploying the yeomanry and the continued restrictions on its recruitment was that the War Office was concentrating on building infantry reserves rather than worrying about the yeomanry.[105] He let slip that if it were not for the cooperation and help the TF associations had provided in raising the New Armies, and how important the TF was in holding the line during the first winter and spring, he would "view with great favour" the amalgamation of the TF and the Regular Army. He conceded that this would not be done "in the middle of a war", but it was an ominous utterance.[106] Members continued to emphasize how the inequity of the promotion system for TF officers, especially those who had been wounded, worked in favour of those who had stayed at home in the 2nd Line. Clearly frustrated by the seeming indifference of the War Office to the entire TF, Captain Amery angrily insisted the depletion of 2nd Line units and divisions meant they could no longer be regarded as fighting units.[107]

As the MPs argued, the 2nd Line infantry dug, route marched, practised Swedish drill, and learned elementary field craft. Troops of 2/21st London went on pre-breakfast running parades

---

101 Ibid., Vol.74, 481-2, 22 Sep.1915. In fact, because GOsC brigades in the 2nd Line were paid only as colonels, costs were not as high as they might otherwise have been.
102 Ibid., Vol. 74, 504, 22 Sep.1915.
103 Ibid., Vol. 77, 536, 563, 668, all 22 Dec.1915.
104 Ibid., Vol. 75, 1781-1783, 16 Nov.1915.
105 Ibid., Vol. 76.699, 1 Dec.1915.
106 Ibid., Vol. 77.539, 22 Dec.1915.
107 Ibid., Vol.77.542, 22 Dec.1915.

both to improve fitness and also because it was thought the runs would enhance officer – men bonding. Before they joined 51st Division, soldiers of 2/5th Lancashire Fusiliers seem to have spent an inordinate amount of time on the Royal Birkdale Golf Course practising entraining and detraining on imaginary trains.[108] It was probably more because there was insufficient equipment to adopt a comprehensive training regime, rather than a deliberate pragmatic policy to establish one of a "steadier and slower description", that persuaded one writer to explain that the "intensive training [for those going overseas] was not pressed so persistently on units of the home army."[109] Pioneer and sniper sections were formed and, with the odd exception such as entrenching tools, most units seem to have been just about fully equipped with personal items by September 1915. Some of the webbing remained of poor quality and was returned to the manufacturers for additional rivets and stitching. By August 1915, a chosen few brigades were issued with Mills equipment to replace the 1914 pattern.

Government pattern GS wagons continued to arrive to replace limbered vehicles, and field kitchens became common sights accompanying troops on the march. Harness also arrived but frequently did so without any instructions as to how they should be fitted. Specialist troops remained largely without their required equipment but made do with what they could acquire. When the required number of horses and limbers were available, sappers built pontoons and trestles, laid wire and drainage pipes, mined, and experimented with pumps. The CRE of 2nd West Lancashire Division complained his field companies were too widely dispersed on coastal duties to perform useful training; his counterpart in 2/1st London Division experienced similar problems but was also on the receiving end of a vitriolic complaint by the infantry. Brigadier General Pleydell-Bouverie, GOC 175 Brigade, railed against the sappers' apparent inability to lay 200 yards of pipe and build two storage tanks. A contractor was brought in to build the tanks to the CRE's design but, after a later conversation with the builder, the brigadier announced the plans and construction were suspect. Troops were warned not to go within 20 yards of the tanks. The brigadier went on to criticize the CRE for taking six months to procure a pump for watering horses, described engineers as "useless," and condemned them as having caused "unlimited and entirely unnecessary trouble." Because the engineers were inept, instead of training their own men the brigadier's officers were apparently spending their time doing RE officers' jobs.[110]

War diary entries during the second half of 1915 are replete with complaints about how the regular posting of officers to the 1st Line was "seriously interfering", "retarding" or "hampering" training." Many 2nd Line COs could not understand and greatly resented why their own subalterns, who knew their platoons and their men, were being deployed rather than trained officers from the 3rd Line. One brigade commander condemned it as an "unnecessary and harmful practice."[111] Nonetheless, as guns and horses became more available there is evidence that infantry brigades conducted a growing number of joint exercises with the artillery, field companies, detachments of cyclist and yeomanry, and sections of a field ambulance. The exercises ranged from nocturnal tactical assaults and testing operational feeding and resupply arrangements, to route marches lasting up to four days. Infantry signallers were trained by sappers of the

---

108 Compiled, *21st London*, p.138; Latter, *Lancashire Fusiliers,* p.87.
109 R.S. Moody, *Historical Records of the Buffs, East Kent Regiment 1914-1919* (London: Medici, 1922), p.79.
110 TNA WO 953007: CRE, Sep.1915.
111 TNA WO 953002: Sep.1915.

divisional signal companies and the drivers by sergeants temporarily attached from yeomanry regiments. The traditional criticism about the weakness of TF NCOs continued but with added purpose because with so many NCOs being posted to the 1st Line, many in the 2nd Line with newly-issued stripes were hopelessly inexperienced. In an attempt to address the problem 185 Brigade secured a number of police instructors from the nearby constabulary for drill purposes.

War diaries make few detailed references to the training but there is the occasional mention of conferences convened by the GOC division to discuss procedures with his GOsC brigades. A War Office training manual issued in September 1914 seems to have been quite widely used by the 2nd Line, as was a Musketry Training Table published shortly afterwards by Northern Command. In between the (usually infrequent) joint exercises, cyclists learned to judge distances and how to map read; gunners practised horse care and management; medical orderlies sterilized and did what they could with ageing surgical equipment. Many orderlies also often worked shifts at local hospitals. Actual and potential NCOs attended special brigade classes and men disappeared on a multitude of courses ranging from cookery to signalling. The supply of artillery pieces barely improved over the winter, and what there was had to be scattered in order to allow the horses to forage. For most battalions the issue of modern service rifles still remained something of a dream. One divisional history points out that owing to the shortage of ammunition and the lack of full sized ranges, when 2/1st Notts and Derby Brigade was sent to crush the Easter Rising, "Only a very small proportion of the men had ever fired a service bullet out of their rifles."[112] When some Lewis guns arrived in the spring, battalions were again reduced in size by the removal of men to form brigade machine gun companies and also for the new trench mortar batteries. The arrival of small numbers of recruits continued to cause disruption to progressive schemes, as did the frequency with which officers were themselves away from their units on courses. Inspections by and parades for important personalities, and regular demands for troops to fill sandbags for 15 days at coastal towns, further disrupted the training process.[113] Rather bizarrely, and probably uniquely, 2/1st North Somerset Yeomanry complained that training was being disrupted because there were many more horses than men to groom them. Despite the shortages, one battalion diarist was convinced his unit was training purposefully and drew attention to the brigadier's comments on "the excellence of its PT and brilliancy of its Bayonet Fighting." Two months later he stated, perhaps with a degree of complacency, "There are no adverse criticisms to be made throughout the Battalion."[114] The OC of one field company also stressed the positive. He decided four months under canvas in "severe" weather at Newhaven had proved "invaluable".[115]

Other tasks that took troops away from more useful training were the constant demand for anti-Zeppelin patrols and the provision of guards to hunt down the alleged hordes of enemy spies infesting East Anglia. Patrols of 2/1st London Division spent much of 1915 reporting the sound of Zeppelin engines but had only rare glimpses of the actual airships themselves. Some of the division's machine guns managed to loose off the occasional burst in an upward direction, the divisional cyclists fired into the clouds, and sappers defused three of the airships'

---

112 Compiled, *59th Division*, p.33.
113 TNA WO 955463: 3/7th Middlesex, Aug.1915.
114 TNA WO 953145: 2/7th Manchester, Aug.1915, Jan.1916.
115 TNA WO 955455: 2/1st Somerset Yeo, Oct.1915; ibid., HQ 2/2 South West Mtd Bde, Oct.1915; WO 955463: 1/3rd Home Co. Field Coy, Dec.1915.

unexploded bombs. Troops were sometimes called out as per the Divisional Emergency Scheme to provide escorts to protect shot down crews from irate civilians. The ancient 15 pdrs were also occasionally used in the anti-aircraft role but most of the alarms and reports of "suspicious" signals and sightings of low trajectory rockets proved to be entirely false.[116]

Until the harvest was in, finding suitable areas on which to conduct the training exercises was always difficult. Depending in which part of the East or South-East a division was stationed, small fields enclosed by hedges prevented troops shaking out into artillery formation, country lanes were sometimes too narrow for the requisitioned carts to transit, and woodland too dense to permit manoeuvre. Open heath land offered good areas for any joint training that might be possible, and for digging. Public parks were made available by corporations and sometimes private estates were offered as training areas, frequently with caveats about the right to shoot game. Exercises were usually by company or battalion but, occasionally, whole brigades could assemble. Even more rarely was the opportunity to conduct a divisional scheme. A combined two-day anti-invasion exercise in October was undertaken by 2/2nd London and 2nd South Midland Divisions but such large scale schemes were unusual and the best most formations could manage were three or four-day divisional tactical exercises without troops. (TEWTs). Towards the end of the year as more equipment began to dribble in, there was a determined attempt to improve and concentrate the training schedules. GOsC brigades were able to show greater interest in how and what their battalions were doing, an interest that according to one brigade created "more zest" within its battalions. The War Office, too, had issued some further training directives including one which stated that as the platoon was the easiest unit to control and supervise in the trenches, there was little need for infantry to train at higher than the company level.[117]

The experience of 184 Brigade demonstrates how difficult it was to train battalions whose composition was so often changed by the drafting of trained men. An exercise held only five months before it sailed for France revealed some alarming examples of inexperience and lack of situational awareness within the brigade. The brigadier was criticised for remaining at HQ when he should have been in the field sorting out the mess created by his battalions, and transport sections were positioned far too close to the front. Some troops either did not draw, or were not issued with, haversack rations, while platoons were prone to bunching, too easily lost direction, failed to reorganize after attacks, and ignored dead ground. Somehow, officers' chargers were picquetted in *front* rather than to the rear of the firing positions. In another exercise a few days later the brigadier turned his fire on his officers and staff for failing to show initiative, for issuing muddled orders, and for not demanding their troops to move quickly enough.[118]

The occasional joint schemes between infantry and cyclists sometimes ended in squabbles about whether the infantry had authority to issue orders to the cyclists. Naturally enough other short-comings also came to light. Communications between brigade HQ and its battalions were at times completely dysfunctional, effective liaison between the different arms almost non-existent, and logistics and sustainment erratic. The yeomanry were guilty of failing to conduct

---

116 TNA WO 952994: CRE, Sep.1915; Various references throughout unit war diaries in WO 953002, WO 953009 Aug-Nov.1915. See Barnes, *The Story of the 2/5th Battalion Gloucestershire Regiment*, p.22 for remarks on the pointlessness of the anti-Zeppelin picquets who were only armed with rifles.
117 TNA WO70/49780: 22 Apr.1915.
118 TNA WO 953 063: 13 and 26 Jan.1916.

efficient reconnaissance, of issuing "ill-considered orders", and of alternating between "wild and unnecessary galloping" and "meandering along roads like weary infantry."[119] In February 1916, 2nd North Midland Division suffered a severe embarrassment when it failed to react to a signal ordering an emergency entrainment exercise. Two telegrams arrived during the night from higher authority to divisional HQ but they were not passed on by what were later described as the "caretakers". The divisional staff only became aware of the orders a matter of minutes before the exercise was due to start. Panic set in when it was realized men, vehicles, and rations could not be assembled, collected and packed before the trains were scheduled to depart. Apologetic phone calls to Eastern Command and presumably rockets fired in all directions followed, but the reputational damage had been done.[120]

It seems unlikely the same division undertook any specialized training for the sort of conflict it was about to experience in April 1916. When deployed to Ireland 59th (2nd North Midland) was engaged in what was effectively a counter-insurgency operation involving house clearing, street fighting, and living in what was at times a hostile civilian environment. Fighting against a small but well-armed and determined group of urban guerrillas who enjoyed good communications and who knew the terrain, cost the inexperienced North Midlanders dear.[121] When only three months away from foreign deployment, 60th (2/2md London) Division was undergoing rather more apposite training for the type of engagements it expected to face in France. It was, however, still some way from efficiency. Three days before Major General Bulfin assumed command the division had undergone a test mobilization. The ASC was employed elsewhere so did not parade, iron rations and field dressings were not drawn, and the intended final concentration in Stisted Park was abandoned owing to inclement weather. In February and March the division attempted several large tactical exercises that met with only luke-warm praise. Troops were felt to require an excessive amount of instruction about what they should be doing and, even after much explanation, orders were still not understood or carried out. Their work was apparently "not accurate enough", fire discipline was poor and the transport "unready". Their drill was "steady" but their officers required "much practice". Despite the division being composed of a substantial proportion of genuine volunteer territorials from some of the capital's most exclusive regiments, there was still "a lot to learn."[122]

In order to build what today would be termed the moral component of fighting power lectures on subjects about the causes of the war and Germany's strategic ambitions were delivered to all arms. These at least allowed some respite from the tediousness of some of the training but the strengths of units within most of the divisions remained woeful. The sense seems to have

---

119 TNA WO 955455: 2/1st Bedford Yeo, Dec.1915; WO 95546: HQ 2/1st London Mtd Bde, Sep.1915.
120 TNA WO 953010: Gen. Staff. Feb.1916; WO 953018: Divisional Train, 29 Feb.1916.
121 There remains some dispute about the division's losses in Ireland. General Sir John Maxwell reported a total of 234 casualties but recent research suggests it was 160. B. Hughes, B. Campbell & S. Schreibman, 'Contested Memories: Revisiting the Battle of Mount Street Bridge 1916', *British Journal of Military History*, Vol.4, Issue 1, Nov.2017, pp. 2-22.
122 TNA WO 953030: 181 Bde, 21 Dec.1915; 179 Bde, Feb.1916 and 8 Mar.1916. A practice alarm in January 1916 for 61st (2nd South Midland) Division, which was to deploy in May, met with similar results. Orderly rooms were understaffed, servants failed to rouse their sleeping officers, or could not find them, essential orders were misinterpreted, men paraded without kit, and ammunition was "misplaced". See WO 953067: 2/4th Ox & Bucks, 5 Jan.1916.

remained that the Regular Army retained its favoured position and that recruitment for the TF was in the hands of "inefficient" people. One GOC brigade recorded his belief that the existing restrictions continued to work against the TF and noted that the only way his division was able to obtain recruits in later 1915 was if recruiters unwittingly broke the regulations.[123] The manpower shortage was addressed by high profile parades, field days and band concerts, as well as sports days and the enrolment of unit teams in some of the local civilian football leagues. With many battalions still at around 300 men such displays and performances did attract some local recruits and, despite 208 Brigade describing the results of one parade as "very meagre", strengths did increase[124]

There are occasional comments in war diaries about the quality of the recruits of 1915. Those to the RAMC were described as "mostly very intelligent" but that the physiques of those in the 3rd Line in early 1916 were "not thoroughly satisfactory."[125] The diarist of 2/2nd London Division thought the type of man enlisting in 1915 frequently wasted his meat and vegetable rations because, when compared to the men's usual civilian diet, the quality of army food was too good and its variety too extensive. Troops of 2/6th Northumberland Fusiliers were praised by the division's AA&QMG for managing to draw fewer rations than the battalion's entitlement, and 2/1st Welsh Field Ambulance bought a second hand sausage machine because it would, it was predicted, save the unit a considerable sum.

As in the pre-war days there were complaints about the length of time it took central authority to reply to divisions' queries and predictable accusations over excessive bureaucracy. This latter submission, however, garnered an unexpectedly sympathetic response. The authorities accepted war diaries had been too diligently written and decreed that if nothing unusual had occurred "Nil" returns could be submitted.[126] All this was, of course, part of the learning process but officers' inexperience and lack of confidence in their new role were sometimes exposed in unforeseen circumstances. When, for example, a CO found himself at the mercy of a civilian railway official, instead of asserting his authority he allowed the "almost insane policy" and "ridiculous blunder" of the official to deprive the brigade of a substantial portion of its equipment.[127]

Throughout the final months of 1915 opportunities for progressive training remained limited. Furthermore, most brigades had gone into billets for the winter. There, because so few doctors and trained RAMC orderlies were available to inspect accommodation, outbreaks of cerebraspinal meningitis, scabies, and measles occurred. Overcrowding and poor hygiene caused scabies to be particularly prevalent. Sulphur fumigations were commonplace and deaths from disease were not unknown. Controlling infectious outbreaks was difficult and did stretch the limited resources of the medical authorities. An outbreak of scarlet fever caused delays in embarkation and there were several instances of units having to leave some of their men in hospital when the division sailed. The dispersal of units during the winter months caused problems with

---

123 TNA WO 953007: Sep.1915.
124 TNA WO 955464: HQ 208 Bde, Oct.1915.
125 TNA WO 952993: ADMS, Aug.1915; WO 953081: 2/5th West Yorks, Jan.1916. Another brigade commander complained of how the "poor physique" of men being sent from the 3rd Line was having "an adverse effect on efficiency." See WO 952976: Sep.1915
126 TNA WO 955464: HQ 68th Division, Oct-Nov.1915. This ruling inspired the supposed diarist of 2/1st South Midland Field Ambulance to write only one entry during the course of four months: "Hostile aircraft flying south-west."
127 TNA WO 955464: 2/1st Welsh Bde, RFA, Aug.1915.

supervision as well as supply and messing. Brigade and battalion reports frequently noted the "inconvenience" of having to visit the dispersed accommodation and of difficulties in maintaining some sort of control over the use and misuse of kit. The Deputy Assistant Director of Supply (DADOS) 2/1st London Division complained about the time he wasted travelling by train between his units because the authorities would not provide him with a car. The consequence of this inconvenience caused the "unwarranted wastage" of equipment and rations.[128] The type of buildings in which one battalion might be accommodated over the winter of 1915-16 ranged from schools, Salvation Army and church halls, to private houses, hotels, sale rooms, warehouses, and drill halls. Those allocated huts often discovered the roofs leaked and that water boilers, if fitted, either did not work or were without fuel. A unit could sometimes be ejected from a group of huts at short notice only for the men to see from their tents those same huts remaining empty for weeks. In January 1916, GOC 178 Brigade recorded his resigned frustration at too many of his men still being billeted in too many unsuitable buildings. His counterpart in 175 Brigade was even more prepared to register annoyance at the system. Colonel Pleydell-Bouverie fumed at what he saw as incompetent officers in other divisions who wanted to hand over "uninhabitable" barracks and where the "gratuitous provision of discomfort" for his troops was creating unnecessary and avoidable hardship.[129]

The difficulties of control and care in these widely scattered and often unsuitable billets were exacerbated by the seemingly permanent shortage of MOs. This was an issue which continued to vex divisions well into 1916. The AA&QMG of 2/2nd London Division expressed his frustration over the unequal pay earned by TF and New Army MOs. This discrimination resulted in a shortage (he claimed) of 16 doctors in 2/3rd Field Ambulance.[130] There was one civilian MO for the entire 2/1st Cheshire Brigade, no doctor could be found within nine miles of 2/5th Suffolk, and South-West Mounted Brigade was so scattered that its units were quartered as far away as 19 miles from the two civilian doctors who comprised its field ambulance.[131] Civilian doctors were criticized by some GOsC for their varying interpretation of what constituted a man's "fitness." They were also roundly condemned for their lack of experience which allowed "absolute children", many with defective eyes and flat feet to enlist. Commanders stressed these recruits were not worth the effort of feeding or training.[132] The inexperience of some MOs was also thought to be why in one artillery brigade there were "abnormal" numbers of men going sick. The less than adequate medical provision was also reflected in a shortage of dentists. In the same way as the 1st Line had been shocked by the numbers of new recruits who required substantial dental treatment, some 2nd Line battalions were equally concerned at the extent of the problem. In October 1915, 2/5th Loyal North Lancashire reported 25 percent of its IS men

---

128 TNA WO 952994: DADOS, Oct-Nov.1915.
129 TNA WO 953024: HQ 178 Bde, Jan.1916; WO 953007: HQ 175 Bde, Sep.1915.
130 The difference was a substantial 14 shillings per day. TNA WO 953026: A&Q, Feb.1916. The OC 2/3rd Field Ambulance had earlier recorded his contention that MOs preferred to enlist as temporary lieutenants in the Regular or New Armies rather than join the TF. The AA&QMG expanded the OC's argument.
131 The problem was resolved in one battalion when Captain Farquhar, a company commander who was also a qualified doctor and commissioned in the RAMC TF, resigned his company command and was immediately re-engaged as the battalion MO. TNA WO 953141: 2/10th Manchester, 2 Sep.1915.
132 TNA WO 955464: 2nd Cheshire Bde war diaries; 2/5th Suffolk, Sep.1915; WO 953031: 180 Bde, Apr-Dec.1915; WO 955463: ADMS, Aug.1915.

would be incapable of proceeding overseas until or unless they had received remedial dental care. Battalion HQ believed the work could be done but, that at the current rate of about 36 treatments per week, the existing work would require at least two months to complete.

In addition to the few available MOs there remained a shortage of officers with knowledge of how army administration worked. One AA&QMG pointed out that any correspondence likely to go as far as the War Office required six copies, one for every office it passed through on its way to Whitehall. This, he believed, was "cumbersome" and particularly unfortunate because carbon paper could only reproduce a maximum of five copies. He claimed his office staff of three officers, one sergeant major, and three clerks had had to respond to 867 pieces of correspondence in a period of two months.[133] The 2/6th Cheshire appealed for an officer and NCO who knew how to pay troops, and there was little idea about how to run courts martial. One South Midland Field Ambulance expressed complete bewilderment at the procedure it was instructed to follow when 26 of its men were charged with refusing to obey an order. The CO sought guidance but it was slow in coming.[134] Divisional HQ of 2/2nd London considered the lack of knowledge of army procedures was "particularly marked" amongst its officers and asked that because the *Army Manual of Military Law* was "so complicated as to be practically useless" a simpler version should be issued. The division also wanted the appointment of a permanent deputy judge advocate to advise on how courts should be run. In particular it also requested instructions on how TF NCOs who were "just capable" in peacetime but later proved "incapable" could be reduced in rank under the Army Act.[135] When one of the division's brigade commanders registered his concern at the number of unauthorized absences amongst his troops, it was put down to the nature of the men's casual civil employment. It was decreed that harsher measures, including short, sharp sentences in detention barracks, would be adopted. On investigation it was discovered there was no such accommodation available. The higher incidence of more ordinary crime was put down to the "lower grade of recruits" and the absence of old soldiers to guide the youngsters during their training period.[136]

In 2/1st London Division cases of insubordination were considered to be far too frequent largely because, it was asserted, officers and NCOs did not understand the need for prompt and "severe" punishments. Members of 2/10th, 2/11th London and the divisional gunners appear to have been the worst offenders but incidences of absence without leave occurred across the division. A surprisingly sympathetic comment in the war diary of the divisional train explained this as the proximity of the men to their homes and their natural desire to visit friends. When 60th (2/2nd London) Division concentrated at Sutton Veny in preparation for deployment official leave was severely restricted. Immediately, the crime rate increased and the incidence of illegal absence soared.[137] The fusilier battalions seem to have had the highest number of men struck off as deserters in 1915 but cases of men signing for one battalion and then disappearing to enlist somewhere else were widespread until 1916.

To add to the existing woes of the 2nd Line, in the early autumn of 1915 a decision was made to reduce the size of its battalions to 600. Together with the constant drain of men to

---

133 TNA WO 953026: A&Q "Statement", Feb.1915.
134 TNA WO 955464: Oct.1915; WO 953051: 2/1st South Midland F. Amb, 27 Sep.1915.
135 TNA WO 953026; A&Q "Statement", Feb.1915.
136 TNA WO 953031: Aug.1915.
137 58th (2/1st London) Division war diaries; Compiled, *21st London*, p.144.

the 1st Line and coming so swiftly after the loss of their HS men to the provisional battalions, this decision constituted another significant blow to unit *esprit*. It is likely that COs did what they could to hang on to their longest serving NCOs and men but it is evident the reduction necessitated the despatch of considerable numbers of officers and ORs to the 3rd Line. In 2nd West Lancashire Division, 4/5th Loyal North Lancashire sent 12 officers and 200 ORs to its 3rd Line; 2/4th York & Lancs, in 2nd West Riding Division, which had posted 226 men to a provisional battalion only a few months earlier, lost a further 248 to its depot. These men were posted away during November and December 1915 and were probably in France by the time the Somme opened. But, even as the former 2nd Line men were settling into life in the 3rd Line, a further decision concerning the composition and purpose of the 2nd Line was being taken.

There was then yet another change of mind on the part of the authorities. Immediately after these departures, and coinciding with December's flurry of parliamentary questions, a circular instruction from HQ Central Force ordered divisions to file up to date reports on their units' fitness to deploy. Compulsory medical examinations for all COs and personnel were ordered, numbers of wagons and horses short of establishment demanded, and reports on the progress of training submitted. The reports themselves have not survived but all battalions in at least six 2nd Line divisions were instructed to be brought to 30 officers and 850 ORs. As some battalions were only at about half strength it was anticipated that many of the men so recently sent from the 2nd Line to the 3rd would now be returned. It was also realized that if the expansion to war strength presaged a move overseas, it was more than just manpower that needed addressing. In 2nd South Midland, for example, in addition to all battalions being below the stipulated 600 ORs, it was also about 300 horses under strength. There also remained significant deficiencies in technical and capital equipment. A divisional ammunition column and other supporting arms had to be raised from scratch, and it was estimated 1/3rd Field Company would require at least a further two months' training before being capable of deployment.

It was not just the 2nd Line, however, that suffered from personnel difficulties. Manpower remained a pressing problem across the entire BEF. Voluntarism had had its day but in a desperate bid to stave of conscription the government had supported the so-called Derby Scheme. Men had been asked to indicate their willingness to serve but to continue in civilian employment until their class was called. Few anticipated this would solve the manpower shortage but Tennant hoped the scheme would at least provide a temporary respite until the country had been persuaded there was no alternative to conscription. The first classes of Derby recruits were called up in late 1915 and began to arrive at 2nd Line units in early 1916. In view of the low current establishments at the start of 1916, numbers of these recruits posted to several divisions were substantial. Their distribution within and without individual divisions was, however, often uneven. For example, in 2/1st London, 175 Brigade took 1,273 Derby recruits whereas 174 Brigade took the relatively low number of 473. One battalion alone in 175 Brigade, 2/11th London, received 424 of the new men. This figure dwarfed the 80 allocated to 2/10th King's in 2nd West Lancashire Division but was modest in comparison to the 614 sent to 2/5th Duke of Wellington's and the 710 accepted by 2/7th Duke's of 2nd West Riding Division. The four battalions of 178 Brigade received an average of 346 Derbyites but, unlike these and many other units, a privileged few battalions were not entirely swamped by these volunteers, most of whom had no former association with any particular regiment or battalion. By levying a unit and company subscription several battalions were still able to choose the type of man they were prepared to accept. Until the introduction of conscription effectively outlawed battalion and company subscriptions, these 1st and 2nd Line battalions very largely continued to receive men from their own 3rd Line. This accounts for the arrival at 2/5th London in February 1916 of 244 men from 3/5th London and another two dozen of its former HS men from the provisional battalion to which they had been posted in 1915. Nevertheless, there are also instances of battalions which had no choice in the matter of who they enlisted receiving drafts in early 1916 from their own 3rd Line: 2/5th York & Lancs took over 200 from its own 3rd Line, and 2/4th KOYLI welcomed back about half of the 260 it had sent to its 3rd Line in November.[138]

The bulk of 2nd Line battalions did, nonetheless, receive large numbers of recruits that did not necessarily originate from within their 1st Lines' usual catchment areas. There also appears to have been a practice in 62nd (2nd West Riding) that required the receiving 2nd Line battalion to send an equal number of its own trained men to the 3rd Line. If that was the case it would suggest the 2nd Line had at least temporarily swapped responsibilities with its 3rd Line. Instead of the 3rd being the unit that trained and then drafted men, in this instance the 2nd seems to have become the training battalion which then passed on qualified men to the 3rd for posting overseas. Because it retarded the possibility of his own battalion going abroad, at least one CO recorded his discontent at such a practice. The CO was supported by his GOC division, Major General Braithwaite, who expressed his "great regret" at the exchange but accepted that it was the result of a growing shortage of eligible men in the West Riding as a whole.[139]

On arrival at battalion HQ, Derbyites were generally placed in separate training platoons and when suitably qualified allotted to companies. Derby recruits often claimed they had been led to believe they could join a regiment of their choice and even be given the option of whether it should be a TF or regular unit within that regiment. When they reported to depots or training camps, however, this assumption was often denied and the men allocated to whichever regiment needed a group of recruits. Whilst appreciated by the senior commanders because they were bringing the divisional units closer towards establishment, these new arrivals generally overwhelmed what was left of the original members. But that, of course, was not difficult. In 2/2nd London Division, 180 Brigade estimated that even as early as March 1915 it had already sent well over 50 percent of its battalions' original members to their 1st Lines; later drafts would further have increased that percentage.[140] Additionally, 2/10th Manchester received not only Derby recruits but also drafts from the Army Reserve of men with a lower medical category; 2/7th Royal Scots took 700 B1 and C1 men from English regiments as well as a substantial group of 18 and 19 year-olds who had been returned from France as under age. These young men were described as "troublesome but useful"[141] An eclectic mix of untrained recruits from the King's Liverpool, Welsh, Dorset, Cambridgeshire and Hertfordshire Regiments was absorbed by 2/4th Ox & Bucks, while several battalions of 2/2nd London Division were brought up to strength with "absolutely first class material" from a number of 3rd Line battalions of the London Regiment.[142] Possibly the most insensitive action on the part of the posting authorities

---

138 These figures were obtained from respective unit war diaries.
139 TNA WO 953090: 2/4th York & Lancs.
140 TNA WO 953031,
141 Mitchinson, *Amateur Soldiers*, p.107; J. Ewing, *The Royal Scots 1914-1919*, Vol. II (Edinburgh: Oliver & Boyd, 1925), p.776.
142 G.K. Rose, *The Story of the 2/4th Oxfordshire and Buckinghamshire Light Infantry* (Oxford: B.H. Blackwell, 1919), p.6; E. May, *Sapper Corporal*, p.22.

was the demand, just after the brigade had sustained significant casualties during the Easter Rising, for all battalions in the Sherwood Foresters Brigade to provide drafts of 200 to their respective 1st Lines . This was described as a "severe blow" and of all the drafts despatched the one which was felt the "keenest."[143]

Another expected source of manpower that could be used to swell numbers in the 2nd Line, and a group to which Tennant had already referred several times, were the men in the HS battalions. During the winter he explained to the House that efforts were being made to persuade men in the provisional units to accept IS before they would be compelled to do so under the terms of the Military Service Act.[144] Although an uncertain number of men did quickly agree to transfers to 2nd Line units it seems likely from the available evidence that the majority of HS troops waited until the change in the law meant their battalions would soon either be disbanded or the men themselves compulsorily transferred. The numbers of men now available for transfer were substantial. For example, while 184 Brigade was fortunate to receive over 1,200 men from its units' 3rd Line battalions in January 1916, 182 Brigade took nearly 1,400 men from a variety of disbanding provisional battalions between March and May. These were in addition to another 360 from the Royal Scots and 2/1st Highland Cyclist Battalion. This meant that although the four battalions in 182 Brigade had received an average of over 170 men from their own 3rd Lines in January 1916, when it left for France five months later almost 40 percent of 2/5th and nearly 60 percent of 2/8th Warwickshire were men from Lancashire and Scotland. Furthermore, almost 35 percent of 2/6th and over 40 percent of 2/7th Warwickshire were Scots, Lancastrians or Welsh. Another substantial percentage of the men originated from Sussex and Hampshire. So numerically significant had been the transfers that Lord Derby travelled to 2/1st Warwickshire Brigade's concentration area to address the Lancastrians now within the formation. He did this in part to empathize with them over their postings to other than their own county's regiments, and in part to wish them good fortune in their adopted units.[145]

The influx of men in the first half of 1916 yet again revived assumptions that the divisions were about to go overseas. Hopes had been raised occasionally if an unexpected draft of recruits appeared, and the surprise arrival of five captains to 2/5th Sherwood Foresters in June 1916 was considered to be positive proof of an imminent move to France.[146] As C-in-C Home Forces, Field Marshall Sir John French travelled widely around the camps on tours of inspections, sometimes taking the opportunity to explain to the men that as there were still inadequate numbers of trained troops for home defence he had been compelled to retain the 2nd Line. Despite 57th Division in February 1916 being ordered to maintain itself at one hour's readiness for immediate deployment overseas – an order that 171 Brigade's HQ considered "inconvenient" because 2/6th King's HQ did not possess a telephone – Sir John told the division's troops in May 1916 that because he had been so impressed by their efficiency they were an obvious

143 Compiled, *59th Division*, p.46; W.G. Hall, *The Green Triangle*, p.36.
144 *Hansard*, Vol. 76, 292, 24 Nov.1915,
145 The various and several groups of numbers given in TNA WO 953054 do not quite add up but the differences are marginal. Lord Derby, who became Secretary of State for War in December 1916, campaigned relentlessly for men recruited in Lancashire to be posted to Lancastrian regiments.
146 P. Davenport & A. Benke (eds.), *The History of the Prince of Wales' Own Civil Service Rifles* (London: Wyman & Sons, 1921), p.230; G. Hall, *The Green Triangle*, p.30.

choice for the task of home defence.[147] The historian of 2/12th London thought differently. He believed 2/1st London Division was kept in the UK because everything that could possibly go wrong during a divisional inspection by the Inspector General Overseas Forces, did.[148] French's comments can be seen simply as attempts to boost morale in divisions whose hopes had been repeatedly raised and then dashed.

By spring 1916, each of the several changes of location undertaken by divisions had been interpreted as the final one before departure. Thousands of men had been sent on so-called embarkation leave more than once. Battalions of 2nd West Riding Division had been sent on what was termed "final leave" in June 1916 when the division was told to mobilize for "immediate service in France." The division was not to deploy for another seven months and, like those in other divisions, many of its men no doubt resented the subsequent accusations of shirkers. Others were apparently ashamed to go on leave because such was their "disgrace" they could offer no acceptable explanations or excuses to the girls they met.[149] The men believed they had been trained to the point of staleness and remained frustrated that their units had not been deployed at their zenith when filled with trained men. "Inspections followed ceremonial inspections with regular monotony," and officers' repeated requests for transfer to the front were usually denied.[150] Some post-war accounts do mention an air of disillusion and even disquiet in some battalions.[151] Many of these volumes were written, however, by officers who had served either from their battalion's beginning or close to it, and probably spoke for themselves when expressing disappointment with the delay. One recalled how despite the many setbacks the constant rumours of deployment continued to raise the spirits and the men remained eager to go.[152] Such sentiments may well have been the case for many but it is equally possible that in the second half of 1916 a proportion of the Derby men and conscripts now filling the ranks of the units were more than content to be kept at home. Two 2nd Line divisions had been sent to France in the summer and one, 61st (2nd South Midland), had been severely mauled at Fromelles. Furthermore, the Somme was well under way and taking its bloody toll. Many men probably felt the writing was on the wall and resigned themselves to the fact it was only a matter of time before they, too, would join the BEF.

In the meantime, the hopes of the enthusiastic continued to be alternatively raised and dashed. The experience of 2/9th Royal Scots would have seemed familiar to several battalions. When it was brought close to strength in mid-1915, rumours of deployment spread and excitement abounded. Enthusiasm waned when drafts left but in early 1916 prospects of France were again considered to be "far from remote." Instead of the battalion leaving, however, another large draft was despatched. Shortly afterwards the arrival of yet more new men again renewed hopes but

---

147 TNA WO 952980: HQ 171 Bde 24 Feb.1916. The 2/6th King's apparently came to an agreement with the owner of a private telephone who lived close to battalion HQ. A. McGilchrist, *Liverpool Scots*, p.193.
148 A. Wheeler-Holohan & G. Wyatt, *The Rangers Historical Records* (London: RHQ, 1921), p.182.
149 E. Godfrey, *The Cast Iron Sixth*, p.54; Wurtzburg, *2/6th King's*, p21; Compiled, *21st London Regiment*, p.141.
150 A. McGilchrist, *Liverpool Scots*, p.193.
151 For example, see F. Skirrow, *Massacre on the Marne* (Barnsley: Pen & Sword, 2007), pp.40-41
152 Wurtzburg, *2/6th King's*, p.15.

these were quickly dispelled when the battalion sent abroad another 300 men in July 1916.[153] Similarly, after taking in about 300 Derby recruits in March 1916, 2/5th Northumberland Fusiliers was ordered in July to despatch 362 of its now trained men to the Continent.[154] Other disappointments had come earlier when, in April 1916, 2/10th King's transferred a large draft to its 3rd Line for so-called final training before the draft was sent on to 1/10th King's.[155] In the spring of 1917, weeks after the flurry of deployment of 2nd Line divisions abroad, units of 2nd Home Counties Division still thought they remained under orders for France. They continued with a programme of "special training" and were up to establishment when, in August 1917, several of the units were suddenly disbanded. COs of those units which survived the cull faced the unedifying task of trying to maintain morale in battalions whose personnel had largely disappeared and whose junior officers were for the large part still merely civilians in uniform.

By 1916, the COs tasked with the difficult job of trying to retain unit establishment and morale were now rather more likely to have been commissioned into the Regular Army than the TF. Percentages of the balance between the two are difficult to establish precisely but it is clear that regular officers who had returned to the UK wounded or invalided were being posted to the 2nd Line. There was still a substantial number of former 1st Line TF officers in command of battalions who had not deployed with their original unit. These officers had subsequently helped to raise the 2nd Line but were now gradually being replaced. Some units were also certainly commanded by 1st Line officers who had been wounded overseas and who brought to their command the invaluable knowledge of active service. Although they did more usually go to the 3rd Line there was also a smattering of wounded NCOs attached temporarily as training staff to the 2nd Line. Because experienced NCOs could act as guide and advisor to any young subaltern or company commander sensible enough to listen, many units would not let a time expired NCO take his release without first having undergone a searching interview with his CO.

There is little extant evidence to explain how and why decisions were made about which of the 2nd Line divisions were to be deployed and which eventually to be broken up.[156] The decision to send some and not others of the 2nd Line undoubtedly depended on three factors: the catchment area of a division; the degree of competition in that area from the New Armies; the casualties sustained by their 1st Line. These assumptions might help to explain why it was decided that the first two 2nd Line divisions to depart should be 60th (2/2nd London) and 61st (2nd South Midland). The latter's parent division, 48th (South Midland), had concentrated in France in April 1915. Having avoided all of the 1915 battles between then and May 1916, when 61st (2nd South Midland) concentrated at Merville, 48th Division had taken relatively few casualties. By the end of March 1915, 47th (2nd London) Division had assembled in France and, apart from playing a flanking role at Loos, had been largely trench holding until May 1916. It had drawn significant drafts from its 2nd Line, but the recruiting situation in London had remained fairly

---

153 J. Ewing, *Royal Scots*, p.779. The 2/7th Royal Scots thought its division's deployment to Ireland in January 1917 spelt the end of any hopes of it being sent to France. Ewing, p.776.
154 TNA WO 955462: 2/5th Northumberland Fusiliers, Mar. and Jul.1916. Among others, 2/7th Lancashire Fusiliers also continued to despatch drafts to its 1/6th Battalion, then in Egypt, until the end of July 1916. See Latter, *Lancashire Fusiliers*, p.89
155 McGilchrist, *Liverpool Scots*, p.192.
156 There is a similar lack of proof to indicate why some 1st Line formations had been sent across the Channel sooner than others.

robust and by transfers from other battalions of the London Regiment, at the general expense of 58th (2/1st London), 60th (2/2nd London) Division had been brought to strength.[157]

Of the other divisions that were later to cross to France, 59th (2nd North Midland) had provided large drafts for its 1st Line to make good losses sustained during its six months in the Salient and at the Hohenzollern; 66th (2nd East Lancashire) continued to send drafts to rebuild 42nd (East Lancashire) during its post-Gallipoli sojourn in Egypt; 57th (2nd West Lancashire) and 58th (2/1st London) had been drained to maintain their first line battalions. These reinforced 1st Lines were later used to reconstitute 55th (West Lancashire) and 56th (London) Divisions respectively.

Whilst the first two 2nd Line divisions to deploy were absorbing their substantial drafts and making their final preparations, Claud Hamilton MP made his derisory comment about the "thousands" of men in 2nd Line units who were of "no earthly use". He even claimed that an order existed which forbade MOs to examine the men for their suitability for overseas active service.[158] Hamilton's assertion about the lack of fitness of substantial numbers of troops had an element of truth because it was undeniable that some B1 category men had been sent to the 2nd Line. These men had been classified B1 for a reason. A rather more sympathetic but still partly inaccurate comment had been made a few weeks earlier. Sir John Walton told the House the TF reinforcement system had "broken down completely" and that it was now time to abandon it entirely and use both 2nd and 3rd Lines purely for drafting. The TF, he insisted, "deserves better."[159] There were many in the War Office who would have agreed with Walton's sentiments about the difficulties in TF drafting and who possibly also felt the force did deserve better. The whole issue of reserves was, however, about to be addressed in an unusually radical manner. Although for the time being the 2nd Line divisions already selected to go would deploy, significant decisions about the future of several of the other formations were about to be finalized.

Both 60th and 61st divisions underwent several months' pre-deployment training on Salisbury Plain. It was common practice for divisions to spend their final training months on the Plain, often technically as part of the Emergency Reserve. While part of Local Forces, Central Force, or later, Home Defence Forces, English 2nd Line divisions had been based either to the north of London, in Kent, or in East Anglia. The 2nd North Midland had moved from the St Albans area to Ireland and then travelled direct from there to Fovant before deploying to France; 66th (2nd East Lancashire) was to forgo time on Salisbury Plain and transited direct from the Bedford area to France. The two Scottish 2nd Line divisions, 64th (2nd Highland) and 65th (2nd Lowland) both moved from Scotland in March 1916 and concentrated around Norwich and Chelmsford respectively. The latter was sent to the Curragh in January 1917 to relieve 59th (2nd North Midland), but both Scottish divisions were among those destined to undergo drastic change by the end of the year. While 64th (2nd Highland) began to have its 2nd Line battalions replaced by graduated battalions of the Training Reserve, it was to survive as a division until the end of the war. A decision had been made, however, to disband 65th (2nd Lowland) completely.

157 Battalions of 60th (2/2nd London) Division had been brought to strength by drafts of up to 300 from their own 3rd Line battalions as well as from other 3rd Line units of the London Regiment. These latter troops should have gone, in theory, to either 56th or 58th divisions.
158 *Hansard*, Vol. 82.129, 4 May 1916.
159 *Hansard*, Vol. 80.1973-4, 14 Mar.1916.

The reasoning behind these decisions was a consequence of nearly three years of total war. By early 1917, the Highlands had been almost denuded of eligible men and the Lowland area was trying to provide sufficient men for too many battalions of too many regiments. Similarly, 63rd (2nd Northumbrian) was trying to sustain its establishment from a catchment area much reduced in potential manpower. In March 1916 the division was barely at two-thirds strength. With its artillery having left to join the Royal Naval Division (RND), by July it was reduced to about half establishment. Competition for recruits from the regiments' many regular and New Army battalions was simply too intense for the four 1st Line TF battalions of the Northumberland Fusiliers and the five of the Durham Light Infantry, as well as their nine 2nd Line battalions, to be maintained. The 1st Line 50th (Northumbrian) Division's losses since its embarkation had been enormous and the 2nd Line had been called upon too frequently to make good those casualties. It sent drafts amounting to 85 officers in May 1915, with two battalions alone each sending almost 240 ORs. In addition, 2/6th Northumberland Fusiliers lost another 371 HS men to 2nd Northern Coast Battalion in May and a further 100 to the 1st Line in October.[160] The division received well over 1,000 B1 recruits in July but it seems likely by the time it despatched a draft of over 600 in the same month, the War Office had already decided 63rd (2nd Northumbrian) should give up the unequal struggle and disband.

The three remaining divisions, 67th (2nd Home Counties), which had twice been warned for Ireland and once for France, 68th (2nd Welsh), and 69th (2nd East Anglian) also recruited from areas where eligible man power had become increasingly limited. As early as September 1915, 2/4th and 2/5th Royal Sussex were ordered to disband. Their HS men were sent to 72nd Provisional Battalion and their IS to the 3rd Line. The two 3rd Line Sussex battalions were then designated as the official 2nd Line units. In December 1915, 2/4th Suffolk was ordered to follow a similar path when its entire strength of 282 ORs was sent to its 3rd Line. The 2nd Line battalion was immediately disbanded.[161] The War Office decided the three divisions should undergo reorganization as part of the wider remodelling of the Training Reserve. Having lost their 2nd Line battalions, by February 1918 they became known simply as 67th, 68th and 69th Divisions.[162]

As the closing weeks of 1916 approached and passed, the five remaining 2nd Line divisions intended for overseas deployment were warned that they would embark in January or early February 1917[163] They had been in existence for two years but there remained an enormous amount to do. Their original troop compositions had changed significantly but a small kernel of originals will have survived. There is evidence to show that drafts did arrive after the huge

---

160 TNA WO 955462: DLI and Northumberland Fusiliers war diaries.
161 TNA WO 952464: HQ 208 Bde, Dec.1915.
162 The formations trained troops of Graduated Battalions of the Training Reserve. The divisions had all disappeared by March 1919.
163 Discussion had begun with the French about the proposed Nivelle Offensive in 1917 and how the BEF would help and cooperate. The French wanted the British to extend their front to the south of the Amiens-St Quentin road in order to relieve French divisions. One of the ways these could be done, so the French suggested, was to speed up the despatch of the remaining 2nd Line divisions. FM Haig agreed in principle to extending his front but only by the end of March rather than, as the French wanted, February. This was partly because, he stated, only two of the divisions would be ready to sail in January. He thought possibly another two would be able to go in February. See C. Falls, *Military Operations France and Belgium, 1917* (London: Macmillan, 1940), pp.40-41.

influxes of Derbyites but the majority of the battalions would have sailed in early 1917 with a good proportion of men who had been in the army for a considerable time.[164] By the second half of 1916, training facilities had improved significantly and much of their equipment was of the same type as that being used in France. Many of the perhaps 80 remaining original volunteers wore stripes and acted as instructors; in some battalions several of the August and September 1914 enlistees were now officers within those same units. By early 1917, these men had been in uniform for at least 24 months and even the Derbyites had been in training for nine months. There may have been some conscripts or young volunteers who had been with their unit for fewer than nine months but these were very much in the minority. Ignoring the small percentage who had joined only more recently, the majority of men in the units had, therefore, been training and messing together for a length of time significantly longer than the ten or twelve weeks most 1916 recruits underwent between enlistment and posting. Many of those men currently being sent to replenish the battalions fighting on the Somme would have, therefore, been in uniform for less time than those Derbyites who arrived at the 2nd Line in February and March 1916.

Some of the earlier training pamphlets and syllabi produced as a result of lessons acquired during the Somme campaign were in circulation and application during the latter stages of the 2nd Line divisions' training. These would have aided the overall development of the individual units' and the divisions' fighting power. The arrival of updated equipment and training procedures promoted improvements in the physical component and the understanding of the changing character of the war. The subsequent growth of associated doctrine helped to develop the conceptual component of fighting power. These advances should have resulted in not only a higher level of skills but also a better developed sense of unit cohesion. The bulk of the men in the divisions about to deploy may not have been genuine territorials but from the evidence available of the origins of men who now comprised them, a proportion of units had retained a sense of locality or at least of regionalism. The divisions' gestation period had been considerably longer and rockier than those of the New Armies but the final product should not have caused any particular worries on the part of the authorities. The units had numbers of men with previous 1st Line trench experience and officers who had served in the ranks overseas and then returned for a commission. Most of the older and less suitable battalion and battery senior officers had been replaced and the divisions were commanded and administered by regulars with recent combat experience. If permitted a period to settle in and acclimatise to the demands of active service, the divisions' fighting power was, on paper, well developed. What the men now had to prove on the battlefield was that their fighting power and capability were sufficient for the task and that the sometimes harsh words used to describe them in parliament were both unwarranted and unjustified.

---

164 There were, of course, exceptions. In October 1916, battalions of 178 Brigade, 59th Division, all received drafts of up to 220 conscripts, most of who originated from London. These troops had only about three months' training before deployment but the young recruits from Yorkshire who had arrived at the battalions in the summer were now regarded as "fully-fledged soldiers." See G. Hall, *The Green Triangle*, p.42.

3

Trench Acclimatization

Divisions usually received about two weeks' advanced notice of the date they would deploy overseas. The intervening time was occupied in a hectic round of completing the required establishments of kit and equipment, and the thousand and one administrative requirements demanded by the War Office. Quartermasters were inundated with forms and a bewildering array of items arriving hourly; one officer believed he signed his name to lists and orders more than 700 times during this period.[1] Although many adjutants and their orderly rooms would already have been performing the tasks for over a year, a circular clarifying what was expected of regimental staff officers arrived in late 1915. This may have helped the staffs but once they left their war stations or final concentration areas, battalions and units fell into the sometimes unsympathetic hands of the officers and staffs of the transport and dock services.

By early 1917, units were well aware of their likely future role and the conditions to be expected overseas. The official sources of information were supplemented by talks from wounded officers and men of their 1st Line, and from visits to the front by many COs, brigade commanders, and occasionally GOC divisions. On return they lectured to their subordinates who, in addition, attended talks by RE and RFA officers who explained what their particular arms could offer the infantry. The opportunity for joint exercises had also increased. These schemes allowed for improved fraternization at all levels between the men of the divisions' different components. By such means inter-branch cohesion and understanding of their respective capabilities added to the development of a division's fighting power.

Once notification of departure had been received arrangements were made for advanced parties to precede the main body. Sometimes the GSO2, a staff captain, and DAA&QMG would constitute the party, often accompanied by up to five officers and 10 NCOs from each battalion.[2] The war diary of 60th Division, however, makes no mention of despatching any other ranks and records only the departure of the GSO3 and 13 other officers, mainly captains, for landing and entraining duties in France. Once abroad, staff captains of the three infantry brigades went on ahead to investigate billeting arrangements.[3] Transport sections of around two officers and 80 men usually travelled separately from the rest of their battalion and sometimes

---

1 G. Hall, *Green Triangle*, p.49.
2 TNA WO 95296: 3 Feb.1917
3 TNA WO 953026: A&Q 15 Jun.1916

from a different port. COs and adjutants sought guidance on many last minute queries, including the rather strange enquiry of what constituted "fully trained" men. Staff of 175 Brigade had doubts about the definition as given in a recent War Office circular and requested the opinion of divisional HQ. (DHQ)[4] On the eve of departure, 2/8th Sherwood Foresters was instructed to transfer 67 men to 2/5th and 2/7th Battalions in order to equalize the sizes of its sister units. As its history explained, "It was an opportunity not to be lost, as no qualifications had been mentioned." When the drafts arrived at their new units the receiving battalions vowed revenge on 2/8th should the situation ever be reversed.[5] Personnel in 58th Division were also ordered to be shuffled from one unit to another and, as a final thought, the War Office instructed battalions to reduce establishment by 10 batmen because the authorities had decided to send only four rather than 10 supernumerary officers with each unit.[6]

Every battalion was allocated two trains as transport from their war station or final assembly area to Southampton. The first two divisions to deploy, 60th and 61st, were fortunate to leave in early summer but the remaining five 2nd Line formations earmarked for overseas were to follow them during the depths of winter. Troops were frequently kept hanging around the docks for hours depending on the condition of the sea or reported sightings of U-boats in the Channel. Battalions of 175 Brigade began moving from Longbridge Deverill on 27 January 1917, with brigade HQ (BHQ) reaching Southampton on 30 January. There, they were informed all crossings had been suspended and the troops made the return journey to camp. They eventually sailed between 3-5 February.[7] The brigade at least had the advantage of a camp to which they could return but units of other divisions were often retained at the freezing docks with only iron rations for sustenance. The half battalion of 2/4th Gloucestershire embarked on the SS *Margeurite* was returned to port for 14 hours after the sea proved too much for the vessel. Fog delayed the departure of some units of 57th Division for two days. The transport section of 2/5th Manchester returned to Southampton after two hours of ploughing through seas in the Solent that were eventually deemed too rough for the escorts. The three officers and 88 men returned to the indifferent facilities of the rest camp for over a week before the section was able to depart.[8] A battalion of the Duke of Wellington's was kept in the UK after its division sailed because one of its members contacted scarlet fever. The Dukes whiled away the enforced wait by creating "disturbances" in Bedford with the military police and troops of 72nd Division.[9] Another battalion's crossing in the same division was rough enough to cause "nearly everyone" to be sick en route. This discomfort was followed swiftly by a severe march in pouring rain up the steep hill to the spartan conditions of a rest camp in Le Havre.[10]

Battalions would usually have a night's rest before enduring the tedious and lengthy journey towards the front's rear areas. Much to their understandable annoyance and frustration units were frequently issued with contradictory orders by staff officers at the camps about times of

---

4 TNA WO 953007: 1 Jan.1917
5 W. Oates, *History of 2/8th Sherwood Foresters 1914-1918* (Naval & Military Press reprint of 1919 edition), p.88.
6 TNA WO 953007: 1 and 8 Jan.1917.
7 Ibid, Jan-Feb.1917.
8 TNA WO 953144: 2/5th Manchester, 4 Mar.1917.
9 TNA WO 953087: 2/6th Duke of Wellington's, 13 Jan.1917.
10 TNA WO 953082: 2/7th West Yorkshire, 8 Jan.1917.

departure and the issue of rations. They were also at the mercy of a French railway system whose apparent deliberate malicious intent was to delay them for hours at Le Havre station and elsewhere. The seemingly endless delays at Le Havre were sometimes filled by the issue of yet more kit. This could range from leather jerkins and fingerless gloves to neck sun shields and box respirators. Generally, however, time was spent simply waiting in the cold and wet. Even when a train arrived and boarding completed, conditions only marginally improved. Trains regularly halted unexpectedly but as no one knew when it might again lurch forward for another mile or two men and animals were forbidden to disembark to stretch their legs or to obtain hot water. One battalion of the King's Own Royal Lancaster (KORL) suffered a 39 hour journey that included only two deliberate stops; 75 percent of the men went without a hot drink for the entire trip. When officers of 171 Brigade demanded the Rail Transport Officer (RTO) at Abbeville do something about insisting on regular stops to water the horses, issue hot drinks and allow sanitation breaks, the RTO managed to persuade the French driver to agree to one halt of 20 minutes. Any more than that, the officer declared, was out of his control.[11]

The lengthy journeys and the winter weather inevitably resulted in the troops arriving at their billeting area late, tired, cold, and hungry. On detraining, troops often had to march several miles to their battalion's allocated village. The newly appointed GOC 66th Division thought the troops he observed were "ragged" and emphasized that officers should set a slower than the officially prescribed pace until the men and their feet grew accustomed to the *pave* roads.[12] Having observed his footsore and chilblained troops slog along mud and slush roads for two days and struggle to push wagons up a steep hill, one battalion commander decided his troops "did not march so well."[13] On arrival at their billets, which were frequently dilapidated and filthy barns largely open to the weather, the men were able to collapse and get what sleep they could. So unpleasant was the weather that at Famechon some men of 2/4th York&Lancs were reported to be suffering from exposure.[14] This was explained not by the men's exhaustion and the chilling cold of the previous few days but because the troops had not hardened sufficiently since leaving their "comfortable" billets in England. Kit inspections to discover what had been lost en route or not previously issued were often held the following day and courts of enquiry looked into all manner of losses and disciplinary incidents. One was convened to investigate the strange case of what had happened to four men and a horse of 2/4th Gloucestershire who had disappeared from their train. Having boarded another train, three of the men turned up later but the fourth man, on who the horse had apparently fallen, was reported to be in a hospital near to the coast.[15]

So far in their journey towards the front, divisional, brigade and even battalion HQ had had little opportunity to assert their authority over their own destiny.[16] They had arrived at their

11   TNA WO 952979: 2/5th KORL, 13 Feb.1917; TNA WO 952980. WD 171 Bde, 14-15 Feb.1917.
12   TNA WO 953120: 7 Mar.1917.
13   TNA WO 953082: 2/7th West Yorkshire, 24 Jan.1917.
14   TNA WO 953090: 25 Jan.1917.
15   TNA WO 953058: 26 May 1916.
16   Whilst on their travels towards the front, battalions issued daily orders covering instructions about clothing, blankets, billets, transport, etc. On the eve of its departure 3/5th Lancashire Fusiliers extended one of its routine issues by telling its troops that if anyone asked them for the name of their battalion or the names of anyone serving in it, they were to deny any and all knowledge and take the questioner immediately to their company commander. See TNA WO 953137: 28 Feb.1917.

allotted corps by means of a system that had evolved since the original divisions of the BEF disembarked in August 1914. Divisional staff had little if any control over where and how its units stayed or travelled. While DHQ might be welcomed by the corps commander and housed in a comfortable billet, brigade units were allocated areas and villages which their own billeting officers often had to find and possibly secure from rival units.[17] One CO and his orderly room staff sat uncomfortably on the steps of a village church with his battalion scattered around the adjacent square to await the arrival of the billeting officer who had managed to get himself lost.[18] The troops may well have cursed the unfortunate officer for his incompetence but the problem was probably created at a higher level. Corps staffs often did not provide guides, or if they did the appointed men usually had themselves only limited knowledge of the area. Furthermore, if a division arrived unexpectedly early or sooner than originally intended, corps' A and Q Branches might be unprepared for them. Brigade staff captains then had the difficult task of securing rations for their units when there were possibly none readily available. This task was made even more difficult because few if any of the staff captains had any experience in such matters. All the company and platoon commanders could do was to see that their men received whatever might be available and try to ensure their soldiers were as comfortable as their billets allowed. It was a harsh and cold introduction to overseas' active service but the divisions cannot be blamed for the difficulties that had to be overcome. Once, however, their brigade units were settled with their host unit for the trench acclimatization process, GOsC and their subordinates could begin to reassert their authority.

When new divisions had been deployed to the Western Front in 1915 and 1916, they were sent to a quiet area of the line and received instruction in the practical arts of trench life by an experienced formation. Once its first units started to leave the UK a division could take up to five days for all of its component parts to reach France. Once there, battalions and other component units could sometimes spend more than a week training and providing working parties in the rear area of its allocated corps before moving forward for their period of acclimatization. The length of time spent under supervision could vary according to local demands but the usual practice was for the division then to assume responsibility for the line where they had received their instruction. The division's senior officers, brigade majors, COs, seconds-in-command, adjutants, transport officers, and quartermasters were usually attached to their equivalents in their hosting divisions for a period of about four days. Company, platoon and battery commanders and their troops could be attached to the experienced units whether those units were in the line, reserve, or support, but would go into the line with that unit when its turn came.

Advance parties of 60th (2/2nd London) Division began to arrive in XVII Corps area on 19 June 1916 but the division's final constituent parts, the three brigade MG companies, did not arrive for another 10 days. DHQ opened on 28 June; 14 days later units of the division began to relieve their mentors of 51st (Highland) Division.[19] DHQ of the other early arrival, 61st (2nd South Midland) Division, left the UK on 22 May 1916; by 29 May its infantry brigades and supporting arms had begun their period of attachment to four different divisions in the Bethune area. On 10 June it began relieving units of 38th (Welsh) Division in and around

---

17 Corps staff mistakenly but frequently allocated the same designated area to more than one battalion.
18 Compiled, *A War Record of the 21st London Regiment*, pp.147-48.
19 TNA WO 95934: XVII Corps, Jun.1916.

Laventie and became responsible for its own sector.[20] Seven months later the newly arrived 57th (2nd West Lancashire) Division occupied much of the same sector of line near Laventie. What were termed "Advanced Tactical Parties" of nearly 300 all ranks from all arms of the division were attached to the New Zealand Division from about 4 February 1917. The intention was that at least five officers from each battalion would be attached to those New Zealand units they would later relieve. The reliefs began to take place two weeks later and, by 25 February, the division had fully relived the New Zealanders and 10 Australian Brigade.[21] Battalions of 58th (2/1st London) Division had a slightly more gentle introduction to trench warfare. Its platoons appeared to have spent longer than the more usual two or three days with their mentors of two 1st Line formations, 46th (North Midland) and 49th (West Riding) divisions.[22]

Most of the other 2nd Line formations had rather more time than did 62nd (2nd West Riding) Division to become acclimatized. DHQ arrived in France on 10 January in the belief it was to become part of Third Army; five days later it was told it had been switched from Third Army to V Corps of Fifth Army. Whereas the other 2nd Line divisions were able to acclimatize in relatively quiet areas, 62nd Division's new corps was fighting in the quagmires of the Ancre Valley and the pulverized ground above Beaucourt and Beaumont Hamel. On 20 January all battalions sent four officers and 16 NCOs, and the RFA 400 gunners, for four days' instruction to four divisions of V Corps. On 21 January all trench mortar batteries were sent on a two weeks' course at Fifth Army School; two days later over 2,300 men of 185 and 186 Brigades began working on roads, dumps, and cable burying. At the same time all of 187 Brigade was told it would not do any training as all of its time would be spent on railway construction and maintenance. After long days of labouring, troops faced the prospect of sleeping in tents, with fuel particularly scarce and night temperatures of -12 degrees Celsius.[23] With only minimal time, and for some units seemingly none at all in the trenches, on 2 February the division was told it would be relieving 32nd Division within the next 10 days. The division's diarist immediately appreciated the likely problems:

> Taking over trenches, or rather shell holes, on the night 12-13 [February] … will be a very high test for our fresh troops who have never been in the line before, except for one night when under instruction in another sector. The tactical situation during the nights of relief will be decidedly delicate for, in addition, our artillery will be relieving that of 32nd and 7th Divisions. Some of the guns, on each night, will not have had the opportunity of registering till the next morning, and the formation of an effective barrage, should the enemy counter-attack, will be uncertain.[24]

20 TNA WO 953033: May-Jun.1916.
21 TNA WO 952964: Feb.1917.
22 Coincidentally, those battalions attached to 46th Division's brigades were in the trenches immediately to the north of where many of their 1st Line battalions in 56th (1st London) Division attacked the Gommecourt Salient on 1 July 1916.
23 TNA WO 953068: Jan.1917.
24 Ibid, 9 Feb.1917.

By logging this apprehension in the diary the division was covering itself to corps and army HQ just in case the relief did go badly. It was an understandable nervousness about the division's first operation and probably a lack of confidence in its abilities to navigate the featureless wastelands to complete a relief at the conclusion of a proposed attack by a brigade from another division. The brigade's final posts and positions were likely to be unknown even to the attacking division's HQ. Major General Braithwaite, GOC 62nd Division, went to see the corps commander, Lieutenant General E.A. Fanshawe, to explain the foreseeable problems but was told the relief could not be postponed. Despite the bewildering complexities of conducting the relief over unfamiliar and contested ground the actual operation went "without a hitch."[25]

On 13 February, a policy whereby brigade majors of 2nd Line divisions deployed to the Somme were replaced by officers who had had experience of the terrain and the fighting resulted in Captain Hoare of the West Kent Yeomanry arriving at 187 Brigade HQ.[26] The brigade was still working on railways and did not move up to the front for the first time until 21-22 February. In the early hours of 24 February, Captain Hoare walked about a mile in front of the brigade's outpost line before encountering any enemy fire. His action confirmed earlier reports that the Germans were retiring along the front of Fifth Army. Orders were quickly despatched from DHQ for 2/4th York & Lancs to advance to the high ground approximately 900 yards ahead.[27] Having spent only about 48 hours in a forward position, over the next two days 187 Brigade led the advance of 62nd Division. Attempts to dig communication trenches to the front posts had long been abandoned by earlier units in favour of laying duckboard tracks across the shell-pocked morass.[28] When 187 Brigade crossed over the former German positions they discovered what roads had existed on maps had been all but obliterated by British artillery; the shin-deep mud made what little was left of them largely impassable. To add to the difficulties, because the mornings were misty, visual signalling was impossible and the length and speed of the advance made telephone communications more problematic than usual. Runners were used to relay information back to brigade and division but, when practicable, 187 Brigade also seems to have improvised by using semaphore between battalions and brigade HQ.

At the start of the advance towards the Hindenburg Line the brigade's entirely green troops had kept pace with those of other divisions on their flanks and had occupied some important tactical positions. When it was relieved on 26-27 February the divisional diarist recorded the brigade's performance had been "most creditable."[29] Unlike its 1st Line formation, 49th (West Riding) Division, that had spent its first nine months abroad line holding, 62nd (2nd West Riding) Division had been thrown into the maelstrom within a month of its arrival. It had been a harsh introduction to warfare on the Somme but the brigades' commanders and troops had adapted quickly to the conditions. In the same way as the other recently arrived 2nd Line divisions, however, 62nd Division was to find the transition from a Home Army formation to a member of the BEF rather more difficult than had the New Army formations. The reason for this additional handicap was the absence of a pioneer battalion.

---

25   Ibid., 14 Feb.1917.
26   TNA WO 953079. 185 Bde, 5 Feb.1917.
27   Falls, *Military Operations 1917*, Vol. I, p.95,
28   Even if they could be dug, floored and revetted, German gunners usually quickly managed to collapse CT heads.
29   TNA WO 953068: 26 Feb.1917.

The need for pioneer battalions to assist and supplement the RE field companies had become apparent in late 1914. The initial eight Regular Army divisions deployed to the Western Front did not have a dedicated pioneer battalion until 1916 but because many of their brigades had TF battalions attached as a fifth unit they possessed the additional manpower to provide working parties. All New Army divisions landed in France or on Gallipoli with a dedicated pioneer battalion and three field companies; the six 1st Line TF divisions that went to the Western Front in 1915 had to wait several months before they were allocated a battalion of pioneers. Furthermore, three of the four 1st Line divisions deployed to Gallipoli had to make do with only two field companies and no pioneer battalion for the duration of their stay on the peninsula.[30] Both 60th and 61st Division crossed to France with three field companies and a pioneer unit but those 2nd Line formations that did not arrive until early 1917 were not allocated a pioneer battalion until the major reorganization of the BEF in February 1918. Why these 2nd Line formations were treated differently in this respect to the New Armies is unclear. There appears to be no extant evidence to explain the discriminatory decision on the part of the War Office but it was possibly a combination of the deteriorating manpower situation, the traditional attitude of the War Office towards putting the needs of the Regular and New Armies before those of the TF, and an assumption that if they were to be largely used only as line holding formations the divisions would be able to do their own pioneer work.[31]

It is likely that the 2nd Line divisions were informed before they left the UK that they would not receive a pioneer unit. This is by no means certain but only one, 66th (2nd East Lancashire), made any comments in the divisional diary about the issue. It is perhaps possible the other four divisions were informed and 66th was not, but five days after DHQ opened in France it noted, "It seems we'll have to go into the line without a Pioneer battalion [and that an application for a one] had been urgently made." Five days later the diary noted First Army had informed the GOC that no pioneer battalion would be made available. This, the diarist believed, created a "serious situation" because the division would be expected to maintain at least 7,000 yards of trenches, numerous strong points and all of the reserve lines within its sector.[32] Pioneer battalions were frequently left in the line to work when their own division was withdrawn to rest so it may have been assumed that when they were in the line field companies and battalions of the 2nd Line divisions would simply have one attached from another division. What was certain, however, was that the infantry would be required to provide even more working parties than would normally be the case. It would also probably explain why 187 Brigade was detailed for railway work rather than undertaking any training or trench acclimatization.

The GOC 66th (2nd East Lancashire) Division, Major General Herbert Lawrence, was clearly disquieted with the way his division had been treated on arrival. Although unpopular with many of his contemporaries, Lawrence was an able commander and spent a good deal of

30 The 42nd (East Lancashire) and 52nd (Lowland) were not to receive a pioneer battalion until they were transferred to the Western Front in March 1917 and April 1918 respectively. In Palestine, the 1st Line 53rd (Welsh) received an Indian Army battalion in 1918; 54th (East Anglian) fought the entire desert campaign without one. A third field company was only allocated to 42nd (East Lancashire) four months after its arrival on the peninsula.
31 K.W. Mitchinson, *Pioneer Battalions in the Great War* (Barnsley: Pen & Sword, 1997).
32 TNA WO 953120: 7 Mar.1917; 12 Mar.1917

his time visiting the front trenches in order to understand the difficulties and problems.[33] He had only taken command of the division two weeks before it left the UK and had been annoyed not only over the lack of pioneers but also because the trench mortar batteries were late in arriving. Furthermore, the machine gun companies, which had also very recently joined the division, were removed shortly before its departure. On arrival in France, and in accordance with recently prescribed strictures, battalions suffered the disruption of a major reorganization of platoons. All reconstituted platoons were allowed only 48 hours in the front trenches with units of 5th Division with before then having to relieve their mentors. The relief was completed within two weeks of the division's arrival but, in even greater haste, 202 MG Company relieved 13 MG Company only two days after the former had reported to DHQ. Probably assuming the corps commander, Lieutenant General Haking, and the Army Commander, General Horne, would be likely see the entry, Lawrence signed off the March war diary with the comment: "These minor difficulties [the lack of pioneers and entirely new MG companies] are of small importance to an old Division, but the fact that in several cases, Battalions carried out difficult moves without 1st Line transport during the period preparatory to taking over trenches for the first time without mistakes, shows promise of good work in the future."[34] Lawrence went on to point out the difficulties the division had experienced in assembling its units during the concentration period, that the original estimation of 7,000 yards of trenches to be maintained was in fact closer to 9,000 yards, and that a battalion of 197 Brigade had successfully repelled a German raid during the fusiliers' very first night in the trenches.[35]

The speed with which the 2nd Line divisions took over their own sectors of front during the brutal winter of 1917 allowed other formations, in theory, greater periods of rest. In practice, however, especially in those areas where the Germans began their withdrawal to the Hindenburg Line, this was rarely the case. Most of the battalions of the 2nd Line divisions arrived with well over 900 men. This made them considerably stronger than other units in their corps but the demands for working parties and attendance at divisional schools eroded the numbers available for trench duty. Although on paper the bulk of the men in units deployed in early 1917 had been in uniform for well over six months before departure, they were still very green. The priority for senior commanders was to continue to train their troops but now with the advantage of doing it in active service conditions. A divisional school which included a section under two Dominion officers devoted to training battalion raiding parties was quickly opened by 57th Division.

On arrival at the corps rear area, senior divisional officers, COs, seconds-in-command, adjutants, and sub-unit commanders were frequently lectured by the GOC corps and sometimes also by his Brigadier General General Staff (BGGS). Precise contents of the speeches are unknown but it is probable that they were aimed at establishing quickly what the corps expected of their new arrivals. Discipline, fighting power, unit esprit and above all imbuement of troops with the offensive spirit would have been among the topics. It would have been made clear to brigade and unit commanders that their key function during the acclimatization process and afterwards was to spend as much time as demands for working parties and line holding permitted in developing the troops' fighting power by progressive training. In a subsequent conference one GOC brigade asked his COs for suggestions as to how a small number of instructional staff could be trained

---

33   Lt. Gen. Sir H.A. Lawrence became Haig's Chief of Staff in 1918.
34   TNA WO 953120: Mar.1917.
35   Ibid.

in each platoon. In response it was agreed that each battalion should form four distinct classes. They would teach tactical bombing, use of the Lewis gun, sniping and scouting, and bayonet fighting. A fifth class was run for platoon commanders and five NCOs selected from each platoon with the object of making each platoon self-sufficient in instructors. Acquiring sufficient instructors to teach the would-be instructors, however, proved to be a challenging process. Divisional schools were also established for certain skills but the lack of trained instructors handicapped progress and efficiency of both these and the brigade schools. One GOC division wistfully signed off a war diary entry that pointed out the lack of experienced instructors with the patently obvious comment of, "These are naturally lacking in this division."[36] The flow of instructional manuals written from lessons learned during the Somme fighting was gathering momentum but training was frequently interrupted not only by the demands of working parties but also by extended periods in the line. For example, in May 1917, 2/4th East Lancashire endured a tour of 23 days in the line, had four days of supposed rest and then went back into the line for another 24 days, In April, 2/9th Manchester was relieved after 31 days and then went back in again for another long tour after only four days in the rear.

So great was the pressure that 187 Brigade cancelled its brigade schools because the demand for railway work took precedence "over all other work or training."[37] The attachment of its NCOs and specialists to other units for instruction was also cancelled. Demands eased a little in V Corps area in April when each brigade of 58th Division was permitted to have one battalion training per day. By the end of the month an unprecedented regime whereby each of the division's brigades was allowed three successive days' training was implemented. This gave some opportunity for men and their units to focus on what they considered to be their real function. In order to achieve some progress until it could establish its own schools, 60th Division sent some of its men to 51st Division's trench mortar, sniper, and grenade schools, but it had managed to open its own PT School by mid-July. When time and demands permitted, brigade grenade schools were often among the first to be established but, in the meantime, only officers were able to attend demonstrations given by corps or other divisions. The CO of 2/4th York & Lancs noted ruefully his "regret that it [a demonstration] was not given to all ranks" because accidents when fusing grenades were commonplace within battalions.[38] In April, while complaining of a lack of drafts and emphasizing how every available man was required for trench maintenance, 66th Division reorganized its brigade training organization but accepted that the introduction of the new system would have to wait until less hectic times. It justified the postponement on the grounds that "units of the division want practical experience much more than theory."[39] Such was the frustration during this initial period for most of the 2nd Line formations that one warrant officer wrote of his battalion's many "useless wanderings" and of how the unit's early weeks overseas convinced him that his "battalion and division generally seemed to be wanted by no one."[40]

As with all new formations, there was a degree of naivety and innocence amongst the men. With understandable frustration the staff officer responsible for 66th Division's war diary

---

36 TNA WO 953120: 30 Apr.1917.
37 TNA WO 953090: 2/4th York & Lancs, 4 Feb.1917.
38 Ibid. 11 Feb.1917.
39 TNA WO 953120: 2 Apr.1917.
40 C.A. Keeson, *The Queen Victoria's Rifles 1792-1922* (London: Constable, 1923), p.294.

recorded troops "do not yet realize the necessity for keeping under cover" and by "wandering about in the open" during daylight gave away the positions of observation posts.[41] With equal innocence and unaware their new position was overlooked by the enemy, 2/15th London marched into Maroeuil with hurricane lamps blazing. It was immediately greeted by a salvo of shells.[42] Despite their earlier attachment to host divisions and supposed familiarity with the line, divisional and brigade staffs still had a great deal to learn on taking over their own sectors. This was not helped by the absence through illness of key staff, the consequence of which for 171 Brigade was a "certain amount of difficulties." Army and corps staffs, however, assumed that as they were working in generally quiet areas the new arrivals would quickly assimilate.[43] Their inexperience, but also their willingness to learn, were possibly two of the reasons why 61st Division, together with the equally untried 5th Australian Division, was selected to undertake the ill-judged assault at Fromelles in July 1916.[44] The reasons for what degenerated into a disastrous attack have been well rehearsed and will not be covered here in depth other than to draw attention to the South Midlanders' failure after only seven weeks in France to seize and hold the enemy's formidable front and support systems.[45]

The attack was originally conceived as an attempt to fix German troops opposite XI Corps and prevent their movement south to the Somme. The planning was rushed, there was hesitancy at First Army GHQ and corps HQ as to the operation's extent and scale, and frequent alterations to the resources allocated. For example, over 2,500 troops of 61st Division had carried up 1,500 gas cylinders to the front lines in June. Once the proposed attack was confirmed some of cylinders were carried back or their gas released to prevent them becoming a hazard in the division's front line. Insufficient artillery, most of which was new to the Western Front, was employed on counter-battery work, cutting the opposing wire, and on destroying the substantial number of concrete machine gun bunkers. This was especially the case for those machine guns positioned in the two German strong points known as the Sugar Loaf and the Wick. To compound these planning errors rather than have the Sugar Loaf, the key to the German front positions, attacked by one brigade it was to be assaulted by troops not only from two divisions but also from two armies. There was no element of surprise (German batteries and machine guns kept the British parapets under constant heavy fire for at least 30 minutes before zero) and the numbers of troops used meant there was no emphatic concentration of force. There was inadequate means of re-supply should success have been achieved and the troops had spent only a limited time in the sector. Patrols and raids to garner intelligence had been largely unsuccessful, no man's land was up to 400 yards wide, and the allotment of liaison officers between the two attacking divisions was insufficient. Dominated by German batteries and observation posts on the Aubers Ridge to the south-east, two major British offensives over the same ground in 1915 had demonstrated how ill-suited it was to frontal assault. The ill-conceived July attack

---

41   TNA WO 953120: 30 Mar.1917.
42   P. Davenport & A.C. Benke (eds.) *The History of the Prince of Wales' Own Civil Service Rifles* (London: Wyman & Sons, 1921), p.238.
43   TNA WO 952980: 171 Bde, 28 Feb.1917.
44   Some of the troops of 5th Australian Division had fought on Gallipoli but the bulk of the division was comprised of previously untried battalions and artillery brigades.
45   With the exception of 21st and 24th divisions, which were thrown ill-prepared into the Battle of Loos with such tragic consequences, New Army divisions were generally awarded something like two months to acclimatize before being used in major offensives.

could and should have been cancelled – the opportunities to do so were there – but General Monro and Lieutenant General Haking decided it should proceed.

Haking later explained that he had been compelled to use 61st Division rather than another more experienced division because it was already manning the sector; this, he wrote, avoided the need to bring in a division even more unfamiliar with the ground. Major General Mackenzie can certainly be criticised for deploying his troops into no man's land only by means of a series of sally ports which quickly became the focus of concentrated enemy machine-gun fire. Mackenzie's brigade commanders carried out his orders but were later to show good practical situational awareness in insisting that once the initial attack had stalled further efforts would be futile. The six assaulting battalions advanced, with 2/6th and 2/7th Warwickshire managing to enter the German trenches, but were cut down in swathes and lost about 50 percent of their personnel. The physical and conceptual components of the division's fighting power were clearly inadequate for the task but their courage and commitment were evident in their attempts to cross no man's land in the face of such intense fire. This, however, was not apparent to Haking. The corps commander knew the artillery was largely untried and thus unlikely to achieve its objectives, but praised 5th Australian Division for its gallantry. He recorded that it was not a lack of bravery that prevented it from consolidating its gains, but its lack of training. The failure of 61st Division was different. In Haking's opinion the South Midlanders lacked sufficient offensive spirit. He complained that some battalions were late in deploying and that others did not rush towards the German lines at the scheduled time. The only battalion, however, that seems to have deployed into no man's land a little late was 2/1st Bucks. Seeing that the sally ports were drawing heavy fire, the CO ordered his men to switch their exit positions and advance instead from a sap a little further distant. When asked by Monro before the assault if he was confident of the resources and troops allocated, Haking expressed his confidence in the ability of 61st Division to achieve its objectives. After the battle Haking noted that a "good" division would have been able to "carry and hold the line." Nevertheless, he concluded, "I think the attack, although it failed, has done both divisions a great deal of good."[46]

Whether Major General Mackenzie actually believed the attack had done his division a "great deal of good" is unclear. In his post battle report he expressed his satisfaction in the way the troops had fought, in the assistance of the artillery, and the manner by which communications were maintained. He accepted that the artillery had been unable to silence the enemy batteries and the machines guns in the Sugar Loaf and the Wick, but stressed that the experience had been a "high test for comparatively inexperienced troops." He would have been reliant on his staff, brigade commanders and COs to report on how the men's morale had been affected by the failure but for his official analysis of the operation he painted a positive picture: "The chief feeling … amongst the men afterwards was anger towards the enemy, and disappointment that they were not allowed to try again, & I am confident that their spirit is a good, or even better, than it was before the attack."[47]

A similarly bright assessment of the morale of the men of 62nd (2nd West Riding) Division was made during its testing time on the Somme. In February, when relieved from their first trench tours, 185 Brigade's men were described as "absolutely exhausted", with some having been

---

46 TNA WO 95165: XI Corps to First Army, 24 Jul.1916
47 TNA WO 953033: 22 Jul.1916

"long without food" because ration parties had not found the posts. Conditions for 186 Brigade "could not have been worse" but the men were "quite cheery" and thought to be "breaking into trench life very well." In an attempt to draw his own conclusions about morale, the brigadier and his brigade major visited all COs in order to ask "very careful and leading questions on all points concerning the health and comforts of the men." In 187 Brigade, spirits were considered to be "splendid" and "extremely high", with the appalling conditions being "borne cheerfully by all ranks."[48] Until Bullecourt in May, the division had little opportunity to demonstrate the quality or otherwise of its training in an offensive operation as its prime function was to engage German rearguards withdrawing across the destroyed zone.

In more settled parts of the front, raids were seen as one of the means of fostering morale and developing fighting power. To GHQ and corps HQ they were viewed as a necessary means to an end and, in the same way as the 1st Line and New Armies divisions, 2nd Line TF divisions were expected quickly to acquire the ways to achieve those ends. There has recently been considerable debate on what constituted the difference between a raid and a patrol. Historians had generally acknowledged that patrols involved intelligence gathering in no man's land and the enemy's forward defences while a raid was a more aggressive and formal affair, usually involving a greater number of men. Their task was to enter the enemy's trenches in order to demolish defences, capture prisoners or collect identification, and generally cause chaos. There is now fairly widespread acceptance that officers at the time drew no great distinction between the two activities; indeed, there is a great deal of overlap in the use of the words. For example, there are frequent references to "fighting patrols" that might not only lie in wait to ambush German patrols but which might also enter the enemy front line. Whatever the difference may or may not have been, activities such as these were aimed to assert dominance over the enemy and limit his activities. When 61st Division joined Haking's XI Corps in mid-1916 it was quickly informed it would be expected to carry out raiding and patrolling.

On 5 June 1916, as preparations for the Somme were proceeding further south, Haking told General Monro, GOC First Army, that he had devised a programme of operations aimed at maintaining pressure on the enemy on his corps' front. All his divisions were ordered to construct models of the enemy trench system opposite their lines; on 14 June a conference of his divisional GOsC was convened to discuss strategy. Between that conference, and another on 30 June which summoned all brigade GOsC to DHQ to discuss raiding policy, 61st Division conducted several raids. Immediately following that conference, brigade commanders cascaded its conclusions to their battalion COs. These discussions presumably examined the results achieved so far and how the process could be improved. Having taken over its own sector of line only just over a week earlier, 2/5th Gloucestershire of 184 Brigade undertook a raid described later as a "sorry tale".[49] The Germans opened a heavy barrage on the Gloucesters' parapets 15 minutes before the British guns were scheduled to fire. At 2230, two reports erroneously claiming the Germans were attacking were received at battalion HQ. This resulted in some of the raiding party being ordered to man the parapet. These men then missed the order to advance because the raid commander mistakenly took his men over seven minutes before the appointed time. The raiders were targeted by front and enfilade machine gun and rifle fire (and possibly also by a

---

48   TNA WO 953079: 17 Feb.1917; TNA WO 953087, 2/7th Duke of Wellington's, 18 & 23 Feb.1917; WO 953090: 2/4th York & Lancs, 24 Feb.1917 and 2/5th York & Lancs, 28 Feb.1917.
49   A. Barnes, *2/5th Gloucester*, p.40.

light field gun embedded in the front line) and were forced to withdraw. The brigadier general's subsequent report related how telephone communications had swiftly broken down, runners were not organized or utilized correctly, and of how lanes had not earlier been cut through the battalion's wire.[50] How or why lanes through friendly wire had not been earlier cleared suggests either an unfortunate naivety or perhaps an excessive wariness of possible German aggression. Six nights later, one company of 2/8th Warwickshire, which as a battalion had spent even less time in the line than the Gloucesters, attempted a raid. The company involved had practised its "manoeuvres" but the enemy was alert and "absolutely ready" for them. As the raiders tried to enter the German trenches, they were "overwhelmed" by "heavy shell and light guns", and then also by an isolating curtain of fire that fell behind them. Initial estimates of the casualties amounted to four dead, 16 missing and 20 wounded. A report explained that the several parties had lost touch with each other and once the German bombardment came down and the withdrawal became evident, some troops ran into uncut wire, some completely lost orientation, and others were confronted by an impassably deep water-filled ditch. The loss of coordination "produced most unfortunate results which could not be rectified and the attack resolved itself into little disconnected parties crawling about in No Man's Land."[51] Why the Germans appeared to have been expecting the raid is unknown – there are no reports of Warwicks men being taken prisoner during the days immediately before the raid – but ignorance of what must have been a significance ditch in no man's land indicates that patrol reconnaissance had been sketchy or that intelligence had been disregarded.

A battalion of 184 Brigade made another attempt the following night and met with the same result. Although the officers and men of the company of 2/4th Ox & B were reported to have fought well and courageously, the brigade commander believed the CO, Lieutenant Colonel Ames, "threw away" the chance of success. Brigadier General Carter criticized Ames for not adhering to the brigadier's instructions about the use of Bangalore torpedoes and for "very injudiciously" ordering the recall when success could still have been achieved. Carter acknowledged that communications had at times broken down and that the covering bombardment lacked sufficient intensity but he was angry because now on two occasions COs had tampered with his "final" instructions and failure had ensued. Carter's attempt to apportion the responsibility for failure on Lieutenant Colonel Ames seems to have back-fired because by the end of the month, both he and Ames had lost their commands.

Before Carter relinquished command, however, there does seem to have been an alteration to the process by which raids were planned. Another of his battalions, 2/4th Berkshire, which had already had one change of CO since it had taken over its own piece of line, undertook what was later described as an "elaborate" and "rather unfortunate raid." The orders received by Lieutenant Colonel Beer stated that he, rather than the GOC brigade, should decide on the numbers and composition of the raiding party, zero hour, points of entry, and how the artillery should cooperate. On 13 July, four officers and 100 men, split into 10 parties, could not find gaps in the German wire and discovered that the men carrying the fuses for the Bangalores had been wounded and left behind. Three of the four officers were also quickly hit but, according to

---

50 TNA WO 953063: 21 Jun.1916. Casualties were recorded as five killed, four missing, and 18 wounded.
51 TNA WO 953054: 28 Jun.1916. Casualties attributed to the enemy barrage in 2/6th Warwickshire were reported as one dead and 17 wounded.

Carter's report, the first wave, which had forced an entry into the German front line under the "galling" fire of four or five machine guns' remained unsupported owing to "a lack of leadership" amongst NCOs of the second wave. Writing before he had received Carter's report and the accusations of a want of initiative on the part of NCOs, Haking congratulated the Berkshires for their "gallant attempt."[52] This had been the Berkshires' first "minor enterprise" and came less than a week before the main attack at Fromelles. It failed through a combination of the CO's excessively and unnecessarily complicated tactical plan, a lack of foresight in not carrying spare Bangalore fuses, the bad luck of having the officers quickly becoming casualties, and the alleged reluctance of NCOs to shoulder the responsibility.

A week before the Berkshires' effort, 183 Brigade had attempted two staggered raids. On the night of 4-5 July, 2/7th Worcestershire and 2/4th Gloucestershire crossed no man's land within two hours of each other with the intention of remaining in the German trenches opposite Fauquissart for one hour. Outlines of the enemy lines had been traced on the practice ground and the companies concerned were drilled over them for two days. Deception was built into the artillery plan by encouraging the Germans to believe the raids would take place elsewhere but, when the Worcesters and Gloucesters left their own trenches at 2220 and 0020 respectively, they quickly ran into trouble. Although the main belts of enemy wire had in places been cut quite well, earlier patrol intelligence had failed to identify numerous wire-filled pits covered with grass and low hung wire in front of the German trenches. There was also a muddy water-filled ditch in front of the parapet that the Worcesters attempted to cross by means of hauling each other out. Fully alerted, the Germans bombed them as they struggled in the mud. Raiders' rifles became clogged and although some of the first two lines fought their way into the enemy trenches, the follow up waves were pinned down close to the narrow gap in the wire by enemy bombing posts either side of it. To add to the chaos, cries of "Retire" shouted by the Germans caused groups of raiders to withdraw. Having expended all their bombs, and in the face of developing German counter-attacks, those who had been fighting at close quarters withdrew to their own trenches. The Worcesters sustained approximately 35 and the Gloucesters about 40 casualties. Although the brigade commander praised the work of Lieutenant Colonel Dorman for his planning and direction of the raid, the enterprise was hardly a success. Artillery and trench mortar cooperation worked well but poor intelligence and a lack of adequate situational awareness resulted in confusion, muddle, and a casualty rate of approximately 30 percent.[53]

Another raid was undertaken in later June by 2/8th Worcestershire. They discovered the enemy front lines badly knocked about and empty. Assuming the Germans had retired to their second line, the raiders explored the deserted trench for about 70 yards in both directions before returning across no man's land little the wiser. The activity was, of course, not all one sided. The Germans welcomed the division to an early display of artillery and small arms prowess by targeting the newcomers' arrival in the front lines with an accurate and heavy bombardment. This was followed by a prolonged and "extremely well aimed" machine gun and rifle barrage that "just topped the edge of our parapet."[54] Nocturnal patrols quite regularly bumped into each other and the Germans did make the occasional raid. One of the most severe occurred on the night 1-2 July 1916. Greater events were taking place to the south when the enemy opened a

---

52   TNA WO 953063: 14 Jul.1916.
53   TNA WO 953058: WO 953060: 5 Jul.1916.
54   TNA WO 953063: 184 Bde, 25-26 Jun.1916.

barrage of heavy shells and shrapnel, later joined by a heavy *minenwerfer* at 0730 on 1 July. This gradually grew in intensity during the day with fire being concentrated on the three forward battalions of 182 Brigade. Communications between the companies of 2/5th Warwickshire were shattered and several fire bays were blown in. One shell exploded the brigade's mining explosive store, which killed several men in the front line, and others destroyed garrisoned saps and bombing posts. Between 2230 and 2300 a party of Germans entered the Warwicks' trenches, bombing dugouts and killing several of the garrisons. It was later assumed they were searching for mine shafts but it appears there were no positive sightings of the group except by one dazed signaller who claimed there had been at least 12 Germans, all over six feet tall. The group seems to have withdrawn across no man's land but because no one at the time knew of their existence and with communications broken, they did not have to pass through any defensive barrage. The Warwickshire later reported 16 dead and 57 wounded. In his subsequent report on the affair, the brigadier general expressed his "regret that a party of Germans should have been able to get into the trenches and out again without loss", but did accept that the concentrated bombardment had been a severe trial for a new battalions. He insisted morale in 2/5th Warwickshire remained unimpaired and that the experience had only whetted the appetite of troops in the two flank battalions "to get at the enemy."[55] As Brigadier General Gordon suggested, this had been a brutal baptism of fire for 2/1st Warwickshire Brigade but, on the whole, and with the exception of the Fromelles attack itself, the division's sector was a relatively quiet one. Until it was relieved by the 1st Line territorials of 56th (London) Division, the South Midland does seem to have dominated no man's land. The Germans did raid and patrol but their aggressive activities were less frequent than the British. In general, they remained more defensively rather than offensively minded. After Fromelles, the division was brought towards establishment and generally maintained a reasonable strength. Having been withdrawn for a short period of training, in mid-November it moved to the Somme.

The other early 2nd Line formation arrival, 60th (2/2nd London) Division, was also despatched to what was initially a relatively quiet sector. Under Lieutenant General Sir Charles Fergusson, XVII Corps had only taken over the sector north of Arras in March. Although there had been some bitter fighting in May on Vimy Ridge, the sector had earned, according to one of the Londoners, something of a "live and let live" reputation.[56] This was not entirely the case as the Germans had developed the practice of firing intense bombardments nightly on the lengthy communication trenches and reserve positions. When making its way up to the front positions for the first time, 2/18th London was caught in one of these bombardments and sustained 35 casualties. As another welcoming gesture, one of the peripatetic German bombardment groups paid the area a visit soon after the division moved into the line. In retaliation, two days later the division's gunners fired their first large scale slow and deliberate bombardment. In possibly not the most impartial manner, this was assessed by DHQ as being "most successful". To make life even more uncomfortable, the Germans also enjoyed observation over the entire divisional front. Mining activity was practiced extensively by both sides and the 1st Line 51st (Highland) Division, whilst not yet having earned the reputation that was later to make it one of the BEF's most formidable divisions, was frequently involved in crater fighting to secure the near lips of

---

55 TNA WO 953033: 182 Bde, 2 Jul.1916.
56 E. May, *Signal Corporal*, p.28.

recently blown mines. It had formed its own Crater Consolidation School to which members of 60th Division were also sent to learn the requisite skills. The Londoners' inexperience became quickly apparent when on 27 July, within two weeks of the division taking over the line, 2/20th London had to make several attempts to secure the lip and consolidate a new crater. On one of the attempts the main party's security was compromised by the failure to place a covering force on one of the flanks.

The 60th Division soon learned the essentials and by early August suggestions were regularly being sent back to brigade and divisional HQ on how similar operations could be improved and honed. Orders were issued by at least one brigade outlining what raids should entail, the rehearsals required, and the tools and equipment to be carried. Once the mine was blown speed, it was quickly realized, was of the essence. If it were a British mine being blown the ground needed to have been fully reconnoitred, the route from the front sap to the probable site of the crater was to be marked by pickets and paper, and previously laid direction tape was to be cut into short lengths to reduce the chance of it being blown away by shell fire. Revetting material had to be ready for immediate fixing because whilst the operation was proceeding, German snipers and trench mortars, if not an assault party, were expected to target the crater.

The division began systematic raiding in August 1916. Although it had already captured a couple of prisoners during a crater fight, its first real "enterprise" was made in less than glorious fashion on 6 August. The raid by 2/13th London quickly degenerated into chaos after the man carrying the reel of tape fell into a shell hole and entangled the tape with his kit. The party pressed on and made its way into a deserted enemy trench. Blocks in place could not be moved or broken because, as the lieutenant reported, they did not possess the appropriate means. It was quickly obvious no prisoners would be taken so recall was sounded and the party, as arranged, split into three sections. One group made it back safely, one had become so disorientated it leapt into other nearby German trenches, and the third found refuge in a shell hole for a day until it was discovered the following night by a patrol sent out to look for it.[57]

One night later a much more organized and choreographed affair was conducted by 2/23rd London. Trench mortars registered on three successive nights where gaps were to be cut in the wire for the raid; other mortars registered on sites up and down the line to aid deception. The wire and trenches opposite the raid's target area were also shelled "casually" from time to time with the object of making it look as if done almost by accident. Howitzers registered on machine-gun posts and communication trenches and a few hours before the raid 4.5 inch howitzers fired 30 rounds on known strong points in the support trench. The GOC brigade had left all tactical details to the CO who, in addition to coordinating the trench mortar and artillery support, also enlisted the assistance of the Lewis guns and rifle grenadiers of 2/24th London. Despite the more thorough preparations and attempts to deceive, the enemy were not fooled and were firing on the debouching saps almost as the first raiders appeared. One bombing group was immediately "demoralized" by the loss of six of its men and as the other groups approached the enemy trenches they found the Germans with bombs laid out on the parapet ready for throwing. Having been blown to pieces the previously laid tape was useless but sufficient gaps in the wire for the parties to make an entry into the trenches were spotted and used. Once in, the raiders threw Mills and incendiary grenades down dugout steps, apparently with some success. When

---

57 Two reports within TNA WO 953030: 179 Bde HQ, Aug.1916.

the recall was sounded, there was great difficulty in persuading the guide rockets to ignite but all save one of the raiders eventually returned with their 12 casualties.[58]

Several other raids during the month also met with equally limited success. Craters and sapheads that were supposed to provide prisoners were found unoccupied, as was a larger attempt by 2/17th London on a stretch of front line of about 130 yards length. Dugouts were bombed but, again, no prisoners were taken. What the divisional history recorded as "the most successful" raid of this period was that by 2/19th London near the site of Watling Crater. Three officers and over 60 ORs spent 20 minutes in the German line, killing a reported 25 of the garrison and taking eight prisoners for a return of only two wounded. September started badly when a so-called "bogus" raid "aroused no enthusiasm" on the part of the Germans and when an attempt by 2/22nd London shortly afterwards miscarried because the party lost their way and ran into strong wire. The men were still trying to find a way through when recall was sounded. A more successful effort was made by 2/15th London. When its companies went into the line a group of two officers and 20 ORs was left behind to practise a medium-sized raid. Under a heavy box barrage, a creeper fired by trench mortars, and with flanks protected by machine guns, the raiders followed a "paper chase" trail to the enemy trenches and seized prisoners. Their return was helped by two decoy lanterns about 500 yards north of their point of re-entry that drew the enemy's "feeble and badly directed" fire. A later report noted German resistance and morale as "low" while morale in the CSR was raised to a "high footing".[59]

Other successful enterprises included a "silent" raid by 2/16th London which took five prisoners and was thought to have killed up to 20 others. The party went over without any support from 18 pdrs because, with the Somme taking priority, First Army had ordered divisions to economize on the use of these shells.[60] Although fired at by a German covering party, the Westminsters pressed on and leapt into the enemy trench only to see many of its garrison already fleeing. The men apparently carried out their demolition tasks with "joyful alacrity" and were back in their own line within 35 minutes.[61] Similarly, one a week later by the London Scots also showed how certain units were acquiring the skills and learning from experience. The lieutenant designated to lead the raid had several times personally reconnoitred the ground, replica trenches were constructed in the rear, Stokes fired rounds to demarcate the position of both flanks, and rifle grenades and searchlights were used as feints further along the line. The raid brought back five prisoners for the loss of six wounded and one missing. The subsequent report highlighted certain useful points for further use. The MO's arrangements were considered sound but evacuation of wounded from the regimental aid post (RAP) to the advanced dressing station (ADS) should have been quicker. This contrasted with the Westminsters' report which thought the "straight run" from the RAP to the ADS had worked well. The London Scots had experimented with different attack formations and finally selected one that allowed the officer in charge to maintain tighter control of the group in the pitch darkness of no man's land. Further assisted by occasional Very lights on one flank which briefly illuminated previously selected landmarks, the entire party was able to enter the enemy trenches as one.[62]

58   TNA WO 953032. 181 Bde HQ, 8 Aug.1916,
59   TNA WO 953030: 179 Bde HQ, 11 Sep.1916; Davenport & Benke, *Civil Service Rifles*, pp. 244-45.
60   TNA WO 95934: XVII Corps HQ, 23 Sep.1916.
61   TNA WO 95179: Bde HQ, 24 Sep.1916.
62   TNA WO 953030: 179 Bde HQ, 30 Sep.1916.

Lessons were also learned and resolutions sought about the use of smoke. Brigadier General Parsons, GOC 181 Brigade, argued that smoke drew a heavier hostile response than would otherwise be the case and suggested instead that the heavies should be reserved for pre-assault counter-battery work. The brigadier general made this suggestion despite a report from one of his COs whose battalion had undertaken a raid the previous night. Raiders from 2/22nd London went over in three groups under smoke and artillery. They easily entered the German trenches and met "extremely slight resistance." The men pushed on, having to be restrained from continuing on to the support line, and only with "the greatest difficulty were persuaded to leave the German trenches" when recall was sounded. A determined and coordinated German barrage did not came down until about 25 minutes after the raiders had disappeared but the CO believed the smoke and decoy barrage fired by the trench mortars had successfully drawn the enemy's artillery and machine-gun fire away from the raiding parties.[63]

In contrast to the boost in morale those successful raids engendered to their respective units, one by 2/21st London "plunged the battalion in gloom." The guns had fired on the enemy wire for four days but a week of reconnaissance by the two officers who would lead the raid discovered only one gap in the wire. When the raiders approached the gap the Germans hurled grenades and smoke bombs to halt the advance. The officer ordered the men to rush the gap but they appeared to "waver" with the result that an officer and NCO were left wounded close to the wire when the rest of the party withdrew. The officer was later brought in but died of his wounds. The brigadier wrote a report that criticised a "lack of dash" on the part of the men and, in an unusually frank assessment of the raid in the later regimental history, the author acknowledged that perhaps the men did show too much hesitation in rushing the gap. He did draw attention, however, to the contemporary assumption that because only one gap had been blown the Germans were bound to be protecting that sector in particular strength. Shortly afterwards the CO went on leave and did not return. The regimental history recorded his "only fault" as being "too kind".[64]

Another raid which also had a negative effect on morale was done by 2/18th London early in October. The enterprise, by three officers and 98 ORs in three parties, was met by a very prepared and alert enemy. It was a bright night and the raiders battled through intense machine gun and rifle fire to reach the enemy trenches. Germans manned the front line with up to six men per bay but many were put to flight and headed for their dugouts. Phosphorous and Mills bombs followed them but when recall was sounded and the survivors regained their own trenches, initial reports stated five dead and 44 wounded. Lieutenant General Fergusson, expressed his satisfaction at the effort made by the London Irish but just over a week later the CO, Lieutenant Colonel Murphy, went on leave to the UK. Murphy returned and resumed command towards the end of October but on 9 November was ordered to report to the War Office. The regimental history believed he had been sent home because he had "struggled too hard" to have the raid of 9 October cancelled and that "his stubbornness in fighting for his battalion resulted in his removal." When he left for home his troops lined the road and the officers, who had dined him out to "express their confidence in his leadership and sympathy

---

63 TNA WO 955032: 181 Bde HQ, 8 Oct.1916, Report by Major Borton; Report by Brig. Gen. Parsons, 9 Oct.1916.
64 TNA WO 953032: 181 Bde HQ, 25 Sep.1916; Compiled, *A War History of 21st London*, pp.157-61.

in his sorrow," themselves hauled his transport out of camp.[65] To make the battalion feel even more aggrieved at the authorities' decision, rather than appoint the second-in-command, or at least another officer from the London Regiment, a major from the West African Rifles was transferred in to command.

Whilst formal raids involved a greater number of men and offered opportunities to enhance a battalion's reputation, patrolling was an every night fact of life. When in the line each brigade would send out up to six patrols every night. Often comprising only one officer or NCO and two or three men, these gathered information on the state of the enemy wire or simply laid up and listened at enemy sap heads or within sound of his working parties. The enemy was reasonably quiet. He, too, sent out patrols but if they bumped into a British squad tended to make off rather than stand and fight. His raids were certainly far less frequent than those of 60th Division and rarely penetrated beyond the British wire. The Germans opposite were largely Saxons, known for their less aggressive spirit than certain other provincial groups within the German Army. They relied more on their artillery and large *minenwerfers*, than regular large scale raids to remind the Londoners of their continued presence. When called upon to repel a raid or seize a crater's lip they generally fought well but the frequency of crater explosions had begun to decline before 60th Division took over the sector.[66] The division maintained a high degree of raid intensity that did, in general, appear to have been effective in gathering identity and intelligence. With the occasional exception the artillery became more proficient in laying box barrages and the trench mortars offered an increasingly secure means of blowing gaps in the enemy's wire. On one occasion, however, the mediums "made such an amazingly bad shoot" that a raid had to be postponed,[67] Small sections of RE often accompanied the raiders to advise or assist in demolition work but most of their field companies' time was spent in improving camps, securing water supply, and building dugouts. Nonetheless, and despite much good work, the sappers could sometimes annoy the infantry. One diarist noted that, "not content with peacefully constructing duckboards" in the rear, "they further undermined us by piercing deep holes in the bottom" of front line trenches.[68]

Drafts arrived reasonably regularly but battalion strengths were well below establishment. Divisions on or about to go to the Somme took precedence for postings but divisions, brigades and battalions up and down the front complained at the quality, origins, numbers, and state of training of the drafts. "A rather poor looking lot" from a variety of London Regiments was taken, for example, by 181 Brigade.[69] For its part, the artillery brigades had not only to maintain their strengths but also underwent a significant alteration in structure and organization. These changes negatively affected the number of available gunners and drivers and also of battery commanders.[70]

---

65 TNA WO 953031: WD 2/18th London Oct. 1916
66 According to XVII Corps WD, excluding camouflets, the number of German and British mines exploded were respectively: 13 and 12 in May; 12 and two in June; seven and three in July. See TNA WO 95943: Jul.1916
67 TNA WO 953032: 181 Bde HQ, 3 Oct.1916
68 Complied, *A War History of 21st London*, p158-9
69 TNA WO 953032: 181 Bde HQ, 20 Jul,1916
70 TNA WO 95943: XVII Corps, 22 Aug.1916. The reorganization of artillery brigades affected all divisions.

Although in relative terms it was not under a great deal of pressure from the Germans, the division learned its trade in the Arras sector. According to 179 Brigade, the raids had been the means of "instilling confidence in the troops," and Major General Bulfin unsurprisingly recorded his belief that the intelligence gathered had been of important use to GHQ and that no man's land had become largely the preserve of the division. Perhaps a more balanced view was later offered by a soldier in the London Irish. He explained that by the time the division left, "We ...had no sense of inferiority or [of] having been dominated – but it is fair to say that the Germans gave no sign of suffering from those feelings himself!"[71] As the summer passed and news from the Somme remained grim, the division assumed that it, too, would head south. It was withdrawn from the line in October for rest and training but its destination was to be Salonika rather than the Somme.

Three of the 2nd Line divisions, 58th, 59th and 62nd, arrived when the line was just about to become fluid. They had, therefore, few early opportunities to conduct formal raids against well constructed enemy trenches. They sent out patrols and there are reports that selected parties did practise raiding skills but they became quickly occupied in the advance towards the Hindenburg Line.[72] In contrast, 57th (West Lancashire) and 66th (East Lancashire) divisions were to remain in the quiet and static areas of II ANZAC and XI Corps for several months.[73] The West Lancashire Division very quickly immersed itself in the philosophy of II ANZAC, producing within days of its arrival a defence scheme that included the creation of what were generally called Fighting Duckboard Parties. These were groups of a minimum of 12 men deployed along the forward positions at a rate of four per battalion front. If the division's posts were entered by hostile raiders the fighting parties were tasked to go out into no man's land and ambush the withdrawing raiders in the flank or rear. The day after producing the paper, DHQ issued another outlining a graduated approach to its raiding policy for the next 30 days. It instructed brigades to conduct small silent raids of about 20 men on 16-17 March. Their objective was straightforward: enter the enemy trenches and kill as many Germans as possible. Then, over the next 10 days parties of 50-60 men from 171 and 172 Brigades were to launch a series of major raids. The culmination of the plan was to be a raid by 250 men of 170 Brigade on the enemy's front three lines in early April. To support the raids, machine and Lewis guns and light trench mortars were detailed to protect flanks, and up to forty 18 pdrs, eight 4.5 inch, and four 60 pdrs were available to provide support. To maintain pressure on the enemy and to aid deception, dummy barrages were to be fired on three nights when operations were not to take place. A Divisional Raiding School was opened immediately to train prospective raiding parties and, until its first students had graduated, patrols were ordered to enter enemy trenches to gather intelligence. These quickly discovered that the German front line was rarely occupied. Because they had been so badly battered by Allied artillery and were frequently flooded the enemy, like the British, tended to hold them either very lightly or not at all. They were used generally only as cover and OPs for sentries. The support and third lines thus became the main lines of resistance.

---

71   TNA WO 953030: 179 Bde HQ, 26 Sep.1916; P.H. Dalbiac, *The History of the 60th Division* (London: George Allen & Unwin, 1927), p.59; E. May, *Signal Corporal*, p.29.
72   The 175 Bde does appear to have conducted four raids all involving about 20 men on 13 March. After that, its battalions quickly returned to "patrolling vigorously" in case of a German withdrawal. TNA WO 953007: 175 Bde HQ, 13 Mar.1917.
73   The 57th Division was transferred from II ANZAC to XI Corps on 25 May 1917.

War diaries suggest that although the intended frequency of raids did not quite materialize several silent raids did take place. Patrol activity was quite intense, with at least one party misjudging the rapidly approaching dawn and becoming caught by the gathering light. A conference of COs was held at the end of the month to discuss a scheme for training a nucleus of instructional staff in each platoon, and on training in general. Training teams were ordered to follow the guidance in four recent centrally issued pamphlets together with significant additional detail covering how and what should be taught. In the meantime, preparations for the raids outlined in the divisional strategy continued. The work of the brigade major of 171 Brigade in the preparation of a proposed raid by 2/7th King's illustrates the effort required to garner and coordinate support. In a period of 14 days, and in addition to his other responsibilities, he held a total of 12 meetings. These included a number with brigade majors from the other two infantry brigades, the brigade major of an artillery brigade, one with an Australian officer experienced in such matters, DHQ, where he discussed his plan in detail with the GSO1 and CRA, and at the divisional school where he observed the raiding party training over practice trenches. With everything seemingly in place, at 1700 hours on 24 March, 2/7th King's was told the raid would take place at 0320 that night. All of the planning and preparations came, however, to naught because the bridge crossing a deep ditch broke at the outset. While the barrage guns continued to hammer away, men in the ditch, up to their necks in icy water, struggled to escape. Orders relayed to the artillery to cease fire were sent in vain and the guns continued unabated. A searchlight was turned on and rockets fired in the hope the guns might get the message. Most of them did manage to cease fire within five minutes but some continued to blast away until another rocket was despatched and the battery finally ceased fire. The raiders, meanwhile, were told to get over the borrow ditch "at all costs" and were told the artillery would recommence the barrage in an hour's time. When told of this at 0348, the artillery demurred and informed 171 Brigade it would not be possible to repeat the barrage. At 0350, brigade HQ ordered the OC raid to bring in the broken bridge and close the sally ports.

Like the first raids by 61st and 60th divisions, 57th Division's initial enterprise thus ended in what was close to tragic farce. The planning had been thorough, experienced opinion was sought and utilized, and the training had been realistic. It had failed simply because a trench bridge had been badly made and because there was no Plan B or built-in contingency. Another raid, three weeks later by 2/10th King's also involved the transport of pre-fabricated bridges. Again, the preparations for what became known as Paynter's Party were thorough but this was the battalion's first attempt and most of the NCOs and men had spent only a few days in the trenches before being sent to the raiding school to practise.[74] It was certainly to be the first time they had come under such intense fire. The raiders crossed no man's land easily with the bridges remaining intact, but as soon as the six parties reached the German wire, they were met by a fusillade of bombs and rifle fire. This disrupted the groups and those which did affect an entry to the enemy front line found it empty; the fire was coming from the wired and barricaded support trench and from the flanks. The raiders never came to close quarters and those that could withdrew when recall was sounded. Of the four officers and 84 ORs who participated, casualties numbered one officer and three ORs killed, one and 26 wounded, and two officers and seven ORs missing. The raid had failed to gain any prisoners or even identify the regiments opposite.

---

74 TNA WO 952985: 2/10th King's, Apr.1917

Brigade HQ decided the failure was not the result of any lack of effort or bravery but because the artillery cover of only about one 18 pdr for every 25 yards had been inadequate. Furthermore, registration had been done hastily and inaccurately and the 18 pdr fire had predictably very limited physical effect on the enemy positions. No guns had been tasked to fire obliquely at the enemy wire and trenches, and the distance between the raiders and barrage had been set at a very distant 100 yards.

Three nights later, 2/7th King's made another attempt and, like the Liverpool Scots, all appeared to be going well until the raiders hit the wire between the unoccupied front trench and the support. On this occasion there were not many Germans in the trench but the few in occupation prevented most of the raiders from bringing the fight to close quarters. No identification was obtained. In an effort to attribute responsibility to other than the planners and the raiders, the failure was blamed largely on the state of the ground. Reports noted no man's land was heavy going and grew worse in the 60 yards before the German parapet. Crossing this required "great physical effort" and subsequently reduced the time available in the German trenches. If patrols had fully reconnoitred the approaches before the raid took place, the poor ground condition should have come as no surprise. Similarly, on the following night an officer and 13 ORs tried to surprise an enemy sentry by passing through two gaps in the wire earlier reconnoitred. They found the gaps but then came across some previously undiscovered belts a few yards behind. The party spent three hours trying to cut a way through before giving up as the wire was "too complicated."[75]

The 57th Division did not manage to capture its first unwounded prisoner until the middle of May, two months into its raiding policy.[76] That month did, however, witness an improvement in technique and successes. The basic tactic used for these more successful actions was to conduct a short, sharp operation that gained an entry into a saphead or post, seized a prisoner, and then scurried quickly back across no man's land. Not all, however, were successful. Three attempts were made by 2/9th King's on successive nights but the raiders still failed to fight their way through the German wire. Similarly, the so-called Roddy's Rumpus was thwarted by a warning from a German patrol in no man's land which caused heavy small arms fire, rifle grenades, searchlights and flares to be brought down on the raiders' likely approaches.

The Germans did not only restrict themselves to the defensive but were also eager to contest the dominance of no man's land. No doubt suspicious of a relief having taken place, only a few days after the West Lancashire took over its sector a German raid snatched a prisoner. Apparently, the sentries realized too late that it was not one of their own returning patrols and allowed the Germans to enter the trench. Some weeks later a small party lay up on the British parapet between two sentry posts and disappeared taking with them an unfortunate subaltern of 2/5th South Lancashire caught whilst doing his rounds. In early March an extremely well executed enemy raid brought reluctant admiration from GOC 171 Brigade. An intense barrage cut communications between the British front and rear trenches; this was followed by a box barrage that further isolated the garrison. Three bombing parties of about 15 men then leapt into the British trench and took 11 men. In view of the embarrassment, Brigadier General Bray recommended that all posts should be kept up to their night strength for at least an hour before

---

75 TNA WO 952976: 170 Bde HQ, 15 Apr.1917.
76 The prisoner was taken captive by 4/5th LNL.

sun set, that front posts should be better wired, and that fighting duckboard parties must immediately counter-attack. These points suggest that on this brigade frontage at least, the divisional defence scheme was not being closely followed. The brigadier general concluded, perhaps with a degree of envy: "The chief factor of the enemy's line of action was the excellent way in which the artillery was handled – its registration was perfect, and the handling of his rolling barrage, which traversed some 3,000 yards, showed a very high standard of efficiency." To demonstrate, however, that the division could redress the balance a small party of 2/5th KORL lay up on the German front line parapet and snatched two unwary Germans, and a fairly large enemy raid at the end of May went wrong when stiff resistance from a small bombing post of 4/5th LNL bought time for the fighting duckboard party to react and counter. A German officer and two wounded men were captured in the British trench. The officer apparently lost orientation and, dragging in one of his wounded men, mistakenly believed he had reached sanctuary in a German trench.

The 57th Division's transfer to Haking's XI Corps was to witness no let up in raiding and patrol activity. As he had been during the summer of 1916, Haking remained anxious to convince the Germans opposite that First Army would launch an offensive. The corps commander drew up various plans whereby posts in the unoccupied German front line should be held for up to 24 hours. General Horne, GOC First Army, was not entirely convinced of the wisdom of such a strategy but agreed to Haking's proposals provided casualties were kept to a minimum. The Germans tended to accept these occasional occupations and because their front line was largely inhabitable contented themselves with regular sweeps of the parapet with machine-gun fire to remind the temporary intruders their presence was known. Nocturnal patrols lay in wait to rush any German patrols or covering parties that crossed their path but most of these generally opted to flee. Consequently, by June, the almost unhindered occupation of no man's land allowed a great deal of reconnaissance work to be done on the state of the German wire, trenches, and tramways.[77] Large, formal raids also continued. A silent raid by 2/4th South Lancashire ran into difficulties when the German first line, that was unoccupied save for bundles of wire, was reached As the raiders attempted to clear the obstacles they were illuminated by searchlights and hit by gas canisters, grenades and small arms fire from the garrison in the support line. Enemy parties worked round the Lancashires' flanks and a 30 minute bombing fight ensued before the raiders could disengage from the carefully staged ambush and return without a prisoner. A major attempt by 165 men of 2/10th King's also failed to live up to expectation. Known as "Dicky's Dash", this large raid also involved RFC support. Three prisoners were hauled from the German positions, but two were killed on the way back and the third was shot when he tried to escape. Casualties among the raiders were heavy, with three officers and 38 ORs killed and nearly 50 wounded for an unsubstantiated claim of 70 German dead.[78] In late July, a company strength raid by 2/4th LNL bumped into a German raiding party and fought a battle in no man's land. What would have pleased Haking, and certainly both the brigade and divisional GOsC about the encounter, was the way the Loyals responded. The brigade report wrote of the Germans showing "far inferior fighting spirit" and, despite being part of a supposed

---

77   For example, see TNA WO 952979: 170 Bde HQ, Daily Intelligence Summary, 24-25 Jun.1917.
78   TNA WO 952984: 172 Bde HQ, Jun.1917; A.McGilchrist, *Liverpool Scots*, pp196-201

sturmtruppen company, of "lacking considerably in morale." In a report despatched to corps HQ, GOC division praised the battalion's "excellent" fighting spirit.[79]

The Lancashire Fusiliers, East Lancashire, and Manchester battalions of 66th Division had been part of Lieutenant General Haking's XI Corps almost since their arrival in France. Quickly adopting their corps commander's philosophy the division had been "making every effort to give the impression we're going to attack."[80] Like the newly transferred 57th Division, its commanders believed they were maintaining morale and developing their units' offensive spirit by means of increased patrolling. One of the divisional staff noted that "units had been a little sticky over patrols at first" but that "great improvements" had been made both with them and with general trench work.[81] The CO of 3/5th Lancashire Fusiliers issued a Special Order by adapting a captured German document to suit his own purpose. The order stressed his battalion's superior fighting spirit and abilities and how it must "annihilate" the enemy should he ever manage to penetrate the battalion's trenches.[82] There will have been men in the ranks who perhaps disagreed with the official capability assessment but any dissent was, understandably, not recorded.

The CO of 3/5th Lancashire Fusiliers appears, like Haking, to have been an advocate of the philosophy which regarded domination of no man's land as the means of developing fighting spirit and morale. Haking's policy of the temporary occupation of posts in the enemy front line was a supplement to a strategy that had long demanded high intensity activity in no man's land. Instructions to ambush enemy patrols, attack his saps and listening posts and undertake frequent raids of up to company strength on his front and support lines had long been in operation. Battalions in the front line were expected to send out up three or four patrols nightly; in early June when the pressure was to be further increased, battalions were instructed to do two silent raids during each of their eight day tours.[83] In the spring and summer of 1917, with elsewhere the Battles of Arras, Messines and Third Ypres to come, First Army's task was principally to maintain pressure on the Germans to prevent them from moving divisions to the more active zones. Although frustrated that his own divisions would not be involved in any immediate major offensive, Haking needed little prompting to instruct his GOsC to continue the strategy of frequent operations to convince the Germans that First Army would also launch a large-scale operation. Major General Lawrence, GOC 66th Division, was equally as enthusiastic as his corps commander. He followed the oft quoted dogma that successful raids "produced their natural effect on the men by inspiring a genuine lust for blood and generally maintaining the high morale of the Division."[84] Although this was the widely accepted view of senior commanders, not all troops subscribed to it. One former officer decided: "It was never ascertained that [raids] produced the effect that was intended, but they were very unpopular with the men as they never failed to draw retaliation from the enemy, the full brunt of which fell on the front line troops."[85] Nevertheless, Lawrence instructed his brigade commanders to look for German posts that could

79 H. Wylly, *The Loyal North Lancashire Regiment* (London: RUSI 1933), pp.191-92
80 TNA WO 953120: 4 Apr.1917.
81 TNA WO 953120: 31 Mar.1917.
82 TNA WO 953137: 26 Feb.1917.
83 TNA WO 952984: 172 Bde HQ, 6 Jun.1917.
84 Ibid., 1 July 1917.
85 A. Barnes, *2/5th Gloucestershire Regiment*, p.40.

be seized and temporarily occupied. There was even a suggestion that 199 Brigade might go for the long contested and previously hugely costly Hohenzollern Redoubt.[86]

Lawrence's division had been finding its feet and gaining experience in the Givenchy area since mid-March 1917 but it could still at times reveal an unfortunate naivety. One battalion was mystified when five men went missing from the Canadian Orchard sector. It came to the conclusion that the men could only have been victims of a raid carried out under cover of a bombardment.[87] There were a few patrol encounters during the month, some of which gained a degree of identification, but most of 2/6th Lancashire Fusiliers' 37 patrols during the month explored no man's land and gained intelligence of the enemy's wire but rarely encountered opposition. By May, fairly small scale raids were becoming more common but, again, the main activity was patrolling. It was not entirely one-sided. After recording statements such as "No man's land is very definitely ours", "patrols showing great enterprise" and "Germans will not patrol or fight in no man's land", the enemy surprised the division by staging several encounters that caused casualties.[88]

The approach of the Messines offensive caused an increase in raid intensity. The division thought itself fortunate to have in the trenches opposite, the "worst [division] in the German Army." Deserters from *80th Division* became increasingly common and told tales of them being kept in the line without relief until they had executed a successful attack.[89] Their resistance to raiders was at times patchy but on others, such as a raid by 2/6th Lancashire Fusiliers on 13 June, they did put up a spirited opposition. There had been so much wire cutting before the raid that the Germans clearly expected an assault and deluged the fusiliers' assembly positions with gas and shells. Wire between the German front and support lines had not been touched by the artillery but having hacked their way through, the fusiliers became engaged in fierce hand-to-hand fighting for 45 minutes in the second and third lines. Strong German counter-attacks then developed up the communication trenches and across the open. The brigadier later wrote of the "grit and determination" and of the "thoroughly workmanlike" behaviour of the fusilier company concerned. All were pleased with the cooperation evident from the nearby battalions which covered the withdrawal and assisted with the wounded. The support of the RE, trench mortars and the artillery, which included a Portuguese battery, was also acknowledged.

A raid by four officers and 185 ORs of 2/4th East Lancashire three days earlier, in close cooperation with 2/10th Manchester, claimed to have killed 160 Germans, and the first carried out by 2/5th Manchester, which was also the division's first large-scale effort, was hailed as "a good model" for such enterprises. The planning, preparations and practices had been meticulous. Blocking and mopping up parties were specifically designated, a specially trained squad tasked to capture a suspected machine-gun position was thoroughly rehearsed, and Lewis guns to cover the flanks were in position. Artillery support, which included smoke and specified lifts in addition to a protective rolling barrage, was fully coordinated. Followed by the mopping up parties, the first wave rushed the enemy near Mad Point and reached their third objective before schedule. Assisted by a party of sappers, the second and third waves dealt with tunnels and dugouts while blocking parties obstructed possible counter-attack routes and maintained

---

86   TNA WO 953120: Divisional Order No.8, 13 May 1917.
87   TNA WO 953137: 3/5th Lancashire Fusiliers, 12 Apr.1917.
88   TNA WO 953144: 2/6th Manchester, 5 May 1917; WO 953120: 16 and 23 May 1917.
89   TNA WO 953120: 12 May 1917.

suppressing fire on Germans to their flanks. Because there was nothing left to blow up, recall was sounded seven minutes early. A post mortem recorded that such raids needed more demolition charges as phosphorous and Mills bombs were not always suitable for clearing dugouts, the dust thrown up by the bombardment had caused problems with direction-keeping, and there had been a tendency to slip towards the smoke on the right. On this occasion the smoke was considered to have been essential because it obscured the German view from their strong points at the Dump and Madagascar Village. Finally, the work of the artillery was thought to have been "excellent" and sure to increase the confidence of the infantry in the arm for future occasions. Of a total of 311 all ranks taking part, the raid effected substantial damage to the German lines for a cost of four killed, 49 wounded, and six missing.[90]

The artillery of the two 2nd Line divisions was, in numbers of guns, up to establishment but the number of corps batteries had been reduced for service elsewhere. The infantry's frustration with the lack of heavy trench mortars and heavy guns is apparent in post-raid reports. Divisional HQ noted that during a raid by 2/5th East Lancashire the Germans escaped through the division's box barrage "as usual" because gun density was insufficient to create an impenetrable curtain of explosives.[91] Haking came under pressure from his divisional commanders to acquire additional heavy trench mortars. He was eventually able to report that five extra guns were to be posted to the corps. The corps commander expressed satisfaction with the way the field ambulances dealt with casualty evacuation and sickness cases that could be treated within divisional areas, and with the manner in which field companies were assisting the repair of damaged trenches, building dugouts, and camp maintenance. Like the infantry, however, the engineers were probably below establishment. Divisions earmarked for Messines and Third Ypres took priority for drafts with the result that 57th and 66th divisions were among those whose strength in the early summer dropped to very low levels. The intensity of patrolling and raids inevitably caused casualties but they were never particularly excessive.[92] Sickness and other reasons for detachment did, however, severely limit trench strengths. For example, 3/5th Lancashire Fusiliers recorded 1,233 and 826 sick in April and May respectively. Of those, only 13 percent of cases were admitted to hospital but when the number of men attached to tunnelling companies, on courses, and involved in administrative and other sundry duties are deducted, trench strengths were often down to a little over 500.[93] Such was the concern that in June the GOC, brigade commanders, and some COs met to discuss what could be done about the manpower problem. Corps mounted troops had already been drafted in for line holding to allow infantry companies time to practise raids but, as platoons remained well below establishment, there was a proposal to amalgamate two companies in each battalion and operate a three rather than a four company unit. Major General Lawrence decided that such a solution should be an absolute last resort and opted instead for maintaining four companies but with them

---

90 TNA WO 953144: 2/5th Manchester, Jun.1917.
91 TNA WO 953120, 30 May 1917.
92 The 66th Division's casualties for June were recorded as "above normal". Totals were: six officers and 57 ORs killed, 21 and 416 wounded, one and 28 missing. Ibid., Summary, Jun.1917.
93 TNA WO 953136: 3/5th Lancashire Fusiliers, Apr.& May 1917; TNA WO 953144: 2/5th Manchester, 1 Jun.1916.

running only two or even one platoon.⁹⁴ "Very welcome" drafts did, however, arrive during June. These allowed battalions to reconfigure their platoons in line with *SS143* and GHQ's *The Organization of Infantry Battalions and the Normal Formation for Attack*. By the end of the month, with 66th Division about to be posted to the coast to prepare for a possible amphibious landing behind Nieuport, several substantial drafts of up to 323 men brought the division much closer to establishment.⁹⁵

The East Lancashire Division had clearly impressed Haking during its time under his command. Only days after its arrival Haking wrote to Lawrence to congratulate the division for not simply relying on the artillery to disperse an enemy raid. Stressing that newly posted formations did not always have the confidence to take on the Germans with small arms, Haking noted "I think the division has started well."⁹⁶ Although it was commonplace to send a division leaving a corps a cable of appreciation for the work done, the wire despatched by Haking to the division went further in its praise and warmth than the usual.⁹⁷ In a corps conference in mid-June he had spoken of the "exceptional results" obtained by the division's raids and of his plans not only for a six division attack against the Fromelles-Aubers Ridge, but also an "exceptionally strong and extensive" raid by 66th Division on Givenchy Hill. This action was to support the general strategy of fixing German divisions and of completely destroying the German front positions to allow their temporary occupation by British forces. Despite the major operations elsewhere, Haking assured his GOsC he would be able to amass considerable additional artillery for the operation.⁹⁸ The raid was approved by General Horne but the East Lancashire Division was transferred before the date pencilled in for the attack.

The division felt it had done well in its first few months. It had served unusually long tours in the trenches, endured regular, heavy shelling, and resisted enemy raids with the loss of very few of its men as prisoners. Although it took some time to become accustomed to the demanded intensity of offensive action, it conducted numerous small and several major raids that culminated in the series of enterprises on 8th, 10th and 13 June. These raids, such as the one executed by 2/10th Manchester, demonstrated the division's progressive tactical development. Lessons had been learned in cooperation, in the understanding of other arms' capabilities, and in the need for flexibility in attack formations. The habit of designating particular groups for specific tasks had become widespread, tactics of how to deal swiftly and effectively with obstacles had been widely taught, and the ways and means of ensuring discipline and coordination when inside the German positions were increasingly apparent in practice. Major General Lawrence, while not the same sort of charismatic and inspirational commander as Solly-Flood, the soon to be appointed GOC of the 1st Line East Lancashire Division, was a thoroughly competent and organized commander. When the division left the sector he signed off the war diary in positive mode. He was pleased with the way the raiding strategy had gone and believed the move to the

---

94 TNA WO 953144: 2/5th Manchester, 12 Jun.1917. Sickness had caused at least one battalion of 57th Division to reduce its companies to three platoons. See H. Wylly, *The Loyal North Lancashire*, p.190.
95 The 323 men went to 2/7th Manchester. Drafts arrived from a number of what could be termed Northern regiments but only a very small number appear to have come from battalions' own feeder units.
96 TNA WO 953120: Haking to Maj. Gen. Lawrence correspondence, 19 Mar.1917.
97 Ibid., 21 Jun.1917.
98 TNA WO 95882/3: XI Corps HQ, 16 Jun.1917.

coast and the prospect of "more extensive and active operations' would continue to improve the division's morale and capability.[99]

It was not until mid-September, three months after 66th Division had gone, that 57th Division left XI Corps.[100] It had been longer in the line than the East Lancashire and had also held a more difficult sector. Haking's comments about the division do not have the same affection as those used for his other 2nd Line formation. While not ever overtly critical he questioned the heavy ratio of officers to other ranks used by the division in its raids and thought it was the consequence of too many small rather than company strength efforts. The division's less ambitious enterprises, he argued, required much less preparation and yielded "insignificant" results in comparison to those undertaken by the corps' other two divisions. After reviewing the number and impressive results of raids by 49th and 66th divisions, he noted that the West Lancashire "have also carried out some successful raids" but did add that it had had "difficulty in getting any of the enemy to stand and fight." This could be seen as veiled criticism of the objectives targeted by the division. Rather than attacking known positions in large numbers that might yield prisoners, the division was perhaps deliberately using smaller parties to go for less contested targets. Having looked again at the favourable activities of the other two divisions Haking, with what might well be interpreted as a sarcastic comment, mentioned he would be "glad if the GOC 57th Division could also bring off one, or perhaps even two, raids in the near future." Because it had such a long front of c.18,000 yards (which required all three brigades to be in the line simultaneously), he seems to have accepted that the division inevitably faced difficulties in permanently preventing the Germans from repairing their damaged wire. Nonetheless, he considered the division's water supply arrangements to be "unsatisfactory" and thought the field ambulances were slow in getting to grips with the scabies situation. There appears to be no extant message of thanks or appreciation for the division in divisional or brigade war diaries when it left Haking's command.[101]

The root of the hesitation apparent in Haking's opinion of 57th Division may have been the result of some loose staff work and a divisional commander who, Haking believed, should have been replaced.[102] The corps commander's much cherished plan for the major attack on the Fromelles-Aubers Ridge had been circulated to all three of his divisions in May 1917. In early June, 57th Division HQ discovered it had somehow managed to mislay its copy. For various reasons the plan was subsequently abandoned by First Army but it is possible that Haking ultimately blamed the division's loss of the plan for the eventual shelving of his corps' ambitious

99 TNA WO 953120: Summary, Jun.1917
100 As with 66th Division, 57th had spent all of its time in XI Corps without the services of a pioneer battalion. Three weeks after it left Haking's command the East Lancashire Division was loaned 10/DCLI (P).
101 TNA WO 95882/3: Report of conference held on 16 Jun.1917.
102 One infantry brigade GOC had already been lost by 57th Division by the time it was transferred to XI Corps. Brig.Gen. Martyn of 170 Bde was probably not sent home on grounds of age. He was technically a 'dugout' and had very limited pre-war combat experience. He was next posted to a largely administrative job in South Africa and was replaced by the CRA of 66th Division, Brig. Gen. Guggisberg. By the end of August 1917, at least 50 percent of the division's infantry COs had also returned to England for other duties.

offensive.[103] Possibly connected directly or indirectly to this was Haking's lack of faith in Lieutenant General Broadwood who, unfortunately for Haking, held equal rank to his corps commander According to one source, when Broadwood protested about the casualties that would inevitably be incurred in what he considered to be a pointless "future attack", Haking reported Broadwood and his division to GHQ for its "lack of fighting spirit."[104] Broadwood died of wounds on 21 June 1917 and, as the only attack proposed since 57th Division's posting to XI Corps was Haking's pet scheme for the six division offensive against the Fromelles-Aubers Ridge, it seems likely it was this proposal that raised Broadwood's ire against his corps commander. Had Broadwood not been killed it is probable Haking would have pressed for his dismissal.[105]

Although Haking may not have been entirely convinced of the division's worth when compared to the other two TF divisions in his corps, the West Lancashire, especially after the June conference, undertook a very similar number of raids to those conducted by 49th (West Riding) and 2nd Division.[106] While the precise terminology of what constituted a raid as opposed to a patrol remains ambiguous, in July, 57th Division carried out over a dozen enterprises that forced an entry to the enemy trenches. The division may not have been able entirely to seize and hold the initiative in order to impose its will on the enemy, but it was rare for any division to be able to do that for any length of time. One incident in June demonstrates its troops did not lack confidence in themselves and their ability to take on the enemy. When a small patrol of 2/5th KORL found itself surrounded by a force three times its size, the troops attacked with "vigour" and fought their way out of the ambush.[107] When it was severely disorganized by a major two-day mustard gas and artillery bombardment of Armentières, 171 Brigade demonstrated similar resilience and fortitude. This was thought to be only the second concentrated use of mustard gas, an evil that was "till then unheard of by us." Reports of its first use at Ypres had only arrived at brigade HQ the night it was relieved and warnings had not yet been distributed to battalions when the attack began. Sixteen officers and 440 ORs of 2/6th King's became casualties yet, only two days later what was left of the battalion, which really amounted to about three platoons, took its place in the line with the almost equally devastated 2/5th King's.[108] From the little evidence available, morale within the division as a whole seems to have been sustained. The division's

---

103 HQ 57th Division convened a court of inquiry on 30 June to investigate the loss. The missing document was eventually discovered in late July. TNA WO 95882. XI Corps, 20 Jun.1917. Some of the detail concerning the issue is cited in M. Senior, *Haking: A Dutiful Soldier* (Barnsley: Pen & Sword, 2012), p.152.
104 Discussion between Basil Liddell Hart and Colonel C. Allanson, 19 Aug.1937. Cited in Robbins, *British Generalship*, p.32. Allanson served as GSO1 under Broadwood and was posted away from the division a month after Broadwood's death.
105 Although a "dug out" at 55 years, Broadwood was not particularly old when he was killed. He was a cavalryman who had ended his pre-war career as Commander of British Troops in South China. He had been appointed GOC 1st Mounted Division in September 1914. When 1st Mounted was converted to a cyclist division in October 1916, Broadwood became GOC 57th Division. He was replaced by Major General R.W.Barnes, also a cavalry man and 10 years his junior. Barnes had been at the front since 1914 and was appointed GOC 32nd Division in Nov.1916. He had returned home sick in late Jan.1917 and on recovery was appointed GOC 57th Division.
106 The 2nd Division relieved 66th Division.
107 TNA WO 952979: 2/5th KORL, 22 Jun.1917.
108 C. Wutzburg, *2/6th King's*, pp.119-26

courts martial and lesser crime statistics are rarely mentioned in unit war diaries but two other generally accepted indicators of poor morale, self-inflicted wounds and cases of trench feet, are noted. Casualties from February to July totalled about average for formations that did not take part in a major offensive. In a division of perhaps 15,000 troops, recorded self-inflicted wounds amounted to only 41 and a there were a mere five specified cases of trench feet.[109]

By the time Third Ypres opened at the end of July, all six 2nd Line divisions had served a degree of apprenticeship. Formal trench acclimatization had been kept to a minimum and the demands of working parties and line holding during the winter months had severely restricted opportunities for battalion and brigade training. Having slogged its way across the Somme heights, and then playing a major role at Bullecourt, 62nd Division had been the most involved in active operations. It was credited with having captured the village but in reality, like units of the 7th Division, it suffered huge casualties for little gain. The division had been forced to attack in the unfavourable ground of a re-entrant and the artillery had proved inadequate for its principal tasks of counter-battery work, wire cutting, and trench destruction. Although not entirely its own fault, cooperation with the Australians on its right and (initially) 4th Division on its left was minimal, the tank support had generally failed to materialize, and the infantry lost direction too readily in clouds of dust thrown up by the artillery. The inexperienced platoons had proved unable to suppress German resistance in its prepared defences and were too prone to go to ground or withdraw when officers and NCOs were hit. In the same way as its 1st Line had lived under a cloud since its attack at Thiepval in September 1916, 62nd Division's performance at Bullecourt was considered by some to have been less than might have been expected even from a 2nd Line formation. While rarely overtly critical the *Official History* implies the division's tactics, its inability to concentrate force, an inadequate barrage, confusion, and perhaps even irresolution in the attacking waves, contributed to its failure.[110]

When it was sent into the rubble of Bullecourt, 58th Division had been more fortunate. As 2/5th and 2/8th London crossed the notorious Red Patch the Germans were in the process of evacuating the remains of their garrison and blowing up former strong points and cellars. Enemy resistance was thus much reduced and deliberately temporary. Unlike the West Riding battalions, the London units were considered to have done well and were praised for what turned out to be a less demanding achievement. The two attacking London battalions had, however, shown initiative, improvisation and flexibility in their assault.[111] Although successful in taking the ruins the division was to remain under frequent and regular shell fire until it moved to a quieter area in July. Having demonstrated the ability to be adaptable and innovative, 60th Division had performed well against a reasonably quiescent enemy, but 61st Division carried with it the stigma of alleged failure at Fromelles. Because its corps commander felt it to be tainted largely by its own GOC, 57th Division's reputation had also suffered. On the other hand, 66th Division

---

109 Ignoring those listed as missing, divisional casualties amounted to: 362 killed, 3379 wounded, and 4971 sick. See TNA WO 952967: A&Q Branch.
110 C. Falls, *Military Operations: France and Belgium, 1917* (London: HMSO, 1940), pp.463-65. The division's casualties had been enormous: almost 200 officers and over 4,000 ORs. A significant but unknown proportion of these casualties must have been inflicted by the division's own barrages falling short. This was not, of course, unique to 62nd Division but reports do suggest that with communications frequently broken the inexperience of the division's artillery did add to the infantry's difficulties.
111 Ibid., p.478.

had been particularly assertive in dominating no man's land and was generally thought to have settled in well and shown potential for future operations. It had been selective in its targeting of achievable objectives and been creative in its use of all-arms cooperation. Because divisions were not self-contained or self-sufficient, sustainment in the field had not been a major issue. The rationing of shells and the reduced size of corps artillery groups occasionally limited the scope and scale of operations but these decisions were made at higher than divisional level. Similarly, rations, the supply of engineering equipment, animal fodder and other essential commodities were governed at corps and army levels. Divisional Q Branches were responsible for the distribution of stores for which they had indented but had only limited control or influence over the quality and quantity that did actually arrive.

The remaining 2nd Line division, 59th (North Midland), had taken over its own part of the line within two weeks of arriving in France. Together with the 1st Line and 2nd Line South Midland divisions it constituted III Corps. The corps' divisions were operating in the area south of the main Amiens-St Quentin road. Both South Midland divisions had endured long winter tours on the Somme, although 61st had not been used in any significant attack since Fromelles. In mid-March the three TF divisions began their operations to follow the German withdrawal towards the Hindenburg Line. For the next few weeks the two 2nd Line Midland formations were to engage in limited open warfare to a greater degree than the other four 2nd Line formations on the Western Front. The North Midland's Division's inexperience during that period was not a major concern but when, at the end of March it came up against fixed defences and was obliged to fight more than scattered rearguards, a lack of synchronicity and coordination between its various arms quickly became apparent.

4

Semi-open Warfare

Those divisions of the BEF involved in the advance to the Hindenburg Line found themselves fighting an unfamiliar type of war. Having spent months or years in the tedium of trench warfare or offensives that could in terms of ground gained be counted in yards, they were now exposed to an enemy who utilized the terrain and rearguards to fight limited delaying actions. These were designed to maximise Allied losses and minimize their own. By the spring of 1917, several of the 2nd Line divisions had acquired some experience and even a degree of expertise in conducting raids but 59th Division had had little opportunity to carry out even a handful of these minor enterprises. In was now to follow a well-organized enemy who knew the ground and who was ultimately to rest his troops in prepared and formidable defences.

The 2nd Line North Midland Division was for a short time the right flank of the BEF. As part of the scheme to relieve French divisions for further offensives, the division concentrated in the rear of III Corps area immediately south of the Amiens – St Quentin road. Only a small proportion of its men and units had had any real time in the trenches under the instruction of either 1st or 50th division before the North Midland took over the line itself on 9 March. Conditions were appalling, with men quickly succumbing to trench foot and sickness. The weather alternated between frost, snow, sleet, hail, and sudden thaws, all of which took their toll on the welfare and health of the men.[1] Two company commanders of 2/6th North Staffordshire were quickly evacuated to the UK and 2/5th Lincolnshire lost its second-in-command, five other officers, and then the MO to hospital. In 176 Brigade, 2/6th South Staffordshire went into the line for the first time on 10 March. When it was relieved three nights later so many of the men were exhausted and sick that it was quickly replaced in its support position by 2/6th Sherwood Foresters and attached temporarily to 178 Brigade. Its CO was immediately relieved of his command and replaced by a major from the Reserve of Officers who had retired as a lieutenant in 1912. The battalion was allowed two days to recover but the event had clearly had an impact at DHQ because on 18 March the unit's officers were addressed by the GOC division himself.[2]

---

1   IV Corps, of which 61st (2nd South Midland) was part, had decided to adopt immediately the French method of dealing with trench foot. This involved foot baths at least every five days with camphorated soap and dried off with talcum mixed with camphor powder. TNA WO 953038: ADMS, 2 Mar.1917.
2   TNA WO 953020: 15 Mar.1917; WO 953024: 18 Mar.1917; WO 953021: 16 Mar.1917.

In view of what was happening further north, the division despatched regular patrols to establish whether the Germans opposite had begun their anticipated withdrawal. So quickly did the enemy eventually depart that when 2/7th Sherwood Foresters went up to relieve 2/4th Leicestershire in the expectation of a simple but uncomfortable trench tour, the Leicesters CO informed the incomers the Germans had gone.[3] Brigades began moving across the former no man's land, with 1st Division on their left and 61st (2nd South Midland) of IV Corps on their right.[4] Although often referred to as "the pursuit to the Hindenburg Line", because there was little intent or expectation that the advancing force would be able to "catch or cut off the hostile force with the aim of defeating or perhaps destroying it", modern doctrine would not recognize the action properly as a 'pursuit'.[5] Furthermore, a pursuit "should, technically, develop from a successful exploitation and commence when the target is demoralized and beginning to disintegrate under pressure."[6] The withdrawing Germans were not demoralized and far from beginning to disintegrate. The attrition on the Somme had caused the High Command to rethink their strategy but the withdrawal was a calculated scheme to save lives and shorten the line. Neither was there any initial opportunity for the Allies to conduct a classic offensive action. This would have included such characteristics as attempts to shock, seize the initiative, take advantage of opportunities to exploit, and maintain a superior tempo and momentum. Because he was conducting a staged withdrawal there were few occasions when substantial physical damage could be inflicted on the enemy and virtually no chance of being able to out manoeuvre him. Coordination and simultaneity between III Corps' three divisions, as well as those of the formations on either side of the corps' boundaries, were essential if there was to be any chance of knocking the enemy off balance and of disrupting his carefully timed withdrawal. Allied objectives were limited to seizing key terrain which, naturally enough was often contested by the Germans, ensuring force protection by advancing the artillery and lines of communication as rapidly as practicable behind the infantry, and concentrating force in case the possibility of tactical exploitation did arise. Because the enemy had so thoroughly and systematically destroyed the land over which he withdrew, until roads had been cleared of obstacles and railways pushed across the devastated zone the British were unlikely to achieve superiority of fires over the ground on which the enemy rearguards chose to fight.[7] Finally, of course, the Allied generals knew that to the rear of the retreating forces lay the Hindenburg Line. Fourth Army may have been advancing but the British were currently concentrating their forces further to the

---

3   Compiled, *The Robin Hoods: History of 1/7th, 2/7th & 3/7th Sherwood Foresters* (Uckfield: Naval & Military Press reprint of 1921 edition), p.312.
4   On 21 March, 1st Division went into corps reserve and was then posted away. It was replaced in III Corps by 48th (South Midland) Division. It was soon joined by 42nd (East Lancashire) Division which meant that III Corps was for a time comprised entirely of TF divisions.
5   Army Doctrine Publications *Operations 0825d;* C. Falls, *Military Operations*, p.169 makes a similar point: "If the pursuer ... cannot ... thrust aside [the] covering forces and attack the main body, there is no real pursuit."
6   ADP *Operations 0825d*
7   The 28th Heavy Artillery Group (HAG) was attached to 59th Division for tactical purposes during the advance. The division's own artillery brigades were completely untried and had only just concentrated at Foucaucourt as the Germans began their withdrawal. It did not fully relieve the artillery of 50th Division until 23 March. TNA WO 953013: CRA, Mar.1917

north in preparation for the forthcoming Battle of Arras.[8] Consequently, when Fourth Army reached the outpost positions of the Hindenburg Line, it would have to halt and dig in. It simply did not possess the ways and means to convert any possible penetration of the enemy line into a breakthrough and, ultimately, a breakout.

In addition to the delayed action mines and booby traps left by the Germans, the Somme river offered another major obstacle to The Advance by III Corps was necessarily slow and deliberate, with troops pausing regularly to dig new lines of resistance. The first units of 59th Division crossed the river close to Cizancourt; by 21 March divisional bridgeheads had been established at Brie and St Christ. These were quickly put into a state of defence in order to protect the engineers building the bridges and the transport required to carry forward the tools and equipment. There was no expectation that the enemy would attack in strength but necessary defensive measures were employed to guard against raids designed to disrupt Allied communications. These all took time and restricted geographical progress to a slow pace.

Sustaining the advance in the face of such demanding man-made and natural obstacles was a severe test for any division but especially for one that had barely had time to acclimatize itself to combat conditions. The process of sustainment, one of the Principles of War, is a means to an end and is integral to maintaining fighting power. If 59th Division could not be adequately supplied its ability to sustain an operation, and when necessary to demonstrate resilience and prolonged capability, would be seriously and possibly fatally threatened. The agility and efficiency of the division depended on the ability of its sustainers to show equal adaptability in the ways and means it could utilize both in the support of an operation and also in the recuperation phase afterwards. Sustainment is not, however, just the provision of combat supplies and combat service support. Because it also involves the evacuation, treatment of, and replacement of the division's casualties, it makes a major contribution to the maintenance of morale..

Towards the end of April, Major General Romer, the recently appointed GOC 59th Division, signed off a report that had presumably been compiled by the divisional AA&QMG. To underscore how great the difficulties of sustainment had been during the advance, Romer highlighted the distances between railhead and the ever moving front. On 18 March, railhead was at La Flaque, with the division's four refilling points only approximately four miles away. By 28 March the refilling points at Prusle were 11 miles from railhead; by 5 April they were 18 miles distant from railhead which, by that time, had advanced as far as Fay. By 19 April the repaired broad gauge had reached Péronne but it was not until May that it was extended to Roisel. To keep the division supplied, horsed transport had to cover the 18 miles along cratered and mined roads on which a brigade of troops laboured to rebuild and maintain. Just before leaving the UK the division had been supplied with hundreds of elderly and "soft" horses taken from 65th (2nd Lowland) Division. The consequence was that in five weeks, 205 of the animals had been struck off strength.[9] The remaining horses were on short forage rations, stricken by the awful weather

---

8   Fourth Army informed its formations on 5 March that it was to lose six siege batteries, two heavy batteries, two HAGs, and three brigades of field artillery to other armies. The units began to leave two days after the Germans had begun their withdrawal in III Corps' sector. See TNA WO 85675.

9   As early as 4 March, only two weeks after the division had left the UK, the Assistant Director Veterinary Services (ADVS) noted the deterioration in a considerable number of horses. He wrote of their "sinking condition." This was not improved by an outbreak of mange in French road labourers' horses which used the same water troughs as some units in his division. To make matters worse, seven

and having to perform more work than would normally be required because additional bridging and RE stores needed to be brought forward. To exacerbate the difficulties, they were also prone to lose their shoes on the inclines of the log roads. The OC of an ASC company in the nearby 61st Division complained that poor systemic organization was forcing "unnecessary work" on his horsed transport with the result that his horses were "done up."[10] During the month, and in addition to those beasts that could be treated by its own Mobile Veterinary Section (MVS), the division evacuated 80 horses and mules to a veterinary hospital.[11]

The sustainment demands of the advance were those required for a mixture of what was both semi-trench and semi-open warfare. Trench stores had regularly to be transported forward because new lines of resistance were so frequently dug, fortified, and then re-established a mile or so further on. Large amounts of artillery ammunition and small arms ordnance also had to keep pace with the guns and infantry rather than be merely dumped at established static points and wait for another transport section to carry them further forward. There were experiments with improvisation in the use of pack animals but, looking on the bright side, Major General Romer could also see an advantage to the excessive work being demanded of the horses. He noted the attrition meant that older animals were being weeded out and that in time the division would thus eventually be equipped with younger and stronger horses.[12] Until sufficient additional beasts might become available, however, the division had to do what it could to maintain deliveries with a constantly diminishing number of animals.[13]

On 59th Division's right flank, and despite its considerable experience in the vagaries of army methodology, 61st (2nd South Midland) Division was having similar problems. The month had started badly for the CRE division because he learned with some concern that timber supplies from Norway and America had been cut off. As soon as the infantry advance began he had ordered his field companies and their attached infantry to salvage pit props from old British and German gun pits. He also persuaded the divisional CRA to sanction the use of artillery wagons to assist in the repair of roads.[14] Furthermore, soon after he had received the bad news about timber shortages he requested permission to have time to train his field companies in pontoon building because, "they have had no practice in this (and no training in Field Engineering) since arriving in France." He had found a suitable site near Chipilly and estimated that if two sections at a time were trained for three days when their company was out of the line, all three of his companies would be fully trained in pontooning by mid-April. He heard officially on 14 March that permission for his scheme had been granted, with the first two sections scheduled to begin training on 22 March. Consequently, when the German withdrawal began four days before the first iteration of the course was due to begin none of the division's three field companies had received training for the essential task that was quickly to be thrust upon them.

   horses of 177 MG Coy had been killed when a roof collapsed on them. TNA WO 953015: ADVS, Mar.1917.
10 TNA WO 953052: No.2 Coy, ASC, 29 Mar.1917.
11 TNA WO 953052: 61st MVS, Mar.1917.
12 TNA WO 953012: A&QM, 24 Apr.1917.
13 The war diaries of 59th Division's ADVS and MVS do not record the numbers of animals treated or evacuated but it was probably similar to 61st Division's figures on its right. On its left, 48th MVS received 96 cases during March, of which 70 were evacuated to No.7 Veterinary Hospital. TNA WO 952753: Mar.1917.
14 G. Rose, *2/4th Ox&Bucks*, p.77 believes the salved logs were never used.

When the withdrawal began, 61st Division was tasked with building four bridges over the Somme and the adjacent canal at Bèthencourt. It was expected that a bridge capable of carrying infantry and field guns could be thrown over the river in two days but first the access roads had to be cleared and repaired.[15] Traffic restrictions and control on lorries and wagons to allow road repairs and filling in of craters remained in place until 25 March. The CRE fought a constant battle with corps HQ for sufficient lorries to bring forward the heavy bridging equipment so necessary to sustain the advance. He was annoyed when DHQ twice failed in its job of providing billets for his sappers at Cizancourt and Tertry, and when a delivery of picks and shovels ordered via the QMG failed to arrive. In view of these setbacks he was, unsurprisingly, none too pleased when divisional staff queried when the bridge he was supposedly building across the Omignon at Tertry would be completed. Lieutenant Colonel Durnford angrily denied he had ever been instructed to build a bridge at Tertry. He went to investigate and on his way was incensed to discover an infantry working party constructing a diversion for artillery around the wrong, unsupported, side of a large crater. Unlike 59th Division, whose three brigades were all ordered to form a pioneer works company, 61st did have a pioneer battalion but the shortage of labour remained critical across all corps during the advance. The CRE's annoyance about the shortages grew even greater when about only half a battalion instead of the promised two full battalions of 35th Division arrived for road repairs one morning at 0200, exhausted and incapable of work.[16]

The CRA of 61st Division had some sympathy for Durnford but stated in blunt terms that the divisional train was "totally incapable" of providing the means of getting rations and forage forward to his batteries. By 19 March two of his RFA brigades were in position to cover the Somme crossings from Epenancourt to Rouy-le-Grand but the question of sustaining them had "assumed serious proportions."[17] As several batteries were entirely without rations it was decided on 20 March to order all horses back west of the old British front line and to supply the men at the guns with what were described as "packs". The following day the line of resistance moved forward and artillery officers began to reconnoitre possible gun positions east of the Somme. The horses had then to be brought forward once more to haul the ammunition wagons and the guns, bringing with them as much fodder as the wagons could carry.[18] The division managed to cope by restricting the daily feed allowance but the problem was made worse when other units were attached to a division for rationing. For example, 59th Division became responsible for a succession of units ranging from a tunnelling company and miscellaneous labour detachments, to 34 Squadron RFC and various types of specialist workshops. Mounted troops of II Corps, whose daily demands required the use of nine of the division's already stretched GS wagons, were also attached to the division for forage and rationing.

---

15   The Germans had exploded mines at many crossroads to create craters of varying size. One company of 2/4th Berkshire was employed filling in a crater near Morchain reportedly 100 feet wide and 30 feet deep. TNA WO 95306: 20 Mar.1917.
16   The battalions which supplied the approximately 600 man working party were two of the remaining bantam battalions in the reconstituted 35th Division. These units were each only about 300 men strong. Detail regarding the RE is taken from TNA WO 953039: CRE 61st Division, Mar.1917.
17   TNA WO 953037: 19-20 Mar.1917.
18   Almost a week later, CRA 61st Division noted "still having good deal of difficulty getting rations up." Ibid., 26 Mar.191.7.

Despite the obstacles and the inexperience, 59th Division's QMG insisted "on no occasion during the advance did units fail to receive their supplies."[19] This is a standard comment found in many war diaries because few QMGs ever admitted their supply system failed. As there do seem to be instances, however, when units did go short it might be questioned whether all units received *all* of the supplies requested.[20] Shell expenditure during the advance was below that of the previous daily average but once the eastward movement was obstructed by resistance from the villages a little to the west of the Hindenburg Line outpost positions, regular and formal barrages again became the norm. Until it moved to another corps, 1st Division's Ammunition Column was put at the disposal of 59th Division, as was the HQ Supply Section of 42nd (East Lancashire) Divisional Train.[21] Once the roads were passable, especially for mechanical transport, advanced ammunition dumps were created in villages to the rear of what was to become the division's front lines. The CRE also managed to secure five lorries for bringing forward engineer supplies but to ease the demand, German wire and timber were used whenever possible. Until lorries were available to carry small arms ammunition and grenades forward, DADOS improvised by carrying what boxes he could in his staff car to the dump at Roisel. Again, division insisted there was "no shortage of important Ordnance stores."

To foster morale during the difficult weather and prolonged working hours, DADOS was able to provide some tents. It was, however, the labours of the brigade pioneer works companies and the town majors installed in the former occupied villages which did most to ease the travails and hardship of the infantry. Town majors decided how many soldiers particular cellars could house and the would-be pioneers then salvaged material from the site to make the subterranean dwellings as habitable as possible.[22] They were even able to erect battalion baths from salved materials in some of the ruins. In addition to passable billets, other significant sustainers of morale were the means of providing regular contact with home and the posting of replacements. Letters and parcels arrived regularly because four lorries were available to deliver a daily average of 280 mail bags from railhead to the units of 59th Division.[23] There was, however, widespread criticism of how drafts were forwarded to units. The QMG 59th Division argued the system by which reinforcements were lorried from La Flaque to the refilling points and then trudged with their new unit's transport section to their battalion only worked because the numbers currently

---

19 The two paragraphs following are taken from TNA WO 953012: 24 Apr.1917.
20 Troops out of the line were able to purchase additional or supplemental rations when 59th Divisional Canteen opened at Bouvencourt on 1 April 1917.
21 A 1st Line TF formation, 42nd Division sailed for Egypt in September 1914. It fought in the Gallipoli campaign from May 1915 until it was evacuated to Egypt in January 1916. It arrived for service on the Western Front in March 1917. The Divisional Train was formed in England January-February 1917 and joined the division in France later that month. The HQ Supply Section attached to 59th Division from 26 March amounted to 36 wagons and limbers, and 74 horses. The personnel and horses will have had even less practical experience than their counterparts in 59th Division. TNA WO 952653: HQ Divisional Train, Mar.1917.
22 Some criticism did come from those who considered that drawing the pioneers and town majors from already under strength battalions was wasteful and unhelpful. This was especially so because there were large numbers of elderly officers in the UK eager for an appointment overseas quite capable of fulfilling the role of town major.
23 Although the TF County Associations had lost just about all of their pre-war responsibilities, many did still have Comforts Committees which sent parcels regularly to their units and formations. These were, of course, particularly valued by soldiers from poorer backgrounds.

involved were so small.[24] Like others in his position, he suggested camps should be built at intervals from railhead towards the forward zone where drafts could acclimatize and rest.

Medical provision was necessarily extemporized during the advance. Huts were quickly erected for an advanced dressing station (ADS) at St Cren and a divisional rest station (DRS) nearby. Together with the three tented field ambulances, these facilities were vital to troops' welfare but, until a corps advanced operating centre (AOC) opened in Péronne in April, 59th Division's wounded in need of an operation had to be carried 20 miles to the nearest casualty clearing station (CCS) at Bray. Despite its very short time in France, there is no evidence to suggest that in comparison to other divisions, 59th Division was unaware of the ways and means of maintaining morale or that it was failing in any its other essential sustainment strategies. To its north, 48th (South Midland) was having a slightly easier time because it crossed the Somme at Péronne and, although devastation was severe in its sector, there were more buildings and villages available as shelter for the troops. The old front lines also lay a little further to the east. This meant that the mileage of roads across the devastated zone requiring repair was not quite so formidable. To the south of 59th Division, 61st Division faced obstacles equally as difficult as its fellow 2nd Line formation. Its Assistant Director Medical Services (ADMS) had cleared the DRS and the scabies hospital at Guillaucourt in preparation for an advance and reconnoitred possible forward sites for his field ambulances and an ADS. These were quickly established by utilizing the devastated site of a former German hospital at Bèthencourt. By 30 March serious and urgent cases were evacuated to Nesle where one field ambulance was functioning as a temporary CCS. By 31 March, an ADS was open at Poeuilly, a main dressing station (MDS) at Tertry and a system of relay posts in place to transfer the wounded expected from 2/8th Warwickshire's attack on the hamlet of Soyecourt.

Two other combat support services essential to sustaining morale were water supply and efficient sanitation facilities. These were largely the responsibility of the divisional CRE, his field companies, and the divisional sanitary section. In addition, corps personnel were also available for testing water quality, advising on the digging of new wells, and the clearing of existing ones poisoned or blocked by the enemy. The sanitary section of 61st Division was something of an innovator in the field of hygiene and waste disposal. Its work had attracted attention from higher authority and, as the advance began, the section was visited by the BEF's Chief Sanitary Officer and the Sanitary Officer of Fourth Army. The senior officers were impressed by the section's record keeping and preventative strategies for infectious diseases, by the experimental nature of the work done in the workshop, and by the detailed reporting and analysis of wells in the former German zones. It was relatively easy during periods of static trench warfare to keep the rear areas clear of refuse and to provide acceptable sanitation and baths in the camps; during the advance, the work was necessarily magnified and more complex. To replace the latrines and baths burnt by the withdrawing Germans in the devastated zone, and to clear the hundreds of wells thought capable of again being utilized, required the construction of new camps and their associated range of incinerators and various types of latrines. The production figures recorded

---

24　In February 1917, 61st Division received only 96 ORs as drafts for its 12 infantry battalions and three MG companies. The reinforcements usually arrived in groups of fewer than 10. See TNA WO 95724: Feb.1917.

by 61st Division's sanitary section, while not excessively different from those of other divisions, demonstrate that it was able to provide those facilities quickly and effectively.[25]

To provide force protection, especially for those troops constructing the regularly advancing system of cruciform outposts, and to pressurize the Germans by keeping in contact with their rearguards, 59th Division formed a mobile column of 2/8th Sherwood Foresters and a battery of 295 Brigade RFA. Because, however, 5th Cavalry Division and subsequently corps cavalry were working in advance of the infantry, the mobile column had little to do. Untested in combat, it was disbanded after an existence of less than a week. It had proved unnecessary largely because the advance was a slow, cautious and measured affair. It was unknown when and where the enemy might choose to stand and fight. When traversing the first 18-19 miles of evacuated territory casualties had been very light, there being few occasions when the infantry came under direct fire from anything other than a distant machine gun and the occasional shell from a 77mm field piece.

German tactics were simple and effective. An enemy prisoner reportedly informed corps HQ intelligence officers that rearguards comprised up to 300 men drawn from each division holding the Hindenburg Line. Their orders were to hold the western edges of successive villages and command the Allies' lines of approach with machine guns and a few pieces of light artillery. The British cavalry was often allowed to pass by unmolested, but the village defenders would then engage the following infantry until just before the anticipated final, organized rush under a creeping barrage. The defenders would withdraw, blowing up or setting fire to what was left of the ruins. Heavier artillery that had previously registered on the village would subsequently shell the vacated site for a day or two. The Germans were also reported to be deliberately showing themselves in the open at ranges of between 1,200 – 1,400 yards in order to give a false impression of their strength.[26] While the Germans may have been under orders to silhouette themselves, the possibly either naive or curious troops of 178 Brigade were condemned by their GOC for "exposing themselves without cause" in the forward positions.[27]

It was recognized that the deliberate lack of prolonged resistance by the enemy would end as the Hindenburg Line and its outposts came within rage of the advancing artillery. It was also expected more formal and determined opposition would be encountered on the ridge lines to the west of the main defensive positions. General Rawlinson, GOC Fourth Army, intended to maintain pressure on the Germans in his sector partly in the hope that an opportunity to break into the main defences might present itself and partly to prevent the enemy from transferring troops north to confront the forthcoming Arras offensive. Rawlinson was a pragmatist and accepted that Fourth Army would play only a supporting role to Byng's Third. He did, however, expect his corps to establish themselves on terrain from which they could observe the Hindenburg Line and from where future offensives could be launched. He instructed his corps commanders to ensure their divisions were able by 8 April, the day before the Arras offensive was scheduled to begin, to have their artillery within range of the Hindenburg Line. The main obstacles to achieving this objective in IV Corps' area were Holnon Wood and Round Hill. It was agreed at a corps conference on 29 March that the most effective way to overcome the wood would be to turn it from north and south. The plan involved 61st Division advancing

---

25   TNA WO 953052: Sanitary Section, Mar.1917.
26   TNA WO 95675: Summary, Mar.1917; WO 953012: A&Q, Intelligence Summary, 30 Mar.1917.
27   TNA 3024: 29 Mar.1917.

along the Omignion Valley from the north while 32nd Division moved up from the south via Savy. This division would work in conjunction with the French move on Dallon and 61st would advance on the right flank of 59th Division. The capture of these villages was about as far as IV Corps expected to advance; III Corps to its north assumed its progress would be halted after the capture of Le Verguier, Hargicourt, Lempire, and Epehy. A series of preliminary shaping operations were planned and undertaken to allow the villages to be attacked using a minimum of infantry and artillery support.

Divisions in IV Corps were ordered to reconnoitre possible enemy positions that would allow machine-gun and rifle fire to be brought down on attackers and to organize fire plans that would neutralize those positions by smoke, artillery, and machine-gun barrages. Coordination between artillery and infantry was to be achieved by the use of flares and rockets to signal the latter's positions. To minimize confusion they were to have only two signals to request artillery fire once the creeping barrages had lifted or stopped: "SOS" and "Lengthen Range". It was anticipated the Germans would continue to hold only small garrisons in the approach villages so the minimum number of infantry thought compatible with the task was to be employed. As IV Corps orders stated, "The fewer men we have under fire means fewer casualties."[28] Modern doctrine would recognize this as 'economy of effort' – the right tools in the right place at the right time.[29] Using its troops sparingly, 61st Division made careful reconnaissance of the projected lines of operation and utilized its artillery, trench mortars and machine guns to work their way through Trefcon, Marteville, Caulaincourt and Vermand against slight opposition. On the extreme left of the division, two companies of 2/8th Warwickshire made its well planned and neatly executed attack on the hamlet of Soyecourt. It was supported by an hour-long bombardment of the hamlet and its wire. This switched to a lift of 100 yards every four minutes until finally settling as a protective barrage 200 yards east of the hamlet. Simultaneously, 59th Division's artillery fired on the wire north of Soyecourt and, on the northern end of the hamlet itself, howitzers split their fire between known machine-gun positions and counter-battery work. Brigade machine gun companies swept the fields to the north and north-east of the buildings. Two companies to the south were ready to act as defensive troops should the Germans attempt a counter-attack from positions north of Vermand.

The two attacking companies moved forward from their jumping off positions east of Poeuilly and took the hamlet and two prisoners against no opposition. Within 20 minutes telephone communications had been established. This was quickly called into use to bring down artillery fire on Montelle Copse concealed in dead ground to the south-east. A German battery hidden in the copse was causing problems to the new garrison. Within another 30 minutes machine guns had been brought forward for defence and a party of sappers supervised consolidation.[30] On 1 April, 2/1st Bucks, who relieved the Warwickshires, began with "the exercise of average ingenuity" to make themselves comfortable utilizing the debris that lay about the ruins.[31] The only slight glitch in the operation had been the initial failure of DHQ to inform the CRE he needed to allocate a section of sappers to accompany the infantry. That mistake was quickly rectified and 479 Field Company despatched six men to assist the Warwickshires.

28   TNA WO 95716: 29 Mar.1917.
29   ADP *Operations, 02A8*.
30   TNA WO 953033: 30 Mar.1917; WO 953057: 2/8th Warwickshire, 30 Mar.1917.
31   TNA WO 953066: 2/1st Bucks, 1 Apr.1917.

Once Soyecourt had been taken it was a reasonably straight forward operation for 59th Division to take Vendelles. Jeancourt lay in a basin to its north, as did Hervilly to Jeancourt's north-west. The few buildings of nearby Hesbécourt straggled up the northern slopes of a valley that led to the high ground topped by Hill 140, Hill 135, Fervaque Farm, Grand Priel Woods, and Le Verguier. The Germans were not expected to offer a great deal of resistance to attacks on the lower villages but the high ground to their east was key terrain. If 59th Division could take Le Verguier, Grand Priel Woods and Fervaque Farm, the way to the final ridges lying in front of the Hindenburg Line would be open. Hargicourt would become untenable to the enemy and, if captured, the Cologne Ridge to its east and Ascension Spur running away to its south-east would give observation over parts of the Hindenburg Line itself. The first, shaping phase of the operations would thus involve taking the villages on the lower ground and then extending up the slopes beyond. These tactical actions were to be the division's first set-piece attempts against what would ultimately be heavily contested terrain.

On the night Soyecourt fell to 61st Division, 177 Brigade of 59th Division despatched patrols from Roisel and Nobescourt Farm to discover whether Hervilly was occupied. At the same time a squadron of corps cavalry penetrated up the Cologne river bank to assess the best approach to Hill 140. Orders issued early next morning confirmed the anticipated attacks on Hervilly, Hesbécourt, Hill 140, Jeancourt, and Vendelles would take place that day (31 March). As opposition was expected to be slight, artillery support was to be relatively thin; only 200 shells of 18 pdr and 50 rounds of 4.5 inch were allocated to destroy or demoralize potential garrisons in each of the two northern-most villages. Unfortunately, communications with the batteries proved not to be as secure as they should have been. A patrol entered the unoccupied Hervilly but had to evacuate it as the British bombardment continued to crash on its ruins. Enemy machine-gun fire also swept the village from the high ground to the north-east and south-east but once requests for the artillery to increase its range did get through, the barrage shifted onto Hill 140 and Hill 135. By 1445, infantry occupied both of the hills, Hesbécourt and Hervilly Wood, but for some reason 48th Division to the north started shelling Hill 140. Appeals to the division were finally acknowledged and the infantry consolidated the captured ground. To the north-east of Hill 140 the ground dropped away to Templeux-le-Guerard; to the south-east of Hill 135, on marginally higher ground, lay the heavily defended Fervaque Farm. Assisted by Lewis gunners and snipers from 2/5th Lincolnshire, 2/5th Leicestershire reached their objectives in the face of a distant enemy presence and began to dig cruciform posts.

To the south of 177 Brigade, Sherwood Forester battalions assembled for their attacks on Vendelles and Jeancourt. The artillery support was, as one observer noted, "lacking in volume"[32] – a mere one battery of 18pdrs and one section of the attached 40th Siege Battery for Vendelles, with one section of 18pdrs to cut wire on the morning of 31 March and one 4.5 inch howitzer battery to hit Jeancourt. The formal bombardment began at 1300 and ceased at 1400 when one company of 2/6th Sherwood Foresters advanced north-eastward from Flechin towards Vendelles. Two other companies advanced across the railway in a north-easterly direction towards Jeancourt and the Jeancourt – Maissemy lane. One company of 2/8th Sherwood Foresters was working to the south of 2/6th and ran into a German barrage targeted on the southern end of Vendelles. The company rushed towards the village cemetery but took some casualties as the

---

32   Oates, *History of 2/8th Sherwood Foresters*, p.98.

enemy kept pace with their progress by lifting and withdrawing their barrage 10 yards at a time. The Germans had clearly anticipated the attack and instead of wasting troops on what was always to be a deliberate withdrawal had evacuated the garrison and relied on the pre-registered shelling to discomfort the attackers. The company of 2/8th met its counterpart of 2/6th and began consolidation. The 2/6th's other two active companies continued on their way towards Jeancourt and the high ground to its south-east. On that higher ground machine guns in two strong points, known as R2b and R9a, could sweep the approaches towards Le Verguier from the west round to the south-east. Jeancourt, which like Vendelles had been evacuated, was taken but when the Sherwoods began ascending the slopes towards Le Verguier and Thierru Copse, and when the other company attempted to move up the Vendelles – Le Verguier road towards the railway cutting, intense fire from the strong points forced them back. Lieutenant Colonel Hodgkin, CO of 2/6th, asked for support and three companies of 2/8th were ordered forward from their holding area east of Bernes. As they approached Jeancourt they found 2/6th withdrawing. Hodgkin had decided the harassing enemy machine-gun fire and artillery prevented his companies from digging in during daylight. As the Germans still had observation over the village he calculated the risk factor and decided it was safer to withdraw and reorganize.[33]

Casualties amongst the two brigades taking part on these small operations had been minimal.[34] Although 2/6th Sherwood Foresters had failed, Brigadier General Maconchy nevertheless congratulated the brigade as a whole on its success in its first action. Despite the problems of coordination with the artillery support, 176 Brigade to the north had managed to secure all of its objectives. The obstacle of Le Verguier, which prisoners implied was garrisoned by up to 200 troops[35] and well protected by dense wire to its west and south, was to continue to be 178 Brigade's objective. There was, however, the possibility of exploiting the success of both 176 Brigade and 48th Division to its north by clearing Hargicourt and getting onto the Cologne Ridge. Templeux-le-Guérard marked the boundary between the two divisions and was soon to be evacuated by the Germans but the enemy garrison at Fervaque Farm was tasked to stay and delay 59th Division's progress. The strong point would have to be taken before 176 or 177 Brigade could descend into Villeret and move up onto the southern end of Cologne Ridge. If that could be achieved, and with 61st Division moving up the Omignon, the Germans would have no option other than to abandon Le Verguier.

On the left of 59th Division's front on 2 April, 177 Brigade pushed into Carpeza Copse and some of the higher ground to its east and south-east. Patrols were sent forward to look at the wire around Fervaque Farm but as the ground occupied by the brigade was considered untenable in daylight it evacuated its gains pending an organized assault on the farm. To the south, 2/7th Sherwood Foresters was ordered to make a hastily arranged attack on Le Verguier from the south with little idea of the ground or definite intelligence of the village defences. Furthermore, the artillery preparation was negligible because reports had come into DHQ that some British troops were actually in Le Verguier.[36] Sensibly, the attack was suspended and no registration on the village by the artillery was allowed until firmer intelligence had been acquired. When

---

33 TNA WO 953024: 178 Bde, 31 Mar.1917; Oates, *History of 2/8th Sherwood Foresters*, pp.101-02.
34 The 2/5th Leicestershire's war diarist recorded one killed, 18 wounded and five missing; 2/8th Sherwood Foresters noted two dead and eight wounded.
35 TNA WO 95675: 2 Apr.1917.
36 TNA WO 953010: 2 Apr.1917.

the reports of British soldiers present in the village were adjudged to be incorrect, the artillery began a one hour bombardment. The delay in confirming the assault would go ahead meant, however, that the infantry's time to assemble at their jumping off points had been compromised. Furthermore, it effectively ruled out any close cooperation with the guns. There was to be no help or demonstrations from 177 Brigade on the left but 61st Division on the right was to attack with 2/1st Bucks on the immediate flank. One and a half companies of 2/7th Sherwood Foresters were tasked to advance from the direction of the Vendelles – Le Verguier road, with C Company undertaking a feint attack along the Jeancourt – Le Verguier road. That company left Vendelles, with almost two miles to cover in the pitch dark and a snow storm, at the same time as the artillery began its "slight and scanty shelling".[37] The company passed through the outpost of 2/8th Sherwood Foresters, shook out into artillery formation and attempted to make its way across country towards the western approaches of Le Verguier. It ran into intact wire and a fully alert German garrison. The company tried to hack its way through the wire but was cut down in numbers and compelled to withdraw into Jeancourt. Meanwhile, in the darkness and appalling weather the main assault force approaching from the south had failed to find the Vendelles – Le Verguier road and had somehow managed to head south rather than north-east. The OC company did eventually realize the mistake, turned his platoons around and marched back into Vendelles. Having identified the correct road, he then headed north-east. By that time any hope of an assault coordinated with the artillery had been abandoned. The platoons pressed on but lost direction as they ran into German fire. Such had been the confusion that even battalion HQ "walked direct into the enemy who had opened fire at very close range."[38] It managed to extricate itself but by 0100 on 3 April, Lieutenant Colonel Raynor acknowledged it was futile to continue the attack and all platoons were recalled to Vendelles.

The assault had been a shambles and things were not about to improve. To the north, 2/4th Leicestershire had made repeated efforts to get through the wire surrounding Fervaque Farm until it was finally told to withdraw at 0330 on 3 April. Another attempt was to be made by 2/4th Lincolnshire at 2115 that night but, despite the knowledge that the farm was well garrisoned and its protecting wire at least 12 feet thick, there was to be only a sparse barrage of one hour by a battery of 18pdrs and a section of 4.5 inch howitzers. The results were predictable and at 0030 on 4 April, 2/4th Lincolnshire was ordered to abandon its attempt. Momentum was, however, to be maintained. Although the attack was later postponed, 2/4th Leicestershire was ordered to move forward and be ready to make an attempt by 0700. Plans again changed and at 0950 the battalion was told to follow closely a 40 minute barrage on the farm. Twenty minutes later a message came through that as 178 Brigade had not taken Le Verguier or Grand Priel Woods the Leicesters should withdraw. The diarist of the Leicestershire was content to lay the blame for his battalion's failure to get into the farm partly on the strength of the wire and partly on 178 Brigade's failure to the south.[39]

It was not only the Leicesters who condemned 178 Brigade. In 61st Division, 2/1st Bucks had already noted its dissatisfaction with the way 178 Brigade had operated. When they began their advance from the railway cutting on 2 April, the Bucks had expected 2/7th Sherwoods to be on their left. The Bucks made good progress towards their objective, the lower part of the sunken

---

37   Compiled, *The Robin Hoods*, p.326
38   TNA WO 953024: 178 Bde, 3 Apr.1917.
39   TNA WO 953022: 2/5th Leicestershire, 2 Apr.1917

Jeancourt-Maissemy lane. They found the Germans "demoralised, running this way and that, and plainly uncertain which avenue afforded them best means of escape." The Bucks, however, realized that their left flank was in the air. Their diarist later recorded that any further advance was thus "out of the question" because "59th Division – whose ideas of cooperation ... appeared then, and subsequently, to be of a very rudimentary nature – revealed no obvious attempt to keep in touch." The Bucks dug in but there was a gap of about 600 yards between their left and the outposts of 2/8th Sherwood Foresters. The following night, and although the wood was well to the left of their battalion front, the Bucks pushed through Caubrières Wood because, the same diarist noted, 59th Division "failed ... to undertake the work."[40]

The next attempt to take Le Verguier was made by 2/5th Sherwood Foresters in the early hours of 4 April. The battalion had moved to Vendelles at dusk on the previous day and, "With the exception of the HQ officers and company commanders nobody knew exactly what was to happen."[41] For those few who were aware of the purpose the objectives were again to be the village, its south-eastern spur, and to make contact with 177 Brigade in Grand Priel Woods. It seems the officers were briefed with intelligence that the enemy expected any attack would come from the direction of Jeancourt; the defences on the village's southern sides were thus assumed to be considerably weaker than those on the west. Why, or if, any officer believed that assumption is unknown but the evidence suggested otherwise. The earlier failed attacks on the village must have been known to 2/5th Battalion but with hindsight and a determination to demonstrate that the battalion was on its mettle, its historian later wrote: "As a fighting force the men were in the pink, their training perfect."[42] As they prepared to advance the men were unaware that what little artillery had been allocated for the attack was to concentrate its fire on the defences *west* of the village. Once the attackers reached its outskirts the guns would lift and sweep the high ground to its immediate north in preparation for the infantry's debouchment from the village to make contact with 177 Brigade. A forward observation officer (FOO) was detailed to remain at battalion HQ as liaison with the guns but it was unlikely that he would, even if runners arrived with such requests, swiftly be able to switch the concentration of fires from the west to the southern approaches.

In front of the battalion, and in the cruciform posts they had dug after their failed attempt the night before, were platoons of 2/7th Sherwood Foresters. Platoon commanders of 2/5th Sherwood were briefed by 0300 and the battalion moved off from Vendelles at 0515. They rested in the railway cutting for 20 minutes and were in position between the northern end of Small Foot Wood and the sunken Jeancourt – Maissemy lane 10 minutes before a zero of 0700. One platoon was detailed to make a diversionary frontal attack from the west 10 minutes before zero against a known machine gun post lying between Thierru Copse and the village. The intent of this deception was to keep the defenders facing towards Jeancourt. Snow began to fall at zero and almost as soon as the companies advanced a German barrage fell on them. At least one machine gun opened up from the north-west and caught them in what was from the village dead ground. Of the 450 who set off at zero, about 150 made it to the sunken lane that runs east-west along Odin's Hollow to the north of Caubrières Wood No.2. Pinned down by HE, shrapnel and machine-gun fire, with the village still about 500 yards away up an open slope, the

---

40   All quotations in this paragraph are from TNA WO 953066: 2/1st Bucks, 1-3 Apr.1917
41   W. Hall, *The Green Triangle*, p.59.
42   Ibid.; TNA WO 953025: 2/5th Sherwood Foresters, 4 Apr.1917.

companies were finally ordered to withdraw. They made their way back to the start line under cover of what had now developed into a blizzard. Casualties had been heavy, with initial reports suggesting 20 dead and over 80 wounded.

The failure was again predictable. There had been no time for any meaningful reconnaissance, the battalion had not seen the ground in daylight, intelligence about the state, depth and alignment of the defences was incorrect, the strength of the garrison was underestimated, the artillery preparation was totally inadequate, and the darkness and weather caused a loss of direction. It was the battalion's first significant action and while the troops may have been, as its historian wrote "in the pink", they were novices in the arts and skills of attacking heavily defended ground. The attack lacked imagination and, above all, appropriate resources. There had been no element of surprise, the deception was unconvincing, force protection was inadequate, there was no superiority of fires and there was no simultaneity with either flank. Instead of being broken, the enemy's cohesion and will would have been strengthened by the knowledge they had continued to thwart attempts to take the key terrain along the entire divisional front.

During the following night, 2/7th Sherwood relieved 2/6th in posts between Jeancourt and the approaches to Le Verguier. The same day, brigade HQ noted that the cruciform posts dug by both 2/5th and 2/6th were of "no value" because they were too far away from the German lines.[43] Disquiet was also expressed by 2/7th Sherwood about the posts vacated by 2/6th because some lay in a valley overlooked by the Germans and others were dug on the forward slope of a bare hill.[44] The excavated chalk showed clearly where the posts were and, unsurprisingly, attracted the attention of the enemy artillery. It was possibly either innocence or simple ignorance of their position *vis a vis* the enemy positions that had allowed 2/6th to dig them in such inappropriate positions in the first place. The following night, 2/7th withdrew a few hundred years and dug a far more sensible and potentially more secure line.

The performance and difficulties experienced by the Sherwood Foresters Brigade were discussed at higher levels. The GOC Brigade, Brigadier General Maconchy, had gone to battalion HQ of 2/7th Battalion as the chaos of its attack on the night of 2-3 April unfurled. On being briefed of the situation by the CO, Maconchy sacked Lieutenant Colonel Rayner and arranged for the second-in-command of 2/8th Sherwood, Major Martyn, to be temporary CO of 2/7th. Maconchy then visited DHQ presumably to advise Major General Sandbach of what he had done. On 5 April, General Romer, BGGS III Corps, paid a surprise visit to 178 Brigade and sacked Maconchy; he was replaced temporarily by Lieutenant Colonel Oates, CO of 2/8th Battalion. Oates was informed his brigade would be required to undertake another attack on Le Verguier in cooperation with 184 Brigade of 61st Division on the night of 6-7 April. A new GOC brigade, Brigadier General Stansfield, had been appointed and duly arrived early on 6 April. Knowing nothing of his brigade or of the terrain he declined to take immediate command and opted to let Oates conduct and manage the attack.[45]

Oates was in a difficult position. He believed that unless the ground to the north of Le Verguier was taken first, any further attack on the village from the south was likely to end in yet another disaster. Corps HQ believed that any further attack by either 176 or 177 Brigade on Fervaque Farm should, however, come *after* rather than *before* Le Verguier had fallen. For

---

43   TNA WO 953024: 178 Bde, 5 Apr.1917.
44   Compiled, *The Robin Hoods*, p.330.
45   TNA WO 953024: 178 Bde, 4-5 Apr.1917; Compiled, *History of 59th Division*, p.54.

Semi-open Warfare 109

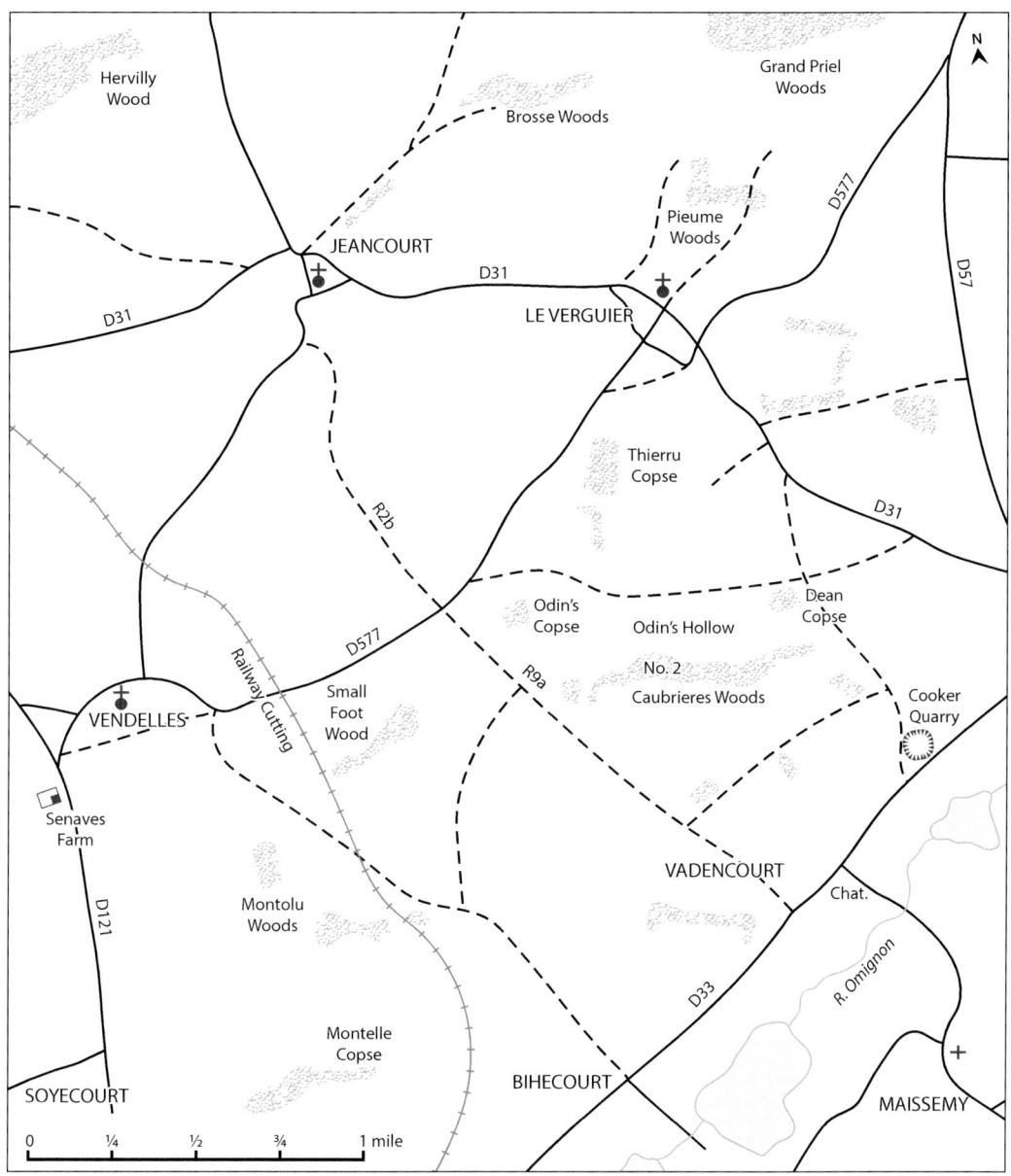

Map 1 184 Brigade attacks, March–April 1917.

that reason corps therefore declined Oates' request even for a demonstration by the adjoining brigade.[46] Apart from being allowed to select which battalion should make the attack Oates' opinion was not sought during what passed for the planning process. He decided his own 2/8th should make the attempt but the reality was that DHQ had presented him with what was effectively a *fait accompli*. He was to direct and command an attack that he considered to be ill-timed, ill-judged and unlikely to succeed. He did agree with one aspect of the plan which allowed for another battalion to bomb its way up the trench that ran on the western side of the Vendelles – Le Verguier road from the site of former German strong point R2b. Oates wanted this assault to act as a preliminary to the main attack but DHQ decided it should be made simultaneously. One company of 2/6th Sherwood Foresters was chosen for the task. The rest of the battalion, with four tubes of 178 TMB and four machine guns of 178 MG Company, was ordered to advance behind 2/8th and wait in Caubrières Wood until called forward. On the right, 2/4th Ox & Bucks, with 2/5th Gloucestershire on *its* right, were to advance with the Oxfords setting the rate and direction of the attack. They were to refuse their left flank to cover the Sherwoods and establish strong points on the eastern slope of the spur. This line of posts would be continued westwards by 2/6th Sherwood.

Artillery support was rather more extensive than on previous attempts. Divisional brigades were belatedly supplemented by corps' heavy artillery and by the brigades of 61st Division. Batteries of 48th Division to the north of 59th Division would also fire on targets around the divisional boundary. Nevertheless, the duration of the bombardment on the enemy wire and suspected strong points was again to be short. After 40 minutes, at 0040 on 7 April, it was to lift and creep back to Le Verguier to cover the projected rush of the infantry. Final orders were issued at 2000. This just allowed time for Major Martyn, who Oates had brought back from temporary command of 2/7th to his old battalion, to brief the officers of 2/8th at Flechin. The companies moved forward at 2100 and were at their jumping off positions on the Jeancourt – Maissemy lane at 2345. All four companies were to be used but in the blackness and rain it was difficult for the two lead companies to keep in touch. Furthermore, B Company also failed to gain contact on the right because the Oxfords' left company advanced more quickly than the Foresters. The lead platoons descended into the valley where 2/7th Sherwood had been so badly mauled five days earlier and became bogged down in knee-deep mud. The British guns were firing short of the wire and to avoid running into their own barrage the Sherwoods stayed in the valley waiting for the barrage to lift at 0040. German machine guns and shrapnel played on them as they attempted to find cover and then, instead of lengthening their range, the British guns brought it back onto their own troops. In the attempt to get away from the shelling one company rushed the wire but found it still unbroken. The men were lashed by machine-gun fire as they struggled through the mud of the bare slope in the hope of finding a gap. In support on the right, C Company despatched a message to battalion HQ stating the Oxfords had withdrawn and that 2/8th was now entirely isolated. Runners sent back to brigade HQ became lost or killed and when one did get through with the message that the British guns were firing short, Colonel Stewart was unable to reach his batteries on the telephone. At 0300 the Brigade Intelligence Officer was despatched to find out what was going on. He returned with the news that 2/8th had dug in on slopes that would in day light be completely untenable and claimed

46   TNA WO 95675: Apr.1917; Oates, *History of 2/8th Sherwood Foresters*, pp.107-14.

he had seen the Oxfords well behind the lines marching back towards their camp in column of fours. Believing the attack had degenerated into yet another catastrophe Oates made the decision to recall both Major Martyn's and Lieutenant Colonel Hodgkin's battalions. The message was received but as the survivors began to withdraw, the British artillery once more shortened its range with the same disastrous results. With their own as well as German shells crashing amongst them, through pouring sleet and gripping mud, what was left of 2/8th Sherwoods struggled back first to Vendelles and then Flechin.[47]

The battalion had done what it could but, again, the conditions and the rushed and inadequate planning had worked against it achieving its objectives. Corps HQ had obviously decided further changes in the division were required and acted. Major General Sandbach was summarily sacked and replaced by Major General Romer who, three days earlier, had sacked Maconchy. The fresh eyes quickly recognized that what Oates had advocated before the attack of 7 April was the correct tactical course. Romer issued orders for an assault to be made by all three brigades on 9 April.[48] He instructed 178 Brigade to bomb up the old German trench alongside the Vendelles – Le Verguier road and push forward from Caubrières Wood. Fervaque Farm was to be captured by 177 Brigade, which was to then press on to the Hargicourt – Villeret road and, if possible, secure Malakoff Farm. In the centre, 176 Brigade was to approach Grand Priel Woods and Pieunel Wood from the west, with one company turning south to enter Le Verguier from the north. The artillery support was to be increased but the duration of the barrage was to be a meagre 45 minutes. This was, however, at least to be supplemented by intense machine-gun barrages on several points and flanks and by trench mortars and rifle grenadiers also targeting pre-selected positions. There was no real attempt to disguise where the assaults would come and no real element of surprise. On the other hand, there was concentration of force and improved all arms coordination to secure key terrain. Should the opportunity arise there were also realistic plans to exploit success and, with the additional fire support, better force protection. Because they involved greater coordination with the divisions to north and south the plans were more extensive and complicated, but they did demonstrate lessons learned and a preparedness to accept calculated risk. Furthermore, brigade commanders delegated some tactical decisions such as how platoons should deploy to battalion COs. The unknown element was, as always, the moral component of the division's fighting power. The operation's outcome depended to a great extent on whether the morale and fighting spirit of the troops themselves had, despite the successive set-backs of the previous eight days, survived reasonably intact.

When the attacking battalions advanced up the slopes they found Fervaque Farm, Grand Priel Woods, and Le Verguier deserted. On the left, 177 Brigade was ordered to advance into Hargicourt and in conjunction with 48th Division was instructed to take both Malakoff and Cologne Farms as well as the Quarries on the eastern edge of Hargicourt. Patrols quickly reported the Quarries had also been evacuated. Platoons pressed on but when at 0430 on 11 April, and again in cooperation with a battalion of 144 Brigade on their left, one company of 2/5th Lincolnshire went for the trench running from Hargicourt to Malakoff Farm while

---

47   Casualties were as follows: five officers and 43 ORs killed; two and 67 wounded. When Le Verguier was evacuated by the enemy, 37 bodies of 2/8th men were recovered close to the wire. Putting aside those who died of wounds, later figures from *Soldiers Died in the Great War* (HMSO) suggest a death toll of almost 50 ORs. Oates, *History of 2/8th Sherwood Foresters*, p.113.
48   TNA WO 953010: Orders No.21 and 22, 8 Apr.1917.

another entered the Quarries, they were met with intense resistance and a ferocious counter-attack. Most of the company near Malakoff Farm was subsequently thought to have been surrounded and captured; the company in the Quarries was badly mauled but some troops escaped. Casualties for what intelligence had suggested should have been two relatively simple operations reached almost 260 all ranks.[49] The two companies involved were formed into one composite unit as trench strength of the battalion sank to about 350 ORs.

Over the next few weeks the division as a whole continued to have a torrid time as it gradually pushed its way towards the main German positions. Cologne and Malakoff Farms were not taken and held for any length of time; the Quarries became a charnel house and were not secured until the end of April; Villeret, Grand Priel and Ascension Farms on the final ridge west of the Hindenburg Line were taken towards the end of the month. Now safely ensconced in their prepared positions the Germans had the luxury of being able to shell at will those positions they had occupied for over two years. Until it moved a few miles north to the Gouzaucourt sector and fell under XV Corps in mid-May, 59th Division remained in the area conducting fighting patrols and improving defences.

Compared to other 2nd Line divisions such as 61st and 62nd, 59th Division's blooding had, perhaps, been relatively tame. It had enjoyed no time to become acclimatized to trench warfare, and the advance across the devastated zone had been uncomfortable, but it had not been thrown immediately into any great pitched battle. The operations in front of the Hindenburg Line had, however, revealed innocence and a lack of preparedness. The often clumsy and predictable attacks against Fervaque Farm and Le Verguier had cost the battalions dear and the authorities had clearly decided the division needed some fresh blood. Sandbach's sacking was a obvious way to invigorate the formation. Having already served as Chief Engineer to Second Army in 1915 and then, after a gap brought back as GOC 68th (2nd Welsh) Division at home, he had taken 59th Division to Ireland. But, his age of 59 was against him. His concurrence to the dismissal of Maconchy as GOC 178 Brigade perhaps saved him for a time but the repeated failures at Fervaque Farm and his flawed plan for 2/8th Sherwood Foresters attack on Le Verguier sealed his fate.

Maconchy had retired from the Indian Army as a colonel in 1914 and was brought back as a dugout in July 1915. He was older than Sandbach and it was his age and lack of imagination in front of Le Verguier that cost him his post. His replacement was the newly promoted Brigadier General Stansfield, an infantryman and 14 years his junior. In view of its inexperience and the number of times it had inflicted casualties on its own infantry, there were changes in the personnel of the division's artillery. In March, the CRA, Brigadier General Ouseley had fallen from his horse and disappeared to a CCS. He was replaced by Brigadier General Cartwright on 28 March but, having commanded the artillery during the worst of the operations in early April, Cartwright was himself replaced just over two weeks later by Brigadier General Stirling.[50] The brigade commanders of 295 and 296 Brigades RFA were also relieved of their commands

---

49 At least 68 of the casualties were later reported as killed. Several others died of wounds in subsequent days.
50 On recovery from his injury, rather than returning him to his old post Ouseley, who was 51 years old, was appointed CRA to 61st Division. The man he replaced, Brig. Gen. R Coates, was three years younger than Ouseley. Brig. Gen. James Stirling was nine years Ouseley's senior and had retired on half pay in 1905.

in April.[51] In mid-April, Brigadier General Charles Humphreys handed over command of 176 Brigade. As this had been the least committed of the division's three infantry brigades in early April it seems unlikely that Humphreys was sacked for poor leadership.[52] Although an infantryman, he was however, certainly inexperienced in command. Furthermore, as he was only three years younger than Sandbach, it is probable that a combination of inexperience, health, and age caused him to return home. Lieutenant Colonels Rayner and Spiers appear to have been the only COs actually dismissed but several others did also return home for reasons of health. There remained, however, at least four genuine TF commissioned COs in the division when it moved in May but, as was common across most of the 1st and 2nd Line TF divisions in the BEF by mid-1917, the majority of COs were regulars with war time experience posted into TF battalions. Similarly, in common with divisions across the BEF, all divisional staff jobs down to and including brigade major remained in the hands of regulars.

Poor staff work and indifferent liaison had caused the division to raise the ire of 48th (South Midland) Division on at least two occasions during April. When the 1st Line division was detailed by corps HQ to take over a section of 59th Division's sector, the latter had failed to give accurate information as to what ground it actually held and the nature of its terrain. On another occasion, when 48th Division was ordered to advance its outposts in cooperation with 59th Division towards the Tombois – Malakoff Farm Ridge, the CO of 1/8th Worcestershire enquired of 2/5th Lincolnshire how the Lincolns intended to conduct their part of the operation. The Lincolns replied they had received no orders to attack and had no intention of doing so. This came as "rather a surprise ... and was very upsetting" to the Worcesters' CO because it meant his men would be exposed on their flank.[53] Reference to what 2/1st Bucks thought of the division's work in April has already been made; 2/4th Oxford made similar comments about 178 Brigade. The Oxfords criticised the Foresters' officers for been too willing to hold their men back before then managing to drive them in the wrong direction and across the Oxfords' front.[54] Complaints such as these are, of course, not uncommon in many war diaries. Battalion diarists frequently claim the reason why an objective was not taken or held was because the unit on its flank had withdrawn prematurely. The North Midland Division was certainly inexperienced but it did provide copious reports and updates on its activities to those divisions on its flanks. It was not so diligent in recording what those divisions sent in reply but it is clear that the division's staff work during April was neither any better nor any worse than that of its neighbours. Its paperwork for reliefs, daily issue of orders and general administration follow the formats in widespread use by 1917. Not all of its unit war diaries are as full as others but all do fulfil the minimum requirements laid down by GHQ.

Major General Romer's task was to stiffen his division and build its self-confidence. He was to remain in command for 14 months and would see the division through its traumatic experience

---

51　Brig.Gen.Coates noted that because 59th Division's artillery had failed to engage some easy targets on its own front, he had directed 61st Division's guns to fire over the divisional boundaries and do the task instead. See TNA WO 953037: 9 Apr.1917.
52　Humphreys had spent some years as Commandant of the School of Music in India. He was replaced as GOC 176 Brigade by Ryvers Currie. He was also an infantryman and had passed Staff College. He had served as brigade major in Irish Command in 1912.
53　TNA WO 952759: 1/7th Worcestershire, *Report on Operations on 13 April 1917*
54　TNA WO 953063: Report by OC A Coy, 2/4th Ox & Bucks, 7 Apr.1917

of the German offensive of March 1918. He assumed command at a time when the division was heavily involved in these untidy small-scale engagements and when trust in all arms cooperation was low. He had not only to command the division and its units but also to manage their cooperation and foster mutual understanding of respective capabilities. Like any commander he had also to show firm and determined leadership. He was not a charismatic leader but began his task by addressing the issue of the poor performance of the artillery.[55] The infantry was asked not to be bitter about or to resent the artillery's recent costly errors but instead to understand and appreciate how inexperienced it was. He also, rather strangely and inaccurately, asserted that the guns had not received any specific order to cut the enemy's wire before 7 April's attack on Le Verguier. Lieutenant Colonel Oates believed the division was "extremely lucky" to have Romer appointed but his period of command had not begun well.[56] Although, as noted above, changes in senior positions had or were about to be made there was to be no instant improvement. The debacles near Malakoff and Cologne Farms when all-arms cooperation was again poor demonstrated how difficult his task would be. He was to be assisted, however, by a lengthy period of relative quiet when the division was able to adopt a more mature perspective and reflect on its early experiences.

Operating on 59th Division's right in April 1917, 61st Division had understandably shown a greater maturity than the North Midland during the advance across the Somme. Although cautious, it was prepared to press on a little more rapidly than 59th Division. To encourage the troops during this difficult period Major General Mackenzie issued an Order of the Day on 31 March. This praised all arms of the division for their persistence, determination, and professionalism. As the division approached the entrenched enemy positions he expressed his confidence that all units would continue to perform well.[57] In reality, the experience gained from its 12 months in France was not always reflected in the way it operated in the area to the immediate west of the Hindenburg Line. It certainly did well in conjunction with 32nd Division in the turning movement that had cleared Holnon Wood, and during the initial moves which had carried it up the Omignon Valley to Vermand. Some of the subsequent actions towards and beyond Maissemy, however, were not conducted with quite the same competence.

On 2 April, the divisional railhead opened at Nesle. This eased transport problems to a degree and allowed the divisional ammunition column to advance to Merancourt. Rationing of daily shell consumption was, however, to be enforced for weeks. Until intelligence clarified the situation there were some contradictory orders about how, tactically, Maissemy should be approached but, while that discussion was underway and the issue resolved, the artillery began its bombardment of the village in preparation for the attack. The village was taken and 2/7th Worcestershire began to consolidate its gains. At about 1630 on 2 April the artillery was called upon to disperse approximately two companies of German infantry reported to be massing to counter-attack the village from its north-east and south-east.[58]

To the left of 183 Brigade, 2/4th Berkshire, with an attached company of 2/5th Gloucestershire, was to take Bihècourt; 2/1st Bucks, on the left of the Berkshire, was to advance from the railway embankment towards the sunken Jeancourt – Maissemy lane. On the left of the Bucks, as we

---

55 Oates, *History of 2/8th Sherwood Foresters*, pp.113-14
56 Ibid.
57 TNA WO 953033: 31 Mar.1917.
58 TNA WO 953037: 2 Apr.1917.

have seen, was 2/7th Sherwood Foresters. The attack was a hastily planned affair, with brigade orders arriving at the two battalions' HQ only four hours before zero. There was no time for any useful reconnaissance (a breakdown in communications meant that the one report which would have been of use arrived too late to be considered) and briefings of officers and NCOs were rushed and incomplete. The refusal of a request by the Bucks for a postponement of the operation caused some "anxiety" amongst its senior officers and, although tapes were correctly laid by the Bucks to the embankment, the two attacking companies were in position only five minutes before zero. A fairly brief and thin artillery barrage, supplemented by one provided by the brigade machine-gun company, was to be laid on the objectives for 40 minutes. Under its protection the left company advanced against little opposition and reached the sunken lane; the right company advanced too quickly and ran into its own barrage.[59] This company took several casualties but also experienced problems with the Berkshires on its right. Having advanced into Bihècourt against slight opposition, the Berkshires sent patrols to discover whether Vadencourt chateau was clear of the enemy.[60] Others, according to the diarist of the Bucks, "filled apparently with enthusiasm at their success" turned left up the Bihècourt-Vendelles lane and made a "regrettable and wholly unwarrantable mistake...which could only have arisen through the failure on the part of BERKSHIRE officers to make themselves acquainted through brigade orders with what was happening on their flanks."[61] Observing troops advancing from left to right across what they thought was their front the Berks opened fire with Lewis guns and rifles on what was actually the right company of the Bucks. It took two to three minutes for the mistake to be realized but several Bucks had been felled by the enfilade fire.[62]

It is easy to understand the vehemence with which the Bucks diary was written, particularly because it was later established that the bulk of the friendly fire casualties were caused by the infantry rather than the artillery. There was little excuse for the Berks to have mistaken the Bucks for Germans: the light was good enough to identify friend from foe from the 200 yards that separated the company of Bucks from that of the Berks. As the two battalions were in the same brigade the mistake could not be blamed on poor communications across an inter-divisional or even inter-brigade boundary. It could simply have been, as the diarist claimed, that the Berks had not been briefed as to who was on their left. Coincidentally, FM Haig and his staff, General Rawlinson and his chief of staff, and Lieutenant General C L Woollcombe, all visited 61st Division HQ that day. Whether or not he knew of the confusion near Bihècourt, Haig expressed his "satisfaction" at what the division had done. Choosing to dismiss the incident as perhaps a vicissitude of war, Brigadier General White, GOC 184 Brigade, added his personal congratulations to the brigade.[63]

Like 59th Division, 61st Division continued over the next few days to pursue its strategy of limited offensive action. Even in the unlikely event that success either side of the Omignon

---

59　TNA WO 953066: 2/1st Bucks, 2 Apr.1917.
60　According to Barnes, *2/5th Battalion Gloucestershire*, p.60, they found the Germans in Bihècourt shaving and eating breakfast.
61　TNA WO 953066: 2/1st Bucks, 2 Apr,1917.
62　Ibid., 1-3 Apr.1917. Bucks casualties were recorded as nine dead and 30 wounded. Neither the Berkshires' war diary nor its regimental history makes any mention of the friendly fire incident. The 2/4th Ox & Bucks history does make an oblique reference to it. See G. Rose, *2/4th Ox & Bucks*, p.81.
63　TNA WO 953033: 3 Apr.1917.

would create an opportunity to exploit (and then only as far as the main Hindenburg Line itself) there were insufficient resources available to IV and III Corps. Manpower was to be conserved and other elements of the physical component of fighting power remained restricted. For example, there was no opportunity for training and, on 3 April, divisional ammunition expenditure was reduced to 50 rounds per day for 18pdrs and 30 for the 4.5 inch howitzers. Appealing targets had sometimes to be ignored lest the available shells proved insufficient in the event of a German counter-attack.[64] Given the shortages of guns and ammunition, other than in very local tactical situations there was little likelihood the division would be able to achieve superiority of fires or concentrate the effects of force to any decisive extent. Its immediate objectives were to pressurize the enemy where and when it could and, by deception, hope to convince the Germans that a major offensive was building in the sector. This might restrict any movement of enemy reserves to the Arras area or to the Aisne. The division, therefore, continued to make progress up the Omignon Valley and the adjoining higher ground. While 184 Brigade had been advancing on the left, on 2 April, 183 Brigade used three battalions to push on to the north-east of Maissemy. Moderate success was achieved and progress was continued on 6 April. The objective was the high ground between Berthaucourt and Fresnoy-le-Petit that, if taken, would allow a degree of observation over sections of the Hindenburg position[65] Under what on this occasion was described as a "perfect artillery barrage", 2/8th Worcestershire took the high ground but came under galling machine-gun fire because, as they reported, 184 Brigade had not kept pace. A barrage was organized to protect the exposed left flank but the crest had to be abandoned and ground lower down consolidated.[66]

At the same time as 183 Brigade was making halting progress towards Berthaucourt, 184 Brigade on its left continued its attempt to gain ground to the south-east of Le Verguier. Once again, the advance ran into previously undetected and uncut wire. The attack, by one company from each of 2/4th Oxford and 2/5th Gloucestershire, advanced under a sparse barrage that repeatedly fell short. Regrouping a little distance from the crest of the spur they rushed forward 80 yards only to be confronted by wire 10 feet thick and five feet high. To illustrate how inaccurate and inadequate the barrage had been, a report emphasized that besides there being no gaps there were not even any shell holes close to the wire. Four machine guns and showers of bombs were turned on the Oxfords as they struggled to cut a gap but as their Lewis guns could not bring sufficient suppressive fire to bear, after a second rush had been attempted and repulsed, the OC A Company consulted with his counterpart of 2/5th Gloucestershire and an officer of 2/7th Sherwood Foresters.[67] The two South Midland companies withdrew to the sunken lane running down to Cookers Quarry and rejoined their support companies.

Patrol activity between lulls in more formal attacks was intended mainly to ascertain the condition of the enemy wire. In particular, the artillery continued to have little success in cutting gaps in the belts protecting a deep and strongly wired trench straddling the Vadencourt

---

64 TNA WO 953037: CRA, 3 Apr.1917.
65 The WDs refer to "Hill 120" but in this case it should have been "Hill 115". The correct Hill 120 lies to the south-east of Fresnoy.
66 TNA WO 953058: 183 Bde, 6 Apr.1917.
67 It will be remembered that the Sherwoods were by now driving across the Oxfords' front. The 2/7th's officer allegedly told the Oxfords' officer he had been waiting for the Oxfords to attack. See TNA WO 953063: 184 Brigade HQ, Report of Operation 6-7 Apr.1917.

– Bellenglise road close to its summit.[68] On receipt of news that Germans in the trench had earlier been seen wearing packs, at 0200 on 9 April a party of 2/4th Berkshire approached the wire, managed to find a way through, and discovered the trench to be empty. The rest of the company was called forward to occupy it while another patrol crept down the slope and found the tumulus 500 yards further on similarly unoccupied. The patrol was forced to withdraw when a large party of Germans were spied about to surround it. In the valley below, Pontru had also been abandoned by the Germans. A sergeant crossed the marshes into Berthaucourt but could find no trace of 183 Brigade on the right. Messages were sent back but such was the poor communication across brigade boundaries that when the Berkshires were relieved on the evening of 10 April there appears to have been no attempt by 183 Brigade to make contact.[69] Inefficient as this suggests, there was an excuse for both 183 and 184 Brigades complaining that the other was not keeping abreast. The difficult lay along the brigade boundary that followed the marshes of the Omignon. It was extremely difficult for infantry to cross the flooded area of the river and during operations there was usually an artillery barrage programmed to drop shells among the reeds to dissuade any adventurous Germans from using the cover to turn a flank. There is no specific mention of officers being sent for liaison purposes to those units across the boundary working on their flanks but by this stage of the war it was generally regarded as a necessary prerequisite to operations. The fact that no knowledge appears to have been shared about their respective positions for almost 24 hours does, however, suggest unnecessarily poor liaison and organization.

Although 61st Division's advance had been slow and unspectacular, it was the progress achieved by the South Midland that helped ultimately to precipitate the German evacuation of Le Verguier. The possession of Fervaque Farm and Grand Priel Woods by 59th Division had also been crucial but it was no coincidence that Mareval Trench and Mareval Copse, as well as the smaller woods on the spur east of Le Verguier, had similarly been abandoned by the enemy. The moves forward from Maissemy had not involved a great deal of fighting but one position where the Germans chose to prolong their defence was at the village of Fresnoy-le-Petit. Like Le Verguier it lay on a dominating position with good fields of fire to the north, west and south. Its chief tactical importance was that it protected the approaches to its neighbour, Gricourt. This village lies in a hollow and was meshed within the Hindenburg system. Tactically, Fresnoy could be held by a small number of men under the protection of guns within the main Hindenburg defences to its rear. The Germans had planned to evacuate the village but opted to make 61st Division work hard before its garrison withdrew to Gricourt.

The German withdrawal eastwards cannot be seen in modern terms as a classic defensive action. Today, such actions are normally defined as moves that will provide the right conditions for future offensive action. They are not synonymous with weakness or defeat but more a means of protecting an existing force in order to buy time or to fix the enemy in one area so that offensive action can be created in another. Characteristically, typical delaying actions trade space for time and reduce the adversary's momentum. The attacker is slowed down, takes losses and is canalized before arriving at the main defence area. During the withdrawal the Germans

---

68   The trench ran through what is today the German cemetery and had several names along its length. North of the road it became Cooker and then Dean Trench, whilst south of it, Mareval gave way to Pontru Trench.
69   TNA WO 953065: 2/4th Berkshire, 8-9 Apr.1917.

had no intention of mounting major counter-attacks – those that were undertaken were local tactical rather than strategic affairs. But the enemy did generally hold the initiative because they decided when the next stage of the withdrawal should commence. The Allies' freedom of action was constricted by an enemy who had organized an all round area defence in order to buy time and limit losses of manpower and materiel. They believed time was on their side: the USA had declared war while the fighting for Le Verguier was underway but the existing US army was tiny in size and with no experience of the type of war being fought in Europe. Russia was undergoing political turmoil, much of which was fostered by German interference, and the unrestricted U-boat campaign was expected to deliver decisive results. By fixing the Allied armies in front of the intended impregnable Hindenburg Line, against which they were expected to hurl themselves and take calamitous losses, the Germans anticipated that defensive action on the Western Front would deliver strategic victory. The defence of Fresnoy, like that of Le Verguier and several other places along the front of Fourth Army were elements of that grand strategic plan.

Fresnoy's first significant mention in IV Corps' orders was made on 5 April 1917. To its right a new line of resistance had just been established by 32nd Division; 61st Division was ordered to align itself with those defences by 0600 on 6 April. There was, however, a caveat. Corps HQ stated that if the trenches running to the west of Fresnoy, across Hill 120 (actually Hill 115) and west of Pontru were strongly held and attacking them would prove too costly, the division should get as close as possible and halt. On 5 April, when a proposed attack by 2/8th Worcestershire on Hill 115 was postponed the artillery demonstrated flexibility and offered to switch the fire plan to cover an approach to Fresnoy instead. This proposal was accepted but when a patrol of 2/6th Gloucestershire subsequently reported the village to be empty, the artillery programme was cancelled. Responding to the patrol's intelligence, two companies of Gloucesters approached the village. Rather than simply occupying a deserted set of ruins, however, they were beaten back by small arms fire. A second attempt met with the same fate. Notwithstanding its earlier stricture, corps HQ now decided that progress by 32nd Division and the French to its south made it imperative the village be taken. An attempt by 2/4th Gloucestershire, that again lacked simultaneity with any other assault along the line, was also repelled. Two companies had assembled north and south of the road leading into the village from the west and strong points had been established in sunken lanes to give supporting fire. Despite the barrage, which began at 2100, ferocious machine-gun and rifle fire hit the attackers and forced them to ground. Several posts were dug successfully about 100 yards from the wire but patrols from these were unable to find any gaps. At 0340 the attack was abandoned.[70] The infantry blamed the failure on the inability of the artillery to cut the wire, a charge that generated an angry response from the CRA. He argued that two clear gaps, one of 80 yards and one of 60 yards had been cut about 100 yards apart. These gaps were apparently later confirmed by patrols. In response to the criticism, the CRA insisted the reason for the failure was not the fault of the guns but the infantry's inability to keep direction and to find the gaps in the dark. "From an artillery point of view" he

---

70 TNA WO 953060: 2/4th Gloucestershire, 5-6 Apr.1917; WO 953058: 183 Bde, 5-6 Apr.1917. One report suggested the Gloucesters managed to reach the village crossroads before being forced back about 300 yards beyond its western edge. This seems unlikely. TNA WO 953033: 7 Apr.1917. Three hours later 2/8th Worcesters failed to take Hill 115.

exclaimed, "it is difficult to realize and understand the desire of attacking against wire at night, especially with only partly trained troops."[71]

DHQ decided a more formal, considered and coordinated plan of attack was required. It was a measured scheme, aimed not at taking a great chunk of territory but to put the brigade in a position from where subsequent attacks could be launched. Six platoons of 2/7th Warwickshire were to advance at 1940 on 8 April to take the village and its trenches as far as the cemetery on its eastern edge. Once those objectives had been achieved, 2/6th Warwickshire would take Hill 120 (Hill 115) to link up with 59th Division on the Omignon and 2/7th Warwickshire in Fresnoy. The artillery cover was to be supplied by the heavy batteries of 62nd and 89th Heavy Artillery Groups (HAGs) as well as seven divisional batteries of 18pdrs and two of 4.5 inch howitzers. Shell allocation was sufficient to allow for up to 390 rounds for the HAG and three rounds per minute for the 18pdrs. During daylight of 8 April, divisional batteries fired on the wire in front of Fresnoy and on Hill 115 while the heavy batteries were to target known strong points in and around the village at zero. In the meantime, machine guns were to be used to keep open gaps made in the wire on the hill. Zero was to be 1900; at 1910 the platoons of 2/7th were to leave the shelter of a bank and advance to the German wire. At 1940 the barrage was to lift and the Warwickshires were to rush a trench running roughly north-south just west of the village crossroads. They were then to establish a post capable of securing control of the road heading south to Fayet. Contact would be made with 32nd Division in a former German trench about 800 yards south-west of the village. For added fire power, machine-gun barrages would cover the right flank and two tubes of the LTB would be available for close protection at the road block.[72]

The six platoons, with another two detailed as carrying parties, and the artillery programme should have been sufficient to overwhelm the garrison estimated at being about 80 men. Strong resistance was, however, maintained for some time. Falling behind the attackers, the enemy barrage caused few problems but north of the village crossroads the Warwickshires discovered the wire to be uncut. Fortunately, the belts were low and not much of an obstacle. German fire from the trench behind the wire was intense. Two reserve platoons were sent up to reinforce the attack after two Lewis gun teams and a bombing section had been "practically wiped out." Although under no great pressure, the Germans eventually withdrew from the trench, crossed the Fresnoy – Berthaucourt road and regrouped in the cemetery. From pre-prepared defensive positions they continued to harass the Warwickshires. South of the crossroads, two attempts to get forward were thwarted by a wall of small arms fire. At 2030 two additional platoons managed to get round the enemy's left flank and by 2300 the enemy fire had slackened. The Warwickshires consolidated the road block and contact was established with 32nd Division by slightly refusing their right flank. On schedule at 0510 on 9 April, 2/6th Warwickshire took Hill 115 and gained touch with 59th Division close to the Omignon.[73]

From the German perspective, the operation had gone well. The British had been forced to expend a considerable number of shells and had lost what turned out to be about 11 dead and over 40 wounded. The defence had further delayed the British advance and compelled the attackers to live and fight in the atrocious conditions for that little bit longer. By holding the key terrain

---

71   TNA WO 953037: CRA, 7 Apr.1917.
72   TNA WO 953054: 182 Bd, .8 Apr.1917.
73   TNA WO 953056: 2/7th Warwickshire. Report on Operations 8-9 April 1917.

and using defence in depth the Germans had forced the British to attack frontally and carry out what were in effect small-scale bite and hold operations. For the British, the final attack on Fresnoy was a good example of how these limited engagements should be conducted. Casualties had not been excessive and the logistical problems of bringing forward guns and ammunition had been surmounted. There remained, however, difficulties with coordination. The two Stokes mortars had not come into action because the mortar teams kept themselves separate from the assaulting infantry and made their own way forward. Its officer had gone ahead without infantry support to reconnoitre and had disappeared. The attached sappers had kept in contact with the Warwickshires and did good work in assisting with consolidation but, once again, there was great difficulty in establishing communication with the batteries. Telephone cables to the rear were laid and maintained but connections via the brigade's forward stations along the metallic circuits and through the switchboards remained tenuous. Lieutenant Colonel Glyn, CO of 2/7th Warwickshire added a polite note of regret about the artillery, suggesting that it was "not as effective as it might be." He had requested a continuation of the protective barrage but all he received in response was a partial one that lasted for only 17 minutes.[74] There was also the perennial problem of a lack of trust between infantry and gunners. Persuading the men to follow as closely behind the barrage as ordered was difficult and the troops were too often correct in assuming that when they reached the wire they would find it uncut. Glyn's comments about the artillery, pertinent as they were, were edited out of reports submitted by both brigade and divisional HQ.

On 9 April, one day later than originally scheduled, Fourth Army began its bombardment of the Hindenburg Line. This coincided with the opening day of the Arras offensive. The two 2nd Line divisions continued to improve their positions until 59th left for Gouzeaucourt and 61st for Arras. Fighting continued in their respective sectors until they departed: 61st Division remained heavily engaged west and north-west of St Quentin; Malakoff and Cologne Farms remained costly sores for 59th Division. By the time they left, fighting strength of battalions in both divisions was generally below 400.[75] The *Official History* later noted that during the advance, it was the "Somme divisions which showed the greatest aptitude and most quickly learnt the new lessons." It was their previous experience under fire which made the difference between them and the newly arrived formations that had, Falls remarked, been "trained mainly for open warfare."[76] This argument does have some credibility because certain neighbouring "Somme divisions" such as 32nd and 48th (South Midland) did show flexibility and adaptability. Their all-arms coordination worked well and at times showed an impressive degree of imagination and innovation. They varied their times of attack and, after consultation with infantry COs, the types and lengths of barrages. In contrast, the war diaries of the two 2nd Line divisions suggest that, for example, it was the divisional commander, his staff and the CRA who decided what sort of barrage should be put down. Because there is no mention that brigade commanders and battalion COs were consulted about what they wanted the artillery to contribute does not mean,

---

74   Ibid.
75   A GHQ letter ordered that no platoon should contain fewer than 28 men. Consequently, several battalions in the divisions were reorganized into three companies with three platoons and one company with two. TNA WO 953065: 2/4th Berkshire, 13 Apr.1917; WO 953066: 2/5th Gloucestershire, 10 Apr.1917.
76   Falls, *Military Operations*, Vol. I, p.162

of course, that they were not involved in discussions, but the fire plans for both divisions generally show a predictable and stylized format. Infantry tactics, especially those of 59th Division, displayed little variation. The repeated failure of the artillery to cut wire and the very infrequent use of the trench mortar batteries during April meant that bunched infantry searching for gaps created excellent targets. The dilemma was whether to assault the entrenched positions in daylight, and thus be easily visible to the enemy, or to attack at night and expect inexperienced and partially trained troops to keep direction and find any gaps in the wire. The artillery of 61st Division was not significantly more able to destroy wire than 59th's, nor to ensure its fall of shot was always where the infantry wanted or expected it to be. Furthermore, all divisions in Fourth Army lacked what they considered to be adequate stocks of ammunition and sufficient support from HAGs to enable effective completion of their tasks. The combat support services of all divisions in Fourth Army were to be severely tested by the conditions under which they operated but, with experienced and able GSO1s, both 2nd Line formations found it no more difficult than other divisions to provide the support.[77]

During these two months of semi-open warfare and limited offensive action, neither of the two 2nd Line divisions was ever in the position to inflict defeat on their enemy through the use or threat of force. Nor were they able to create the conditions for freedom of movement and manoeuvre. Opportunities to surprise or shock the enemy were constricted to time rather than place and it was generally the enemy who maintained the initiative and dictated where engagements should occur. Lessons learned by the army during the Somme fighting about simultaneity of actions were not always evident and coordination with other formations was not sufficiently utilized in order to establish or maintain tempo or momentum. These were not entirely the fault of either division because much of the direction came down from corps HQ. Nonetheless, there does seem on occasions to have been an absence of effective liaison or cooperation. Like any newly arrived formation, 59th Division had a great deal to learn but, unlike most others, it was thrown almost directly into active operations. It did have some very unfortunate encounters during this initial period and, as one of its unit historians later noted, "Once more [it] apparently failed to carry through a definite piece of work entrusted to it." He went on to qualify this by stating, "The truth is that…it was given an impossible task to perform."[78] The tasks were not "impossible" but they were very challenging for any inexperienced formation. The division learned through experience that knowledge would be gained from undergoing hardship and difficulty. But by the time it reached St Julien in September it had had time to train in and adopt the new skills laid out in recent training manuals. The South Midland Division also had a reasonably quiet interlude near Arras before it, too, would take part in Third Ypres. It would need to muster all the collective lessons gained from Fromelles, the Somme and the spring advance to cope with the conditions and demands of the Ypres Salient. Of the other 2nd Line divisions still on the Western Front, only 62nd was to avoid Third Ypres. For 57th, 59th and 66th divisions the operational confusion of the Salient was only to add to the tactical difficulties encountered when fighting their first major set-piece battles.

---

77 Lt. Col. R St G Gorton (59th Division) and Lt. Col. Sir Hereward Wake, Bt (61st) had both passed Staff College and had held a variety of administrative and staff positions. By March 1917, both had been in post with their respective divisions for over 12 months.
78 W. Hall, *The Green Triangle*, p.86.

5

Offensive Operations I: Third Ypres – The Middle Weeks

In addition to the operations undertaken by Third, Fourth and Fifth armies in the advance towards the Hindenburg Line, 1917 was a year of major Allied offensives. Improved strategic and operational coordination between the Allies allowed the British and French armies on the Western Front to pursue an aggressive strategy aimed at further attriting the Central Powers. Debate continued amongst senior commanders as to whether a breakthrough and breakout remained a feasible proposition, or whether a series of 'bite and hold' operations would in the long term prove more successful and less costly in Allied lives. Haig and Fifth Army GOC, General Herbert Gough, still thought in terms of the Clausewitzian concept of decisive battle; Generals Rawlinson and Plumer favoured the more deliberate step by step wearing down process. The six 2nd Line TF divisions on the Western Front were well represented in the BEF's major offensives of 1917: five were involved in Third Ypres, three at Cambrai, and two at Bullecourt. None, however, took any part in the operation at Messines.[1]

The objective of modern offensive operations is to defeat the enemy by the use, or the threat to use, physical force. Commanders seek to create the conditions for freedom of movement and manoeuvre, break or reduce the enemy's cohesion and will, and confuse and disrupt his understanding of the strategic, operational, and tactical situation. The main characteristics of offensive actions involve surprise, shock, agility, and superior tempo. Inflicting physical damage assists the process but, in addition to firepower, simultaneity and coordination of force and effort also help to disorientate and prevent the enemy from mounting a coherent response. Great War generals would have recognized these characteristics. The difficulty was, however, that whereas in most previous conflicts one army was able to out-manoeuvre the enemy by turning his flank, the trench system precluded that possibility in at least the opening stages of a battle. The proponents of a strategy of breaking in, breaking through, and then breaking out argued that overwhelming physical force had thus to be applied in order to neutralize or dislodge and disperse the enemy. Only then would a war of manoeuvre and the opportunity to inflict a crushing defeat again become a possibility.

The doctrine produced during and after the Somme campaign looked towards the return of manoeuvre but was pragmatic enough to appreciate the difficulties thrown up by trench

---

1   The Battles Nomenclature Committee termed the fighting around Bullecourt as 'Flanking Operations in the Arras Offensive.'

to trench attacks. By laying down revised and often new operational and tactical skills, and explaining how they could be taught to and absorbed by commanders and troops, training pamphlets were intended to offer a degree of central direction in how operations might be conducted. They were to be the means by which German defences could be breached in depth; in the ensuing disruption of enemy forces, exploitation would then follow. Like any doctrine, however, the pamphlets were not intended to be taken as the last word in tactical development. They were provided as a framework by which commanders could train their units and sub-units and emphasized the necessity of all-arms coordination and the integration of new forms and weapons of attack. Debate and experimentation were not prohibited but the pamphlets produced in late 1916 and early 1917 were the product of experience and analysis of the fighting on the Somme. For the development of the infantry's offensive skills, *SS143* was the most important. It laid down formations for attack, a new structure for platoons (which was now formally recognized as the primary offensive sub-unit) the weapon balance within platoons, and the tactics considered most likely to achieve success in both trench to trench attacks and open warfare. Training programmes and schedules were also laid down but, again, although the underlying principle of the pamphlets was to ensure a degree of uniformity in training and tactical action, commanders were encouraged to adapt the tactics demanded by the situation and the ground. Above all, *SS143* was a pamphlet based on the realities of the Western Front and of the limitations of the army's capability in 1917.

One of the accepted realities of that capability was the perceived quality of junior officers. By 1917, probably the majority of company commanders had been in post for fewer than 12 months. The high casualty rate meant promotion was often rapid but the frequent consequence was that in comparison to the regular sub-unit commanders of 1914, many company commanders of 1917 lacked tactical knowledge and were reluctant to use initiative. Platoon and section commanders were often even more limited in their skills and their self-confidence to command and lead their troops. Although made at a time when the division's deployment to France was still two months away, Lieutenant Colonel Allanson's assessment of 57th Division's officers' map reading abilities was possibly accurate but, and certainly of equal importance, was the belief that many officers and NCOs were considered incapable of effectively teaching their troops.[2] In an attempt to counter this, a plethora of brigade, divisional, corps, and army schools had sprung up since 1916, with the latter two types specifically tasked to improve the instructional abilities of junior officers and NCOs. These schools and the training regimes of the officer cadet battalions at home undoubtedly improved the capabilities of young officers. One later history recorded how necessary this process had been: "It was interesting to note how many of the young Platoon Officers, soaked in trench warfare, behaved when set a simple exercise in open warfare."[3] Useful and essential as these courses were, the officers' remaining limitations were, however, highlighted in a training programme devised by 61st Division's 184 Brigade.

Because he thought his majors and captains were "not sufficiently educated" to teach their own men, Brigadier General White advocated reversing the normal procedure of conducting

---

2   H. Davies (ed.) *Allanson of the 6th* (Lowesmoor: Square One Publications, 1990). Diary entry 3 Dec.1916 claimed the quality of the officers was so poor it "rendered them unfit to command a platoon or read a map." Lt. Col. C.J.L. Allanson, of 6/Gurkha Rifles, was GSO1 57th Division from July 1916 until July 1917.

3   Barnes, *The Story of The 2/5th Gloucester*, p.66.

company and platoon training as a precursor to battalion and brigade schemes. By means of staff rides and TEWTS over a four day period he wanted COs first to teach their company and platoon commanders and senior NCOs the skills of open attack and wood and village fighting. Once they had mastered the principles, they would in turn teach their section leaders by the same means. Battalion schemes, followed by company training, would then take place. White believed that, "Once the captains and other officers have seen the whole programme they will more easily realize the nature of their duties."[4] Although a dug out who had retired from the army in 1900, White had been in post since September 1916 and was to remain in command until wounded in March 1918. As an experienced commander he would have had a good understanding of the strengths and weaknesses of his brigade and of its junior commanders. Experimentation and innovation were encouraged within limits by senior authority but White, like his counterparts in other brigades and divisions during the build up to involvement in Third Ypres, faced serious problems about how and where the training could be done.

In the weeks preceding their withdrawal from the line in preparation for their participation in the battle, the 2nd Line divisions received an influx of new junior officers from the cadet battalions at home. Welcome as these officers were, many were quickly sent away on courses and were thus frequently unavailable to train their own platoons. For example, in August, 2/5th North Staffordshire had 40 officers on strength but only 22 were with the battalion; its sister battalion 2/6th North Staffordshire had a mere 14 of its on-strength officers actually serving with the unit. Brigadier General Cope pointed out how difficult it was to train the brigade when so many officers (and men) were away. Commanders and their units, he wrote, "had little chance of becoming mutually acquainted" and were thus unable to share knowledge and experience. The process of engendering mutual trust suffered as the consequence.[5] When 58th Division joined Ivor Maxse's XVIII Corps in late August, several of its battalions were ordered to send all company and platoon commanders to a three day course at the corps school. There they were lectured by Maxse himself on what he expected of them as leaders and commanders and on the tactics to be employed in their forthcoming attacks. Once the *SS143* method of attacking strong points had been explained and taught, an instruction from GOC 61st Division ordered all platoon commanders to devise their own training scheme by which the theory could be put into practice. Because they needed to be able to think on their feet in action, DHQ believed there was little point in battalion or company commanders inventing plans in training and handing them down to their subalterns. The platoon commanders would know their commander's intent and were then expected to use a degree of initiative, or mission command, to achieve them. The senior officers would be available during training to advise when necessary but their principle role was to ensure the platoon commanders were asking themselves the right questions about how to deploy their sections, secure their gains, plug any gaps, protect their front and flanks, and bring up the right tools and ammunition. Once they were aware of the problems, the junior commanders could think about plausible solutions.[6] Rather than retaining the company messes that had prevailed since the division arrived in France, its prolonged period of training

---

4   TNA WO 953062: 184 Bde, Appendix XVI, 26 Jun.1917.
5   TNA WO 953020: 176 Bde HQ, Summary, Aug. 1917. Cope replaced Brig. Gen. Currie, who had been appointed Commandant of the Junior Staff Officers Course, Cambridge, in mid-August.
6   TNA WO 953034: Appendix III, 10 Aug.1917. The Appendix states, "The corollary of delegation of authority is intelligent supervision." According to Stacke, *The Worcestershire Regiment* (Worcester:

allowed 58th Division to introduce battalion messes. Operations and lack of accommodation had earlier prevented battalion messes but the opportunity was seized as a means of allowing the units' officers to get to know each other, foster coherence, and exchange tactical ideas and philosophies.[7]

The company and platoon commanders were, of course, the officers with whom the other ranks came most into contact. Divisional and brigade commanders were seen only occasionally on parades and schemes; even battalion commanders could be reasonably remote figures to the men. The role of the junior commanders in the maintenance of morale was thus crucial. Modern doctrine emphasizes how, because the human element is the least predictable aspect of conflict, the moral component of fighting power is key: it drives the army's ability to get its personnel to operate and fight. Command at any level "requires an understanding of desired results, doctrine...missions and priorities."[8] The three constituents of command are recognized as decision-making, leadership, and control. These elements overlap and influence each other, but a commander's ability to harness these constituents is a major factor in all three components of fighting power. Because they are so intimately connected to their troops the example and leadership shown by junior commanders can significantly affect that platoon's or company's willingness to fight. In 1917, as today, these mostly young officers had to demonstrate their own professional competence and motivate their men through positive and inspired leadership. They had to show confidence, resolution, personal courage, fair and astute judgement, possess good communication skills, show humility and, when necessary, be creative and original. If sufficient of the commanders in the battalions of the 2nd Line had not been able to offer these characteristics, and if a significant proportion of them were as bad as Allanson asserted, it seems likely that the morale and resolution of their men might well have cracked during their time at Ypres.

The numbers of soldiers within the companies and platoons commanded by the junior officers and their predecessors had in some 2nd Line divisions been substantially depleted during the previous months. Drafts had been sporadic and few. At the end of June 1917, when 61st Division began its pre-Third Ypres training, the fighting strengths of the four battalions of 182 Brigade were all below 30 officers and 620 ORs; after a month's respite from the trenches, all battalions had increased to over 900 ORs. Several battalions of 58th Division were below 400 ORs when they left the Havrincourt sector for their training grounds in the north. Other divisions had been more fortunate in remaining reasonably strong. The average August strength of battalions in 176 Brigade of 59th Division was a little over 700 and when they came out of the line to begin their training period, the battalions of 170 Brigade of 57th Division were all over 35 officers and close to or even in excess of 900 ORs. The increase in troops during the training period was welcomed but it meant that once the nucleus personnel had been withdrawn, which was usually comprised of experienced men who had served in the battalion for some length of time, and the other non-front line personnel are discounted, possibly 40-50 percent of the attackers were men who had only recently been posted to the battalion.[9]

    Cheshire & Sons, 1929), p.287. Lt.Gen.Sir Herbert Watts, GOC XIX Corps, insisted 61st Division's officers repeatedly chant the maxim.
7 TNA WO 952992: A&Q, 3 Aug.1917.
8 Army Doctrine Publication, *Operations*, 0620.
9 In the case of 2/1st London Division, this percentage could be even higher. In August one battalion received drafts totalling 528 other ranks

Drafts could arrive from just about any regiment's training battalions. Unit war diaries are generally quiet about their troops' origins but it is known, for example, that 2/5th London received over 30 men from its 3rd Line and for some unknown reason the diarist of 2/7th Worcestershire decided to note it had received over 50 men from 8/Suffolk.[10] Most of the war diary entries, however, simply state the arrival and numbers of drafts. This is no different from the majority of diaries written by officers in non-2nd Line divisions. As the adjutant or officer responsible for writing up the diary may well himself have been posted into the unit from another regiment, recording the origins of drafts was perhaps considered to be unimportant. What was important, however, was to persuade the men that their new battalion was their new 'home'. Their morale, and thus their potential fighting power, was affected by the way they were treated, how well their welfare was protected and, despite their likely lack of regimental and geographical enlistment homogeneity, the degree to which they perceived they were appreciated

All pre-war Territorial Force divisions were, naturally enough, originally designated by the area from which they were raised. In early 1915. the War Office allocated numbers to the original 14 divisions and the 2nd Line formations. These were largely related to the order in which they deployed overseas. Twelve divisions of the New Armies were similarly identified by their national, regional, or provincial origins. This practice of local identification continued at a sub-divisional level when the Pals units were raised for the Fourth and Fifth New Armies. Throughout the war, Lancashire regiments were more fortunate than most in having a strong champion in Lord Derby who, despite the advent of conscription, tried to ensure Lancashire men were posted to Lancashire units. This applied to both New Army and TF units. Compared to several other units, the Lancashire Fusilier battalions in 66th Division were fortunate to receive a steady flow of officers and men from the regiment's reserve battalions. This helped to perpetuate the territorial identity of those battalions, a feature that was emphasized by many COs. On Minden Day, Lieutenant Colonel Arthur Bates, CO of 3/5th LF, issued a message in which he "congratulate[d] all ranks on having the privilege of fighting as Lancashire Fusiliers."[11] Although Major Generals Lawrence and Barnes, GOsC 66th and 57th divisions respectively, do not seem to have followed Major General Jeudwine's and later Major General Solly Flood's example of deliberately and openly encouraging the 'Lancashireness' of their 55th and 42nd Divisions, when they became involved in Third Ypres the two 2nd Line Lancashire divisions do seem to have retained a high degree of regional and territorial identity.

Yet, maintaining morale involves more than trying to ensure personnel from the same region serve together. As it was the first time since their arrival that the divisions had been able to spend a significant amount of time out of the line, the training period before Third Ypres was used to develop morale by means of sports and recreation. Brigade Recreation Committees were established in some divisions and brigade sports and horse shows were commonplace.

---

10 This mention of 8/Suffolk may have been a clerical error. The battalion, then in 18th Division, was not disbanded until February 1918. There is no mention in its, or the division's A&Q's, diary of it transferring men in June or July.

11 Lt. Col. Bates was a long-serving TF soldier. After some time in a Hampshire Volunteer Battalion, he joined the London Rifle Brigade (LRB) in 1900. He rose to command the battalion during its almost complete annihilations in 2nd Ypres and then again at Gommecourt on 1 July 1916. He was invalided home in August 1916 and on recovery was appointed CO of 3/5th LF a few weeks before it sailed.

Battalion sports were popular, with a company points scheme fostering a competitive spirit and aiding bonding. Divisional and sometimes battalion concert parties entertained the troops in open air performances; troops of 61st Division were even able to bath four times in the space of about three weeks. Health, fitness and morale in 66th Division was considered to be good and enhanced by issuing passes for the local villages and towns. Officers in 2/10th Manchester paid for ten cornets to help with the formation of a battalion bugle band and COs in 170 Brigade were told it was "impossible to underestimate the value of music" for morale. They were urged to get their men to sing, whistle and even blow penny whistles when on the march.[12] The health of the troops in 59th Division was, however, not considered to be as good as "it should have been." This may have been indicative of questionable morale or simply the result of serious outbreaks of PUO in some battalions. Its cause was blamed on the camps' "inadequate facilities" for bathing, ironing and laundry.[13] Initially, the ADMS disagreed with the MO of 2/5th Sherwood Foresters, who believed the battalion's poor health was the result of the "foul state of the camping ground." The ADMS "found no cause for complaint" and blamed it on the lack of attention being paid by the troops to the latrines and soak pits. He ordered the horse lines of 2/1st Field Ambulance to be moved further away from the cookhouse but was sufficiently concerned about the length of the division's sick list to discuss the matter with DMS Fifth Army. The outcome was an increased emphasis on improving latrines, water supply, baths and general cleanliness within the camps and also on the need to provide more fresh vegetables and a greater variety in rations. Like all divisions, whether regular, New Army or 1st Line, the 2nd Line TF formations were at the mercy of corps HQ as to where they were to train but there were opportunities for ADMS to ameliorate conditions within the camps. ADMS 59th Division felt "much good" would come from his meetings with the division's quartermasters but the reality was that the onus to make improvements still lay with battalions. Their capacity to do this remained limited.[14]

Securing adequate training grounds was often problematic. An officer of 2/1st London Battalion noted "very little ground available" and a staff officer in 66th Division of "congestion" making it difficult to obtain "good" training areas.[15] Growing crops exacerbated the problem and until the harvest, finding sufficient space to conduct brigade manoeuvres was in some places impossible. Nevertheless, the divisions had to make the best of the areas and the time they had been allocated. And the time did vary considerably. The shortest period of pre-offensive training was that allotted to 66th Division.[16] The formation had spent several months on the coast and had been earmarked for the proposed August offensive against Nieuport. When out of the line, battalions and field companies had been training in pontoons and bridging, ferrying units across the Yser, building light railways, and road construction. When it became obvious at the end of August that the offensive had been abandoned, 3/5th Lancashire Fusiliers recorded it

---

12   TNA WO 953141: 2/10th Manchester, Sep.1917; WO 952976: 170 Bde HQ Training Circular No. 3, Aug.1917.
13   TNA WO 953014: ADMS, Sep.1917.
14   Ibid.
15   TNA WO 953001: 2/1st London, Sep.1917; WO 953120: 13 Aug.1917.
16   There were exceptions within the division. Some battalions in 199 Brigade appear to have spent only about six days in the line, although their training period was interrupted by the need for working parties. One company of 2/8th Manchester was, for example, attached to the RE for most of September.

as a "matter of great regret" but noted the "augers [for an offensive elsewhere] are too clear for anyone to mistake them."[17] The division moved from La Panne to the Ypres area at the end of September. Some battalions managing only between four and five days of intensive training in preparation for assaulting enemy positions across a morass of broken land rather than practising for a river crossing in small boats. In contrast to the minimal period afforded 66th Division, 58th Division enjoyed over three weeks uninterrupted (save for the weather) training in August near Arras. Some battalions then had up to a further ten days before moving into the line. Although not as long as the London division's time, 57th Division had a lengthy period before it undertook its attack in late October but, as was common for the artillery, its batteries were loaned to other divisions and thus had less time in the rear than the infantry. About a month was given to 59th Division to prepare for its late September attack but, like the artillery, its field companies were also often either attached to divisions closer to the front or spent their time improving camp facilities in the rear. Occasional route marches and wagon drills were about the extent of the sappers' specified training. Field companies of 57th Division did do a little better by having time for sports and taking part in practice attacks with their respective brigades. MG companies usually had about the same length of training time as battalions. They practised gun and barrage drills and spent endless time on the causes and clearing of stoppages. When possible, the divisional light trench mortar batteries, machine gunners, sappers, signallers, and ASC companies all took part in divisional combined arms tactical exercises.

Where and when they could, the infantry followed the training regimes passed down to them from corps HQ or the now widely available doctrinal pamphlets. Several war diaries make direct reference to the publications, one brigade HQ insisting, for example, "every officer" should read *SS135* and *SS148* "continually"; others note instructions taken on board from sources such as divisionally generated circulars and memos from Fifth Army.[18] The great bulk of battalion diaries refer in different but identifiable ways to the standard drills laid out in *SS143*. Their platoons rehearsed advancing across shell-broken ground, pushing forward patrols, night reconnaissance, relieving scattered posts of other units in forward areas, consolidation, and rapid wiring. Night exercises in laying assembly tapes by compass, forming up for dawn attacks, capturing pill boxes, intensive digging, large scale trench to trench attacks, and deploying from columns into waves and artillery formation were all undertaken. "Fostering of the offensive, bloodthirsty spirit"[19] was done by frequent bayonet drills and, in the attempt to get men to think in terms of using their rifle rather than resorting to bombs, musketry was high on the list of priorities. NCOs and officers listened to lectures by RE officers on basic field engineering before cascading the knowledge to their platoons; conferences for brigade and unit officers were held frequently at brigade and divisional levels to discuss programmes and progress. Brigadier General Stockwell from the 1st Line 55th (West Lancashire) Division, lectured to officers from all units of 61st Division on what they could expect of the ground and enemy tactics when they entered the battle. In turn, the South Midland's DAQMG visited Stockwell's division to hear

---

17 TNA WO 953137: 3/5th LF, 31 Aug.1917.
18 TNA WO 952977: 170 Bde HQ, Oct.1917; WO 953138: 198 Bde HQ, Oct.1917; WO 953034: Jul.1917; WO 953025: 2/6th Sherwood Foresters, 1 Sep.1917.
19 TNA WO 953141: 2/10th Manchester, 10 Aug.1917.

of its experiences and to take notes on the methods and administration of supplies and transport in Fifth Army area.[20]

Conferences of senior divisional officers hammered out how the training was to be conducted. Several war diaries note how the refined German defensive tactics had necessitated a change in the way the enemy lines were to be assaulted, and recorded how their units trained for the task.[21] Most divisions seem to have been given a reasonably free hand from their corps commanders and were able to devise their own schemes. One brigade of 57th Division developed a comprehensive scheme that was circulated among other brigades. This stressed the need for the men to be smart and clean and to turn out for a quick pre-breakfast parade to practise rapid loading and section drill. Training had to be conducted with "dash and keenness" and with no "perfunctoriness"; any "loafing or want of keenness" was to be "instantly punished" by an extra hour's drill. The number of hours to be spent in the four basic platoon skills was precisely detailed, with further emphasis on deploying from artillery to open warfare formations. At least two daily PT sessions of 15 minutes each were to be conducted, as were frequent close order drills with limited rest periods. The GOC brigade insisted that as the "hours are short" all ranks must "put their backs into it" and, to prevent men from hanging around during the training periods, every future session was to be rehearsed during the previous afternoon by officers and senior NCOs. While those rehearsals were underway the troops were engaged in sports or practising for the inter-platoon and inter-company competitions. These included skill at arms, guard turn out, target shooting, bayonet fighting, and cross-country running. On a lighter note, they could also involve wrestling on mule back.[22] Another frequently mentioned competition across several of the divisions was the packing and carrying of the Yukon pack.[23] The South Midland Division embodied this within a broad scheme of competitions including one that embraced physical fitness as well as infantry skills aimed at improving the leadership and command of NCOs. Company officers could play no part and were warned against surreptitious involvement. Other instructions banned the practice of using sappers to teach the infantry how to build deep dugouts, and insisted officers were to ensure that "the discipline of sleep" should be enforced. "There is nothing more important", it stressed, "than insisting on rest during fighting."[24]

Unit war diaries of both 59th and 66th divisions are generally brief on the types and methods of training conducted. There are references to practising attack formations but it is probably safe to assume that in the time available their battalions underwent the same sort of basic skills training detailed in *SS143* as those in other formations. Brigadier General Guggisberg, GOC 170 Brigade, was, however, prepared to go further and criticized the attack formation described in *SS143*. Guggisberg, who had been appointed to 57th Division in May 1917 from his post as CRE 66th Division, saw what he considered a serious flaw in the official text.[25] Whilst instructing that every battalion in his brigade must be able to shake out into any formation

---

20 TNA WO 953036: A&G, 10 Aug.1917
21 For example, see TNA WO 953020: 176 Bde HQ, 28 Aug.1917.
22 TNA WO 953020: 176 Bde HQ. Aug.1917
23 These packs were proving their worth for carrying up both rations and ammunition. With their bent backs, stout stick and slouching gaits, one later history described the carriers as resembling "aged mendicants". Oates, *2/8th Sherwood Foresters*, p171
24 TNA WO 953034: Appendices Jul.1917.
25 TNA WO 952976: 170 Bde HQ, Synopsis of Training, 28 Aug.1917.

quickly and efficiently, and that the "best" formation depends on the ground to be covered, he argued that the attack formation detailed in *SS143* meant that when the second line joined the first, the platoons and sections invariably became mixed. This, he wrote, meant section commanders lost control of their men. His scheme, which he considered to be "superior in every way both for trench to trench attack and for open warfare", was intended to restore control to junior commanders and thus allow initiative and flexibility. Each section in the platoon could, he reasoned, still be covered by another and could be more quickly deployed from artillery formation. He did acknowledge that ground conditions and enemy responses might compel local commanders to adapt accordingly but ordered that all his battalions should rehearse the formation whenever possible. On wet days, visual aids could be used.[26] He also urged junior commanders to show invention when it came to positioning Lewis guns. The stereotyped idea of placing the guns on the flanks had, he wrote, to be "knocked on the head ... it might sometimes be the best place to use it, but it might also be where it already is. Any section [of the platoon] can be used anywhere – the 'anywhere' being the place most suitable for it – and this place changes with the ground." Guggisberg's thesis of enlightened ideas ended with an exhortation to his men. There was "absolutely nothing to fear" from counter-attacks provided Lewis guns and rifles were kept clear of mud and placed in "brave men's hands." Should any men be seen to be falling back, the wave behind should move forward and, he instructed, "charge the enemy with a cheer." The principles upon which his officers and men were to act were clear: "Get to the objective with dash and rapid action; mop up well; stick to what you have won with all the grit in you; be prepared to turn your hand to anything, no matter what wave you belong to."[27]

Guggisberg's GOC division, Major General Barnes and his GOC corps appear to have been willing to allow their brigadiers their head in the training programme. There are no direct references to Guggisberg's programme in the divisional or the war diaries of the other two brigades, but it is likely that a similar, if not Guggisberg's actual, scheme was adopted by 171 and 172 Brigades. The programme which had possibly been devised by a single CO or by the GOC of one brigade, was adopted by the rest of the 2nd South Midland Division. Battalions spent specified times on route marches, PT, bayonet fighting, mopping up, rapid wiring, and box respirator drills while senior officers took part in skeleton attacks and TEWTS. These dealt with not just the attack itself but cooperation with the machine guns and trench mortars, carrying parties, contact aircraft, and how to deal with prisoners. In the same way as brigades in other divisions, battalion commanders were urged to stress to their junior commanders the necessity of sending clear and regular reports back to battalion and brigade headquarters.[28]

---

26 Ibid. GOC 58th Division convened a conference of officers on the Canal Bank to discuss whether a changed company organization was needed to counter the new German defences. His brigadier generals decided the formation suggested in *SS143* – the one in which the men had been most recently trained – would still be the most effective. Strangely, however, there is nothing in the minutes of the discussion about platoons and sections being tasked for specific objectives. Neither is there mention of companies leapfrogging each other. TNA WO 952987: Notes on Divisional Conference, 30 Aug.1917. Furthermore, there is nothing in the Corps war diary to point to Maxse or any of his staff having played any part in the debate.
27 TNA WO 952976: Synopsis of Training, Aug.1917.
28 Barnes, *The Story of The 2/5th Gloucester*, p.66; TNA WO 953063: 184 Bde HQ, Jul.1917 Appendices; 2/4th Berkshire, Jul.1917.

GOsC of several divisions across the BEF were sometimes instructed by their corps commanders as to the actual methodology and content of their training schemes. Having taken part in a major battle and having earlier spent time out of the line training, VIII and later XIX Corps HQ may have thought 61st Division was capable of devising its own training schemes based on *SS143* for Third Ypres.[29] But, as three of the other four 2nd Line formations tasked to be involved in the Salient were facing their first battle and, if there was some doubt in the minds of the authorities about the capability of the divisions, it might be expected their corps commanders would pay close attention to the divisions' training programme. There is little to suggest, however, that II ANZAC showed any real interest in the training programmes of 59th or 66th divisions, and no hard evidence to show that V or XIV Corps had any significant input to 57th Division's training period.[30] The exception is the involvement shown by Lieutenant General Maxse of XVIII in the development of 58th Division's efficiency and fighting power.

Never a man to hide long in the shadows or refrain from voicing an opinion, Maxse had been promoted to command XVIII Corps in January 1917. He had brought with him from 18th Division his zeal for, and concern with, the training of troops. This is evident in his corps war diary. This is probably the most detailed of any in recording the daily activities of its commander. In modern parlance, Maxse targeted all three components of fighting power by lecturing frequently at his corps school and issuing pamphlets on subjects ranging from the role and operational leadership of commanders, through to tactics, weaponry, discipline, and morale. Maxse presumably knew 58th Division was to come under his XVIII Corps some time before the formal date of 24 August. The division had been transferred from V to IV Corps in early July and at the end of the month swapped with 9th Division from XVII Corps when it moved to the training area at Fosseux. It remained with XVII Corps for nearly all of the first three weeks of August but, on 18 August, DHQ was told to prepare to join XVIII Corps within days. The division had assembled near Poperinghe by 25 August and on the night of 28-29 August relieved 48th Division in the St Julien sector. Besides being delighted to be relieved, the bemused diarist of 1/7th Worcestershire recorded the "most astonishing" spectacle of the relieving London battalion entering the trenches in full marching order.[31]

---

29 In July the division was issued with 'Training Instructions GC32/1'. This effectively amounted to a description of what its future objectives would be and an outline of the scheme of attack. The division was instructed to "… immediately complete its training in … trench attacks under a barrage and open warfare advance against enemy rearguards." TNA WO 953034: Jul.1917

30 The North Midland Division was to remain under II ANZAC for only five days; the East Lancashire Division came under its command on the same day that corps HQ took over the sector formally held by V Corps. II ANZAC had been in the Messines area for months and had enjoyed only a few days rest and recuperation before moving north to Ypres. With 66th Division having been holding the line and training near the coast before joining II ANZAC, there had been, therefore, little opportunity to liaise and familiarize. Similarly, 57th Division had only concentrated in XIV Corps area on 22 October. The next day 170 Bde moved up to the line and on 26 October the division carried out its attack. Interestingly, after the war the battalion history of 2/6th King's Liverpool recorded that Ivor Maxse attended 57th Division's training exercises before it joined XIV Corps. His presence apparently "produced considerable animation on the part of those involved." There is no mention in the very detailed XVIII Corps war diary, however, that Maxse ever attended these manoeuvres or even inspected brigades or battalions of the division. Wurtzberg, *2/6th King's*, p134

31 TNA WO 952759: 1/7th Worcestershire, 28 Aug.1917.

The arrival of the London Division boosted Maxse's command to five divisions: 39th Division had been taken over by XVIII in January 1917, 51st and 11th divisions had joined it in June, and 48th Division in July. All of these divisions had experienced the worst of the Somme but were allocated about the same amount of time for training as the considerably more innocent 58th Division.[32] Their officers attended courses and lectures at XVIII Corps School, listened to lectures delivered by Maxse and brigade commanders from within the corps on their battle experience as well as on subjects such as artillery and infantry cooperation. Senior commanders gathered regularly at corps HQ to discuss training schemes and spent a good proportion of their time watching and analyzing the performance of their brigades on the training ground. The training periods allocated for 39th Division lacked some of the continuity of the other divisions but overall there was no great difference between the time spent out of the line by the corps' five divisions during the preparatory period.[33] The field companies of 58th Division were fortunate in securing a longer period of training than their counterparts in the other divisions but, unlike the others, the London Division was still without its own pioneer battalion. Maxse does not appear to have believed the 58th required his special attention because he failed to visit the division any more frequently than he did the others under his command.[34]

Brigadier General Freyberg, GOC 173 Brigade, noted that the first three weeks of August were spent training "under Maxse's direction".[35] This may well have been the case but the "direction" was generally from afar rather than by close and frequent personal supervision. At the time, Maxse was heavily involved in conducting his corps' August attacks and the first recorded meeting with 58th Division's GOC, Major General Fanshawe, was a gathering of all five of his divisional commanders on 31 August. That does not necessarily mean he had not had previous but unrecorded meetings because there is the well-known but undated greeting of Maxse to Freyberg in August of, "I hate you gallant Brigadier Generals... what the devil do you know about training men?"[36] He made a recorded visit to 175 Brigade immediately before the first of a series of raids and small advances undertaken by that and 174 Brigade in early September, and then a number of routine visits to DHQ and brigade HQ in advance of and following the division's first major engagement on 20 September. The evidence suggests, therefore, that Maxse held no particular concerns about 58th Division's efficiency and fighting power.

---

32 The following detail is taken from the various divisions' war diaries and from XVIII Corps WD, TNA WO 95951. Whether Maxse's peremptory demand for GOC 39th Division to prepare and submit a scheme for an offensive operation for the right division of the corps within 24 hours was a testament to his faith in the division and its staff, or a means of keeping it on its toes, remains open to question. TNA WO 952566, 22 Jun.1917

33 F Brewsher, *The History of the Fifty-First (Highland) Division 1914-1918* (London: Blackwood, 1921) pp.196-98 noted the division had six weeks to prepare. Maxse is recorded as having shown the "greatest interest" in the division's training and details the replica enemy trench systems constructed in the rear.

34 It is known that together with Gough, Maxse did on one occasion watch 174 Brigade at training before 20 September. F. Maurice, *History of the London Rifle Brigade* (London: Constable 1921), p.294.

35 During this period the division remained technically part of XVII Corps.

36 P. Freyberg, *Bernard Freyberg, VC* (London: Hodder & Stoughton, 1991), p.110. By the time Freyberg met Maxse, the former had already been wounded several times and awarded the VC.

Part of the sector occupied by 60th (2/2nd London) Division during its short sojourn on the Western Front. Now bisected by the A26 (right) the Vimy Ridge woods are in the distance. Visited frequently by patrols and raiders of both sides, the area in front of the woods was littered with mine craters. The track was originally sunken, with dugouts in its bank.

The site of the much contested Red Dragon Crater looking south towards the tree-lined La Bassée Canal. Throughout the spring and early summer of 1917, 66th (2nd East Lancashire) Division persistently raided the enemy lines opposite.

As they followed the German spring withdrawal towards the Hindenburg Line, the Somme's meanders and marshes to the south of Péronne caused engineering and sustainment problems for 59th (2nd North Midland) and 61st (2nd South Midland) divisions. Huge numbers of RE and infantry were employed in bridging and road building to maintain communications with the advancing brigades.

German resistance deliberately stiffened once the isolated hamlet of Soyecourt, west of Vendelles, had been occupied by 2/8th Warwickshire. Although still following a strategy of fighting only delaying actions, the enemy garrisons of the remaining fortified areas west of the Hindenburg Outpost Line offered a more protracted defence.

Commanding the crest of the ridge west of Hargicourt the trees (centre) mark the site of Fervaque Farm. The green troops of 177 Brigade made repeated but badly planned and unsuccessful attacks on the well-protected farm. The Germans eventually voluntarily withdraw from the ruined buildings to the prepared defences of the Hindenburg Line farther east.

The village of Le Verguier, 2,500 yards south of Fervaque Farm, was also one of the fortified locations tasked with slowing and attriting the British divisions during the enemy withdrawal. The church and water tower are visible (centre) and Odin's Hollow drops away to the front of the camera. The attacks on the village in appalling weather by the Sherwood Foresters were ill-conceived and costly.

Hargicourt Quarries. The trees cover the extensive quarries on the lower slope of the Cologne Ridge. During the late spring of 1917, these and neighbouring quarries were the scene of intense fighting between the Germans and 59th Division. The ridge was finally taken in the summer. In early 1918 it was within 66th Division's Forward Zone.

Working on the right flank of 59th Division in April 1917, 61st Division assaulted the strong defences which ran north-south through the (now) German cemetery on the crest of the ridge. They protected the approach to the main Hindenburg Line at Bellenglise. In March 1918 this sector, including Cooker's Quarry in the foreground, formed part of 24th Division's defences.

The low lying, marshy and in places flooded Omignon Valley necessarily canalized some of 61st Division's attacks towards Vadencourt and Pontru. Maissemy church steeple appears above the trees (centre left and left of the pylon). German resistance here remained deliberate until they implemented the next stage of their planned withdrawal.

Following its disastrous attack at Fromelles, and despite its better showing during the German withdrawal, 61st Division's reputation suffered a further blow during its stay in the Salient. Attacks against Pond, Keir, and Gallipoli Farms, as well as the Battery Position, were difficult and costly. Pond Farm is left, with a small roadside shrine in front and St Julien behind.

Schuler Farm (centre) was the objective of 55th Division and to the right was the site of Keir Farm. The enemy in the pill boxes on the Battery Position and in Gallipoli Farm brought devastating fire to bear on 61st Division's troops as they attacked towards Keir Farm and Kansas Cross.

Gallipoli Farm, with the Battery Position just to its right. Keir Farm was in the near foreground. The poet Ivor Gurney of 2/5th Gloucestershire was gassed in this area in September 1917.

The inter-divisional boundary of 58th and 59th divisions for the attack on 26 September. The higher ground in the distance is the stretch of Gravenstafel Ridge between Boetleer and Korek. The former site of Riverside is centre and that of Nile, the objective of 2/12th London, is just off left. The Hanebeek drains right – left beyond the harvested field of maize.

The ground attacked by 59th Division on 26 September, with Dochy Farm in the foreground. The division's final objective was close to where the New Zealand memorial now stands. The poly tunnels occupy the former site of Otto Farm, with the Enclosure beyond it on the slope of the Gravenstafel Ridge.

The view from the Belle Vue Spur over the Ravebeek valley towards the start line of 66th Division on 9 October. The farm on the right is Laamkeek, with the area known as Marsh Bottom beyond. Waterfields is centre, with the poplars at Tyne Cot Cemetery behind.

East of Nobles Farm looking south to the trees of Poelcapelle British Cemetery. With Nobles Farm off right and Spider Crossroads behind and left, 173 Brigade attacked from right to left. The Fusilier battalions' objectives on 26 October lay north and south of the Poelcapelle – Westrozebeke road.

Looking west from Spider crossroads. The spire of Poelcapelle church is left, Requete Farm left of centre, and Bescote Farm on Hill 19, right. This is the ground attacked by 57th Division in late October.

With Poelcapelle church and village on the right and Gloster Farm at the end of the lane on the left, 2/8th London formed up in this area for its attack on Cameron House and Papa Hill.

Taken from the same position near Tracas Farm as the previous photograph but looking east. The former site of Cameron House is about where the white gable end of the house centre left now stands. The almost indiscernible rise of Papa Hill is further on and roughly to the right of the large white barn in the far centre. The diversionary attack by 2/8th London on 30 October met with the same fate as earlier ones.

Looking south from the sunken lane east of Graincourt held by 2/7th Sherwood Foresters and two companies of 2/4th Lincolnshires during the withdrawal to the Flesquieres Line on 5 December. Flesquieres church is in the far distance to the left of the right windmill. The western edge of Orival Wood is on the left of the photo. The Sherwoods with the Lincolns to their east, withdrew up the slope towards the main British line.

South and west of La Vacquerie, Village Road on the right runs away towards Flag Ravine and Fifteen Ravine Cemetery. The original front British trenches of 20 November opposite the Hindenburg Line ran from right to left about half way down the lane but with the Germans counter-attacking from the south 183 Brigade improved hastily dug trenches on the reverse slope in the fields on the left.

Emden Trench and Emden Support, the front lines of the extended Hindenburg Line Position east and north of La Vacquerie, ran through the copse in the centre towards the camera. These trenches were heavily contested by 182 Brigade until they were forced back and onto Welsh Ridge itself.

The German front lines of Corner Trench and Corner Support ran south to Welsh Road, west of Corner Work. Corner Work itself lay across Welsh Road about where the field of grass joins the ploughed field near the seven spindly trees.

The north-eastern slope of Welsh Ridge, taken from close to where Ostrich Trench joined Emden Support. Ostrich Trench then ran down the slope towards the thin line of tress on the right. On the high ground behind those trees, which mark the line of the A26 *péage,* sits Lateau Wood. British FOOs had a very restricted view of this area whereas German observers in Lateau Wood had an excellent panorama of the battle.

Pontefract Trench, the front of 59th Division's Battle Zone, extends away from the camera towards Ecoust St Mein's church tower on the far left. The white buildings on the right are the silos just to the south of Bullecourt. The railway embankment is off camera to the right. The photograph was taken at about the spot where the long communication trench (Sidney Trench) crossed Pontefract Trench as it cut north-eastwards towards Horseshoe Support in the Forward Zone.

With Riencourt-les-Cagnicourt in the distance, and taken just north of the railway embankment, the chalk track ran up to Horseshoe Support. Horseshoe Redoubt lay further along the track towards Riencourt. This area was the western end of 178 Brigade's Forward Zone.

From north-east of Vaulx-Vraucourt along the Hirondelle Valley, with Vraucourt Copse on the right. Noreuil Switch, which connected the front and rear of 59th Division's Battle Zone ran just below the crest of the higher ground of the Noreuil Spur on the northern slope of the valley.

The Forward Zone of 66th Division from Pimple Post east by north of Templeux Quarries. Malakoff Wood is in the far centre distance and Ruby Wood on the Cologne Ridge to the right. Hargicourt lies in the valley just off camera to the right, with the A26 *péage* cutting north-south to the east of the village.

The village of Fresnoy-le-Petit caused problems for 61st Division both in April 1917 and March 1918. The photograph looks west from 250 yards south of the village crossroads over the rear of the division's Forward and the front of its Battle Zones. Otter Copse is left and the high ground of Bayley Hill in the distance. Fresnoy Redoubt, where Lieutenant Ker won his Victoria Cross, was just off camera to the right.

In clear visibility, 58th Division's defenders of *Ferme Rouge* Locality (white buildings extreme left) and Triangle Locality (close to the hamlet of Caniers (right) would have had excellent targets as the enemy advanced towards them across the rolling fields from the camera position immediately west of Travecy.

Ferme Rouge (left) and its adjoining posts and fields of wire were elements of 58th Division's Battle Zone. A counter-attack from its defences by two platoons of 3/London delayed the enemy for a time but the fog helped the Germans to press on westwards towards the canal.

The northern part of 66th Division's Battle Zone. Carpeza Copse is right, the woods of Templeux Quarries and Hill 140 in the far centre, and Hill 135 on the left. Three of the unfinished redoubts, Trifle, Trinity, and Trinket, lay in the centre, with Upstart just off right.

Taken from the site of Trinity Redoubt on Hill 140 looking north over the Cologne. The trees in the far left distance line the eastern edge of Templeux Quarries. Sherwood Trench lay just over the crest in front of the trees and Bolsover Switch ran down the field to their right and on into Higson's Quarries.

From Trinity Redoubt looking north across the Cologne Valley and into 16th Division's area. Although the enemy was fairly quickly through 66th Division's Forward Zone and into its Battle Zone, once 16th Division's front had broken the East Lancashire Division was compelled to withdraw towards its Green Line.

Roses Valley, east of Selency, with the A26 embankment at the far end. The communication trench Ivry Alley ran along the bottom of the valley, with the Vickers and Lewis guns of Ellis Redoubt garrisoned by 2/8th Worcestershire sited on the banks to right and left. The *péage* now covers part of the eastern end of the former redoubt.

Sitting on the ridge immediately west of Hervilly and Jeancourt, Nobescourt Farm became the focal point of 66th Division's withdrawal and temporary home to several HQ. Divisional and brigade staff attempted to coordinate the withdrawal of what was left of the division whilst at the same time units of 50th Division began to arrive in the area.

His influence and insistence that his ideas and principles on how the division should train and prepare are, however, clear.[37]

The drafts arriving at the 2nd Line divisions during the preparatory period for Third Ypres followed the procedure common in many divisions. They were assessed at the divisional depot or reception camp with the rawest being put through an intensive period of musketry and basic skills before being despatched to brigades and thence to battalions. After the war one CO told the official historian that from early 1917, GHQ never understood "with what poor, untrained material we were fighting."[38] This opinion reflected a widespread belief throughout the BEF but, as in all generalisations, the reality was that not all drafts were as poor as others. Like most divisions, the 2nd Line formations themselves had no effective influence at the Base Camps as to who they received as replacements. Nonetheless, 2/1st London Battalion, for example, reported that the more than 500 men it received in August were of "very good appearance" and showing signs of becoming "very useful men." It was initially a little disappointed with another 100 taken from the Divisional Depot Battalion early in September because they required "considerable training." It was more encouraged a week later, however, because those recruits were now "showing up well [with] quite a considerable number of useful NCOs amongst them."[39] In October the Lancashire Fusilier battalions in 197 Brigade would have been pleased to receive drafts from their 19th Battalion, a pioneer unit from which men of the highest medical category were being culled for the conventional infantry. On the other hand, 2/5th Manchester was disappointed to receive 48 men in a large draft who had to be sent to the Brigade Recruit School as "untrained".[40] Comments such as these were widespread across a BEF in which men from the Highlands with three months' training were exchanging their kilts for standard drill trousers of English regiments, and where Londoners were discarding trousers for kilts. In 1917, however, there is no evidence to suggest that 2nd Line divisions were being singled out to receive men of lower medical category or those with poorer military skills.

It is difficult to know how confident the troops of the 2nd Line divisions were in their training as they assembled on the tapes for their first major attack. The diarist of 2/8th London struck a positive note when he thought the performance of one platoon during a raid in early September "showed how complete their training had been." Yet, when 61st Division, the first of the 2nd Line divisions to undertake a set piece attack in the Salient assembled, the nature of the ground, the resolution of the German defenders, and the failure of the offensive so far to have secured any significant territorial gains would have been well known. Although morale in the British divisions fighting in Flanders never actually broke, the battle was to prove its nadir. The troops, their equipment, the support of the other arms and the tactics to be employed may have been well practised and efficient, but offensive action required more than the coming together of fighting power and operational design. The doctrine, learned and rehearsed, was current and considered appropriate to the task facing them. But the infantry had also to be confident that their officers' training and initiative were sufficient to allow amendment to the doctrine should

---

37 See TNA WO 953001. For example, one entry on 1 Sep.1917 notes, "Training carried out on the lines laid down by GOC Corps."
38 Colonel F M Birch to Cyril Falls, 24 Sep.1938. TNA CAB 45/116. Quoted in Robbins, *British Generalship*, p.85.
39 TNA WO 953001: 31 Aug, 1 Sep, 8 Sep.1917.
40 TNA WO 953136; WO 953144: Oct.1917.

the unexpected occur. Furthermore, the troops had to overcome doubts created by earlier experiences when interlocking elements of the application of physical force by combined arms had not worked efficiently and effectively. They also knew that fortune had to be with them. By the time the 2nd Line divisions entered the battle the dream of a breakthrough and breakout had been shattered. The divisions' capability and resolution, their tactical acuity and overall fighting power were to be tested in battles of unrelenting attrition and of engagements of limited but ferocious 'bite and hold'.

All of the 2nd Line divisions' engagements to be examined have several features in common with each other as well with the experiences of most of the 1st Line, Regular and New Army divisions that fought in Third Ypres. The battle is remembered for its atrocious weather and the consequent physical conditions created in the area by one of the wettest summers and autumns on record. Clausewitzian frictions were ever-present and added considerably to the existing difficulties of the planners, staffs, and troops. Fighting power and efficiency was affected by the almost ubiquitous mud, the troops' mental and physical exhaustion, the artillery's unsteady firing platforms, disjointed and disrupted communications, the problems of resupply, and the fortitude of the German defenders. Another factor common to the overwhelming majority of Allied attacks during the battle was the inability to deceive or surprise the enemy. To achieve surprise, current doctrine advocates the use of secrecy, concealment, speed, intelligence, security, originality, novel technologies, unfamiliar activity, and audacity in order to confuse, paralyse or disrupt effective decision making on the part of the enemy. It can be generated through unexpected timing or an unexpected direction or method of attack. It is used to undermine an enemy's cohesion and morale and can produce potent psychological reactions. But, the reaction is usually transient because shock and confusion recede over time. If aggressive exploitation does not follow swiftly, the initial reaction can often be quickly checked. The introduction of gas at 2nd Ypres and the first tanks on the Somme in September 1916 both produced shock and confusion but on neither occasion was there either the will to exploit further or sufficient resources to maintain momentum.

Deception is closely allied to surprise and can be an integral part of it. By deliberately allowing the enemy to witness false activity or, alternatively concealing the reality, the enemy may be induced to act against his interests. The idea is to "...make the enemy very certain, very determined, and very wrong."[41] Chinese attacks were used on occasions during Third Ypres, and demonstrations and limited operations were undertaken by Third and Fourth Armies as diversions. Yet, the reality was that the German High Command and its troops on and around the Passchendaele Ridge knew the high ground was the ultimate British objective. There had been much debate during and since the Somme about varying the timing of zero hours and the pros and cons of long, short, or even no preliminary bombardments. For the British and Dominion forces, a basic difficulty was that the enemy had observation over most of their assembly areas and the contested ground. With the exception of its actual hour of assault any attack was, therefore, difficult to disguise. The corps and divisional commanders of the 2nd Line divisions, like those of all others operating in the Salient, showed little imagination when it came to selecting

---

41 B. Whaley, *Stratagem, Deception and Surprise in War* (Cambridge, Massachusetts: Massachusetts Centre for International Studies, 1969).

the hour of attack. Only on one occasion did a 2nd Line formation ignore the usual and generally predictable time of an hour or so either side of dawn.

The conceptual component of fighting power had been examined and developed in the 2nd Line units during the preceding months but conditions in the Salient differed considerably from those anticipated in the training manuals. Training for some divisions had, as we have seen, been patchy but other elements of the physical component, especially the accumulation of guns and munitions, were thought to be more than adequate for the expected task. This assumption was to prove false but the most challenging aspect of the campaign was the maintenance of the moral component. Troops could justifiably ask why they were repeatedly expected to advance into gales of howling lead in such demanding conditions while, despite the exhortations of their leaders and commanders, the end of the war appeared to be no closer. Conditions in the rear offered little in the way of comfort for rest and recuperation and the regular arrival of drafts, albeit usually small in number, continually undermined the integrity of the units' original coherence. Furthermore, it was widely known that the German U-boast campaign was causing hardship to their families and that Russian resolution to continue fighting was waning. With the exception of 58th Division, which achieved a significant success in a major coordinated offensive operation on 20 September, the 2nd Line divisions, like many of their neighbouring formations, were largely tasked to undertake smaller and less well-publicized attacks. Whether set-piece battle or limited operation, and whether experienced or novice formation, the prevailing conditions posed similar challenges to all divisional staffs, sub-unit commanders, and often newly arrived privates. War diaries of several 2nd Line units mention the eagerness with which their men were reported to be looking forward to fighting their division's first set-piece battle. This may or may not have been an accurate assessment but given the character of the fighting and the overall current strength and training state of the BEF, we should expect to see little real difference between the achievements of the 2nd Line divisions and those of the already battle-tested formations.

As part of XIX Cops, 61st (2nd South Midland) arrived from its training area and moved into the line east of Wieltje between 17-19 August. On 19 August orders were issued for the South Midland and 15th Divisions to attack on 22 August in conjunction with XVIII Corps on the left and a cooperating II Corps on the right. The formation selected to undertake the attack on 61st Division's front, 184 Brigade, relieved two battalions of 183 Brigade in the forward positions during the early hours of 20 August. It was the first time 2/1st Bucks and 2/4th Ox & Bucks had seen the sector and thus had extremely limited time to reconnoitre possible routes across no man's land or visibly to identify German strong points and their platoons' objectives. Neither is there mention in the sources of the troops having been able to study any replica model of the German positions. Instead, officers were told they must point out the objectives to their men. How this was to be done is unrecorded. In what are for war diaries unusually emotive terms, the diarist of 2/1st Bucks recorded 21 August as being "a strenuous day for everyone, organizing and preparing the battalion to reach that pitch of perfection required for the great day." He then described 22 August as, "The day for which the whole battalion has waited and trained incessantly, the day of attack. Everyone was in position, knowing exactly what he had to do, and not a soul but was confident that the battalion would do its utmost to succeed."[42]

42 TNA WO 953066: 21-22 Aug.1917.

The tactics employed were straightforward and followed a pattern that, in the fourth week of the campaign, was becoming common. The Bucks on the right had one company in each of the first and second waves; the remaining two companies constituted the third and fourth waves. The Oxfords assembled slightly differently: three companies formed the first and second wave and the final company the third. Instead of the more usual practice of the leading waves halting and consolidating the first objectives to allow the following waves to leapfrog on to the second and third, the leading waves were to press on to the final objective and leave the mopping up to platoons of 2/4th Berkshire. The Bucks were allocated eight platoons of Berks and the Oxfords five. Their task was to pass through the other two battalions' companies and rush their allocated strong points. If they could not capture the positions they were to keep the enemy fire suppressed so as not to constrain the advance of the Bucks and Oxfords. Each platoon of the Berks was to have two sappers attached, one of whom carried a charge to destroy pill box doors. The two lead battalions were each to have four machine guns and two Stokes as additional fire protection. For two days before the attack, corps heavy artillery had been following the usual scheme of targeting known enemy strong points and pill boxes. Although impressive visually and audibly, DHQ pragmatically assessed the barrages' destructive effect on concrete positions as "probably very small." The heavy artillery also conducted counter-battery work assisted by air observation and claimed to have neutralized 46 hostile batteries. The divisional artillery fired the creeping and protective barrages at what was by then the usual rate of advance and duration, and eight tanks were allotted to help neutralize strong points. Because tanks tended to "wander at will" troops were warned not to follow or take direction from them and were instructed to get their bearings from the smoke barrage, identifiable roads, and known enemy positions. Officers were told to ensure they knew the compass bearings of their objectives and their names as indicated on maps. A machine-gun barrage was to be fired by 40 guns over the heads of the attacking troops who were to advance with three days' rations.[43] Although the advantages of each man carrying two water bottles into battle were by this time well understood, 184 Brigade could only note it was "trying to get an additional" canteen for each man. Two bottles and three days' rations was becoming usual practice because men in scattered posts could then provision themselves rather than having to rely on the unlikely ability of nocturnal ration parties to find them. They were also to carry three pairs of socks, with another pair waiting for them at the QM stores when relieved. Rum, however, was only to be issued if the CO believed conditions warranted it. Divisional orders specified that communications, which by this stage of the battle usually involved power buzzers, buried lines, signalling lamps, pigeons, and dogs, were to be as laid down in *SS143*. A contact patrol aircraft (CPA) from 21st Squadron RFC was to be alerted by flares and Watson fans.[44] To warn against lingering too long on captured positions, troops were explicitly informed the Germans "don't like the bayonet" and "losing the barrage means

---

43 These were known as "barrage rations" and consisted of: 1lb biscuit, 1lb preserved meat, tea, sugar, and jam. One tin of stew was provided for four men and a tin of milk for 12.
44 Watson fans were pleated canvas discs about 12 inches in diameter, white on one side and dark hued on the other. Troops were supposed to spin them over and back repeatedly to signal their position to aircraft.

Offensive Operations I: Third Ypres – The Middle Weeks   137

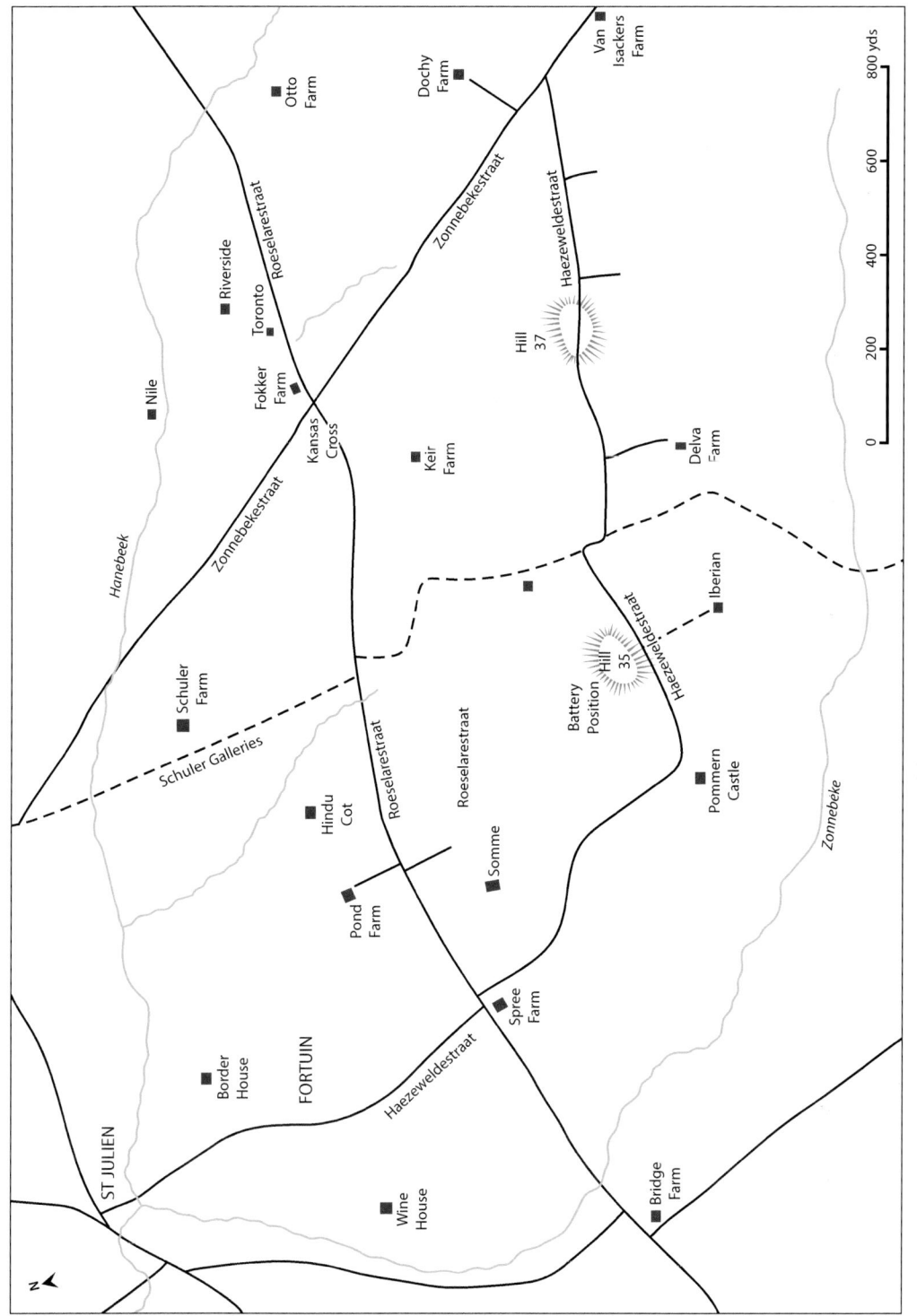

Map 2 Third Battle of Ypres, August 1917.

disaster." Finally, the Bucks battalion was told to maintain momentum and not to wait for the Oxfords who were likely to be held up by the enemy garrison in Pond Farm.[45]

The assembly, covered by "strong patrols" of the units to be relieved, went according to schedule and the barrage opened on time. The Bucks on the right made good initial progress, with the Berks platoons following behind to take strong points known as Somme and Aisne. On their right 15th Division failed to take Gallipoli and Hill 35. This meant machine-gun fire from those positions ripped into the flank of 184 Brigade and allowed the enemy to retake Aisne. Unconfirmed reports, later to be recognized as unfounded, suggested some Bucks had crossed the Winnipeg – Zonnebeke road and established posts some score of yards east of Kansas Cross. On the left, the Oxfords moved past Hindu Cot and took the right sections of Schuler Galleries but the garrison in Pond Farm held out and fired into the rear of the Oxfords and the Berks. The forward platoons of Oxfords soon lost touch and remained out of contact until a message finally arrived at brigade HQ reporting that only three men were holding the captured sections of Schuler Galleries. The 1st Line Warwicks of 143 Brigade on the left failed to take Winnipeg so several platoons of 2/5th Gloucestershire were sent up to help plug the gaps and protect the flanks of the two lead battalions. The Gloucesters had lost men on the way up owing to an apparent instruction direct from Fifth Army ordering them to advance through the German counter-barrage at a time when, according to 184 Brigade, their move was premature and unnecessary. Three messages failed to get through to one company of the Gloucesters that should have moved to support the Bucks' right flank but, at the third attempt, platoons of another company rushed Pond Farm and the garrison finally surrendered. It was quickly retaken by the enemy and then recaptured again during the following night. A strong counter-attack seemed to be developing from the direction of Wurst Farm in the afternoon of 22 August but this was broken up by the artillery. Further ferocious attempts by the Germans to retake Somme and Hindu Cot failed but they did succeed in recapturing the earlier lost sections of Schuler Galleries and the much contested Pond Farm. Brigade HQ learnt of the loss of Pond Farm at about 0400 and ordered its recapture because its German garrison could again fire into the rear of the brigade. Three platoons of 2/6th Gloucestershire, one of the two battalions of 183 Brigade attached to 184, retook it at a cost of 40 casualties at 0800 on 23 August.

This had not been a major attack, the main activity on the Ypres front then being a little further to the south, but it had been a fairly significant operation by four divisions of two corps. It had been an organized and planned enabling operation designed to establish better jumping off positions for the next large attack scheduled for early September. The failure of 15th, 61st and 48th divisions to achieve and hold their objectives[46] led to a succession of smaller, often uncoordinated attempts to establish themselves on what had been the objectives for 22 August. In preparation for the next attacks the divisional field companies and pioneers continued their work of improving tracks and consolidating posts. The CRE reported that as the ground was making it virtually impossible to get wiring stores forward, DHQ had to decide whether they wanted Somme and Pond Farm to be wired. He outlined the problems his engineers would

---

45 On 19 August, 2/4th Gloucester had attacked (and possibly taken part of) Pond Farm to support an operation by 48th Division on its left. Wire and heavy fire forced the Gloucesters to withdraw.
46 On the left of 48th Division, 11th Division did make more ground than the other three formations but the failure of 48th to keep abreast meant that the right of 11th did have to withdraw from some of its gains

have to overcome if they were to repair a bridge over the flooded Steenbeek in time for the next operation, and also pointed out that 15th Division's failure to take Gallipoli and Hill 35 had created yet more work for his own field companies. The engineers borrowed two dozen mules from the infantry to carry stores forward (the mule convoys stampeded when they were caught in a barrage during the attack on Aisne) and all available lorries were impressed to bring up duckboards, fascines and sleepers to extend and repair existing tracks.[47] Two small platoon-sized attacks on the concrete pill box at Aisne were to be made before the main operation began in conjunction with 48th and 15th divisions but these met with little success. The Germans were alert and anticipated the enterprises and although one section reached the position, it could not open the rear door and withdrew.[48] An attempt on the Schuler Galleries and several nearby strong points also failed.

The next significant attack was scheduled for 27 August. By the early hours of 24 August, 183 Brigade had relieved 184 Brigade in the line with its GOC under instructions from DHQ to keep two of his battalions as fresh as possible for the attack. To help to confuse the enemy, smoke and a practice barrage would be fired in the days preceding the assault but there were an almost bewildering number of changes to the original orders concerning the number of companies to be utilized and how they would be deployed. When the GOC brigade expressed doubt about whether his two front battalions, 2/8th Worcestershire on the right and 2/4th Gloucestershire on the left, would be fresh enough to rush the Schuler Galleries and the strong points to its right, a degree of rationalization set in. Presumably in consultation with corps HQ, Major General Mackenzie decided the objectives for 27 August would be reduced; another attack planned for two days later would then complete the operation. The artillery and machine-gun barrages were as per the current norm, but instead of following the usual pattern of the heavy artillery firing generally slow, deliberate bombardments on strong points and block houses, it conducted shorter but more intense and concentrated shoots on known sites. The field artillery fired 30 minute HE and shrapnel searches for machine-guns posts to a depth of 3,000 yards behind the German front positions as well as the usual nocturnal harassing and interdiction shoots. Each battalion was to have two light trench mortars attached and the usual means of communications were expanded to include the provision of signal rockets. There were doubts as to whether the four allocated tanks would be able to cross the Steenbeek but if they could they were to be used for mopping up. Even if they did manage to arrive, however, troops were instructed to "act as if the tanks were not present." Specific parties under "very able" NCOs were selected to liaise with 143 Brigade of 48th Division at Winnipeg and with 44 Brigade of 15th Division at Gallipoli. Finally, and for what seems to have been the first time for 61st Division, each of the assaulting battalions was to have an artillery liaison officer attached.

47 Field companies and pioneer battalions of most divisions took pride in recording the yardage of duckboards laid in 24 hours. Their achievement varied according to the degree of shelling, the numbers of infantry assisting the sappers, and the nature of the ground. Those recorded by 61st Division are about average for the divisions working in the Salient in August.
48 It is unknown whether on this occasion a sapper with explosives had been detailed to accompany the assault platoon.

Until 0900 on 27 August, when corps HQ decided the ground was drying sufficiently for it to go ahead, the operation had remained in doubt.[49] Companies of the Gloucesters and Worcesters had become mixed up in the dark at Spree Farm but managed to sort themselves out and were in position by 0330. They then lay out in flooded shell holes until 1355 when they attacked, just as heavy rain and gale force winds began. These blew in a swirling thick mist that quickly made observation virtually impossible. The rain ruined the smoke candles and the troops were hit immediately from the front and right flank by fierce enemy fire. The barrage was quickly lost, Lewis guns and rifles were swiftly clogged, and platoons and sections lost each other in the mud. The extreme left, which had been instructed to be prepared to help 143 Brigade take Winnipeg, did reach its objective but along the rest of the brigade's front the advance stopped about 100 yards short of its targets. The 1st Line Warwickshire battalions on their left had bogged down short of their objectives and 44 Brigade on the right had again failed to take Gallipoli and the so-called Battery Position on Hill 35. The reserve companies of the Worcesters and Gloucesters were ordered up but the futility was quickly realized and the orders cancelled. The initial estimate of casualties amounted to about 30 percent of officers and 50 percent of other ranks.

The two lead battalions of 183 Brigade swapped places with the two that had been in support. They next immediately swapped with the two Warwickshire battalions attached from 182 Brigade, but the relief of 183 by 182 was postponed from the intended night of 29-30 August to the one following. To exacerbate further the frustrations and difficulties of relieving scattered posts in such conditions the already tired troops of 183 were informed that the light railways which had been supposed to take them to the rear had instead been commandeered for transporting ammunition. The replacement buses had also been cancelled so battalions were told to march to Ypres Asylum on the west side of the town and pick up the broad gauge. Any "very tired" men who could not manage to march to the Asylum were instructed to get to St Jean where they were "certain to pick up a lift up to 0300 as long as there [were] not too many."[50]

There was to be something of a pause between the larger set-piece battles in early September, but Fifth Army wanted a degree of tempo to be maintained. Certain tactical positions were ordered to be captured by 61st Division in preparation for the next set-piece operation. The divisional front was extended to what had been the left of 15th Division with the result that the much contested Hill 35, its Battery Position, and Gallipoli now fell opposite its sector. In addition to these positions, Aisne, the strong points around Cross Cots, and the Schuler Galleries and Farm were to be taken by 182 Brigade "without delay." The subsequent assaults on Hill 35 and Aisne give the impression of the GOC division and brigade going through the motions to demonstrate they were attempting to carry out their commanders' intent but at the same time accepting they would probably fail. Their paramount concern seems to have been conserving their men. Rather than conducting formal attacks with sufficient concentration of infantry force to take and consolidate any ground or positions won, the attacks took on more of the character of piecemeal assaults whose instigators had little faith in their likelihood of success. One company of 2/5th Warwickshire tried to rush Hill 35 at 0430 on 1 September but failed in the bright moonlight and sodden ground. Another tried again at 2200 only to be hit by heavy fire

---

49   This decision presumably involved coordination with the other corps involved in the attack and Fifth Army HQ. One hundred gas projectors discharged canisters on Cross Cots at 0400hrs.
50   TNA WO 953034: 30 Aug.1917.

from the Battery Position and Aisne. A small simultaneous demonstration on Aisne apparently did nothing to suppress the fire of its garrison on the company attacking Hill 35.

Repeated attacks over the next few days on the hill and Aisne by single companies similarly failed to provide any success. The tactics employed and the deployment of the platoons and sections in these attacks varied slightly but they usually involved *SS143*'s approach of suppressing fire from two sections while the other two tried to work around to the rear. The artillery programmes also varied to a degree but essentially they involved a box barrage of shrapnel and smoke fired by about 25 percent of the field pieces with the remainder of the 18 pdrs and howitzers concentrating on the SOS lines. Frustrated at the lack of progress corps HQ ordered another combined attack on the Battery Position in conjunction with 42nd (East Lancashire) Division. The artillery preparation for 6 September followed the usual pattern but staff now believed that as they had corrected the previously erroneous locations of the concrete emplacements on the hill the fall of shot would prove more effective. One company of 2/5th Warwickshire was allocated to make the assault. The morning attempt failed, as did another later the same evening. To the right, 42nd Division failed to take and hold Iberian (which was connected to Hill 35 by a trench) and the positions known as Beck and Borry. As in his reports for the earlier attacks, Brigadier General Sackville-West praised the efforts of the men but believed a "lack of leaders" once the officers and NCOs had become casualties led to failure.[51]

At noon on 7 September, V Corps relieved XIX Corps but 61st Division remained in the line. Immediately orders were issued to withdraw any troops within 250 yards of the Battery Position so that a steady bombardment could be put onto it. Two hundred gas projectors were fired on Cross Cots while gas and 4 inch Stokes targeted Gallipoli. Heavy artillery fired on the Battery Position for two days simultaneously as field artillery fired short but intense barrages on the pill boxes' support trenches. Machine-gun barrages sprayed the hill while other guns targetting German positions on the flanks of the crest. The variations in the artillery programme were inventive and the weight of fires should have been sufficient to at least have disabled the garrisons in the trenches linking the former gun pits and the interval concrete machine-gun emplacements. Two companies of Oxfords were tasked for the attack scheduled for 1600 on 10 September. As they assembled during the night they were heavily gassed by their own side and hit by artillery firing short. Like the seven previous attempts by the brigade on the position, the attack failed. The enemy infantry in the trenches had not been subdued by the barrages and those in the pill boxes were untouched. Just as the Oxfords were about to rush the positions they were disconcerted by a line of Germans "suddenly appearing" in front of them and firing at point blank range. Despite the attention of the heavy and field artillery the garrisons at Aisne and Iberian poured fire from the flanks and three enemy aircraft harassed the attackers from the air. Within minutes all Lewis guns were clogged and an enemy box barrage came down around the hill.

One of the company commanders involved left an excoriating account of the assault. He described the spirits of the troops before the blue on blue gassing as "excellent" and "optimistic" but that the effect on morale of the mistake (which had been caused by "criminal negligence") "was as pitiable as it was justified." He did not condemn the artillery for the shorts, accepting that worn barrels were a fact of life, but described the assault as "an object lesson

---

51   TNA WO 953054: 182nd Bde HQ, 4 Sep.1917; 9 Sep.1917.

in the squandering of our efforts in attack...Operations upon a general scale having failed to capture all three positions [Iberian, Gallipoli and Hill 35] it was fantastically hoped that each could be reduced separately ... [because they supported each other]..it was not feasible to hold any without holding all." Success, he thought, had been "impossible."[52] The GOC brigade's report was not as ferocious in its condemnation but did criticize some of the tactics employed and, by implication, the training. The brigadier thought good discipline allowed the troops to assemble undetected and that the counter-battery work had been effective. He was less content with the absence of British aircraft to protect ground troops from marauding enemy air, and with the quality of the artillery barrages. He wanted the field artillery to ensure they actually fired the number of shells per minute ordered and to deliver a mix of HE and shrapnel. He thought more gas and smoke should have been applied on the flanks and that the infantry could have made a more "judicious" use of smoke grenades. This would have helped to create surprise and cause the Germans to fire through a fog. He did consider the use of only two companies to have been correct, especially as "an attack by three times [the 170 actually used] would scarcely have had any better results under the circumstances." He argued more could have been done to neutralize enemy positions supporting the main objective but, like Captain Rose, did criticize the attitude of some of the men. Brigadier General White noted that a "vigorous attack by men who mean to get there" would have produced better results; Rose thought too many of his soldiers had gone to ground too readily and that consequently "less was done by the men than the conduct of their leaders deserved." These assessments are perhaps supported by the number of casualties. Despite the recorded intensity of the enemy's machine-gun and rifle fire, in addition to his accurate protective and box barrages, the Oxfords' reported casualties amounted to under one third of those involved.[53]

This failure was to be the last attempt by the division to advance its line during Third Ypres. On the orders of Fifth Army, planned operations for further attacks on Aisne, Gallipoli, and the Schuler Galleries by 183 Brigade were shelved by corps HQ on 11 September.[54] Instructions were issued to the brigade in the line to do what they could to link up shell holes as assembly positions for the relieving division's attempt on the Battery Position and Schuler Galleries. Between 13-15 September, the incoming 55th (West Lancashire) Division relieved the South Midlanders and 61st moved down to Third Army in the Arras sector. The division's three weeks in the Salient had been costly and the ground gained minimal.[55] The two attacks in August were later to warrant no more than a footnote in the battles and engagements list, and the September

---

52 G. Rose, *2/4th Ox&Bucks*, pp.131-40.
53 *Soldiers Died* records 15 of 2/4th Ox & Bucks kia on 10 Sept.1917.
54 In his diary entry of 11 Sep.1917, Haig noted that in a conversation with Lt. Gen. Fanshawe, the latter had told him 61st Division had been in the line for three weeks and its troops were thus "not fresh enough to undertake the attack on Gallipoli etc." Fanshawe was inclined not to attempt any more of these "minor enterprises." Haig then saw Maj. Gen. Mackenzie who said he was "anxious to take Hill 35 before going out of the line and was confident his men could take it." Haig replied that it was "primarily" for Mackenzie and Fanshawe to decide whether these small operations should take place. G. Sheffield & J. Bourne (eds.) *Douglas Haig: War Diaries and Letters 1914-1918* (London: Phoenix, 2006) pp.323-24
55 TNA WO 953036: A&Q, 14 Sep.1917. The total of killed, wounded and missing in the division for 21 Aug-14 Sep.1917 was given as 3,101. DHQ (WO 953034) gives 129 officers and 3,110 ORs for 17 Aug-15 Sep.1917.

attempts on the Battery Position took place before the official opening of the Battle of the Menin Road. The division did not, therefore, appear in the lists of those that fought in the campaign's principal and better known battles. It was used instead in attempts to advance the line by taking tactical objectives that might have influenced the outcome of the subsequent larger offensives. On reflection, one officer wrote that the division suffered as a consequence of Fifth Army's mistaken operational methods: "By attacking spasmodically we play the enemy's game…the nibbling tactics passed down from above, inadequate cooperation by the divisions fighting side by side with us and the failure of our artillery to hit the pill boxes…further combined to paralyse efforts which, had they been directed to more easy tasks would …have earned for the Division the highest military success."[56] The difficulty for 61st Division, as for all divisions in the Salient, was to identify what might have been "more easy tasks." Once the decision to continue the battle towards the Passchendaele Ridge, despite the weather and the subsequent deteriorating conditions had been made, there was no real alternative to trying to slog through the quagmire in the hope that attrition might cause a collapse of the German forces. The desired strategic end state of the capture of the Roulers railway hub, and even perhaps liberation of the Belgian Channel ports, remained the ultimate prize but the operational objective of the ridge became Haig's obsession. His subordinate commanders, Plumer and Gough, were thus obliged to concentrate as much force as they could assemble and direct it towards this operational end. The ways and means employed were brutal and costly but, given their commander's intent they had to devise, within their operational restrictions of manpower and overall sustainment, how Haig's desired strategic and operational end states could best and most efficiently be achieved.

In autumn 1917 the role of corps HQ was largely that of a conduit to pass on instructions from Montreuil[57] and army HQ to divisions. Some GOsC corps, such as Maxse, took a great personal interest in the perceived quality of the divisions under their command, while others, such as Lieutenant Generals E.A. Fanshawe and H.E. Watts of V and XIX Corps respectively, applied a slightly lighter hand. These commanders were more prepared to allow their divisional commanders a freer rein in the ways employed to achieve the desired ends. This did not mean that Major General Mackenzie of 61st Division and his GOsC brigades were able to devise and implement radical methods because they did remain constrained by the means they had available.[58] If they believed the ground or local circumstances warranted it they could, however, employ means that did not come directly from doctrinal manuals. They had control over their divisional artillery and were free to ask for additional help from the batteries of neighbouring divisions. They could also request the corps heavy artillery target selected sites and make suggestions as to how the heavy batteries could be used more effectively. Brigadier General Spooner, GOC 183 Brigade, believed German defence in depth could be overcome if the heavy artillery concentrated not so much on the enemy's rear positions but on the ground and the pill boxes

---

56 G. Rose, *2/4th Ox & Bucks*, p.130.
57 The old town of Montreuil housed the General Headquarters of the BEF from March 1916 until early 1919.
58 It was pointed out earlier that on 22 August Fifth Army instructed a support battalion to move forward at a time which the GOC brigade conducting the attack thought was misjudged. DHQ also recorded that the time set for zero on 27 August was "at the wish of GOC XVIII Corps." See TNA WO 953034. As this was a combined attack by three corps, simultaneity and cooperation were important but Maxse had long been advocating afternoon, rather than morning attacks. The tone of 61st Division's comment may imply discontent with this decision.

to be attacked. Yet, to avoid these becoming simply area shoots and creating additional terrain problems for the infantry, the guns would have to be directed by FOOs in the infantry lines connected by wire to the batteries. Spooner thought that if the pill box garrisons realized they were becoming singled out by the heavy artillery they would abandon the concrete and shelter in nearby trenches or shell holes; there they would become exposed to shrapnel. Like many other commanders, Spooner also argued for more realistic rates of lifts for creeping barrages. There had to be, they argued, more frequent halts in the barrages to allow time for mopping up and reorganization of platoons and companies. The infantry accepted that unstable firing platforms and worn barrels caused shorts and thus casualties, and even that it took considerable time for messages instructing the guns to lengthen their range physically to reach the batteries. What they did resent, however, was the unrealistic speed by which the creeping barrages advanced. Smoke was also regarded as a mixed blessing: it could blind the defenders but also added to the problems of direction-keeping. One observing officer of 2/7th Warwickshire noted that a smoke barrage on the enemy line created "a fine spectacular effect – but without military use."[59]

Sustaining the supply of ammunition to the guns was a major logistic difficulty and largely beyond the control of the divisional staff. Transport from railhead to divisional dumps and refilling points along choked roads frequently targeted by long range German guns, was partly the responsibility of army and corps staff. Getting the shells forward from those points to the guns themselves was the job of the men and pack animals of the divisional ammunition column (DAC). There is no record of 61st Division's batteries ever running short of shells but there are occasional references to possible restrictions.[60] Nevertheless, the divisional artillery did generally perform as well as the conditions allowed. It (unusually) received praise from 184 Brigade for the more realistic pace and accuracy of its barrage on 22 August, and during the preliminary barrage for 10 September FOOs in observation posts were acknowledged to have conducted a "deliberate and carefully observed bombardment."[61] It did show flexibility and variety in the way it laid barrages before and during the three main attacks, and placing artillery liaison officers with each assaulting battalion was a sensible move. Cut wires, enemy counter-battery shoots, and smoke-reduced visibility, however, made mistakes inevitable.

In addition to the divisional artillery, certain corps batteries could at times be placed under the direct command of Major General Mackenzie and his CRA. Gas discharges came under control of corps HQ but divisional staff organized the machine-gun barrage and in conjunction with GOsC brigades decided how the LTM batteries might be best utilized. Lessons were learned and assimilated. For example, a report on the attack of 22 August by the OC 182 MG Company noted several faults with his crews, particularly their proclivity to become "excited" which resulted in excessive rates of fire and a lack of fire discipline. He blamed himself for not having withdrawn the guns when the barrage was completed but took heart from the reports of prisoners who claimed the machine-gun fire had "considerably harassed them."[62] Communications, as always, had proved problematic. DHQ utilized the practices laid down

---

59   TNA WO 953056: 2/7th Warwickshire, 4 Sep.1917.
60   For example, practice barrages were occasionally cancelled and field artillery batteries were warned to be prepared to fire a mixture of HE and shrapnel if no smoke shells were available. TNA WO 953034: 4 Sep.1917
61   TNA WO 953034: 7 Sep.1917.
62   TNA WO 953034: Report by Capt. Dann, 23 Aug.1917.

in *SS148* and instructed that reports should be sent back every 30 minutes until zero+2 hours and, from then on, every two hours. These were in addition to those ordered to be despatched which recorded any observed movement of enemy forces. One attacking battalion noted that its wires were cut 90 percent of the time, and brigade HQ complained that its signallers had had insufficient training on amplifiers. DHQ reported that not one pigeon returned with a message during the attack of 27 August. Runners, therefore, with their inherent difficulties remained the primary source of intelligence reporting.[63]

Divisional and brigade commanders could also consider and decide which attacking formations the infantry should adopt. *SS143* was available as a framework but could be modified. The nature of the ground, of course, disrupted assembly positions and progress across no man's land. Because experience showed that squads and platoons became hopelessly split and mixed, 61st Division's brigades did vary the shape of their assault formations. After its attack on 27 August, 183 Brigade reported the state of the ground and clogged weapons meant emplacements could not be dealt with in "the orthodox manner."[64] This presumably means the methods prescribed in *SS143*. One officer commented that the methods of attack conducted in the spring and summer proved impracticable and although the need for change was quickly recognized, troops trained in the *SS143* methods, "were slow, in action, to adopt the new ones requisite."[65] His brigade commander was clearly thinking along similar lines.[66] Brigadier General Spooner questioned the suitability of the wave and worms approach because it diluted the concentration of force. It had been developed for trench to trench attacks but because the enemy occupied shell holes as well as emplacements, he believed the attackers would suffer unduly from the flanks and too much of the force would be directed against what might in the end prove to be unoccupied shell holes. Although he did not specify their weapon composition and mix, he advocated the use of small, scattered and largely independent groups. The drawback was, however, that units did not have the time to train their men as thoroughly as the methods required. "Such [well-trained] men", he added, "are not easy to find at the present time." One way around overcoming the shortage of sufficiently skilled men was, Spooner argued, to have groups of skirmishers to clear out shell holes following groups of four sections allocated to take a particular strong point. The largest group within the four would attack the rear while the other three suppressed fire from front and flanks. The manoeuvring to position had to be done under smoke (and possibly gas) and in harmony with both the creeping shrapnel barrage and another fired by the heavy artillery on nearby strong points. This latter bombardment was to be aimed at preventing garrisons firing through the smoke onto the assaulting parties. Once the rear party had rushed and gained access to the strong point the skirmishers would advance beyond the position to establish a fixed line to repel counter-attacks and prepare a new jumping off line for the next phase. The storming parties would then consolidate the captured strong points and shell holes as other units passed through. If "every kind of mechanical means of destruction" such as tanks, gas, boiling oil, liquid fire, burning phosphorous, and smoke were used Spooner believed fewer men would be needed than was currently required by the more conventional method. A further recommendation concerned command and control. Spooner argued tactical control would be more effective

---

63 TNA WO 953056: 2/7th Warwickshire, 7 Sep.1917; WO 953034.
64 TNA WO 953063, Lessons Which May be Drawn from Recent Operations, n.d.
65 G. Rose, *2/4th Ox & Bucks*, p.130.
66 TNA WO 953063: 183 Bde, Lessons Which May be Drawn from Recent Operations, n.d.

if at least 50 percent of the officers engaged were kept under shelter at brigade HQ and sent up as needed or later to reorganize scattered groups.[67]

The division did certainly demonstrate adaptability in its attack formations and methodology. In the light of additional intelligence and discussion, 183 Brigade amended its attack instructions for 27 August four times. Equally important, the brigade staff managed to distribute the final set to all companies in sufficient time for the assaulting platoons to be appraised of them.[68] On 6 September, 2/5th Warwickshire's CO specifically asked for no preliminary bombardment for the evening attack on the Battery Position. He intended to advance his assaulting platoons onto the position in the dark in the hope of catching the garrison by surprise. On another occasion the attackers tried to manoeuvre around the site and attack simultaneously from all directions. The tactic might have worked had the sections not been halted by fire from the site's adjoining and covering emplacements. But, however much commanders might try to innovate and improvise, the basic obstacle of crossing the broken and flooded ground remained constant. Several reports record that troops were thwarted as much, if not more, by small garrisons in shell holes rather than by the concrete pill boxes.[69] The occupied shell holes were difficult to identify until fire came from them and with Lewis guns, rifles and, perhaps above all grenade launchers unusable, clearing those staggered and mutually supporting defences was always difficult. Troops often claimed they were only defeated by the mud but the enemy's counter-attack or local support troops had to contend with the same difficulties. Mud was a major contribution to the division's lack of territorial gains but so, too, was the inability of the heavy artillery to silence fire from the concrete structures. The dilemma for commanders was whether to concentrate greater physical force at particular points in the hope of overcoming the enemy by mass, or whether doing so would simply add to the casualty lists. Commanders have to consider the requirements and relative priority between individual engagements and actions, and the conservation of fighting power for future use. Economy of effort has to be judicious, with commanders ensuring they do have "the right tool in the right place at the right time" in order to achieve "the right result."[70] In September, GOC 182 Brigade thought that the right tool was used in the wrong way, at the wrong time, and in the wrong place.

Brigadier General White believed 61st Division's attacks, together with those of its neighbouring divisions, were "somewhat premature." He considered the attack deployment by which 2/4th Berkshire was split up into platoons to assist the lead battalions as moppers up was mistaken. These platoons, he argued, felt that they were not working for their own comrades and fell under no real distinct command. If three battalions were to be used in the attack, a three battalion front would have better suited the purpose and overall efficiency. The timing of the operations was unfortunate because on the three occasions 61st Division attacked the weather was against them. It rained on the Germans, too, but apart from their counter-attack troops, the defenders were static and generally in semi- or prepared positions. The attackers' restricted mobility doomed them to failure but Fifth Army believed the initiative had to be retained

---

67   Given the difficulties of getting forward through a counter-barrage, the high rate of officer casualties and the frequent complaint that men went to ground too readily when their officers were hit, this final recommendation seems particularly unhelpful.
68   TNA WO 953058: Various orders for the attack dated 23-26 Aug.1917.
69   For example, report by 2/8th Warwickshire, 4 Sep.1917. TNA WO 953057.
70   Army Doctrine Publications, *Operations*, 02A8

and the pressure maintained. The weather was beyond human control but the objectives of the attacks were not. The slightly raised site of the Battery Position on Hill 35 gave observation over the largely flooded Hanebeek Valley. To support and supply their positions close to the Winnipeg-Zonnebeke road, Germans had to descend the Gravenstafel Ridge[71] and cross the valley. If the 61st or other divisions took those enemy positions to the south of the stream they were then faced with having to cross that same quagmire in the opposite direction before next beginning the gentle ascent of the ridge. Brigadier General White saw the obvious advantage of concentrating the attacks on the western end of the ridge around Vancouver, Springfield and Winnipeg; their capture would allow a turning operation around von Tirpitz Farm and then an advance along the slightly drier and higher ground. This manoeuvre would cut off the enemy positions south of the Hanebeek. Commanders have to accept and take calculated risk but the repeated slogging against positions such as the Battery Position, Aisne, Kansas Cross and Gallipoli were instinctive rather than calculated. As a consequence, they did little to foster one of the crucial elements of fighting power – morale.

The maintenance of morale is closely allied to resilience, sustainment and the retention of an offensive spirit. Resilience is the degree to which troops and their equipment remain effective in challenging conditions and combat. Sustainment, as we have seen, involves the physical and psychological sustenance of personnel, the maintenance of their equipment and materiel, the provision of combat supplies and support services, the evacuation and treatment of wounded, and the supply of drafts. Morale is often difficult to assess but as the *Official History* pointed out, the "strain of fighting with indifferent success [during Third Ypres] had over-wrought and discouraged all ranks…Discontent was general."[72] Many personal testimonies of those who fought at Third Ypres bear out this assessment. The conditions worked against the precept that to maintain morale soldiers are provided with the best chance of success and survival, that their task is justified and necessary, and that they are valued and protected by their commanders. Because it spent a reasonably limited period in the Salient, 61st Division did not suffer especially harshly. Several war diaries write of the men's gallantry and determination and of some of its units being so eager to advance they had to be preventing from going through their own barrage.[73] Another even claimed that on the return to the rear after the 22 August attack, the filthy and exhausted men were so "excited and full of their experiences that the camp resounded with laughter well into the morning."[74] By contrast, another wrote of the "futility" of continuing the attack on 27 August and of the men "feeling themselves powerless to advance."[75] The opinion expressed by the company commander of 2/4th Oxford about the lack of drive of some men was noted earlier.

By supplying all troops with the rations and ammunition laid down in the official tables the divisional quartermaster was confident he had done all he could to equip the troops fully and thus play his part in maintaining morale. In addition to the usual three days' barrage rations, he supplied two lemons and two water bottles per man. One Tommy cooker for eight men was

---

71 In several war diaries Gravenstafel Ridge is also called Aviatik or Wurst Farm Ridge. The hamlet of Gravenstafel lies around the crossroads on which the New Zealand Memorial now stands. Aviatik and Wurst were two farms further west along the ridge.
72 J.E. Edmonds, *Military Operations France and Belgium 1917*, Vol. II (London: HMSO, 1948), p.209.
73 TNA WO 953063: Report on Operations of 22 Aug 1917.
74 TNA WO 953066: 2/1st Bucks, 22 Aug.1917.
75 TNA WO 953058: 183 Brigade report of 22 Aug.1917,

also provided but after the battle it was thought one cooker to six men and more tea and less bully beef would suit them better.[76] The men will have appreciated the attempts to supply them with the necessities, and for the hot soup on the way back from the line, but they would have expressed less gratitude for the appalling state of the camps and lack of bathing facilities in the rear. Neither would they have appreciated the staff mix ups over the supposed provision of buses to get them away from the Salient.[77] On one occasion a simple expedient proved beneficial. One battalion was treated to a concert with free beer and cigarettes; on the following days the queues at sick parades were comparatively short.[78] As far as can be ascertained, overall, morale within 61st Division was probably no better or worse than in any other division in the area.

With understandable pride and a degree of equally understandable bias, Captain Rose believed that if the division won any credit from Third Ypres, it had been earned by his own 184 Brigade. He added, "improvement in morale flowed from this great battle." Even allowing for somewhat tainted post-war reflection, that may have been the case, but as far as "success" was concerned, 61st Division had little to cheer about. On no occasion, despite sometimes several repeated attempts, did it take and hold all of its objectives. Battalions often managed to get close to and even temporarily occupy some of the objectives, but the final gains were never more than a few yards of devastated ground, the almost indistinct rubble of a former farm house, or a stinking and flooded concrete pill box. Although the terrain 2,000 yards either side of the division's front was not completely identical it bore many of the same characteristics; it was those same characteristics that caused similar failures in mid-to late August and early September to the divisions attacking in those sectors. The 1st Line 42nd (East Lancashire), the performance of which had caused some concern during its first months on the Western Front, was used only once in what was a fairly minor but failed attack before being withdrawn from the Salient. Repeated attacks by the other 1st Line formation in Maxse's XVIII Corps, 48th (South Midland) were repulsed east of St Julien before it finally managed to edge forward sufficiently to secure Triangle Farm, Springfield and Winnipeg. Despite its losses at Loos, the Somme and Arras, 15th (Scottish) Division was still considered to be a good, solid formation but it could make little progress towards Hill 35 and Gallipoli. Operating on the left of 48th Division, the K1 formation, 11th (Northern) Division, with the experience of Gallipoli, the Somme and Messines under its belt, did have rather more but still very limited success. In what were the most trying and arduous of conditions, in what were intended to be series of purely attritional battles against a well-armed, organized and supplied enemy, and in what were its first set-piece major engagements since Fromelles 13 months earlier, 61st Division did about all that could have been expected of any division.

The next 2nd Line division chronologically to play an offensive role in Third Ypres was 58th (2nd London) Division. All three of its brigades, together with several tanks, conducted their last large scale pre-battle training exercise on 21 August. The divisional conference on the Canal Bank on 30 August has already been noted and on the same night, having just relieved 48th

---

76   TNA WO 953036: A&Q, 23 Aug.1917; WO 953063: 184 Bde, Lessons which may be drawn from recent operations, Sep.1917.
77   Ibid. 15 Sep.1917.
78   Ibid. Sep.1917. Sick rates were recorded as "very good", with the highest daily number of those evacuated being 66. One battalion described its men as "in poor condition but morale is good." TNA WO 953056: 2/7th Warwickshire, 10 Sep.1917.

Division, a patrol discovered four men of the supposedly relieved Warwickshire stuck fast in a shell hole. As corps HQ had instructed each battalion in the line to conduct at least one "enterprise" during its tour, 175 Brigade was tasked quickly to take Spot Farm and the much contested former civilian cemetery close to Winnipeg. On 4 September Spot Farm was discovered to be unoccupied but the next series of raids and small attacks did not bode well. There had been much initial confusion about a proposed operation by 2/12th London before the OC of the company designated for the task finally called it off at short notice. This at least demonstrated that both the CO and the GOC brigade were prepared to back the judgement of the man on the spot who believed too much haste in preparation was condemning the operation to failure. This followed on from some other attempts that also met with considerable difficulties. For example, the Queen Victoria's assaulting party for an attack on the cemetery and Winnipeg was gassed and shelled by its own side and had its officers and NCOs killed or wounded very early on.[79] Another attempt, by 2/8th London, was detected as the platoon formed up and although it secured some "useful" intelligence on the shell hole defences, failed to take a prisoner.[80] A few days later 2/1st London attacked Winnipeg from Springfield with one company and again made no gains. The battalion did, however, later manage to repel an attack on Springfield by an estimated 200 Germans.[81]

These small scale assaults aimed largely at improving future jumping off positions or straightening the outpost line were not particularly costly but were frequently futile. The London Division had begun to alternate with 48th Division, which had suffered similar difficulties in its numerous attempts in August and early September. After the war the historian of 2/6th London recalled how the battalion learned "with astonishment" that it was to do a raid against what was known as the Blunt Salient and concluded that it was "foredoomed to failure, and should never have been attempted."[82] The writer's vehemence can be understood but these operations were executed as attempts to maintain a degree of tempo until the next major offensive was launched on 20 September. They can be identified as enabling actions. These link several tactical actions together to gain intelligence about enemy dispositions and intent, provide early warning of enemy actions in order to protect the force, and as necessary preparation for future offensive operations. The reconnaissance value of these actions does seem to have been valid. In particular, identifying pill boxes (some of which were well camouflaged in and by the mud) and occupied shell holes was undoubtedly useful. By establishing defended outposts the main positions were protected from sudden counter-attacks or raids.

The attack of 20 September, in which the division did particularly well, has been fully documented and the purpose here is merely to draw out some of the more important points of why success was achieved. The operation serves as an example of what commanders and planners today sometimes use as a rational sequence for their decision-making process: Sense; Warn; Consider; Decide; Execute.[83] Evidence from the extant planning and orders suggests that the

---

79   C. Keeson, *Queen Victoria's Rifles*, pp.332-34.
80   TNA WO 953006: 2/8th London, 10 Sep.1917.
81   TNA WO 953001: 2/1st London, 14 Sep.1917.
82   E. Godfrey, *The Cast Iron Sixth*, pp.141-42.
83   Army Doctrine Publications, *Operations*, 0605. Briefly, this involves: the ability to sense or anticipate the need for a decision; those who will depend on the decision should be warned so that they can sense their own decision-making requirements; collect and analyze intelligence to think through the

staff of 173 Brigade followed a similar scheme and may well also have used a process resembling today's Decision-Action Cycle. This is the classic OODA (Observe, Orientate, Decide, Act) Loop – a means by which a course of action is decided upon, a plan drawn up, and then put into operation.[84] Major General Fanshawe's original plan submitted on 4 September involved a two brigade attack, each with two battalions up on a two company front. This was altered to a one brigade attack on a one battalion front supported on the right flank by one battalion of another brigade. Although it is unclear whether Fanshawe devised the alternative on his own volition or whether Maxse had instructed him to think again, DHQ discussed the revised plan on 13 September.[85]

The final plan involved some differences from the norm in the artillery preparation and in the tactics employed by the infantry. Corps HQ believed the success of this quite complicated turning movement was a consequence of the infantry's "vigorous and incessant" use of the rifle to repel enemy counter-attacks, the new tactical schemes for dealing with strong points and consolidated shell holes, the so-called "draw net" programme of the artillery that did much to demoralize the enemy as well as cause him many casualties, and the use of 3 inch mortars.[86] In 173 Brigade, the four companies of 2/4th London, each of 100 men, reported that its success in working on the right flank of 174 Brigade and the left of 55th Division was because it had trained understudies for all commanders down to section level and, because it had adapted its attack formations to the ground state, sections and platoons arrived at the designated objectives as formed bodies. The successful diversion created by the Chinese attack of 2/3rd London was also credited.[87] Signalling worked with "perfect smoothness", aided by the personal initiative of a soldier from 2/4th London who moved his poorly placed visual signalling station to be a better position. The brigade's only one small hitch occurred when the platoon sent to help 55th Division secure Schuler Farm was hit by machine-gun fire and halted. The farm was taken the next day by 164 Brigade.

The main attacking force (174 Brigade) executed a leap-frogging advance on its one battalion front. Unsurprisingly, its battalions were very satisfied with the result. In its subsequent submission, 2/5th London hailed its success, despite there being "mebus in every direction," and in conditions where their physical objectives "could only be guessed at."[88] A note by 2/6th London thought the supplemented rations of additional sandwiches, chocolate, and sardines were "greatly appreciated", and a report by 2/8th London believed the formation adopted by its front

problem; make a decision which is unambiguous and not open to interpretation; confirm the degree of direction, time, and resources to be used; define a way of measuring progress, and what may come or be required next.
84   Ibid., 0602.
85   On what appears to be the only extant copy of Fanshawe's original submission, Maxse made only one annotation. He agreed with Fanshawe that Schuler Farm had to be taken by the right division before 58th Division attacked. TNA WO 952987: 4 September 1917. One of the several later very important alterations was the acceptance that because the area was a swamp there should be no attack up the Hanebeek Valley. The GOC 175 Bde had already instructed his COs to foster their troops' morale by emphasizing the thoroughness of their training and how the operation was part of a great advance. The brigade was to be told that it had been allotted the most difficult and thus the most honourable task. TNA WO 953007: 175 Bde HQ, 6 Sep.1917
86   TNA WO 95952: Appendix II
87   TNA WO 952999: 173 Bde HQ, Report on Operations 19-21 September 1917.
88   TNA WO 953005: 2/5th London, Report on Operations of 20 September 1917.

platoons whereby two sections extended to form a skirmishing line had worked very well. The forming up had been handicapped by a ditched tank straddling the duckboard track and a halted ammunition train across it further up. This had forced troops to climb over its trucks and continue along the greasy duckboard behind a slow, heavily laden group of machine gunners and their carriers. Nevertheless, little time was lost and by zero everyone was in place. The attack commenced under what was universally applauded as an artillery barrage "beyond all praise."[89] The guns were similarly praised for inflicting "sanguinary losses" on the enemy when he massed for a counter-attack.[90]

The conceptual component of fighting power is developed by learning from past experience. By the autumn of 1917, brigadiers (or their brigade major) were responsible for composing a critique of the last operation so that future operations could be better informed. GOC 174 Brigade's report on 20 September's operation made the usual points about ground lines and cables being useless compared to buried and ditched ones, how dogs needed to be "honed" for at least five days so they could become used to the sound and proximity of the barrage, and how the infantry should not be burdened with unnecessary tools. It was also thought the RE should concentrate on making shelters and clearing out pill boxes for accommodation rather than helping the infantry to consolidate shell holes. Points about the need to use the rifle and bayonet rather than the Mills bomb, and how men should be trained to keep close to the barrage were, as usual, noted. Brigadier General Higgins did, however, add a few suggestions that were not as commonplace. For example, the fact that 16 men per battalion had been specially trained to carry ammunition for the MG company was considered to have been far more successful than the usual practice of simply detailing a platoon hours before an attack. In addition he made practical points about the loss of sign boards and that flares used to signal the CPA should be wrapped in waterproof paper. But he did also draw attention to something which had been either a planning omission by the staff, or a failure on the part of the support battalion to carry out its orders. Higgins pointed out that the battalion should have had fatigue parties standing by to take forward supplies as soon as the objectives had been secured.[91]

Brigadier General Worgan of 173 Brigade[92] went a little further in his practical suggestions on improvement. He believed ammunition boxes of 500 rounds were too heavy and unmanageable for the conditions, and the 1914 pattern leather pouches still worn by many of the 2nd Line battalions were impractical and needed to be replaced. Freyberg thought poor training was still resulting in too much ammunition being wasted and considered the use of rifle grenades against strong points and shell holes to be "invaluable." He did also recognize the current anxiety that putting too much emphasis on the use of the hand grenade involved a "loss of dash." He also laid stress on one major concern which had been raised several times before by other divisions. Like many of his counterparts, Freyberg was anxious that the ways and means of infantry-artillery

---

89 TNA WO 953005: 2/6th London. Report on Operations 20-21 September 1917.
90 TNA WO 952987: 21 Sep.1917. The battalion history of 2/7th London provides a graphic account of the bombardment, describing it as "one of the most extraordinary sights of the war." Compiled, *The History of the 7th (City of London) Battalion*, p.73.
91 TNA WO 952987: Report on the Capture of the Langemarck Ridge 20-22 September, 29 Sep.1917
92 Once the wounded Brig. Gen. Freyberg was evacuated, 173 Bde came under the temporary command of Lt. Col. W. Dann. On 3 Oct.1917, Dann went back to his battalion and Brig. Gen R.B. Worgan became GOC 173 Bde. He put his name to the report outlined below.

communications had to improve. This would allow a quicker response from the gunners for them to bring back a barrage, to inform them swiftly that a barrage was no longer required, or to warn them if they were firing short. Everyone from general to private knew this had to be done. The challenge which was beyond the capability of *any* one division, was how to develop the technology required to ensure communications were reliant and robust enough to achieve it.[93]

Lieutenant General Maxse was equally pleased, describing the battle as "the most successful" fought by XVIII Corps during its five months in Flanders.[94] The deliberate limiting of objectives had struck "a great blow" at the enemy's morale by "destroying their faith in the counter-attack." There had been "careful selection" of where to place the 40 machine guns for the barrage, of where gas should be laid, and of the decision to put smoke around Wurst Farm. It was always going to be a "difficult operation" for the three battalions that had to wheel under the barrage and for the fourth which had to perform a holding action on the western slope. Nonetheless, tactical positions of importance were taken by effectively assaulting the Langemarck – Gheluvelt Line from the rear. Maxse also made points about mission command and of brigades knowing the commander's intent. The emphasis he placed on thorough preparation and training was partly to ensure that all commanders knew what their objectives and responsibilities were. To underline the point he adopted a fairly hands-off approach to the operation itself. He stressed the "responsibility for using the reserves" lay with the commander(s) of those reserves – in this case the two GOsC brigades involved – rather than corps HQ. The inference was that provided corps and DHQ were satisfied their subordinates knew what was to be achieved, neither the corps nor the divisional commanders should interfere with decisions made by the man on the ground. Although on many occasions senior commanders found it difficult to adhere to this doctrine there is nothing to suggest that in this operation either Fanshawe or Maxse over-ruled decisions made by the two brigade commanders. Brigadier Generals Freyberg and Higgins no doubt appreciated this freedom of action but, as the former himself acknowledged, "success [was] due more than anything else to the determination of the individual and the initiative of Junior Commanders."[95]

There was to be another operational pause between the Battle of the Menin Road and the next projected advance on 4 October later to be known as the Battle of Broodseinde. Major General Fanshawe's 58th Division was again to be involved in a further advance along the Gravenstafel Ridge and also to act as flank guard to another 2nd Line division, 59th (2nd North Midland). This division had spent a month in training but once it moved into the forward zone time became short. The battalions of 178 Brigade had only one day in Brandhoek to study the large model of the area to be attacked and to practise how it should be done. One officer later wrote: "The whole affair was very rushed, and there was practically no time to explain matters to the men."[96] As this was the first time the division had taken part in what DHQ called "any

---

93 TNA WO 952987: Notes and Suggestions by 173 Bde on the operations of 20 Sep.1917.
94 The other attacking division of XVIII Corps, the 1st Line 51st (Highland) operating on the left of 58th, had also made good ground. Quotations in the paragraph come from TNA WO 95952: XVIII Corps, General Remarks.
95 TNA WO 952987: Notes & Suggestions on recent operations East of St Julien, 173 Bde report, 8 Oct.1917.
96 W. Oates, *2/8th Sherwood Foresters*, p.159.

large battle", the lack of specific preparation time could have proved costly.[97] As part of V Corps, on 24 September, 59th Division relieved 55th (West Lancashire) in the area to the right of 58th Division. On *its* right, 3rd Division, which was also new to the area, relieved 9th (Scottish) Division. The North Midland Division's front ran roughly from Gallipoli Copse in the south, over Hill 37, down to Cross Cots and through Kansas House, Keir Farm and Schuler Farm. Under the command of Major General Jeudwine, the 1st Line 55th Division was held in high favour by some senior commanders. After his division had won the ground on 20-21 September, Jeudwine submitted two comprehensive reports. Perceptive as they were, however, even if either report had been seen by Major General Romer, GOC 59th Division, it would have been too late for them to have had any impact on 59th Division's tactical approach to its first major battle.[98]

The divisional artillery had gone into the line earlier in the month under orders of other divisions. It had fired in support of the attacks of 20 September and, on 25 September, fired its own trial barrages to register on the junctions with the divisions on its flanks. In response, the Germans fired area shoots that caused some casualties including the OC of one RFA brigade. Corps heavy artillery was in position to fire "crashes" on identified strong points and the rate and placement of the creeping and protective barrages was circulated to infantry brigades. The fire power supporting V Corps' two attacking divisions on a front of about 3,000 yards was impressive: 59th and 3rd Divisions' own artillery was supplemented by that of 9th and 42nd Divisions, eight army brigades of RFA and 38 siege and heavy batteries.[99] The divisional signallers had been burying additional cables and testing lines taken over from 55th Division as well as coordinating with 21 Squadron RFC to fix an aircraft message and dropping station. There appears to have been a shortage of Watson fans but "if available" two were to be allocated to each platoon.[100] MG companies had relieved their counterparts in 55th Division on 24 September and reconnaissance parties had located future battery positions once the objectives had been secured. By 21 September, all three field companies had returned from attachments elsewhere and were again under the command of the CRE. The pioneers of 9th Division, 9/Seaforth Highlanders, had been borrowed in lieu of the lack of the division's own pioneer battalion. Battalions involved in the attack spent 24 September equipping while officers attended several meetings with their COs, and the COs with their brigadiers. COs and OsC companies were instructed "as far as possible" to get in touch with their counterparts of the units on their flanks, especially during the longer pauses in the barrage. The divisional staffs had convened their own meetings to discuss administrative and service arrangements ranging from the provision of soup

---

97 TNA WO 953010: 29 Sep.1917.
98 Briefly, Jeudwine argued that the principles of the training regimes were fine, but that troops needed far more time to practise them. He thought the German defence in depth would usually mean that all three brigades would be needed to fight a battle on a two brigade front and that all commanders should be expected to act at once on their own initiative without having to wait for orders. He doubted whether the "great disintegration" of platoons and sections over broken ground was fully appreciated and pointed out that many German strong points had been taken by individuals who had become separated from their leaders. He also made suggestions as to how the barrage and artillery-infantry cooperation could be improved. TNA WO 95748: 25 Sep.1917.
99 The diarist of 2/4th Leicesters recorded: "Our barrage continued practically all the day with an intensity hitherto unprecedented." Ferocious as it undoubtedly was, it should be remembered that the battalion had so far experienced few barrages. TNA WO 953022: 26 Sep.1917.
100 TNA WO 953021: 2/5th N. Staffordshire, 21 Sep.1917

kitchens and sanitation, to replacement clothing and policing issues. All appeared to be in place for what might today be termed *almost* to have been a 'hasty attack.' These aim to defeat the enemy by trading mass for time in order to seize what might be a fleeting opportunity. Although arrangements were ready and this was to be a partly coordinated attack with adjoining divisions and corps, there was no opportunity to exploit a fleeting opportunity because none existed. Fifth Army was in reality only maintaining a limited degree of offensive action while Second Army was preparing a much larger blow. This larger affair, the Battle of Broodseinde, would today be classified as a 'deliberate attack.'[101]

In accordance with one of the fundamental Principles of War, the infantry's plan was kept simple. There was little chance of securing any real surprise but 59th Division was to be protected by 175 Brigade of 58th Division on its left and by the advance of 8 Brigade, 3rd Division on the right. Its own attack was to have 177 Brigade on the right and 178 on the left. Both brigades would have a two battalion frontage, with two companies up. To strengthen the offensive capability, each of the assaulting brigades was to have a battalion of 176 Brigade attached. The four lead battalions were to gain and consolidate the Red Line and at zero +100 minutes, the other two battalions in each brigade would leap frog and advance to the Blue Line. Once that was secured and consolidated by previously tasked parties, a few additional posts were to be attacked. The capture of Dochy Farm and the spur to the north-west was considered to be of "special importance." This meant that in total, the depth of the advance was intended to be between 600-700 yards. LTMs and sections of RE were attached to each battalion and each brigade was to have four tanks to assist; they would cross the front line at zero + 10 minutes and make for known strong points. Once the final objectives had been taken the tanks were rather optimistically ordered to patrol along the front to cover the consolidation parties. There was some delay in issuing orders regarding the precise assembly areas but they were distributed in time for all units to be in place for when the barrage opened at 0540. On one of the only two recorded reconnaissance by officers squeezed in on 25 September, the CO, adjutant and OsC companies of 2/5th Lincolnshire recorded they could not see their objectives because the land was swathed in mist. Furthermore, not all of Hill 37 was actually thought to be in British hands. Mist fell again during the night of 25-26 September and remained until well after zero.

The assaulting battalions lined up on the tapes and discs but, as one later account testified, the ground made textbook formations "impossible and the advance looked more like a football crowd than an attack in blobs."[102] In contrast the battalion working to the immediate right of the "football crowd" thought the formation was "quite satisfactory." It acknowledged that the line of skirmishers was "at times very energetic and difficult to maintain" but that the sections in file kept fairly well together and did not deploy until the objectives were reached.[103]

---

101 The object of a "deliberate attack" is to defeat the enemy with an emphasis on massing fighting power at the expense of time. The debate about the seven week delay between the success at Messines and the opening of Third Ypres, which many historians regard as a major operational error, continues. Some argue that the advantage of committing to an immediate "hasty attack" at Ypres while the Germans were still recovering from Messines, out-weighed the disadvantages of waiting and conducting the later "deliberate attack". The delay gave the Allies, but also the Germans, time to reorganize and mass force.
102 W. Hall, *The Green Triangle*, p.109. The tapes and discs were removed once the troops arrived to avoid them being seen by observing Germans.
103 TNA WO 953023: 2/5th Lincolnshire, hand-written report, 3 Oct.1917

Initially, the attack went well. Covered by a barrage that advanced at a slow rate and gave sufficient time for companies to reorganize, consolidate, and for other battalions to pass through, considerable progress was made. "Resistance", according to one report, "was easily overcome."[104] Intelligence began to filter back to DHQ at about 0720 and reported that when the barrage paused on enemy strong points, sections had worked around and then rushed them once the shelling moved on. Some blockhouses were reported to have been "knocked to pieces", with one on 2/5th Lincolnshire's front described as "non-existent."[105] Everything went according to schedule. When the Blue Line was taken, and a report received that 58th Division had taken its first objectives, Major General Romer ordered his companies to continue on to the division's final objectives of Otto Farm and Riverside.[106] These were reached and taken but when the protective barrage began to fall short, Riverside was evacuated and things began to go wrong.

What precisely happened is unclear because all diarists were understandably reluctant to admit that it was troops of their own battalion that first began to withdraw. The process by which Otto Farm was to be captured had earlier caused disagreement between GOC 178 Brigade and Lieutenant Colonel Gadd, CO of 2/5th Sherwood Foresters. The GOC had told Gadd to use only two platoons whereas Gadd, who reluctantly had to fall in with his GOC's wishes, believed it would take two companies. The day before the attack, Gadd had sent his adjutant to 2/5th Lincolnshire, which was tasked to be on the Sherwood's right flank, to discuss how the position should be secured. The CO of 2/5th Lincolnshire did not think his own forces were sufficiently strong to offer significant support to any Foresters' garrison in Otto Farm and the matter was sent up to their respective brigadiers. They, according to Gadd, devised a coordinated scheme to ensure the Foresters' right flank was protected. As intended, 2/5th Sherwood passed through 2/6th Sherwood when the latter had reached its second objective and moved on to take the Enclosure and Otto Farm.[107] B Company took the Enclosure but owing to the dust, smoke, mist, and enemy fire, the two designated platoons of C Company tasked to take Otto Farm were so weak that the OC Company collected as many of his company, no matter from which platoon, he could find and took the farm. The garrison, which amounted to only 15 men, then made touch with 2/5th Lincolnshire on their right but when the Germans opened fire on the Lincolns' line, that battalion withdrew 500 yards. What was left of C Company of 2/5th Sherwood formed a defensive flank and awaited events. When the OC went again to the Lincolns to ask why they had withdrawn, the Lincolns' officer said that Otto Farm was beyond his objectives and he did not want to extend his line that far forward. A small counter-attack against Otto was repulsed in the afternoon but at about 1700, British troops on both flanks began to withdraw. With the enemy threatening its right rear, the farm was evacuated. The garrison withdrew about 100 yards and formed a defensive flank facing roughly east

---

104 TNA WO 953010: 26 Sep.1917.
105 TNA WO 95748: 26 Sep.1917; WO 953023: 2/5th Lincolnshire. The diary also dryly noted that captured blockhouses "came in for more than usual attention and seem to be places to avoid." Opinion was divided as to whether blockhouses could be more of a hindrance than a help to their new occupiers.
106 Orders for 178 Bde included: "Otto Farm will be captured and held at all costs." TNA WO 953024: Order No.52, 23 Sep.1917.
107 Otto Farm was to have been smothered by a box barrage of gas and HE from the outset. The intention was that its garrison would be "utterly fed up by the time C Company got there." W. Hall, *The Green Triangle*, p.105.

Although impossible to prove emphatically, it might have been this withdrawal from Otto Farm which precipitated the more general one along the corps' front. About the same time as Otto was evacuated, German infantry were seen advancing towards Riverside. A counter-attack by these troops drove 58th Division from Aviatik, and Vale and Dear houses. On the left of the division's front, 2/7th Sherwood signalled there was no enemy approaching its positions but reported that for "some unknown reason... our troops on the extreme right and left" were retiring. The difficulty comes with the interpretation of "our" and "extreme". On the right, 8 Brigade of 3rd Division had not made good ground and did withdraw some distance; on the left, 58th Division had certainly retired. If "our" and "extreme" refers to the adjoining divisions, then 59th Division might appear blameless. But, if they refer to more immediate troops and their positions, 59th Division, although specifically which of its battalions remains unclear, did undoubtedly become involved in the withdrawal. On the division's own "extreme right", 2/4th Leicestershire recorded that "owing to a misunderstanding" some troops in the brigade sector did withdraw. This, the diarist acknowledged, lead to a "more or less general retirement along the whole front" but one that, he noted, involved "very few men" of the battalion.[108] In its report, 2/5th Lincolnshire claimed a "few men of an unknown regiment" and 8 Brigade did withdraw and that "a general retirement seemed imminent." It insisted its own front posts had not been affected but that the cause had not been "discovered."[109] The diarist of 2/8th Sherwood noted it was the "battalion on our right" (the very same 2/5th Lincolnshire) that withdrew and insisted "our men did not give at all."[110] At 1850, DHQ recorded that some advanced posts of 177 Brigade had given way but that the counter-attack "does not seem as serious as first thought."[111] The two battalions of 176 Brigade in reserve to the front two brigades (2/6th North Staffordshire with 178 Brigade and 2/6th South Staffordshire with 177 Brigade) were sent forward but, 35 minutes earlier, 177 Brigade had noted some of the carrying parties of the brigade's "reserve battalion" – which is difficult to identify positively – had begun to retire.[112] In its log timed at 1850, DHQ noted that shelling of the support lines caused "portions of North and South Staffs" to withdraw from Keir Farm and Pommern Castle. This, it believed, was the result of "the loss of commanding officers and to the lack of previous experience in the troops themselves."[113] Without naming any battalions, 178 Brigade HQ also considered the retirement was "chiefly among the supporting troops."[114] One of the brigade's battalions, 2/5th Sherwood, recorded it was the enemy counter-attack and barrage on Dochy Farm on its right at about 1700 that began the "retrograde movement" but did acknowledge some of its men were also caught up in the withdrawal. Most of them, it was recorded, only withdrew about 300 yards to the supporting troops but 15 of them went back as far as Wieltje.[115] What is of more importance than identifying which particular battalion may have begun the withdrawal is the fact that the enemy counter-attack, whose troops descended the Gravenstafel Ridge in massed ranks "almost

---

108 TNA WO 953022: 2/4th Leicestershire, 26 Sep.1917.
109 TNA WO 953023: 2/5th Lincolnshire. Report, 3 Oct.1917.
110 TNA WO 953025: 2/8th Sherwood Foresters, Report, n.d.
111 TNA WO 953010: 26 Sep.1917.
112 TNA WO 953022: 177 Bde., Action East of Ypres, 26 Sep.1917.
113 TNA WO 953010: 26 Sep.1917.
114 TNA WO 953024: 178 Bde HQ, 26 Sep.1917.
115 TNA WO 953025: 2/5th Sherwood Foresters, Report on Operations, 26 Sep.1917.

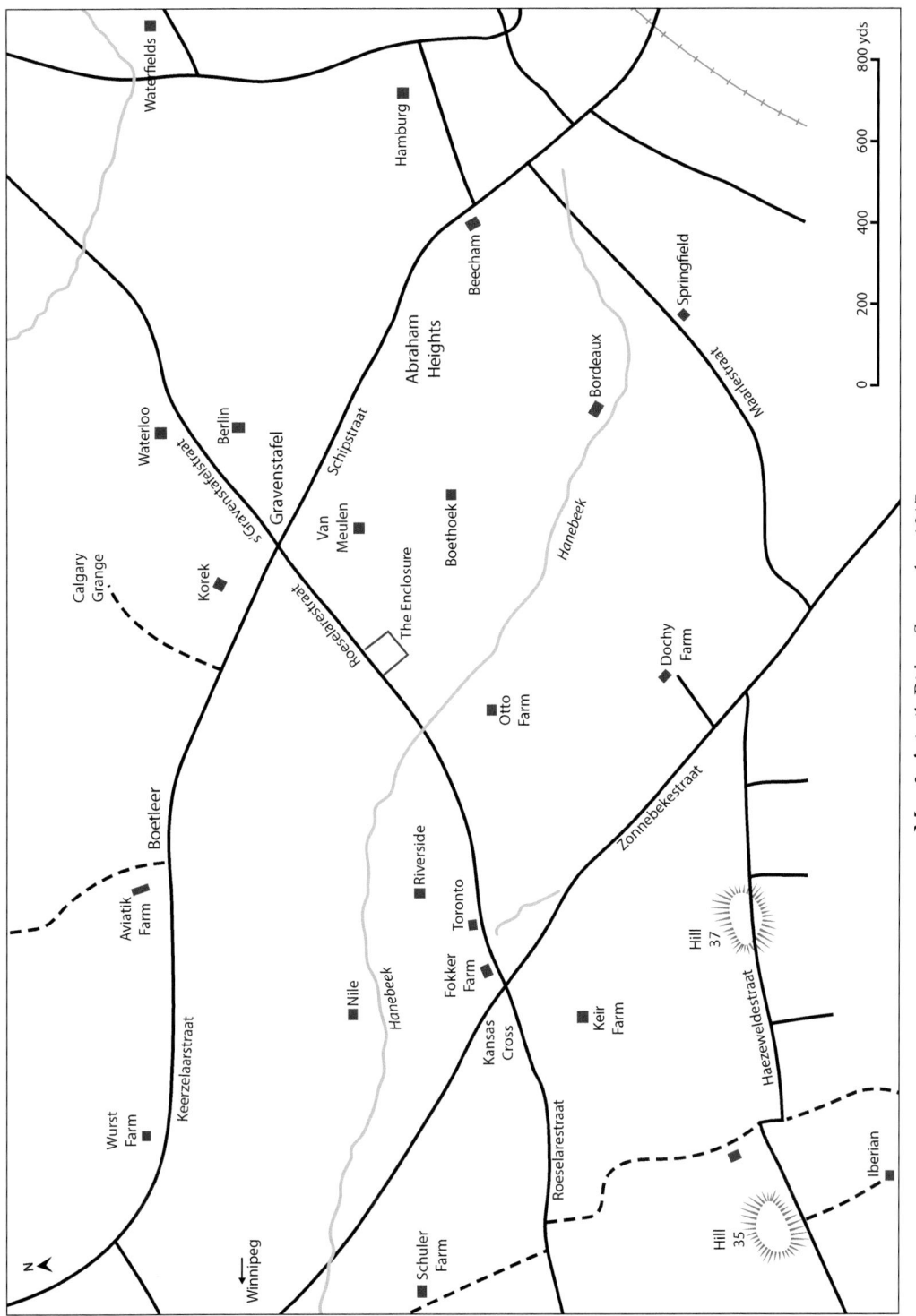

Map 3 Aviatik Ridge, September 1917.

shoulder to shoulder", was destroyed by the combined attention of the artillery and machine guns.[116] By about 2000 hours all the division's earlier gains, with the exception of Otto Farm, had been reoccupied.

The night of 26-27 September passed reasonably quietly but at dawn a heavy German bombardment opened. It continued during the day on the support line and drew the rueful comment from DHQ that "our counter-batteries were not altogether able to cope with [it]."[117]

The intensity of enemy fire drove the garrison out of Dochy Farm by mid-day but it was reoccupied later in the evening. The quality of the German barrage fired soon after the attack began on 26 September was admired by at least two of the division's officers. One thought it "a clever bit of work" in the way it followed behind the British creeping barrage as the latter rolled over the German positions. The tactic demonstrated the enemy was "careless of his own infantry" but it did inflict casualties on the advancing skirmishers and blobs.[118] By dusk of 27 September, when the shelling again intensified, 59th Division's line ran from a little south of Aviatik, down to the Hanebeek north of Riverside, across the low ground to Dochy Farm and then back to van Isackere Farm where it met with troops of 3rd Division. Artillery broke up a German counter-attack of two to three companies advancing down Hill 40 on 28 September and the forward and rear divisional positions were shelled and gassed on the night of 28-29 September. The assaulting brigades were relieved that night by 176 Brigade but as the Sherwood Foresters trudged back to Wieltje, 2/8th Sherwood discovered that owing to what was perhaps wilful but pragmatic leadership, another battalion was in occupation of its allocated area. The men collapsed and fell asleep in widely scattered groups. When the area was later drenched in gas many could not be found to be awoken. The MO treated over 100 cases the following day.[119]

Shortly before the 26 September assault, the boundary between 58th and 59th divisions was altered in order to alleviate the need for 59th Division to operate on both sides of the flooded Hanebeek. In accordance with an inter-corps decision, during the night of 27-28 September, 2/6th North Staffordshire crossed the marsh to occupy positions evacuated by the relieved 58th Division. The London Division was withdrawn after its attack which, in contrast to its assault six days earlier, had not gone entirely to plan. Two battalions of 175 Brigade, with another in support, were to drive along the Gravenstafel Ridge from the existing front line about 200 yards east of Stroppe Farm. They were to push through Aviatik, Vale and Dear Houses and as far as the ruins that had earlier constituted the hamlet of Boetleer. From there, the objectives swung south to join with 59th Division around Riverside and Nile on the Hanebeek. Although it was thus tasked to take ground, the attack was primarily to protect the left flank of 178 Brigade. The left of 175 Brigade's front, held by the attached 2/2nd London, was to remain where it was; further left, 11th (Northern) Division was to conduct a Chinese attack. This "demonstration" was designed to attract enemy fire away from the main assault and was to be made more

---

116 Compiled, *The Robin Hoods*, p.366.
117 TNA WO 953010: 27 Sep.1917.
118 W. Oates, *The 2/8th Sherwood Foresters*, p.167; Compiled, *The Robin Hoods*, p.363.
119 Oates, p.173. Enemy aircraft over the back areas added to the misery. On 29 September, 178 TMB, for example, lost 13 killed and 10 wounded from hostile bombing in Vlamertinghe. See TNA WO 953010.

convincing by smoke laid around Winchester Farm and Wallemolen.[120] Three companies of 2/12th London were to advance on the right and gain touch with 2/7th and 2/8th Sherwood Foresters; 2/9th London, with a company of 2/12th attached, would advance on the left. In support was 2/10th London. At least one officer of 2/12th had visited the battalion HQ of both Foresters' battalions on 25 September to liaise and arrange rendezvous points. Both attacking London battalions were in position in time for zero but, like the Sherwoods on their right, were handicapped by the thick mist. Messages arrived at brigade HQ within two hours indicating that Aviatik and Vale House had been taken and that 2/12th was in contact with 178 Brigade across the Hanebeek. A CPA message timed at over four hours after zero reported it had seen flares at Dear and Vale Houses, Aviatik, and Winzig. A fairly limited German counter-attack at 1045 was repulsed by the artillery but when larger numbers began to mass on the left of 2/9th London, another SOS was fired and two companies of 2/10th were sent up to bolster the line of posts. At 1540, 2/12th reported all was in hand at Aviatik but it had become clear that Boetleer had not been taken. Division ordered troops to push on towards that objective but 20 minutes later changed its mind because the large counter-attack that had helped to cause the withdrawal of some of 59th Division's troops was also affecting the right of 175 Brigade. The attack was repulsed and 58th Division had effectively protected the left of 178 Brigade. It did, however, remain short of its final objectives.

The *Times History of the War* later described 175 Brigade's battle as "one of the most bitterly contested in the Ypres Salient."[121] "Bitter" it certainly was, but if "one" infers a relatively limited number in total, the comment is something of an exaggeration. The two attacking battalions did suffer considerable losses but compared to those of the nearby battalions of 59th Division, they escaped reasonably lightly.[122] There is nothing to suggest that the failure to secure all objectives was the result of irresolution on the part of the companies. Later criticism centred on what were thought to have been several unnecessary communication errors, and a badly executed barrage which had spread confusion. The Queen Victoria's of 2/9th London had been instructed to establish a relay signalling station at Cluster Houses. For some reason this was not done. This caused delays in passing messages on to brigade HQ. On the morning following the attack, a brigade staff officer discovered two signallers of 2/12th manning what should have been 2/9th's station. Their lamp, however, was aligned at "a point in the sky" rather than towards their battalion HQ. Lamps at two other relay stations were also later found to be poorly aligned.[123] These errors meant that during the attack the only visual contact available between brigade HQ and the two forward battalions was by a FOO's lamp at battalion HQ of 2/9th aligned towards Cheddar Villa. Furthermore, although the HQ of both battalions were in very close proximity, the brigade signalling officer discovered there was no signals cooperation between the two. "Initiative", he thought, "seemed to be lacking very much."[124] There is little excuse for

---

120 "Demonstrations", as opposed to "feints", are intended to distract the enemy without seeking contact. Both of these types of "offensive action" can contribute to "fixing" the adversary and are meant to have a psychological as well as a physical impact.
121 Quoted in C. Keeson, *Queen Victoria's Rifles*, p.351.
122 The operation cost 2/9th London about 70 dead. With roughly 20 dead, 2/12th was not as heavily affected.
123 TNA WO 952987: 175 Bde HQ, 'Notes on Signalling Communication, 25-28 Sep.1917', 5 Oct.1917.
124 Ibid.

the failure of 2/9th's to carry out the order and for two battalions in the same brigade not to have coordinated their signal traffic. The high casualty rate among officers of 215 MG Company was blamed partly on the signalling failures, as well as the volume of smoke and dust.[125] There was further criticism about the poor performance of power buzzers, the unreliability of pigeons, and the under usage of dogs.[126] The battalions were not, however, blamed for not using the available rockets. They had only been issued a mere two days before and there had been "no time to experiment or learn how to use them properly."[127]

At the conclusion of the operation there was general satisfaction with the way the troops had been briefed. Good quality maps and photos had been supplied by XVIII Corps. Other factors that were also thought to have worked well were the replacement of the greatcoat by leather jerkins, the (now usual) issue of two water bottles, the detailing of one man per platoon to strip the dead of ammunition, and the appearance of a CPA hours earlier than scheduled. What did cause some anxiety, however, was with the way the tapes had been laid and the usual complaint that there was no adequate way of stopping the barrage. One report notes that the jumping off tapes were supposed to have been laid by the RE but owing to snipers and other difficulties they appear to have been placed instead by junior officers and NCOs of the attacking battalions. This was "particularly unfortunate" as it was one of the reasons given for a later loss of direction by 2/9th London.[128] The complaint about there being no light signal to instruct a cessation of the barrage was an oft-repeated expression of frustration. The lack of any universally adopted signal caused unnecessary wear and tear on the guns, wasted ammunition, and frequently led to confusion on the part of the infantry. The creeping barrage's rate was thought to have been suitable for the ground conditions but what was described as "a mistake" by Brigadier General Jackson was the decision to have the protective barrage fired at the start of the operation. This gave away the position of the assault's left flank and was mistaken by some of 2/9th London for the creeping barrage. They consequently veered off direction and offered German machine-gunners in Winchester and Albatross Farm the tempting target of their flank. The creeping barrage, it was suggested, should have been prolonged and sent across to the north of the Stroombeke in conjunction with 11th Division's demonstration.[129] This would have kept the Germans guessing a little longer as to the true direction and objective of the operation.

Maintaining direction, as so often proved to be the case over such featureless ground, also caused problems. In the heavy mist 2/9th London suffered "a serious" loss of direction when going for Aviatik. There was divided opinion about why compasses did not always behave in the attack: some blamed the proximity of iron in the air and the ground; some the metal of the user's

---

125   TNA WO 952987: 175 Bde, 'Report on Operations on Aviatik Ridge, 26 Sep.1917', 2 Oct.1917. During the day, 215 MG Coy had one officer and four ORs killed and three officers and nine ORs wounded. The high numbers was thought to be because the Vickers were sent forward before it was ascertained whether the infantry actually occupied the guns' intended positions.
126   TNA WO 952987: 'Notes on Signals Communication, 25-28 Sep.1917', 5 Oct.1917. There was widespread concern about the real value of messenger dogs. C .Keeson, *Queen Victoria's Rifles*, p.351 recalled, "Our dogs simply ran around in circles and failed to start."
127   TNA WO 953007: 175 Bde's answers to a series of questions. Dated 13 Oct., but referring to the attack of 26 Sep.
128   TNA WO 952987: DHQ containing 175 Bde's 'Report on Operations on Aviatik Ridge, 26 Sep.1917', 2 Oct.1917.
129   Ibid.

steel helmet; others the junior officers for first not allowing their compasses to settle. On 26 September, those platoon officers who did wait until the compass stopped spinning discovered they had lost their platoons in the mist.[130] A serious and totally understandable consequence of the issue became apparent when the brigade handed over to II ANZAC on 28 September. When 176 Brigade extended its hold north of the Hanebeek on the night 27-28 September, it claimed the line was 250 yards west of where 175 Brigade had reported it to be. The brigadier questioned the officers of the two London battalions and even took them back up to the front positions. Once there it was realized they had mistaken Olive House for Dear House and Clifton House for Aviatik. This embarrassing and "serious discrepancy" was reported to corps HQ.[131]

For its part, 59th Division, which had been transferred to II ANZAC, was to remain only a short time in the line before being withdrawn. It could feel pleased with its performance in its first real battle but had suffered heavy casualties. It had made a little more progress than the nominally still regular 3rd Division on its right had achieved over similar terrain, and had fended off the counter-attacks, losing only two forward positions in the process. The pace and format of the barrage had been "very suitable" and there had been no difficulties in maintaining contact with it. Nevertheless, and as usual, formations did lose some cohesion and direction as they advanced. The inevitable result was confusion and the mixing and separation of platoons. The haste in assembling had caused some difficulties with the taping procedure, the consequence being that COs had had no time to ascertain whether the tapes were actually where they were supposed to be. One CO argued that had there been greater time to accustom themselves to the terrain and area, it would have been possible and useful to have plotted the fall of the enemy's counter-barrage. Communications presented their predictable problems, with all lines destroyed and the pigeons unreliable. The need for a sizeable pool of good runners, with relay posts at no more than 100 yards, was advocated by at least one CO.[132]

The tactics employed in the advance had thus generally worked well. Several battalions later reported they had suffered only light casualties on the way to their objectives. It was once they had reached them, and during the consolidation period and after, that casualties mounted.[133] DHQ recorded the totals for 20-30 September as: 32 officers killed, 105 wounded and seven missing; ORs were 470, 2,194 and 438 respectively. In 178 Brigade, the four Sherwood Forester battalions lost an average of 14 officers and 331 ORs; in 177 Brigade, 2/5th Lincolnshire suffered 50 and 51 percent casualties of those officers and men who were engaged. At least two COs were wounded and evacuated and the adjutant and a number of other officers of 2/8th Foresters were sent up from the battle surplus during the evening of 26 September to replace

---

130 Interestingly, in a report of 2 Oct.1917, Brig.Gen.Jackson, GOC 175 Bde, thought the loss of direction was the consequence of helmets and shot disturbing the needle. In another report, written less than two weeks later, he thought it was the lack of training and the consequent failure of officers to give the compasses time to settle which caused the problem. He bemoaned the unavailability of the more reliable oil compasses. TNA WO 953007. Included in answers to questions posed by 58th Division DHQ dated 12 Oct.1917
131 TNA WO 952987: DHQ, '175 Bde Report on Operations on Aviatik Ridge, 26 Sep.1917' 2 Oct.1917 insert.
132 TNA WO 953023: 2/5th Lincolnshire, 3 Oct.1917 report.
133 Corps noted what must have been an unlikely report that one unidentified battalion had reached its final objective with only one casualty. TNA WO 95746: Report on Attack of 26 September 1917.

those who had been shell shocked and wounded. These high levels of losses indicate some of the dilemmas posed by the use of bite and hold tactics. Seizing only a small area of ground and then smashing the inevitable German counter-attacks with massed artillery and machine-gun fire was clearly having a dreadful effect on German manpower levels; report after report stressed how the ground was carpeted with German dead. But the cost to the Allied divisions was also severe. The area taken was so compact that once the objectives were secure there was little chance of thinning out the line. As those figures for 59th Division testify, German artillery could cause equal havoc on what was a closely defined and densely populated collection of shell holes. Attrition could work both ways.

Although still formidable, the number of available German guns and their ammunition supply was inferior to that of the British and Dominion forces in the area. British counter-battery fire and long range targeting and bombing of communication centres was having an effect on German sustainment but was not achieving the devastating results anticipated. On 4 October, for example, the Germans fired off the equivalent of 30 ammunition trains worth of shells.[134] Furthermore, they had easy targets. British rear areas and railheads were well registered by German aircraft and long range guns; British field artillery was hauled forward between battles to new firing positions that were often in full view of enemy observers. The enemy did employ counter-battery fire but tended rather to concentrate on targeting the infantry than the guns. In 59th Division, three of B/296 Brigade RFA's 18 pdrs were knocked out and three of its ammunition pits blown up on 28 September. Nevertheless, for its extended stay in the forward area, the divisional artillery lost only six officers killed and nine wounded and, respectively, 19 and 112 ORs. The enemy re-worked his defensive doctrine several times during the campaign and although losses were to a degree ameliorated, the fires brought to bear on attacking British infantry from his artillery and machine guns consistently carved great swathes through the advancing waves, worms, and blobs.

The attacks by 58th and 59th divisions of Fifth Army on 26 September were on the flank of the major effort by Second Army known later as the Battle of Polygon Wood. There was nothing particularly complicated about the tactics employed by the two 2nd Line divisions – both were broadly frontal attacks with only a limited amount of tactical manoeuvre to suppress hostile strong points. The maxim of "keep it simple" could easily be applied, as could the intent of seizing key ground. Given the high casualty rolls, particularly in 59th Division, operational superiority of fires was not achieved. German casualties were also high but there seems not to have been a great difference in the respective numbers sustained. There had been little attempt to achieve surprise along the front – the heavy and varied bombardments indicated the British would continue to attack but the Germans did not know the precise dates. What they could anticipate, however, was that when an attack came, zero was more than likely to be between 0530 and 0630.

The principle of "exploit success" was also abandoned in favour of the concept of bite and hold. There was never any intention or indeed expectation that the German defences would suffered a major collapse and allow through the British cavalry. The concept of concentration of (infantry) force on 58th Division's front – in effect about half a brigade – could hardly be applied. Haig continued to urge Gough and Plumer to be prepared to exploit any success but both knew the

---

134 N. Lloyd, *Passchendaele: A New History* (London: Penguin, 2017), p.234.

limitations imposed on each successive attack. Had the unexpected happened and the Germans around Otto Farm and Boetleer fled at the approach of 59th and 58th divisions, there was little either of them could have done to exploit that success. There were no other divisions in close support to get up and through, and the artillery would have been left behind. Even if they had secured the Gravenstafel crossroads, their forward posts would have been exposed in an awkward and potentially deadly salient.

The two 2nd Line divisions which fought in the late September battles had followed the existing doctrine. Their pre-battle orders are littered with references to the doctrinal pamphlets which laid down, for example, how communications, machine-gun companies, LTMs, infantry formations, and even the battalions' battle surplus were to be disposed or applied. The divisions had been allowed a reasonable amount of time to train in the new methods and prepare for the attacks but sufficient time for reconnaissance and to become familiar with the terrain was denied to 59th Division. The men in both divisions were reported as being in high spirits, Maxse himself having written a particularly glowing tribute about the qualities of 2/8th London and of the other London battalions as a whole.[135] Senior commanders congratulated 59th Division's troops for their fighting spirit and for their enthusiasm to want to press forward through their own barrage.[136] Yet, perhaps, all was not quite so pleasing. Questions will have been asked, but no extant answers survive, about the retirement of the North Midlanders during the German counter-attack. With the exception of its artillery and a few other units which followed a little later, 59th Division was taken out of the area and relieved the Canadians in the quieter sector around Lens. While some British divisions were returned several times to the Salient, 59th Division was not to see the area again. The London Division was pulled out for about three weeks' rest, training and recuperation, during which time Major General Fanshawe was sacked and returned to the UK. Maxse's plaudits for the individual units did not extend to the divisional GOC and at least on one occasion to some of his officers.[137] Nevertheless, despite the disappointing result of 26 September the division had generally done comparatively well. It had made rather better progress over very much the same ground as had sapped the strength of 48th Division since August. It was noted earlier that the 1st Line South Midland had slogged away against the Triangle, Mont du Hibou, Springfield and Winnipeg on several occasions and suffered badly until those positions were finally taken. The attack by 58th Division on 20 September had shown rather more finesse in execution than the more frontal and predictable attacks by 143, 144 and 145 brigades.[138] The London Division had earned its rest but was soon to return to the sloughs north-east of Ypres under a new commander.

135 J. Baynes, *Far From A Donkey: The Life of General Sir Ivor Maxse* (London: Brassey's, 1995), p.178.
136 TNA WO 953023: 2/5th Lincolnshire. Handwritten report on operations; WO 953012: A&Q, Message from Gough, 7 Oct.1917.
137 Maxse allegedly once described the division's officers as being far too kind and polite when giving orders. Rather than generating the atmosphere of a "Sunday school", he wanted them to "cultivate a vocabulary" and swear. F. Maurice, *History of the London Rifle Brigade*, p.295.
138 This is not, of course, an attempt to demean the efforts of 48th Division. Severe problems were also experienced by 58th Division when it attacked Winnipeg and its supporting pill boxes. Furthermore, 48th Division attacked in worse weather than the London Division did on 20 September. The 1st Line South Midland Division did, however, tend to adhere to the more formal and usual methods of attack. See, K.W. Mitchinson, *The 48th (South Midland) Division 1908-1919* (Solihull: Helion, 2017), Chapter VII.

6

Offensive Operations II: Third Ypres – The Latter Weeks

As 59th (2nd North Midland) Division left II ANZAC, another 2nd Line division, 66th (2nd East Lancashire) and the 1st Line 49th (West Yorkshire) came under the corps command. There is no extant source explaining why these two divisions were put into the same corps at this time and in this particular area. A sceptic might argue that it was more than a simple coincidence. Since its arrival in France in April 1915, 49th Division had earned an undeserved but lingering reputation as a TF division that had not done particularly well. It had spent 1915 holding the line in the Laventie and Ypres areas rather than taking part in any of that year's offensives. On 1 July 1916, it was thought by some to have been reluctant to act swiftly enough to support 36th (Ulster) Division in its attack on the Schwaben Redoubt. It was later officially criticized for its failure to make any impact on the enemy lines opposite Thiepval Wood on 3 September 1916. Since then it had spent its time in the Somme, Arras, La Gorgue, and Coxyde Bains sectors. Before moving to the coast in preparation for the proposed but then abandoned amphibious landing, 66th Division, as we have seen, had been active in the Givenchy and Cuinchy sectors. It was decided the two divisions were to be used in what was a predictably doomed attack across the swamps lying at the foot of the Passchendaele Ridge. It was almost as if the staffs at GHQ studied their ORBATS for two divisions that had not yet done a great deal but which were capable of providing a flank to draw fire from the Australian divisions pushing towards the ridge. The unfavoured 49th and the untried 2nd Line 66th divisions appeared to fulfil the requirements.

The Battle of Broodseinde on 4 October and subsequent days had gone remarkably well. This relative success had inspired Haig to increase the operational tempo; the usually cautious Plumer had uncharacteristically agreed. The plan was to advance with another three days of outright offensive action on 9th, 12th, and 14 October. II ANZAC was somewhat incredulously optimistic: "It was considered that the disorganization of the enemy offered a considerable chance of exploitation of success." This caused the staffs to draw up plans to "concentrate the cavalry and for the rapid entrainment of lightly equipped Brigades of Reserve Divisions should opportunity offer."[1] The short time between the subsequent proposed attacks presented the staffs with major difficulties in working out train timetables and added to the complications of 49th and 66th divisions relieving the New Zealand and Australian brigades in the trenches. On the night 5-6

---

1 TNA WO 951032: 5 Oct.1917.

October, 199 Brigade of 66th Division relieved two brigades of 3rd Australian Division; the divisional artillery moved from XV Corps and began taking positions in the forward area on 7 October. Command of the line passed to 66th Division on 6 October, the same day as 198 Brigade moved into a bivouac area near Potijze.

An additional and what seemed almost insurmountable problem was the state of the roads and tracks leading towards the front. In Poperinghe, the nodal point for transport of II ANZAC, XVIII and part of I ANZAC heading east, traffic congestion had reached alarming proportions The GOC 66th Division, Major General Lawrence, resented the order that on 29 September had meant his field companies and attached pioneer battalion worked under corps rather than divisional command.[2] This left him with only three sections of Australian engineers. Under corps control his own three field companies worked on slab roads around Wieltje and Bridge House. The usual practice for road building was for a number of sections to be allocated a given distance to construct in a given time. For example, 432 Field Company laid 100 yards in three days with 90 sappers. They completed the section of road to Spree Farm in the allocated time, while 430 Field Company completed its designated section forward from Wieltje a day early.[3] Huge numbers of infantry, especially Lancashire Fusiliers from 197 Brigade were also working on roads, tracks and at railheads. If the campaign had not already turned into a battle where logistics were likely to hold the key to success, the middle period of October was to prove it to be the case.

Furthermore, if there was a campaign fulcrum to Third Ypres, it could probably be identified as being the battles of 9 -11 October. Fortune had favoured the British attempt on 4 October because, with their forward positions packed with troops about to launch their own large scale attack just as the British barrage fell, German casualties were exceptionally high. Furthermore, the weather held for a good few hours. German High Command again adjusted its defensive doctrine in the light of the battle but in some ways the greatest danger to the German positions had passed. Winter was approaching and even if the Allies did gain the ridge there was little else they could do until at least the spring. The difficulties of bringing forward the guns and ammunition for the 9 October attacks were proving severe enough; to have to bring them up further across the flooded morass for any attack eastwards from the ridge itself would only exacerbate the problems. Nonetheless, Field Marshal Haig was adhering to the principle of selection and maintenance of the aim. There was little of strategic value to be gained by persevering with the campaign but Haig ordered its continuance because he needed to demonstrate to the Allies and to the politicians at home that it had actually achieved one of the original objectives. The idea of a breakout continued to be a chimera to most of those who appreciated the severity of the logistical, geographical, metrological, and physical problems. Nevertheless, as the plans had been laid to continue the offensive, 66th Division did what it could to organize its brigades and supporting units in as efficient a way as the conditions permitted.

The objectives of 49th and 66th Divisions included the Belle Vue Spur, a particularly well defended zone. The spur effectively guarded the western approaches to the ridge and had the swamp created by the destruction of the Ravebeek's banks lying at its foot. There were substantial numbers of concrete enemy pill boxes protected by thick belts of wire; three fresh

---

[2] The pioneers of 10/DCLI (P), had, since July, been attached from 2nd Division
[3] TNA WO 953125: CRE; 430 F .Coy; 431 F .Coy; 432 F. Coy war diaries, WO 953129 and WO 953130.

enemy divisions with additional machine guns had also just arrived in the sector. If the British attack was to be successful, the infantry would have to wade through the swamp, ascend the lower parts of the ridge, and hope the artillery had destroyed the wire and silenced sufficient of the machine guns in the shell holes and concrete to allow progress. The objectives had been explained to the senior commanders at a divisional conference on 30 September; 197 Brigade was to attack on the right and 198 on the left. Each brigade was to have a lead battalion, 3/5th Lancashire Fusiliers and 2/9th Manchester respectively. These were tasked to take the Red Line on a four company front. Two further battalions, each on a two company front, would then leapfrog the leads and pass on to the Blue Line. The barrage was to open 150 yards in front of the start line and progress 100 yards every six minutes; the protective was to fall 200 yards in front of the Blue Line. The now usual machine-gun barrage would fire on selected positions and each battalion tasked for the Blue Line was to have two machine guns and one LTM as close support. Brigadiers were warned to ensure their start lines were taped and marked as straight lines and to instruct their COs to establish their battalion HQ far enough forward to be able to control local eventualities. The divisional boundary was readjusted slightly which meant that on 6-7 October, 198 Brigade shuffled a little left to take over part of 147 Brigade's front. GOC 199 Brigade expressed his discontent that this was the third successive night 2/5th and 2/8th Manchester had been involved in moves. It was, he said "an extremely difficult operation [and the] men were beginning to suffer severely from fatigue."[4]

The assembly could not have been more chaotic. Corps HQ recorded the difficulties but it should have done more to ensure there was sufficient accommodation for the attacking brigades in the assembly positions on Frezenberg Ridge. One GOC brigade offered veiled criticism against the staff because by the time 197 and 198 arrived in the area, most of the space not occupied by batteries was taken by reserve brigades and signallers.[5] This, noted DHQ, had a "very deleterious effect throughout the operation."[6] The staff was also at fault for not having informed the brigades where the camp for battle surpluses was to be housed. Troops were consequently sent on successive wild goose chases in the search for its location.[7] Unit transport was frequently stuck waiting for shelling to lift on the road ahead or kept waiting at rendezvous point for guides who turned out to be "entirely illusory and non-existent." It had been decided troops should not go east of the ridge in daylight so the two brigades of 66th Division crowded onto the sodden ground already filled with heavy batteries. There was little or no shelter from rain that fell according to one source with "almost tropical violence."[8] With field kitchens held up in traffic jams some battalions had no hot food and, "to add to the pleasantness", the area was subjected to fairly regular "violent shell storms" from enemy counter-battery fire.[9] One unit also seems to have been lacking in elements of its equipment. It was instructed to rectify the shortages by plundering any local salvage dump.[10]

---

4 TNA WO 953141: 2/10th Manchester, 6 Oct.1917
5 TNA WO 953120: Lessons Learnt From Operations SW of Passchendaele. Report by 198 Bde, 17 Oct.1917.
6 Ibid., Report by 199 Bde, Account of the Action East of Ypres 9 October 1917, 11 Oct.1917.
7 For more alleged shortcomings on the part of staffs, see TNA WO 953137. WD 3/5th LF Oct.1917, Appendix 3.
8 TNA WO 953120: Report by 198 Brigade for Operations 10-11 October 1917, 13 Oct.1917.
9 TNA WO 953141: 2/10th Manchester; 2/9th Manchester.
10 TNA WO 953137: 3/5th LF, 8 Oct.1917.

By this stage of the campaign the question of when attacking brigades should be moved forward had been well discussed but not resolved. Divisional HQ thought 24 hours should be sufficient when broken ground was to be covered but the decision not to move east of Frezenberg in daylight complicated the matter. Depending on the distance to be traversed and the state of the ground, opinion varied between those who thought it would be better to move up during the night before the night of an attack, and those who recommended troops moving to a position close to the final assembly position only the night before. The remaining distance would then be crossed during the night of the attack itself. Although troops would not be fresh or properly rested given either of these options, DHQ argued they were preferable to moving to the jumping off line over dreadful ground against time during the night of the attack itself. Corps HQ, however, decided differently.[11]

There had been little opportunity for any reconnaissance by officers and NCOs and it was only on 8 October that units were informed zero was to be 0520 on the following day. Such was the confusion on the Frezenberg Ridge that although some taping parties are known to have left for the front during the afternoon of 8 October, it seems unlikely that all succeeded in fulfilling their task. The march up was a nightmare. Battalions were informed that Australian engineers would act as guides for the approach march. In the event, not all of these turned up. Some guides disappeared from the columns en route while others simply indicated the tape was continuous and said another guide was waiting further up. At 1745, 198 Brigade began it approach march from the 'camp', followed 15 minutes later by 197. Only one track was allocated to each brigade; on each there was intermittent shelling and returning working parties and pack animals attempting to move in the opposite direction. Men lost touch, fell unnoticed into shell holes, and simply became lost in the dark. Lieutenant Colonel Bates, CO of 3/5th Lancashire Fusiliers, the lead battalion of 197 Brigade, arrived at the end of Jack Track at 0515 virtually alone. He waited in vain for any of his own battalion or any others of the brigade to turn up. Convinced the attack had been called off he telephoned brigade HQ for confirmation. Brigade said the battalions were on their way and that he should send forward any troops that did arrive, irrespective of to which battalion they belonged. If there were no others available he was told to use 2/7th Manchester, which had been holding the line in the sector. Above all, he was instructed to get in touch with 198 Brigade on the left and the Australians to the right.[12]

Initially, 198 Brigade had faired rather better. It had been well guided with the lead battalion, 2/9th Manchester in position by 0320; its support battalion, 2/4th East Lancashire, was there by 0510. Only two platoons of 2/5th East Lancashire had arrived by zero and there was no sign of 2/10th Manchester. The CO of 2/4th East Lancashire used his initiative and deployed his own battalion across the entire brigade front in support of 2/9th Manchester. It advanced at 0520, followed intermittently by increasingly exhausted dribs and drabs of the rest of the brigade. About half way to the Red Line they ran into difficulties when crossing old German trenches

---

11 In 49th Division, 148 Bde also believed the assaulting troops should have moved up to the assembly lines 24 hours earlier than they did. TNA WO 952768: 13 Oct.1917
12 One battalion of 199 Bde, 2/7th Manchester, went forward and cleared part of what later became Tyne Cot Cemetery. Its battalion HQ at Beecham had been destroyed by a direct hit on 6 October. At the time, the CO was at a brigade conference but in his absence and with the adjutant incapacitated, the signals officer, a lieutenant, organized the defence against a subsequent German infantry attack and called up support from 2/5th Manchester.

and the marsh, and quickly began to lose the barrage. Machine guns and snipers from the rear edge of Augustus Wood, Crest Farm and Laamkeek hit them from the left where 49th Division had failed to get forward any real distance. The brigade went to ground 2-300 yards behind the Red Line's protective barrage and waited for its next lift. Some East Lancashires tried to push forward when the pause was over but were again halted by machine gun and rifle fire. To their right, 197 did have men of 198 Brigade become attached but there was no real contact with the latter brigade as a cohesive unit. Lieutenant Colonel Bates was instructed to push all available troops forward to the final objective in the afternoon and although successful for a time, with no sign of 198 Brigade, 197 fell back to the Red Line. What Bates described as "a stream" of men on his left withdrew even further but he and the adjutant stopped the flow within their immediate area. Despite using "extreme measures", however, Lieutenant Colonel Hobbins of 2/7th Lancashire Fusiliers failed to halt a similar movement in his sector of the front.[13] Manchester battalions of 199 Brigade in support were also suffering badly and, as evidence of equal confusion and halting progress on the other side of the divisional boundary, two companies of 1/5th KOYLI had become lost and attached themselves to 2/8th Manchester. Most of 2/8th Manchesters' runners had become casualties when their shelter was demolished by a direct hit and for much of the morning the battalion had been herding stragglers of 197 Brigade forward towards their own units. Instead of moving forward as instructed during the afternoon, 2/5th Manchester, whose runners had also all become casualties, apparently opted to stay on the Heights of Abraham. On the night of 9 October, therefore, it meant a much weakened 2/8th Manchester covered a front of about 800 yards. During the night, corps and DHQ tried to find out who was where and what the line held actually was.[14] Gradually, intelligence filtered back, especially when the CPA reported next morning. It was discovered the line ran roughly from the railway crossing north-east of the cemetery, through Hillside Farm to Augustus Wood, and finally to the road crossing the Ravebeek near Waterfields. That evening, what was left of the division was relieved by 3rd Australian and made its way back through Ypres to rest. Initial casualty returns recorded total losses of killed, wounded and missing as: 121 officers and 3,225 ORs. Together with those of the other TF division, these men had fallen in the brave attempt to gain their objectives against what were impossible odds.[15]

Understandably, post-battle reports emphasized the appalling physical conditions but also drew attention to the haste with which the plan was devised, the lack of time for sufficient reconnaissance and intelligence gathering, and the inadequacy of the barrage. Although on paper the number of artillery pieces supposedly available was about average for such an operation,

---

13 In his report, GOC 197 Bde insisted the withdrawal by 2/7th LF was "not dictated by the actions of the enemy." TNA WO 953120.
14 There were later reports that patrols from two battalions of the division entered Passchendaele village but withdrew some distance to the west fairly swiftly. In its WD, 49th Division noted that about 60 men of the East Lancashire Division entered the village at 1735 hrs. TNA WO 952768.
15 Haig put something of a gloss on the operation when he noted: "66th Division took all its objectives – 49th gained all except a small piece on the left." See Sheffield & Bourne (eds.) *Douglas Haig*, p.335, diary entry 9 Oct.1917. The distribution of casualties indicates how mixed up battalions and brigades had been. What began as essentially a two brigade attack was quickly to involve all three: 197 Bde took 38 percent of total casualties, 198 Bde 37 percent, and 199 Bde 25 percent. Subsequently, 197 Bde received 40 percent of the awards. Casualties for 49th Division were initially recorded as 105 officers and 2,472 ORs. TNA WO 952768.

the number of guns that were actually brought to bear was far below that. Traffic congestion in and around Ypres and on the Frezenberg road meant that, for example, only one battery of 331 Brigade RFA was in action on 9 October. The division's other brigade, 330 Brigade RFA, succeeded in bringing up 68 percent of its field guns but was firing them from positions in full view of the enemy and at the extreme range of 18 pdrs.[16] As gun platforms continued to sink into the mud accuracy was jeopardized and fire intensity limited while they repositioned. Unlike 49th Division, which reported the barrage as being so thin the troops on the ground had not be able to discern when its lifts had actually taken place, 66th's divisional report claimed the barrage had been "good...dense and accurate." It did also believe, however, that the counter-battery work had had little effect on the German barrage and that the creeping barrage was too fast for broken ground.[17] This, it was suggested, needed longer and more frequent halts. It was also thought gas should have been more widely used to neutralize enemy battery positions. It was later claimed that no gun was forced to reduce its rate of fire owing to insufficient shells, but the reduced number of guns meant, of course, that fewer shells were required.[18] The East Lancashire's DAC used nearly 300 horses and pack animals night and day from its dumps near Frezenberg to carry up approximately forty-five thousand 18 pdr shells during its nearly three weeks in the Salient.[19] The attacking brigades do seem to have appreciated the quality of the barrage but at this stage of the campaign and for the operation's intended objectives, there were just not sufficient guns available for any attack to have a reasonable chance of success. On 9-10 October there were enough to break up the few and small scale German counter-attacks but not enough to protect the infantry on their way to the objectives or to cover them as they consolidated and conducted reliefs.

Many of the other points brought out in reports reiterate what had been said before by senior officers in many divisions involved in the battle. Everyone saw the need for duckboard tracks to be laid swiftly behind advancing troops and that existing ones should have permanent repair parties at regular intervals. There was also a wide consensus that animals and relieving troops should not use the same tracks as men going towards the lines. Signalling remained problematic, with more complaints about the under use of pigeons, the inoperability of power buzzers, the time taken to establish visual signalling stations, and the lack of ready replacements for lost or damaged lamps.[20] The inability of some forward units to signal for the SOS again came under censure, particularly if insufficient flares had been available for issue. There was general agreement about the need for two or three days' rations to be provided but the weight of men's loads could be reduced by replacing some of the larger shared tins of meat with lighter ones and by reducing the percentage of men carrying shovels. Weight could be further reduced, it was argued, if the men left behind all cleaning and shaving kit. There was also debate about how many rounds should be carried – some advocated as few as 120, others as many as 170. The value of forward Lewis guns was widely appreciated but the division had obviously been unhappy

---

16 TNA WO 953127 and TNA WO 953128: 330 and 331 Bdes RFA.
17 TNA WO 952768: 148 Bde report, 13 Oct.1917; TNA WO 953120: 198 Bde report, 13 Oct.1917.
18 TNA WO 951032: II ANZAC, 31 Oct.1917.
19 TNA WO 953128: DAC, 8-27 Oct.1917.
20 TNA WO 953130: 66th Division Signal Coy. Oct.1917. Because so many pieces of signalling equipment were damaged when men carrying them stumbled and fell, the OC Coy suggested to Second Army Signals HQ a special pack should be designed to lessen the effects of jolting.

with the way the machine-gun companies had been deployed and how their orders were issued. LTMs were thought "invaluable" to advancing troops and had to be kept as mobile as possible but they frequently arrived with too few bombs. They were thought to be at their most useful when pushed forward after consolidation to act as a supplement to the protective barrage. The great difficulty with both machine guns and LTMs, however was their need for large carrying parties to serve them.[21] The divisional report suggested pre-tasked brigade carrying parties of up to 120 men would lessen the need for men to be withdrawn at short notice from battalions.[22]

The process of issuing orders was also thought to need revision. DHQ complained that "authorities", by which it presumably meant corps staff, waited too long before despatching orders to formations. By the time DHQ had issued them to brigades, and they in turn to battalions and subsequently companies, there was usually little opportunity for reconnaissance or meaningful briefings. While Major General Lawrence and his GOC brigades fully understood the need to seize any opportunity to exploit success, they recorded that hurried and inadequate preparations "minimized the chance of success."[23] More time to prepare would also allow better selection of sites for brigade HQ. Too often the places chosen did not have relatively safe approaches, were not easy to find, and were under enemy observation. There needed to be more time and more RE and pioneers available to make captured former German pill boxes habitable and appropriate as forward HQ. Another source of grievance against the divisional staff was their apparent reluctance to decide soon enough in advance how many officers and other ranks would be withdrawn from battalions in order to man the divisional dumps and perform divisional administrative and other related duties.[24] A further constant source of irritation, again reiterated in the divisional report, was the annoyance generated in battalion and brigade HQ by the arrival of a breathless runner from higher authority with a pointless message. In the midst of battle, with shells smashing into the HQ area, there was little more frustrating than a demand for an immediate response confirming the number of surplus bayonet fobs in a unit.[25] There was nothing particularly original in the reports submitted within the division but as this was the East Lancashire Division's first real battle its senior officers clearly felt they needed to emphasize that it was not the fault of their men that the attack made only limited gains at such tremendous cost.

Several of the division's war diaries praise their men for their fortitude and courage in even attempting to deliver the attack.[26] While stressing the chaos of the assembly march, the thinness of the barrage, the conditions "which did not add to moral"(sic), and the ensuing confusion

---

21 Machine guns could fire off prodigious amounts of ammunition. For example, 48 guns were available to the division – 16 for the assaulting brigades and 32 for the barrage and supporting fire. If the SOS was signalled, all guns would rapid fire for 10 minutes and then fire 50 rounds per minute for 20 minutes. The usual procedure was to dump 10,000 rounds per gun at battery positions.
22 TNA WO 953120: Various reports within DHQ WD
23 Ibid
24 TNA WO 953120: Observations on Recent Operations, Report by 197 Bde, 15 Oct.1917 in divisional war diary.
25 For example see, G. Chapman, *A Passionate Prodigality* (London: Buchan & Enright, 1985) p.199 and E. Blunden *Undertones of War* (London: Penguin, 1984), p.48.
26 In an almost at times surreal account of the operation, the MO of 3/5th LF wrote of the "cheeriness and pluck" of the wounded and how he was also "impressed...by the number of men who had lost their false teeth." TNA WO 953137: 3/5th LF Oct.1917, Appendix 9

of which units were where, Lieutenant Colonel Bates also mentioned the draft of "apparently inexperienced men of a Labour Battalion." He argued that their arrival on the eve of the assault was one of the reasons why the attack did not gain all objectives.[27] These 339 men from 19/Lancashire Fusiliers were distributed amongst the four Lancashire Fusilier battalions in 197 Brigade. This New Army battalion had been converted to pioneers in July 1916 and then joined 49th Division the following month. Like most pioneer battalions in 1917, many of its fitter and higher medical category men were posted to infantry units and replaced by RE of a lower category. Those who had been with the pioneer battalion for a reasonable period would have spent a good proportion of their time training as conventional infantry as well as on engineering skills. Furthermore, they would have served longer in the line and under fire than many of the infantry in their division. Those fusiliers who arrived at 197 Brigade might not have spent as much time as their new comrades in training specifically in how to "rush" pill boxes, but they should not have been as naive as Bates inferred them to be. Besides, given the ground to be crossed and the intact wire and still functioning machine guns, there was little opportunity for anyone to "rush" or "pounce" on pill boxes as the doctrine prescribed.

Bates's comment about how morale was affected by the conditions is echoed elsewhere in other reports. He wrote, "If the circumstances had been normal, the Brigade would have done itself credit." This was a sentiment felt by others within both 66th and 49th Division. It believed the demoralization and disorganization caused by snipers and machine guns operating from shell holes was "greater than usual." This was, the report asserted, because there was a lack of control by junior officers and NCOs. Too many experienced section commanders, it was believed, had in the past become casualties or gone home for commissions.[28] Few diaries of 66th Division record the number of NCOs lost to commissions and, as the battalions had only been overseas for eight rather than the 32 months of 49th Division, there had been far fewer casualties. Nevertheless, the same point was thought to apply. The diarist of 197 Brigade concluded, "The men were excellent and if led by experienced officers will achieve great results."[29] The troops and their commanders were certainly inexperienced but even Field Marshal Haig was reported to have "much appreciated their fighting spirit." Major General Lawrence later remarked that he had been asked by the corps commander two nights before the attack if he thought his division would be able to do it. He is reported to have replied: "If it were humanly possible the 66th Division would do it, and they did." He added that the higher authorities appreciated the

---

27   TNA WO 953137: Report by Lt. Col. Bates, 14 Oct.1917. As his own former battalion had been considered for conversion to pioneers in 1915, Bates should have known that 19/LF was a pioneer and not a "Labour Battalion". The two units were very different things. By indicating that it was a "labour Battalion", and thus that its men were not of A1 medical category, Bates may have been seeking an additional explanation for the brigade's partial failure. It was perhaps ironic that in their first engagement as conventional infantry the newly-arrived fusiliers were fighting alongside their former (ie. 49th) division. See K.W. Mitchinson, *Pioneer Battalions in the Great War* for further discussion on the quality, training and work of pioneer battalions.
28   TNA WO 952768: 49th Division, 148 Bde Report, 13 Oct.1917. The GOC wrote that on average the brigade lost four NCOs per week for commissions. Furthermore, when it was on the coast, between 19-17 July, the brigade suffered over 2,000 casualties. Large drafts of officers and men "who didn't know each other" arrived shortly before the October assault.
29   TNA WO 953120: Summary to Reports on Recent Operations, 197 Bde HQ, 15 Oct.1917.

difficulties to be overcome so the success was "all the more remarkable and praiseworthy."[30] Lieutenant Colonel Bates summed it up succinctly: "Seldom I suppose has any attack been carried out under less favourable conditions."[31]

The next two occasions which 58th Division was employed occurred during diversionary operations or feints. On the first occasion it worked alongside another 2nd Line formation, 57th (2nd West Lancashire), which was making its debut in a major battle. In order for feints to be successful the attack needs to be conducted with sufficient vigour for the enemy to be convinced it poses a major theat. Several of the Principles of War apply: deception in order to achieve surprise; protection of your own force; the seizure of key ground; achieving fire superiority; concentrate the effects or the threat of force, and keeping it as simple as practicable. On 26 and 30 October the plans were exceptionally simple: advance to contact and draw the enemy's attention away from the main operation – ie the Canadian Corps' attack on the Passchendaele Ridge. One soldier of 2/6th London quickly realized the essence and the purpose of his attack: "It was to draw fire from the Canadians [and it] didn't matter twopence whether we reached our objective or not."[32] It is difficult to disagree with this contemporary assessment of the attacks. The objectives were inconsequential, the tactics predictable, the concentration of infantry force was, mercifully, very restricted, there was little attempt to secure what in any way could be described as sufficient force protection and, as this was a deliberate diversion, there was no attempt to deceive the enemy. The only troops it may have deceived were any of those of 58th, 63rd, 50th and 57th divisions naive enough to imagine the attack was likely to achieve anything significant. The same effects could have been achieved by a Chinese attack and a series of prolonged creeping barrages and deliberate targeted shoots by the heavy artillery. Instead the two 2nd Line divisions were among others tasked to provide men in the vain hope of diverting attention away from what would clearly be the more important assault to the south-east.

When 57th Division joined XIV Corps, the corps had just undergone a transition. At the start of October it had comprised the Guards Division, two Regular Army divisions (4th and 29th) and 17th (Northern) Division. By the middle of the month is consisted of the less august 34th, the former bantam 35th, the 1st Line 50th (Northumbrian) and the 2nd Line 57th Divisions. At a corps conference on 18 October, Lieutenant General Earl of Cavan outlined his corps' tactical policy and what he expected of its divisions in the coming weeks. He emphasized the need for discipline in the attack to prevent "over-enthusiastic moppers-up" joining up with the lead troops, and for officers and NCOs to ensure their sections assaulted the pill box actually allocated to them rather than one that just happened to be close by. He stressed how duckboards must be pushed forward on the night of the battle, optimistically insisted more use should be made of LTMs, and ordered that troops must be instructed to show themselves to CPAs. When consolidating shell holes he wanted men to be spread out and to arrange themselves in depth rather than bunching together in a few positions. This latter practice made it easier for junior commanders to assert control but resulted in higher casualties. He, like many others, believed the rifle had "come into its own again" and warned against battalions issuing bombs rather than

---

30   TNA WO 953137: 197 Bde HQ, Oct.1917.
31   TNA WO 953137: Diary of Messages sent to and from Brigade Headquarters from 8-10 October 1917.
32   E. Godfrey, *The Cast Iron Sixth*, p.256.

additional rounds to their men before an attack. The morale impact of hot food was underscored as was the practical need for troops to keep their weapons covered for as long as possible.

As with all divisions within the corps, 57th Division would have been under no misapprehension as to its purpose. The four battalions of 170 Brigade, its MG company, LTM team, 502 Field Company, and 3/2nd Field Ambulance had been undergoing repeated training schemes all based very much on the principles and format of the attack to come. On the division's arrival the corps' line was expanded from a two to a three divisional front; on 22 October, 34th and 35th divisions attacked, but met with little success. By 24 October the front was held by 35th Division on the left, 50th in the centre and 57th on the right. Orders had been received the day before that they were to attack in conjunction with First French Army and XVIII Corps. On the left, 35th Division was to establish a defensive flank rather than make a frontal attack, but 50th and 57th divisions were to advance to contact. On the West Lancashire's front, 170 Brigade was to deploy 2/5th LNL, with 173 Brigade of 58th Division on its right, 2/4th LNL in the centre and 4/5th LNL on the left. The close support battalion, 2/5th KORL, was to position itself about 200 yards in front of the former British line to provide immediate support to any of the front three battalions. There was a sensible degree of mission command as the CO of 2/5th KORL was ordered to act on his own initiative and then inform brigade HQ of what he had done.

Most of 57th Division's artillery had been in the line since 8-9 October. It had been supporting attacks of neighbouring divisions and firing its own destructive and harassing shoots ever since. The battery areas were concentrated in the swamps around the Steenbeek and on the marginally firmer ground near Langemarck. The number of guns tasked to provide the bombardment for the 26 October attack was substantial but not overly generous partly because re-supply remained supremely problematic.[33] The wagon lines were nine miles behind the batteries and to replace the daily expenditure of 2-300 rounds, shells were brought up day and night by pack animals. Decauville railways were available only to supply guns above 18 pdrs. The policy of maintaining 1,000 rounds per 18 pdr at their position thus put an immense stain on the supply system. Of necessity, the batteries were kept as close to the plank roads as possible. This severely limited the availability of possible gun positions. Wooden base platforms laid in the mud sank under the guns' weight and recoil, with the mud in "one typical case" managing to swallow five successive layers of platforms.[34] The gunners worked in the open, with little protection against rain or shells and under regular gas and HE bombardments.[35]

---

33 The assault was to be preceded by a 48 hour bombardment. Every 18 pdr gun had a daily allowance of 300 shells and every 4.5 inch one of 250 rounds. The programme for that stage of the campaign was fairly typical. It was a mixture of timed and irregular shoots on specific areas and targets and creeping barrages which swept forwards and back. Seventy-eight 18 pdrs were tasked for the creeping barrage fired from zero, with another 38 as well as twenty-eight 4.5 inch howitzers allocated to the standing barrage. One 18 pdr and one 4.5 inch battery were allotted "special tasks" and another six guns allocated to fire smoke. The corps heavy batteries were slightly more limited in number than in previous similar attacks. In a typical creeping barrage, each 18 pdr would fire up to four rounds per minute.
34 TNA WO 952968: CRA 57th Division, 31 Oct.1917.
35 When divisional artillery was in the line for extended periods gun crews were sometimes pulled out of the forward zone to rest at the wagon lines for 24-48 hours.

RE field companies were fully engaged in taping assembly lines and in continuing to make new, or improve existing roads, tramways and tracks. Given the working conditions, unsurprisingly some of the latter were considered by one particularly critical OC to have been "very roughly laid."[36] Infantry working parties carried up 900 duckboards as far as Ferdan House on the night preceding the attack but could take them no further owing to the ferocity of a German bombardment. Dumping them as close to the line as possible was in accordance with the policy of swiftly extending the tracks across captured ground following an attack. Pioneers and sappers also brought up pickets and wire to defend the anticipated gains. The ADMS and his OsC field ambulances busied themselves organizing and inspecting evacuation routes, ensuring sufficient supplies were on hand and detailing the numbers and working areas of SBs.

Despite the sound administrative and preparatory arrangements, and the very limited objectives, the attack was a disaster. Orders made it clear that the attackers were to form three distinct lines of defence on their objectives but sensibly accepted that it would be folly to try to construct any actual strong points at least for the time being. The only objectives eventually taken and held were Rubens and Memling Farms, a distance respectively of 350 and 200 yards from the start line. The reasons for the failure are not difficult to discern. Some of the assembly positions were not where they should have been, two of the three attacking battalions quickly lost the barrage, and the leading waves quickly came under fire from machine guns in shell holes far enough forward to have escaped the barrage. Fire from previously unreported pill boxes also cut swathes through the advancing sections, the idea of using LTMs to put down an intense close support barrage at zero on selected strong points had been abandoned and, in addition to the ground-based fire, the advancing troops were strafed by low-flying enemy aircraft. Officers and anyone seen pointing or appearing to give orders were swiftly sniped, insufficient moppers up remained when the survivors reached their allotted pill boxes, and the left flank was particularly exposed because 149 Brigade failed to advance any distance. Finally, several of the covering machine-gun teams were quickly neutralized[37] Casualties were so severe that the support battalion had to send up companies and platoons to fill gaps and reinforce the forward units. It suffered almost as many casualties as the attacking three.

On the division's right flank to the south, 173 Brigade of 58th Division had an equally difficult time. The divisional boundary and objectives lay from about Spider Crossroads down through Whitechapel, east of the slight knoll at Papa Farm, and past Tournant Farm to Source Farm. The junction with 63rd (Royal Naval) Division lay just south of Moray House. The brigade was to attack on a two battalion front, each with four companies up. The third battalion was to pass through, with the fourth acting as the counter-attack unit. The brigade had been conducting intensive platoon, company, battalion, and then brigade schemes for three weeks and had taken over the line from 54 Brigade, 18th Division on 25 October. This was Maxse's old division and its 53 Brigade had undertaken a successful albeit limited attack three days earlier. This assault had demonstrated sound economy of effort, an appropriate concentration of force, surprise, flexibility and security, all of which was based on sound intelligence. The brigade had used fewer troops than was normally the case for such an attack but had allowed plenty of time for

---

36 TNA WO 952973: 502 Field Coy, 25 Oct.1917
37 One gun of 170 MG Coy and most of its crew was destroyed whilst moving up to the front. A shell exploded an 18 pdr shell dump as the crew passed. The company lost another two guns during the attack. TNA WO 952979, 25-26 Oct.1917.

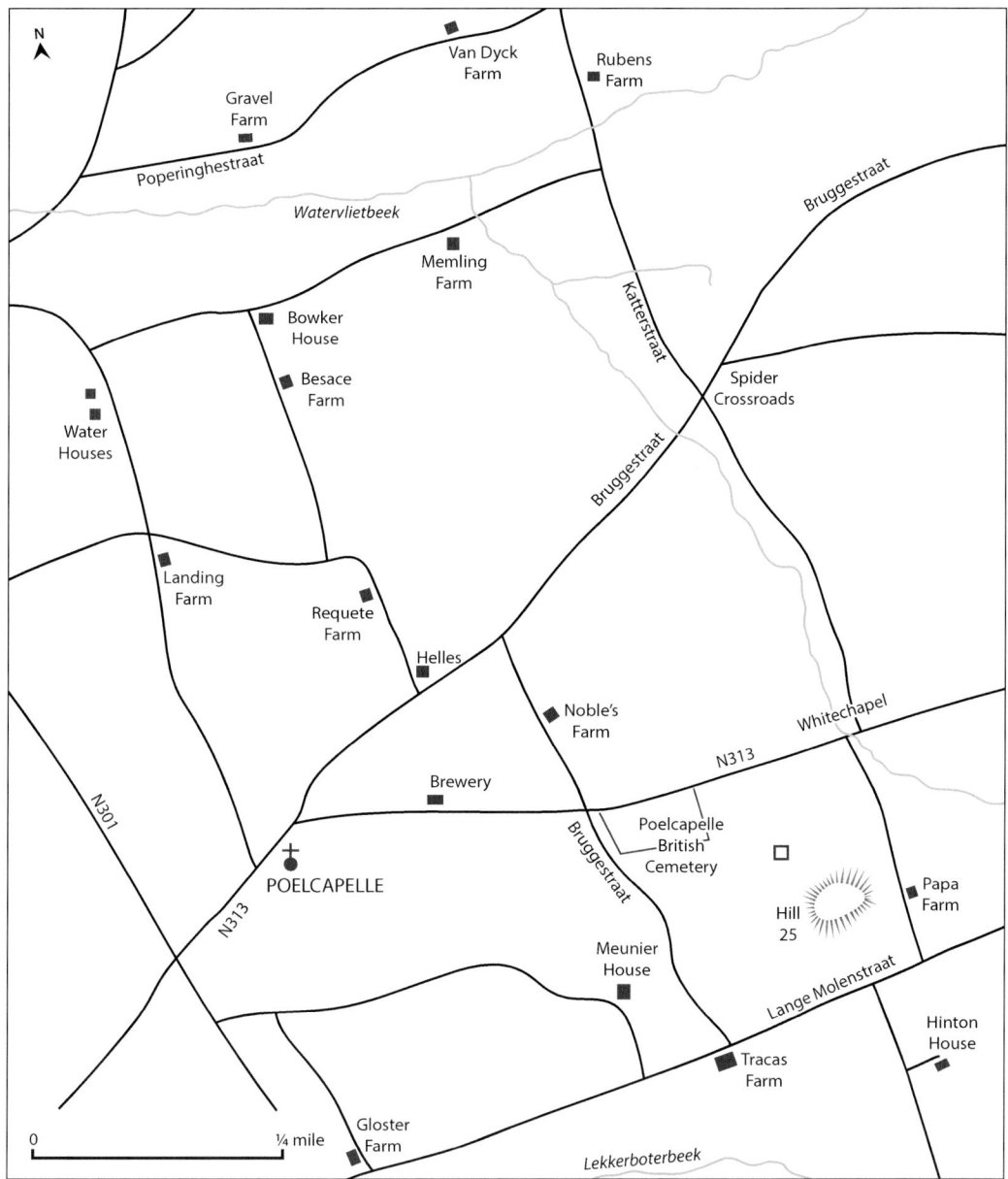

Map 4 Poelcapelle sector, October 1917.

reconnaissance, chose carefully the time when the assaulting battalions moved into the front line, checked its forming up tapes in daylight, and had worked in close cooperation with the FOOs and batteries. It was a textbook little attack but made easier because it involved pinching out a small salient in the enemy positions. As both formations were part of Maxse's XVIII Corps, it is likely 53 Brigade's planning and subsequent success was known to the staff of the London Division. The latter's attack, however, was not to be quite so straightforward.

The artillery barrage in support of the four 2nd Line City of London Fusilier battalions was slightly heavier than that enjoyed by 57th Division. The 48 hour bombardment involved moving barrages, counter-battery fire, destructive shoots on strong points and general harassing fire on the rear areas and likely assembly positions. The creeping barrage was to be fired by 16 brigades of field artillery and eight groups of heavies, a total of 421 guns. The orders described the artillery support as "being on the same lines as previous attacks", there being only a few minor tactical changes to the intensity of the protective barrage. The number of guns intended for the machine-gun barrage and for the consolidation period were not as many as that provided for 57th Division but, if requested, 63rd Division to its right was able to bring supporting fire to bear over the divisional boundary. The administrative arrangements such as ration and water dumps, RAPs, SB relay posts, stragglers' posts, the availability of drying rooms and the location of cemeteries appear to have been in place and the by now usual exhortations by company commanders to make sure their men fully surrounded enemy pill boxes, minimized movement in forward positions before zero, and had dulled their helmets with mud, delivered.

The assembly was difficult but the two forward battalions and the following third were in position well before zero at 0540. Instead of a forming up tape illuminated by luminous discs one battalion had to make do with pages torn from flimsy field message pads. The two lead battalions were, however, able to advance on time as the barrage broke. Because XVIII Corps had learned from earlier attacks that German posts were often closer to the British positions than had been thought, the corps' forward posts were withdrawn shortly before the attack. The barrage then fell on the now vacated ground and progressed hopefully to destroy any possible advanced enemy positions. Despite the number of accumulated guns the barrage was described later as "thin and too fast." Troops were delayed and disrupted by having to pull comrades from the mud and then by the German counter-barrage and machine-gun fire that was ranged to fall on what had been their own former forward posts. Some advance was, however, made. Several mebus evacuated by the enemy when threatened from the rear, were captured by 2/3rd and 2/2nd London but, at 0710, the first German counter-attack fell and forced the survivors back virtually to the start line. In the early afternoon orders were despatched instructing 2/1st and 2/7th London (which was attached to 173 Brigade as reserve) to relieve the three assaulting battalions as quickly as possible. The two battalions relieved the three fusilier units and command of the divisional front subsequently passed to 174 Brigade on 28 October.

The day 174 Brigade took over the line, its 2/6th and 2/8th London were told they were to be used to advance across the same ground as 173 Brigade's assault in another attempt to draw fire from the Canadians attacking on the right. The assault was to be made on 30 October but there was some uncertainty as to where the line taken over by the brigade actually lay. A message from 2/7th London on 28 October, for example, stated that instead of it being garrisoned by one of its own platoons, Nobles Farm was still in German hands. As this position would have enfiladed the forming up line it necessitated a late change of orders at a quickly convened divisional conference. One company of 2/6th was tasked to attack the farm and the several pill boxes to its south-east.[38] These included an artillery programme of protective and creeping barrages supported by "smothering fire" on known machine-gun positions, tracks and likely assembly points. In addition, periodic shoots were to sweep forwards and back over the enemy forward zone.[39] There was also to be a box barrage around Nobles Farm until zero+20. If the wind was blowing from a suitable direction a smoke screen was to be laid to cover the approaches to the farm. Finally, 12 machine guns under the direct control of DHQ were allocated to barrage and consolidation fire. Having originally stipulated the attack should be made in two bounds, corps HQ then delegated authority to DHQ to decide the number of phases and the formations to be adopted to reach and secure the objectives. The Post Office Rifles (2/8th London) were tasked to take and then form three lines of defence around Moray House, Minton Farm, Papa Hill, and Cameron House. The capture and retention of Papa Hill (in reality just a slight mound) was considered to be "of special importance."[40] When the attack began, the experience of so many previous attempts by a multitude of divisions of all kinds repeated itself. On the right, three battalions of 63rd Division made little progress and because 57th Division to the left did not attack, 2/8th London achieved little.[41] Nobles Farm was taken by 2/6th London but German counter-attacks and heavy machine-gun fire drove 2/8th from most of the meagre ground it had taken. When it was relieved at 2200 that night, for a cost of over 250 casualties, the survivors of 2/8th London were virtually where they had been at 0540.[42]

The attacks by the two 2nd Line divisions in October had on both 26 and 30 October achieved marginally more than by those on their flanks. Nevertheless, their success was limited and they, like the majority of divisions, contributed little of a decisive nature to the overall campaign. One diarist summarized 30 October's attempt as: "... a repetition of what has been so frequently experienced [and that 58th Division's effort near Nobles Farm] demonstrated the fact that to expect troops to attack across deep and clinging mud is to expect the impossible."[43] Divisional HQ endorsed this opinion: "Power of manoeuvre was nil ... neither FIRE NOR MOVEMENT was possible, and any prospects of success under the conditions were nil."[44] Following an attack the next day on one of the enemy-occupied mebus near Nobles Farm by a platoon of 2/5th London, DHQ announced it was "unlikely" the division would be required to undertake any more offensive operations.[45] This was swiftly confirmed by GOC corps but which added the

---

38   The orders for this task were issued at 2048hrs on 29 October, nine hours before zero. It probably took at least two hours for the orders to reach the company detailed for the job but the message did add: "The Colonel understands the OC Coy is acquainted with the situation and means of attack." Nevertheless, the time allowed to brief the platoon and section commanders and organize their respective directions of attack was very limited. TNA WO 953005: 2/6th London, hand-written message, 30 Oct.1917.
39   As an apparent concession to the conditions, the creeping barrage was timed to lift 100 yards every 12 minutes. However, this was to prove too swift.
40   TNA WO 952987: Orders issued on 28 Oct.1917.
41   It appears that although there was no formal cooperation between 57th and 58th divisions about an attack by the former, two platoons of 2/6th King's were trying to occupy Memling and Reubens Farms when 58th Division's barrage opened. The platoon attacking Ruebens Farm was "practically wiped out" by the Londoners' bombardment. See Wurtzberg, *2/6th King's Liverpool*, pp.142-43.
42   Some reports give zero as 0550.
43   TNA WO 95952: 30 Oct.1917.
44   TNA WO 952987: Report on Operations on 30 October 1917, 28 Nov.1917.
45   Ibid., Division Orders, 31 Oct.1917.

qualification that if Major General Cator believed any "local adjustments ... were desirable" they would be sanctioned.[46] The division was to stay in the same area for the next two weeks until being relieved and withdrawn to rest and reorganize.

With the exception of the advance on 20 September, 58th Division had not done well in terms of territorial gains during its stay in the Salient. Like the other 2nd Line divisions, it had probably done all it could to achieve greater success and if there were officers and men within the division who reflected on the experience they might have felt a degree of satisfaction. The staff had given considerable thought as to how the forming up process could be improved with the result that on both occasions in late October the men had been led to positions by guides who had accompanied the taping parties. Luminous discs had been used, and lamps and guards stationed at selected positions where parties were likely to take wrong turns. This organization had allowed 2/8th London to assemble "in good condition" and, apparently, in a "cheerful" frame of mind. To assist in making the assembly as easy as possible, the attacking companies also carried only 50 rounds.[47] Where it went wrong, however, was that corps HQ remained convinced that the best time to attack was dawn. The enemy had grown used to this practice and was always on particular alert. Furthermore, the men attacked half frozen and on empty stomachs; troops of 2/2nd London, for example, had not had any hot food or drink for about 19 hours. One report noted, "This fact alone takes the starch out of the strongest heart." The divisional report went on to add that it did not believe "the importance of a full stomach and [the dangers of] a daylight attack in winter are sufficiently realized" by corps' staff.[48] The war diaries do not question the resolution of the men, insisting their courage and determination were "beyond reproach." They also praised the efforts of junior officers and NCOs in using initiative.[49] Staff captains and battalion QMs did what they could to aid the men on return from the line, with 2/7th London despatching forward transport line details to carry the packs and Lewis guns of the returning companies and issue them with a tot of rum. Further back there was hot soup and lorries to take them to Siege Camp. More hot food was provided there and clean underwear laid out in each tent.[50] But, despite the sound efforts of the staff, the haste with which the attack on 26 October was organized meant that confirmation of zero, barrage tables, situation maps and flares were not available to battalions until about eight hours before the attack was scheduled to begin.[51]

The attacks had again been made more difficult by the predictable breakdown of communications. These arrangements were largely out of the control of brigade and battalion HQ who had to make the best of the atrocious conditions. Its hurried takeover of the front was condemned by

---

46 TNA WO 95952: 31 Oct.1917. On 7 Nov. a patrol of one officer and 20 men of 2/10th London captured 22 prisoners and killed an estimated 20 more in a hand-to-hand encounter in return for only two wounded. Despite it occupying equally appalling ground, 63rd Division on the immediate right was to make two more attacks before 6 Nov.
47 TNA WO 952987: *Preliminary Report* by Lt. Col A.D. Derviche-Jones; WO 953006: 2/8th London orders for 30 Oct.1917.
48 TNA WO 952987: Divisional report on 16 Oct.1917; WO 953001: 2/2nd London, 26 Oct.1917.
49 TNA WO 95952: XVIII Corps WD, 26 Oct.1917. Statements such as this are found in many battalion and brigade war diaries.
50 Compiled, *The History of the 7th (City of London) Battalion, The London Regiment* (OCA: Sun Street, 1946) p181
51 TNA WO 953001: 2/2nd London, 26 Oct.1917.

173 Brigade because it meant its signallers knew little of the existing circuits and lacked the time to test them adequately. Neither had they had the opportunity to reconnoitre fully the positions or to get the lamps correctly aligned. Only one of its power buzzers worked and there was no accommodation available for the other. "Confusion reigned" when uncharted buried cables were cut, runners were compelled to crawl with their messages, and saturated pigeons were incapable of flight. DHQ recorded, "More difficulty was experienced in maintaining communications… than I have hitherto experienced during the War."[52] On 30 October, after zero, divisional and brigade HQ received no information from the attacking battalions for over seven hours. This was not excessive in comparison to other divisions, several of which commented on the lack of Watson fans for contacting the CPA and of the awkwardness, unreliability and weight of the rocket apparatus.[53] One brigade (174) also complained of the cumbersome nature of the Lucas system and recommended the use instead of the Bleriot light as being more suited to the conditions. All of the brigade's Orilux and Lucas lamp bearers and all of its pigeoneers had become casualties. Only five company signallers remained active at the close of the operation.[54]

The Post Office Rifles' post-battle report noted the impossibility of using stretcher bearer parties in the quagmire and thought the use of corrugated sheets dragged by ropes or some sort of mud sledge would be more practical for evacuating the wounded.[55] A report by 2/2nd London was more forthright and complained that there should have been a large relay post of RAMC bearers close to the assembly positions. Once the battalion bearers had become casualties, it stated, the lack of nearby RAMC personnel resulted in there being a "practically negligible" number of evacuations.[56] Everyone knew how difficult it was for stretcher parties to get the wounded away but the lack of what was perceived to be an adequate number of RAMC bearers was considered to be an inexcusable omission and one likely to affect troop morale and resolution.

Lieutenant Colonel Richardson also commented on the proclivity of the heavy batteries consistently to fire short and of how the creeping barrage was so "poor" that only with "the greatest difficulty" could officers identify the lifts. The shrapnel barrage was described as "hardly discernible" and DHQ's report suggested troops would not have been able to keep up with the creeper even if it had progressed at the unheard of rate of 100 yards in 30 minutes.[57] Corps HQ recorded that because it was "impossible" to keep up with the barrage the men did not even attempt to do so. Instead, "Their efforts were mainly employed in endeavouring to extract each other out of the mud."[58] The artillery was also criticised for keeping the protective barrage stationary for too long; the infantry preferred it to search repeatedly backwards and forwards across its beaten zone. During its long pauses, and because it lacked the intended intensity, enemy scouts were able to shepherd up counter-attack troops in small columns and wait for

---

52   TNA WO 952987: Report on Operations on 30 October 1917.
53   Message rockets were supposed to be fired from battalion HQ in the direction of Pheasant Farm. There, two men were detailed to dig them from the mud. Their range when fired from an angle iron of 45 degrees was about 2,250 yards.
54   TNA. WO 953003: 174 Bde HQ, 2/8th London report.
55   TNA. WO 952993: ADMS. Col. J. Houghton advised there were 10 mud sledges available for casualty evacuations at the tramway terminus. Oct.1917.
56   TNA WO 953001: 2/2nd London, 31 Oct.1917.
57   Ibid; TNA WO 952987: Report on Operations on 30 October 1917.
58   TNA. WO 95952: XVIII Corps, 30 Oct.1917.

the opportunity to pass through the barrage. German counter-attack tactics largely involved first bringing up a line of skirmishers under an "exceptionally vigorous and effective" machine-gun barrage before next passing the main body of troops through the skirmishing line. The British infantry thought this an effective method, made easier by the faults inherent within their own artillery barrages.[59] Snipers were also able to filter through the barrage and pick off the advancing troops as they struggled through the mire. To add to the misery of the attackers, the German barrage was fired to follow a little behind the British creeper and thus on the areas where the advancing platoons were struggling to make progress.

In common with most formations and units, 58th Division HQ thought another reason why its battalions failed to achieve their objectives was because the attack on one or other, or often both flanks, had failed to keep abreast. The West Lancashire Division was blamed for allowing 58th Division's left flank on Spider Crossroads to become exposed. This had allowed the enemy to drive round behind the foremost advance of the London Division, cut off the forward posts and roll up its attack along its northern portion. As this counter-attack was being pressed home, a large number of Germans debouched from the sunken lane running between Whitechapel and Papa Farm with the intent of retaking Meunier Farm. Only the timely arrival of elements of 2/4th London and 206 MG Company, as well as the fact that the Germans were now as equally exhausted as the London battalions, prevented a further withdrawal to the west.[60] While there is truth in the assertion that the right of 57th Division did not get up, the left of 58th Division did not do a great deal better.

The primary reason for the failure of these last attacks by the 2nd Line divisions was, of course, undoubtedly the mud. Its ubiquitous presence impacted on both the operational and tactical conduct of the campaign. It affected the artillery's fire density, clogged individual weapons, prevented efficient communications, and disrupted sustainment. It also demanded huge amounts of labour to curtail its most pernicious effects. About 1,000 men of 58th Division were permanently struck off fighting strength "to compete with the mud," Again, like so many other divisions, DHQ advocated the formation of more labour battalions to ease the work burden of the infantry. The mud caused senior officers to recommend that tactical objectives should be limited to 200-400 yards from the start line and believed it was imperative men should advance in extended order rather than in blobs or small columns. There was also, again, the sensible call to limit the amount of kit to be carried by the leading troops.[61] Yet, no matter how realistic the designated objectives, how thorough the training, how well nurtured unit will and cohesion, and how comprehensive the materiel of the physical component, the mud and the resilience and adaptability of a determined enemy condemned the campaign to failure. Furthermore, the campaign as a whole also failed ever to achieve certain pre-requisites that would today be considered essential to ultimate success in offensive operations.

Almost from the start of the campaign there was a fundamental imbalance between the ends to be secured and the ways and means of achieving them. The desired strategic end state of the capture of the Channel ports and the collapse of the German field army was too ambitious for the means provided by the physical component and for the existing state of the conceptual

---

59   TNA WO 952987: 173 Bde, Operations Report 25-27 October 1917.
60   TNA WO 952987: Report on Operations on 26 October 1917.
61   TNA WO 952987: 173 Bde Operational Report On 25-27 October 1917; DHQ Report on 26 October 1917.

component. It was pointed out earlier that the main characteristics of offensive action are surprise, shock, seizing and retaining the initiative, agility, superior tempo, and keeping the enemy off balance. All these elements can be identified within the Allied campaign but, with hindsight, within two days of the start of the battle it became apparent that Haig's grandiose scheme of a break in, break through and break out was unlikely to be achieved. Moreover, although the subsequent bite and hold attritional operations did make territorial progress, they were ill-suited to the terrain and the enemy's possession of the higher ground. When the battle became bogged down, the Allies could never concentrate sufficient fires or forces to overwhelm the defenders and allow a significant advance across the ineluctable morass.

Strategic and operational success also necessitates the destruction or neutralization of the enemy's centre of gravity. In the Great War, Germany's centre of gravity was the German Army. Only when that was smashed was there a possibility of victory. The decisive conditions required to achieve this objective were not yet in 1917 attainable. German manpower proved to be adequate to maintain their front (and even to dispatch divisions to support the Austrians at Caporetto) and the integrity of their lines of communication and industrial capacity were sufficient to ensure their sustainment. Allied troops were never able to establish effective battlefield mobility nor adequately suppress enemy firepower. Although Plumer introduced a greater degree of pragmatism and realism to the campaign Allied operational planning offered few alternatives to repeated frontal assaults. Their purpose was to effect deep and multiple penetrations but any dreams of developing such actions into envelopment, double envelopment, or encirclement, remained illusory. The successful turning movement by 58th Division on 20 September was a rare exception. Tactical improvements and the emphasis placed on logistics and formation *roulement* did allow greater territorial gains but enemy observation made surprise difficult to achieve and the conditions prevented any substantial tactical or operational flexibility. Corps commanders did allow divisional GOsC a degree of autonomy in respect to artillery and machine-gun barrages and the size of the formations or units to be employed in attacks. Yet, the prevailing conditions and poor communications with forward units meant that even if operational branches and sequels had been built into the planning they generally remained impossible to implement with sufficient speed.[62]

By the time of the possible campaign fulcrum, two of the five 2nd Line divisions engaged in Third Ypres had yet to become involved. Excluding the Dominion divisions, the BEF had 52 divisions on the Western Front available for the campaign. Of those, 41 were used in specified battles, three were involved in engagements that were not officially 'actions' within Third Ypres, and eight were not used within the later determined official dates of the battle. One of those was the 2nd Line 62nd Division. This meant that 83 percent of available 2nd Line divisions were actively utilized in the campaign.[63] Of the 41 divisions deployed, a total of 58 percent (24 divisions) were used in either one or two of the battles within the campaign; only 10 percent (four

---

62   Branches and sequels are contingency provisions built into lines of operation in anticipation of unexpected opportunities or reverses.
63   The percentages of the different types of divisions used in specified battles to those which were ultimately available were: Regular 80 percent; New Army 81 percent; 1st Line 66 percent. The figures are calculated from E.A. James, *A Record of the Battles and Engagements of the British Armies in France and Flanders, 1914-1918,* (Aldershot: Gale & Polden, 1924).

divisions) were used either five or six times. Of the five 2nd Line divisions, one, 58th Division, was used three times and the other four either once or twice.

These figures offer no real guide to the discussion of whether 2nd Line divisions were considered to be of lesser value than other formations. If they were thought to be have been of a lower quality it might be expected they would have been used more often because they were perhaps considered expendable. The fact that 58 percent of all types, but that 80 percent of the available 2nd Line divisions was used once or twice might suggest this was the case. The figures are, however, far from conclusive. When considering its overall war time reputation, the inclusion of 58th Division in the same group as those possibly elite formations which at Ypres were also used on three occasions, hardly suggests it should be regarded as a full-fledged member of that band.[64] Neither is it possible to determine the 2nd Line's worth by comparing ground gained during attacks. Few divisions captured any significant amount of ground after 31 July and those working on the flanks of the 2nd Line formations during their attacks generally did no better and no worse than the 2nd Line ones themselves: 3rd, 9th, 50th, 63rd, 48th, 42nd, and 49th divisions struggled as badly as the 2nd Line formations alongside them.

The insufficiently developed conceptual component and the inadequate physical component of the 2nd Line's fighting power were mirrored across all divisions serving in the Salient. What is more difficult to determine is whether the moral component was also lacking across the BEF. If the fostering of morale, will, and cohesion of units is neglected, no amount of resources will compensate. Without a sense of being valued, men will generally not fight with as much commitment. The year 1917 was a poor one for the Allies, with the post-Nivelle French mutinies and the disturbances at the Etaples Base Camp in September exacerbating the existing strategic and operational difficulties. The 2nd Line divisions appear to have done as much as was within their power to enhance morale by the provision of baths, the regular issue of clean underwear, and by attempting to make camp and recreational facilities as comprehensive as possible. These all helped but, as always, it was the comradeship developed within platoons, companies, batteries, and battalions that proved crucial. The responsibility for this lay with the officers and with their ability to make their men feel appreciated and that the job they were doing was worthwhile. To be able to do this presupposes that the officers themselves felt valued and were thus sufficiently enthused to motivate their men. Brigadier General Borrett, GOC 197 Brigade, believed the "inexperience and want of leadership" was crucial to his brigade's failure to hold on to its gains and stressed that although the men were "excellent" they were not being "as well handled as they deserve."[65] In 57th Division, Lieutenant Colonel Hitchins, CO of 2/5th LNL, complained that many of his officers had been too long without leave, a factor that was bound to affect morale.[66] But issues such as these were not restricted only to 2nd Line divisions. Major General Barnes called a meeting of his COs in order to explain that XIX Corps had written to complain that officers attending the corps school were "showing an unsatisfactory spirit [and] did not appear to be recovering" from their recent experiences. Barnes insisted he did not think

---

64   There seems no discernible logic in the decisions made about which divisions should be most frequently used. The four most used formations were three not particularly renowned New Army divisions, and one Regular division.
65   TNA WO 952120: 197 Bde, Summary To Report on Recent Operations, 15 Oct.1917
66   TNA WO 952965: Proceedings of Divisional Conference (A), 15 Nov.1917. At the time of the letter, XIX Corps (Lt. Gen. H.E. Watts) comprised 17th, 18th, 35th, 50th, and 57th divisions.

the criticism was aimed at any of *his* divisional officers but wanted to warn his COs of "what might happen in the future." Forewarned, they would be in a position to "prevent the spirits of their officers from getting depressed."[67] Across the BEF as a whole the training of junior officers was causing as much concern to the authorities as the training received by other ranks.

Mention has been made earlier of how some divisional commanders deliberately fostered regional identity as a means of developing fighting spirit and *esprit de corps*. As with most divisions in 1917, the territorial identity of the 2nd Line formations and units continued in general to grow rather than to diminish. Before they began to suffer losses during Third Ypres, both of the 2nd Line Lancashire divisions had retained a good degree of their 'Lancashireness'. They had received large drafts of re-rolled men formerly of the RASC as well as recruits trained by the East Surrey Regiment,[68] but the Lancashire Fusilier, East Lancashire and the Manchester Brigades of 66th (2nd East Lancashire) Division, for example, also received considerable drafts of men from the King's Liverpool and other Lancashire regiments. In contrast, it is evident that even when 59th (North Midland) Division landed in France it was barely a formation composed of men from the North Midlands. An average of 33 percent of the fatalities from across its three infantry brigades in its first three months in France came from outside their battalions' traditional recruiting areas. During its five days of fighting in September, the percentage of fatalities born or resident outside the North Midlands rose to over 50 percent of the total. For both those periods of action at least a third of those fatalities originated from London. To describe the division as in all but name another 'London Division' would be an exaggeration but it is clear that if North Midlanders actually did form the majority in the division, it was a bare majority. In comparison, and despite drafts from the training battalions in 64th (2nd Highland) Division and the former members of the Huntingdon Cyclist Battalion, 58th (2/1st London) very much retained its London identity. Most of its battalions received drafts from training or reserve battalions of other London battalions or from those traditionally recruited in the Home Counties. Less than 20 percent of the division's fatalities in September and October came from beyond the Greater London area. Like its 2nd North Midland counterpart, when it arrived in France, 61st (2nd South Midland) Division was also a very much diluted division of South Midlanders. The Warwickshire Brigade landed having already received very large drafts from the Royal Sussex, Hampshire, King's Liverpool, and Welsh Regiments, as well as significant numbers of re-rolled Highland Cyclists. These influxes meant that in the two lead Warwickshire battalions at Fromelles in July 1916, 44 and 37 percent of the fatalities did not originate from Warwickshire. On their arrival in France the division's other two brigades were a little more 'local' but had received drafts from a variety of regiments geographically dispersed from Lancashire to Devon.[69] During the advance across the devastated area and its work along the Omignon in the spring of 1917, fatalities from outside their regiments' usual catchment areas across 182 and 184 brigades averaged 32 percent. In the August and September fighting around Ypres this figure soared to 67 and 70 percent in some battalions of those same brigades.

---

67 Ibid.
68 The 130 recruits from the East Surrey who arrived in mid-September were later described as "a fine body of men." Wurtzberg, *2/6th King's Liverpool,* p.133.
69 The 'outside' fatalities of the two lead battalions of both 183 and 184 brigades at Fromelles averaged 24 percent.

The 2nd Line divisions were not alone in experiencing regional dilution. With drafts arriving at divisions during the winter months from the reorganized Training Reserve it was more a case of serendipity rather than calculation as to whether replacements had any territorial link to their new battalion or division. Strengths were gradually increased but rest was not always immediate. Both 66th and 58th divisions stayed in the Ypres sector for some weeks and 57th Division returned to it in December. After a quieter few weeks with First Army, 59th Division went to the Cambrai area and, together with 61st Division, became involved in that battle's later actions. The only 2nd Line division not to have a role in Third Ypres was 62nd (2nd West Riding). The division was heavily involved in offensive operations at Cambrai and then, after a period of training, it moved to the Oppy – Gavrelle sector.

The major role played by 62nd Division on the opening two days of the Cambrai battle contributed to what was, to date, one of the BEF's most successful days of the war. The detail and course of the battle are generally well known so all that needs to be added here is to underscore how 62nd Division, working in close cooperation with tanks, broke through the Hindenburg Line and advanced a distance of about 7,000 yards. The preparation for the operation and the opening stages fulfilled many of the elements of the Principles of War and the prerequisites for successful offensive action. The operation demonstrated maintenance of the current aim of attriting German resources and manpower, security, surprise, concentration of force, a degree of flexibility, and some innovative means of cooperation. Ultimately the offensive failed, owing largely to misjudgements in planning, sustainment and high level staff work, an overly ambitious expectation of what armour might achieve, and the inability to prevent the rapid reinforcement of German front line formations. Efficient staff work, sound training, effective leadership, and good cooperation between supporting and supported arms, allowed the West Riding Division's troops to fight their way through several major physical obstacles and to secure their objectives in the first few hours of battle. The division later became embroiled in the bitter struggle for Bourlon Wood. Exhausted and depleted after its two periods of assaults, the division left the area towards the end of November. In comparative terms, the division had done well, winning the praise of corps and army commanders as well as that of Sir Douglas Haig. It had, as several soldiers were reported to have said, "Wiped out [the disappointment of] Bullecourt."[70] The other 2nd Line divisions had experienced mixed fortunes and had not had the opportunity during their offensive operations in 1917 to achieve decisive, or with the exception of 58th Division on 20 September, even significant, success. The 2nd Line West Riding Division had begun its set-piece offensive campaigning with an indifferent showing at Bullecourt. It ended the year at Havrincourt with what had been an initially spectacular example of successful offensive action.

---

70 E. Wyrall, *The Story of the 62nd (West Riding) Division 1914-1919*, p.109.

7

Defensive Operations I: Rearguards

The transition of the BEF from offensive to defensive operations during the winter of 1917-18 was brought about by several strategic and operational factors. The only really positive outcome of the year for the Allies was the knowledge that US manpower and industrial resources would become increasingly more evident as 1918 progressed. Allied forces were not in a position to threaten the enemy's centre of gravity – the German field army – and would not be until the Germans had expended a considerable proportion of their reserves and materiel in a series of spring offensives. The Allies thus found themselves forced into active defensive operations from the middle of March 1918 and were not able until July to establish the decisive points and conditions required as pre-requisites for a return to the offensive. Two 2nd Line divisions, however, were somewhat unexpectedly required to become involved in defensive operations during the later stages of the Battle of Cambrai. With the culmination of the British divisions by about the third day of the battle, the initiative and momentum was lost and the battle again became another of bloody attrition for possession of key terrain. To the surprise of many, but by no means all of the British senior commanders, the enemy seized the initiative on 30 November and launched what was at first a devastating counter-attack. The two 2nd Line divisions, 59th and 61st, were rushed to the area and fought what were largely improvised defensive engagements in a bid to halt the German counter-offensive.

Modern doctrine identifies three types of defensive action: mobile, area, and delay.[1] Mobile aims to destroy the enemy by means of fixing him to deny him freedom of manoeuvre whilst a counter-attack is prepared and resourced. Area defence, which often contains elements of mobile defence, aims to defeat an attack by denial of ground through the concentration of force and counter-mobility effects such as field obstacles. Ideally, the enemy's advance will initially be slowed by canalizing his forces and by fighting holding and blocking actions to weaken and inflict losses before he reaches the area defence. When the enemy has been baulked and exhausted by the area defence, the defender will launch a counter-attack. Delaying actions are those whereby a force trades space for time. In so doing, and as the enemy's lines of operation and communication lengthen, momentum and tempo will diminish and his forces suffer losses. The defender's object is for this point to be reached before the withdrawing force has become decisively committed. The process of withdrawal requires a high degree of coordination in the

---

1   Army Doctrine Publications, *Operations*, 0829.

command and control of the various elements of the defending force but the object is, again, to secure time to concentrate forces that will subsequently be used to counter-attack a weakening enemy.

Whether in defence or attack, and with emphasis sometimes shifting on some of the constituent elements, the Principles of War still apply. The German counter-attack near Cambrai was designed to surprise the British forces and by means of shock action, simultaneity, and considerable air and artillery cooperation, dislocate and break the cohesion and will of the already weakened British divisions. The Germans were able to concentrate significant forces for the attack but the offensive was met and eventually contained by rapidly organized defensive positions, hasty and effective cooperation at divisional, brigade, battalion and company level, flexibility in deployments, a necessarily restricted but adequate economy of effort, and improvised methods of sustainability.

The defending forces were able successfully to apply the necessary Principles of War and within a few days managed to halt the German assault. Elements of all three types of recognized defence were also apparent during this approximate six day period of intense fighting. The principal difference between the modern doctrinal concept and that which prevailed in the fields west of Cambrai in December 1917 was, however, that the former almost always uses defence as a prelude to attack.[2] In the December 1917 scenario the British commanders decided that their defensive action was to secure a defendable line on chosen ground that could be held by a minimum number of men. There was no presumption or intention that the ground yielded should be regained in the near future by counter-attack. This decision was made on purely pragmatic grounds but, in the same way as it was in partial contradiction to modern doctrine, it was also partly at variance with the doctrinal framework for defence laid out in *Field Service Regulations I.*

Naturally enough, *FSR I* emphasizes the importance of using manoeuvre to secure defensible ground; this should allow the defender to economize his own resources whilst wearing down the enemy's. [3]The occupied ground will ideally have been previously reconnoitred; air and cavalry would keep the defenders informed of the routes and speed of the approaching forces. The defending commander should try to ensure he distributes his own forces to cope with the options open to the enemy and that his troops have good fields of fire over land on which his infantry and artillery could cooperate to the maximum. He should pay special attention to his flanks and to the possibility of receiving enfiladed fire. His rearward communication should be secure and by adroit tactical decisions should try to secure and maintain his freedom of manoeuvre. When the correct balance between the opposing forces is adjudged to have been reached, the defence will attempt to regain the initiative by launching a counter-offensive with reserves husbanded or concentrated in the rear. Thus, an essential element of British doctrine was the emphasis on the need to counter-attack in order to disrupt the enemy and seize the initiative. Selecting the moment to do this is a crucial aspect of command, leadership and management. Like all divisions, the two 2nd Line formations involved in this stage of the Cambrai offensive were acting under the command of army and corps HQ; the divisional commanders' freedom of action was therefore somewhat limited. Nonetheless, they were expected to apply their forces with guile

---

2   As Third Ypres had so aptly demonstrated, launching counter-attacks whilst fighting an essentially defensive battle was a fundamental element of current German doctrine.
3   *FSR I,* (1912 edition) pp.140-46.

and efficiency in order to frustrate and wear down the enemy's will to continue his offensive. The two divisions were, however, compelled to fight different types of defensive battles. The North Midland Division fought a delaying action before withdrawing over terrain, which should have largely aided the offensive force, to prepare defensive positions; while 61st Division had to hold its ground by means of constant local counter-attacks and frequent redistribution of units.

Towards the end of November, with a warning that it would probably be used in the exploitation stage of the Cambrai operation, 59th Division (but not its artillery brigades) was ordered south from the Vimy sector.[4] Its brigades had been training in open warfare, with officers having conducted several staff rides in schemes involving the pursuit of a withdrawing enemy. The division had spent a few weeks in the area during the summer so it did have an idea of the terrain but until senior officers had conducted some reconnaissance the lines and positions following 20 November's attack were unknown. On 26 November, GOC 176 Brigade and several of his senior officers visited the forward positions of 29th Division between Marcoing and Masnières. During the following day several other officers were taken by CRE 20th Division through La Vacquerie towards Lateau Wood. The North Midland's field companies were quickly put to work and three battalions of Sherwood Foresters were placed under the command of 6th, 20th and 29th divisions. Some of this work involved digging on Highland Ridge. On 30 November two of the battalions working on the ridge and eight machines guns were attached for tactical purposes to 6th Division. On 27 November, 176 Brigade had been placed temporarily under command of the Guards Division and began relieving Guards units in the Bourlon Wood area. The line taken over was vague and consisted largely of posts scattered amongst the shattered trees and undergrowth. On 30 November, 177 Brigade assumed command of the Flesquières sector with the instructions that the village was to be organized for all round defence and to be "held at all costs." In the early afternoon, IV Corps had also ordered DHQ to reconnoitre existing gaps in the wire protecting what was now the British-occupied Hindenburg Line. Ominously, it was told to prepare notice boards and signs in case a withdrawal was ordered.

By the time DHQ received this order, it had already been warned that creating a defended flank on Highland Ridge was "of vital importance"; the two Sherwood Forester battalions on the ridge now attached to 6th Division were immediately instructed to establish the flank's defences.[5] To the north-west, Brigadier General Cope's 176 Brigade assisted in the repulse of an enemy attack that developed from Fontaine-Notre-Dame against the division on its right. It then itself came under considerable shell fire. On taking over from the Guards on 28 November, Cope had expressed concern about his position to Major General Romer. With a good degree of foresight Cope believed that because it provided such a difficult physical obstacle, any attack by the Germans would, of necessity, by-pass Bourlon Wood. Cope predicted the Germans would simply drench the wood with gas and shell and attack round its sides. Corps HQ had ordered formations to maintain as large a mobile reserve as possible so, having observed the condition of the wood and the potential channels of advance to its north and south, Cope petitioned

---

4 The division's artillery brigades waited another week before they, too, moved to the south-east. Their HQ opened at Haplincourt on 2 December and came under the command of 56th (1st London) Division.
5 Two brigades of artillery were to be moved to the south-east of Trescault to assist the Foresters in their task. For the next three days 2/5th Sherwood Foresters stood to but was rarely troubled other than by shell fire.

Romer to allow him to deploy only two companies inside the wood. Most of the rest of the brigade would then be available for conducting counter-attacks. Romer agreed to the proposal but corps HQ refused to sanction it on the grounds that as the wood was such key terrain, two battalions rather than two companies should be positioned within its confines. The two selected were 2/6th North and 2/6th South Staffordshire; their respective 2/5th Battalions formed flank guards and acted as reserves. As Cope had predicted, the wood was subjected to intense gas and shelling, with the enemy attacks largely trying to outflank and envelope the high ground. The two 2/5th Battalions repulsed several German assaults by sound application of Lewis guns and rifle fire, and by skilful positioning and use of their reserve companies. The two 2/6th Battalions inside the wood, however, unable to remove their respirators safely for about 36 hours, suffered badly from the effects of the gas. When relieved both battalions had been reduced to well under 200 rifles.

The morale, disciple and leadership of any battalion sustaining close to 400 gas casualties was likely to be a cause for concern to the authorities. There is no evidence that the bulk of the men in the two 2/6th Battalions were deliberately negligent in donning their respirators or that their gas drills had been inadequately practised. A very high proportion of the battalions' officers were also evacuated. This suggests that those affected by the gas were genuine casualties rather than those who had purposefully delayed applying their respirators.[6] But it is perhaps worth noting that when 2/4th Lincolnshire went into the wood two days later, and was also heavily gassed, it claimed to have suffered no casualties. If corps HQ had been prepared to heed the advice of the two senior commanders on the ground, casualties amongst the two 2/6th Staffordshire battalions might well have been substantially reduced.

In its sector, 176 Brigade had done well during the opening surge of the German counter-attack. It was relieved by 177 Brigade on 1-2 December.[7] The Sherwood Forester battalions of 178 Brigade remained working or attached to other divisions during the same period but, as one officer recorded later, "For many days our men lived in a constant atmosphere of strain... Move and counter-moves following each other in rapid and bewildering succession."[8] On 30 November, 2/6th Sherwood Foresters' attachment to 6th Division was switched to attachment to 20th Division. Initially the battalion remained in reserve to the north-east of La Vacquerie but when 12th Division on its right was attacked, and with orders from 59 Brigade that the Hindenburg Line was to be "held at all costs", it repositioned its companies and prepared to face the advancing enemy. Two companies were "greatly impeded" by troops of 12th Division flooding back from the front positions and seeking shelter in the Foresters' trenches. The CO's account stresses that it was only by good leadership and command by two of his own company commanders that the withdrawing troops were re-organized and possession of the Hindenburg Line retained. Two further platoons of the Sherwoods were sent to assist another battalion but a

6   The belief that it was the extreme density of the gas, which remained trapped in the still heavy undergrowth of the wood, rather than any other factor is supported by figures. For example, 19/London went into the wood with 15 officers and more than 600 men. Two days later it came out with five officers and 65 ORs. TNA WO 952738: 1/19th London (St Pancras). In effect, 141 Bde was all but incapacitated.
7   L/Cpl. John Thomas of 2/5th North Staffordshire was awarded the Victoria Cross for his work on 30 November.
8   W. Hall, *The Green Triangle*, p.127.

shortage of bombs added to the difficulties of halting the Germans who were progressing up the old trench systems. The last platoon of 2/6th Sherwood's reserve company was sent forward to contain the advance and for the time being the enemy's attempt to cut off the Flesquières Salient had been thwarted. After the battle, GOC 60 Brigade despatched a wire to 59th Division's HQ praising the "splendid soldierly qualities" of the battalion and of how its "dogged determination and fine spirit" had contributed significantly to delaying the German advance.

Another unit of 59th Division, which in its case unexpectedly found itself in the thick of the action, was 470 Field Company. The unit was marching to rejoin the division from detached work but when passing through Gouzeaucourt on 30 November, was ordered by Major General de Lisle, GOC 29th Division, immediately to organize the defence of the town. The order came too late because Germans had already entered its ruins. Under the command of Major Robinson the company joined a group of about 30 pioneers of 11/DLI who, under their CO, had withdrawn to the south-west of the town. The sappers only carried 50 rounds each but more ammunition was brought up in his car from Fins by Major Conlan, the Senior Supply Officer of the Divisional Transport Train. Together with other small parties of transport sections, traffic police, headquarters details, and even some American railway engineers, the mixed groups fought a delaying action until the Guards arrived to eject the enemy from Gouzeaucourt. The sappers of 470 Field Company later apparently joined with three companies of a Guards' battalion and advanced with them towards Quentin Ridge.[9]

The Germans in the Gouzeaucourt sector showed little inclination to attack with any vigour beyond the town and once the British counter-attack was launched withdrew swiftly to Gonnelieu. In these opening three days of the German counter-attack, 59th Division had been used to plug gaps by attachment to the severely tired and depleted divisions in the forward zones. Several of these divisions had launched the initial offensive on 20 November and had remained in the line ever since. The North Midland's personnel had showed sufficient flexibility and produced efficient enough staff work, despite the disruption and confusion caused by the German thrust, to enable its units to deploy where they were ordered and to remain just about adequately sustained. The positions occupied and the defence of them were of necessity extemporized and not always well-sited, but in the following days the division became engaged in a more formal and organized area defence. This tactical operation initially gave ground but at the same time staged rearguard actions calculated to gain time for the preparation of more substantial defences to the rear.

With the exception of the artillery brigades, most of the division's other supporting arms, including the three field ambulances, had travelled with the division. As the German counter-attack had thrown the existing medical evacuation system into disorder, the division's ADMS was compelled on arrival to show considerable command and initiative. Colonel Lindsay quickly

---

9   TNA WO 953010: 30 Nov.1917. The field company's war diary contains little detail of the engagement (WO 953017) but that of 11/DLI (WO 952108) gives an almost blow-by-blow account. W. Miles, *Military Operations France and Belgium 1917*, Vol. III (London: HMSO, 1948) p.188, states the "rather indifferent musketry" of the mixed groups of British defenders. The account in the divisional history, (Compiled, *59th Division*, p15 of the supplementary section), written by the company's second-in-command, notes that "although ... unused to the use of rifles" the company managed to repulse several attacks. Personnel of field companies were supposedly obliged to fire a short course annually. It is perhaps worth noting that subsequently, 470 Field Company did undergo training in the use of Lewis guns and instruction from 175 MG Coy in January and February 1918.

decided Third Army's evacuation system was "poor," ambulance trains were not operating as scheduled, and many of the motor ambulances designated to run between field ambulances and CCS had been diverted to other uses. When yet another ambulance train failed to arrive at Trescault to evacuate the waiting 600 wounded, and as appeals to IV Corps for cars, lorries and buses met with no response, Lindsay took matters into his own hands. This was easily justified by the fact that telephone contact with corps and DHQ had been lost in the afternoon of 30 November. He liaised with 47th Division's ADMS to secure the services of some of the London Division's MOs and orderlies and requisitioned all available wheeled transport from both divisions. The ADS managed to start evacuating the wounded by about 2200 on 30 November; on the following day Lindsay went looking for more transport to clear the 450 cases from the ambulances and MDS. He discovered 24 cars and immediately took them under his command. They fought their way through traffic jams near Metz and Gouzeaucourt and, by 2030 on 1 December, the MDS was cleared of wounded for the first time since 0900 on 29 November.[10]

On both 3 and 4 December, conferences were held at V Corps HQ under the corps commander, Lieutenant General E.A. Fanshawe. Just as the first meeting convened, 59th Division reported hostile bombing parties working their way towards the division's positions near Bourlon Wood. Attending the conference, Major General Romer and his counterparts from other divisions discussed the order for a retirement that had been passed down from Third Army. Maps showing divisional boundaries and possible rearguard positions were examined. On the following day, the GOsC were joined by their GSO1s to hammer out administrative details for the withdrawal. In consultation with GHQ, Third Army had decided that the Bourlon salient was untenable and that a line on the Flesquières Ridge would be a more secure and defendable area to spend the winter. The news came as a relief to the men of 177 Brigade then occupying the gas soaked positions in Bourlon Wood. After dark on 4 December, following another enemy gas barrage on the wood, pack ponies and limbers were brought up and loaded with stores. Leaving a rearguard platoon to fire at intervals, the three front line battalions withdrew their posts' garrisons and made their way independently across country in the direction of Flesquières. So quietly and efficiently was the evacuation executed that the Germans were completely unaware of the movement. The few casualties incurred by 177 Brigade's battalions were from random rather than organized shell fire.[11]

Most of 177 Brigade retired to the new or improved trenches dug by battalions of the division in and around Flesquières. Such was the need for flexibility, particularly since the two gassed 2/6th Staffordshire battalions had been virtually incapacitated, that units in all three infantry brigades were attached to other brigades as well as other divisions. For example, in 178 Brigade 2/5th and 2/8th Sherwood Foresters had been attached to 6th Division. On 2 December, 2/5th re-joined its own brigade but three days later was returned to 6th Division with express permission from V Corps that it could be deployed east of its corps' boundary. The 2/7th Battalion was

---

10 TNA WO 953014: ADMS, 29 November-1 December 1917. The account by the ADMS 47th Division, Colonel Gibbard, while not quite as dramatic as Lindsay's, does state that despite some of his MOs working at the Flesquières MDS, responsibility for evacuating the wounded lay with 59th Division. Gibbard had lost seven of his MOs as a result of the gas bombardment on Bourlon Wood on 30 November. Report by Gibbard, WO 952714: 17 December 1917.
11 TNA WO 953023: 2/5th Lincolnshire, 4 Dec.1917.

attached to 177 Brigade and was to be that brigade's principal rearguard battalion during the withdrawal to Flesquières .

In a partially sunken lane running from the south-east corner of Graincourt in a slightly northern and easterly arc down to a solitary farm house at La Justice, north of Orival Wood, the battalion, with company strengths of only about 100, was to be supplemented by two companies of 2/4th Lincolnshire. Their role was to garrison the sunken lane (known as the Yellow Line) as other battalions of the division withdrew through it. They were then to hold the lane until enemy pressure made their position untenable. The field of fire from the lane was not ideal and there were no established trenches in the immediate vicinity. The night of 4-5 December was spent erecting wire and deepening shelters but in front of the lane the physical defensive obstacles remained minimal. The officers knew that when the order to withdraw to the main Flesquières defences was given, any survivors would have to ascend the gentle slope across an open area of land until they reached the new front line. The 1st Line 47th (2nd London) Division was on their left and 6th Division on the right.

By 0250 on 5 December the main body of 59th Division's infantry had cleared the Yellow Line and by 0725 all V Corps' divisions and attached artillery were reported to be in their new positions on the Flesquières Ridge. In the sunken lane, things were relatively quiet during the daylight hours. Enemy troops were seen debouching en masse from Bourlon Wood and Fontaine-Notre-Dame and his artillery registered on what was now the temporary British front line. During the night, and to its surprise, DHQ "discovered" that 6th Division had evacuated its stretch of the sunken lane and withdrawn the considerable distance to the Hindenburg Support Line. There is no evidence that 6th Division attempted to inform the North Midland of its decision or of there being any officers detailed for liaison work between the two formations. On receipt of the unexpected news, DHQ ordered 2/7th Sherwood to throw back a defensive flank on its right to conform with 6th Division's movement. A series of posts was hacked out in the frozen ground and occupied by dawn but there had been no time to lay more than the thinnest screen of protecting wire. DHQ had instructed Lieutenant Colonel Martyn, CO 2/7th Sherwood Foresters and the two attached Lincolnshire companies, to decide himself whether he should reinforce his outposts in the sunken lane with a reserve company or, alternatively, to select the moment when the line should be withdrawn to the main defences. Martyn elected to withdraw one of his own and one of the Lincolnshire companies to form the right defensive flank. This eventually managed to re-establish contact with 6th Division. Two machine guns were sent up from reserve to assist the rearguard but soon after they were in position Martyn received disconcerting news from the London battalion on his left. A major of 1/15th London reported that the Germans had penetrated his positions and were advancing towards Flesquières. The major wanted to form a defensive flank on the Sherwoods left but, as the enemy penetration appeared to be on a narrow front, he and Martyn decided only to position some Lewis guns to protect the gap.[12] Anxious to hold the Yellow Line for as long as possible to allow

---

12 With eight Vickers attached, 1/15th London formed 47th Division's covering party. It began to withdraw from the sunken lane when Germans infiltrated Graincourt on its left. TNA WO 952727: 140 Bde, Report on Operations December 1917.

those troops that had withdrawn through it to settle into the main line, Martyn, detailed a carrying party to take additional ammunition to the London battalion.[13]

The German assault was preceded by a bombardment that began at about 1430. After an hour of heavy fire on the outposts, the SOS was fired when eight waves of infantry formed up and began to advance towards the sunken lane. Another force approaching from the north-east headed towards the slit trenches in front of Orival Wood. Martyn had no telephone contact with brigade HQ but did have communications with his company commanders. Weight of numbers and a delay of about 30 minutes before the artillery responded to the SOS forced Martyn to begin considering a withdrawal. On his right, his own D Company and one of 2/4th Lincolnshire's companies bore the initial brunt of the attack and gradually fell back from their positions east of Orival Wood. A bayonet charge against the beet factory close to the junction of tracks east of Flesquières halted the Germans for a time but numbers told.[14] Martyn next ordered his centre and left companies to pull back to Flesquières across the 1,500 yards of open ground. This withdrawal, which conformed with a similar movement by 1/15th London, was protected by the SOS barrage and 16 machine guns of 200 MG Company firing over the defenders' heads.[15] Staff work had previously identified specific routes to be followed by the Sherwoods and Lincolnshires as they withdrew to Flesquières . These routes not only avoided masking the fire of the defenders in the main defences but also fortuitously missed the worst of the German barrage and overhead fire. During this manoeuvre the battalion sustained fewer than 20 casualties. With German losses later reported to have been over 1,000, the enemy began digging in a few hundred yards to the north of the main defensive lines protecting Flesquières. The fighting soon died down. The North Midland Division was to remain in those defences until a few days before Christmas. Its troops became occupied in nocturnal patrolling, the occasional raid, and maintenance work on the trenches. Because battalion strengths were already low and made worse by the virtual loss of the two 2/6th Staffordshire battalions, a composite brigade was formed.[16] In the deepening winter weather the division settled back into trench routine and reflected on its work during the defensive action.

The division had completed its tasks to time and with a reasonably small number of casualties.[17] The initial evacuation from Bourlon to the prepared line above Flesquières was conducted efficiently and with little molestation from the enemy. The responsibility for deciding the actual time of the retirement had been passed down by V Corps to DHQ, and, in turn, DHQ to brigade HQ, and brigade to the local commander, Lieutenant Colonel Martyn. Corps had also ordered staffs of 47th and 59th divisions to liaise with each other to discuss the timing of the

---

13   A. Maude, *The History of the 47th (London) Division,* (London: Amalgamated Press, 1922) p131, notes that the penetration had been made because the "outposts of the division on our right" (i.e., 59th Division) had been driven in. Only 200 men of 1/15th London were tasked to hold the covering position which stretched west and east of Graincourt.
14   One company of 2/5th Leicestershire also assisted in this counter-attack against the beet factory.
15   TNA WO 953017: Vickers guns fired over 40,000 rounds during the German attack "inflicting enormous casualties."
16   The composite brigade consisted of three battalions of 178 Brigade and the two 2/5th Staffordshire battalions.
17   TNA WO 953012: A&Q gives divisional casualties for 1-8 December as: 11 officers and 208 ORs killed; 55 and 1,009 wounded; two and 94 missing. At least 600 of the wounded were gas casualties.

withdrawal. They were then to inform V Corps heavy artillery as to their decision.[18] Sustainment seems to have been adequately organized and resourced, with no reported shortage of rations and ammunition. The transport section's nightly journey from the divisional dump through Gouzeaucourt and up towards Flesquières may have been "full of thrills" and the rations may have arrived in a "terribly squashy condition" but the only direct reference to them not arriving at the right place and time came a few days after the withdrawal.[19] When battalions had been relieved and returned to the Havrincourt Wood area for rest, there appears to have been the odd, but inevitably predictable confusion with accommodation and cookers, but improvised sail baths were quickly rigged and fresh underwear and clothing issued.[20]

Communications had, as usual, been severely disrupted, but it does seem strange that Martyn was reportedly out of contact with brigade HQ during the entire process. It is likely that runners did manage to inform brigade at times as to the progress of the withdrawal because such messages are extant. It may be that they arrived *after* rather than *during* the process owing to the German artillery and machine-gun barrages. There was clearly good support work from the MG company and the division also had the assistance of 6/South Wales Borderers, pioneer battalion of 25th Division, when preparing the Flesquières' defences. The rearguard had liaised well with 47th Division on its left but it is unknown precisely what arrangements were made with 6th Division to its right.[21] The principal problem experienced during the operation was the slow response to the SOS requested by 2/7th Sherwood just after 1500 on 6 December. Reports suggest that the artillery did not open fire for 30 minutes after the call went up. It may be that the rifle grenades then used by Third Army to call down the SOS barrage were not seen by the FOOs in Flesquières.[22] Nonetheless, from their position of advantage they would have experienced the German bombardment and would probably have been able to see the attacking enemy waves as they approached the sunken lane. At 1520, a Royal Artillery FOO did report that British troops were retiring past Orival Wood and heading for Flesquières; this may have been the actual prompt for the SOS barrage to open.[23] While it was attached to 20th Division, 2/6th Sherwood Foresters had complained of a "complete lack of artillery support" on 1-2 December. The German attempt on those particular days was not especially threatening. The delay of 30 minutes on 6 December was potentially more catastrophic.

The war diaries of the divisional CRA and his RFA brigades are sometimes unclear and confusing in their detail for this period.[24] The division's own two brigades of field artillery were under the command of 56th and 51st Divisions, about three miles to the left of 59th Division. At different times during the withdrawal period CRA 59th Division, who had his advanced

---

18 TNA WO 95748: Appendix 15.
19 W. Oates, *2/8th Battalion Sherwood Foresters*, p.209.
20 TNA WO 953025: 2/6th Sherwood Foresters, Dec.1917; W. Hall, *The Green Triangle*, p.134; Oates, pp.206, 209.
21 It is difficult to imagine that for such an important and potentially difficult operation some unrecorded (or now possibly non-extant) liaison did not take place. Furthermore, Miles, *Military Operations 1917,* Vol. III, p260 notes, "special measures were taken to ensure that the closest liaison should be preserved between the left of 6th Division and the flank of the 59th."
22 Miles, *Military Operations*, p.266, fn.
23 One report, however, recorded the barrage as opening at 1505 (CRA) while DHQ opted for the rounded "3pm".
24 TNA WO 953013: CRA 59th Division; WO 953016: 295 and 296 Bdes, RFA war diaries.

HQ in Flesquières and his rear HQ in Trescault, commanded Army RFA brigades and others drawn from 61st (South Midland), 51st (Highland), Guards, 2nd Cavalry, 6th, and 62nd (West Riding) divisions. It was some of these brigades, together with those on the left under 47th Division's direct command (as well as the corps heavy artillery) that covered 59th Division's withdrawal.[25] The brigades were divided into Left and Right Groups, each with allocated zones of fire but the crucial grid square covering the area south of Orival Wood appears to have fallen between the two groups' zones. If that was the case, it might explain why the response to the SOS was delayed. When it did open, however, it was devastating. The heavy artillery's FOO estimated that his guns had "caught and wiped out" 2,000 Germans east of Orival Wood.[26]

At the instruction of IV Corps, Major General Romer submitted a narrative account of the period leading up to and of the withdrawal itself. He later also produced an appendix that included some thoughts about the operations as a whole.[27] There is, however, no deep analysis of the events and Romer drew only two recorded conclusions from the withdrawal and the wider defensive operation. Having decided that the security of his HQ in Trescault, "was at one time decidedly precarious" he considered the "chief lesson" to be drawn was not to position DHQ too close to the front lines. His other conclusion concerned the use of machine guns. He believed so much time and theory had been expended on the development of machine-gun barrages that there was now a risk of "losing sight of the supreme value of the gun for direct fire." Emphasizing the vital role played by the guns during the withdrawal Romer asserted that because they had proved so useful to the infantry, battalions no longer resented having to provide 32 men as belt fillers and carriers.

The division's task had not been a particularly difficult one. It had played its part in a withdrawal to a winter line that could be adapted to a system of defence in depth. By means of trading space for time, the initial withdrawal from Bourlon Wood, and then the delaying action of 6 December, had given the opportunity for troops in the rear to improve the defences and for the artillery to reposition. As *FSR I* states, the object of the encounter was not to achieve a decisive result but to prevent the enemy from gaining ground to manoeuvre and secure a position where he might be able to turn the flanks of the prepared defences. The initial positions in the sunken lane did not offer particularly good fields of fire but once those defenders were ordered to retire, the ground over which the enemy advanced did allow the division's artillery support, machine gun and rifle fire to take a significant toll. On its left, the lie of the land meant the Germans did have more of an opportunity to manoeuvre; consequently, the hugely under strength 47th Division did experience rather more difficulty. The companies of 1/15th London had been all but surrounded and had to fight their way out against severe opposition. This had an impact on the timing of Lieutenant Colonel Martyn's decision to withdraw. The

---

25 TNA WO 952711: 47th Division; WO 951591: CRA 6th Division. The two RFA Bdes of 47th Division were not actually in a position to cover their own division until 11 December. On 4 December, CRA 59th Division reported "batteries retired behind Flesquières Ridge" (WO 953013); at 0550 on 5 December, V Corps noted 59th Division had "all guns in position." (WO 95748). When he wrote: "The 59th Division withdrew some of its batteries behind the Flesquières Ridge at dusk," Miles, *Military Operations*, p.263 may have taken these references to mean 59th Division's *own* rather than *attached* artillery brigades.
26 TNA WO 95748: 6 Dec.1917
27 TNA WO 953010: Summary of Operations November 27 to December 7 1917, 12 Dec.1917; Part II of the Report – Remarks (n.d. but Dec.1917)

principal object of the delaying forces' one recorded organized counter-attack (near the *raperie*) was to gain time to disengage. On the right, and having been continuously in the line since 20 November, 6th Division was exhausted and extremely weak. Its divisional history does not mention the withdrawal but its war diaries record the problems it had in disengaging and in containing the pursuing Germans. To the left of 47th, 2nd Division had a fairly easy withdrawal from the Yellow Line but its troops had been exceptionally busy in digging new main defences to the rear. When 59th Division left V Corps it departed with three satisfying references and the expectation of a substantial period of rest.[28]

Once withdrawn from the Ypres sector in late September 1917, 61st Division returned to the Arras area. There it spent the next two months in and out of the line around Fampoux and Roeux. On 20 November it discharged smoke and used dummies as a diversion for the attack at Cambrai and was warned on 27 November that it would be moving in three days' time. The division had conducted nine major raids in the previous four weeks, all of which had penetrated the enemy trenches and demonstrated sound all-arms coordination. It left the sector with a ringing endorsement of its efficiency by the corps commander and travelled towards Bapaume in the expectation of joining V Corps and being utilized to exploit the recent gains made towards Cambrai. When it detrained at Bapaume, however, the disruption and near panic caused by the German counter-attack on 30 November became immediately apparent. A wire from Third Army informed DHQ that the division was to join IV Corps and would be bussed to Ruyaulcourt. The three infantry brigades were to have concentrated in Metz, Fins, and Heudicourt by 0700 on 1 December. What they were to do once there was somewhat vague. They were ordered to be ready to reinforce the divisions of either IV or VII Corps currently in the line, or to support an attack on Villers-Plouich.

The infantry brigades negotiated their way through traffic congestion and had concentrated around the designated area by about 0300. Such was the confusion on the ground that three of the battalions of 184 Brigade at Fins had no billets allocated; in Metz, 183 Brigade despatched mounted patrols to try to discover what was happening. Having battled through the chaos, the transport and cookers arrived some hours later. At mid-day, a staff officer of III Corps arrived and instructed the division to relieve 20th (Light) Division with one brigade in the forward zone. DHQ queried this order with IV Corps, who told the division to do nothing except to send officers from one brigade to reconnoitre 20th Division's line just in case a relief was ordered. Almost immediately DHQ was indeed instructed to lend one brigade (183 Brigade) to 20th Division of III Corps with the other two brigades remaining under IV Corps. Two battalions of 184 Brigade were next ordered to support the Guards Division but, having marched off, they were quickly recalled.[29] After dark 183 Brigade's battalions began to relieve the right sector of the Light Division's very tired and very under strength units.[30] The relief was done "under

---

28 These came from 18 Brigade of 6th Division, 60 Brigade of 20th Division, and one from the corps commander who praised its work and expressed the hope the division would sometime again come under his command.
29 Besides being warned to support the Guards Division, the situation was so unclear that 184 Bde was also ordered to be ready to support Secunderbad Cavalry Bde. TNA WO 953065: 2/4th Berkshire, 2 Dec.1917
30 Having been so reduced in numbers, 20th Division's field companies were in the line acting as infantry. Between 20 November-8 December 1917 the division lost just under 3,000 all ranks. W. Miles, *Military Operations*, p.382.

great difficulty." There was no 'line', no forward wire, an acute shortage of grenades, CTs led from one side's shattered trenches to the other's, and several posts were entirely isolated from their company HQ.[31] The following day, 182 Brigade began relieving troops of 20th Division's left sector in the forward positions north of la Vacquerie and on the slopes of Welsh Ridge. Battalion COs had attended a conference at brigade HQ in the morning of 2 December and during the late afternoon their companies began moving up from Gouzeaucourt Wood. This proved difficult because movement orders had either been undelivered or divisional and brigade staff work was not sufficiently coordinated. In the resultant confusion one of the battalions was almost requisitioned en route by the brigade major of 184 Brigade. This officer told the CO that his unit's orders had been changed and GOC 184 Brigade now wanted the battalion to move further south. The CO sensibly declined because the brigade major had no written orders to that effect and went to find Brigadier General White for clarification. During his search he telephoned his own GOC brigade for instructions and was told by Brigadier General Evans to carry out his original orders.[32] The battalion continued on its way up Welsh Ridge.

Further uncertainty came later that day when Brigadier General Evans met with a senior officer of 20th Division to discuss reliefs. When the latter said he wanted 182 Brigade to extend further to its right, Evans pointed out that as he knew nothing of the line, none of his officers having been able to do a daylight reconnaissance, he would pass the issue up to DHQ. He suggested giving 183 Brigade, which had now been in the line for 24 hours, one of his own battalions to cover the proposed extended right sector. This was agreed and 2/5th Warwickshire came under 183 Brigade from 2100 that night. This sensible initiative did not solve the problem of where his remaining three battalions should deploy. As DHQ 20th Division was ignorant of the locations of some of its own posts as well as those of the enemy, Evans decided to put 2/7th and 2/8th Warwickshire in what were surmised to be the forward positions. Each battalion was to have one company of 2/6th in support. Patrols were then despatched to investigate whether there were any undiscovered posts of 20th Division further east. Evans later reported how his battalions were "under very disadvantageous circumstances" and somewhere between 1,000 and 500 yards to the rear of the completely unfamiliar 'line' they thought they should have relieved.[33] The brigade's posts ran approximately north-south, east of la Vacquerie until they met the detached 2/5th Warwickshire and 2/6th Gloucestershire of 183 Brigade. With Gonnelieu having fallen to the enemy, 183 Brigade's front turned almost 90 degrees west, a little to the south and about 900 yards east of la Vacquerie. West of this salient, the line ran roughly parallel to and north of the Péronne – Cambrai road. Because the line was so close to the main road there was little opportunity to develop any sort of defence in depth to the south of the village.

31 TNA WO 953060: 2/4th Gloucestershire, 1 Dec.1917
32 TNA WO 953054: 182 Bde HQ. Report by 2/7th Warwickshire. The staff work of 184 Bde was perhaps not all it should have been. When 2/4th Oxford was instructed to move up to the forward area the brigade major did not detail a route. Its officers therefore led their companies by compass bearings. See TNA WO 953067: 1 Dec.1917
33 It took 2/7th and 2/8th Warwickshire over two hours to establish exactly where their own inter-battalion boundary was located. On its left flank, 2/8th Warwickshire discovered its posts were about 500 yards north of the supposed boundary between 29th and 20th divisions. No confirmation of the relief had arrived at DHQ but at 0700 on 3 December, 61st Division assumed command of the sector. What was left of 59 Brigade, 20th Division amounted to 350 rifles. They remained in reserve to 61st Division for 24 hours. TNA WO 953034: 2 Dec.1917

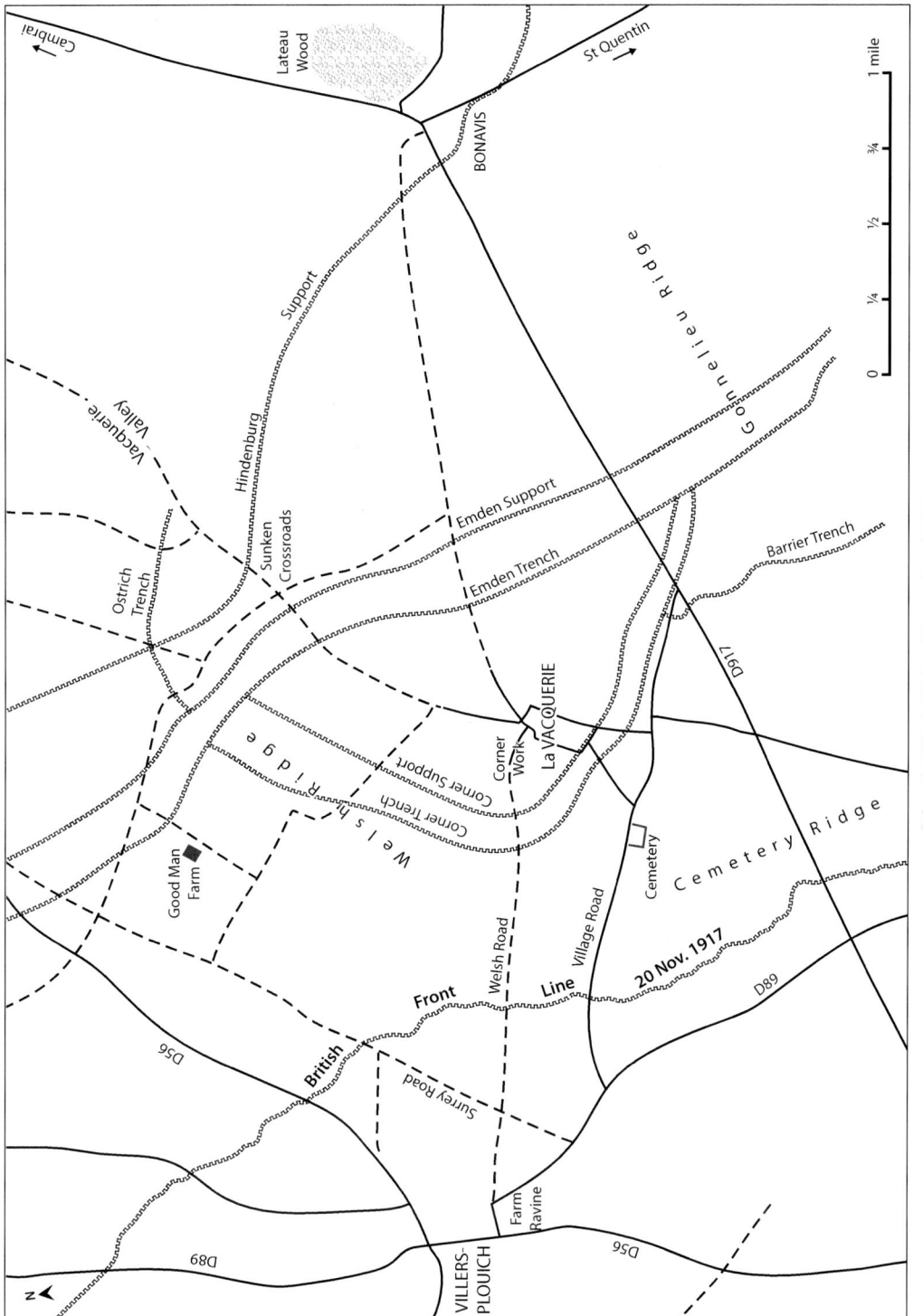

Map 5 Welsh Ridge, December 1917.

III Corps instructed 183 Brigade to push closer towards the road to give it a little more room to create posts but this was never to be a practicable solution to the village's defence. On less than ideal defensive ground, two stretched and under strength brigades were tasked to defend over 5,000 yards of intermittent line against three German divisions.

Over the next few days, 61st Division was to experience some of the most bitter and prolonged fighting seen on the Cambrai front. It was on the receiving end of repeated German attacks designed to occupy the tactically important high ground of Welsh Ridge. In some sectors the German counter-stroke had petered out on the second day but here, as 59th Division had encountered at Bourlon, the fight continued. Two of 61st Division's brigades, 182 and 183 brigades bore the brunt of the fighting that frequently degenerated into hand-to-hand contests in a maze of almost obliterated trenches. In the early hours of 2 December the enemy launched a series of attacks against 183 Brigade's salient to the east of la Vacquerie.[34] These were repulsed but in the afternoon an intense bombardment fell on the two Gloucestershire battalions in front of the village. Large numbers of Germans attacked in waves over the open ground, probably as an intended diversion from other groups bombing their way up the trench system. The enemy attacking over the open were repulsed with heavy losses but those who worked their way up the trenches were more successful. The hardest hit was 2/6th Gloucestershire. Facing overwhelming numbers and with bombs almost exhausted, battalion HQ burnt all papers and tried to re-establish a line on the eastern edge of the village. Touch with 2/4th Gloucestershire on its right had been lost (2/4th subsequently formed a defensive flank facing north-east) and, after dark, 2/6th's HQ was over-run and the CO killed. The Germans took and occupied about 500 yards of the former Hindenburg front system but the two Gloucestershire battalions managed to regain touch with each other and, overnight, with companies of 2/8th Worcestershire. Darkness also allowed rations, water, bombs, and ammunition to be brought up by specially designated sappers and TM battery personnel. One company of 2/8th Worcestershire had attempted a counter-attack late in the evening but as this was only partially successful two companies were warned that another attempt would be made the following morning. In a change of mind, however, 183 Brigade decided the newly-arrived 2/5th Warwickshire should instead regain the Gloucesters' lost trenches. The Warwicks had no time for a reconnaissance and knew nothing of the ground. Adopting what was described as the "normal attack formation of 61st Division" two companies advanced, seemingly without any artillery preparation or cover, just as a heavy bombardment came down on their lines.[35] German infantry fire from troops massing for their own attack swept through the waves, knocking over all officers and NCOs of the two companies. The attack withered and died.

---

34 The area in which 61st Division became involved is what G.C. Wynne, *If Germany Attacks: The Battle in Depth in the West* (London: Faber & Faber, 1940) pp.141-43, called the "Hindenburg Position". It was an improved sector of the Hindenburg Line where two additional lines, one running through la Vacquerie and another, including Emden Trench and Emden Support, were constructed 500 yards behind on the reverse slope. By adding these lines, German artillery observers had a much improved view of their forward defences. British FOOs had very poor observation over much of the contested area.

35 TNA WO 953056: 2/5th Warwickshire. Report by Lt. Col. Coates, Appendix II, 30 Dec.1917. As the battalion's signallers had managed to salvage only about 300 yards of telephone wire, all communications during the attack had to be carried by runners.

The fighting then took on something of a repetitive and predictable nature. Supported by what was at first only a very weak artillery group, and with no cooperation from air, 61st Division was subjected to increasingly intense German bombardments.[36] These were followed by waves of successive infantry attacks. Adhering to current doctrine, 182 and 183 brigades launched often company-sized counter-attacks that, on several occasions succeeded in regaining trenches or posts. These were, however, often only to be lost again in subsequent German assaults. Remnants of the two Gloucestershire battalions of 183 Brigade were forced from la Vacquerie village some hours after the failed attack by the two companies of 2/5th Warwickshire. When Lieutenant Colonel Coates of the still-attached but mauled Warwickshire battalion "looked for support" among the Gloucesters for a counter-attack, he recorded there were "no troops available." Later, Coates insisted it was the Gloucesters', rather than his own battalion's line that had broken. There was, he said, "no backward movement of my troops."[37] Ferocious fighting continued on the western edge of the village in and around a strong point called Corner Work. Its garrison of sections from several battalions hung on grimly until relieved after two days by two companies of 2/4th Berkshire. After the enemy had later all but surrounded the site, the Berkshires abandoned the position and appear to have fought their way out. The evidence about its actual loss is unclear and vague but there was no serious attempt to retake it. Resistance was, however, continued in the Hindenburg Support trenches immediately to its west and north.

Because the fall of la Vacquerie exposed 2/7th Warwickshire to German fire from their right rear, the battalion was forced to withdraw from Emden Trench. Other companies of 2/7th and 2/8th Warwickshire in the former but now largely flattened German communication trench known as Ostrich Avenue then endured a series of attacks over two days and themselves launched almost as many counter-attacks. Inspiring leadership by one company commander in particular, adroit handling of any available reserves, and dogged perseverance and bravery by a dwindling number of men kept the trench in 182 Brigade's hands until relieved. An area close to the crossroads of two sunken lanes about 1,800 yards north of la Vacquerie and just north of Emden Trench and Emden Support was also lost and retaken several times. Corner Support, which ran roughly south-west – north-east just below the eastern crest of Welsh Ridge saw fierce and bloody fighting for two days. By this time the Warwickshire battalions were much reduced and "getting very tired."[38] The struggle continued until 36th (Ulster) Division, which had been bringing battalions into the line and acting in support of 182 Brigade since the night of 4 December, assumed command of the northern divisional sector on 6 December. The southern section was taken over by 184 Brigade. Its troops were set immediately to wire and strengthen the new line.

The enemy's failure by the evening of 6 December to secure the crest of Welsh Ridge marked the end of the German counter-stroke. Fighting continued on a much reduced and intermittent scale until the enemy made another serious attempt to take the ridge at the end of December. The significance of 61st Division's sustained effort to defend la Vacquerie and, in particular the ridge, lies in the fact that they were crucial to the security of Byng's newly-established Winter

---

36 TNA WO 953034: On 2 Dec. DHQ noted that the division's artillery support consisted of only four 6 inch howitzers and two "weak and tired" RFA brigades of 20th Division. A third RFA brigade was brought up on 4 December.
37 TNA WO 953056: Report by Lt. Col. Coates, 8 Dec.1917
38 TNA WO 95303: 4 Dec.1917

Line. Haig had visited Byng on the morning of the failed counter-attack by 2/5th Warwickshire, the same day as the village fell, to discuss a withdrawal to a more favourable position. Byng had selected his proposed rear line before he met Haig and reportedly informed him "he had no particular anxiety concerning the position about la Vacquerie and on Welsh Ridge."[39] It is understandable that Byng was indifferent about who controlled the village (and explains why III Corps told Major General Mackenzie only to counter-attack if the enemy tried to progress west out of the village) but it is more difficult to agree with Byng's assessment about the worth of the higher ground. The ridge held significant tactical importance and, if lost, would threaten the security of the intended Winter Line by improving observation over sections of it.[40]

The crest was successfully held by the division partly because it followed the methodology suggested in *FSR I* of dividing a front into unit sections.[41] Around la Vacquerie and on Welsh Ridge the 'section' constituted a battalion. The extent of the section's front depended on the lie of the ground and how this might impact on the ability of the battalion CO to control his zone of command. The defensive positions manned by the division's brigades were largely those occupied, often in haste or necessity, by those brigades the South Midland battalions had relieved. As always, in most sectors there were areas of special tactical importance. These included higher ground, sunken lanes, former German bunkers, and even trench junctions. With the objective of disrupting and disorganizing enemy attacks battalions did establish advanced posts where and when they could but there were insufficient men available to create any real defence in depth. This was further confounded by the layout and direction of the pre-existing trench system. This rarely assisted the defenders and a lack of time and tools to dig more suitably aligned trenches meant that brigades were compelled to fight in positions that were not necessarily suited to their purpose. Unlike 59th Division, 61st Division did not have a prepared line on which to fall back and although there are no recorded instances of garrisons being ordered to "hold at all costs" or "to the last man and round", the troops would know there was little of any substance behind the main line of resistance other than what the brigades and, more importantly individual battalions, had managed to retain as a reserve.[42] *FSR I* advocated the creation of a local reserve by every section for the purpose of counter-attacking on the initiative of section commanders. These attacks, according to *FSR I*, were necessary to keep alive an offensive spirit in the defenders, to "exhaust the enemy, draw in his reserves" and, in theory, to prepare for an offensive. As was pointed out earlier, however, in 61st Division's case an offensive was neither intended nor contemplated.[43]

Corps and DHQ allotted objectives and directed the movement of divisions and brigades while GOsC brigades decided which battalions were to be in the line and which in support. In

39 W. Miles, *Military Operations*, pp.257-58.
40 At 1300, Mackenzie enquired of corps HQ whether he should use 184 Bde to retake the village and was told to hold fire. At 1330, corps HQ received a wire from DHQ that three companies were on their way to clear the southern part of the village. DHQ later reported the enemy had failed to advance from the village but that the three companies had been unable to eject them from it. TNA WO 953034: 3 Dec.1917; TNA WO 95677: 3 Dec.1917
41 *FSR I* (1912 edition) pp.142-43.
42 The one known example of an uncompromising order was to a platoon of 2/5th Warwickshire which was instructed to hold its section of trench "with the bayonet." TNA WO 953056: Report of 8 Dec.1917, Appendix I
43 *FSR I*, (1912 edition) p.145.

this defensive action on the ridge, the conduct of the battle was largely reactive and devolved to the control of COs and their sub-unit commanders. There are ten recorded occasions between 2-7 December when battalions or companies were attached to other brigades or to battalions within their own brigade. This required COs and OsC companies to be adept, willing and flexible enough to work with possibly previously unknown officers from other units for periods of between days to hours in "situations…and [in] methods of fighting [which were] new to most."[44] Platoon and company commanders holding battalion flank positions had always to liaise with their counterparts in other units but on the ridge there were several occasions when companies of one battalion were inserted between two of another as counter-attack or support troops. For example, a composite company created by amalgamating remnants of 2/5th Warwickshire of 182 Brigade, was collected by 183 Brigade and sent to 182. Brigadier General Evans, GOC 182 Brigade, who had been previously unaware of the company's existence, sent it as a support company to 2/8th Warwickshire. This set in train a series of subsequent moves during the night of 4-5 December of other companies of different battalions to different brigades. These were kept either in support or thrown piecemeal into counter-attacks in alliance with their host unit.

In engagements such as those on the ridge, it is the training and ability of junior officers to command and lead which inevitably comes to the fore. With one exception, post-battle reports praised the junior commanders for their initiative, boldness, and leadership qualities. The work of Major Lefroy in organizing and leading his own company, as well as men attached from two different regiments in a series of counter-attacks around Ostrich Trench, warranted mention in the *Official History*.[45] There is the possibility that a second lieutenant of 2/4th Gloucestershire who came out of la Vacquerie with 20 of his men might have acted prematurely,[46] but the only undoubted criticism of a junior commander was one who was deemed "incapable of controlling or leading his men."[47]

The mention of one officer who did not fulfil expectation does not mean, of course, that the behaviour of all others was exemplary. They were as prone to exhaustion, shock, and fear as the men they commanded but leadership demanded they hide or disguise them more effectively. Given the often hand-to-hand character of the fighting and the intensity of the enemy barrages it is not surprising one CO grew increasingly concerned about the effect the battle was having on the mental and physical state of the men his officers commanded.[48] His report does, nonetheless, go on to praise the troops' endurance and their "unbeaten demeanour." The moral component of the division's fighting power is difficult to assess as there are few extant reports that refer to the concept's several elements. Evacuation of the wounded, an important element of men's morale, seems to have worked rather more smoothly than the system managed by 59th Division. Transport and additional stretcher bearers appear to have been organized and

44 TNA WO 953054: Bde HQ. Report by Lt. Col. W. St John, CO of 2/7th Warwickshire.
45 TNA WO 953056: 2/7th Warwickshire, *Report on Operations 3-7 December 1917;* W. Miles, *Military Operations*, p.269.
46 TNA WO 953056: 2/7th Warwickshire. *Report on Operations*. It is equally possible that the mention of 2Lt Reggie was in praise of his leadership in managing to get his men out of the la Vacquerie before it fell. There was, however, also a note that men of 183 Brigade came into the Warwicks' trenches saying they enemy had broken through. They were, apparently peremptorily, "Ordered back to their sector."
47 Ibid. The unnamed officer had apparently only been posted to the company the previous night.
48 TNA WO 953054: 182 Bde HQ. Attachment to report by Lt. Col. W. St John, n.d. but Dec.1917

employed effectively because reports stress that RAPs and the ADS were cleared quickly and efficiently.[49] Proficient divisional and brigade staff work also aided the maintenance of morale and welfare – bathing allocations are known to have been swapped to advantage and fresh clothing and hot food in Havrincourt Wood were on hand for relieved troops. A successful counter-attack by one company of 2/5th Gloucestershire, which had lost 16 men killed and 54 wounded four days earlier when an ammunition dump exploded, was taken as evidence that morale had been unaffected by that particular "disaster."[50]

If the troops' morale was not considered to be a particular problem, their skills were certainly called into question by at least one CO. He asserted that what faults there may have been on the part of the men was attributable to the doubtful efficacy of their training. Referring to an incident concerning 182 Brigade on 4 December, Lieutenant Colonel St John considered some lost trenches "might have been retaken." This ambiguous statement was followed by one that offered greater clarity. Unless officers led the way in bombing encounters, and themselves threw bombs – a practice which for some reason he considered to be "unsound" – St John believed his men suffered from "a lack of push." Compared to the enemy, who threw their bombs with "great accuracy" his men's fighting power was "severely hampered" by their poor bombing technique. Furthermore, several attacks, he thought, would not have materialized if the men had not interpreted the lift of the German barrage and the start of the infantry's advance as a signal to take cover. Had the defenders opened Lewis and rifle fire earlier than they did, greater damage, he asserted, would have been done to the enemy's cohesion and will.

Throughout this period vital elements of the division's physical component were undoubtedly inferior to those of its opponent's. In particularly the shortage of Mills bombs caused the brigades to fight at a serious disadvantage. There had been no time to establish divisional dumps and those of 20th Division were virtually exhausted. St John later reported that had he not been able to acquire a "small supply" before his battalion moved up, "disaster would have befallen us." Similarly, on its way up to the line, 183 Brigade thought itself fortunate that it was able to draw two extra bandoliers of SAA and an equally small number of additional bombs. The critical shortage of bombs was eased to a degree by the salvage of German stick grenades but it was not until the worst of the fighting was over that divisional dumps were established. Until then, company strength carrying parties, supplemented by any available sappers and TM crews, took up as many SAA boxes, bombs, Lewis gun pans and Very lights from improvised dumps as they could find. The corps CE (chief engineer) had been of little help to the CRE when the latter pressed his superior for assistance in finding sites for his dumps. In the end the CRE had to secure the site for a light railway siding to feed the divisional dump by dealing personally with the "Railway people."[51]

At times, all-arms cooperation during the defensive battle was not as efficient as it should have been. The British air component was dismissed as being all but non-existent and there was

---

49 See TNA WO 953038. The division's three field ambulances took over the corps' main dressing station and 20th Division's medical posts and lines of evacuation. The ADMS, Lt. Col. C.Howkins, regularly visited all sites and stations.
50 TNA WO 953036: A&Q, 8 Dec.1917; WO 953066: 2/5th Gloucestershire, 3 Dec.1917. A. Barnes, *Story of 2/5th Gloucestershire*, p.79.
51 TNA WO 953040: 9 Dec.1917. Because the site eventually found was outside the corps area, CE Corps washed his hands of the matter and said he was unable to help.

considerable criticism of the artillery.[52] Several commanders reported the "weak" or "slight" response of the guns, the "lack of neutralizing fire", that shells were "always short" and of "no" or "late" replies to SOS signals. It is evident that German batteries fired more frequently and with more effect but 61st Division's own guns can be exonerated because they had not travelled to the Cambrai sector with the infantry. Its artillery brigades were not transferred to III Corps until 12 December and it was only two days later that CRA 61st Division assumed command of the groups covering 61st Division's infantry. During the period of intense fighting the infantry had been under the protection largely of 20th Division's artillery. These brigades had been in the line almost continually since late October. Their batteries were under strength, with their men exhausted and the guns worn. The Germans had massed a superior number of guns in preparation for their counter-stroke and were able to retain fire supremacy over the subsequent days of their operation.[53] The enemy tactic of maintaining tempo with massed and diversionary attacks meant 61st Division had to fill its own trenches with as many men as could be prudently gathered. These positions were precisely registered by the German guns whose fire intensity wreaked havoc on the South Midland's brigades. By the time the division's own guns had arrived in the line and registered, the battle's intensity had diminished. The infantry undoubtedly suffered from a lack of sufficient artillery protection and assistance but its disquiet about that inadequacy could not be targeted at the division's own gunners.

Another example of inter-arms cooperation that did not work quite as it should have was the division's experience with tanks. On 3 December, 16 tanks had been made available to 61st Division by III Corps. These were to be used in counter-attacks in the event of the enemy assaulting Beaucamp Ridge. In the afternoon of 3 December the tanks were ordered to move 1,000 yards forward from their leaguer on the eastern side of Havrincourt Wood.[54] For some undisclosed reasons, but to the obvious annoyance of DHQ, "This order OC Tanks failed to carry out."[55] This displeasure was clearly passed on to OC tanks by corps HQ because the following day eight were moved to the immediate east of Beaucamp village. Although the value of tanks in the type of fighting being waged would have been limited, especially as the brigades' experience in tank-infantry cooperation was negligible, the division did not suffer from their early absence because the enemy made no serious attempt on Beaucamp Ridge.

Air, tanks, and to a lesser degree artillery, came under the control of corps HQ rather than DHQ; the division's machine-gun companies did fall under the command of divisional and brigade HQ. Machine-gun sections generally worked in close cooperation with the infantry – a section of which was often tasked with protecting the guns and their crews – and the artillery. This frequently involved firing barrages in conjunction with the RFA brigades as well as routine

---

52 War diaries of some of the division's units mention the frequently unopposed strafing and bombing runs of enemy aircraft. The only known occurrence of a friendly aircraft having an influence on 61st Division's battle was a wire from III Corps. In consequence of a pilot's report, corps HQ instructed the division to occupy posts which gave observation down Vacquerie Valley. TNA WO 95677: 5 Dec.1917
53 It was widely thought the Germans also used British 18 pdr pieces and their shell stocks which had been captured on 30 November.
54 TNA WO 95677: 3 Dec.1917
55 TNA WO 953034: 3 Dec.1917. OC tanks may well have had entirely valid reasons for not immediately obeying the order. By that stage of the battle tank crews and machines were at a premium. Most of what personnel remained was formed into composite crews.

nocturnal shoots of anything between 4-8,000 rounds. All three of the division's companies were engaged 1-6 December and suffered casualties but their presence was not of critical significance.[56] They could be useful against the attacks coming over the open but were of marginal importance in the bombing attacks that worked up the trenches. OsC sections were expected to use their initiative to support the infantry but one battalion CO was clearly unimpressed by their work. He claimed the brigade's company was "valueless to us" and believed they were allowed only to fire on SOS lines rather than on targets of opportunity. He suggested that a certain number of guns should be placed under the direct command of battalion COs and asserted that he had been unable to ascertain successfully whether certain guns had actually fired at all.[57] In the confusion of battle the CO may have been unaware that in the late morning of 4 December DHQ ordered all guns in the front line to be withdrawn to the support positions. This was a rational move because if the forward positions fell, the guns would then be able to bring cross fire on all likely approaches. The absence of the guns in the front zone may have coloured the CO's judgement as to their actual worth[58] but, as always, keeping the guns supplied with ammunition proved difficult. Parties managed to bring up adequate supplies of rations and water for 182 MG Company but owing to the "impossibility" of obtaining carrying parties from the infantry the company struggled to sustain its ammunition supply.[59]

Compared to other divisions in II Corps, 61st had had a difficult time but, in some respects it did enjoy several advantages over most of the other engaged divisions. It had gone into the line at a critical time, fortunately largely into the positions in which it was to stand and fight, with its brigades' fighting strengths reasonably strong. Before its arrival in the sector it had been line holding with short periods of rest since September.[60] Nonetheless, it sustained considerable casualties and had fought an improvised defensive battle with ingenuity and fortitude.[61] Most importantly, it held the crucial ground at a time when other divisions were shattered and exhausted. Its two flank divisions, 6th and 29th divisions, had been in the line since 20 November.[62] The 2nd Line 61st Division's defensive action on the ridge allowed these two regular divisions to withdraw from their exposed positions with reasonable cohesion and integrity. Welsh Ridge had been secured at least for the time being and the other withdrawing divisions of Third Army were now inside the Winter Line. Major General Mackenzie clearly

---

56 For example, 183 MG Coy lost four officers and 42 ORs on 3 December and had seven of its guns knocked out. TNA WO 953062.
57 TNA WO 953054: "General" comments in Report on Operations by Lt. Col. W. St John.
58 There is some confusion as to how this order was carried out. Some or all of 183 and 184 MG Coys' guns were withdrawn on 4 December but 182 MG Coy recorded that as a result of the forced withdrawal by battalions of 183 Brigade on its right, it took four or its guns *forward* from their reserve positions in the Hindenburg Line. TNA WO 953062; WO 953057.
59 TNA WO 953057: 4 Dec.1917.
60 See TNA WO 953034. On 1 December fighting strengths of 182 and 183 brigades, the two brigades which were to be most heavily involved over the following days were: 88 officers and 1,850 ORs and 93 and 1950 respectively. W. Miles, *Military Operations*, p.269, fn gives 182 Bde's casualties as 52 officers and 710 ORs.
61 See TNA WO 953034. The division's total battle casualties for 1-7 December were initially recorded as, 99 officers and 1800 ORs
62 The relief of 29th Division began on 4-5 December but 6th Division was to stay in the line until 9-10 December. The reliefs of 12th and 20th divisions, the other two formations of III Corps which had attacked on 20 November, were completed by 2-3 December.

thought the division had done well. He addressed all units, either on special parades or by letter, expressing his appreciation of their work. As he said, "The task of taking over an unknown front, from troops actually engaged with the enemy, was very difficult."[63] That task had certainly been exacerbated by the poor positional reports 20th Division and elements of 12th Division had been able to provide on relief.

Although not excessive, the number of casualties necessitated the reorganization of several battalions into two companies. Drafts did begin to trickle in but until the division was relieved on the night 22-23 December, numerically reduced battalions were compelled to hold extensive frontages. When battalions of 184 Brigade, for example, relieved the remnants of 182 Brigade they subsequently held fronts of up to 1,000 yards. The divisional artillery was to stay in the line for an additional few days before it rejoined the infantry and other arms in the area of the Somme. Later in the month it was warned it would be going to the front opposite St Quentin to take over trenches from French units. On 21 March 1918 and the following days, the division was to fight another and even more ferocious defensive battle against an enemy determined to break through and bring the war to a swift conclusion.

63 TNA WO 953054: 10 Dec.1917 and Appendix XI

8

Defensive Operations II: Preparations for Battle

Much has been written about the events of 21 March 1918 and the subsequent withdrawal of parts of the BEF from its forwards positions. The initial success of the German attack is usually ascribed to the dense fog, an overwhelming artillery bombardment, the attackers' numerical superiority, a misunderstanding and misapplication of the ways and means of the British strategy of defence in depth, a breakdown in the command structure, and the failure of some defenders and their commanders to demonstrate sufficient fortitude in the face of what was an anticipated onslaught. There are elements of truth in all these assertions but we should also add the difficulties created by the haste with which Fifth Army took over a section of line ill-prepared for defence, the very recent and disruptive re-organization of British divisions, and the fact that there had been little thought given to training in defensive tactics by an army that had spent the previous three years on the offensive.

Current operational planning comprises several crucial and inter-related concepts.[1] These include identifying and targeting the enemy's centre of gravity, providing sufficient resources to protect your own vulnerabilities, formulating an achievable military and political end state that will secure national or alliance cohesion, and providing adequate means to secure that desired objective. Planners will identify a series of decisive points and conditions which must be achieved during the course of the campaign, design a sequence of lines of operation with alternative branches and sequels that will allow those decisive points and conditions to be secured, and apply operational art. In preparation for his Spring Offensives General Ludendorff amassed what might have been adequate resources, and also identified the alliance as the enemies' potential weakness and centre of gravity. His desired end state was to defeat the Allies before substantial numbers of Americans arrived to swing the balance of forces in the Allies' favour. He and his staff will have identified a series of decisive points and conditions including, for example, the seizure of particular tactical and strategic positions to inhibit the Allies' defence and sustainment operations, as well as the lines of operation required to achieve those goals. Finally, he was to apply his interpretation of today's concept of operational art. This involved the direction of his resources in a series of successive hammer blows designed to split the alliance both politically and militarily.

---

1   *Allied Joint Doctrine for Operational Level Planning* (NATO, 2013), (AJP-5).

If Sir Douglas Haig viewed the forthcoming German offensive through an identical lens, he would have been confronted with a series of similar and yet, as the defending force, dissimilar problems. There was growing evidence that a major enemy attack would come in March but there was no certainty as to where the blow or blows would fall. Haig and his political masters appreciated that Germany's centre of gravity was its army and the army's relationship with the nation. If "Prussian militarism" were smashed, Germany would collapse. Despite the arguments between so-called Easterners and Westerners, the bulk of Allied resources had been geared to achieving that desired political and military end state. Protecting their own centre of gravity – ie alliance cohesion – was of paramount importance but it was only after the offensive had opened that the Allies accepted there had to be one supreme commander to coordinate the Allied armies and their strategy.

Haig and his staff had previously discussed schemes for a planned withdrawal if necessary by Fifth Army but it was believed First and Third armies would be able to hold the offensive in their respective defensive zones.[2] In that sense, there were few alternative sequences and phases available to commanders if things went wrong in those sectors. Neither, when it came to it, was there any inbuilt contingency when Fifth Army fell back beyond its anticipated new line of resistance. Counter-attacks schemes had been prepared and rehearsed but when the momentum and tempo of the enemy's thrusts swept away and beyond the prepared scenarios, there was no real Plan B. Gough and his corps commanders lost control of the battle and were unable to regain the initiative until the enemy's forces had effectively culminated.

If his armies were initially to contain and then eventually defeat the offensive, Haig's own decisive conditions and subsequent lines of operation would have included such elements as the construction of widespread ground-based physical defensive obstacles arranged in depth, sufficient active and silent artillery brigades positioned in secure areas, and numerous well-protected machine-gun and TMB emplacements with weapons able to sweep and bombard potential avenues of approach. In addition, there would have to be reliable and resilient communications between all levels of command and control, the ways and means to deploy large numbers of infantry and artillery reinforcements at short notice to pre-prepared positions, the ways and means seriously to disrupt and even destroy the enemy's logistical capability, and be confident that his own army's morale was sufficiently strong to withstand a prolonged enemy offensive and possible strategic withdrawal. He would also have had to create the circumstances that would allow himself, his commanders, and his forces to cooperate and coordinate actions with those of the French.[3] Like all of his subordinate commanders, the GOsC of the four 2nd Line divisions in the front zones, and also Major General Braithwaite of 62nd Division whose brigades were to be thrown into the maelstrom on 26 March, knew an attack was coming. They had been in almost daily receipt of sheaves of orders and doctrinal pamphlets explaining how the offensive was to be halted. Their task from January-February onwards was to disseminate the commander's intent and prepare their divisions' terrain and men for the defensive task to come. When the attack came, and with communications from DHQ to corps and army often severed, the GOsC would have to prioritize what effects they could generate along their own lines of operation with whatever forces they were able to control. With as great a degree of operational

---

2   J.E. Edmonds, *Military Operations 1918,* Vol. I (London: Macmillan, 1935), pp.96-99; Edmonds, *Military Operations, France & Belgium 1918, Appendices*, Appendix XII, 4 Feb.1918.
3   Ibid. Appendix VI, 14 Dec.1917.

synergy and simultaneity as could be applied they would also seek to coordinate those actions with any other organized forces which remained in contact on their flanks.

British defensive doctrine had emerged in the post-Somme period but had only been codified with any real coherence in late 1917. Although its appearance provided essential guidelines, theories and practices for an army forced to confront the unexpected realities of fighting defensive battles in the near future, its tardy appearance gave little time for its strategic, operational, and tactical elements to be fully understood by those who were to operate under its aegis. Elements of *FSR(2)* were to remain equally essential reading for commanders about to face the forthcoming test but their over-riding concerns were the absence of physical defensive obstacles in some parts of the front, insufficient manpower to rectify those deficiencies, and the lack of time for their men to become accustomed and trained for a system of defence that was both largely unfamiliar and widely disliked.[4]

The conceptual component of British fighting power in early 1918 had been heavily influenced by German defensive doctrine. The enemy's development of defence in depth supported by strong and swiftly organized counter-attacks had frustrated many of the British assaults during Third Ypres and later at Cambrai. The resultant evolution of British defensive doctrine was a combination of lessons learned from bitter and costly experience, captured German doctrinal documents, and the consequence of assessments of the state of British force preparedness and defences in late 1917 and early 1918. A GHQ memo of December 1917 explained the principles on which an accepted period of British defensive posture should be laid. The document emphasized the need for such components as three successive areas or zones of defence, economy of effort, the timely employment of reserves, and the construction of protective shelters and posts. It advised on the role of the artillery and machine guns and reiterated the need for constant aggressive patrolling and raiding. Frequent rehearsals of counter-attacks over ground likely to be contested, and the "maintenance of confidence and fitness of the troops" were also to be prioritized.[5] One of the elements of the modern conceptual component is the requirement to understand the character of the war being fought. That had been relatively simple enough to comprehend while the Allies concentrated on the offensive. With the enemy now about to revert to the offensive, the character had changed. The BEF was compelled to undergo a fundamental shift in strategy. The ends remained the same but the ways and means of achieving the desired ultimate victory was to go on the defensive and let the enemy do the attacking.

The GHQ memo was not a prescriptive list of how it expected the armies and corps to conduct themselves but did make it clear that commanders and staffs of those higher echelons should base their own preparations around this set of principles. There had to be, for example, positions and accommodation prepared for the likely emergency arrival of additional artillery and infantry to a corps area, but armies and corps were largely allowed to decide how divisions were to hold their own stretches of front. In acknowledgement of how the composition of armies and corps changed frequently, GHQ did insist, however, that the plans drawn up by corps should be accepted as instructions by incoming divisions. Army HQ were ordered to coordinate their corps' defence schemes, and corps were to ensure their own divisions' preparations were mutually compatible. Both army and corps were responsible for overseeing and ultimately

4 Ibid. See Appendix IV, 24 Nov.1917; XIII, 24 Jan.1918; XI, 1 Feb.1918 for concerns over manpower, etc.
5 Ibid. Appendix VI, 14 Dec.1917

supervising divisional schemes of work and allocation of labour for the construction of artillery and machine-gun sites, OPs, belts of wire, and switch trenches.[6] Although this supervision, and in parts direct control from higher authority, did impact on the ability of GOsC divisions to decide how and where their brigades should fight, it did also enforce a sensible degree of influence and balance over the importance of subordinates knowing their commander's intent and on how they should and might use their ways and means to achieve operational objectives.

During the regular meetings between Haig and his GOsC armies, as well as the subsequent conferences between the army commanders and their GOsC corps, it became clear that there were differences in how GHQ doctrine was interpreted. Haig suggested the artillery should reduce its rate of fire so as not to provoke retaliation and interference with the work on defences. General Gough, GOC Fifth Army, and 58th Division's staff in particular, welcomed this suggestion but because the defences of Third Army had been established for significantly longer the strategy was not so imperative for 59th Division. Both armies, however, had to either adapt and add to existing defences or, in the case of the southern divisions of Fifth Army, begin almost from scratch. Fifth Army's Defence Scheme was consequently something of a hybrid and rather more complicated than that of Third Army's. What evolved was essentially a cross between a present-day mobile and an area defence. Haig's strategy of defence in depth combined a fixing element to deny the enemy freedom of manoeuvre and, by concentration of force and counter-mobility effects such as wire and funnelling, to deny him ground, slow him down, and inflict losses. Enemy exploitation would then be frustrated by counter-attack. The defence schemes needed to provide sufficient fire zones in which the enemy would be canalized and destroyed.

There was much discussion and passing of memos between Gough and GHQ over whether and when a withdrawal to the line of the Somme and the Péronne bridgehead might become imperative. GHQ believed the most southerly 12 miles of Gough's front – including 58th Division's sector – was "unlikely to be the scene of a serious hostile attack."[7] It did nevertheless want the principles of defence of Fifth Army to be similar to those of the other armies – i.e. to fight in the Battle and Rear Zones but to avoid using large reserves (which did not exist anyway) to recover them should the zones be lost. Gough was more than concerned about the state of his inherited defences and reported his front lacked adequate railways, tramways, labour, RFC squadrons, road materials, and RE companies. Even in the unlikely event that all of his requests for additional resources were met, he still believed stretches of his Battle and Rear Zones would remain in a parlous state until the end of March. In addition to the poor state of the defences, the manpower available to Gough to defend his extended front was extremely limited. The idea of a withdrawal to the Somme and even the Tortille (north of Péronne) had come from him but was also endorsed by GHQ.[8] On the positive side, the defended areas of 66th Division (XIX Corps), and to a lesser extent 61st Division (XVIII Corps), already had considerable defensive obstacles *in situ*. On assuming responsibility for those sectors the two divisions aimed to improve them further by constructing additional strong points, redoubts and switches.

---

6   Ibid.
7   Edmonds, *Military Operations 1918, Appendices*, Appendix XII.
8   Ibid., Appendix XII and XI.

210 Of No Earthly Use

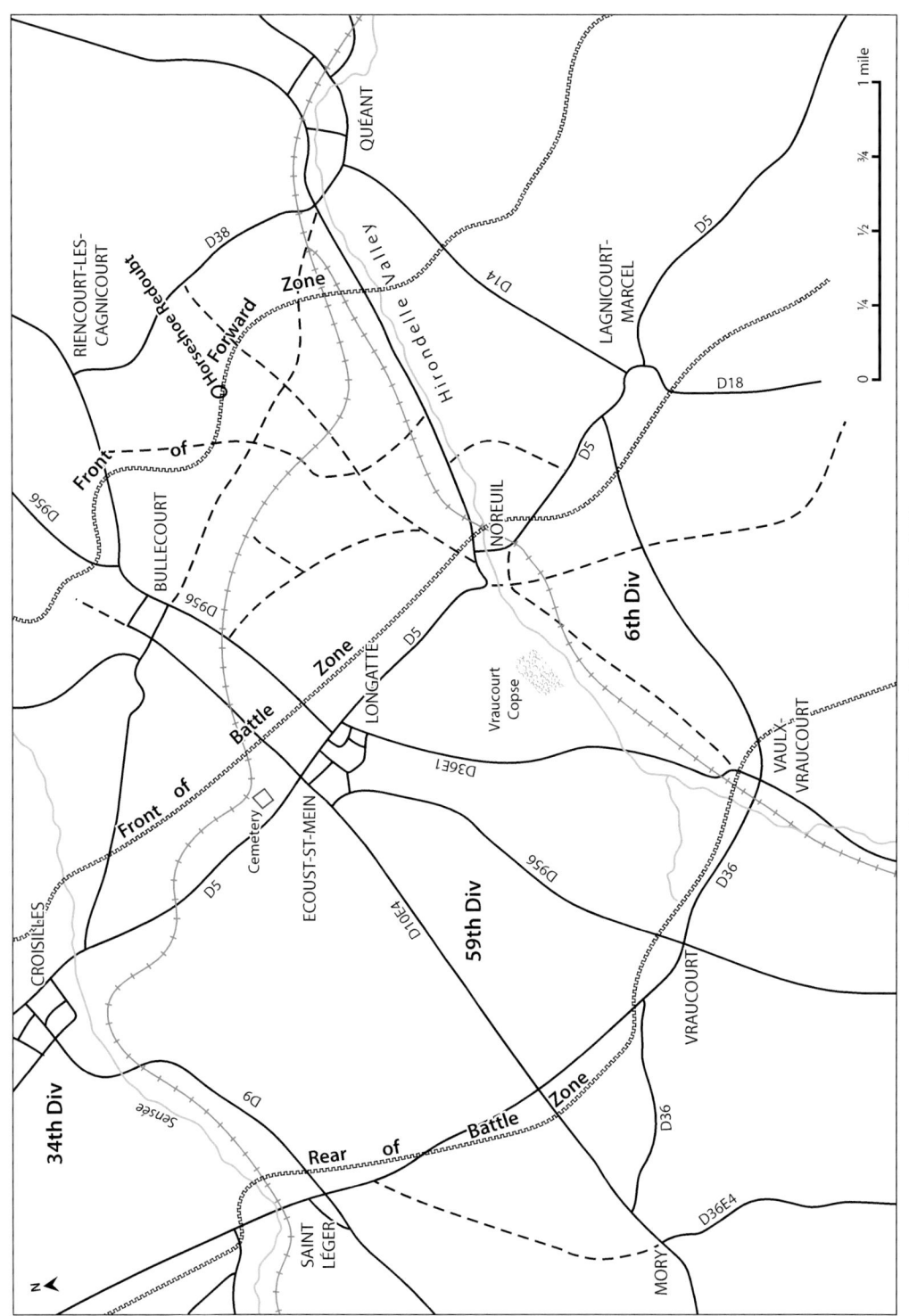

Map 6 Ecoust-St-Mein, March 1918.

Third Army's defence scheme was rather more straightforward.[9] As one of three divisions in VI Corps, 59th Division took over sections of the former Hindenburg Main and Support Lines near Bullecourt. The army's scheme included exhortations to pay special attention to the security of its junction with Fifth Army, to the positions and protection of OPs and TMBs, and warnings about placing field guns too far forward. Arrangements had to be in place to prepare alternative positions for every existing field artillery battery as well as those for the arrival of reinforcing artillery brigades. Signals had to be agreed for SOS barrages and how and when counter-preparation barrages should be fired. Effective anti-tank measures had also to be devised and acted upon. Despite these strictures, however, corps HQ insisted the allotment of fixed artillery positions should not "too much" cramp the initiative of battery commanders. They, it was asserted, should be prepared to vary their dispositions if "the direction of the attack changed" from that contemplated in the corps' plan. According to the corps' scheme (which ran to 46 pages) 59th Division's role was to hold "at all costs" the Longatte Spur and the spurs north of Noreuil and Ecoust.[10]

When it took over the Bullecourt – Noreuil sector in mid-February, 59th Division held it on a three brigade front. All brigades had two battalions up and one in reserve. It was on this basis that the first divisional defence plan was drawn up but, on 2 March, what had been the left brigade sector was taken over by 34th Division. From then on, 59th Division held a two brigade front. This, of course, necessitated changes to the original defence scheme. Its three brigades were instructed to produce their own schemes, all of which were based heavily on the divisional plan. For example, that the prime purpose of the Forward Zone was to make the enemy commit large forces and expend significant quantities of ammunition in taking it was precisely reiterated in 178 Brigade's scheme. Brigade HQ believed the zone should be thinly held and did not intend to launch any large-scale counter-attacks from the rear should it fall. There were to be plenty of Lewis guns, particularly to protect the flanks, and communication trenches were to be wired and used if necessary as fire trenches. Junior commanders were urged to deliver counter-attacks rapidly and not to retire purely because their flanks had been turned. If the ground could be held they were to fight for it. It was beholden on junior commanders, however, to make judgements and not to fritter away reserves in counter-attacks that were unlikely to succeed. To enforce this philosophy, COs were instructed to set problems and scenarios for their subordinates to analyze and solve. Pre-arranged plans had to be thoroughly rehearsed and platoons designated as counter-attack units had to be familiar with trench exists and the ground over which they would operate.[11] The plan submitted by 177 Brigade specified how it would use its reserve battalion in coordination with a prepared artillery programme to counter-attack two tactically important trenches from three possible starting points. The brigade plans also reiterated the belief that machine guns were the "backbone of the infantry defence." Crews were warned not to fall back "because they are the framework" on which the defence was built. The brigade used the divisional scheme to detail the grouping of machine guns, the position of TMs, locations of divisional, brigade and battalion bomb dumps and ration stores, signal arrangements, and routes to and from the three defensive systems.[12] Although not all possible examples are extant,

---

9   Ibid., Appendix XIV.
10 Ibid., Appendix XV.
11 TNA WO 953024: 178 Bde Defence Scheme; n.d. but Feb.1918.
12 TNA WO 953022: 12 Mar.1918.

it seems that the nine battalions were also instructed to develop their own defence scheme. The plan drawn up by 2/5th Sherwood Foresters detailed the size of its counter-attack unit and the circumstances under which it was to be used, what troops should do if enemy tanks appeared, and how the transport section was to operate if an attack occurred. The plan was updated and amended regularly as and when more posts were created in the Forward Zone.[13] When the attack came, there is strong evidence to demonstrate that the division's units had rehearsed well and that they adhered to the prepared plans and arrangements until circumstances forced a widespread withdrawal.

The three 2nd Line divisions serving under General Gough were part of what was generally perceived as an unhappy and disjointed army. The relationship between Fifth Army's senior commanders and staff with its corps and divisional commanders during Third Ypres is widely thought to have been toxic. Gough and Major General Malcolm, his Chief of Staff, drove their commanders and troops hard and were prepared to sack those whom they felt were not up to the task. There were rumours in October 1917 that because his regime was considered to be so unpopular, Gough himself was about to be degummed. He survived the rumours and, to the surprise of some, also retained the services of Major General Mackenzie, GOC 61st (2nd South Midland) Division. Mackenzie apparently himself believed he would be sacked following his division's unsuccessful attacks on the Battery Position in September.[14] In December, Gough lost the services of Malcolm largely because Malcolm's presence at army HQ was considered by some of his superiors to be too disruptive. He was appointed GOC 66th (2nd East Lancashire) Division in XIX Corps and was thus again to come under Gough's command.[15] Malcolm's now immediate superior, Lieutenant General Watts, had been criticised by both Gough and Malcolm during Third Ypres but, with Haig's support, had retained his command. Haig thought Watts to be a "fine leader" but a "distinctly stupid man" who lacked imagination.[16] At about the same time, 58th (2/1st London) Division came under Lieutenant General Richard Butler. He was formerly Deputy Chief of the General Staff and was generally thought to be a difficult man. Haig was disappointed to lose Butler but although Gough had a low opinion of him, Butler was appointed to Fifth Army as GOC III Corps in January. Another of Gough's GOsC corps was Lieutenant General Ivor Maxse. Maxse, a man who Gough respected and appreciated, had retained command of XVIII Corps since its creation in January 1917. This corps now included Mackenzie's 61st Division.

The length of Fifth Army's front and the few divisions allocated to defend it, created problems for GOsC corps and divisions when they drew up their defence schemes. Both Maxse and Butler believed their inherited Battle Zones were too linear and preferred instead a system of strong

---

13   TNA WO 953025: 2/5th Sherwood Foresters, 15 Feb.1918.
14   I.F.W. Beckett, 'Gough, Malcolm and Command on the Western Front' in B. Bond et al, *Look to your Front: Studies in the First World War* (Staplehurst: Spellmount, 1999), pp.2-12. Opinions do vary and there is substantial evidence to show that becoming an element of Fifth Army was not as universally hated as is sometimes believed. There is, however, considerable evidence to suggest that it was far from being the most popular of the five British armies, and that Gough and his staff were distrusted and disliked.
15   Gough was clearly annoyed at Malcolm's removal and at the refusal of GHQ to replace him as Chief of Staff with Gough's preferred choice. Sir H. Gough, *Fifth Army* (London: Hodder & Stoughton, 1931), p.223.
16   S. Robbins, *British Generalship*, p.54.

points, preferably linked, to increase depth and make better use of the restricted manpower. A series of redoubts, they believed, would add strength to the rear edge of the Forward Zone and the forward part of the Battle Zone. Maxse's divisions commanded good fire zones in all areas but Butler's stretched III Corps, and especially 58th Division, relied on the marshes of the Oise to restrict the areas likely to be attacked. Issued only 11 days before the German attack commenced, III Corps Defence Scheme was an expansion of a series of "Principles" laid down on 27 January and the result of meetings between Butler and his divisional commanders.[17] It covered the familiar material such as signalling and artillery arrangements, how the line was to be held, medical provisions, demolition schemes for bridges, administrative details for accommodation, ammunition and ration dumps, the role of the reserve brigade, and counter-attack plans. This latter section went into very detailed tactical arrangements for several possible scenarios and laid clear the responsibilities of GOsC brigades and COs for organizing counter-attacks.

Major General Cator, GOC 58th Division, issued a preliminary divisional scheme on 21 February. Further amendments were issued on the way the line was to be held as work on the Forward and Battle Zones progressed.[18] The formation to be most heavily involved on 21 March, 173 Brigade, produced its own scheme and assessment of the likely scenarios probably very shortly afterwards.[19] Cator had instructed 173 Brigade, positioned north of the Oise, to have one battalion in the Forward Zone, one in the Battle, and one in reserve behind the Green (Rear) Line. In effect, this meant that 2/2nd London, 206 MG Company and six LTMs in the Forward Zone were to hold a front of about 7,000 yards. As it was impracticable to hold this as a continuous line, one defensive post in each company area was to be a keep, "capable of holding out indefinitely." Platoon and section positions were organized in depth in a chequer board pattern sited to cooperate with the machine guns. The Forward Zone was "to be held to the last", with nominated platoons tasked to deliver immediate counter-attacks. Rather than wait for higher approval, their commanders were instructed to act on their own initiative. Company defence schemes were subsequently drawn up detailing how counter-attack platoons were to rehearse certain scenarios. Once these and the battalion schemes had been approved by GOC brigade they were to be "rigidly adhered to and taken over on relief." Troops were to be informed there would be no support from the Battle Zone unless the GOC brigade specifically gave permission for platoons there to advance to the Forward Zone.

This, the division's left brigade, did not, however, expect to be attacked. If it were, it was assumed it would be only a diversion from a larger assault on the centre and right brigades, or on 18th Division to the left. This was to prove a desperately false assumption but was a prime reason why the brigade's reserve battalion, which was meant to be helping in the construction of the Battle Zone's defences, was lent for three weeks to 174 Brigade. On taking over the sector, 173 Brigade had pointed out that the existing French defences were neither strong enough nor suited to the number of men available to garrison them. Consequently, until sufficient progress had been made on strengthening them, training was deemed to be "subservient" to providing

---

17 TNA WO 95674: III Corps Defence Scheme, 10 Mar.1918.
18 TNA WO 952988: 21 Feb.1918. Amendments, 28 Feb.1918.
19 TNA WO 953000: 173 Brigade Defence Scheme, n.d. On 6 March, 174 Bde issued its Defence Scheme. This replaced that produced by 90 Bde which 174 Bde had inherited. Unit COs were instructed to go through the new scheme with their company OC and draw up their own based on the brigade's plan by 13 March. TNA WO 953006: 2/8th London, Mar.1918.

working parties.[20] Furthermore, patrolling was to be restricted to dead ground and canal crossings; the artillery was limited to firing only on SOS lines, counter-battery programmes, and retaliation shoots. Harassing fire by machine guns was not allowed in case it revealed the guns' positions and drew an enemy response.[21] This was a sensible policy while strong points were constructed, cables laid, relay and visual signalling stations established, and forward artillery positions prepared. Nonetheless, when the Germans struck, the brigade's defended localities remained incomplete. With a trench strength of only 22 officers and 585, 2/2nd London was stretched very thinly across the enormous frontage of its Forward Zone. Even if the defences had been further advanced the weak battalion would still have struggled to contain and repel the enemy assault.

On the left of Butler's III Corps was Maxse's XVIII Corps, with 61st Division as its left flank formation. The corps' three divisions relieved the French forces in mid-January and soon afterwards produced a defence scheme. This included a Forward Zone comprised mainly of posts rather than connected trenches, supported by a mobile reserve and a series of keeps. In common with those of other armies and corps, Maxse stipulated that the distance between the Forward and Battle Zones precluded any immediate counter-attacks coming from the latter and that any launched by counter-attack units from within the Forward Zone were to be on the initiative of their own commanders. Like those of III Corps to the south, the defences inherited by XVIII Corps were inadequate and work was immediately set in train to improve and develop them. The three zones were to be adapted to provide defence in depth with divisions responsible for developing the Forward, corps the Battle, and Fifth Army the Rear Zones.[22]

As an enthusiastic believer in the value of thorough training, Maxse organized several corps conferences to discuss strategy and training programmes. He accepted that intensive training could not begin until the Battle Zone had been completed which, he predicted, would be within the second week of March. Subsequent to Maxse's meetings, Major General Mackenzie convened divisional conferences to disseminate the commander's intent and to discuss policy and priorities for his three brigades. Readjustments of the line in early February necessitated another series of meetings involving COs, brigade majors, and staff captains. These conferences were supplementary to courses on defence at the corps school designed for officers from GOsC brigades down to platoon commanders. These occasions were somewhat irreverently described by one officer as opportunities to "worship at the shrine of Maxse."[23] Based on papers issued in mid and late January, 61st Division produced its own defence scheme on 2 March. This was very similar to that issued by corps HQ, including a section stating that construction of defensive works was to take priority over training and recreation. There were also sections dealing with anticipated scenarios on its particular front.[24] One of these was a scheme to regain an important area of high ground just beyond the division's northern boundary. If 24th Division,

---

20 So incomplete were the inherited defences that as late as 20 March, the CRE, senior commanders, and divisional staff were still deciding on where to build positions to defend the tactically and strategically important village of Condren. TNA WO 952994: Mar.1918.
21 TNA WO 953000: 173 Brigade Defence Scheme.
22 TNA WO 95953: XVIII Corps Instructions for Defence, 10 Jan.1918.
23 G. Rose, *2/4th Ox & Bucks*, p.159.
24 One copy of the early instructions can be found in TNA WO 953061: 1/5th Gordon Highlanders, Feb.1918.

on 61st Division's left, was forced to withdraw along the Omignon Valley, enemy possession of Spooner Redoubt would threaten to expose the South Midland's flank. The remarkably detailed scheme looked at the possibility of a two battalion counter-attack from the Battle Zone. This was in theory to be supported by four 18 pdr batteries, one 4.5 inch, three 6 inch, and one 9.2 inch howitzer batteries, and eight machine guns firing an overhead barrage in advance of the infantry. The artillery programmes were clearly laid out with various amendments should the intended number of guns tasked for support become unavailable. This was to be one of the few prepared schemes put partly into operation during the initial German attack.

All of the division's brigade sectors were also issued with exceptionally detailed defence schemes.[25] Among other things these gave the positions of posts, strong points and trenches, numbers and types of available guns, rates of fire, and the locations of various HQ. They also stressed the need for initiative and responsibility down the chain of command, insisting that all officers to platoon commanders, "must have a clear idea of what he means to do, and a cut-and-dried plan of action in the event of the enemy penetrating his front, right and left." All scenarios were to be practised by day and night at least once during every tour in the Forward Zone. At the next level of command down, individual battalions also devised schemes based on the wider divisional plan. In February, 2/4th Berkshire received a copy of the divisional plan and had produced its own scheme by 6 March. In the meantime, OsC companies had reconnoitred the positions mentioned in the larger scheme and with their companies began practising their emergency occupation. The CO explained the plan to all officers who, with their platoon sergeants, then reconnoitred the Forward and Battle Zones. By mid-February a training schedule had been drawn up and NCO classes for instruction begun. The CO lectured all officers and NCOs on 'The Defence Scheme of the Battle Zone and the Forward Zone' on two successive days in March. When in the line, aggressive patrolling and intelligence gathering was carried out nightly. As intelligence of the probable date of the attack grew, and as it became more likely that on that day the battalion would be used in a counter-attack role, on 20 March company officers and NCOs reconnoitred the Battle Zone sector between Spooner Redoubt and Holnon Wood. This was the area that the divisional scheme had pin-pointed as the sector where the proposed two battalion counter-attack was most likely to be executed.[26]

The potentially vulnerable area on the left of 61st Division was manned by 24th Division which, together with 66th Division constituted Lieutenant General Herbert Watts' XIX Corps.[27] The East Lancashire Division had handed over its Zonnebeke sector on 10 February and moved to Proyart, east of Amiens. It trained there until 27 February. It was then ordered

---

25 TNA WO 953055: 182 Bde, 61st Division Right Sector FZ Defence Scheme and amendments; WO 953059: 183 Bde, Defence Scheme for Left Sector.
26 TNA WO 953065: 2/4th Berkshire, Feb-Mar. 1918. It seems likely that other battalions in 184 Bde would also have developed their own unit plans on the orders of either brigade or DHQ. On the right of 61st Division, and also in XVIII Corps, was 30th Division. In its review of the fighting in March it stressed the "inestimable value" to its troops of rehearsing counter-attacks over the ground most likely to be contested. (TNA WO 952313, Narrative of the 30th Division 21-30 March 1918, n.d.). The detail of both 61st and 30th divisions' Defence Schemes and their frequent references to rehearsals and constant intelligence gathering in their war diaries may well have been deliberate in order to appease the ever-watchful Maxse.
27 1st Cavalry Division near Roisel was also at the disposal of XIX Corps.

216　Of No Earthly Use

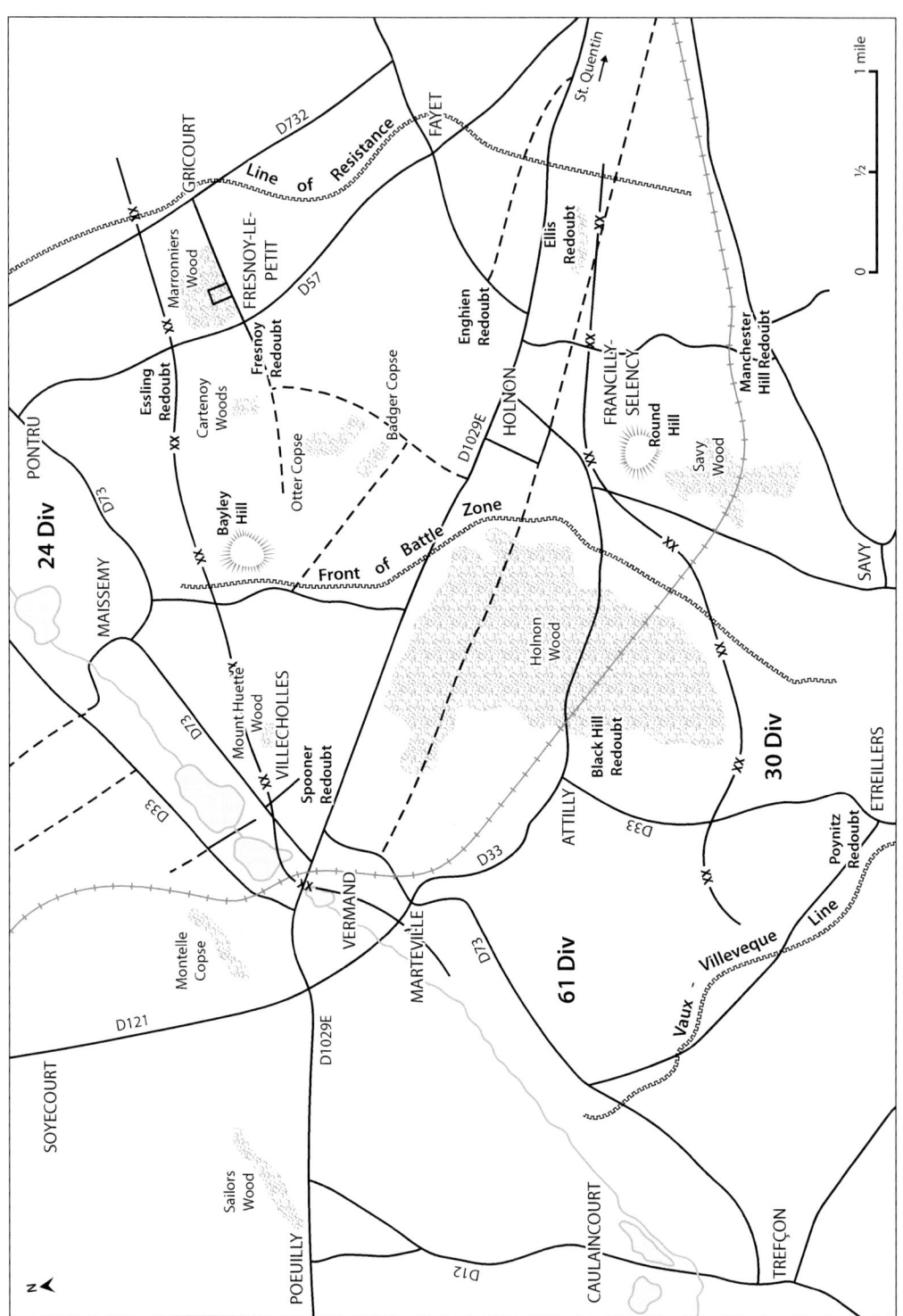

Map 7 Holnon sector, March 1918.

to relieve 24th Division "in accordance with the Cavalry Corps Defence Scheme."[28] The relief was completed on 1 March, with 2/7th Lancashire Fusiliers immediately being welcomed to the area by an unpleasant German raid.[29] On 11 March, and presumably under instruction from corps HQ, DHQ decided that until it could fully assess the situation and terrain it would continue to use the existing Cavalry Corps Defence Scheme and modify where necessary.[30] There were some immediate alterations of artillery programmes but the main change came on 19 March when corps HQ announced there was to be a building programme in the Battle Zone of 12 company-sized redoubts.

Major General Malcolm was reasonably relaxed about the threat of a major offensive on his divisional front. He believed the main enemy blow would fall elsewhere but that his 66th Division might have to make a partial tactical withdrawal without even fighting. He gave his GOsC infantry brigades one day to consider possible scenarios and to suggest where, in the case of withdrawal, the forward positions and flanks should be established. At a conference on 13 March the senior officers discussed the strengthening of posts, which positions should be retained and which abandoned, barrage arrangements, MG positions, and the role of the RE and pioneers. To improve liaison and appreciation of other arms' capabilities, the CRA invited infantry brigadiers to visit the heavy artillery's counter-battery office to gain understanding of its operational and analytical methods. Although this was almost still a week before corps HQ announced the construction of the 12 redoubts, it was obvious much work was needed on the already existing defences. Malcolm instructed brigades to practise manning battle stations but insisted only officers and NCOs should be used in what were essentially TEWTs. This, he insisted, would allow work on the defences to proceed unhindered.[31]

As XIX Corps' war diary does not contain a fully revised defence scheme it seems likely that the amended Cavalry Corps scheme was still in place on 21 March.[32] Given Malcolm's character and record as a senior staff officer it is very likely, however, that he instructed his GOsC brigades to produce schemes for their own sectors. There are no extant copies of any which might have been produced by 198 and 199 Brigades but 197 Brigade has left a brief description of how it was to defend the neighbourhood of Templeux-le-Guérard. This area was in the division's Battle Zone and was divided into three sectors, the strongest of which was Templeux Quarries. This collection of large excavations and spoil tips was to be defended by a combination of two companies of pioneers, one section of a field company, some attached infantry, and

28 TNA WO 953121: 27 Feb.1918.
29 Coincidentally, the division's sector was very largely that fought over by 59th Division in April-May the previous year.
30 According to one post-war source, 66th Division inherited "a golf course, an officers' club with garden, a very fine battalion officers' mess and theatre, but the defences which everyone wanted to see were difficult to find." Compiled, *A History of the East Lancashire Royal Engineers* (Private publication, n.d.) p.238.
31 TNA WO 953121: Notes on the Defence of the 66th Divisional Front, 12 Mar.1918; Conference of Senior Officers, 13 Mar.1918.
32 A Defence Scheme was produced by 24th Division (TNA WO 952192, 30 Jan.1918) but the division later slipped to the south vacating part of its former front which was then occupied by 66th Division. There are similarities in 24th Division's scheme with the way by which 66th Division later held the three zones. As Major General Malcolm is known to have discussed changes to 24th Division's plan with his GOC bdes and staffs it is probable that he adopted the existing plan and issued amendments where necessary. TNA WO 953121, 4 Mar.1918

any Lancashire Fusiliers of the battalion manning the Forward Zone who may have been forced back. The strong point, which was spread over a considerable area and controlled access along the Cologne Valley towards Roisel, was "expected to hold out for at least 4 or 5 days."[33]

By opting to go on the defensive and await a major enemy offensive the BEF had, at least temporarily, abandoned the initiative. *FSR(2)* acknowledged that going on the defensive depended upon the "strategical situation" but that if it was necessary, the commander should attempt to manoeuvre in order to occupy more easily defendable ground. There he would wait for the situation to change to his advantage before switching to the offensive.[34] Above all, "The choice of a position and its preparation must be made with a view to economizing the power expended on defence in order that the power of the offensive may be increased."[35] In March 1918, the BEF had little alternative other than to wait for the assault on ground they already occupied. Behind both Third and Fifth Armies' fronts lay the devastated zone. This area severely hampered communications but did offer some tactical and operational advantages to the defender rather than the attacker. As manpower was at a premium it had been tacitly decided that when an attack came certain areas might be relinquished in order to minimize losses and cause additional operational difficulties to the enemy. Although some sectors where the 2nd Line divisions were to fight offered good fields of fire, with the possible exception of 59th Division, the defenders were spread thinly over long sectors. In addition to 2/2nd London's 7,000 yards of front, the three forward battalions in 61st Division all had fronts of about 2,000 yards; the three of 66th Division all approximately 1,800 yards; the two battalions of 59th Division's two forward brigades each defended roughly 1,100 yards.[36] Even if the necessarily altered and partially new elements of the conceptual component of fighting power had been understood, disseminated and practised by the formations of the BEF, the troops faced a daunting prospect. For over three years their commanders had been used to being on the offensive and doctrine had developed to enhance the prospects of success. But defence, especially on the scale and the ways and means by which it was to be fought, was new and demanded a difficult mental readjustment.

To exacerbate the difficulties of adjusting to a changed conceptual method of waging war, the physical component of British fighting power was also under pressure. The influx of German divisions from the Eastern Front meant the Germans opposite British Fifth and Third Armies had at least the temporary advantage in guns and manpower. Furthermore, another crucial factor in the physical component is the ability of units, once the character and the tactical and operational methodology have changed, to absorb new doctrine and organizations that reflect those changes. A later report by the Director of Military Operations (DMO) emphasized that

---

33 TNA WO 953135: Templeux and Defences, 17 Mar.1918. This scheme was amended three days later to detail the tactics to be employed should the enemy make a surprise attack with tanks. (197 Bde Order No.7, 20 Mar.1918). At the divisional conference on 13 March, Malcolm had "deprecated" the unconfirmed report of tanks opposite the divisional front. On 11 March, an intelligence report had noted "a motor, shaped like 2 railway trucks joined together, with conning tower, 3 masts and appeared to have wheels." TNA WO 953121: 11 Mar.1918.
34 Today, that phrase would encompass consideration of the strategic realities of the military and political situation.
35 *FSR* (1912) p.140.
36 A former officer of 2/5th Gloucestershire summed it up nicely: "The holding of such an extended line so lightly was probably a necessity, but to say the least, it was audacious." A. Barnes, *The Story of the 2/5th Gloucestershire*, p.82.

the lack of time given to British units to rest and train had been a major factor in the German successes of March and April 1918. Major General Dawnay claimed that it took a minimum of six weeks of training to bring a division to a satisfactory level of efficiency.[37] The reasons why divisions were not awarded that amount of time were numerous but of the four 2nd Line divisions engaged on 21 March, only 59th Division had enjoyed, as a division, Dawnay's six week period of training in the three months before the German offensive.[38] In the same period, 58th, 66th and 61st divisions had, respectively, four, two and one week of uninterrupted training and rest. Moreover, even when the divisions did have the limited opportunity to train, the training itself was not particularly tailored for the forthcoming task.

The GHQ memo of December 1917 instructed divisions out of the line to study, utilize and incorporate into their training regimes the philosophy contained within two captured German documents on defensive strategy.[39] Another pamphlet specified by the memo was a piece of British doctrine first issued in June 1917 and revised in January 1918. This was known as *SS152*.[40] The document ran to 94 pages and effectively laid out a syllabus and uniformity of doctrine for what should be taught across the BEF in army and corps schools. None of the war diaries of the 2nd Line divisions go into any great detail about what their troops did during their training periods but it is likely they used *SS152* as the basis of their programmes.[41] In addition, there were many other doctrinal pamphlets available covering other aspects of defence, force protection, communications, tactical schemes, sustainment, weapons training, infantry cooperation with air and artillery, and even recreational training. The 2nd Line formations rarely mention the pamphlets and generally simply state the troops did PT, musketry, close order drills, specialist training, open warfare schemes, and counter-attack practice.[42] There is occasional mention of, for example, fire control competitions, instruction in the use of German machine guns, staff rides of the Battle Zone for senior officers, and advance guard actions against a retreating enemy. Only one diary, however, specifically states troops undertook "training in defence."[43]

---

37 IWM, Maxse Papers, Box 69/53/14, File 59. Quoted in R. Bryson, 'The Once and Future Army', in B.Bond, et al, *'Look to your Front', p49*
38 Depending on when they were relieved in the line, some battalions even managed a seven week period of training.
39 These were published as *SS561* and *SS621*
40 *SS152. Instructions for the Training of the British Armies in France*, and by March 1918 known as *Instructions for Training within Schools at GHQ, Army and Corps Level*.
41 Unfortunately, few BEF divisions went into the same expansive detail about their training regimes as the 1st Line 42nd (East Lancashire) Division. TNA WO 952646 catalogues and lists the doctrinal pamphlets (including *SS152* and *FSR*) to be used, what the various supporting arms will do, and how the infantry will practise forming defensive flanks, defend tactical localities, and mount both small unit and more methodical large-scale counter-attacks. The probable reason for the unusual amount of detail was the division's GOC. Maj. Gen. Solly-Flood was renowned as one of the great trainers of the BEF.
42 A run of eight miles, to be completed within 1 hour 20 minutes, was organized by 177 Bde. A "small" percentage of 2/4th Lincolnshire's troops did it in the time allowed and only 47 of 2/5th Lincolnshire. Given the taxing conditions endured by the troops in the trenches of Cambrai in mid-winter, this is hardly surprising. TNA WO 953023: Jan. war diaries of the two battalions.
43 TNA WO 953121: 25 Feb.1917. When 197 Bde practised a scheme, its machine-gun company fired ball ammunition into the ground. According to the observer, it was more realistic than the usual rattles and drums. See WO 953022: 2/5th Leicestershire, Jan. 1918

Throughout the diary entries is the consistent theme that training was frequently done in relays, compromised by the need to provide working parties and interrupted by the weather.[44] There is clear evidence that GOsC divisions did take cognizance of the GHQ memo's insistence that senior officers should repeatedly explain the new system of defence in depth to their men. They were also ordered to stress that an enemy offensive would give troops an excellent opportunity to inflict heavy losses. Gough and corps commanders were regular visitors to divisions' training areas and their Battle Zones and may even have attended the several lectures given by divisional and brigade GOsC to officers and NCOs on the defensive arrangements. At an army commanders' conference in early February, Haig emphasized the need for officers to make men familiar with the system and with their role in defence in depth. This message will have been passed down at meetings such as the four-day session held by XVIII Corps for divisional, brigade, and unit commanders two weeks later.[45] Although only one battalion recorded a lecture given by one OC on lessons learned from the previous trench tour, it is likely that other battalions also arranged similar sessions. It is impossible to know how effective the training had been but when the four 2nd Line formations were attacked on 21 March their training had probably been no more adequate or inadequate than the divisions on their flanks. Major General Dawnay's post-operation report states that less than 50 percent of divisions in action on 21 March had enjoyed even four, rather than the prescribed six, weeks training.

Many of the infantry may not have entirely understood or liked the defence in depth system but they would have been aware of the number of divisional artillery brigades, machine guns and trench mortars available to support them. On the other hand, they would have had little if any idea of what additional infantry, artillery, tanks and air were likely to be tasked as divisional reinforcements. Troops have to have confidence in the adequacy of the physical component in the supporting arms if they are to fight well. They would know they were spread sparsely on the ground and that losses during 1917 had been huge. Some in 61st and 58th divisions may have taken solace in the belief that as the areas now occupied by XVIII and III Corps had been relatively quiet for a year, if Fortune smiled, they might not be much affected by any possible offensive. They would imagine the main British forces to be concentrated in the more vulnerable areas where much of the 1917 fighting had occurred. Although the enemy opposite Fifth Army was to amass a superior number of artillery brigades, Gough's artillery in all calibres was not especially weak to fight a defensive battle.[46] Broad gauge railways had been laid across the devastated zone and many battery positions were linked to railhead by light railways or motorized transport. Artillery sustainment was thus not considered to be a major problem. On the other hand, once bridges, railways and roads had been demolished, any enemy opting to attack across that zone would find sustainment problematic.

Because the number of Fifth Army divisions and attached labour units was restricted, the demand for working parties was insatiable. The reaction of XIX Corps to the state of the defences taken over was typical of other formations in Fifth Army. They were described as

---

44 TNA.WO 953035: 12 Mar.1918. For example, 61st Division had three battalions garrisoning the FZ, three working in the BZ, two companies of each were training rather than working, and three in reserve. These three undertook often interrupted training and recreation.
45 TNA WO 95521: Record of Conference of Army Commanders, 16 Feb.1918; WO 95059: 183 Bde, 16 Feb.1918
46 See J. Edmonds, *Military Operations*, pp.126, 130

"unsatisfactory", not organized for defence in depth or "in a backward condition." The defences south of the Omignon in XVIII Corps' area were adjudged to have been devised without any thought about how they might coordinate with those of XIX Corps to its north.[47] Amongst the many other concerns all corps were very apprehensive about the limited amount of buried cabling. The East Lancashire Division employed a cavalry pioneer regiment and elements of 9 Cavalry Brigade on cabling fatigues, but while 61st Division managed to get cables to their redoubts buried to a depth of eight feet, a seam of rock two feet below the surface meant 58th Division's engineers could only bury a main cable to that meagre depth for a run of 300 yards before, fortunately, the seam disappeared. The North Midland Division inherited a comprehensive communication system in its sector but opted to improve it further by running additional cables to relay stations and by increasing the numbers of amplifiers and power buzzers linking DHQ to its units. It utilized parties of about 500 men nightly to dig a major cable trench from Mort Homme to Ecoust but, anticipating it would not be completed by the time the offensive started, made alternative arrangements that later managed to keep DHQ in touch with the right brigade at Vraucourt for much of 21 March.

In addition to the crash construction programme of redoubts by XIX Corps, as late as 5 March, 66th Division found it necessary to instigate a building programme of OPs in the Rear Zone. Construction seems not to have begun until 9 March, possibly owing to debate about their design, but the work was done hand-in-hand with the preparation of reserve artillery positions in the Battle Zone and sites in the rear for the arrival of any reinforcing brigades.[48] Extensive arrangements were developed by 61st Division for the duties of FOOs if the enemy attacked in fog and by the end of January every one of its batteries had a direct line from each battalion HQ to the 18 pdr battery covering that battalion's front. Third Army ordered all batteries or lone 18 pdrs within 300 yards of the forward line to be wired in; all single 18 pdrs or captured enemy 77mm field pieces positioned to fire within 1,000-1,500 yards of the front system were to be camouflaged. These guns were to have 300 stored rounds and those designated silent were only to be fired *in extremis*. Whether the wiring of the forward guns was completed or even attempted by 59th Division is unknown but the division's artillery did regularly fire its "Strafe Programmes" on known enemy positions and rear areas in conjunction with its machine guns and TMs.[49]

---

47 TNA WO 95962: Report of Operations 21 March-5 April 1918.
48 In addition to these sites, the field companies were also in the process of constructing a series of dugouts for up to 150 men; 1/5th Border (P) was building another six large dugouts to house up to 300 men for the artillery and medical services; the attached 258 Tunnelling Coy was building a further nine large garrison dugouts within the divisional area. TNA WO 953125: 12 Mar.1918, Appendix 4.
49 The artillery of 59th Division consisted of 295 and 296 Bdes RFA, supplemented by 26 Army Bde (less one battery as a mobile reserve) and the divisional TMs. The brigades were arranged in two groups in liaison with the two infantry brigades in the front system. The guns were positioned in two valleys running away from the front towards the Battle and Rear Zones. The corps heavy artillery and the Army Bdes were in addition to the divisional brigades and were generally but not inevitably under corps rather than divisional command. For example, 61st Division, was clearly informed by XVIII Corps that if it were attacked, the attached XIV and LXV Heavy Artillery Bdes would come under division rather than corps command. TNA WO 953035, 3 Mar.1918.

All four 2nd Line divisions had their artillery sustainment arrangements organized and in place by mid-March. There are odd indications from corps and divisional sources which suggest ammunition use was not to be unnecessarily profligate in the pre-offensive period but, on the whole, supplies of the different shell calibres were adequate to provide frequent bursts of harassing fire, counter-preparation shoots, and responses to SOS requests.[50] The guns of 296 Brigade RFA in 59th Division fired nearly 1,300 rounds in a six burst counter-preparation Schedule B programme on the night of 15-16 March, over 1,100 during the following day, and 1,000 on the next.[51] As late as 20 March, XVIII Corps ordered "every available gun" of 61st Division to fire a prolonged concentrated shoot on some approximately 500 suspicious "objects" opposite its front. There are no reports of the shoot having to be restricted owing to ammunition shortages.[52] Corps defence schemes required divisions to ensure their DACs had full details of where dumps were located, alternative routes to and from them, positions and systems in use at railhead, and locations and capacities of refilling points. Numbers and types of guns and shell availability per gun were regularly updated. Details of rates of fire for different calibres, SOS lines and signals, counter-preparation schemes, and who could be responsible for calling down which particular type of barrage, were all in place.[53] Corps defence schemes usually specified liaison arrangements for artillery cooperation in the cases of major counter-attacks and also emphasized the importance of coordination between OsC batteries and their FOOs. CRA 61st Division was involved in a Mutual Support Scheme with the artillery of neighbouring divisions but as this was a common practice and not always logged in war diaries it is probable that the other three 2nd Line divisions were also party to similar arrangements. No restriction was placed by VI Corps on the number of shells fired in the weeks before 21 March. During that period it managed to destroy several large enemy shell dumps identified by aerial reconnaissance. Neither did the corps stint on the use of gas in counter-preparation shoots. In contrast, XIX Corps decided that as its supply of gas shells was limited, those available should be held in reserve.

Working parties in all 2nd Line divisions were engaged in constructing machine-gun emplacements within the Front and Battle Zones. Divisional defence schemes decided how many guns, usually in pairs or four-gun batteries, should be in which zones and how many kept in reserve. In March, some of the 2nd Line division's machine-gun companies were still in the process of being amalgamated into divisional machine-gun battalions. As drafts and COs often new to the divisions were still arriving for these battalions, the units needed time to bed down and reach establishment. In consultation with GOsC brigades, RE, pioneers, and attached infantry were tasked to build the camouflaged emplacements and wire them in. In 59th Division, 59 Bn MGC deployed three eight-gun batteries in camouflaged positions in the

---

50 VI Corps Defence Scheme noted that concentrated counter-battery shoots could not be undertaken by several batteries at the same time because it would use too much ammunition and give away the position of those batteries. J. Edmonds, *Military Operations 1918*, Appendix 15.
51 TNA WO 953016: 296 Bde RFA. On 18 March the heavy artillery on the division's front fired 2,000 rounds as a counter-battery shoot on enemy guns behind Riencourt.
52 The "objects" were thought to be a new type of mobile ammunition transporters capable of sustaining the artillery in open warfare. TNA WO 953035: 13 and 20 Mar.1918
53 Intelligence updates caused regular amendments to divisions' defensive and offensive fire programmes. These changes often necessitated a re-scheduling of ammunition requirements and types.

Second System to support any counter-attack launched by the reserve brigade. Its other guns were arranged in batteries in trench, pit, or well-constructed champagne emplacements.[54] The extent of the divisional front meant that the full establishment of 60 available guns, plus four in reserve, were positioned to defend the more important tactical features to a depth of 6,000 yards. Emplacements had 15,000 stored rounds per gun and practice alarms were held every 48 hours.[55] The East Lancashire Division was not as fortunate. With its fourth company yet to appear the battalion possessed only 48 guns. Furthermore, men who had been transferred from the infantry in February were only partially trained and 60 more who had been transferred only ten days before had received no training of any note. The division did have an additional eight guns attached from the cavalry but the nature and extent of the divisional front meant that not all of its limited number of guns could be positioned in pairs. Moreover, the shortage meant that their barrage positions had to be very close to their actual battle positions. This was not always ideal. On 6 March, about 50 percent of the incoming guns took over positions vacated by the previous division, all of which it was subsequently discovered were known to the German gunners. The guns held a slightly greater numbers of belt boxes in reserve than those of 59th Division.[56]

Divisional TM batteries were also still in the process of forming. They were written into army, corps and divisional defence schemes with the specific role of infantry support. They were to be used when the enemy was massing for attack or if he had already occupied sections of the British system. Their daily function was to force the enemy to repair his wire and to blow gaps in it to allow the passage of raiding parties. Third Army stipulated batteries should be no closer than 500 yards from the front posts or line and ordered the construction of emplacements for two 6 inch Newtons close enough for them to fire on any 500 yard length of enemy-occupied British line. This was a fairly widespread policy across Fifth and Third armies. Two Newtons of 61st Division were positioned in a forward redoubt, each with specified targets on anticipated German forming up areas. In addition, four LTMs were placed in both the Forward and Battle Zones. The Newtons of X/66 TMB of 66th Division were deployed with four in the Forward, six in the Battle, and two in the Rear Zones. Like the machine-gun battalions, the most pressing problem for the batteries was the lack of experience among many of the crews. All personnel of Y/66 TMB were sent to Second Army School for almost a week in early March; 59th Division sent its crews to Third Army School in relays during January and February.[57] Several crews were also engaged in constructing their own emplacements and in fusing French 2 inch mortar bombs for anti-tank minefields. As this area of defence came under the aegis of the RE, and after two men were killed on one day in mid-March whilst fusing the bombs, CRE 61st Division expressed to corps HQ his growing concern about the unpredictability of

---

54 The emplacements came in a variety of forms. Champagne emplacements, for example, were mined dugouts, often 20 feet deep, with tunnel access and vertical climbing ladders to the individual gun positions.
55 TNA WO 953017: 59 Bn MGC, Mar.1918. Of the 60 guns, 28 were deployed within 2,000 yards of the front line. The deployments in all divisions depended on the terrain and the completeness or otherwise of the Front and Battle Zones. For example, 61st Division placed 12 in the forward areas of the Forward Zone, 20 in the rear of the Forward Zone (mainly in the redoubts), and 24 in the Battle Zone. The remainder were in reserve. See WO 953049: 61 Bn MGC, 1 Mar.1918.
56 TNA WO 953121: Narrative of Operations, Appendix 27, 7 Apr.1918.
57 TNA WO 953128; 1-6 Mar.1918; WO 953059: 83 Bde, Mar.1918.

the French bombs. Responding to these worries, XVIII Corps prohibited their further use and ordered all existing minefields to be fenced off.[58]

Corps HQ expected battalions in Forward Zones to adhere to guidance within *SS119* and *SS195* by undertaking regular patrols and raids.[59] Those of 58th Division rarely encountered any Germans and found many of the enemy's posts unoccupied. Standing patrols went out nightly, some in the hope of ambushing enemy parties and others in liaison with neighbouring battalions. The swamps in front of 173 Brigade offered little scope for patrolling but during March, and somewhat to the alarm of those who predicted no enemy attack would be able to cross them, the swamps began to dry out. On moonlit nights so-called "visiting patrols" and others tasked with gathering specified intelligence on particular areas of front were despatched by 61st Division.[60] On one night, 197 Brigade sent out 14 patrols in addition to its standard listening excursions but, as 4/Lincolnshire reported, it was suspected the enemy had been ordered not to engage with British patrols in case of disclosing identification of newly-arrived divisions. Raids did secure some important intelligence about enemy reliefs but they were not always successful. Displaying a considerable degree of naivety that is difficult to understand in an experienced 1st Line battalion, 1/8th Argyll & Sutherland Highlanders tried and failed twice. Raiders from 2/4th Berkshire found enemy trenches unoccupied; when they made a second attempt they were successfully driven off.[61] In 66th Division, one by 199 Brigade was abandoned when the alert sentries quickly raised the alarm, but a silent one on 19 March by 2/4th Leicestershire secured one prisoner. Another by 2/7th Manchester succeeded in capturing two prisoners but, to the disgust of the interrogators, the Germans were described as "extremely unintelligent."[62] A raid in early March by 5/North Staffordshire captured four prisoners, and a large raid by 240 men of 2/6th Warwickshire on 20 March took between 12 and 15 captives and three machine guns.[63] Securing prisoners was not, however, all one way traffic. Soon after it arrived in the sector, 61st Division lost two men in separate enemy raids and also held a court of enquiry to discover how 2/5th Warwickshire had twice been raided successfully in January.[64]

Infantry fatigue parties generally worked under the supervision of officers or NCOs of the divisional field companies. CRE divisions consulted with the commanders of divisional units to decide where emplacements, horse lines, medical facilities and OPs should be sited. In addition to this work, all divisional defence plans had an active role for the field companies should the signal to MBS be transmitted. The time allowed to sappers to practise infantry skills was,

---

58 TNA WO 953040: 14 Mar, 18 Mar.1918. Very sensibly, CRE laid down strict regulations about how minefields should be laid. He stressed they should be of uniform pattern along the whole divisional front.
59 By early 1918, these two doctrinal pamphlets about the importance of active patrolling should have been familiar to battalions
60 TNA WO 953055: 182 Bde, 22 Feb.1918
61 TNA WO 953059: 183 Bde, 18-19 Mar.1918; TNA WO 953065: 2/4th Berks, 17-18 Mar.1918
62 TNA WO 953121: 10 Mar.1918; Daily Intelligence Report, 10 Mar.1918
63 TNA WO 953056: 2/6th Warwickshire, 20 Mar.1918. Word that the Warwickshires were thought to have captured men from four different regiments spread quickly. Four miles to the south, 36th Division, which had fired a diversionary barrage in support of the raid, believed this confirmed an enemy attack was imminent. It fired an additional barrage on the German forward positions in case enemy infantry were preparing to assault. WO 952494: CRA, 20 Mar.1918.
64 TNA WO 953056: 2/5th Warwickshire, Jan.1918.

however, limited. Those of 59th Division were given some instruction in machine gun and Lewis gun drills in February but one OC complained that any sort of training was proving difficult owing to the time having to be spent on improving billets and baths. The thaw and regular bursts of shelling meant huge lengths of trenches had to be reclaimed, new stretches dug and fire-stepped, and elephant shelters built in the forward areas. Wiring, however, was allotted precedence over all other work.[65] Lieutenant Colonel Durnford, CRE 61st Division, felt particularly aggrieved at the shortage of available transport and materials. He complained that a shortage of trains from corps dumps forwards was seriously depleting stock at the divisional dumps and asked for 12 more lorries per day to be supplied. Corps supplied an additional two. When he complained of a shortage of steel and other materials for gun positions in the Battle Zone, he was told instead to concentrate on making emplacements in the Forward Zone. He also criticised the handling process at the corps dump which was, he argued, making his men work an excessive 14 hours a day. To make matters worse he was then instructed to build an additional redoubt (Ellis) as well as improve and expand those known as Essling, Enghien, Manchester Hill, and Fayet. Durnford's annoyance increased yet further when Maxse visited the area and declared he would have preferred the redoubts to be about half the size they were.[66] Durnford demanded adequate supplies of timber and camouflage netting to complete the tasks only to be told by the OC RE corps dump on 19 February that he had already drawn his month's supply of materials. Unsurprisingly, Durnford resisted attempts by 172 Tunnelling Company to purloin some of his materials on the argument that as he was only able to draw 40 of his required 100 mining frames per day, he had none to spare. On 20 March, he was at least able to record that wiring of Ellis Redoubt would be completed that night.

Many as his complaints were, Durnford believed corps HQ most egregious behaviour came over the construction of huts. Sections of one of the division's field companies had for some time been erecting Nissan huts in Marteville. By mid-February, 39 huts had been delivered, many with parts missing. Twenty-seven had been erected. When Maxse visited the site he observed many of the huts were not the statutory 25 yards apart and ordered several to be demolished and reconstructed elsewhere. Durnford's anger is obvious from the war diary. He recorded that the huts had been erected on sites allotted by AA&QMG, who had acted on the orders of DA&QMG XVIII Corps. The latter had inspected the sites during the construction process and the camp was visited frequently by CE XVIII Corps and his staff. With all the other demands for skilled labour, the demolition of the huts was for Durnford the last straw.[67]

Divisional cyclists were frequently pressed into labouring work but, in February, the four 2nd Line divisions in Third and Fifth armies did finally receive their own pioneer battalions. Useful as this was, rather than bringing with them a wealth of engineering or construction skills,

---

65   TNA WO 953015: CRE, Jan.-Feb.1918. 20,000 yards of double apron wire was reported by the division to have been laid in one week.
66   As a consequence of Maxse's visit, Ellis was built to a more compact design than those already constructed.
67   TNA WO 953040: Feb.1918. Durnford was clearly concerned that his men in the field companies were working 14 hour per day. He was also equally concerned about the lack of work done by the division's pioneer battalion and told its CO to ensure his men worked a full eight hour day. Transport shortages were being felt right across the BEF. On one day alone, 66th Division's ammunition column provided sufficient wagons to supply 200 loads of RE material in addition to those used for its normal ammunition replenishment. See WO 953128: DAC, 19 Mar.1918.

three of the four pioneer battalions had only just been converted from conventional infantry units. The exception was 1/5th DCLI which was not raised as a pioneer battalion but had been converted in the UK and sailed in that capacity with 61st Division. When 1/4th Suffolk, 6/7th RSF and 1/5th Border arrived at, respectively, 58th, 59th and 66th Divisions, not only did they know almost nothing about pioneering duties but also resented having been demoted, as they saw it, to a form of lesser battalion. The first task of CRE 66th Division was to find a training ground for the men of 1/5th Border. Here they were lectured and introduced to their new job and instructed in some of the skills they were immediately to need.[68] The pioneers were quickly put to work but whereas battalions originally raised as pioneers in 1914 and 1915 were in theory obliged to consist of 50 percent skilled men and 50 percent used to working with pick and shovel, the new conversions would have contained very few skilled men. They worked on roads and digging duties and although valuable to their divisions they could not perform much of the skilled work undertaken by the hard-pressed field companies. There is no suggestion that the 2nd Line divisions were singled out to receive battalions less able to undertake pioneering duties or to receive units which were not necessarily from the TF. This was simply part of the major reorganization and restructuring of the BEF. New Army and TF battalions across the five armies were being disbanded, amalgamated, re-rolled, and transferred, frequently irrespective of their origins, to other divisions or brigades.[69]

It was noted earlier that part of the sustainment process – the business of maintaining a force by enhancing and prolonging its capability and resilience – is that of medical provision. By early 1918, the ADMS of all 2nd Line divisions had been in France long enough to have become familiar with how the medical system worked and its importance to troop morale. The system was to be severely tested during the withdrawal but on the eve of battle there appear to have been no obvious shortcomings in the relevant sections of the divisional defence schemes. Preparations made by ADMS 58th Division, Colonel J.Houghton, were typical of those made by all, rather than just 2nd Line, divisions. He met regularly with DMS Fifth Army, DDMS corps, his own OsC field ambulances, and with GOsC brigades and the GSO1 to discuss likely needs and provision. He frequently visited field ambulance and ADS, and selected sites for new or alternative ones should a withdrawal occur. He discussed with battalion COs what medical provision was possible in keeps and strong points and made arrangements for which types of cases should be sent to which ambulances or CCS. As it was common practice for incoming units to relieve the departing ambulances in their existing positions, the division's three ambulances tended to occupy sites previously used by the French. Houghton reported that all preparations, as laid out in the Defence Scheme, had been completed by 18 February.

The 2nd Line divisions' administrative and resupply arrangements, as well as the physical components of fighting power as a whole, were indistinguishable from those of the regular and New Army divisions on their flanks. Brigade strengths and artillery establishments were very similar, with none of those formations reporting significant shortages of anything other than RE materials. Brigades had schemes to ensure how rations brought up to dumps on light railways or lorry transport were distributed to battalions; battalions had standing orders for which wagons and limbers should be ready to move and what was to be carried on them. Field kitchens

---

68 TNA WO 953125: Feb.1918; WO 952402: 1/5th Border, Feb-Mar. details the lectures received and the battalion's training programme.
69 K.W. Mitchinson, *Pioneer Battalions in the Great War*, Chapters, 11-12.

had to be capable of moving at short notice, sufficient horses and harness were to be available, and adequate numbers of rations ready for issue at battalion stores. Standing orders were in place to ensure water bottles were always filled.

Provost and straggler posts were organized in the same manner and format as other divisions, and artillery and TMs regularly fired similar types and lengths of bombardments as neighbouring formations. All DACs across all armies drew as regularly from corps' reserve dumps as well as their own. Defence schemes were completed and submitted at about the same time by all divisions in Third and Fifth armies and were all as comprehensive as each other. There was little difference in the numbers of active patrols and raids undertaken and, unlike 30th Division on the right of 61st Division, none of the 2nd Line formations noted the need for "drastic changes" in their training programmes.[70]

Troops working on the Battle Zone defences and holding the Forward Zone frequently saw their senior commanders and staffs wandering about inspecting progress. With the exception of Major General Malcolm, who had arrived at 66th Division in December, the GOsC divisions for the four 2nd Line formations about to face the onslaught had all been in post for a considerable time. On 1 March, most of Major Generals Cator, Romer, Mackenzie, and Malcolm's infantry brigade commanders had also been with their divisions for, in some cases, years. Only two of the 12 had served with their brigades for fewer than seven months. There were, however, to be two changes on the eve of battle: Brigadier General Jackson left 175 Brigade to command 50th Division on 19 March; Brigadier General Travers, GOC 199 Brigade, was sent home and replaced by the division's CRE, Brigadier General Williams.[71] In common with most divisions across the BEF, none of the infantry brigadiers was a territorial, although CRA 66th Division, Brigadier General Birtwistle, unusually, was.[72]

All four GSO1s had been to Staff College, with two of them having been with their divisions since early 1916. Lieutenant Colonel Mangles had arrived at 58th Division in November 1917 but Livesay, who had retired from the army in January 1914, only reported to 61st Division on 16 March. Similarly, two of the four AA&QMG had been with their divisions since 1916, with the other two having joined theirs in 1917. The CRA and CRE all had considerable experience but with Williams' promotion to GOC brigade, the acting CRE 66th Division on 21 March was a captain. One unusual promotion had been that of H.G. Howitt to Brigade Major of 184 Brigade. Although such positions were still almost exclusively the preserve of regular officers, Howitt was a territorial and a businessman.[73] Howitt, together with one AA&QMG, one CRE, and Brigadier General Birtwistle, were the only representatives of the TF in the non-unit staffs of the four divisions.

There was still, however, a sprinkling of original territorials among the officers and other ranks. A percentage of the senior NCOs and some privates transferred from the recently amalgamated

---

70   TNA WO 952313: Notes of the Divisional Conference, 19 Jan.1918.
71   See M. Middlebrook, *The Kaiser's Battle* (London: Penguin, 1983) p.129. Travers' brigade major recalled the peremptory dismissal of his commander. Maj. Gen. Malcolm apparently sacked Travers at one hour's notice. He told him he was too old for the test to come. Travers was 51, which was not an overly excessive age for a GOC brigade. Williams, his replacement was 14 years younger.
72   In August 1914, Birtwistle had been a major in VI Lancashire (Burnley) Battery in the East Lancashire Division.
73   G. Rose, *2/4th Ox & Bucks*, p.148.

1st Line battalions will have been originals, as were some of the junior officers who had been commissioned from the ranks of 1st Line units. There was still even a small number of men who had enlisted in the 2nd Line in the early months of the war and subsequently escaped being drafted overseas to other units. Although very much in the minority there were a few TF commissioned officers as COs and second-in-commands within the four divisions. The percentage of TF officers holding the two senior positions in the 40 battalions (including the pioneers) was probably a little below 10 percent. Two other TF COs had recently gone back to the UK and another, who had just returned to resume command of his battalion, was sidelined. Major General Malcolm and Brigadier General Borrett considered the present incumbent to be "more satisfactory."[74] The senior TF officers who remained had usually been captains or lieutenants in (what became) their 1st Line in August-September 1914. They included Lieutenant Colonel A.R. Richardson of 2/2nd London, Major T.J. Biddolph, acting CO of 6/Lancashire Fusiliers, and Major W.G. Oates second-in-command of 2/8th Sherwood Foresters. Oates was soon to be promoted to command of 2/4th Berkshire.

The Regular COs were drawn from a wide variety of regiments. Most were commissioned between about 1895-1902 but others were younger and had been lieutenants or captains on the outbreak of war. Three were from the cavalry, one had come via the Canadian Militia, one from the British Militia, two from the Special Reserve, and at least one from the Reserve of Officers. One had served his entire career in the Indian Army, while others came from regiments such as the Suffolk, Royal Fusiliers, Royal Irish, and "Kill Boche Jones" from the King's Own Royal Lancaster.[75] At least five of the non-TF COs had once served as adjutants to yeomanry or TF units and they, like those who came as COs of 1st Line battalions to command the now amalgamated battalions, would have an idea of the ethos and character of TF units. Any originals of the 1st Line who came with their COs on amalgamation would also have brought something of that character with them but with so few genuine pre-war and 1914-15 territorials having survived the many drafts to the parent battalions before 1917, the 1st Line originals may barely have recognized the 2nd Line as being TF formations.[76] The TF officers who remained with the 2nd Line as COs did try to perpetuate the TF ethos of paternalistic command within their battalion but, with most of the COs being either regulars or New Army, their particular style of command was very much a reflection of their own beliefs and character. These could range from the obviously caring, compassionate, almost collegiate method of Lieutenant Colonel C.B.Benson of 2/6th London and the inspiringly enthusiastic Lieutenant Colonel J.H.Dimmer VC of 2/4th Berkshire, to the unintentionally distant and unpopular Lieutenant Colonel W.St. John of 2/7th Warwickshire. St.John was clearly an awkward individual "who never seemed to

---

74   Lt. Cols. W. Coape Oates and G. F. Collett of 2/8th Sherwood Foresters and 2/5th Gloucestershire respectively, were on sick leave in the UK. Lt. Col. G. Roberts was the unfortunate CO of 2/8th Lancashire Fusiliers whose services were no longer required. The division asked Fifth Army what they should do with him. The CO who replaced him was a regular. See TNA WO 953123: 28 Feb.1918

75   The nickname of Lt. Col. A.D. Derviche-Jones, CO of 2/8th London. C. Messenger, *Terriers in the Trenches. The History of the Post Office Rifles* (Chippenham: Picton, 1981), p.73.

76   Technically the divisions were 'TF' in name only. The county associations had lost responsibility for raising and training them in 1916. Most of their members, as we have seen, were either Derby men or conscripts.

get on with anyone," and was apparently able effortlessly to alienate his subordinates. He was, however, "fully aware of his unpopularity [and] no one regretted it more than himself."[77]

The COs' styles of command, leadership and management were tested in an unusual fashion before the German offensive began. Like all British divisions, the 2nd Line formations had undergone a substantial emotional and morale-sapping blow with the reduction to three battalions per brigade. This in turn caused a significant alteration in brigade and divisional relationships. Of the four 2nd Line divisions in Third and Fifth armies, the worst affected was 61st Division. Because its 1st Line was in Italy the possibility of amalgamating battalions was impracticable. Consequently, six battalions were disbanded, one was moved to a different brigade, and an entire brigade of 1st Line Highland battalions was transferred in from 51st Division. Middlebrook comments that the Highlanders did not like serving with the 2nd Line but, possibly reflecting on the division's difficult time during Third Ypres, one of its members thought the Scots would "probably stiffen us up a little."[78] In 58th Division, three battalions were broken up in addition to six amalgamations, whereas 59th and 66th divisions each had three battalions disbanded and three and two, respectively, amalgamated. Drastic as these changes were, compared to some of the New Army divisions the 2nd Line formations were rather more fortunate. The personnel of the disbanded units were posted very largely to battalions of their regiment or as large drafts to the same entrenching battalion.[79] Morale and unit cohesion was bound to have been affected by these changes but possibly not as significantly as in some other formations and units.

Today, the moral component of fighting power is acknowledged to be built on motivation. Motivation is the enthusiasm to fight and is a product of influences such as effective leadership, fair and firm discipline, confidence in the equipment and training, an understanding of why you are fighting, and an appreciation of what is required of the individual soldier. Motivation, in turn, influences that intangible force, morale. Morale sustains people in difficult situations and is stimulated by conviction, success, and the men's confidence in themselves and in their superiors as soldiers. It is also driven by a sense of belonging and of being valued. Soldiers who had lost their battalion in February 1918 by disbandment or by amalgamation needed to acquire a new sense of belonging. They may have been drafted in platoons or even sections but it was to a new battalion (or even a new regiment) that may have done things very differently. As many of the troops were disgruntled by the changes it became the responsibility of their new commanders to exercise leadership so as to minimize their effect on morale.

BEF morale in early 1918 was already delicate. Although discipline had not broken and fighting spirit had not been destroyed, the conditions and casualties of Third Ypres, together

---

77 E.Godfrey, *The Cast Iron Sixth*, p.152; D.W. Cuddeford, *And All for What?* (London: Heath Cranton, 1933), p.71. Cuddeford was St John's adjutant and wrote of the CO's "adverse influence" on the battalion, pp80-1. Lieutenant Colonel John Dimmer had been commissioned into the KRRC in 1902. He won his VC at 1st Ypres. Dimmer's motivational philosophy is clearly apparent in many of his routine daily orders. See, for example, his Orders of the Day when the battalion was out at rest in Feb.1918. See TNA WO 953065.

78 M. Middlebrook, *The Kaiser's Battle*, p.92. C. Falls *The Life of a Regiment: The Gordon Highlanders in the First World War 1914-1919* (Aberdeen: AUP, 1957), p.175, makes a similar point when describing the departure of 1/5th Gordon Highlanders for 61st Division.

79 Entrenching battalions were really holding units. Surplus men were retained in them until reinforcement drafts were needed elsewhere.

with the disappointment of Cambrai and a harsh winter, had affected morale. It was pointed out earlier that falling under the command of General Gough and Fifth Army could also have affected the morale of three 2nd Line divisions. The reputation Gough and his staff had gained on the Somme and at Ypres lived on in memory.[80] Battalion COs and their subordinates had to motivate the new arrivals by demonstrating professional competence, decisiveness, confidence, communication skills, and humility. Leadership, as well as management and command, was required to make the new men feel welcome and comfortable with their changed surroundings. Unfortunately, although the 2nd Line war diaries record the farewell parades to those battalions being disbanded or transferred,[81] there is no mention of how the arriving units were greeted. Many brigadiers and COs in other divisions are known to have paraded the men and addressed them as, for example, fellow riflemen, fusiliers, or Lancastrians, and to have stressed any historic links between their old and adopted battalions. This approach will have appeased many but there were others who resented the disruption and the vagaries of the army. Their morale would have suffered accordingly.

Long after the war one officer of 2/5th Manchester, 66th Division recalled: "Morale wasn't high. Everyone was tired of the war. If we'd had the guts we'd had eighteen months earlier the Germans would never have knocked a hole in the line as they did that time."[82] Despite Haig's diary entry which (mistakenly) claimed that 66th Division had gained all of its objectives on 9 October 1917, that Lieutenant General A.J. Godley had (probably for political reasons) thanked it for being "an efficient and dependable division," and how Gough later remembered it as being "animated by a great spirit of comradeship, cheerfulness and esprit de corps," Major General Malcolm had probably been placed in command to shake it up.[83] Beyond 24th Division on Malcolm's right, was 61st Division, one of two formations singled out by him for an indifferent performance on 6 September during Third Ypres. Further south still lay 58th Division, whose training methods under Major General Fanshawe are thought to have annoyed Maxse at Ypres. Fanshawe had been sacked and now both Gough (and Maxse) had faith in the division and in Cator, its GOC.[84] Romer's 59th Division had not done well in its earliest engagements, had very limited success in its one attack at Ypres, but had executed a limited text-book withdrawal at Cambrai.

Together with the regular and New Army divisions, the 2nd Line formations were to fight a defensive battle against an enemy using several elements of what today constitutes the

---

80 See FN.14 of this chapter.
81 For example, see detailed plans for the farewell parade to the disbanded 3/5th Lancashire Fusiliers by 197 Bde in TNA WO 953135: 12 Feb.1918.
82 M. Middlebrook, *The Kaiser's Battle*, p.332-33. This is possibly an accurate assessment of his unit's morale, but Lt. R.A. France's battalion had only been in France for 12 rather than the 18 months he mentions. It is, of course, possible that France had been posted into the battalion from elsewhere.
83 Sheffield & Bourne (eds.) *Douglas Haig*, 9 October 1917, p.335; TNA WO 953121: Lt Gen. Godley (GOC XIII) to DHQ correspondence, 16 Feb.1918. Privately, II ANZAC had been less than complimentary about the supposed state of 66th Division's posts when it was relieved by 3rd Australian Division on 10 Oct.1917; H. Gough, *The Fifth Army* (Hodder & Stoughton, 1931), p.223.
84 Maxse's belief in 58th Division had not been diminished by its less successful attacks in late September and October. When XVIII Corps moved to the St Quentin area Maxse had asked Gough to allocate the division to his corps. Gough declined the request.

Manoeuvrist Approach.[85] Although his intelligence gathering system was not particularly efficient, Ludendorff understood the contemporary politico-strategic and operational situation. He concentrated force; employed deception; secured simultaneity and superiority of fires; aimed to seize the initiative; used shock action to try to break cohesion and will; ensured tactical and operational flexibility; maintained a fast tempo to disrupt and disorganize, and intended to exploit to achieve the elusive 'decisive victory'.[86] In opposition were the British divisions, ensconced in their "bird cages" with defences which, whilst not complete, were strong.[87] Although some local commanders believed their Forward Zones were held too densely at the expense of their Battle Zones, manpower was spread sparsely. Nonetheless, the Forward and Battle Zones, sited on generally favourable ground, were protected by mine fields, wire obstacles and, usually, well-armed redoubts. Those positions were supported by adequately resourced artillery brigades registered on probable approaches and counter-battery targets. Doctrinal pamphlets and voluminous defence schemes explained how the tactical defence of the positions should be conducted. The training may have been badly disrupted and insufficient in practice but all brigades had held several full rehearsals of manning battle positions. The troops were familiar with the ground and the defences and knew what was expected of them. Morale was probably not particularly high but, like their comrades in neighbouring divisions, troops in the 2nd Line formations should have been reasonably confident. If Clausewitzian frictions could be kept to a minimum, the defences were sufficient to disrupt and contain the attack in the Battle Zones. Moreover, the opportunity was there for the troops to deliver the same sort of punishment on the enemy as his in-depth defences at Ypres had earlier inflicted on them.

---

85 ADP, *Operations*, Chapter 5
86 Ludendorff is generally criticized for having altered his operational focus and objectives once the offensive was underway.
87 The oft-quoted comment made by a long-serving NCO: "[defence in depth] don't suit us. The British Army fights in line and won't do any good in these bird cages." J. Edmonds, *Military Operations 1918*, p.258. The most outstanding deficiencies on Fifth Army's front were a shortage of buried cables and insufficient numbers of shell-proof shelters.

9

Defensive Operations III: Battle, 21-22 March 1918

As the opening two days of the German offensive were conducted very largely in the prepared defensive positions of Fifth and Third Armies, and because two of the 2nd Line divisions were initially engaged for fewer than two days, only the activities of the four 2nd Line divisions in those first 48 hours will be considered here. This is a rational parameter because, with the exception of the battered 177 Brigade, 59th Division's surviving infantry was withdrawn from the line on the night of 21-22 March; what was left of 61st Division, was pulled temporarily into reserve only a day later.[1] The other two 2nd Line formations involved, 58th and 66th Divisions, fought protracted rearguards and delaying actions during the rest of the month and into the next. These engagements, however, better reflected the characteristics of open warfare rather than the defence of designated zones with pre-determined defensive schemes and garrisoned by organized formations. Consequently, many of the withdrawal actions after 22 March were frequently fought by *ad hoc* brigades and smaller formations hastily assembled to confront particular events and emergencies created by a pursuing enemy.

The hazards of what was at times a chaotic withdrawal necessitated extraordinary courage, leadership, and command from all involved, The surviving evidence suggests that many members of the two 2nd Line divisions were not lacking in any of those virtues. But, because they were not always fighting as formed or discrete divisions, beyond the first two days their overall effectiveness as *divisions* is difficult to assess. There will be some mention of the work of 62nd Division in the later days of the first German offensive but attention will concentrate on evaluating how far the four participating divisions acted on 21-22 March in accordance with existing doctrine and their particular defensive schemes.[2] The analysis will also include discussion on how those divisions demonstrated the effectiveness of their fighting power during the initial 48 hours of defensive action.

The general narrative of the German offensive is well known and will be covered here only briefly.[3] The Army Groups of Crown Prince Rupprecht and the German Crown Prince,

1   The divisional units did, however, return to action almost immediately, although not always under direct divisional control.
2   Less its artillery and some of its RE, 57th Division remained in Army or Corps Reserve during the Battle of the Lys.
3   For what is still probably the best and most readily accessible account of the Germans' preparations, intended strategic, operational and tactical objectives, and their deception plan, see J. Edmonds,

consisting of (south to north) *Eighteenth Army* (von Hutier), *Second Army* (von der Marwitz) and *Seventeenth Army* (von Below), were deployed opposite British Fifth and Third Armies. Generally speaking, the deployment density of German divisions was least in the south and greatest in the north. This roughly matched the dispositions of the two British Armies. At about 0614 on 21 March, 173 Brigade of 58th Division was the first British formation to be assaulted by the enemy infantry.[4] Protected by the mist and assisted by the almost dry beds of the Oise and adjacent canal, the Germans stormed through or past many of the scattered posts but did meet significant resistance in the Forward Zone west of La Fère and from the garrison of Travercy Keep. During the afternoon and evening, determined enemy attacks against Fargniers in the Battle Zone were repulsed. Further north, 2/4th London contained the enemy within the front sector of the Battle Zone having earlier contributed to the initially successful defence of the threatened divisional boundary with the right flank of 18th Division. Nonetheless, and despite there having been no attack against the two London brigades south of the Oise, both General Gough and Lieutenant General Butler knew III Corps would have to withdraw, as previously planned, behind the Crozat Canal. This manoeuvre was completed during the night and the bridges blown. On 22 March, soldiers of 8/ and 3/London resisted several attempts by the enemy to cross on the demolished bridges but, by the end of the day, weight of numbers had secured a German bridgehead over the canal between Tergnier and Quessy. The London Division's five battalions south of the Oise had seen little activity during the two days but as French troops of 125th Division were now arriving into the division's sector as reinforcements, at 2100 on 22 March, 58th Division fell under French command.

In Maxse's XVIII Corps, three battalions of 61st Division in the Forward Zone were all but destroyed by the bombardment and infantry assault. Fresnoy was lost by about 1330, but both Ellis and Enghein redoubts were thought to have held out until the late afternoon. The enemy was certainly assaulting the Battle Zone by 1400. The left flank had been compromised by the enemy's penetration of 24th Division's defences close to the Omignon Valley but the 1st Line Scottish battalions of 183 Brigade threw back a defensive flank and maintained possession of the important redoubt on Mill Hill to the south of Maissemy. With good fields of fire and the dispersing mist, 182 and 184 brigades defended the Holnon plateau relatively easily. Repeated assaults against 183 Brigade and the right of 24th Division continued, however, to threaten the division's left flank. A counter-attack by two companies failed to relieve the pressure but the fighting died down overnight. Early on 22 March the enemy attacked again and gradually forced their way south to threaten both 182 and 184 brigades. Concerned by the withdrawal of elements of both 24th Division and 183 Brigade, the penetration of parts of 30th Division's Battle Zone on the right and by III Corps' difficulties further south, XVIII Corps was ordered to withdraw to the barely existing Green Line. Closely pressed by the enemy the three brigades of 61st Division fought difficult rearguard actions until their remnants reached the Green Line, passed through the recently arrived 20th Division, and into reserve. As the *Official History* later suggested, had the brigades been allowed to hold their positions until dark, as their officers believed was feasible, the withdrawal would have entailed far fewer casualties.[5]

Military Operations, pp. 135-60.
4   Ibid., p.166, fn.1.
5   Ibid., p.275.

To the north of 24th Division, the battalions manning 66th Division's Forward Zone had, like those of 61st Division, all but disappeared. It is clear that many of the various battalions' posts resisted but by 1100 the enemy was in front of the Battle Zone. The villages of Templeux-le-Guérard , Hargicourt, and Villeret were harshly contested but as 16th Division on the left began to fall back along the Cologne Valley, 197 Brigade lost the important position of Templeux Quarries. This combined blow allowed the enemy to penetrate the more open ground to the west. Tenacious defence by 9/Manchester and 2/7th Manchester towards the centre of the divisional front slowed the German advance as reserves to the rear were organized. While the village of Le Verguier, garrisoned by 24th Division held, the rear defences of XIX Corps' Battle Zone were reasonably intact. Once the village fell, together with further enemy advances through Grand Priel Woods and along the Cologne Valley, the withdrawal of 66th, 24th and 16th divisions became inevitable. The East Lancashire Division was ordered back to the Green Line. Counter-attacks by cavalry and tanks were undertaken on 22 March but in accordance with Gough's instructions, Lieutenant General Watts ordered a fighting withdrawal through the newly arrived 50th Division. Resistance by elements of 66th Division, cavalry, and 9/R. Sussex (the battalion in corps reserve) continued once the withdrawal began from the rear of the Battle Zone at about 1400. Several platoons of Lancashire Fusiliers and Manchesters are known to have fought on until surrounded or wiped out. One German thrust towards Hervilly was thwarted for a time but, with the division's, and thus the corps', left flank thoroughly exposed the enemy pressed on towards the Green Line. Like most sections of this supposed defensive position, the line boasted few wire obstacles and trenches of only 20 inches deep. During the night of 22-23 March the division tried to organize what it could of its tired and depleted strength but, with the enemy through sections of the Green Line, and with XVIII falling back on the right, those elements of 66th Division that could be contacted were ordered to continue the retirement through what had been deemed the southern section of the Péronne bridgehead. There, they manned positions on the west bank of the Somme between La Chapellette and Eterpigny. Although it had already lost possibly over 70 percent of its fighting strength the division was not relieved until early April.

The final 2nd Line division involved in the opening two days was 59th. The four battalions in the Forward Zone, two of 178 and two of 176 Brigades, were hit accurately by the enemy barrages and then assaulted by overwhelming numbers of German infantry. Two battalions of Sherwood Foresters, 7th and 2/5th, as well as 2/6th South Staffords and 5/North Staffords, suffered huge losses. With little knowledge of what was happening in the Forward Zone, the one remaining battalion of each brigade manning the Battle Zone remained largely in ignorance of the direction from which Noreuil, Longatte, and Ecoust might be attacked. Enemy advances down the Hirondelle Valley, which was just inside the adjoining 6th Division's (IV Corps) boundary, exposed the Foresters' right flank and allowed the Germans to swing northwestwards up the Noreuil – Longatte road to take the front sections of the Battle Zone from the south and rear. By about 1330, all six battalions of 176 and 178 Brigades had virtually ceased to exist as fighting units; 177 Brigade was ordered forward to man the rear defences of the Battle Zone. Two of its battalions detached companies to attempt counter-attacks towards Ecoust and Noreuil but both ran into heavy German resistance and lost the equivalent of about two companies. With 6th Division to the south also under great pressure and with the Foresters' brigade overwhelmed, hordes of Germans poured towards Mory across largely open ground. Frantic defence by officers' servants, cooks, pioneers, and gunners acting as infantry, inflicted heavy

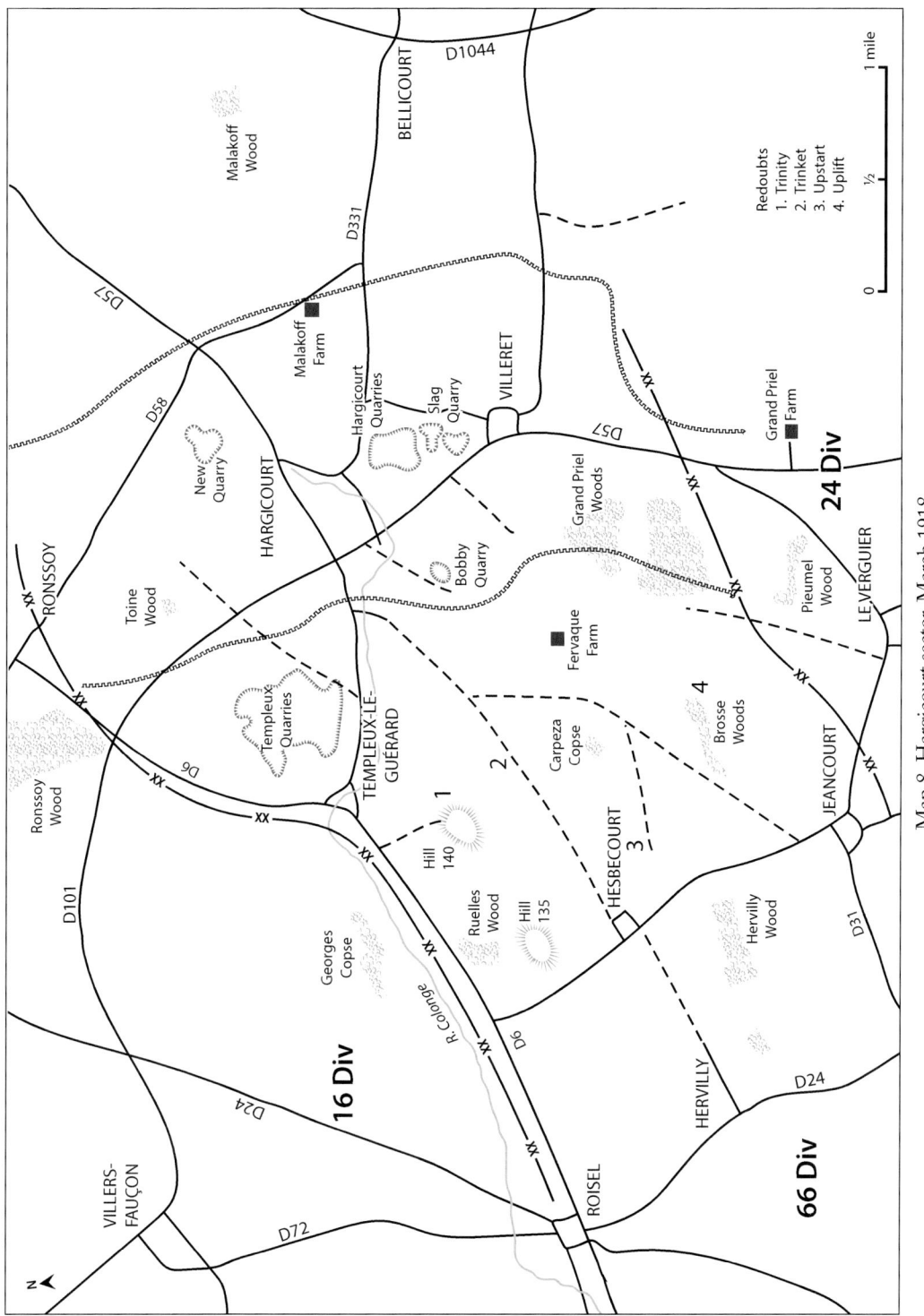

Map 8 Hargicourt sector, March 1918.

losses until elements of 40th Division began to arrive. By 2200, 177 Brigade, whose fighting strength was probably little more than a battalion, one machine-gun company, and approximately 15 undamaged guns of the divisional artillery, had been temporarily transferred to 40th Division. They remained in the line while the few unwounded survivors of 59th Division's other units withdrew into reserve.

Strategically and politically, Allied commanders knew they were buying time until the Americans could enter the field in decisive numbers. The defensive actions of March and April had this objective in mind as well as the assumption that once the offensive had been halted at the cost of exhausting German manpower and materiel reserves, the initiative would again pass to the Allies. The British corps had done as much as the weather and manpower allowed to apply the principles behind both contemporary and modern defensive doctrine. There was to be an emphasis on offensive local counter-attacking to regain the initiative, the defences were constructed in depth with zones of all round defence, and positions were designed to offer mutual support to increase the strength and flexibility of the defence. Where it was feasible, concealment and deception had been used to deny the enemy the advantages of understanding the extent and nature of the British defensive system.

The prisoners taken during a raid of 20-21 March by 2/6th Warwickshire had confirmed what many British intelligence officers had already surmised. Heeding corps HQ warnings, two of the 2nd Line divisions decided not to despatch working parties to the Forward and Battle Zones after dark. Some listening patrols of the other two divisions were warned not to venture beyond the British wire but others crept further forward. Despite having reportedly been "very vigilant", patrols of 2/6th Sherwood Foresters somehow missed hordes of German assault troops laying out in no man's land. At 0345, however, a returning patrol of 2/8th Lancashire Fusiliers reported a heavy concentration of troops in the trenches opposite its right company. The CO sensibly asked for a pre-emptive barrage, a request to which the GOC brigade agreed. The artillery responded and after about 30 minutes the fusiliers' CO wired that he thought the guns had probably done enough. The GOC brigade demurred and ordered the bombardment to continue. This firing was still underway when the German barrage opened at 0435.[6]

All divisions had repeatedly rehearsed the requirements for MBS.[7] At 0120 on 21 March, XVIII Corps ordered the artillery of 61st and 30th divisions to fire a pre-emptive bombardment between 0230 and 0407. Having received intelligence from the Warwickshires' raid, at 0218 corps HQ wired its divisions that the enemy was expected to attack in the early morning. It next ordered a test MBS for 0435, the same time as the German barrage opened. The 'test'

---

6   There is some difference in the WDs about when the German barrage opened and when the various DHQ received the MBS signal from their corps HQ. The breadth in time across the four corps in which the 2nd Line divisions served was approximately 30 minutes.

7   MBS applied to all supported and supporting arms. For example, GOC and ADMS 66th Division had inspected all MDSs, ADSs and field ambulances in the few days before 21 March. They "expressed satisfaction" with the medical arrangements under the division's defence scheme as partially inherited from the Cavalry Corps. Under the now expanded scheme certain facilities such as baths had to be converted to medical use and some field ambulances from general purpose to specialist functions. Liaison was made with the light railway system and transport parks, and selected field ambulances had to be emptied of scabies and other non-urgent patients. Walking wounded posts were established and manned with orderlies. TNA WO 953126: ADMS; WO 953131: 2/1st and 2/2nd East Lancashire field ambulance war diaries.

was rapidly changed to an order to execute the full and actual programme. One source in 58th Division notes that "Prepare for Attack" was issued by III Corps as early as the afternoon of 20 March but that the actual signal to MBS was not sent until 0515 the following morning. The division's infantry brigades had previously prepared their own texts that enabled, according to one report, 173 Brigade to send its signal as early as 0420. The dugout housing the brigade exchange had, however, received a direct hit in the first few minutes of the shelling which resulted in the signal being sent by runner. It is unknown when 2/2nd London's HQ in the Forward Zone received the message but it noted that by 0630 all communications to the rear had been cut.[8] It is probable that, like the CO of 2/4th London in the Battle Zone who did not receive the message until 0830, Lieutenant Colonel Richardson used his initiative and ordered his companies to stand to by at least 0530.

In 59th Division, 6/7th RSF (P) was also at stand to by 0530. This followed a night when the CO, adjutant, and all other available officers had wielded spade and pick alongside the battalion's working parties to emphasize the sense of urgency to complete the defences.[9] Given that the defence plan had been long in place, it seems remiss that on their return to camp the officers were then apparently briefed as to the "course to be taken should the battalion...go into the line."[10] The division's two forward brigades were already in the Forward and Battle Zones, the third moved to its prescribed positions by 0530. The nucleus machine-gun teams were galloped up to their reserve positions on the battalion's limbers also according to schedule. Miles to the south, 2/5th Gloucestershire of 184 Brigade, already on alert to move at short notice, reportedly left its billets in Attilly within five minutes of MBS being received and made its way to its Battle Zone positions in the Holnon Defences. Despite having to march through woods soaked in gas and deluged by high explosive its diarist recorded "very few casualties". In 183 Brigade, 1/9th Royal Scots also escaped lightly in reaching its reserve position behind Holnon Wood by 0850; 1/8th Argyll and Sutherland Highlanders was not so fortunate, suffering 40 casualties as it made its way to the Battle Zone. With telephone communications broken by 0500,[11] runners from 199 Brigade HQ successfully reached the two Manchester battalions in the right Forward and Battle Zones of 66th Division. Setting off for its five hour march to the Battle Zone, troops of 2/7th Manchester were compelled to wear respirators. In 198 Brigade, the companies of 9/Manchester also began the trudge up to their support positions in the rear of the Battle Zone in gas masks. On the way the battalion collected a stream of stragglers making their way back from

---

8 This is likely to have been a diarist's error and was probably meant to read 0530.
9 The enemy bombardment on this front was recorded as beginning at 0500. TNA WO 953011: Narrative of Operations on 21 March 1918.
10 TNA WO 953017: 20-21 Mar.1918. There are no earlier references in the war diary as to meetings concerning the battalion's role in the forthcoming offensive. Unrecorded conferences may well have taken place and the implication in the quotation a matter of unfortunate expression. In similar apparently unprepared vein, however, the day before the offensive began the CO of 1/5th Border (P) received a wire from DHQ outlining the different scenarios in which his reserve company, currently in divisional reserve, might be used. TNA WO 952402: 20 Mar.1918.
11 The other division in XIX Corps, 24th, seems not to have sent out its MBS signal until 0525. TNA WO 952192: Narrative of Operations, 21 March-6 April 1918. On 66th Division's other flank, brigades of 16th (Irish) in VII Corps sent their signal at 0520. TNA WO 951956.

the forward area. These troops were organized into a reserve company for any counter-attack that might become necessary.[12]

There was no unnecessary delay or significant difference in the time it took the battalions and support units' of the four 2nd Line divisions to begin and complete their movement towards their battle positions. The time at which the MBS signal arrived clearly did vary among the separate corps, but only one division in the four corps containing the 2nd Line formations appears to have pre-empted its arrival by an early precautionary manning of its Battle Zone and reserve positions.[13] As per the defence scheme, artillery liaison officers (LOs) reported to their respective infantry brigade HQ largely according to schedule but having LOs in position did not guarantee the guns could respond quickly to calls for assistance from the infantry. A swift response relied on functioning communication systems. Without them, commanders' overall situational awareness would be severely restricted and command and control thus dangerously jeopardized. If the British formations' various defensive schemes were to be effective in defeating the German offensive, continuous contact between corps, division, brigade, and battalion HQ had to be maintained. Only if the various systems of visual and wire communications worked efficiently could senior commanders make timely and adroit decisions about when and where reserves should be deployed. Similarly, the most suitable artillery programme required by the infantry could be brought down at judicious moments. If, on the other hand, the enemy bombardment was successful in severing a high enough percentage of cabling and in destroying sufficient equipment and runners, British commanders' ability to influence the battlefield could be fatally curtailed.

The working parties had done what they could but on 21 March there were still too few cables buried in sufficiently deep trenches. Generally speaking, the further north a division's sector was, the more buried cable it was likely to have. Staffs of both 61st and 66th divisions later confirmed that communications had been the "weakest link" in their divisional schemes. Yet, as the East Lancashire Division did not expect any serious attack on its front, and because the terrain "lent itself extremely well [for the] very complete system" of visual communication in operation, one officer did not believe the division would be handicapped too severely.[14] The officer's optimism was quickly shattered when his communications system was challenged by its first test in the early hours of 21 March.

With the fog putting paid to any possible visual communication from forward to rear positions, and with most telephones and power buzzers inoperable, runners and pigeons were the principal alternative means. Some war diaries mention the work done by several individuals who braved the tumult of the shelling and enemy troops only to arrive with intelligence which was often long out of date. A pigeon sent from one of 59th Division's forward battalions reached 178 Brigade HQ within an hour while one of the few runners who survived the journey took

---

12 TNA WO 953143: 199 Brigade, Narrative of Operations; WO 953121: Report on Operations of 9/Manchester.
13 TNA WO 951874: Report of Operations During the Period 21-31 March 1918. Like 58th Division, 14th (Light) Division, also in III Corps, received the Prepare for Attack signal at 1140 on 20 March. On receipt, the GOC Division visited his three brigades and ordered all forward posts in the Battle Zone to be manned by 0001 on 21 March. Unless the attack actually came, the troops were to be stood down at 0630.
14 TNA WO 953121: Narrative of Operations, 21 March-31 March 1918.

two. Staff of 66th Division thought pigeons were the more efficient means and later asserted there were not enough of them available. Divisional HQ was particularly frustrated when a bird carrying a message from 9/Manchester struggled in only to discover that a lack of discipline, opportunity, or thought on the part of the sender resulted in the message offering no indication of the time it was despatched.[15]

If there appeared to be little happening on their own front junior sub-unit infantry commanders despatched patrols to seek intelligence and contact with neighbouring troops. Some will have inevitably bumped into enemy soldiers and were killed or captured, but others did return with sometimes pertinent information. Patrols of 2/5th Lincolnshire attempting to discover what was going on in the Hirondelle Valley met huge numbers of the enemy coming towards and around them; 1/5th Gordon Highlanders despatched at least one patrol to try to make contact with 72 Brigade of 24th Division on its left; 58th Division ordered 2/4th London to gather any information it could on what was happening at Travercy Keep, and requested 18th Division to assist in the quest. Brigade majors and other staff went backwards and forwards continuously between their battalions, brigade, and DHQ to seek orders and relay information. Even if either were forthcoming, getting those orders or information to or from the forward areas was often impossible. A post-battle analysis of the communication difficulties experienced by VI Corps underscored the necessity of buried cables, buried junctions of important overhead permanent routes, and the importance of formation HQ being sited close to communication centres.[16] A similar report from 61st Division acknowledged how difficult maintaining contact between forward units, artillery groups, and infantry brigade HQ had been, and advocated a much increased use of horses by brigade staffs and battalion HQ.[17] How practical the use of horses in forward positions would have been is questionable but they might have proved beneficial in maintaining contact between brigade HQ and DHQ.

Inter-divisional and corps-divisional communications remained largely secure during the opening day but there were obvious delays in getting information back to the higher formation commands from their own most forward troops. The diarist at XIX Corps noted the arrival of "vague and conflicting reports" and only received the first confirmation of an infantry attack on its two divisional front at 1100.[18] Divisions within the same corps updated their neighbours fairly frequently and from mid-morning onwards the various divisional HQ provided a reasonably regular flow of intelligence even across inter-corps boundaries. Not all of the information passed on was, unfortunately, necessarily encouraging: 16th Division, on the left of 66th, admitted frankly that it had little idea of what was going on along its front, and 18th Division's replied in the negative to 58th Division's query about whether it could confirm that it was actually in touch with troops of the latter division. Limited communications did, therefore, continue to influence the outcome of the battle on all divisional fronts. Non-2nd Line formations were affected as badly as the 2nd Line divisions themselves. What mattered was not the *division* but the time a formation had had to prepare protection for its communication systems and the intensity and accuracy of the enemy barrage on those particularly vulnerable points. The degree

---

15 TNA WO 953121: Narrative of Operations.
16 TNA WO 95773: Notes on Communications During Recent Operations.
17 TNA WO 953059: 183 Bde Report on Operations, 21 March-3 April 1918.
18 TNA WO 95962: Report on Operations of XIX Corps.

of disruption in a division's fighting power certainly varied across Third and Fifth Armies but *all* divisions experienced severe difficulties with their communications.

The guns of the front line divisions fired a programmed shoot of harassing artillery and machine-gun fire at some time during the night of 20-21 March. Both 59th and 61st divisions had conducted major gas shoots on their fronts the night before. This was followed by the XVIII Corps wire at 0120 on 21 March mentioned above ordering its three divisions to fire the intense bombardment on enemy positions from 0230-0407. About 25 minutes after the programme was completed the German barrage began. In response, 61st Division commenced its first counter-preparation, which was also the signal for FOOs to make their way to their allocated OP or liaison HQ. Disruption followed almost immediately because a direct hit on the Forward Exchange at Maison Garde cut off the Left Group HQ from all of its batteries. All guns of all divisions in VI Corps, including the previously silent batteries, were ordered to double the intensity of their harassing shelling and to fire their counter-preparation programme at intervals during the night until 0440. Thus, 59th Division had been firing its counter-preparation Schedule B for some two hours when the German bombardment began. In response to the enemy shelling, and before it had done any significant damage to the signal cables, the CRA was able to instruct the guns to switch to the programmed Schedule A. Counter-preparation began again at 0500 and the counter-battery schedule was put into operation at 0540.[19] Given the knowledge that the enemy was likely to attack that morning and that the unprecedented barrage had opened at 0440, this was either a hesitant response by corps HQ or a measured strategy designed to conserve ammunition until the infantry attacked. It was possibly the latter as XVIII Corps did not order its divisional counter-preparation programme until 0505, and XIX Corps until 0515. However, in the latter corps at 0450, 66th Division did begin firing on the SOS lines of its centre and right brigades. Because SOS visual or wired signals might not be seen or received by their intended recipients to the rear, this was a rational extension of the pre-emptive barrage it had begun earlier in front of its left brigade. In III Corps, 58th Division had also fired a counter-preparation bombardment from 0345-0404 and immediately recommenced the programme when the German bombardment began at 0420.[20] The artillery of probably only one other division in Fifth Army acted any more promptly than the East Lancashire and London. Without waiting for the MBS signal 36th (Ulster), the southernmost division in XVIII Corps, opened fire on its SOS lines immediately the German bombardment began at 0435.

As "many" of 61st Division's batteries were in their alternative positions when the bombardment began they were not too severely affected by the German shelling.[21] In 59th Division's area, the gas deluge was recorded as having caused "few" casualties and with having "little effect" on neutralizing its batteries.[22] While it may not have been entirely successful in achieving those objectives, the enemy bombardment did play a crucial role in preventing an entirely effective artillery response. At least two of the four corps containing 2nd Line divisions stipulated that Intermittent Signal Relay Posts should be manned in the event of fog until a senior officer

---

19 On the immediate right of 59th, 6th Division did not begin its counter-preparation programme for another 35 minutes. TNA WO 951584
20 TNA WO 952995: 290 Bde RFA.
21 TNA WO 953035: Narrative of Operations, 21 March-2 April 1918.
22 TNA WO 95773: VI Corps.

at the group OP was satisfied the SOS signal could be seen by the established infantry relay posts. Whether this was done by all divisional groups, or whether the men detailed for the task managed to make their way safely through the enemy barrage, is unknown. It is certain that some of the buried cables running along the Hirondelle Valley and into 59th Division's Battle Zone survived until well into the morning. Similarly, although several in 61st Division's sector were cut by 0945, those linking the artillery and infantry brigade HQ to at least one of the redoubts remained intact until about 1600. Other lines from brigade to battalion HQ in the Battle Zone remained in operation all day. The extent and ferocity of the opening German barrage meant, however, that it did severely disrupt British communications: 58th Division lost direct contact with 2/2nd London in 173 Brigade's Forward Zone by 0630; 66th Division with its three forward battalions by 0610; 59th Division with its right brigade's front two battalions by at least the same time. Contact between a division's artillery groups and their batteries were cut swiftly with what in several cases proved ultimately to have dire consequences. For example, 61st Division's groups' HQ lost touch with their batteries by 0715 – which one officer with some understatement believed caused "great inconvenience"[23] – while 66th Division recorded all communications forward of its groups' HQ were cut soon after 0440. Another officer in 61st Division noted that the frictions created "considerable difficulties" in regulating the pre-arranged bombardment schemes. This would certainly have been the case but even firing blind the shelling will have caused some disruption to the assembling and advancing Germans and added to their difficulties of keeping direction.[24]

From very early on, therefore, brigade and battery commanders were largely compelled to act on their own initiative. Until 58th Division's guns received definite information that the German infantry was assaulting the Forward Zone, commanders remained very much in the dark. The OC 290 Brigade RFA was asked to put down what was more or less a speculative protective barrage on the canal crossing points at about 0700; 61st Division decided to fire its second counter-preparation programme at 0910 on targets suggested by prisoners captured by 2/6th Warwickshire the previous night. The preventive bombardment for 66th Division's Battle Zone was fired as early as 0700 despite the fact battery commanders did not know whether any of the division's Forward Zone positions were still intact. Although a late amendment to 61st Division's defence scheme had ordered the issue of SOS flares to all section commanders, they still had to get permission from their platoon commander before firing them. This permission would have been impossible to secure in the fog and in areas where section posts in the Forward Zone were spread thinly. In the unlikely event that they were not already firing on their own SOS lines, in theory, artillery group commanders could also call for reinforcing fire from batteries in another group within its own or even neighbouring division.[25] Additionally, batteries were allowed to fire at alternative targets during the intervals within normal SOS barrages but even in ideal circumstances this would have involved delays because messages would have to be passed back and guns switched from their normal barrage lines to those now being requested.

23 TNA WO 953035: Narrative of Operations.
24 Ibid.
25 TNA WO 952313: 30th Division. This mentions the Inter-Divisional Mutual Support Scheme which describes the means by which 30th Division could call down 61st Division's artillery to support its own guns, and visa-versa. Both divisions were in XVIII Corps.

Amidst the ferocity of the enemy bombardment and an absence of firm intelligence OC batteries had to use instinct, empathy and a degree of guesswork as to what and where they should be firing. As the morning progressed, and with still little information coming back from the Forward Zones, brigades began to reduce their rates of fire so as to conserve ammunition until a time when they were sure of using them on observed, lucrative targets. At 1030, 66th Division ordered its artillery to slacken to a slow rate. After the division's three infantry brigadiers had reported they had not yet received any confirmed intelligence of an enemy infantry assault, XIX Corps ordered only one section per battery to maintain its counter-preparation fire.[26] Liaison officers stationed at OPs and battalion HQ did what they could to report back what was happening but until about noon few of the messages despatched succeeded in reaching group HQ or batteries. One of the few that did come through arrived from the liaison officer stationed at battalion HQ of 2/6th South Staffordshire. He reported that he was now entirely alone and that once he had burnt all confidential papers and destroyed the communication equipment he would attempt to break out and rejoin his battery.[27]

The disrupted communications continued to blight the possibility of fighting a coherent defence throughout the opening and subsequent days. The German barrage was described as "extraordinary" in its depth and violence, and a considerable amount of "promiscuous" shelling on the rear areas persisted throughout the day.[28] Heavy counter-battery work was continued by both sides but when the British artillery was informed of soft targets it fired with often devastating effect. The RFA brigades of 58th Division repulsed three major attacks as the enemy approached the canal crossings and another on 22 March when the Germans attempted to cross at Tergnier. Guns of 59th Division had "a tremendous effect" when they fired on Germans debouching from Noreuil, and batteries of 66th Division did "great execution" on enemy troops emerging from the ruins of Templeux-le-Guérard. By the early afternoon many batteries were firing over open sights as hordes of Germans approached their positions.[29] Some guns fired off their entire stocks and were then disabled or blown up. Many gunners continued the fight with Lewis guns and rifles. One RFA lieutenant organized his own men, a group of infantry stragglers and 100 partially trained machine-gunners to delay for a considerable time Germans advancing along the Hog's Back. The crews of B/330 were last seen resisting with rifles and bayonets as the enemy entered their gun pits, and a message reached 61st Division's CRA reporting the enemy to be "all among our guns."[30] Breach blocks were removed if the guns could not be withdrawn but some in the forward areas were captured intact.[31] The anti-tank guns in particular were often surprised in the fog and. if the gunners were unable to destroy them, they were turned on their former owners.[32] By the close of the first day crews of two batteries of 290 Brigade, 58th Division, are known to have blown up all of their guns but 59th Division had managed to save 20 of its 18 pdrs and 4.5 inch howitzers. At least 24 of 61st Division's 18 pdrs

---

26 TNA WO 953121: Narrative of Operations
27 TNA WO 953020: 176 Bde, Report on Operations
28 TNA WO 953037: 21 Mar.1918; WO 953011: CRE report.
29 'Open sights' usually meant firing at targets at a range of between 1,000-1,500 yards, well within the effective range of the German MG08/15 light machine gun carried by German *sturm* battalions. The effective range of the 18 pdr was about 6,000 yards.
30 TNA WO 953020: 176 Bde, Report on Operations; WO 953124: CRA, 21 Mar.1918.
31 TNA WO 953024: 178 Bde, Report on Operations 20-21 March 1918.
32 TNA WO 953121: Report on Operations 21-22 March of 9/Manchester.

and seven of its 4.5 inch were saved, but 66th Division lost 21 of its 18 pdrs.[33] Yet, amidst the chaos and uncertainty, 61st Division even managed to coordinate a barrage to support a counter-attack in the late afternoon of 21 March. Severe as these losses of the 2nd Line divisions were, they were not exceptional.[34] With the help of 1/8th Argyll & Sutherland Highlanders, 61st Division's gunners were able to recover a number of their abandoned guns near Mount Huette early on 22 March.[35]

As the afternoon of 21 March wore on it became clearer about where the enemy had succeeded in penetrating the Battle Zone. The Forward Zone and the Line of Redoubts had been lost along most of the two armies' fronts but until confirmation of which units were still fighting was received, the various divisional HQ faced a dilemma. That confronting DHQ of 61st Division was typical of other formations along the entire front. The buried cable to Ellis Redoubt had been cut by 0945 and few of the runners despatched to regain contact ever returned. At 1052 it was decided to put down the pre-arranged barrage for the defence of the redoubts but, at 1340, 2/6th Warwickshire asked for the protective barrage covering the Battle Zone to be fired. DHQ refused the request because it had no information that the Battle Zone was actually under attack and decided all available guns were needed for the continued defence of Ellis. Just over two hours later, and still with little news of what was happening at Ellis coming through, DHQ opted to put down the Battle Zone barrage. This meant "the artillery defence of Ellis was consequently abandoned." Two runners were despatched to Ellis to tell any of the surviving garrison to fight their way out. The runners managed to get no further than Holnon.[36] Similarly, once it was convinced the Forward Zone was lost, 66th Division ordered D/86 Brigade RFA to fire the 2,000 previously hoarded gas shells into Hargicourt and then, having informed the two flank divisions of its intent, put down the Red Line Barrage on 197 Brigade's front.

With the increasing loss of guns and growing numbers of enemy penetrations into sections of the Battle Zone, the artillery was forced to retire. The guns of III Corps were ordered to withdraw over the Crozat Canal during darkness. The loss of officers, NCOs and the reduced number of available horse teams created leadership and organization problems but, with the infantry helping to manhandle the guns to positions from where the teams could limber up, the 18 pdrs were in position by dawn.[37] By continuous fire during the late afternoon two sections of B/295 and a section of 117 Battery,[38] all previously silent, prevented the enemy debouching from Vraucourt Copse and restricted the German advance down the Hirondelle Valley. The guns were withdrawn only when their crews were convinced there was no British infantry still in front to protect them.

Once assessments had been made about how many guns were still operable, all artillery groups attempted to re-organize during the night of 21-22 March. Some sections and batteries

---

33 TNA WO 952992: CRA; WO 953013: CRA; WO 953031: CRA; WO 953127: 330 and 331 Bdes RFA. In March 1918, British divisions had two brigades of RFA, each with three batteries of six18 pdrs and one battery of six 4.5 inch howitzers. This gave a divisional total of 48 guns.
34 In neighbouring divisions, 177 and 189 Bdes RFA of 14th Division lost the enormous total of 44; 30th Division at least 12; 34th Division 18 either damaged or destroyed; 36th Division at least 12.
35 There is some variation in the numbers of guns recovered. J. Edmonds, Military Operations, p.177 claims it was ten; other sources note the total as nine.
36 TNA WO 953055: 182 Bde 21 Mar.1918.
37 J. Edmonds, *Military Operations*, pp.209-10.
38 117 Bty was part of 26 Army Brigade RFA

were swapped between groups to even up numbers; other sections were amalgamated to form one effective but composite battery.[39] When they had some idea of what was available, staff officers went in search of infantry brigades or battalions to coordinate and arrange provisional SOS lines for the hours of darkness. By early morning the Left Group of 61st Division had repositioned and reorganized itself sufficiently to put down barrages on the first of the enemy morning attacks on Mill Hill. By the same time, 66th Division's groups had occupied new positions from where they had registered on revised SOS lines on the rear sectors of the Battle Zone. They quickly began to fire programmes on suspected German positions and assembly areas and at 0700, what was left of the groups opened the protective barrage on the newly registered line.[40] Within 80 minutes, however, it became clear that the line would be breached. With the enemy by then within 800 yards of the guns, the batteries were ordered to withdraw. Two batteries each placed one gun on high ground to cover the continuing infantry withdrawal; other commanders were told to use their judgement and to support their infantry "according to circumstances."[41] The CRA later praised the work and initiative of OC batteries and the men who "adapted themselves to the moving warfare in a very short space of time."[42]

Despite the obvious efforts of the artillery to liaise with the infantry overnight, post-battle reports do offer some criticism. One battalion of 182 Brigade claimed that as it withdrew, "not a round of shells had been fired on the enemy."[43] The DHQ was also clearly unhappy with the way corps HQ handled the artillery during the later stages of the withdrawal. The divisional staff felt artillery-infantry cooperation, especially in the preparation of counter-attacks, had been very poor. Major General Mackenzie reiterated the point about artillery staff officers making insufficient use of their horses and believed the two RHA batteries of 2nd Cavalry Division allotted to the South Midland during the battle, were "admirable and showed what could be done in this respect." More controversially, Mackenzie went on to complain that his ability to decide how the divisional artillery should be used had been usurped by corps HQ.[44] This was an unusual accusation and one that seems difficult to justify from the surviving evidence. Unsurprisingly, it was vigorously refuted by XVIII Corps.[45] Corps' schemes specified where any available reinforcing brigades could be deployed but, with the existing communication difficulties and the fluidity of the front, arriving brigades did not always manage to arrive at the positions where the planners intended them to deploy.[46] Provided corps HQ was in contact with them, corps would decide what the brigades should do – remain as discrete units or be split up amongst the existing divisions. During the night of 21-22 March, XIX Corps (and possibly others) quite rightly ordered the surviving groups of its divisions to withdraw to specified positions. Furthermore, it was the job of corps HQ, especially at a time of considerable confusion, uncertainty and disruption, to coordinate its arms and try to maintain force cohesion. Similarly, it was also within the remit of

39 TNA WO 953037: CRA, 21 Mar.1918
40 TNA WO 953059: 183 Bde Report on Operations; WO 953124: CRA, 22 Mar.1918.
41 TNA WO 95312: CRA, 22 Mar.1918
42 Ibid.
43 TNA WO 953056: 2/7th Warwickshire, *Narrative*.
44 TNA WO 953035: Preliminary Notes.
45 Ibid. Reply from XVIII Corps, 11 Apr.1918.
46 The number of guns arriving could be substantial: two brigades of RGA came into XIX Corps area during the night of 21-22 March. These reinforced the corps' original three heavy brigades. J. Edmonds, *Military Operations*, pp.282-83.

corps HQ to decide where and what bombardments should be conducted by the heavy artillery. The work of the divisional RFA brigades was left to the discretion of the divisional GOC and his CRA.[47] There are no extant instances of GOC 61st Division being instructed by corps HQ to order his artillery to do something that Major General Mackenzie had not already instructed it to do. Even if it had, the problem would have been getting that order through to DHQ, and then on to one or more of the division's groups. There may have been some unrecorded instance which particularly aroused Mackenzie's ire but there is nothing in the war diaries to suggest XVIII Corps frustrated or thwarted a divisional order, or even attempted to question the actions of its GOC.[48]

The various divisional defence schemes deployed the two medium trench mortar batteries of six 6 inch Newtons in the Forward and Battle Zones and, in particular, as part of the defensive arrangements for the redoubts. The accounts differ but it is probable that if two barrels were positioned within a redoubt complex they may have held an arsenal of about 450 rounds. The guns had been registered on certain points in the enemy line and would themselves have alternative positions. Three of the six in the front part of 66th Division' Battle Zone were destroyed during the bombardment; the remainder were thought to have continued firing until the enemy were 50 yards away, and then blown up.[49] It is likely those in the Forward Zone were quickly over-run. Four of 58th Division's were recorded as "captured" and two of 61st Division's 6 inch and two of the 3 inch barrels were thought to have been destroyed during the early bombardment. One officer's report describes how he and a crew spent two hours digging themselves out of their collapsed dugout before then assisting some infantry with their one remaining gun and fighting until surrounded. Another account tells of the crew of a light mortar fighting from house to house in Templeux-le-Guérard, Those crews which escaped were sent to work, as per the prepared schemes, in the divisional ammunition dumps.[50] Until exhausting their shells or over-run, the mortars will have fired blind against their registered targets. This will have caused some casualties and disruption to the assaulting troops but, the weapons' lack of mobility and possibly restricted crew observation, as well as the likely early destruction of their ready dumps, meant they would have exerted only limited impact.

Aimed primarily at making it easier for the mortars to work with the two artillery groups, the reduction of a division's trench mortar batteries to two was one element of the developing integrated defence system. Useful as the TMBs were, however, the machine guns of the divisional MGC battalion also worked in close conjunction with the artillery and should have exerted a more decisive impact on the assaulting forces than mortars could ever achieve. The machine-guns' fire programmes were frequently included as integral elements of the field artillery's barrage schedules. They were registered on assembly areas to provide harassing and interdiction fire as well as sited to sweep approaches to the British wire. Like the TMBs they could respond

---

47 See, for example, VI Corps orders for the shoots to be conducted during the night of 22-23 March in TNA WO 95773
48 Although unusual, Mackenzie's anger was not unique. Maj. Gen. Deverell, GOC 3rd Division which, like 59th Division served in VI Corps, also complained strongly about the actions of the corps heavy artillery. After Lt. Gen. Haldane had told Deverell "the facts", the criticism was later toned down. Ibid.
49 TNA WO 952996: 18-21 Mar.1918; WO 953128: X/66 TMB and Y/66 TMB.
50 TNA WO 953135: 197 Bde, 21 Mar.1918; WO 953128: X/66 TMB; WO 953045: X/61 TMB.

immediately to SOS calls and on their own initiative open intermittent fire on their registered barrage lines. Even if the fog prevented visual observation of enemy troops the crews could fire blind on expected enemy avenues of approach. A crucial aspect of the day's fighting was how effective the machine-gun companies were and how efficiently the reserve guns were handled.

One company of 58th MGC and a detachment of another were attached to 173 Brigade. Three further guns were rushed up towards St.Firmin Keep and fired off 3,000 rounds when news of the keep's encirclement reached DHQ. What happened next is unclear but it seems that one gun at least escaped from the Forward Zone and withdrew to join two others near *Ferme Rouge*, an area that DHQ had previously identified as a potential weak spot. Here, the guns helped to hold off huge numbers of the enemy for two hours. They, or possibly *it*, then withdrew again to join a company of 2/4th London near Quessy. In a prescient tactical move another report suggests that at about 1930, OC A Company was ordered to remove all his surviving guns, which might have amounted to eight, to the west bank of the Crozat Canal.

The number of crews of the recently constituted 61st Bn MGC who were later reported missing[51] indicates that those in the Forward Section must have been over-run in the early morning fog. But, about noon, six guns in the Battle Zone were able to bring fire onto Germans advancing over nearby Manchester Hill. After pouring devastating fire into those waves they switched targets to lash masses of the enemy moving down the Holnon-Savy road.[52] There was considerable transfer of the reserve guns during the day, with several sections moved to support counter-attacks, some to replace losses in the Battle Zone, others to sweep areas of dead ground where the enemy was known to be massing, and some to give covering fire during the withdrawal. The reserve guns of 66th Division also seem to have been used as effectively as the circumstances and intelligence allowed. With only three companies and thus 48 rather than 64 available guns (plus the eight on attachment from the cavalry) the anticipatory deployment of reserve guns was perhaps more important than for other divisions. By nightfall, 15 guns remained in action, 25 had been destroyed by shellfire, five wrecked by their own crews, eight simply "missing", and three still in reserve. Eight of the original reserve guns had been allotted definite positions in the Battle Zone. According to one report these, and those others that survived 21 March, did "great execution" on 22 March and held the line with "no great difficulty." There was also enough flexibility to allow every non-Forward Zone gun to move at least once during the day. For example, several had been moved up from the rear to support the defence of Templeux village during the afternoon of 21 March..[53]

Little is known of what happened to the three forward companies of 59th Bn MGC. Their deployment, thought at the time by DHQ to have been unsatisfactory, meant they were probably hit very hard in the opening bombardment. It was believed that some crews fought on with borrowed Lewis guns and even revolvers, but those in the Battle Zone did certainly inflicted

---

51 TNA WO 953049: 61 Bn MGC. The diary records 14 officers and 320 ORs as missing. The number given as missing is considerably larger than the battalion's recorded strength at the end of February. At the beginning of March the diary noted no battalion staff had yet been appointed.
52 If accurate, this report of 61st Division's machine guns firing on the Germans advancing round Manchester Hill must have been seen as a target of opportunity. Later, 30th Division claimed that its 24 guns in the Battle Zone were hardly affected by the enemy bombardment, and that only four of its guns were put out of action during the day. TNA WO 952313.
53 TNA WO 953135: Summary of Operations; TNA WO 953121: Narrative of Operations.

massive casualties on Germans emerging from Ecoust and Longatte. B Battery claimed to have shot down about 1,500 on the Hog's Back, and C Battery "virtually demolished" a further two battalions. Eventually, shrapnel fire and a threatened turning movement by the enemy from the south forced the crews to withdraw. The survivors were joined near Mort Homme by about 100 partially trained machine-gunners and some gunners of the artillery despatched forward as platoons of infantry.[54] DADOS did manage to send up four replacement guns, oil, and 60,000 rounds, most of which were used to cover the withdrawal of what was left of 59th Division's infantry.[55]

Much of the work done by the forward sections of machine-gun battalions of the 2nd Line, as, indeed, all machine-gun battalions in all divisions, went largely unrecorded. They probably did inflict substantial casualties on the advancing Germans but the work of the battalions was later not without criticism. Brigadier General Spooner, GOC 183 Brigade, later reported that he believed machine-gunners were imbued with the concept of never allowing themselves to be in a position where they might lose a gun. This, he argued, had led to a preoccupation with identifying their possible line of retreat. The implication of this suggestion was that concern about the issue took precedence over the need to concentrate fire on the enemy. Spooner considered the changes to the structure by which machine guns operated had failed and recommended they be taken back, "as in the old Regular Army," under battalion control. He considered the German tactical method of bringing forward wheeled machine guns in their skirmishing line, with the infantry then building up their line on them, to be a superior model. This proposal might have necessitated a temporary devolution of tactical command to a battalion CO but Spooner's suggestion of a return to permanent decentralization was out of step with contemporary doctrine. Moreover, and in contrast, all infantry commanders of 66th Division praised the work of the machine-gunners. The MG battalion's CO thought his battery commanders had in fact given too *little* thought to their line of retreat and that had it not been for the "astonishingly bad" and "contemptible shooting" of the German machine-gunners fewer crews would have escaped. He emphasized the need for more training at moving targets lest his men became "as bad as the Germans."[56]

The roles to be played in the defence schemes by the field companies and pioneers varied from the demolition of bridges to providing additional infantry cover for selected areas of defence. The devolved responsibility for demolishing bridges was more complex than it might have been but once the remnants of 173 Brigade had crossed the Crozat Canal, 58th Division's RE destroyed all in its sector.[57] Sappers of 66th Division's did not have any major hitches until 23 March when they found themselves having to improvise to complete the destruction of one which had been left partly intact by other engineers.[58] The field companies of 61st Division had prepared charges for all bridges in their sectors and when relieved handed them over to

---

54 TNA WO 953017: 59 Bn MGC, Notes on the German attack.
55 DADOS sent another eight guns on 22 March.
56 TNA WO 953121; Appendix XXII. MG Bn report, 7 Apr.1918
57 The demolition of one bridge even had to be finished off by hand.
58 This was a bridge over the Somme in Péronne. As all of its detonators had been destroyed by a bomb, sappers of 432 Field Company resorted to spraying petrol on the bridge and setting light to it. TNA WO 953125: CRE, 23 Mar.1918

20th Division for demolition.⁵⁹ Other tasks for RE on 21 March included 61st Division's 476 Field Company laying wire around Black Hill Redoubt until it was ordered to cut gaps in the Army Zone wire to allow access for withdrawing troops. On their way to the Army Line two sappers of 479 Field Company were detailed to blow up an ammunition dump in Attilly. This task was abandoned when too many Germans were found to be barring the way.⁶⁰ Sections of 58th Division's 504 and 511 Field Companies joined with 18/Entrenching Battalion in digging sections of the Green Line, while other sections, with what must have been a remarkable degree of *sans froid*, continued to build shelters and boxes for Strombos horns.⁶¹ In the evening of 21 March, two sections of 432 Field Company of 66th Division were attached to 199 Brigade and ordered to man "such defences as existed" in Jeancourt. Despite the obvious importance of Le Verguier's tactical position, Jeancourt's defences offered no defensive obstacles or positions facing that village. A lack of time was cited for the failure to rectify this omission. It might have been expected that two divisions within the same corps should have cooperated rather more fully to ensure adequate defences were in place to cover their divisional boundary. Nonetheless, the sappers were later praised for rendering "valuable assistance" to the infantry before being ordered to conduct a fighting withdrawal to the Green Line.⁶² The large numbers of engineers of all four divisions who fought as infantry met with varying fortunes. In 59th Division, apart from one officer and six sappers who eventually managed to fight their way down a switch trench, 470 Field Company in Noreuil was reported as having "fought to the last."⁶³ Sappers of 503 Field Company fought alongside 8/London and 2/2nd London on the canal bank, while 20 men of 479 Field Company were detailed to fight their way through to Enghien Redoubt with a similar number of 2/4th Ox&Bucks.⁶⁴ Two of the sections were then ordered to assist 2/4th Gloucestershire in any way they could but were later withdrawn to Beauvois to cut more gaps in the Army Zone wire.

With three of the four pioneer battalions of the 2nd Line formations only recently converted to their new role, they might have been expected to fight well as conventional infantry. Two battalions, however, played fairly minor parts on the opening day: one company of 1/4th Suffolk doled out "considerable execution" alongside 173 Brigade at Quessy; one company of 1/5th DCLI fought as *bona fide* infantry whilst attached to 183 Brigade.⁶⁵ The other two battalions were more considerably involved. In the early afternoon 6/7th RSF moved up to a switch trench near Vraucourt and within 20 minutes of arriving was firing into waves of advancing Germans. For the next 18 hours the battalion was at times out of touch with both flanks and under fire from British heavy and field artillery. It kept its snipers active in preventing enemy patrols emerging from Vraucourt Copse and even managed to bring up an additional three Lewis guns from their anti-aircraft positions in the rear. The battalion maintained a steady fire into apparently never ending masses of Germans heading for Mory and remained in the line under 40th

---

59   TNA WO 953047: 479 Field Company RE, 22 Mar.1918
60   TNA WO 953046: 476 Field Company, 21 Mar; TNA WO 953047, 21 Mar.1918
61   TNA WO 952996: 504 and 511 Field Companies, 21 Mar.1918
62   TNA WO 953130: 432 Field Company RE, 21-22 Mar.1918.
63   TNA WO 953011: Narrative of Operations.
64   By the time this relief column had been organized, the task was deemed to be impossible and cancelled. TNA WO 953048: 479 Field Company, 21 Mar.1918.
65   TNA WO 952996: 1/4th Suffolk, 21 Mar.1918; WO 953050: 1/5th DCLI, 21 Mar.1918.

Division when most of what remained of 59th Division was relieved. Its CO was wounded on 23 March and his successor, Lieutenant Colonel Wilkie, later claimed that because it fell under the command of other formations the battalion never received its due credit for halting the enemy advance "at a crucial time."[66] In 66th Division, 1/5th Border had an equally torrid experience. Two companies in Templeux Quarries fought into the early afternoon. By about 1400 the site was entirely surrounded and only three officers and 36 men escaped to join the remaining company west of Templeux village. The remnants fought a rearguard action in Roisel on 22 March before withdrawing through 50th Division and reassembling at Cartigny.[67]

In optimum circumstances the movement of additional machine-gun teams, pioneers and field companies to support the infantry should have been a relatively straight forward affair. Deployments for most of the likely scenarios had been worked out in the defence schemes, as had those for the moves of reserves and counter-attack battalions. The intensity of the enemy bombardment and the early break down of communications meant that many aspects of the pre-arranged schemes became immediately redundant. Consequently, commanders on the spot rather than those at corps HQ had to adapt to the unexpected and improvise. Corps commanders controlled the deployment of reserve divisions or brigades towards the front, but it was divisional, and below them brigade, commanders who made decisions as to where their own reserve battalions or companies would be most effectively deployed. This required not only instinctive and almost anticipatory situational awareness but also acuity and agility of thought, flexibility, and the physical means of disseminating the orders to those involved in their execution.

During the battle's early stages, and while it seemed to those in the rear to be reasonably static, corps HQ played an influential role in the defensive operation.[68] When, for example, Major General Mackenzie informed XVIII Corps that he was unhappy with the situation on the left of his Battle Zone and had moved 2/4th Berkshire forward from Marteville, corps HQ agreed that Mackenzie could use the Berkshire to restore the Battle Zone. A caveat was added, however, that any other battalions available were not to be interpolated unless agreed to by corps HQ. It was for this reason that Mackenzie declined requests later in the day from 182 Brigade HQ and 2/6th Warwickshire for another battalion (presumably 2/7th Warwickshire which was near Holnon as brigade counter-attack battalion) to be put into the Battle Zone to beef up 2/6th Battalion's right company.[69] On 22 March, it was corps HQ that decided how 30th Division's 17/King's should be used by 61st Division and that also concurred with Mackenzie's proposal to move 1/9th Royal Scots from Holnon Rear Defences to Villeveque so as to cover the division's left flank on the Omignon Valley. After being informed by Mackenzie that the enemy was "streaming down" the northern side of the valley, it was again corps HQ that ordered

---

66 Post-war but undated letter from Wilkie to the Army Historical Branch. See TNA WO 953017. Wilkie was a fairly rare example of an officer commissioned into the TF being in command of what was an amalgamated battalion of two New Army units.
67 TNA WO 952402: 1/5th Border, 21-22 Mar.1918.
68 See, for instance, the number of wires sent from VI Corps HQ to its three divisions during 21 March in TNA WO 95773. When the withdrawal began in earnest and communications became even more strained, corps HQ found it increasingly difficult to make decisions and influence the battle. See Ian F. W Beckett in *Look To Your Front*, pp1-12
69 There had been little real activity on 2/6th Warwickshire's position in the Battle Zone but its right company had suffered severely during the bombardment. TNA WO 953055: 182 Bde.

a general retirement to the Vaux-Villeveque Line.⁷⁰ It was XIX Corps HQ that controlled where the arriving 50th Division and 1st Cavalry Division, which was already in corps reserve, should deploy. The separate formations of 1st Cavalry Division were then placed by corps at the disposal of 66th Division. Similarly, six companies from 73 Brigade were in corps reserve and were detailed only to be used for the defence of the six redoubts in the Battle Zone. They came under 66th Division's control from their time of arrival in the divisional sector but, should the need arise, only corps HQ could order their use beyond the Redoubt Line.⁷¹

Decisions by GOC divisions to move reserves had to be made in sufficient time for the messages to be sent, received, and for the troops concerned to move to their allotted position. Major General Romer, GOC 59th Division, knew by 1030 that heavy fighting was going on in the Forward Zone and that Noreuil in the Battle Zone was already under pressure. Romer's reserve formation, 177 Brigade, was four miles away from the Battle Zone but was not ordered forward to take up positions in its Intermediate Line until 1215. With hindsight, if two advanced companies from two of the three battalions had been despatched as soon as it had become clear Noreuil was under severe threat, they may well have arrived in time to offer substantial help in the Battle Zone to 2/5th Sherwood Foresters and 2/6th North Staffordshire.⁷² On the division's left, Major General Nicholson, GOC 34th Division, acted extremely swiftly in response to received intelligence. Realizing that 59th Division's front had been broken and that enemy forces were likely to advance north-westwards behind his own front positions, at 1000 Nicholson enacted a pre-arranged and rehearsed plan that involved the realignment of 102 Brigade and the movement of reserves to guard against that contingency.⁷³

Although largely uninformed of what was happening on 173 Brigade's front, Major General Cator acted promptly to send two companies of 3/London to stiffen 173 Brigade's Battle Zone. Then, after a little more time for thought, he issued a pre-emptive order to move four machine guns of Dismounted Cavalry Brigade to Triangle Locality lest the enemy utilized nearby dead ground. Wary of corps' strictures about how battalions in the Forward Zone could not rely on support from the Battle Zone, Cator refused a request from the hard-pressed CO of 2/2nd London and 173 Brigade HQ for two companies of 3/London to conduct a counter-attack in the Forward Zone. As per corps' orders, however, he did agree to allow two of its platoons to counter-attack in *Ferme Rouge* Locality which was inside the Battle Zone. Nonetheless, he did delay until 2015 before ordering 8/London to move from distant Pierremande, south of the Oise, to assist the virtually broken 173 Brigade. He next issued further warning orders for 18/Entrenching Battalion, currently working on the Green Line and, when it arrived, for a regiment of 3rd Cavalry Division. In view of what had happened to 173 Brigade, it was not

70   TNA WO 953035: 22 Mar.1918; WO 953036: 22 Mar.1918.
71   TNA WO 95962: 21-22 Mar; WO 953121, 21-22 Mar.1918.
72   This assertion is, however, open to some debate. Order times and movements for the counter-attack given in 177 Bde's Report on Operations (TNA WO 953022) are at significant variance with those in Edmonds, *Military Operations*, p.233 and also the war diaries of 2/4th Leicestershire (WO 953022) and 2/5th Lincolnshire (WO 953023) Those in VI Corps war diary more closely reflect those of 177 Bde. It may be that Romer acted rather more swiftly than some sources indicate.
73   J. Edmonds, *Military Operations*, p.236. The efforts of 34th Division to halt the attacks on its right and 59th Division's left flank were costly. Two-thirds of 102 Bde became casualties and three companies of 25/Northumberland Fusiliers which counter-attacked towards Ecoust disappeared. See TNA WO 952436.

until almost 2200 that he rather belatedly decided to use 120 all ranks currently attending the Divisional Signal School to defend the Condren canal crossings.[74]

Major General Malcolm of 66th Division faced a marginally more difficult conundrum than Cator. Malcolm's entire Forward Zone fell quickly and with the enemy by 1100 attacking all along the front of his Battle Zone, with his left flank under severe pressure and the right of his right flank division having already fallen back, he had to make difficult decisions about where to send his reserves. He knew 9/Sussex in corps reserve was manning the barely constructed redoubt line in the rearmost part of the Battle Zone, and that from the afternoon onwards could call on the support of 2 Dismounted Brigade of 1st Cavalry Division. He had also been told that 5th Tank Battalion had been tasked for counter-attack purposes and would be arriving at Nobescourt Farm during the night. In the centre of the divisional front Malcolm believed the German assault appeared "irresolute and disorganized";[75] here he contented himself with moving up the reserve companies of 2/7th and 2/6th Manchester. On the left, one company of 9/Manchester, 180 troopers of the cavalry and (according to one source) one company of 2/5th East Lancashire, were sent forward to reinforce the Sussex in the partially built redoubts. In order to allow guns and troops to reorganize on the Brown Line Malcolm ordered all forward posts to be held as long as possible. There was also thought given to using tanks to retake Fervaque Farm in the hope of re-establishing contact with the left of 24th Division north of Le Verguier. This scheme was sensibly abandoned and Malcolm concentrated instead on holding the centre and left. Along the Cologne Valley, the left flank of 197 Brigade remained exposed and, at about 1800, Brigadier General Borrett sought permission to evacuate Templeux village. Aware of 16th Division's withdrawal north of the stream, Malcolm nevertheless replied that corps HQ required army HQ approval for such a move. This was granted at 1850. Its attached troops and the remnants of 197 Brigade then fought a fighting withdrawal to Roisel. Although parts of his Battle Zone had been lost, by using his own reserves and those later made available by corps HQ, Malcolm believed the division's position remained reasonably satisfactory. The day had opened disastrously but by the morning of 22 March, Malcolm somewhat optimistically claimed that although his division was "disorganized and rather exhausted", the attack had been "completely broken" and the battle was at a "standstill."[76]

At lower levels of command, battalion, company, and platoon commanders, often out of contact with any other officer, had to make tactical decisions about how to employ what the bombardment had left of their commands. The dire position confronting 59th Division in the morning and afternoon of 21 March required unit and sub-unit commanders sometimes to take instant decisions about where to position their men. Several days before the offensive opened Lieutenant Colonel Gadd, CO of 2/5th Sherwood Foresters, had expressed disquiet about how strongly the Forward Zone of 178 Brigade was held. He argued that it should be thinned and greater weight put instead into the Battle Zone.[77] His battalion was in support on 21 March but the standing orders preventing any counter-attacks from the Battle Zone meant he could not advance before, or until, troops of 177 Brigade had moved up to the Battle Zone to replace his. All he could do was to call forward his own reserve company and try to discover what was going

---

74   TNA WO 952988: Narrative of Operations.
75   TNA WO 953121: Narrative of Operations.
76   Ibid.
77   W. Hall, *Green Triangle*, p.154.

on to his front. Events remained unclear until huge numbers of Germans appeared on either side of his battalion HQ. He gained contact with 2/7th Sherwood Foresters and, until about 1400, the two COs believed the advance had been stopped.[78] Having regrouped the Germans attacked again and destroyed Gadd's command.

On the division's left front, Brigadier General Cope, GOC 176 Brigade, asked DHQ to send up two companies of 177 Brigade to replace two companies of 2/6th North Staffordshire, the support battalion in the Battle Zone. Despite the standing orders, he wanted to send the two companies of North Staffords across the gap between the Battle and Forward Zones.[79] Telephone communications were down so a runner was sent to DHQ but, probably unknown to Cope, two companies of 177 Brigade had already been ordered forward to occupy the second line of the Battle Zone west of Ecoust. Before any answer arrived at 176 Brigade HQ, however, the enemy was through the Forward Zone in considerable force and had attacked the two North Staffordshire companies just as they were about to counter-attack eastwards. With his CO already dead, Major Keating of 2/6th North Staffordshire had now to turn intended attack into hasty and desperate defence. Keating and his men, confronted with constant explosions and dense phosphorous smoke from a nearby dump hit during the bombardment, were compelled to wear gas respirators for two hours. There was no communication with any other company or battalion, and no possibility of obtaining any SAA and Lewis drums. He held a post on the railway embankment in front of Ecoust and was frequently over-flown by enemy aircraft which dropped flares over his position. He sent out runners in pairs to contact other companies and seek reinforcements, but none returned. As sparse information came in and with the enemy hitting him from all directions Keating did what he could to shuffle his dwindling platoons and sections around. The aim was to fight their way to the higher ground near the civilian cemetery but, with wheeled enemy machine guns being run up towards him and ammunition almost exhausted, he and his 12 surrounded survivors surrendered.[80]

At least one of Keating's runners must have reached brigade HQ because DHQ placed 1/East Lancashire of 34th Division at the disposal of GOC 176 Brigade. The plan, rapidly extemporized rather than one taken from the defence scheme, was for a coordinated counter-attack using one battalion of 177 Brigade and 1/East Lancashire to retake sections of the Battle Zone. The attack was cancelled, however, because the East Lancashire proved too slow in assembling its companies and 2/4th Leicestershire was unable to reach its supposed jumping off point beyond the Third Line.[81] By mid-afternoon enemy forces were pouring along the spurs and up the Hirondelle Valley. It was now that 6/7th RSF (P), together with transport details, cooks, and batmen were rushed up hurriedly from the rear to join the eight machine-gun crews of 59th Bn MGC.[82] On their right, 6th Division was being equally hard-pressed. Its GOC, Major General Marden, ordered a reserve battalion across from the centre towards the Hirondelle Valley. Shortly afterwards, an opportunity arose for a counter-attack up the valley but the designated battalion took too long to get into position and the chance evaporated[83] Strangely,

---

78   TNA WO 953025: 2/5th S. Foresters.
79   TNA WO 953020: 176 Bde, Report on Operations.
80   TNA WO 953021: 2/6th N. Staffordshire. An Account of Events 21 March by Major Keating.
81   TNA WO 953022: 176 Bde, Report on Operations.
82   Ibid.
83   TNA WO 951584: 21 Mar.1918.

Marden seems not to have known until almost mid-afternoon that the reserve battalion of his 16 Brigade, much closer to where the counter-attack was supposed to have been made, remained almost intact and available.[84] A confused period followed which allowed a "serious gap" to develop between 59th and 6th divisions. A meeting at about 1930 between a brigade major of 59th Division, Brigadier General Dobbin, GOC 75 Brigade, and two battalion COs of 40th Division, discussed the situation but the gap of about 500 yards remained unfilled. Fortunately, fighting eased off during the night, although the enemy did make some attempts to bomb down a trench towards a block established earlier by 6th Division. At 0055 on 22 March, Marden, who by this time was fully appraised of the tactical situation and of the state of his division, telephoned Romer and asked if 59th Division could make an attempt to work southwards and get in touch with 6th Division's left. With what little remained of 177 Brigade constituting virtually the whole division, Romer replied his division was in the process of being relieved by 40th Division.[85]

As every divisional commander and his staff appreciated, counter-attacking was an integral element of any defensive operation. *FSR(2)* and *SS152* made this very clear. If they were to adhere to current thinking and strategy, commanders knew they were expected to plan for and execute counter-attacks in order to "keep alive the offensive spirit in the defender."[86] Numerous counter-attacking scenarios were, as we have seen, spelt out in divisional defence schemes but, as always, sufficient elements of the ways and means to effect those offensive actions had to be in place. Many pre-arranged and rehearsed schemes of where reserves and counter-attack companies or battalions should be placed and operate came to nothing once the enemy attack began, But, even with communications down, artillery support in doubt, and units not in the prescribed position, local commanders in the 2nd Line divisions were equally aware as their counterparts in other formations that they were expected, as stipulated in the existing doctrine, to use their initiative and launch vigorous counter-attacks to disrupt enemy forces and retake positions of tactical importance.

During the afternoon of 21 March, General Gough spoke to his four GOsC corps. Using words and phrases that could have been taken directly from *FSR(2)* he informed them that his intent was now one of fighting a series of delaying actions.[87] He explained the strategy would involve halting the Germans whenever possible, forcing them frequently to redeploy, not to hold on unnecessarily to any position, especially if it was of little tactical or operational importance and, above all, to avoid what he called the "complete annihilation" of his army.[88] While these actions were being fought, French and British reserves would be moving up to hold an agreed line. When the time was right, and with the enemy forces having culminated, the Allies would turn defence into attack. Manoeuvre and counter-attack were to challenge the initiative and force the enemy off balance. Fifth Army was thus to stage a fighting withdrawal on what were essentially text book lines. Having learned their commander's intent, GOsC corps disseminated it to their subordinates.

---

84 Ibid.
85 Ibid, 22 Mar.1918
86 *FSR* (1912), p.144.
87 See Chapter 7 for more on the nature of delaying actions.
88 H. Gough, *Fifth Army*, p.264; J. Edmonds, *Military Operations*, pp.205-08.

There must have been many local and often spontaneous counter-attacks attempted in the Forward Zone, knowledge of which died with their participants. It is known, for example, that a post in Ellis Redoubt had been regained from the enemy before the redoubt itself fell. The CO of 2/6th Sherwood Foresters attempted to organize a last-ditch bayonet charge but "could not assemble the men," and 2/6th South Staffordshire recorded that it despatched patrols to determine whether a counter-attack was feasible. Owing to intense enemy pressure, its CO decided against the action.[89] Understandably, more is known about those counter-attacks which took place within the Battle Zone. A locally organized attack by two platoons of 173 Brigade on the Distillery failed through lack of numbers and support. Two companies of 6/Lancashire Fusiliers successfully cleared Templeux village of the enemy but were then forced to retire to a sunken lane where they held out for nearly 24 hours. Three platoons of 2/7th Warwickshire are known to have disappeared when they counter-attacked near Holnon, and another attempt by the same battalion marshalled a counter-attack force but decided the "operation was not possible."[90] These and other known attacks took place from the mid-morning onwards but, through a combination of inadequate intelligence and often no artillery support, they generally failed. The war diary of XIX Corps records that several such attacks were made by troops of 66th Division in previously determined positions and specifically detailed for the task. Some of these were assessed as having had "some success."[91] If this is an accurate assessment of any of the division's attempts, they have elsewhere gone unrecorded.

As the mist cleared and the situational awareness improved, the objectives of the enemy thrusts on XVIII Corps' front became more apparent. The German advance down the corps' boundary astride the Omignon Valley threatening the right of 24th and left of 61st divisions was met by a counter-attack taken almost exactly from 61st Division's defence scheme. It was mentioned earlier that without first securing the approval of corps HQ (which came later), Major General Mackenzie moved 2/4th Berkshire from its MBS position in Marteville railway cutting towards the left flank of the division's Battle Zone. The objective was to recover that part of the Battle Zone on the high ground south of Maissemy in order for 24th Division, in whose sector Maissemy lay, to counter-attack the village itself. Four machine guns from divisional reserve were positioned to cover possible enemy approaches from Maissemy, at 1400 the division's Centre Group fired a preliminary barrage, and at 1545, sections of three batteries of 306 Brigade RFA began laying a creeping barrage. The heavy artillery was supposed to have cooperated at 1645 but this does not appear to have materialized. Led by the mounted Colonel Dimmer[92] two companies of Berkshires advanced and for a time were successful in recapturing some of the ground. Eventually, however, the Germans attacked again, threw the

---

89   TNA WO 953055: 182 Bde; WO 953025: 2/6th S. Foresters, Narrative; WO 953020: 176 Bde Report on Operations.
90   TNA WO 952998: WO 953140: 6/Lancs. Fusiliers, 21 Mar.1918; WO 95056: 2/7th Warwickshire narrative.
91   TNA WO 95962: Report on Operations of XIX Corps.
92   There was later some dispute about whether Dimmer was actually mounted when he led the attack. One report suggests he was leading two companies towards the assembly area when they ran into enemy forces. Caught by surprise, he had no time to dismount. See J. Edmonds, *Military Operations*, pp.201-02 and correspondence from Captain Whitfield, 1 Sep.1925 in TNA WO 953065: 2/4th Berkshire.

Berkshires back and made yet another assault on Spooner Redoubt. The Berkshires tried again the following day and met with the same result.

The prepared plan had included a scheme for cooperation between the artillery and the machine-gun battalion, and the Berkshire clearly believed coordination with the neighbouring division had been secured. Nonetheless, the resources for conducting the counter-attack remained inadequate for their intended purpose. There is little doubt that the Berkshires fought bravely but the supporting barrage was indifferent, enfilading fire could not be suppressed, and there were simply too many Germans in the way for two companies with no reserves to retain any recaptured ground. A larger but equally ill-fated attempt to regain lost ground in the Battle Zone was made by 177 Brigade during the afternoon of 21 March.[93] Reference to Major General Romer's possible delay in ordering forward the battalions of 177 Brigade has already been made. The original plan, a form of which did exist in the defence scheme, was for 2/5th Lincolnshire to occupy the intermediate line in the Battle Zone west of Noreuil, and 2/4th Leicestershire to defend the same line behind Ecoust. The advance, which soon technically developed into a counter-attack because the enemy was already in possession of the objectives, was conducted without any artillery cooperation. It is probable that being unsure of where their own two front brigades actually were, Romer and his staff refused a barrage in case it fell on the Staffordshires or Foresters. Running into severe machine-gun and small arms fire inside the Battle Zone, 2/5th Lincolnshire took shelter in a trench which, as they began to receive fire from all directions, was necessarily manned on both sides. The companies were all but wiped out. The other battalion, 2/4th Leicestershire, fared little better. Galling fire fell on the lead company as it approached Ecoust across open ground. Its survivors fell back to join the rest of the battalion in the Third System.[94] Meanwhile DHQ, in ignorance of the disaster unfolding on the two battalions, ordered 4/Lincolnshire, which had moved to the Third System, to advance further forward and take position to the right of its sister battalion which, DHQ assumed was in the Support Line of the Second System. Once in position both battalions were then intended to counter-attack the Firing Line of the Battle Zone. Fortunately, DHQ learned of the enemy's presence in the Second System and cancelled the proposed counter-attack before it was launched to what would have been certain calamity.[95] Like the attempt by 2/4th Berkshire, the plan was in accordance with current thinking and reflected the commander's intent but the lack of up-to-date intelligence meant that the resources, or means, that could and should have been brought to bear, were not.

The VI Corps war diary records very little contact with 59th Division during the course of the day. There is mention at 0930 of the infantry attack on the division and then silence until 1345 when a message from DHQ confirmed the enemy was advancing down its right flank area. There was no indication given of how far the penetration had reached. Another wire at 1518

---

93 TNA WO 953022: 177 Bde, Report on Operations.
94 M. Middlebrook, *The Kaiser's Battle* pp.251-52 provides some first-hand accounts of this operation. See fn. 72 above for the contradictions over timings.
95 TNA WO 953022: 177 Bde. Report on Operations. An account by 4/Lincolnshire mentions that the brigade's other two battalions received the order to occupy the Second System at 1200, and that it (4/Lincolnshire) was ordered to occupy the Third System. It then asserts that at 1400 it was instructed, in conjunction with 2/5th Lincolnshire, to counter-attack Pontefract and Dewsbury Trenches. Fortunately this order was, however, "cancelled almost as once as it was realized the operation was impracticable." TNA WO 952590: Account of Operations 21-25 March 1918.

informed corps HQ that 6th Division had fallen back almost to Vraucourt and that the enemy was attacking all along the North Midland's front. Another wire, 12 minutes later, indicated the division was now on the Reserve Line of the Third System. There is no mention of any order from corps HQ instructing the division to counter-attack but in its later *Report of Operations*, it describes 177 Brigade's counter-attack and adds: "I had intended to throw in a brigade of 40th Division to regain Ecoust Switch and the Second System but the brigade moved too slowly and the opportunity had gone."[96] The indication of minimal communication between corps HQ and 59th Division probably has more to do with written messages being lost than indifferent staff work on the division's part. That the division remained in regular contact with 34th and 6th divisions is evident in those two formations' war diaries.

On the morning of 22 March, a counter-attack that did temporarily halt the enemy advance was the result of a coordinated affair by 61st Division and 17/King's, a battalion of 30th Division released from XVIII Corps reserve. The King's battalion was put at the disposal of 184 Brigade, part of whose Battle Zone had been penetrated. On the right of 2/5 Gloucestershire, 2/6th Warwickshire cooperated when one company of the King's and the Gloucestershires drove the enemy from the captured trench. Despite this local success, shortly afterwards came the signal for a general withdrawal along the corps front. As one officer later observed, isolated counter-attacks "rarely achieved anything significant."[97] When successful they may temporarily have boosted morale but, on 21 March, they generally achieved little more than weaken an already stretched the defence. Moreover, whether they may even have boosted morale is open to question because when used as tactical ploys in delaying actions, counter-attacks are not intended or expected to achieve any decisive result. Perhaps, however, the most illustrative example during the first two days of an attempt at extensive cooperation by a 2nd Line formation was a counter-attack undertaken in 66th Division's sector.[98]

By the early morning of 22 March, most parts of Major General Malcolm's Battle Zone were still contested. Malcolm knew overnight moves had brought up tanks, additional heavy artillery, another cavalry brigade, and the infantry brigades of 50th Division to within striking distance of the front. Welcome as they were, these additional forces were of no immediate help to the remnants of 197 Brigade who were "blown out" of the Brown Line at 0745. What little was left of the brigade was ordered to join with 15/Hussars from Roisel, half of 15/Entrenching Battalion, and the one remaining company of 1/5th Border (P) to regain the ground. On the right, 198 Brigade, including 9/Sussex which was still holding out in two redoubts, was ordered to support the attack with any reserves it could muster. The Hussars, elements of the Lancashire Fusiliers, and Borderers launched their attack and drove the Germans back along the Roisel-Templeux road. Because, however, runners failed to find or reach both the Sussex and the Entrenching Battalion there was no support on their right. At 1100, the enemy burst through another section of the Brown Line. In response, 199 Brigade managed to coordinate a counter-attack with tanks, dismounted cavalry and elements of its own battalions. This was partially successful but failed to force the enemy entirely from the key terrain of Hervilly Wood. Even so, a substantial part of the Brown Line was still held by the division and at 1130 the first battalion of 150 Brigade, 50th Division, arrived on the scene. This was the "crucial moment"

---

96 TNA WO 95773: Report of Operations of the VI Corps.
97 TNA WO 953121: Report of Operations of 9/Manchester.
98 TNA WO 953121: Narrative of Operations, 22 Mar.1918.

when Malcolm believed the battle had come to a "standstill". He later claimed that if two fresh battalions had been pushed through either side of Hesbécourt they would "undoubtedly have been able to regain the whole of the Divisional Battle Zone with very little resistance."[99] This was clearly an over-optimistic assertion but at the time of writing Malcolm was able to make the claim safe in the knowledge that corps HQ had decided not to engage the newly-arrived troops in counter-attack operations. In accordance with Gough's order, corps HQ had opted instead to fight a delaying action whilst withdrawing through 50th Division's positions on the Green Line.

During the first two days of the offensive, the four 2nd Line divisions had thus, like every other division in Third and Fifth Armies, executed a number of counter-attacks either as prescribed in their defence schemes or, more usually, as extemporized necessities. Comparing the number of counter-attacks per division would be futile because it would not be comparing like with like: length of frontages, the numbers and relative strengths of battalions in the Forward and Battle Zones, the availability of reserves, the numbers of enemy divisions engaging, and so on, varied from division to division. Of those divisions adjoining, within the same corps, or in close proximity to the 2nd Line formations, 16th Division is known to have countermanded an intended counter-attack by 1/RMF because the battalion was too slow in moving towards its assembly position. As we have seen, a similar fate happened to one proposed by 6th Division for a battalion of 75 Brigade, and the one by 25/Northumberland Fusiliers of 34th Division in support of the North Midland met with disaster. Two battalions of 30th Division, 19/King's and 2/RSF, launched two successful operations in the early hours of 22 March; another by a battalion of 18th Division captured a substantial number of prisoners. DHQ then cancelled a proposed attempt by 7/Queens to regain its Forward Zone.[100] One attempt of limited size by a battalion of 36th Division failed to eject the enemy from 107 Brigade's Battle Zone, but perhaps the most surprising is mention by 24th Division of it having to cancel a counter-attack on Maissemy by two companies of 9/East Surrey because 61st Division "could not assist in the operation."[101] The cancellation was logged at the very time Colonel Dimmer's two companies of 2/4th Berkshire were fighting to the south of Maissemy as a prerequisite for 24th Division's supposed attack on the village.[102]

Late in the evening of 22 March, the much depleted 173 Brigade of 58th Division came under command of 125th French Division. The division's other two brigades had seen little fighting and remained intact. While trying to get in touch with 18th Division on its left, 173 Brigade held the line roughly Condren-St Quentin Canal-Viry Noreuil. On 24 March, pressure on the French forces caused 173 Brigade to withdraw across the Oise. The Germans made no attempt to contest the crossing and from then until 1 April, when the process of relieving the division began, there was little further fighting. The division went to a sector east of Amiens and reorganized.

99 Ibid.
100 TNA WO 951956; WO 951584; WO 952436; WO 952313; WO 952017.
101 TNA WO 952492: Account of Operations; WO 952192: Narrative of Operations 21 March-6 April 1918, 24th Division.
102 This apparent contradiction could be the result of errors in the loggings of wires and messages received and sent. Other timings in the report are, however, consistent so in this instance mistakes are unlikely to be the cause.

Without what remained of its artillery and the much reduced 177 Brigade, 59th Division withdrew to Bouzincourt on 23 March.[103] The CRE reported there "was a total absence of anything like a disorderly retreat or rout" and "a total absence of stragglers."[104] Given the chaos of the preceding two days this is likely to have been a somewhat rose-tinted impression. A rout it was not but the absence of stragglers is harder to accept. Some battalions had been without relief from working parties or in the line for over three weeks, they had been tried beyond measure, and had often been without officers during the withdrawal and fighting.[105] By the end of the month the division was with Second Army at Proven. The pioneers of 6/7th RSF (P) were relieved on 24 March and 177 Brigade was clear of the line by 26 March. It rejoined the division four days later.[106]

By late morning of 22 March, DHQ 61st Division was increasingly worried about the situation on its left. At 1215 it wired XVIII Corps to say that if the enemy could not be checked on the north side of the Omignon, the division would have to retire. HQ of 183 Brigade had reported "large numbers" of troops of 24th Division and some of its own Argyll & Sutherland Highlanders pulling back from Villecholles. Attempts were reportedly being made to organize defences at Vermand and Marteville. Within 30 minutes corps HQ had replied and laid out the method and disposition of the brigades on completion of a retirement to the Vaux-Villeveque Line.[107] Orders were distributed to the three brigades and by 1740 they were all reported to be on the new line. This appears to have been done in good order, with companies of three battalions covering the withdrawal of their respective brigades. There had been some earlier confusion when 182 Brigade spoke to 90 Brigade on its right with a view to cooperating; 90 Brigade replied that as it had received no orders it would stay in its current positions.[108] The two Warwickshire battalions, one of which had seen very little fighting in its Battle Zone, were told troops of 20th Division would be in the new line. When the Warwickshires arrived, without tools and little ammunition, they found no troops and some very shallow trenches. Almost immediately the enemy approached "in masses". Despite tapping into a discovered buried cable, 2/7th Warwickshire could not get in touch with brigade HQ and although each of the three artillery groups was supposed to be covering its own infantry brigade, there was no artillery support. The trench to the Warwickshires' right was empty and the retiring troops of 30th

---

103   VI Corps recorded it could not extricate 177 Bde because it was so "deeply involved" in the operation of 40th Division. Its removal would have jeopardized the corps right flank. TNA WO 95773, 23 Mar.1918.
104   TNA WO 953011: Report by CRE; WO 953011: CRE report.
105   TNA WO 953022: 2/4th Leicestershire, 21 Mar.1918.
106   The artillery of 59th Division was not relieved. As the months passed and most units of the division were reduced to cadre, 295 and 296 Bdes RFA remained attached to other divisions. They did rejoin the reconstituted 59th Division later in the year.
107   Although the actual instruction had come from Gough, three weeks later Maxse explained why he had ordered the withdrawal: "The choice lay between sacrificing the 61st Division in its Battle Zone or withdrawing it to conform to the deeply penetrated British line on its left." TNA WO 953055. Maxse account dated 10 Apr.1918
108   TNA WO 953055: 22 Mar.1918. When 182 Bde HQ queried the issue with 61st Division HQ it was told 30th Division had ordered 90 Bde to withdraw at the same time as 182 Bde. J. Edmonds, *Military Operations*, p.274, notes 2/Bedfordshire of 90 Bde had conducted six local counter-attacks in its Battle Zone during 22 March. The battalion war diary (WO 952333) does not record these counter-attacks but 90 Bde is thought to have been in, and behind the Green Line by 1700.

Division "refused to occupy it." Enemy aircraft overhead were clearly spotting for their artillery and when troops on their left fell back their own almost non-existent trenches were quickly caught in enfilade. The men began to withdraw in an action "which was quite impossible to check" until the GOC brigade and his staff managed to halt it near Foreste.[109] In the early hours of 23 March the three brigades, "much attenuated in numbers and to a measure disorganized" crossed the Somme and, temporarily and briefly, went into reserve.[110] It was not until 2 April that the division, having had units attached to other formations and suffered an estimated 272 officers and 5,661 ORs casualties, was finally relieved.[111]

In the words of 66th Division's official narrative, the withdrawal was conducted "without the slightest difficulty, the enemy being too demoralized and tired to make any attempt to follow up our men who simply walked back over the open ground." They passed through the Green Line manned by 50th Division about 5,000 yards to the rear.[112] In reality it was not quite as simple as stated, with the enemy constantly pressing and harassing the rearguards. The division headed to the south of Péronne, its part in the operation far from over. With the three brigades totalling an estimated 50 officers 1,500 ORs it fought a series of running battles during its westwards retirement.[113] Rarely fighting as a discrete formation the division was finally withdrawn to rest on 2 April.

If we are to believe all that was written soon after the battle, the 2nd Line divisions, as did all formations, fought with exceptional gallantry, high spirits, and "to the finish." Congratulatory and 'thanks' messages flooded into DHQ from the C-in-C downwards. Some individual units, including 2/5th Gloucestershire, were singled out for special praise.[114] Possibly with a nod to internal alliance relations, General Barthelemy thanked 58th Division for '*la bravoure des battaillons Anglais,*' while Brigadier General Stansfield despatched a heart-felt hand written message to survivors of his 178 Brigade. His sentiments were echoed by Lieutenant General Haldane, the GOC corps, who reiterated the "very gallant stand against overwhelming numbers…supported by tremendous artillery … in as trying circumstances as can possibly happen in war."[115] The fighting spirit and powers of endurance of 66th Division were recorded by XIX HQ as "beyond all praise" and, as the wounded Major General Malcolm was in the process of being evacuated, he wanted his division to know "we have not asked for relief or assistance… a proud record."[116] Lieutenant General Maxse offered some warm praise to 61st Division when he wrote of it having "established a high reputation for its fighting qualities and gallant spirit" but the division's own GOC, Major General Mackenzie went further in an Order of the Day. He wrote of the "glorious way" the division had fought, how it was soon to receive a special mention in an

---

109 TNA WO 953056: 2/7th Warwickshire.
110 TNA WO 953035: Narrative of Operations. Individual brigades had a fighting strength of around 600 all ranks.
111 Ibid.
112 TNA WO 953121: Narrative of Operations.
113 Ibid
114 Including Arthur Conan Doyle, *The British Campaign in France and Flanders, January-July 1918*, Vol. 5 (London: Hodder & Stoughton, 1919).
115 TNA WO 952988: Correspondence dated 16 Apr.1918; WO 953025: Correspondence dated 30 Mar.1918; WO 953022: 2/4th Leicestershire correspondence dated 30 Mar.1918
116 TNA WO 953121. Correspondence dated 31 Mar.1918; WO 953126: ADMS wire dated 29 Mar.1918

official despatch, and of how it had never left its ground until ordered to do so. He assured his men that they had had a "better reward than any that can be given you in the consciousness of duty nobly done." The despatch mentioned by Mackenzie, that he valued "more than anything else," was despatched by Gough's. The army commander wrote: "No division did better or even as well as yours."[117] A less dramatic but equally telling valediction came from the war diary of 2/4th Berkshire. The diarist noted the battalion had "annoyed the enemy to the fullest possible extent."[118]

General Gough was to bear the ultimate responsibility for the apparent collapse of Fifth Army. He was made the scapegoat but fervently contested his dismissal and agued, with much justification, that Fifth Army withdrew largely according to a prepared plan. The real culprits, he argued, were the politicians who had deprived the BEF of sufficient troops to defend its extended front. General Byng's Third Army, much stronger than Fifth in terms of numbers of divisions for its length of front, was not so severely condemned for its withdrawal. While the enemy offensive was underway divisional war diaries, as always, were keen to make the point that it was not their troops but those alongside them who had given way or showed a less than resolute determination to hold their ground. This was sometimes certainly the case. The language used is often, for obvious reason, somewhat opaque but the implication is usually clear. In Third Army, 59th Division, which was probably the hardest hit of any under Byng's command, believed it was the left of 6th Division on its right that allowed the enemy to penetrate the Hirondelle Valley and roll up the North Midland's right. The valley itself was 6th Division's responsibility and in the fog 59th had little chance of stemming the enemy hitting its right brigade.[119] Both of 6th Division's forward brigades were forced back but the use of words in its war diary implies that rather than the pressure exerted directly on its own two brigades, the reasons for the withdrawal of its forces were the actions of 59th Division on the left and 51st Division on its right.[120]

In III Corps, by nightfall of 21 March, 18th Division was also registering concern about the situation on its flanks. As we have seen, on its right 173 Brigade of 58th Division had suffered badly in the initial stages and, as it was exposed to repeated attacks from the south, 18th Division's 55 Brigade had been forced to form a defensive flank. On 18th Division's left, 14th (Light) Division was hit particularly hard and was pushed quickly back to its Battle Zone. Despite the pressure on its northern and southern flanks, some of 18th Division's posts in the Forward Zone were still holding out. To emphasize its own relative security, the division recorded that if the situation on its flanks had been better, it was a "reasonable assumption" that an organized counter-attack by its husbanded reserves would have regained its entire Forward Zone.[121] On the left of 14th Division, 36th (Ulster) also blamed the Light Division for its enforced withdrawal. This move affected 30th Division on the Ulster Division's left and then,

---

117 TNA WO 953055: 182 Bde narrative by Maxse, 10 Apr.1918; Ibid, wire dated 24 Mar.1918; A. Barnes, *The Story of the 2/5th Gloucester*, p. 97.
118 TNA WO 953065: 2/4th Berkshire, 30 Mar.1918.
119 In January, Third Army had described the junction of VI and IV corps as not "entirely satisfactory." TNA WO 95369: 6 Jan.1918.
120 TNA WO 951584.
121 TNA WO 952017.

also, 61st Division.¹²² The New Army 30th Division did not directly blame the South Midland and accepted that its own left was compromised.¹²³ Although acknowledging that some of 183 Brigade had withdrawn from the division's extreme left, 61st recorded it was largely the German thrust down the Omignon Valley in 24th Division's sector which necessitated its own retirement to the Green Line. For its part, 24th Division expressed confidence in its ability to hang on to Le Verguier provided 66th Division was able to hold its Battle Zone. It was with some misgivings, therefore, that it noted the withdrawal of the Manchester battalions just north of Le Verguier. Soon afterwards the village fell but, by that time, the divisional boundary north of the village had been successfully penetrated on either side.¹²⁴ In a not entirely fair assessment, 66th Division felt it was compelled to order its southern flank's troops to conform with 24th Division's withdrawal. The division quickly appreciated the danger on its left as 16th Division was forced back north of the Cologne and, of course, 197 Brigade had suffered badly in relinquishing its hold on Templeux village and the Quarries. As the newly attached cavalry moved up from the rear, the division was in the process of organizing the counter-attacks from Roisel.¹²⁵ Nonetheless, whilst acknowledging that its own 7/Royal Irish Regiment was being rolled up from the south, that its two RFA brigades had lost all of their guns, and that 1/R. Munster Fusiliers had failed to assemble for a counter-attack, 16th Division recorded that the left of 66th Division had given way. As the result, it noted, its own right was being attacked by tanks and enfiladed from the East Lancashire Division's sector.¹²⁶

Leaving alleged or proven inadequacies aside, the four 2nd Line divisions had fared better than many other formations. At the close of 21 March, 66th, 61st and 59th divisions were all still holding positions within their Battle Zones; the remnants of 173 Brigade had lost their Battle Zone but had, as ordered, withdrawn to defensive positions behind the Crozat Canal. Along the front of the two armies several divisions had lost considerably more.¹²⁷ Casualties had been enormous and although a huge casualty list does not necessarily mean the men "fought to the last", 59th and 66th Divisions suffered the highest and third highest numbers respectively of all formations involved that day. Lieutenant Colonel Gadd's earlier concern that the Forward Zone was too strongly held at the expense of the Battle Zone proved to have been justified. Troops of the two front Sherwood Foresters battalions were either killed, wounded, or quickly surrounded. As the Germans swept into and around their positions, they were left with the option of surrendering or dying at their posts. Initial returns late on 21 March gave the combined number of survivors of those two battalions as 59 ORs. Gadd's battalion. 2/5th Sherwood, had just three ORs at the first roll call. The Foresters' Brigade casualties were recorded as 88 officers and 1,899 ORs. Casualties in the three Staffordshire battalions of 176 Brigade were noted as 70 officers and 1,683 ORs. The reported strength of 2/5th Lincolnshire on the morning of 22 March consisted of five officers and 80 ORs.

---

122 TNA WO 952492: Account of Operations.
123 TNA WO 952313.
124 TNA WO 952192: Narrative of Operations.
125 TNA WO 953121: Narrative of Operations.
126 TNA WO 951956: 22 Mar.1918.
127 These ranged from the 1st Line 51st (Highland) to 14th (Light), 16th (Irish) and 36th (Ulster) New Army divisions.

At the beginning of March the strength of the three Lancashire Fusilier battalions of 197 Brigade amounted to 166 officers and 3,025 ORs. Like most battalions in the BEF, the Fusilier units were, on paper, over-strength as a result of the recent amalgamations and disbanding of battalions. A substantial percentage of battalion members, however, were not trench strength. Consequently, on 21 March the three battalions each had probably about 650-700 all ranks in the trenches.[128] By the end of the month the brigade's casualties were recorded as 81 ORs killed, 32 officers and 299 ORs wounded, and 1,644 ORs missing. There was a similar raft of statistics for 61st Division which, in overall casualties, was not far behind those of 59th and 66th Divisions. Before 21 March, trench strengths for most of the division's battalions were no larger than 700 all ranks, which gave average brigade trench totals of around 2,000. Estimated casualties for the 10 days' fighting were noted as 63 officers and 1,700 ORs for 184 Brigade, and 59 and 1,690 respectively for 183 Brigade.

These early totals were rough estimates and many of the missing men did turn up later or were discovered to be in hospital. Large numbers of the missing were also prisoners of war (PoW). It is difficult to be precise on how many men did surrender when, dazed from the bombardment and finding themselves surrounded or out of communications and ammunition, decided further resistance was futile. Undoubtedly, in the opinion of others some did surrender too quickly. In what may have been a case of self-justification, Captain Saxon of 9/Sussex acknowledged that two platoons of 2/6th Manchester fought "splendidly" alongside his men in Trinket Redoubt but condemned other troops of 66th Division as "swine" for surrendering too swiftly. This, he wrote, exposed his left flank and compelled him and his men to surrender.[129] Later reports and published accounts understandably insist the men fought to the end but that, equally understandably, was not always the case. Three examples of battalions in the Forward Zone of 61st Division, illustrate the point. At 2100 on 21 March, one officer and six ORs of 2/8th Worcestershire reported to 182 Brigade HQ.[130] They were thought to be the battalion's only survivors. Well into the night a few more stragglers arrived back which allowed the diarist later to write that the battalion had 19 officers and 566 ORs missing.[131] The regimental history[132] quotes Major Davies, OC of the company garrisoning Ellis Redoubt. He believed that casualties in his company were 60 percent, of which 40 percent were killed. There were, apparently, "comparatively few wounded as the casualties were mainly bullet wounds to the head." The final totals recorded in the war diary were nine officers killed and 12 captured, and 560 ORs missing. After the war, figures showed that the battalion's four companies had lost a total of only seven officers and 19 ORs killed. Those figures actually account for fewer casualties than those reported for Major Davies' own single company. They confirm that men in the other three companies must have surrendered, albeit perhaps wounded, in large numbers. In 183 Brigade, 1/5th Gordon Highlanders held the Forward Zone. Late on 21 March, the battalion reported

---

128 In 59th Division, 2/5th North Staffordshire recorded a strength of 46 officers and 1,039. Of these, 17 officers and 175 ORs were away from the battalion for one reason or another. TNA WO 953021. 2/5th N.Staffs, 30 Jan.1918
129 TNA WO 952219: 9/Sussex. Captain Saxon wrote this report in Dec.1918 on his return from captivity in Germany.
130 J .Edmonds, *Military Operations*, p.176, fn. 2.
131 One officer and 18 ORs were also known to be wounded and in field ambulances behind the lines.
132 H. Stacke, *Worcester Regiment in the Great War*, p.326.

its casualties as 24 officers 575 ORs missing. Figures after the war show the number of fatalities to have been two officers and 33 ORs. In contrast to these two battalions, whose companies outside of their redoubts were probably overwhelmed in the fog, the other Forward Zone garrison, 2/4th Ox&Bucks, with one company in Enghien Redoubt, had five officers and 88 ORs killed. Tragic as these figures are, they are small in comparison to those registered in 59th Division. The division lost particularly severely because it faced probably the heaviest attack on its corps' front. It did, nonetheless, still manage to delay the enemy long enough for 40th Division to move up from reserve.[133] The two battalions of 178 Brigade and two of 176 Brigade in the Forward Zone, suffered a total of 452 OR fatalities. This gives an average fatality loss of 113 per battalion compared to the average of 49 in the three Forward Zone battalions of 61st Division.[134]

Middlebrook calculated that four divisions had more than 2,000 men taken prisoner on 21 March. Heading Middlebrook's list was 59th Division with an estimated 3,142 troops captured, largely from the division's nine brigaded battalions. That figure is 750 greater than the next largest loss, that of 36th (Ulster) Division. There are, however, no other 2nd Line formations within the top four divisions.[135] Two of the four pioneer battalions, 1/5th Border and 6/7th RSF, lost as heavily as many conventional infantry battalions. Sappers in several of the field companies, many of which were involved in fighting as infantry, also lost considerable numbers. Fatalities, however, were not huge: eleven certainly died in the three field companies of 66th Division on 21-22 March; two ORs were thought to have been killed in 59th Division's three field companies; and four in 61st Division's three. The numbers of wounded and missing increased the totals to: three officers and 72 ORs missing from 59th Division's companies, and one officer and 40 ORs from 66th Division's. Early casualty returns for gunners and drivers in the RFA brigades confirm the fact that many guns in the forward positions were fought very much to the last. The combined totals of casualties in the two RFA brigades of 61st Division were 11 officers and 144 ORs, which included seven officers and 60 ORs missing. The total casualty list in the two RFA brigades of 66th Division was 294.

In the later defence of his leadership and of his command Gough wrote that Watts' XIX Corps faced "perhaps the most serious prospect" on Fifth Army's front. Gough described the corps as consisting of "two weak divisions", with 1st Cavalry Division in support and 50th Division too far away to be of any help until at least the second day.[136] In fact, 66th Division was not, as indicated above, particularly weak – its own DHQ declared it was "well up to strength."[137] Fearing that voluntarily to jeopardize its hold on terrain that had been costly to capture might affect morale, and because they considered that 66th Division was unlikely to be attacked in strength anyway, Watts and Malcolm took a calculated risk and maintained a strong

---

133 In a hand-written letter of gratitude to his command, Brig. Gen. Stansfield, GOC 178 Bde, wrote that it had taken the Germans four hours to advance 2,500 yards. The diarist of one of Stansfield's battalions thought it had taken the enemy eight hours to penetrate 2,000 yards. TNA WO 953025: 2/6th S. Foresters. Letter dated 30 Mar.1918; Ibid., 2/5th S. Foresters, Mar.1918.
134 For further discussion on casualties see Appendix 1
135 M. Middlebrook, *The Kaiser's Battle*, p.321. The calculations are 36th lost 2,392, 14th lost 2,238, and 6th Division, 2,116 as POWs.
136 H. Gough, *Fifth Army*, p.267.
137 TNA WO 953121: Narrative of Operations. At the end of February the division's infantry strength was recorded as being only 323 troops below establishment. WO 953123: A&Q, 28 Feb.1918.

garrison on the Cologne Ridge.[138] This restricted the number of troops available for the Battle Zone. When, on 21 March the gamble failed, the Forward Zone garrisons lost heavily. To the south, Maxse's three divisions of XVIII Corps were confronted by eight German divisions with another six in close support. Despite the imbalance of forces, 61st Division was able to demonstrate considerable resilience in order to hold on to all but the extreme left of its Battle Zone. Its flexibility and adaptability, like that of 66th Division, became especially apparent during the withdrawal and the delaying action phases post-22 March. As we have seen, Gough was loud in his praise for what his corps commanders and divisions had achieved during the first two days and directed his criticism towards GHQ for its lack of grip and situational awareness. Although when as Gough's Chief of Staff Malcolm had sometimes openly aired his views, it was rare for GOC corps publically to discuss or log criticism of individual divisions. In two of the very few recorded exceptions, Watts expressed some disappointment with the way 50th Division had fought, and Haldane had clearly been wary of how 41st Division might perform.[139] None of the 2nd Line divisions received anything other than praise for their defensive work.

In some respects the German infantry tactics played into the hands of the defenders. Many reports wrote of "dense" masses of the enemy "streaming" across the terrain in waves towards the Battle Zone. Provided there were still machine guns and artillery able to respond, they presented supreme targets. There is praise for the way the enemy used valleys and depressions to work their way forwards and for how effectively they deployed their mobile machine guns. There was praise, too, for the way they operated their signal lights to call down artillery support, and also for the regular presence of German aircraft. There were accounts of attempted deception with enemy troops dressed as British soldiers[140] but there is no mention in the war diaries of the 2nd Line formations and units of the use by the enemy of infiltration tactics. This might be simply because the fog in the Forward Zones prevented the defenders from becoming aware of the tactic being employed. When fighting in what were often cases of isolation, it would have been difficult for the garrisons of posts to distinguish infiltration from conventional assault. When the fog lifted and the German follow up and support troops were seen advancing towards the Battle Zone, with lines of skirmishers followed by platoons in artillery formation or waves, the defenders saw what they believed to be a more-or-less traditional German tactical attack.

It was against dense masses, advancing sometimes shoulder to shoulder, that 62nd (West Riding) Division was pitted 26-31 March. The division had come out of the line near Arras on

---

138 They believed that because the eventual capture of the ridge in 1917 had cost several British divisions so much blood, morale would suffer if it were voluntarily abandoned.
139 TNA WO 95962: 22 Mar.1918. H. Gough, *Fifth Army*, p.74 was more generous to 50th Division. He believed the division must have been tired after its journey to the front and implicitly criticized GHQ for having removed its GOC only days before. Lieutenant General Haldane was unusually open with his thoughts when he heard IV Corps on his right was to receive 41st Division. The formation had just returned from Italy and, Haldane thought, "seems a rather doubtful asset…It is reported to be in indifferent form and given to exaggerate the situation unfavourably." WO 95773: Extracts from Haldane's Diary, 25 Mar.1918.
140 Several units claim they saw Germans dressed as British troops. Major Keating, however, was sure that with sandbags on their helmets and with pack and equipment arranged in such a way, "they could easily be mistaken for our men." TNA WO 953021: Correspondence in 2/6th N. Staffs war diary; WO 952988: Wire dated 25 Mar.1918. As late as 25 March, 58th Division was convinced Germans dressed as British officers were spreading "panic" amongst civilians and "false information" to British troops. See WO 952988: 25 Mar.1918

23 March and in the very early hours of 25 March was ordered to march south to Ayette and then to Bucquoy. Later that same day, 185 and 186 brigades were to the east of Achiet-le-Petit. Such was the confusion and the exhaustion of the divisions that had borne the first blows of the offensive that little hard intelligence was forthcoming as to what 62nd Division might have to face. Later that night, with 187 Brigade marching to rejoin the other two brigades, the division was ordered to form a defensive line running roughly Bucqouy – Puisieux. For the next five days what might be termed either a prolonged delaying action, or more probably a desperate last ditch defensive battle, was fought by the division in conjunction with the 1st Line 42nd (East Lancashire), the New Zealand Division, and a brigade of Australians. When it was relieved on the night of 31 March, first estimates put its casualties at 98 officers and 2,084 ORs.[141]

In the division's narrative of the operation,[142] frequent mention is made of the tremendous effect of concentrated rifle and Lewis gun fire on the enemy. Assault after assault, sometimes aided by the guns of the RFA brigades, was broken up by these weapons in which, the report stressed, the men had acquired new confidence. The role of the newly-organized MGC battalion was also praised, with batteries of guns under disciplined fire control pouring thousands of rounds into the advancing enemy.[143] Often unaware of where the front line actually was, the 18 pdrs sensibly aimed to fire the barrage about 300 yards in advance of where it was thought to be. This left the rifles and Lewis guns to destroy survivors of the massed hordes between the trailing edge of the barrage and the division's wire. Communications remained the ever-present problem but with two infantry brigades sharing one HQ, signallers could concentrate on keeping only one main line working back to DHQ. With the destruction of dumps and the intensity of ammunition discharge, sustainment was a major problem.[144] There were shortages, particularly of rifle grenades and Stokes bombs and, again, the superiority of the German stick grenade and the skill behind its thrower was acknowledged. There were enforced changes in brigade and battalion commands[145] but in managing to overcome the communication difficulties the division worked in close liaison with its neighbours. In addition to demonstrating endurance, discipline, and considerable tenacity, it conducted counter-attacks and limited staged withdrawals. The division had done well at Cambrai in an operation for which it had trained extensively; the defensive battle in the Bucquoy – Puisieux – Rossignol Wood area was unrehearsed and improvised but devastatingly efficient. Unsurprisingly, IV Corps wired its grateful appreciation.[146]

---

141 TNA WO 953072: A&Q. The return gives: 14 officers and 225 ORs killed; 57 and 1,289 wounded; 18 and 570 missing; nine officers wounded at duty.
142 TNA WO 953070: Narrative of the Operations, 22 Apr.1918.
143 Two squadrons of machine guns from an unnamed source were attached to the division from 27 March. In addition, E. Wyrall, *The Story of the 62nd (West Riding) Division*, p,149, tells the story of how the Commandant of the Machine-Gun School in Camiers, Colonel (later Field Marshal) Edmund Ironside, turned up at Maj. Gen. Braithwaite's HQ on 26 March with about 100 trained machine-gunners. He offered the services of his men to Braithwaite who immediately and gratefully accepted.
144 TNA WO 953072: 29 Mar.1918.
145 GOC 187 Bde went sick before the battle. Lt. Col. Barton was placed in temporary command but he, too, went sick quickly under the strain. He was replaced by the CO of 2/7th West Yorkshire. Two battalion COs were killed and three wounded.
146 TNA WO 953070.

Post-battle reports by the other four engaged 2nd Line formations generally contented themselves with a narrative of events and of how courageously their men countered the onslaught. Some officers did, however, realize that aspects of the defence could have been better executed. There were the familiar complaints of poor communications, especially between artillery and infantry, trench warfare was thought to have made troops over-sensitive about their flanks, and the signal for a section of men to withdraw to give depth to a defence was often seen as a signal for all to follow suit. The men were thought to have fought and rallied well but, as was so often recorded, were "lost" and showed little initiative if their officers became casualties.[147] The RFC was frequently criticised for its apparent absence, and there were complaints about the lack of mobile troops such as cavalry and armoured cars.[148] One report noted there was insufficient attention and care given to the possibility of enemy troops moving up valleys – merely occupying and defending the adjoining heights was not enough[149] – and the CO of 66th Battalion MGC wrote a treatise on how the use of his arm could be improved. His recommendations ranged from stressing the need for more training, to the positioning and use of reserve guns, emplacements, tactics, and how instead of trying to save the weapon, guns should be fought until "the last moment" and then destroyed.[150] One OC field company that had been much engaged in the Battle Zone even noted it was "next to impossible" to get additional trained Lewis gunners and pointed out that new guns came up so clogged with grease as to be useless. The grease, he stressed, could only be efficiently removed by skilled men.[151] A report by GOC 6th Division, on the right of 59th, could probably be applicable to all divisions. Major General Marden thought there were too many unprotected machine-gun posts and section dugouts, that poor fire control resulted in significant ammunition wastage because every Lewis and rifleman fired at "every man in sight," and that not enough use was made of Stokes and rifle grenades. He criticized the lack of training, especially in how specifically to fight a rearguard action, and the absence of sufficient switch lines. Yet, as had been demonstrated in the local counter-attacks, he acknowledged the men had showed "splendid spirit".[152]

Another aspect of the battle that met with at least one GOC brigade's disapproval was the manner by which the medical provision operated. Brigadier General Spooner wrote that the arrangements were "not good." He claimed he never saw any bearer companies working in the Forward Zone and thought the ambulance cars should have been driven further forward. Undue pressure, he argued, was therefore brought to bear on the regimental SBs. Stragglers too often also seized the opportunity to carry back the wounded and then did not return to the fight.[153] If he ever saw the report, Spooner's own ADMS would have argued that shelling prevented the SBs from getting into the Forward Zone and also severely restricted the movement of

---

147 TNA WO 953059: *Remarks* by Brig. Gen. Spooner, 6 Apr.1918
148 TNA WO 953035: Preliminary Notes on Points that have come to notice during recent Operations by Lt. Col. R. Livesay, GSO1 61st Division, 4 Apr.1918.
149 Ibid.
150 TNA WO 953121: Report by Lt. Col. W.J. Woodcock, 7 Apr.1918.
151 TNA WO 953130: 432 Field Company, 66th Division.
152 TNA WO 951584: Points by the GOC, 6 May 1918. Marden thought officers and men assumed fighting a rearguard simply meant falling back from one trench to the next.
153 TNA WO 953059: GOC Bde's Remarks. It is unlikely Brig.Gen.Spooner actually visited the Forward Zone during the day. His brigade HQ was in the rear of the Battle Zone in Mount Huette Wood.

ambulances. The light railway used for conveying wounded from Foreste to Ham had worked well but shelling on the Attilly-Marteville road closed it to traffic for hours. Eventually three cars carrying additional SBs managed to open a bearer post in Attilly, but one of the cars was quickly destroyed. Transport difficulties also caused problems for ADMS 66th Division. He lost one car in Hesbécourt but managed to get three lorries sent from DDMS XIX Corps soon after noon. All available transport held by 2/1st East Lancashire Field Ambulance was quickly despatched to Bernes but nothing could get up the Roisel-Templeux road until 22 March. Three horse-drawn ambulances and three cars succeeded in running the gauntlet in the afternoon and evacuated the wounded trapped in Hesbécourt. In attempting to establish a degree of order from the closure and evacuation of his field ambulances, detached sections, ADSs, and MDSs, the ADMS issued very clear and precise instructions about where the three ambulances should be by the early hours of 23 March and which sorts of wounded the various units and stations were all to treat. ADMS 59th Division knew little of what was going on in the front of his Battle Zone because his deputy, several runners, and the reserve SBs failed to get through to the ADSs in Noreuil and Ecoust. The Decauville railway running down the Hirondelle Valley was out of action by 0900 and when the CCSs moved from Grévillers and Achiet-le-Grand to Albert, there were insufficient cars to maintain a steady flow of evacuees over the now greater distance. Four additional lorries were fairly quickly acquired from Third Army. The numbers of wounded coming through for treatment and evacuation had, however, reduced by the evening because the enemy had over-run the ground where so many of them lay.

The pressure on the field ambulances in all divisions to clear the casualties as efficiently and quickly as possible meant orderlies and clerks collated only approximate numbers of evacuated wounded. Unlike the other 2nd Line formations, 58th Division's three field ambulances were barely stretched on 21 March and the subsequent few days: 2/1st Home Counties Field Ambulance had only 600 sick and wounded pass through its hands in the 10 day period until 31 March. Once 2/2nd Home Counties had, as according to the defence scheme evacuated its sick early on 21 March, it returned to working on dugouts, bemoaning the fact that the RE were unable to help as much with the task as they had hoped.[154] The ADMS spent the first part of the day quietly examining men of 16/Entrenching Battalion for medical fitness, although he did visit his ambulances during the afternoon. There is nothing in the records to suggest that the medical systems and personnel of the three most active 2nd Line divisions were any less prepared or able to deal with the unfolding disaster than the Regular or New Army divisions working alongside them. Three of the four ADMS made the point in their diaries that everything was already in place for the presumed enemy offensive and, that when it did burst upon them, their implemented plans and actions adhered to the agreed corps and divisional schemes.[155]

---

154 2/1st London Division's three field ambulances were posted to 56th Division when the original 1st London Division reformed in France in February 1916. The three 2nd Line field ambulances of 67th (2nd Home Counties) Division were sent to 58th (2/1st London) as their replacements.
155 TNA WO 953038: ADMS 61st Division; WO 953051: 2/1st, 2/2nd and 2/3rd South Midland field ambulance war diaries; WO 953216: ADMS 66th Division; WO 953011: ADMS 59th Division; WO 953014: 2/1st, 2/2nd & 2/3rd North Midland field ambulance war diaries; WO 952997: 2/1st and 2/2nd Home Co. field ambulance war diaries; WO 952993: ADMS 58th Division. Precise figures for wounded are impossible to find but at a very rough estimate, the field ambulances of the three northernmost 2nd Line divisions all appear to have dealt with about 600 patients until 0600 on

If there were any great failings of leadership or courage in the four 2nd Line divisions, they have gone unrecorded.[156] Later divisional and regimental histories retold stories of unquestionable bravery, command and endurance: Lieutenant Colonel Dimmer's arguably foolhardy leadership as he advanced mounted towards the enemy; Brigadier General Stirling, also mounted, encouraging his gunners as shells crashed around the gun positions; when out of communication with his seniors, Major Ackerman, using his initiative to handle his guns "superbly"; the leadership and command of Second Lieutenant Shankland and CQMS Riding of the Lancashire Fusiliers, and the bravery of Major Trench of 2/5th Sherwood Foresters to cite only a few.[157] Overall, ten Victoria Crosses were awarded for work on 21 March; two of them went to officers of 61st Division.[158] The majority of officers and men of the 2nd Line, like the bulk of those in the other divisions, were prepared to resist so long as they felt duty compelled and their ammunition lasted. If and when they believed there was little point in continuing to fight and honour had been satisfied, they surrendered.

Had the modern understanding of Jomini's Principles of War and the concept of fighting power already been formulated, the troops might have realized they had at times employed limited offensive action to contest the initiative; demonstrated flexibility in organization and deployment; attempted to cooperate with neighbouring forces and, when appropriate, had applied economy of effort to provide virtual force security. There had been attempts to concentrate infantry force but, in the Forward Zones of some corps that concentration had been carried too far. In the rear area of Fifth Army there had been too little. That, however, was the fault of GHQ and corps operational planning rather than GOC divisions. Because there had been insufficient time and opportunity to train, the conceptual understanding amongst the troops of defence was probably hazy and possibly misunderstood. Other than manpower, elements of the physical component were generally well developed and resourced. The moral component – why the men were still prepared to fight – held until events compelled alternatives. Yet, after the trials of Third Ypres and a long winter, morale was undoubtedly low. While it is impossible to describe it as a *decisive* friction, without the fog they might have held and attrited the assault in the Forward Zones for a longer and more devastating period. Then, as anticipated in the planning, it might have been broken in the Battle Zone.

22 March. Six RMOs of 66th Division were reported missing and 2/3rd North Midland F. Amb. lost 44 ORs. All were presumed to be prisoners of war.
156 Only one of the 26 divisional commanders on that day was sacked.
157 Compiled, *The 59th Division*, pp.641, 62; J. Latter, *Lancashire Fusiliers*, pp.296-97; G. Hall, *Green Triangle*, p153
158 For their work during the offensive, VCs were awarded to the following: in 61st Division to 2Lt. J.C.Buchan, 1/8th Argyll & Sutherland Highlanders and Lt.A.E.Ker, 61 Battalion MGC. In 62nd Division to Lt.Col. O.C.Watson, 5/KOYLI, and Pte T.Young, 9/DLI.

Conclusion

According to modern UK doctrine, every land force has four inherent attributes: soldiers, presence, persistence, and versatility. These qualities underpin a force's relative strengths and limitations. Although a land force's persistence and presence is often necessary to secure an eventual military and political outcome, because it relies on human initiative, enterprise, and intelligence, its primary attribute is its soldiers.[1] Versatility comes a close second because it requires forces to be capable of adapting swiftly and effectively to changing situations. Land forces must, therefore, learn quickly and be able to alter plans and scenarios accordingly.[2] As in all BEF divisions on the Western Front, commanders and soldiers of the 2nd Line formations needed to demonstrate a thorough understanding of, in particular, the first and last of the four presumed attributes. Similarly, through their training, equipment, organization, management, leadership and command, the divisions embraced the three components of modern fighting power. If the 2nd Line divisions were to become of some worth to the Allied war effort, like all constituent parts of the BEF they would have to develop structures and identities capable enough for them to cope with the need sometimes to adjust the balance between those three components. Without this appreciation and the requisite support from higher authority, the 2nd Line's force development and future utility would have remained questionable. In that scenario the divisions would indeed have been of "no earthly use."

Unit cohesion of many 1st Line TF battalions had been badly affected before and during the Somme; the original *esprit* of the Pals battalions of the New Army was also largely destroyed during the campaign. With so few 1914 enlistments remaining in their battalions by mid-1915, and with the subsequent constant turnovers of personnel, 2nd Line units had had little consistent opportunity to build a deep *esprit*. Since under-developed cohesion often influences the quality and extent of personal and unit morale, *esprit* is an essential element of the moral component of fighting power. However, with war diaries and later histories reluctant to suggest that morale was rarely other than entirely sound, it is difficult at this distance to assess its quality with any real accuracy.[3] Various factors such as the incidence of crime and the length of sick parade queues are frequently cited as indicators of morale but they offer only a partial picture. Some war diaries do make occasional references to courts martial, and one soldier of

---

1 *Joint Doctrine Publication 0-20: Land Power* (Shrivenham; DCDC, 2017), 3.11
2 Land forces today must be sufficiently versatile to reconfigure quickly for scenarios ranging from peace support and humanitarian assistance, through counter-insurgency and counter-terrorism campaigns, to state-on-state war.
3 Personal correspondence and memoirs can give some indication of how morale varied but they are generally less than entirely reliable sources.

a 2nd Line division, Private William Smith of 3/5th Lancashire Fusiliers, was shot by firing squad. Others, including Smith's two comrades who deserted with him, had narrow escapes and had their sentences commuted to penal servitude and then suspended.[4] There were similar cases in other 2nd Line divisions, as there were in all formations.[5] After the war the alleged lack of morale was identified as a reason why men succumbed to shell shock. When Brigadier General Burnett, who had gone to France in 1914 as CO of 2/Gordon Highlanders, was asked by the Shell Shock Committee for his observations on the phenomenon, he related the usual belief that shell shock was virtually unknown amongst the regular soldiers of 1914 and 1915. After taking command of 186 Brigade, 62nd (2nd West Riding) Division in December 1917, he quickly became convinced that *esprit de corps* in his 2nd Line TF brigade was consistently worse than it had been in his highlanders' battalion. This was quite possibly true but comparing a regular battalion of 1914 with a largely conscript formation of 1918 was hardly comparing like with like. Burnett went on to assert that "after sustaining casualties in action it was always harder to get second line battalions trained up again." Quite what he meant by that statement is somewhat open to question because many factors could contribute to difficulties in getting a unit "trained up again." The only recorded evidence Burnett offered in support of his theory was that, provided the pre-war platoon commander of a regular battalion "did not go back with a nervous breakdown, very few of the men would." That, he intimated, was not the case in his wartime 2nd Line brigade.[6]

The physical and conceptual components of the 2nd Line divisions' fighting power developed along the same lines as those of other divisions of the BEF. Individual divisions had little say in manning levels and equipment supply but did have a degree of control over aspects of training. What evidence there is suggests there was no distinction made between the different types of division as to the length of periods allocated to rest and training. The time available depended entirely on the exigencies current in the relevant army and corps sectors. How the available training time was actually spent was, however, more likely to be determined by the division and brigades, rather than by higher authority. The C-in-C's intent and the desired operational and strategic ends were known, and the tactical doctrine was widely disseminated. It is probable, therefore, that although few war diaries precisely specify the content of their training regimes, 2nd Line divisions were unlikely to have followed any radically different path from those of other formations. All divisions were expected to make their training as practical and extensive as possible because this helped to provide both the "forcing function for wider innovation and adaptability" and also the context to develop leadership skills in dynamic scenarios.[7] The difficulty of finding time to undertake meaningful training was, however, the problem shared

---

4   J. Putkowski & J. Sykes, *Shot at Dawn* (London: Leo Cooper, 1990), p.216.
5   For example, four men of 2/5th Gloucestershire were not as fortunate as Smith's associates. In September 1917 they were tried under a catch-all provision of the Army Act and sentenced to penal servitude or hard labour for between 18 months and six years. P. Scott, 'Law and Orders: Discipline and Morale in the British Armies in France, 1917' in P. Liddle (ed.) *Passchendaele in Perspective: The Third Battle of Ypres* (London: Leo Cooper, 1997), pp.349-68.
6   War Office, *Report of the War Office Committee of Enquiry into "Shell Shock"* (London: HMSO, 1922), p45
7   *Joint Doctrine Publication 0-20: Land Power*, 3.11. In the words of Maj. Gen. Hull, GOC 56th (1st London) Division, "It is all very well to teach a subaltern how to take his men bathing, but what if crocodiles turn up?"

by all divisions of the BEF. GOsC armies and corps could exhort their subordinates to implement the content of the ever-expanding range of new or revised doctrinal pamphlets but unless those same senior commanders could manage their armies and corps sufficiently to create time for training, the exhortations would remain vacuous. The development of their fighting power, therefore, depended on having sufficient opportunity for uninterrupted, realistic training.

There would have been little excuse for the 2nd Line formations not to have been at least averagely effective divisions. Unlike the New Army and 1st Line TF divisions, rather than having to adjust the tactics and organization they had been taught in the UK to the realities of warfare on the Western Front, the 2nd Line (with the exception of 60th and 61st divisions) had the advantage of having been trained in at least some of the tactical doctrines learned from the Somme. The main flood of doctrinal pamphlets appeared after the divisions had sailed, but it is clear from several war diaries that once issued they were circulated widely to the various DHQ. The divisions adopted the common practices of using the divisional reinforcement camps as finishing schools for drafts, and divisional and brigade schools for specialists. Training competitions were also organized to encourage skills and platoon bonding. There is also considerable evidence to confirm that officers engaged in post-exercise discussions to analyze how they and their troops had performed. Officers and other ranks attending corps' schools would also have the benefit of discussing with those from other divisions which practices and tactics had worked in the field, and which had failed. The learning process was thus both lateral and horizontal.

At the operational level, corps or army HQ dealt with overall allocation and direction of resources and the wider ways and means of concentrating force to destroy the enemy's will and cohesion. At the tactical level, DHQ concerned itself with how to allocate sufficient manpower and local fires to ensure success in raids and attacks. When the planning processes for what were conventional attacks underestimated the amount of force and fires needed by 59th and 61st divisions in April and September 1917 respectively, failure ensued. In contrast, 58th Division's attack on 20 September worked successfully with a minimum number of men because DHQ had analyzed the available intelligence and devised an innovative plan which caught the enemy by surprise. In defensive operations, well positioned posts, effective cooperation with the TMs and artillery, and rehearsed drills were designed to be able to shatter the cohesion and will of any enemy raid, attack or counter-attack. The defence schemes devised by the 2nd Line divisions for halting the expected enemy offensive in early 1918 were all very similar to those of other divisions. All were signed off by their respective corps HQ.

The prepared schemes aimed to maximize the effect of the often limited firepower and manpower resources by defence in depth and close cooperation between all arms. Successful cooperation relies on mutual trust and goodwill, a common aim, a clear division of responsibilities, and a thorough understanding of the capabilities and limitations of other arms. Following Third Ypres, the BEF's infantry was cynical but also realistic about the limitations of the artillery and about the utility of tanks and air. Nevertheless, in divisions that had nurtured an understanding of respective capabilities there was also a trust and belief that the supporting arms would do what they could to assist the infantry. On 21 March, the infantry may have cursed their own artillery for dropping shells short but, deadly as the fire was for many, the infantry might have appreciated the artillery's communication and targetting difficulties. It would, however, have been little consolation for troops such as those of 66th Division on the slopes above Jeancourt to have known their counterparts in other divisions were also being shelled by friendly fire.

What doctrine describes as economy of effort – the ability to decide when, where, and which resources should be used – is crucial to the success of any activity. Furthermore, it is central to the conservation and balance of a division's fighting power. Corps and above decided on the operational or strategic scale of any campaign or major operation, but it was usually DHQ which decided on force size and the capability needed to undertake the multitude of enterprises and patrols conducted during trench tours. Like staffs in all divisions, those of the 2nd Line could seek advice from others and also learned from experience. Not all raids were executed in the manner planned, as several of those conducted by 60th, 57th and 66th divisions showed. Yet, as both staff and troops became more familiar with the available ways and means of raiding, 2nd Line battalions proved to be as effective as those of most other British divisions.

Surprise is another of the essential Principles of War. It embraces elements such as secrecy, concealment and audacity to confuse or disrupt effective decision-making by the enemy. Any confusion or doubts generated in his mind will assist in undermining his cohesion and morale. Corps instructed divisions to conduct frequent raids but often delegated to DHQ decisions of precisely when they should take place. Depending on the type of raid and the tactics and resources allocated, surprise was, therefore, frequently possible. It was more difficult, however, to secure surprise in large and often coordinated attacks. Too many British attacks during Third Ypres were timed to begin within a 90 minute period around dawn. A preliminary bombardment usually gave away the approximate location, although not the precise time of the infantry assault. With the Germans expecting an attack at or around the 'usual' time, their troops were standing to and their own bombardment was brought down to disrupt the advance. Decisions about timings were generally made by corps, with DHQ having little input. Only once during the campaign was a 2nd Line division able to attack at an unexpected hour and was thus able to gain the advantage of surprise. Yet, as was the case for most of the post-31 July attacks, by the time the infantry had struggled across the mud of no man's land, the enemy was fully alert and all benefit of surprise had been lost. On 21 March 1918, the enemy used surprise to good effect. Most parts of the Forward Zones of 58th, 59th, 61st and 66th divisions were over-run quickly, although not as swiftly as several others of Fifth Army. Nonetheless, garrisons in those four 2nd Line divisions' Battle Zones were able to withstand the initial shock and rally sufficiently to hold onto their zones until the end of the first day. The initiative still lay with the enemy but a degree of command and control had been reasserted within the 2nd Line formations. Their cohesion and will had been shaken but not entirely shattered.

DHQ was also largely responsible for the efficient operation of a division's sustainment processes. The ability to sustain a force involves the physical and psychological sustenance of personnel as well as the proper supply and maintenance of their equipment. As such, it is a critical enabler of fighting power. Formations and units considered it a point of honour to ensure combat supplies and service support were available and arrived regularly. Not all of these elements – especially the swift replacement of casualties – were under the immediate control of DHQ, but divisional staffs were expected to manage the provision of rations, replacement clothing, billeting, recreation, and bathing. The war diaries of the 2nd Line units demonstrate that staff captains, transport sections, pioneer squads, sappers, and cooks of their units were as good, and as fallible, as those of other formations. That two brigades of 66th Division lay exposed with no shelter and no hot food for nearly four days on the Frezenberg Ridge was not so much the fault of the divisional staff but the result of a decision made by corps HQ.

The very small number of senior 2nd Line divisional officers sent home suggests the authorities were generally content with those they appointed to command the formations overseas. In the first 12 months of their service in France, the nine 1st Line divisions had four GOsC divisions removed for reasons other than health or promotion. During their first 12 months overseas the last six New Army divisions to deploy had three GOsC removed;[8] the seven deploying 2nd Line divisions had two. At the next level of command – brigadier generals serving as CRA and GOsC infantry brigades – five are known to have been sent home as unsuitable for command.[9] Despite the civil organizational and administrative experience that many war time commissioned officers could offer to divisions, with the exception of Howitt in 61st Division, the position of brigade major remained very much the preserve of regular officers. Similarly, the three GSO1s in all divisions were regulars. That did not mean, of course, that they were all inherently efficient but the staff work apparent in the war diaries follows the expected procedural formats and method. There are few examples of the divisions' sustainment processes having come under exceptional strain.

When they departed for France the large majority of 2nd Line battalion COs, as well as what must have been a good proportion of their junior officers commissioned from the ranks, already had first-hand experience of active service conditions. The replacement of TF COs by Regular Army officers in 1st Line units had been in progress since 1915 but there did still remain a respectable number of them in early 1918. In 2nd Line units, however, by mid-1917, TF-commissioned COs had virtually disappeared. Most of the TF officers had gone in the occasional post-engagement culls, and the authorities had certainly taken advantage of advanced age or questionable health. By the time of Third Ypres, the majority of unit commanders of the five 2nd Line divisions involved in the campaign were Regular Army officers appointed on merit.[10]

The practical experience of the other rank returned wounded of the 1st Line or New Army who deployed with the 2nd Line would have been essential to the informal instruction of the newer recruits. By the time the divisions sailed, the majority of their personnel had actually

---

8   The divisions were the 31st, 34th, 35th, 39th, 40th, and 41st.. All deployed between January and June 1916.
9   The five were: Brig. Gens. Martyn (170 Bde); Carter (184 Bde); Maconchy (178 Bde); Hunt (173 Bde) and Travers (199 Bde). A further 16 were replaced after having been killed, died of wounds, wounded or sick. In addition, 11 others were replaced for unspecified reasons. Six of these are known to have been promoted. Why the remaining five were replaced remains unclear but it seems likely that some, for example Stewart (183 Bde), were also dismissed.
10 The three or possibly four remaining TF COs included Richardson of 2/2nd London, Bates of 3/5th Lancashire Fusiliers, and Preece of 2/8th London. Bates had been commissioned into the London Rifle Bde in 1900. Richardson had fought in South Africa, while Preece had joined the Rifle Volunteers on retirement from the Army in 1902. He transferred to the TF when it formed in 1908. These officers had been joined by regulars and war time commissioned men from the New Armies. Some of these, such as Perry of 2/4th KOYLI, were young in comparison even to the reducing average age of lieutenant colonels. Gasson of 2/4th LNL had spent 10 years in the ranks before being commissioned. He had served as both staff captain and brigade major before being appointed CO in mid-1917. Thorn of 2/6th South Staffordshire had retired from the army as a subaltern in 1908 and by 1918 was a little older than the majority of COs. Marchant and Hodgkin of 2/4th South Lancashire and 2/6th Sherwood respectively, had served with Hussar regiments. These two COs as well as at least another two, had served as pre-war adjutants in TF regiments. As a further link to the TF, at least two battalion seconds-in-command had been pre-war TF officers. The greatest concentrations of TF commissioned officers tended to be medical officers in the field ambulances.

been in the army for longer than most of the conscripts then being sent as drafts from the 3rd Line or Training Reserve. Several of the units in the deploying divisions were still recognizable as having been filled principally by men drawn from their 1st Line divisions' customary recruitment areas and, despite the later arrival of drafts, they did retain something of a wider regional or geographical identity. But, as in most overseas divisions, that identity had been substantially diluted.[11] Moreover, with an ever-diminishing proportion of genuine TF officer and other rank enlistees, the divisions retained little of their original TF ethos and character. In the same way as divisions of the New Armies, they developed identities of their own.

The War Office's policy of replacing senior TF and officers was undertaken partly because it believed unit efficiency would improve if stiffened by regular officers, and partly because it was conducting a strategy aimed at forging one, unified army. Rather than maintaining the current complicated structure of three constituent parts, the authorities wanted to amalgamate those three elements into one homogenous organization. Although the War Office and politicians knew they had to tread warily along that path until peace was secured, limiting the retention of a separate TF identity was integral to that process.

This ambition to meld a national army was logical but the political and military pragmatists knew that achieving the objective might adversely affect civil and military morale. The government did not wish to annoy the TF county associations any further by ruling out a reconstituted post-war TF. With the huge losses suffered by the French Army and its demand that the British take over a greater length of front, more divisions were needed in France. Since their creation the 2nd Line formations had helped to serve an important purpose in reassuring a home populace periodically alarmed about the threat of invasion. As there was in reality little if any possibility of invasion, the authorities sought the means of reinforcing the BEF. By the close of 1916 the War Office had reined in the unwieldy and independently minded Volunteer Training Corps, created the Royal Defence Corps from the National Reserve and supernumerary companies, and was well on the way to organizing the new Volunteer Force.[12] As the restructuring of the training process proceeded, the government believed there were sufficient uniformed men at home to convince the population of its security. The opportunity was there to send abroad the remaining viable 2nd Line divisions.

This deployment was an important gesture for trust and for alliance cohesion. Only 4th Canadian and 3rd Australian Divisions had arrived in France since the last of the New Army formations landed in June 1916. The French had been unsettled by the six-month gap between the arrival of 40th Division and the deployment of the five 2nd Line divisions between January and March 1917. Even if in their early years of existence they had been of little military value, the departure of the 2nd Line was a necessary military and political statement. It reassured the French by reaffirming British commitment to the Western Front and also increased the options available to Allied planners preparing for the 1917 campaigning season.

Major Claud Hamilton's May 1916 comment in the Commons about the perceived quality and potential use of the 2nd Line TF divisions had resonated with many both inside and out of the army. Indeed, by mid-1916, so little progress had been made with their development that the divisions did appear to have been born to fail. The disaster suffered by 61st Division at Fromelles

---

11   See Appendices I and II
12   For a discussion on the anti-invasion forces, see K W Mitchinson, *Defending Albion: Britain's Home Army 1908-1919* (Basingstoke: Palgrave Macmillan, 2005).

in July and 60th Division's short sojourn on the Western Front seemed ostensibly to confirm their limited utility. The South Midlanders were accused of a wanton lack of fighting spirit but the battle had been ill-conceived and inadequately resourced.[13] It would stretch credulity to imagine that any division, let alone an entirely green one, could have done significantly better than 61st. The division demonstrated a growing maturity as it followed the German withdrawal across the devastated zone in the spring of 1917. It showed tactical flexibility and although there were occasions when the division's liaison methods and situational awareness were not all they might have been, its supported and supporting arms adapted quickly and effectively to the changed operating environment. It certainly did not do well during Third Ypres, attracting criticism especially for its repeated failures to take the Battery Position but it fought doggedly in the brutal counter-attack on Welsh Ridge. In March 1918, some of the troops in the Forward Zone might not have resisted as strongly as was expected, but conditions were against them. Battalions in the Battle Zone and those in support fought well, especially when compared to some of the divisions to their south. Its soldiers' resilience was particularly apparent during the period of withdrawal in late March. Despite its solid performance during that operation, its failures at Fromelles and Ypres, however, seem to have stigmatized the division's reputation. According to one assessment, it could be included in the bottom six British divisions with lower than average reputations.[14]

The seemingly early transfer of 60th Division to Salonika was not the result of a poor showing on the Western Front. On arrival in France many of the division's units were still filled with intelligent men of the clerical classes; probably the majority were also genuine territorials. They did not take part in any battle in the Arras sector but were clearly eager to learn from their mentors, and raided prolifically. The division later went on to win plaudits for its activities in Palestine.

Having been thrown, almost on arrival overseas, into the final stages of the Somme campaign, and onto some of its worst terrain, 62nd Division experienced a difficult introduction to operations. Its advance struggled in the mud to maintain communications and to assert its collective fighting power, but it achieved the limited objectives asked of it. The division had very much to learn on the job but its inexperience does not appear to have caused its corps commander undue concern. Reflecting on its experience at Bullecourt, the division appreciated its performance had not been particularly impressive. One soldier in another division of the same corps wrote that 62nd Division's "washout" had been entirely predictable and that he was "not surprised at that division's [failure]."[15] In defence of the division, Walker asks, "But what hope could there be for this second-line territorial division when even a crack division like the 7th could not shift the enemy from Bullecourt?"[16] Walker clearly believes 62nd was not of the same quality as 7th Division, an understandable assumption given 62nd's inexperience. Nonetheless, the statement

---

13   Outspoken criticism had come from Lt. Gen. Haking and the Australians.
14   D. Tattersfield, *Divisional Usage in the BEF on the WF 1916-1918*, Unpublished MA, Univ. of Birmingham, 2006.
15   Papers of Pte A P Burke, Imperial War Museum. Quoted in J. Walker, *The Blood Tub: General Gough and the Battle of Bullecourt, 1917* (Staplehurst: Spelmount, 1998), p.153. Burke was in 20/Manchester, 7th Division.
16   Walker, p.186. In theory, 7th Division was a regular division but it had exchanged one of its brigades for a New Army brigade in 1916. It was an 'efficient', rather than a 'crack' formation.

is pejorative in that it implies that any 2nd Line formation was inevitably to be of inferior worth than other divisions. The West Riding's remarkable success in the opening stages of Cambrai redeemed its earlier reputation but its brigades made little headway in its later and somewhat stereotyped attacks against Bourlon Wood. It fought a very effective rearguard and defensive battle in late March, and was used extensively during the Hundred Days.

Until 1918, 57th Division's only real battle experience had come at Third Ypres. Its attack was a diversionary affair, with little expectation of territorial gain. Furthermore, because it did poorly over ground where other divisions had already fared badly it would be invidious to offer any worthwhile assessment of its performance. After that operation the division occupied quieter sectors but there is no evidence that the authorities deliberately refrained from using the division because they considered it to be of lower than average quality. It was probably just fortunate to escape the German offensives but was used quite consistently between August and November. It suffered at Riencourt and Hendecourt in late August from poor intelligence and some confusion with internal communications, but demonstrated good all-arms coordination in its attacks on the Drocourt-Queant Line and the Canal du Nord.

In its advance towards the Hindenburg Line during the enemy's withdrawal, 59th Division showed considerable caution. The supporting arms did adjust to the changing environment and were able to sustain the advance by demonstrating adaptability and innovation in dealing with disrupted transport systems. The division's attacks on Le Verguier were rushed, inadequately planned and naive; those on and around Hargicout were predictable and unimaginative. Coordination of resources both within and beyond the division was poor and there had been far too little consideration given to likely frictions. Nonetheless, the division fought well in March 1918. In the *Official History,* Edmonds' account of its operations verges on the apologetic, almost as if he had not expected the division to perform as well as it did.[17] Quite rightly he later lauds its actions as one of the most effective formations on 21 March. It was partly because it fought so well in March and April that it was destined to be temporarily reduced to cadre.

On its arrival in France the deployment of 66th Division to a reasonably quiet area gave the opportunity for its units to bond in an active service environment. It undertook a substantial number of raids and then moved to the coast where it trained for a complex amphibious operation whilst at the same time holding a contested line. Its attack at Ypres in October was handicapped by inadequate and unrealistic planning, mismanagement of resources, overly ambitious objectives, and the exacting physical conditions. That some battalions of the attacking brigades even managed to reach the jumping off line demonstrated stubborn determination. If a party reached the crest of the ridge, as some reports suggest, it was a remarkable achievement for an untried division over atrocious terrain. On 21 March, the division made a disastrous start but as the day wore on its surviving units rallied and offered a fairly solid resistance. During the chaos of the withdrawal towards Amiens, what was left of the division was largely organized into *ad hoc* groups that, although exhausted, fought a number of sometimes effective rearguards and counterattacks. Under the command of the maverick Major General Bethel it played a major part in the Hundred Days.

The timing of 58th Division's attack on Bullecourt proved fortuitous, and it subsequently reaped the plaudits. Similarly, John Lee noted that an important factor in its success on the

---

17 J. Edmonds, *Military Operations*, p.228, fn. 4.

Gravenstafel Ridge on 20 September 1917 was because, unlike some of the other formations involved that day, it was fresh.[18] There is a strong element of truth in that claim but the success was also the result of thorough training and innovative planning. It had clearly benefited from the doctrinal lectures and strictures offered by Maxse, but the operation planning was completed largely by its own commanders and staff. The division did not do so well a few days later on the Hanebeek or in October near Poelcapelle but, again, few divisions in that sector did. Like 57th Division and other formations in that northern area of the Salient, it was used in diversionary actions. Fortunately, the numbers of men involved were kept deliberately low but the brigades and supporting arms had to survive the testing rigours of the winter in unforgiving conditions. It made steady but unspectacular progress during the Battle of Amiens but lost heavily in clearing the enemy from Epehy in September. It can be considered to have been a good, possibly average division – well organized and disciplined, able to adopt new tactical concepts and adapt older ones. It was also a formation which, despite Maxse's sometimes insulting words about its officers, was well led and managed under Major Generals Fanshawe, Cator, and Ramsay. One historian seems almost surprised to note "the apparent ease with which a second-line Territorial division" could adapt so readily to mobile all-arms warfare.[19]

The reduction to cadre of two overseas 2nd Line divisions,[20] the conversion of others in the UK to training formations, and the disbanding of several in Home Forces, probably added to the general perception that the divisions were of dubious value. Of the six 2nd Line divisions in France in May 1918, 33 percent were reduced to cadre. This was slightly higher than the 28 percent of New Army divisions, and substantially higher than the 10 percent of 1st Line TF divisions on the Western Front.[21] In line with the changes underway in the training structure there was a sound rationale behind the decision already taken by May 1918 to convert or disband several of the home-based 2nd Line divisions. The changes were extensive and far-reaching but rather than disband the 3rd Line TF groups and absorb them into the wider Training Reserve, the War Office chose to retain them. By mid-1916 the TF county associations had reluctantly and resentfully lost almost all of their traditional administrative responsibilities. The decision to reconstitute only one of the 1st Line formations in France and maintain the other nine, in addition to the concession to retaining the 3rd Line groups as an essential element of the training

---

18 J. Lee, 'Command and Control in Battle: British Divisions on the Menin Road Ridge, 20 September 1917' in G. Sheffield & D. Todman (eds.), *Command and Control on the Western Front* (Staplehurst; Spellmount, 2004), pp. 119-39.
19 P. Simkins, 'Building Blocks: Aspects of Command and Control at the Brigade Level in the BEF's Offensive Operations, 1916-1918' in Sheffield & Todman (eds.), pp.141-71.
20 The unfortunate 59th Division was reconstituted twice during 1918. In its final form it was filled with garrison guard battalions as a B Division. Although unrecognizable as a TF formation, it did again take part in active operations. The reconstituted 66th Division also became a shadow of its former self. It lost seven of its March 1918 battalions, receiving the South African Brigade, three Irish and one King's Liverpool battalions as their replacements. Most of 62nd Division's February 1918 battalions were retained but by the middle of the year the division did include battalions of the London, Devonshire and Hampshire Regiments. It, too, was heavily engaged in several of the major battles of the final stages of the war. With only one newly imported battalion, 57th Division almost kept its February 1918 configuration until the end of the war. Similarly, 58th Division also underwent only one fairly minor change to its infantry composition.
21 The only 1st Line division to be reduced to cadre and then reconstituted was 50th (Northumbrian) Division. It lost all of its TF battalions.

reforms, can be seen partly as sops to the associations. The remaining links between the 1st and 3rd Lines and their county associations were more emotive than practical but the retention of an identifiable 3rd Line and the associations' new responsibilities for the Volunteer Force were hints that when the war was concluded the TF would remain extant.[22] Once those concessions had been granted, it was then politically easier to transform or disband the home based 2nd Line divisions. Criticism of the War Office's attitude to the auxiliary continued to be aired in the Commons but even the TF's supporters realized that certain parts of the country were running out of would-be recruits. They accepted that the Home Forces and the training system needed reform and, with the 3rd Line now saved, they were pragmatically amenable to letting some of the 2nd Line divisions disappear. To these informed individuals the disbanding would be viewed as the elimination of a (regretfully) unnecessary burden on a system in need of overhaul. To the less well informed it was yet another act by an ungrateful War Office against an organization that had exceeded the expectations of even its most ardent supporters.[23]

One supposed contemporary orison, often ascribed to (more than) one senior commander, asked that the Regular Army should be "saved from the New Army and the Territorials." This is sometimes altered to "the New Army and the Second-Line Territorials," and often cut to just "the Territorials." The precise authenticity of the quotation is in doubt but, if true, it does portray the view of the TF as a whole held by many War Office and Regular Army commanders. The TF movement had long been used to criticism and even in the pre-war period had in response developed a self-deprecating humour. The troops used their regimental acronyms or poetic doggerel to invent new names which reflected the ridicule to which they were often subjected.[24] At least one division believed the authorities were generally unsympathetic to its worth because it was given "an unduly large share" of what it called the "dirty work of demonstrations, secondary operations and taking over and holding nasty parts of the line."[25] Such a claim is difficult to reconcile with the facts. With the exception of 57th (2nd West Lancashire) Division, until April 1918 the 2nd Line divisions were as active or inactive as most British formations on the Western Front.[26]

Middlebrook noted that the 2nd Line divisions were "known somewhat derisively as 'Conscript Divisions'".[27] In the minds of some MPs, War Office officials, and elements of the press, the divisions may have seemed to be the scrapings of the barrel. To some, the name '2nd Line' could have suggested 'second rate' or 'second division' but, by March 1918, conscripts were probably in the majority in all British divisions. This is one of the reasons why the 2nd Line divisions' fighting power and battlefield performance were no better or no worse than the majority of British formations. With the exception of 62nd (West Riding) Division they do not figure in historians' lists of the most frequently used and most reliable divisions, but neither do the bulk

---

22 Essentially, all that remained for associations to do in regard to their TF units was to administer separation allowances and maintain the comforts funds.
23 The fates of the various home-based divisions are outlined in the Introduction.
24 For example, 2/5th London Rifle Brigade became 'Loungers Round Britain'; 61st Division became 'The Sixty-Worst'.
25 Brig. Gen. R. White, quoted in Rose, *2/4th Ox&Bucks*, p. xiii.
26 According to the criteria of the Battles Nomenclature Committee, between its arrival in February 1917 and 27 August 1918, 57th Division was engaged in 'battles' for only 11 days.
27 M. Middlebrook, *The Kaiser's Battle*, p.91.

of British divisions.[28] By the time they were deployed they were equipped as well as any other division and trained and fought according to current doctrine. They could be innovative and predictable, dogged and casual, but they were prepared to learn from their experiences and from their mistakes. The 2nd Line had its detractors and in its early years certainly deserved some of the criticism directed toward it. While the War Office remained unsure of what it wanted from the reserve, its divisions appeared to absorb an unjustified amount of resources which could have been used more advantageously elsewhere. As a supposedly trained anti-invasion force it was unconvincing, and its uncertain future was a constant frustration for its supporters. Nevertheless, once the War Office had decided how the 14 divisions could contribute to the war effort, whether that be at home or abroad, the 2nd Line divisions ceased to be "of no earthly use." They became instead integral cogs in the increasingly tactically and operationally astute BEF.

---

28 D. Tattersfield, *Divisional Usage*.

Appendix I

2nd Line Division Casualties, March 1918

Accurate and precise casualty totals are, essentially, impossible to obtain. Although, however, there are incongruities and abnormalities in the *Soldiers Died in the Great War* rolls (*SDGW*), they are a reasonably reliable source for fatalities; when used alongside the Commonwealth War Grave Commission's registers they become even more so. The *Officers Died* rolls (*ODGW*) give a good guide but as many officers were attached to regiments and battalions other than their own, it is not always possible to ascertain precisely how many officers were killed whilst serving with any one particular unit. The figures below are taken from unit war diaries which did include the names of attached officers and the regiments from which they came.

The number of casualties reported by any unit and formation were initially, of necessity, speculative. As men were discovered to be in hospital and as stragglers returned to their units, the numbers could change daily. Below is a table compiled from an undated return of 58th Division and information gleaned from *SDGW*, *ODGW* and CWGC registers. It serves to illustrate how tentative the early returns were.

Casualties in 173 Brigade, 58th Division, 20 Mar-3 Apr.1918[1]

Battalion	Rpt Killed 20/3/-3/4/18		Rpt Wounded 20/3/-3/4/18		Rpt Missing 20/3/-3/4/18		Actual Fatalities 20/3/-3/4/18	
	Off.	ORs	Off.	ORs	Off.	ORs	Off.	ORs
2/2 Lond	0	7	2	26	19	585	1	46
3/Lond	2	9	4	37	12	299	5	69
2/4 Lond	0	37	10	123	6	217	0	69
8/Lond[2]	1	8	2	25	10	288	3	81

1 TNA WO 952988.
2 NB: 8/London was in 174 Bde.

On 20 March, the war diary of 2/2nd London, which was 173 Brigade's battalion in the Forward Zone, recorded a trench strength of 22 officers and 585 ORs. At 1015, on 21 March the war diary noted that the adjutant and 41 ORs 'constituted the remnant of the battalion.'[3] The transport section and the battle surplus will also have rejoined the battalion at some stage. There is, therefore, incongruity in the figures because the total of ORs 'missing' is the same as the recorded trench strength. Nonetheless, the relatively low number of fatalities suggests that owing to the dense fog garrisons in the widely dispersed platoon and section posts were either unable or unwilling to offer a determined and prolonged resistance.

Although compiled equally soon after relief, in 62nd (West Riding) Division, 5/Duke of Wellington's submitted its casualty return for ORs for the period 24-31 March 1918. It recorded 31 killed, 115 wounded and 56 missing.[4] *SDGW* has 52 killed or died of wounds during the period. This suggests that if the original figure of 31 deaths was accurate, 38 percent of the missing were also actual fatalities. Using 2/2nd London's figures, only 8 percent of its missing were fatalities. The number of troops who became prisoners, albeit as perhaps wounded must, therefore, have been substantial.

The table showing 66th Division's reported casualties demonstrates how all arms of the division suffered during the three week period. Drafts rushed out from the UK began to arrive at the division towards the end of March. By that time the division had withdrawn to the Hangard area and was still fighting. The attrition had been severe. For example, on 1 March the strength of 197 Brigade had been 166 officers and 3,025 ORs[5]. Only 2/8th Lancashire Fusiliers had under 50 officers, with all three battalions comprising over 900 men. On 31 March, total brigade strength had fallen to 42 officers and 943 ORs. Brigade HQ estimated casualties in its three battalions were in the region of: 81 ORs killed; 32 officers and 299 ORs wounded; 1,644 all ranks missing.[6]

66th (2nd East Lancashire) Division: Reported Casualties 21 March- 13 April 1918[7]

Unit	Killed		Wounded		Missing		Total	
	Offs	ORs	Offs	ORs	Offs	ORs	Offs	ORs
330 Bde RFA	1	16	6	51	8	65	15	132
331 Bde RFA	4	35	6	96	3	31	13	162
X Bty TMB	-	-	1	6	1	7	2	13
Y Bty TMB	-	1	-	2	-	40	1	43
430 F.Coy	1	2	1	32	-	11	2	45
431 F.Coy	-	6	1	13	-	12	1	31
432 F Coy	-	10	2	22	1	17	3	49
6/Lancs F.	3	30	19	218	15	333	37	581
2/7 Lancs F.	3	30	13	125	20	473	36	628

3   TNA WO 953001.
4   TNA WO 953085.
5   Including the brigade LTM battery and brigade MG company. The reorganization of the brigade's MG company into an element of 66th Bn MGC was begun a few days later.
6   TNA WO 953135.
7   TNA WO 953121.

Unit	Killed		Wounded		Missing		Total	
	Offs	ORs	Offs	ORs	Offs	ORs	Offs	ORs
2/8 Lancs F.	-	30	10	46	22	624	32	700
9/Manc	5	20	16	213	3	390	24	623
4/E.Lancs	2	6	13	29	21	628	36	663
2/5 E.Lancs	5	44	10	134	16	516	31	694
2/5 Manc	2	3	8	22	23	670	33	695
2/6 Manc	5	50	11	171	14	300	30	521
2/7 Manc	4	80	11	136	16	321	31	537
66th MGC	2	9	7	58	7	205	16	272
5/Border (P)	2	17	8	102	13	345	23	464
F.Ambs	-	-	2	-	1	58	3	66
TOTALS	39	392	152	1516	188	5081	379	6989

NB: The TOTALS also include casualties in the DAC, Signals Coy, Div.Train, 254 Employment Coy, 198 and 199 LTMB and Div.HQ.

The three tables below showing officer casualties on 21-22 March may or may not give some indication of how hard battalions fought. Fatalities among the three Sherwood Foresters' battalions of 178 Brigade are particularly high. The South Midland Division suffered about the average fatality rate experienced by British divisions in Third and Fifth Armies, with 2/8th Worcestershire and 2/4th Ox & Bucks, each with one company in Ellis and Enghien Redoubts respectively, sustaining an understandably higher rate. The other battalion in the Forward Zone, 1/5th Gordon Highlanders, seems to have been especially fortunate.

Given the ferocity and intensity of the enemy attack on 66th Division, its fatalities are relatively low. Battalion HQ of 2/8th Lancashire Fusiliers was captured intact, the staff not having known that the infantry assault had even begun. Platoons and HQ of 2/5th Manchester, also in the Forward Zone, in Villeret and on Cologne Ridge, must have been infiltrated or overwhelmed without having had either the will, or opportunity, to offer much of a defence. The losses taken by battalions in the Battle Zone indicate the considerable resistance shown later in the day and until the withdrawal on 22 March.

Officer Casualties 21-22 March 1918[8]

Officer Casualties in 59th (2nd North Midland) Division:

Battalion	Reported Killed	Reported Wounded	Reported Missing	Actual Fatalities 21-22 Mar.18
2/6 S.Staffs*	0	1	23	4[9]
5/N.Staffs*	1	2	20	8[10]
2/6 N.Staffs	0	2	22	4
4/Lincs	3	3	0	3
2/5 Lincs	1	6	11	4
2/4 Leics	2	6	10	5[11]
2/5 S.For	0	2	29	8
2/6 S.For*	0	2	32	8
7/S.For*	1	2	22	10
6/7 RSF (P)	4	4	5	4
TOTALS	12	30	174	58

NB: * indicates battalions in the Forward Zone at 0400 on 21 March 1918

Officer Casualties in 61st (2nd South Midland) Division[12]

Battalion	Reported Killed	Reported Wounded	Reported Missing	Actual fatalities 21-22 March 1918
2/6 R.War	2	7	7	2
2/7 R.War	2	8	5	1[13]
2/8 Worc*	2	4	23	7
1/9 R.Scots	2	13	2	0
1/5 G.High*	3	5	16	2
1/8 A&SH	2	10	7	1[14]
2/4 R.Berks	2	8	3	2
2/4 Ox&B*	2	Unknown	2	5
2/5 Glouc	2	Unknown	2	3
TOTALS	19	55	67	23

NB: * indicates battalions in the Forward Zone at 0400 on 21 March 1918

---

8   TNA WO 953012.
9   One of the missing died in German hands Jul.1918.
10 One of the missing died at home Dec.1918.
11 One of the missing died in German hands Nov.1918.
12 See TNA WO 953055, 3056, 3059, 3065, 3066, 3067; *Officers Died in the Great War* (London: HMSO, 1921).
13 Of the two reported dead on 22 March, one died on 23 March and the other on 11 April. Two of the missing DOW later in March.
14 Two of the missing DOW on 23.Mar.1918.

Officer Casualties in 66th (2nd East Lancashire) Division[15]

Battalion	Reported Killd	Reported Wounded	Reported Wounded and Missing	Reported Missing	Actual Deaths 21-22 Mar.
6/Lancs Fus.	2	18	3	12	4[16]
2/7 Lancs Fus.	3	7	3	14	3[17]
2/8 Lancs Fus.*	0	5	1	19	0[18]
9/Manchester	5	11	0	2	5[19]
4/E.Lancs*	1	7	0	22	5[20]
2/5 E.Lancs	4	6	0	11	5[21]
2/5 Manchester*	0	2	0	18	0[22]
2/6 Manchester	3	3	0	8	0[23]
2/7 Manchester	1	8	0	12	3[24]
5/Border (P)	2	2	0	10	2[25]
TOTALS	21	69	7	128	27

NB: * indicates battalions in the Forward Zone at 0400 on 21 March 1918

15   TNA WO 953121.
16   One of the wounded and missing died in German hands 13.Apr.1918; one of the missing was KIA on 28.Mar.1918.
17   Two of the reported dead did not die; two of the missing were KIA on 21.Mar.1918 and two more died in German hands in Apr.1918. One of the missing died at home in 1920.
18   None of the wounded and missing or missing are known to have died.
19   Neither of the missing were killed.
20   Four of the missing were KIA on 21.Mar.1918; one DOW in German hands; one was KIA on 26.Mar.1918
21   One of the missing was KIA on 21.Mar.1918; one died in German hands
22   None of the 18 missing are known to have died.
23   None of the 8 missing are known to have died.
24   Two of the missing were KIA on 21.Mar.1918; one was KIA on 24.Mar.1918.
25   One of the missing died in German hands in Dec.1918.

Appendix II

Origins of Other Rank Fatalities, November-December 1917

Several mentions have been made in the text about the personnel composition of the 2nd Line divisions. It was noted in Chapter 7, for example, that over 50 percent of 59th Division's losses at Ypres came from outside the battalions' traditional recruiting areas. About one-third of that percentage was men who originated from London. In the spring of 1917 in 61st Division, an average of 32 percent across 182 and 184 brigades came from outside the battalions' catchment areas; at Ypres this figure in some battalions rose to 70 percent of their total fatalities.

The tables below show the fatalities of the two 2nd Line divisions which played a considerable defensive role at Cambrai. The percentage of 'outside' fatalities had grown, but not hugely. If we ignore the very low losses of 2/4th Leicestershire, 2/5th and 2/8th Sherwood Foresters of 59th Division, and 2/7th Worcestershire, 2/4th Ox & Bucks and 2/1st Bucks in 61st Division, the averages for the two divisions are 41 percent and 54 percent respectively. The fatalities show that drafts to 2/5th Warwickshire originated from 16 different regiments; those to 2/6th Warwickshire from 13; those to 2/7th Warwickshire from 10. The drafting regiments were spread across all regions of Great Britain. The result was that roughly one half of the men in a battalion or brigade did not have any direct link to the area or region from which their battalion had been originally raised.

59th (2nd North Midland) Division

Battalion	Killed Nov-Dec 1917	Percentage of total not B/E/R in county[1]
2/5 N. Staffs	28	46%
2/6 N. Staffs	70	46%
2/5 S. Staffs	34	56%
2/6 N. Staffs	97	47%
2/4 Lincs	18	56%
2/5 Lincs	23	30%
2/4 Leics	8	63%
2/5 Leics	15	15%

1   B/E/R: Born, Enlisted, Resident.

Battalion	Killed Nov-Dec 1917	Percentage of total not B/E/R in county[1]
2/5 S.For	7	0%
2/6 S.For	38	39%
2/7 S.For	30	30%
2/8 S.For	7	14%

61st (2nd South Midland) Division

Battalion	Killed Nov-Dec 1917	Percentage of total not B/E/R in county
2/5 Warwick	52	56%
2/6 Warwick	54	76%
2/7 Warwick	53	51%
2/8 Warwick	15	73%
2/4 Gloucs	61	28%
2/6 Gloucs	76	47%
2/7 Worcs	12	-
2/8 Worcs	28	54%
2/4 Berks	37	51%
2/5 Gloucs	76	47%
2/4 Ox&B	6	17%
2/1 Bucks	5	80%

Origins of Other Rank Fatalities: March 1918

The reorganization of divisions and the reduction in the number of their battalions was completed largely, but certainly not exclusively, by the transfer of men from one battalion to another of the same regiment. If the amalgamated battalions had been composed of men from their regiment's usual catchment areas then the 'new' battalion should have reflected the traditional territorial affiliation. That, however, was not the case in many of the reformed brigades and divisions.

Nonetheless, the tables below show the 2nd Line fatalities of March were fighting in divisions which had regained something of their territorial identity. With the exception of 8/London, which had enlisted Post Office workers from across the country since at least August 1914, 58th Division remained very much a London formation, 59th Division and the two original brigades of 61st Division now had a higher percentage of 'local' men than they had possessed at Cambrai and, with the exception of two battalions, 66th Division remained very much composed of Lancastrians. Most of those who did not come from within the county, however, originated from nearby towns such as Stockport.

58th (2/1st London) Division

Battalion	Killed 21-22 Mar.1918	Killed 23-31 Mar.1918	Percentage of total not B/E/R in Gtr London
2/2 London	28	46	11%
3/London	41	69	7%
2/4 London	49	69	12%
8/London	53	81	62%
6/London	7	18	8%
7/London	12	12	21%
9/London	3	16	11%
2/10 London	2	10	0%
12/London	5	4	33%
4/Suffolk (P)	1	10	

59th (2nd North Midland) Division

Battalion	Killed 21-22 Mar.18	Killed 23-31 Mar.18	Percentage of B/E/R in county	% with links to divisional area	% of dead with no link to divisional area
5 N.Staffs	74	77	72%	12%	16%
2/6 N.Staffs	86	121	41%	20%	39%
2/6 S.Staffs	99	105	33%	30%	36%
4/Lincs	31	40	53%	7%	40%
2/5 Lincs	44	50	73%	5%	22%
2/4 Leics	19	84	52%	14%	33%
2/5 S.For	104	113	63%	6%	31%
2/6 S.For	124	125	68%	7%	25%
7/S.For	155	161	70%	5%	25%
6/7 RSF (P)	32	41			

61st (2nd South Midland) Division

Battalion	Killed 21-22 Mar.18	Killed 23-31 Mar.18	Percentage of B/E/R in county	% with links to divisional area	% of dead with no link to divisional area
2/6 Warwick	38	67	43%	6%	51%
2/7 Warwick	26	64	50%	13%	37%
2/8 Worcs	19	63	60%	11%	29%
2/4 Ox&B	88	103	60%	14%	26%
2/5 Gloucs	26	85	70%	9%	21%
2/4 Berks	23	32	38%	22%	40%
1/9 R.Scots	24	113			
1/5 G.High	33	36			
1/8 A&S.High	80	112			
1/5 DCLI (P)	15	43			

66th (2nd East Lancashire) Division

Battalion	Killed 21-22 Mar.18	Killed 23-31 Mar.18	Percentage of total not B/E/R in Lancashire
6/Lancs.Fus.	65	16	29%
2/7 Lancs Fus.	94	19	33%
2/8 Lancs.Fus.	53	9	53%
9/ Manc.	79	20	23%
4/E.Lancs	104	12	17%
2/5 E.Lancs	57	64	21%
2/5 Manc.	57	14	35%
2/6 Manc.	64	55	28%
2/7 Manc.	93	20	48%
1/5 Border (P)	61	20	

Bibliography

Archival Sources

Permission to quote from original documents has been granted by the relevant authorities. My thanks are due to the National Archives, the Liddell Hart Centre for Military Archives at King's College, London, and various county record offices.
The National Archives (TNA): War diaries of corps, divisions, brigades and units in WO 95 classification
Liddell Hart Centre for Military Archives, King's College, London: Papers of Sir Ian Hamilton
County Record Offices: Territorial Force Associations Minute Books; Cambridgeshire, Derbyshire, Durham, Leicestershire, Lincolnshire, Manchester, Northumbria, North Yorkshire, Nottinghamshire

Official Publications

AAP-6(V) NATO Glossary of Terms and Definitions
Army Doctrine Publications, *Operations* (*ADP*) E-2 (Shrivenham: DCDC, 2010)
Allied Joint Doctrine for Operational Level Planning (NATO,2013) (*AJP-5*)
Joint Doctrine Publication 0-20: Land Power (Shrivenham; DCDC, 2017)
War Office, *Report of the War Office Committee of Enquiry into "Shell Shock"*, (London: HMSO, 1922)
War Office, *Field Service Regulations (1909)* (London: HMSO, 1914)
SS series of instructional pamphlets issued by the War Office 1916-18
A.F. Becke, *Order of Battle of Divisions*, (*ORBAT*) Part 2B (London: HMSO, 1936)
J.E. Edmonds, *Military Operations France and Belgium 1917*, Vol. II (London: HMSO, 1948)
J.E. Edmonds, *Military Operations France and Belgium 1918*, Vol. I (London: HMSO, 1935)
C. Falls, *Military Operations France and Belgium 1917*, Vol. I (London: HMSO, 1940)
E.A. James, *A Record of the Battles and Engagements of the British Armies in France and Flanders, 1914-1918* (Aldershot: Gale & Polden, 1924)
W. Miles, *Military Operations France and Belgium 1917*, Vol. III (London: HMSO 1948)
Hansard Parliamentary Debates, Fifth Series

Divisional, Regimental, Unit Histories, Autobiographies, Biographies

C.T. Atkinson, *The History of the South Wales Borderers* (London: Medici, 1931)
O. Bailey & H. Hollier, *'The Kensingtons', 13th London Regiment* (London: OCA, 1936)

P. Bales, *The History of the 1/4th Battalion, Duke of Wellington's Regiment* (Halifax: Edward Mortimer, 1920)
A. Barnes, *The Story of the 2/5th Battalion Gloucestershire Regiment 1914-1918* (Gloucester: Crypt House Press, 1930)
J. Baynes, *Far From A Donkey: The Life of General Sir Ivor Maxse* (London: Brassey's, 1995)
E. Blunden, *Undertones of War* (London: Penguin, 1984)
B. Bond et al, *Look to your Front*: *Studies in the First World War* (Staplehurst: Spellmount, 1999)
F. Bewsher, *The History of the 51st (Highland) Division 1914-1918* (Edinburgh: William Blackwood & Sons, 1921)
G. Chapman, *A Passionate Prodigality* (London: Buchan & Enright, 1985)
C. von Clausewitz, *On War* (London: David Campbell, 1993)
Compiled, *59th Division 1915-1918* (Chesterfield: Wilfred Evans, 1928)
Compiled, *A War Record of the 21st London (First Surrey Rifles)* (London: Skinner, 1927).
Compiled, *The Robin Hoods: History of 1/7th, 2/7th & 3/7th Sherwood Foresters* (Uckfield: Naval & Military Press reprint of 1921 edition)
Compiled, *The History of the Old 2/4th (City of London) Battalion the London Regiment* (London: Westminster Press, 1919)
Compiled, *A History of the East Lancashire Royal Engineers* (Private publication, n.d.)
Compiled, *Historical Records of the Queen's Own Cameron Highlanders*, Vol. III (London: Blackwood & Sons, 1931)
Compiled, *The War History of the 1/4th Battalion, The Loyal North Lancashire Regiment* (Preston: Toulmin & Sons, 1924)
Compiled, *The History of the 7th (City of London) Battalion, The London Regiment* (OCA: Sun Street, 1946)
A. Conan Doyle, *The British Campaign in France and Flanders, January-July 1918,* Vol. 5 (London: Hodder & Stoughton, 1919)
D.W. Cuddeford, *And All for What?* (London: Heath Cranton, 1933)
P.H. Dalbiac, *History of the 60th Division (2/2nd London)* (London: Allen & Unwin, 1927)
P. Davenport & A. Benke (eds.) *The History of the Prince of Wales' Own Civil Service Rifles* (London: Wyman & Sons, 1921)
H. Davies (ed.) *Allanson of the 6th* (Lowesmoor: Square One Publications, 1990)
C.H. Dudley Ward, *Regimental Records of The Royal Welch Fusiliers 1914-1918* (London: Forster Groom, 1928)
J. Ewing, *The Royal Scots 1914-1919*, Vol. III (Edinburgh: Oliver & Boyd, 1925)
C. Falls *The Life of a Regiment: The Gordon Highlanders in the First World War 1914-1919* (Aberdeen: AUP, 1957)
P. Freyberg, *Bernard Freyberg VC* (London: Hodder & Stoughton, 1991)
E. Godfrey, *The Cast Iron Sixth* (London: Stapleton, 1930)
H. Gough, *Fifth Army* (London: Hodder & Stoughton, 1931)
W. Hall, *The Green Triangle: Being the History of the 2/5th Battalion Sherwood Foresters (Notts and Derby) in the Great European War 1914-1918* (Letchworth: Garden City Press, 1920)
J.Q. Henriques, *The War History of 1st Battalion the Queen's Westminster Rifles 1914-1918* (London: Medici, 1923)
H. Jomini, *The Art of War,* (London: Greenhill Books, 1992)
C.A. Keeson, *The Queen Victoria's Rifles 1792-1922* (London: Constable, 1923)

J. Latter, *The History of the Lancashire Fusiliers 1914-1919* (London: Gale & Polden, 1949)
I. Liberty, *A Record of the 2nd Bucks Battalion TF 1914-1918* (Chesham, n.d.)
P. Liddle (ed.) *Passchendaele in Perspective: The Third Battle of Ypres* (London: Leo Cooper, 1997)
J.H. Lindsay, *The London Scottish in the Great War* (London: HQ, 1925)
N. Lloyd, *Passchendaele: A New History* (London: Penguin, 2017)
A. Maude, *The History of the 47th (London) Division* (London: Amalgamated Press, 1922)
F. Maurice, *History of the London Rifle Brigade* (London: Constable, 1921)
E. May, *Signal Corporal: The Story of the 2nd London Irish Rifles (2/18th London Regiment) 1914-1918,* (London: Johnson, n.d.).
A.M. McGilchrist, *The Liverpool Scottish 1900-1919* (Liverpool: Henry Young & Sons, 1930)
C. Messenger, *Terriers in the Trenches. The History of the Post Office Rifles* (Chippenham: Picton 1981)
M. Middlebrook, *The Kaiser's Battle* (London: Penguin, 1983)
K.W. Mitchinson, *Gentlemen and Officers: The Impact of Experience of War on a Territorial Regiment 1914-1918* (London: Imperial War Museum, 1995)
K.W. Mitchinson, *Defending Albion: Britain's Home Army 1908-1919* (Basingstoke: Palgrave Macmillan, 2005)
K.W. Mitchinson, *The Territorial Force at War* 1914-1916 (Basingstoke: Palgrave Macmillan, 2014)
K.W. Mitchinson, *Amateur Soldiers: A History of Oldham's Volunteers and Territorials 1859-1938* (Oldham: Jade, 1999)
K.W. Mitchinson, *Pioneer Battalions in the Great War* (Barnsley: Pen & Sword, 1997)
K.W. Mitchinson, *The 48th (South Midland) Division 1908-1919* (Solihull: Helion & Co., 2017)
R.S. Moody, *Historical Records of the Buffs, East Kent Regiment 1914-1919* (London: Medici, 1922)
W. Oates, *History of 2/8th Sherwood Foresters 1914-1918* (Uckfield: Naval & Military Press reprint of 1919 edition)
F. Petrie, *The Royal Berkshire Regiment 1914-1918* (Reading: The Barracks, 1925)
J. Putkowski & J. Sykes, *Shot at Dawn* (London: Leo Cooper, 1990)
S. Robbins, *British Generalship on the Western Front* (London: Frank Cass, 2005)
G.K. Rose, *The Story of the 2/4th Oxfordshire and Buckinghamshire Light Infantry* (Oxford: B.H. Blackwell, 1919)
M. Senior, *Haking: A Dutiful Soldier* (Barnsley: Pen & Sword, 2012)
G. Sheffield & J. Bourne (eds.) *Douglas Haig: War Diaries and Letters 1914-1918* (London: Phoenix, 2006)
G. Sheffield & D. Todman (eds.), *Command and Control on the Western Front* (Staplehurst; Spellmount, 2004)
F. Skirrow, *Massacre on the Marne* (Barnsley: Pen and Sword, 2007)
H. Stacke, *The Worcestershire Regiment* (Worcester: Cheshire & Sons, 1929)
J. Walker, *The Blood Tub: General Gough and the Battle of Bullecourt, 1917* (Staplehurst: Spellmount, 1998)
A. Wheeler-Holohan & G. Wyatt, *The Rangers Historical Records* (London: RHQ, 1921)
C. Wurtzburg, *The History of the 2/6th Battalion 'The Kings' (Liverpool Regiment) 1914-1919* (London: Gale & Polden, 1920)
H. Wylly, *The Loyal North Lancashire Regiment* (London: RSUI, 1933)

G.C. Wynne, *If Germany Attacks: The Battle in Depth in the West* (London: Faber & Faber, 1940).
E. Wyrall, *The Story of the 62nd (West Riding) Division 1914-1919* (London: Bodley Head, 1924)
E. Wyrall, *The Die-Hards in the Great War* (London: Harrison, 1930)

Journal Articles

B. Hughes, B. Campbell, S. Schreibman, 'Contested Memories: Revisiting the Battle of Mount Street Bridge 1916', *British Journal of Military History*, Vol.4, Issue 1, Nov. 2017.

J. Lee, 'Command and Control in Battle: British Divisions on the Menin Road Ridge, 20 September 1917' in G. Sheffield & D. Todman (eds.), *Command and Control on the Western Front* (Staplehurst; Spellmount, 2004).

Lt. Col. A.F. Mockler-Ferryman, 'The Collection of Material for a Regimental Record of the War', *RUSI Journal*, 63.449

P. Scott, 'Law and Orders: Discipline and Morale in the British Armies in France, 1917' in

P. Liddle (ed.) *Passchendaele in Perspective*: The Third Battle of Ypres (London: Leo Cooper, 1997)

P. Simkins, 'Building Blocks: Aspects of Command and Control at the Brigade Level in the BEF's Offensive Operations, 1916-1918' in Sheffield & Todman (eds.), *Command and Control* (Staplehurst; Spellmount, 2004)

Theses & Dissertations

D. Tattersfield, Divisional Usage in the BEF on the WF 1916-1918, Unpublished MA, Univ. of Birmingham, 2006

Index

General Index

Achiet-le-Grand, 267
Achiet-le-Petit, 265
Aisne (area), 116
Aisne (farm), 116, 138-42, 147
Albatross Farm, 160
Albert, 267
Amery, Capt. (MP), 48
Armentieres, 92
Arras, 78, 83, 85, 87, 97, 102, 116, 120-122, 128, 142, 148, 164, 195, 264, 275
Attilly, 237, 248, 267
Aubers Ridge, 91, 92, 73, 90
Augustus Wood, 168
Aviatik, 147, 156, 158-161

Bapaume, 195
Battery Position, 140-43, 146, 147, 212, 275
Beaucamp Ridge, 203
Beaucourt, 68
Beaumont Hamel, 68
Belle Vue Spur, 165
Bernes, 105, 267
Berthaucourt, 116, 117, 120
Bethencourt, 99, 101
Bethune, Maj.Gen. 38
Bethune, 67
Bihecourt, 114-16
Boetleer, 158, 159, 163
Bourlon Wood, 184, 187, 190-94, 198, 276
Bouzincourt, 258
Bridge House, 165
Brie, 97
Broodseinde, Battle of, 152, 154, 164
Bucquoy, 265
Bullecourt, Battle of, ix, 75, 93, 122, 184, 211, 275, 276

Burke, Pte A, 275

Cambrai, Battle of, 122, 18-87, 195, 198, 203, 208, 219, 230, 265, 276, 285, 286
Cameron House, 177
Caporetto, Battle of, 181
Carpeza Copse, 105
Carr-Gomm, (MP), 48
Cartigny, 249
Caubrieres Wood, 107, 110, 111
Caulaincourt, 103
Chief of the Imperial General Staff, 37
Church Lads' Bde, 33
Cizancourt, 97, 99
Clausewitz, C.von, xi, 122, 134, 231
Cluster Houses, 159
Cologne:
    Farm, 111, 114, 120
    Ridge, 104, 105, 264, 282
    Valley, 218, 234, 251
Commanders:
    Haig, FM Sir D, xii, 62, 71, 115, 122, 142, 143, 162, 164, 165, 168, 171, 181, 184, 200, 207, 209, 212, 220, 230
    Army – Gens: J.Byng, 102, 199, 200, 260; H.Gough, 122, 132, 143, 162, 163, 207, 209, 212, 220, 230, 233, 234, 253, 257, 258, 260, 263, 264; I.Hamilton, viii, 38, 40, 41, 45; H.Horne, 71, 86, 90; C.Monro, 41, 74, 75 ; C.Plumer, 61, 122, 143, 162, 164, 181; H.Rawlinson, 102, 115, 122
    Corps – Lt.Gens: R.Butler, 212, 213, 214, 233; Cavan, Earl of, 172; E.Fanshawe, 69; C.Fergusson, 78, 81; R.Haking, 71, 74, 75, 77, 86- 92, 275; J.Haldane, 245, 259, 264; I.Maxse, 124, 130-32, 143,

148, 150, 152, 163, 174, 176, 212-15, 225, 230, 233, 258, 259, 264, 277; H.Watts, 125, 143, 182, 212, 215, 234, 263, 264 ; C.Woollcombe, 115

Divisional – Maj.Gens: F.Adam, (Brig-Gen) 23; R.Bannatine-Allason, 45; R.Barnes, 92, 126, 130, 182; C.Barter, 41, 42; Barthelemy, 259; W.Braithwaite, 45, 57, 69, 207, 265; R.Broadwood, (Lt.Gen.), 92; E.Bulfin, 45, 52, 83; A.Cator, 178, 213, 227, 230, 250, 251, 277; W.Cavaye (Brig.Gen), 23; H.Fanshawe, 132, 150, 152, 163, 230, 277; H.Lawrence, 70, 71, 87-90, 126, 165, 170, 171; H.Jeudwine, 126, 153; H.MacCall (Brig.Gen.), 23; C.Mackenzie, 24, 74, 114, 139, 142-44, 200, 204, 212, 214, 227, 244, 245, 249, 254, 259, 260; N.Malcolm, 212, 217, 218, 227, 228, 230, 251, 256, 257, 259, 263, 264; T.Marden, 252, 253, 266; C.Romer, 97, 98, 108, 111, 114, 153, 155, 187, 188, 190, 194, 227, 250, 253, 255; A.Sandbach, 45, 108, 111-13; A.Solly-Flood, 90, 219; G.Stockwell (Brig.Gen), 23

Brigade – Brig, Gens: A.Birtwistle, 227; O.Borrett, 182, 228, 251; J.Burnett, 270; W.Evans, 196, 201; B.Freyberg, 132, 151, 152; A.Gordon, 78; F.Guggisberg, 91, 129; G.Hunt, 273; A.Macfie, 46; W.Maconchy, 105, 108, 111, 112, 273; A.Martyn, 91, 273; R.Ouseley, 112; G.Paynter, 46; G.Pleydell-Bouverie, 49, 54; Hon.C.Sackville-West, 141; J.Stirling, 112, 268; A.Spooner, 143-45, 247, 266; T.Stansfield, 108, 112, 259, 263; J.Travers, 227, 273; C.Watts, 46; R.White, 115, 123, 124, 142, 146, 147, 196, 278; G.Williams, 227

GSO1 – Lt.Cols: C.J.Allanson, 92, 123, 125; Blair, 25; A.Dunlop, 45; R.St G.Gorton, 121; R.Livesay, 227, 266; R.Mangles, 227; P. Marling, VC, 25; H.Wake, 121

AA&QMG – 23, 25, 53, 54, 55, 64, 97, 225, 227

CRA – 34-36, 84, 91, 96, 98, 99, 112, 116, 118-20, 144, 173, 193, 194, 203, 217, 222, 224, 227, 240-45, 273, Brig. Gen.A.Birtwistle, 227; R.Coates, 112, 113

CRE – 227, 242, 247, 258; Lt.Cols: G.Durnford, 99, 225

Jnr staff officers – Capt.Hoare, 69; Capt.H.G.Howitt, 227, 273

Adjutants – 27, 44, 46, 47, 64, 65, 67, 71, 228, 273

ADMS – Lt.Col. J.Houghton, 179, 226; Lt.Col. Lindsay, 189, 190

ADVS – 35, 97, 98

Unit/sub-unit: Lt.Col.Ames, 76; Lt.Col.Bates, 126, 167, 168, 171, 172, 273; Lt.Col.Beer, 76; Lt.Col.C.B.Benson, 228; Lt.Col.Carr-Gomm (MP), 47, 48; Lt.Col.Coates, 198, 199; Maj.Davies, 262; Lt.Col.A.D.Derviche-Jones, 178, 228; Lt.Col.J.H.Dimmer VC, 228, 229, 254; Lt.Col.Dorman, 77; Lt.Col. Dunfee, 26; Lt.Col.Fraser, 27; Lt.Col.Gadd, 155, 156, 251; Lt.Col.Glyn, 120; Lt.Col. Gordon-Clark, 27; Lt.Col., Hitchins, 182; Lt.Col.Hobbins, 168; Lt.Col.Hodgkin, 105, 273; Maj.Keating, 252, 264; Maj. Lefroy, 201; Lt.Col.Maclean, 26; Lt.Col. Martyn, 108, 110, 191, 192, 193; Lt.Col. Murphy, 81; Lt.Col.Oates, 108, 110, 111, 114, 228; Lt.Col.Prince, 26; Lt.Col.Raynor, 106; Lt.Col.A.A.Richardson, 179, 228, 237, 273; Capt.Saxon, 262; 2Lt.Shankland, 268; Lt.Col.Spiers, 113; Lt.Col.W.E.St John, 201, 202, 204, 228; Maj.Trench, 268; Lt.Col. Watts, 27; Lt.Col.Wilkie, 249; Lt.Col. Wilton, 27

Command, xi, xii, 16, 23, 26, 27, 46, 47, 60, 113, 114, 123-25, 129, 145, 152, 173, 186, 188, 189, 200, 201, 206, 207, 215, 228-30, 238, 251, 263, 268, 273

Commons, House of, vii, 29, 274, 278

Concentration of force, xiii, 73, 111, 145, 174, 184, 185, 209

Condren, 214, 251, 257

Contact Patrol Aircraft, 130, 136, 142, 153, 203

Cooperation/liaison, 51, 73, 107, 113, 117, 121, 139, 144, 191, 193, 217, 221, 222, 224, 236, 238, 240, 242, 275

Corner Work, 197, 199

Courts Martial/Enquiries, 55, 66, 93, 224, 269, 270

Coxyde Bains, 164

Crozat Canal, 233, 243, 246, 247, 261

Cuinchy, 164

Dawnay, Maj.Gen (DMO), 219, 220

Dear House, 156, 161

Decauville, 173, 267

Derby, Lord, 36, 58, 126

Derby Scheme/Derbyites, 48, 56-60, 63, 228
Dochy Farm, 137, 154, 156-58
Doctrine:
   Delaying actions/rearguards, 95, 117, 185 *passim*, 232, 253, 256
   Field Service Regulations, xi, xii, 186, 194, 200, 208, 218, 219, 253
   Fighting Power, viii, xii, xiii, xiv, 52, 63, 71, 74, 75, 97, 111, 116, 125, 126, 131, 133, 134, 146, 151, 154, 182, 202, 208, 218, 226, 229, 232, 240, 268-72, 278
   Manoeuvrist Approach, xiii, 231
   Modern Publications, xi, xii, 96, 125, 146, 149, 185, 186, 208, 268, 269
   Offensive, xii, xiii, 96, 115, 117, 121, 133, 159, 181, 184
   Principles of War, xii, xiii, 97, 154, 172, 184, 186, 268, 272
   SS Pamphlets, xii, 90, 123, 124, 128, 129, 130, 131, 136, 141, 145, 224
Drafts, 16, 21, 23, 28, 36, 39-44, 48, 57-63, 65, 72, 82, 89, 90, 100, 101, 125, 126, 133, 135, 147, 171, 183, 184, 205, 222, 228, 229, 271, 274, 281, 285
Drocourt-Queant Line, 276

Economy of effort, 103, 146, 174, 186, 208, 268, 272
Ecoust-St-Mein, 211, 221, 234, 247, 250, 252, 255, 256, 267
Egypt, 15, 16, 22, 46, 60, 61, 100
Etaples, 182
Eterpigny, 234

Fargniers, 233
Fauquissart, 77
Fayet, 119, 225
Ferme Rouge, 246, 250
Fervaque Farm, 104-06, 108, 111, 112, 117, 251
Fins, 189, 195
Flechin, 104, 110, 111
Flesquieres, 187, 189-194
Fontaine-Notre-Dame, 187, 191
Foreste, 259, 267
Francilly-Selency, 216
Fench, FM Sir J, 58
Fresnoy-le-Petit, 116-120, 216
Frezenberg Ridge, 166, 167, 169, 272
Fromelles, viii, 59, 73, 77, 78, 90-94, 121, 148, 183, 274, 275

Gallipoli, 22, 34, 43, 45, 61, 70, 73, 100
Gallipoli Farm, 138-42, 147, 148, 153
Gommecourt, 68, 126
Gonnelieu, 189, 196
Gouzeaucourt, 120, 189, 190, 193, 196
Graincourt, 191, 192
Grand Priel Woods, 104, 106, 107, 109, 111, 112, 117, 234, 235
Gravenstfel Ridge, 147, 152, 155-58, 163, 277
Grevillers, 267
Gricourt, 117, 216

Hamilton, C, (MP), vii, 61
Hanebeek, 137, 147, 150, 157-59, 161, 277
Hargicourt, 103-05, 111, 234, 235, 243
Havrincourt, 125, 184
Havrincourt Wood, 193, 202, 203
Hervilly Wood, 104, 109, 234, 235, 256
Hesbecourt, 104, 104, 235, 257, 267
Heudicourt, 195
Hill 135, 104, 235
Hill 140, 104, 235
Hill 35, 137-42, 147, 148, 157
Hill 37, 137, 153, 154, 157
   Hindenburg Line , ix, 69, 71, 83, 94-97, 100, 102, 104, 112, 114, 116-18, 120, 122, 184, 187, 188, 191, 197-99, 204, 211, 276
Hindu Cot, 137, 138
Hirondelle Valley, 234, 239, 241, 243, 252, 260, 267
Hohenzollen, 61, 88
Holnon Wood, 102, 114, 215, 216, 233, 237, 243, 246, 249, 254
Home Service, viii, 16, 21, 30, 31, 36-38, 41, 44, 47

Iberian, 137, 141, 142, 157
Imperial Service, 15, 37
India, viii, x, 15, 22-24, 45, 46, 113
Indian Army, 25, 70, 112, 228
Ireland (Easter Rising), viii, 23, 35, 52, 60-62, 112

Jeancourt, 104-10, 114, 235, 248, 271
Jomini, H, xii
Joynson-Hicks (MP), 29, 47

Kansas Cross, 137, 138, 147, 157
Keir Farm, 137, 153, 156, 157
Kitchener, FM, 15, 17, 20, 23, 29

Laamkeek, 168
La Chapellette, 234
La Fere, 233
Langemarck, 152, 173
Larkhill, 34, 35
Lateau Wood, 187, 197
La Panne, 128
la Vacquerie, 187, 188, 196-201
Laventie, 68, 164
Le Havre, 6, 66
Lemons, 147
Lempire, 103
Le Verguier, 103-12, 114, 116-18, 234, 235, 251, 261, 276
Lloyd George, D, 19
Longatte Spur, 210, 211, 234, 247
Lucas Lamps, 179
Ludendorff, E, General, 206, 231

Madagascar Village, 89
Maison Garde, 240
Maissemy, 104, 107, 109, 110, 114, 116, 117, 216, 233, 254, 257
Malakoff Farm/Wood, 111-14, 120
Marcoing, 187
Mareval Copse, 117
Marteville, 103, 216, 225, 249, 254, 258, 267
Masnieres, 187
Memling Farm, 174, 175, 177
Messines, Battle of, 40, 87, 88, 89, 122, 131, 148, 154
Metz-en-Couture, 190, 195
Meunier Farm, 175, 180
Military Service Act, 58
Minton Farm, 177
Mockler-Ferryman, Lt.Col.A.E., ix
Morale/cohesion/*esprit*, viii, xi-xiii, 22, 27, 31, 36, 41, 44, 48, 56, 59, 60, 63, 64, 74, 75, 78, 80, 81, 87, 91-93, 97, 100, 101, 108, 111, 122, 125-27, 131, 134, 141, 147, 148, 150, 152, 161, 171, 173, 179, 180, 182, 186, 188, 201, 202, 204, 206, 207, 226, 230, 231, 244, 256, 263, 264, 268-72, 274
Moray House, 174, 177
Mort Homme, 221, 247
Mory, 210, 234, 248

Nesle, 101, 114
Nile, 137, 157, 158

Nieuport, 90, 127
Nobescourt, 104, 251
Nobles Farm, 176, 177
Noreuil, 210, 211, 234, 242, 248, 250, 255, 257, 267
Norwich, 22, 61

Oise, 213, 233, 250, 257
Olive House, 161
Omignon Valley, 99, 105, 109, 114-17, 119, 183, 215, 221, 233 249, 254, 258, 261
Orival Wood, 191-94
Otto Farm, 137, 155-58, 163

Papa Farm/Hill, 174, 175, 177, 180
Passchendaele/Ridge, 134, 143, 164, 166, 168, 172
Patrolling – *see* Raiding
Peronne, 97, 101, 196, 209, 234, 247, 259
Pierremande, 250
Pigeons, 136, 160, 161, 169, 179, 238, 239
Poelcapelle, 277, 175
Polygon Wood, Battle of, 162
Pommern Castle, 137, 156
Pond Farm, 137, 138
Pontru, 117, 118, 216
Poperinghe, 131, 165
Potijze, 165
Poeuilly, 101, 103, 216
Puisieux, 265

Quessy, 233, 246, 248

Raids/Patrols, Chapter 3 *passim*, 50, 96, 97, 104, 105, 111, 112, 115, 118, 128, 132, 149, 195, 224, 227, 271, 272, 276
Ravebeek, 168
Recruiting, 15-17, 19, 20-22, 36, 38, 39, 60, 183, 285
Redoubts:
    Black Hill, 216, 248
    Ellis, 216, 225, 233, 243, 254, 262, 282
    Enghien, 216, 225, 248, 263, 282
    Essling, 216, 225
    Fresnoy, 216
    Manchester Hill, 225, 246
    Spooner, 215, 216, 255
    St.Firmin, 246
    Travercy, 233, 239
    Trinket, 235, 262

Reubens Farm, 177
Riencourt-les-Cagnicourt, 210, 222, 276
Rifles:
   Japanese, 32, 33
   Lee Metford, 32, 33
   Lee Enfield, 32, 33
Riverside, 137, 155-58
Roisel, 97, 100, 104, 215, 218, 235, 249, 251, 256, 261, 267
Royal Military College of Canada, 45
Rupprecht, Crown Prince, 232
Ruyaulcourt, 195

St Albans, 40, 41, 61
St Christ, 97
St Julien, 121, 131, 137, 148, 152
St Quentin, 62, 94, 95, 120, 205, 230
Salisbury Plain, 61
Savy, 103, 216, 246
Schools of Instruction, 71, 72, 123, 219, 271
Schuler Farm/Galleries, 137-40, 142, 150, 153, 157
Siege Camp, 178
Smith, Pte W, 270
Somme, Battle of, xii, xiii, 56, 59, 63, 69, 72-75, 78, 80, 82, 83, 93-97, 120-23, 132, 134, 148, 164, 208, 230, 269, 271
Somme, (farm), 137, 138
Somme, River, 97, 99, 101, 114, 209, 234, 247, 259
Southampton, 65
Soyecourt, 101, 103, 104, 109
Spider Crossroads, 174, 175, 180
Spot Farm, 149
Springfield, 147-49, 163
Staff College, 23-25, 45, 113, 121, 227
Steenbeke, 139, 173
Stroombeke, 160
Stroppe Farm, 158
Sugar Loaf, 73, 74
Surprise, xiii, 73, 108, 111, 121, 122, 134, 142, 154, 162, 172, 174, 181, 184, 186, 271, 272
Sustainment, xiii, 51, 94, 97, 98, 101, 143, 147, 162, 180, 181, 184, 193, 206, 219, 220, 222, 226, 265, 272, 273
Templeux-le-Guerard, 104, 105, 217, 218, 234, 235, 242, 245, 246, 249, 251, 254, 256, 261
Tennant, H, (MP), 18, 29, 48, 56, 58
Tergnier, 233, 242
Tertry, 99, 101

Thierru Copse, 105, 107, 109
Tortille, River, 209
Trefcon, 103
Trenches:
   Cooker, 117
   Corner Support, 197, 199
   Dean, 117
   Ecoust Switch, 256
   Emden/Support, 197-99
   Mareval, 117
   Ostrich Trench/Avenue, 197, 199, 201
   Pontru, 117
Trescault, 187, 190, 194

Vadencourt, 109, 115, 116
Vale House, 159
Van Isackere, 158
Vendelles, 104-11, 115
Vermand, 103, 114, 216, 258
Victoria Cross, 25, 132, 188, 228, 229, 268
Villecholles, 216, 258
Villeret, 105, 111, 112, 234, 235, 282
Villeveque, 216, 249, 250, 258
Vimy Ridge, 78, 187
Volunteer Decoration, 26, 27
von Tirpitz Farm, 147
Vraucourt, 221, 248, 256
   Copse, 210, 221, 243, 248, 256

Walton, Sir J (MP), 61
War Office, vii, viii, ix, xii, 15-21, 25-32, 36, 38, 39, 42, 46, 48, 50, 51, 55, 61-65, 70, 81, 126, 270, 274, 277, 278, 279
Waterfields, 168
Watson fan, 136, 153, 179
Welsh Ridge, 196-200, 204, 275
Whitechapel, 174, 175, 180
White City, 22, 31
Wick, The, 73, 74
Wieltje, 135, 156, 158, 165
Winchester Farm, 159, 160
Winzig, 159
Winnipeg, 138-40, 147-49, 157, 163
Wurst Farm, 138, 147, 152, 157

Yate, Col. (MP), 48

Zeppelins, 50, 51
Zonnebeke, 138, 147, 215

Index of British, Dominion, and Empire formations and units

Bantam Battalions: 20, 99, 172
British Expeditionary Force: ix, xi, xiii, 17, 40, 41, 56, 59, 62, 67, 69, 70, 95, 113, 131, 133, 135, 143, 181, 182, 185, 206, 208, 218, 219, 225-27, 229, 260, 262, 269, 270, 271, 274, 279
Armies:
    Regular: vii, viii, x, xi, xiv, 15, 17, 18, 20, 21, 23-25, 27, 46, 48, 53, 60, 70, 172, 247, 273, 278
    New/Kitchener: vii, viii, xiv, 15, 16, 17, 18, 21-24, 27, 29, 30, 38, 42, 47, 48, 54, 60, 63, 70, 75, 126, 273, 274
    Territorial: viii, 41
    First: 34, 42, 70, 73, 75, 80, 86, 87, 91, 184
    Second: 45, 112, 154, 162, 169, 223, 258
    Third: 68, 142, 190, 193, 195, 204, 209, 221, 223, 260, 267
    Fourth: 96, 97, 101, 102, 118, 120, 121
    Fifth: 68, 69, 122, 127-29, 138, 140, 142, 143, 146, 154, 162, 206, 207, 209, 211, 212, 214, 220, 226, 228, 230, 240, 253, 260, 263, 264, 268, 272
Artillery:
    Batteries: VI (Lancs), 227; 40 Siege Bty, 104; 117 Bty, 243 ; Portuguese, 88
    Brigades: 26 Army Bde, 243; 2/5 London Bde, 34; 2/4 Welsh Bde, 34; 86 Bde, ; 117 Bde, ; 290 Bde, 35, 240; 295 Bde, 102, 258; 296 Bde, 162, 222, 258; 306 Bde, 254; 330 Bde, 169; 331 Bde, 169
    Heavy Artillery Groups: 106; 28th HAG, 96; 62nd HAG, 119; 89th HAG, 119
Cavalry/Yeomanry:
    Divisions: 1st, 215, 250, 251, 263; 2nd, 194, 244; 5th, 102
    Brigades: 2 Dismounted Bde, 251 ; 9 Bde, 221; 2/1st London Mtd Bde, 35; Secunderbad Bde, 195; S-W Mtd Bde, 54
    Regiments: Bedford Yeo, 52; 15/Hussars, 256; N.Somerset Yeo, 50; Sussex Yeo, 33; W.Kent Yeo, 69
Corps:
    Cavalry, 217, 236
    III, 94-97, 103, 108, 116, 195, 198, 200, 203, 204, 212-14, 220, 233, 237, 238, 240, 243, 260
    IV, 95, 96, 102, 103, 118, 131, 187, 190, 194, 195, 234, 260, 264, 265
    V, 68, 72, 131, 141, 153, 190, 191, 192, 193, 194, 195
    VI, 211, 222, 239, 240, 245, 249, 250, 255, 256, 258
    XI, 73-75, 83, 86, 87, 90, 91, 92
    XIV, 131, 172
    XVIII, 124, 131, 132, 135, 143, 148, 152, 160, 173, 176, 178, 179, 209, 212, 214, 215, 220-22, 224, 225, 230, 233, 236, 240, 241, 244, 245, 249, 254, 256, 258, 264
    XIX, 125, 131, 141, 143, 182, 209, 212, 215, 217, 220-22, 234, 237, 239, 240, 242, 244, 250, 254, 263, 267
    I ANZAC, 165; II ANZAC, 83, 131, 161, 164, 165, 169, 230
Divisions:
    Guards, 172, 187, 195; 1st, 96; 3rd, 153, 154, 158, 161, 245; 6th, 45, 187, 188, 190, 191, 193, 194, 195, 204, 234, 240, 252, 253, 256, 257, 260, 263, 266; 9th (Scottish), 131, 153; 11th (Northern), 138; 12th (Eastern), 188, 205; 14th (Light), 243, 260; 15th (Scottish), 138, 139, 140; 16th (Irish), 234, 239, 257, 261; 18th (Eastern), 126, 131, 174, 213, 233, 239, 257, 260; 20th (Light), 187, 188, 193, 195, 196, 199, 202, 205, 233, 248, 258; 24th, 214, 215, 217, 230, 233, 234, 239, 251, 254, 257, 258, 261; 28th, 45; 29th, 187, 189, 204; 30th, 215, 227, 241, 243, 246, 256, 257, 258, 260, 261; 32nd, 68, 92, 103, 114, 118, 119; 34th, 211, 243, 250, 252, 257; 35th, 99, 173; 36th (Ulster), 224, 243, 257; 39th, 132; 40th, 236, 253, 256, 258, 263, 274; 41st, 24, 264; 42nd (East Lancashire), 100, 141; 43rd (Wessex), 22; 44th (Home Counties), 22, 24; 45th (2nd Wessex), 25; 47th (2nd London), 41, 42, 190, 193, 194; 48th (South Midland), x, 60, 96, 98, 101, 104, 105, 110, 111, 113, 120, 131, 132, 138, 138, 139, 148, 149, 163, 182; 49th (West Riding), 43, 68, 69, 91, 92, 164, 165, 167, 168, 169,

171, 182; 50th (Northumbrian), 62, 95, 96, 172, 173, 182, 227, 234, 249, 250, 256, 257, 259, 263, 264, 277; 51st (Highland), 41, 43, 45, 49, 67, 72, 78, 132, 152, 193, 194, 229, 260, 261; 52nd (Lowland), 43, 70; 53rd (Welsh), 22, 70; 54th (East Anglian), 22, 70; 55th (West Lancashire), 61, 126, 128, 142, 150; 56th (1st London), 61, 68, 78, 187, 193, 267

57th (2nd West Lancashire), 22, 58, 61, 65, 68, 71, 83-87, 89-93, 121, 123, 125, 126, 128, 129, 131, 172, 173, 176, 177, 180, 182, 184, 232, 272, 276, 277, 278

58th (2/1st London), 22, 23, 25, 35, 39, 49, 50, 54, 55, 59, 61, 65, 68, 72, 83, 93, 124, 125, 128, 130-32, 135, 148, 150, 152-56, 158, 159, 161-63, 172, 173, 174, 177, 178, 180-184, 209, 212, 213, 219, 220, 221, 224, 226, 227, 229, 230, 232, 233, 23-39, 240-42, 245, 246-48, 257, 259, 260, 264, 267, 271, 272, 276, 277, 280, 286, 287

59th (2nd North Midland, x, 52, 58, 61, 63, 83, 94-108, 110, 112-15, 117, 119, 120, 121, 125-29, 131, 152, 153, 154, 156, 158, 159, 161-63, 164, 183-85, 187, 189-95, 198, 200, 201, 209-11, 217, 218, 219, 221-23, 225, 226, 229, 230, 232, 234, 236-38, 240, 241, 242, 245-50, 251-53, 255, 256, 258, 260, 261-63, 266-68, 271, 272, 276, 277, 282, 285-87

60th (2/2nd London), x, 52, 55, 60, 61, 64, 65, 67, 70, 72, 78, 79, 82-84, 93, 271, 272, 275

61st (2nd South Midland), viii, x, 52, 59, 60, 61, 65, 67, 70, 73-75, 84, 93-96, 98, 99, 101-06, 108, 110, 112-15, 117, 118, 120-48, 183-85, 187, 194-96, 198, 199, 200, 203, 204, 209, 212, 214, 215, 218-27, 229, 230, 232-34, 236, 238-49, 254, 256-59, 261-64, 266, 267, 271-75, 278, 283, 285-87

62nd (2nd West Riding), x, 57, 68, 69, 74, 83, 93, 112, 119, 121, 181, 184, 194, 207, 232, 264, 265, 268, 270, 275, 277, 278, 281

63rd (2nd Northumbrian), ix, 35, 44, 45, 62

63rd (Royal Naval), 62
64th (2nd Highland), 25, 61, 183
65th (2nd Lowland), 45, 61, 97
66th (2nd East Lancashire), 61, 66, 70, 72, 83, 87, 89-93, 121, 126, 127-29, 131, 164-66, 168, 169, 171, 183, 184, 209, 212, 215, 217-19, 221, 223-27, 229, 230, 232, 234, 23-50, 252, 254, 256, 259, 261-64, 266-68, 271, 272, 276, 277, 281, 282, 284, 286, 288
67th (2nd Home Counties), 22, 35, 60, 267
68th (2nd Welsh), 31, 35, 53, 62, 112
69th (2nd East Anglian), viii, 35, 62
3rd Australian, 165, 168, 230, 274; 5th Australian, 73, 74; 2nd Canadian, 35; New Zealand, 68, 147164, 265

Entrenching Battalions: 229; 15th, 256; 16th, 267; 18th, 248, 250

Infantry Brigades: 2/1st Cheshire, 54; Gordon, 23; 1 London, 15; 5 London, 42; 2/1st Manchester, 26, 19; 2/1st Notts & Derby, 58, 108; 2/1st Staffordshire, 39; 2/1st Warwickshire, 78, 183; 8 Bde, 154, 156; 44 Bde, 139, 140; 53 Bde, 174; 54 Bde, 174; 59 Bde, 188, 196; 73 Bde, 250; 75 Bde, 253, 257; 143 Bde, 138, 139, 140; 170 Bde, 83, 125, 127, 129, 173; 171 Bde, 66, 73, 83, 84, 85, 92; 172 Bde, 83; 173 Bde, 132, 150, 173, 174, 176, 179, 213, 214, 224, 233, 237, 246, 247, 248, 250, 254, 257, 260, 261, 280; 174 Bde, 56, 132, 132, 150, 176, 213; 175 Bde, 49, 54, 56, 65, 132, 149, 154, 158, 159, 161, 227; 176 Bde, 95, 105, 111, 113, 125, 154, 156, 158, 161, 187, 188, 252, 261, 263; 177 Bde, 104, 105, 106, 108, 111, 154, 156, 161, 187, 188, 190, 191, 211, 232, 214, 236, 250, 251, 252, 253, 255, 258; 178 Bde, 33, 54, 56, 63, 95, 102, 106, 108, 11-13, 152, 155, 156, 158, 159, 161, 188, 190, 192, 238, 251, 259, 263, 282; 179 Bde, 83; 180 Bde, 40, 57; 181 Bde, 81, 82; 182 Bde, 58, 78, 125, 140, 146, 196, 199, 201, 202, 205, 244, 249, 258, 262; 183 Bde, 77, 114, 116, 117, 135, 138-40, 142, 143, 145, 146, 147, 195, 196, 198, 199, 201, 202, 204, 233, 237, 247, 248, 258, 261, 262; 184 Bde, iv, 51, 58, 75, 76, 108, 109, 115, 116, 123,

135, 136, 138, 139, 144, 148, 195, 196, 199, 205, 227, 237, 256, 262; 185 Bde, 50; 186 Bde, 75, 270; 187 Bde, 68, 69, 70, 72, 75, 265; 195 Bde, 46; 197 Bde, 71, 133, 165, 166, 167, 168, 171, 182, 217, 224, 234, 251, 256, 261, 262, 281; 198 Bde, 44, 165, 166, 167, 168, 237, 256; 199 Bde, 88, 127, 165, 166, 168, 224, 227, 237, 238, 248, 256; 208 Bde, 53; 10 Aust, 53

Infantry Regiments/Battalions
  Argyll & S.High, 1/8th, 224, 237, 243, 258, 268
  Border, 1/5th, 221, 226, 237, 249, 256, 263
  Buckinghamshire Bn, 2/1st, ix, 74, 103, 106, 107, 113, 114, 115, 135, 147, 285
  Cambridgeshire, 57
  Cameron High, 1/4th, 27; 2/4th, 27
  Dorset, 57
  Duke of Cornwall's LI, 1/5th, 226, 248; 10th, 91
  Cheshire, 2/6th, 39, 55
  Duke of Wellington's, 2/5th, 56; 2/6th, 65; 2/7th, 65
  East Kent, 2/5th, 44
  East Lancashire, 1st, 252; 2/4th, 43, 72, 88, 167; 2/5th, 44, 89, 167, 251
  East Surrey, 9th, 257
  Gloucestershire, 2/4th, 65, 66, 77, 118, 138, 139, 196, 198, 201, 248; 2/5th, 39, 47, 75, 87, 110, 114, 116, 120, 123, 138, 202, 218, 228, 237, 259, 270; 2/6th, 118, 138, 196, 198
  Gordon Highlanders, 20, 23; 2nd, 270; 1/5th, 214, 229, 239, 262, 282
  Highland Cyclist, 58, 183
  Hertfordshire, 57
  King's Liverpool, 1/6th, 27; 1/9th, 27; 2/5th, 92; 2/6th, ix, 20, 29, 39, 58, 59, 92, 131, 177, 183; 2/7th, 84, 85; 2/9th, 85; 2/10, 39, 56, 60, 84, 86; 17th, 249, 256; 19th, 257
  King's Own Royal Lancaster, 2/5th, 66, 86, 92, 173
  King's Own Yorkshire LI, 1/5th, 168; 2/4th, 38, 57, 273
  Lancashire Fusiliers, 2/5th, 33, 41, 49; 2/6th, 26, 88; 2/7th, 19, 60, 168, 217; 2/8th, 19, 228, 236, 281, 282; 3/5th, 66, 87, 88, 89, 127, 166, 167, 230, 270, 273
  Leicestershire, 2/4th, 96, 106, 153, 156, 224, 250, 252, 255, 258, 259, 285; 2/5th, 104, 105, 192, 219
  Lincolnshire, 2/4, 106, 188, 191, 192, 219; 2/5th, 95, 104, 111, 113, 154, 155, 156, 161, 190, 219, 239, 250, 255, 261
  London, 3rd, 233, 250, 287; 8th, 248, 250, 286, 287;1/12th, 27; 2/1st, 56, 127, 133, 149; 2/2nd, 248, 280, 287; 2/3rd, 150; 2/4th, 29, 21, 26, 150, 180, 233, 237, 239, 246; 2/5th, 43, 57, 93, 126, 150, 177, 278; 2/6th, 19, 149, 150, 151, 172, 177, 228; 2/7th, 33, 151, 176, 178; 2/8th, 93, 133, 149, 150, 163, 176, 177, 178, 179, 213, 228, 273; 2/9th, 39, 159, 160; 2/10th, 159, 178; 2/11th, 55, 56; 2/12th, 19, 39, 59, 149, 159; 2/13th, 26, 79; 2/14th, 80, ; 2/15th, 39, 73, 80; 2/16th, 39, 80; 2/17th, 32, 80; 2/18th, 38, 46, 78, 81, 82; 2/21st, 37, 46, 48, 81; 2/23rd, 19, 79; 2/24th, 79
  Loyal North Lancashire, 2/5th, 33, 173, 182; 4/5th, 85, 86, 173
  Manchester, 2/5th, 65, 88, 89, 90, 133, 167, 168, 230, 282; 2/6th, 88, 251, 262; 2/7th, 50, 90, 167, 224, 234, 237; 2/8th, 127, 166, 168; 2/9th, 43, 72, 166, 167; 2/10th, 19, 43, 44, 54, 57, 88, 90, 127, 128, 166, 167
  North Staffordshire, 5th, 224, 234; 2/5th, 124, 188, 262; 2/6th, 95, 124, 156, 158, 250, 252
  Northumberland Fus., 45; 2/5th, 60; 2/6th, 53; 25th, 250, 257
  Ox&Bucks LI, 2/4th, 52, 57, 76, 98, 110, 113, 115, 116, 135, 142, 147, 196, 214, 227, 248, 263, 278, 282, 285
  R.Berkshire, 1/4th, 27; 2/4th, 21, 27, 39, 76, 99, 114, 117, 120, 130, 136, 146, 195, 199, 215, 224, 228, 249, 254, 255, 257, 260
  Royal Munster Fus., 1st, 261
  Royal Scots, 20, 26, 58; 1/7th, 43; 1/9th, 237, 249; 2/7th, 57, 60; 2/9th, 59
  Royal Scots Fus., 6/7th, 226, 237, 248, 252, 258, 263
  R.Sussex, 183; 2/4th & 2/5th, 62; 9th, 234, 251, 256, 262

R.Warwickshire, 2/5th, 78, 140, 141, 146, 196, 198, 199, 200, 201, 224, 285; 2/6th, 76, 119, 224, 236, 241, 243, 249, 256, 285; 2/7th, 58, 74, 119, 120, 144, 145, 148, 196, 199, 201, 228, 244, 249, 254, 258, 259, 285; 2/8th, 58, 76, 101, 103, 146, 196, 199, 201
Sherwood Foresters, 2/5th, 19, 43, 58, 107, 127, 155, 156, 187, 212, 250, 251, 261, 268; 2/6th, 95, 104, 105, 110, 128, 155, 188, 189, 193, 236, 254, 273; 2/7th, 96, 105, 106, 107, 108, 110, 115, 116, 156, 191, 193, 252; 2/8th, 65, 102, 104-08, 110-12, 114, 129, 152, 156, 158, 159, 190, 228, 285
South Lancashire, 2/4th, 86, 273; 2/5th, 85
South Staffordshire, 2/5th, ; 2/6th
Suffolk, 228; 1/4th, 226, 248, 287; 2/4th, 54, 62; 2/5th, 32, 54; 8/Suffolk, 126
Welsh, 57
West Yorkshire, 2/5th, 53; 2/6th, 19; 2/7th, 65, 66, 265
Worcestershire, 1/7th, 113, 131; 2/7th, 77, 114, 126, 285; 2/8th, 77, 116, 118, 139, 198, 262, 282
York & Lancs, 2/4th, 47, 56, 57, 69, 72, 75; 2/5th, 47, 57, 75
Yorkshire (Green Howards), 2/4th, 20, 33; 2/5th, 20

Central Force: 17, 32, 34, 35, 38, 41, 56, 61

DADOS: 54, 100, 247
Divisional Ammunition Columns: 56, 114, 116, 144, 245

Home Commands: 40; Eastern, 52; Irish, 113; Northern, 50

Machine Gun Companies/Battalions: 222, 223, 245-47, 252, 265, 266, 281, 282

Militia: 23, 26, 46, 228; Canadian, 228
Mobile Veterinary Section: 98

National Reserve, 26, 274

Pioneers: 70, 71, 100, 138, 170, 171, 174, 217, 217, 222, 226, 228, 234, 247, 249
Provisional Battalions: 56, 57, 58, 62, 244, 37, 38, 44, 47

Reserve of Officers: 95, 228
Rifle Volunteers: 19, 26, 46, 47
Royal Army Medical Corps: 53, 54, 179
Field Ambulances: 17, 41, 45, 49, 53, 54, 55, 89, 91, 101, 127, 173, 174, 189, 190, 202, 226, 236, 262, 267, 273
Royal Defence Corps: 274
Royal Engineers: *See* CRE
Field Companies:173, 17, 33, 41, 42, 49, 50, 56, 70, 82, 89, 98, 101, 103, 127, 128, 132, 138, 139, 153, 165, 174, 187, 189, 195, 217, 221, 22-26, 247, 248, 249, 263, 266
Signal Companies: 50
Tunnelling Companies: 89, 99, 225
Royal Flying Corps: 86, 99, 136, 153, 209, 266

Sanitary Sections/Officers:
Special Reserve, 101, 102

Tank Battalions: 5th, 251
Territorial Force
County Associations: ix, x, 15-20, 21, 25, 26, 28, 47, 100, 228, 274, 277, 278; Co.of Durham, 38; Derbys, 20; East Lancs, 16, 20, 39; Northumbria, 39; North Yorks, 20; Staffordshire, ix
Training Reserve: 61, 62, 184, 274, 277
Trench mortar batteries, 110, 158, 223, 245, 281, 281

Volunteer Force: 274, 278